C000283553

# Supervision

## QUALITY, DIVERSITY, AND TECHNOLOGY

## SECOND EDITION

*Samuel Certo*
Crummer Graduate School of Business at Rollins College

***IRWIN***
Chicago • Bogotá • Boston • Buenos Aires • Caracas
London • Madrid • Mexico City • Sydney • Toronto

©The McGraw-Hill Companies, Inc., 1994 and 1997
*All rights reserved.* No part of this publication may be
reproduced, stored in a retrieval system, or transmitted,
in any form or by any means, electronic, mechanical,
photocopying, recording, or otherwise, without the prior
written permission of the publisher.

**Irwin Book Team**

Publisher: *Rob Zwettler*
Sponsoring editor: *Karen Mellon*
Marketing manager: *Michael Campbell*
Project supervisor: *Beth Cigler*
Production supervisor: *Bob Lange*
Designer: *Matthew Baldwin*
Coordinator, Graphics and Desktop Services: *Keri Johnson/Elm Street Publishing Services, Inc.*
Director, Prepress Purchasing: *Kimberly Meriwether David*
Compositor: *Times Mirror Higher Education Group, Inc., Imaging Group*
Typeface: *10/12 Janson*
Printer: *Times Mirror Higher Education Group, Inc., Print Group*

**Library of Congress Cataloging-in-Publication Data**

Certo, Samuel C.
    Supervision: quality, diversity, and technology/Samuel C. Certo.—2nd ed.
    p. cm.
    Originally published: Supervision: quality and diversity through leadership.
    Includes index.
    ISBN 0-256-20805-0
    1. Supervision of employees. 2. Diversity in the workplace.
    I. Title.
    HF5549.12.C42 1997
    658.3′02—dc20                                              96–17363
*Printed in the United States of America*
    2 3 4 5 6 7 8 9 0 WCB 3 2 1 0 9 8 7

2299/C

# Supervision

**QUALITY, DIVERSITY, AND TECHNOLOGY**

*To Trevis*
*—One who doesn't need the footsteps of others to move forward*

# *Preface*

As with the first edition, this book prepares students to be supervisors and is based on the premise that the supervisor's job has never been more exciting or challenging than it is today. Important organizational variables such as the nature of the workforce, computer and communication technology, and the design of organization structures are changing perhaps more rapidly than at any other time in our history. With this changing situation in mind, *Supervision: Quality, Diversity, and Technology* has been developed to help students learn how to be successful supervisors.

My personal philosophy concerning the character of a high-quality supervision text remains unchanged. A worthwhile supervision text must meet the criteria not only of containing important theoretical material but also of facilitating student learning and the instructional process. The overwhelming success of the first edition of this book is an expression of support for this philosophy. The following sections explain how this new edition was carefully crafted to reflect this philosophy even more than the first edition.

## Overview of Text Development

### *The Foundation*

The first edition of this text provides a solid foundation for the second edition. The first edition evolved from careful and conscientious planning. A survey was mailed to instructors of supervision courses and supervisors nationwide to gather information about what would be needed to develop the highest-quality supervision learning package available in the marketplace. The main themes generated from the results of this survey were then summarized and presented to a focus group around the country for refinement and expansion. Supervision professors and practicing supervisors then acted as individual reviewers to help fine-tune my book plan, and they were the final advisers before writing began. An illustration depicting the focus of various professionals during the development of this text is presented in Figure A.

## ▇ FIGURE A

*Supervision:* **The Professional Team**

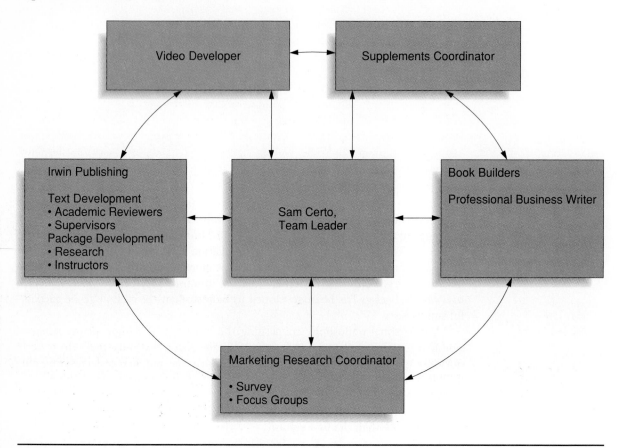

### This New Edition

*Supervision: Quality, Diversity, and Technology* is divided into five main parts: "What Is a Supervisor?", "Modern Supervision Challenges," "Functions of the Supervisor," "Skills of the Supervisor," and "Supervision and Human Resources." The following sections describe the parts and chapters of the second edition and pinpoint new text features and relevant second edition reviewer comments.

Part One, "What Is a Supervisor?", is new to this edition and consists of only the first chapter, "The Role of the Supervisor." It is aimed at providing the student with a thorough introduction to supervision before embarking on a more detailed study of the supervision process. *Reviewer highlight: The explanation both of the skills and of the degree of importance of human relations is very complete.*

Part Two, "Modern Supervision Challenges," represents a significant new reorganizational thrust to the book. Chapter 2, "Ensuring High Quality"; Chapter 3, "Working with Teams"; and Chapter 4, "Meeting High Ethical Standards," discuss the supervisor's critical role in the organizational quest for building quality into all phases of operations, the characteristics and types of groups and teams and their importance in supervision, and the relationship between ethics and supervision. Chapter 5, "Using Modern Technology," is a new chapter, added to give students an understanding of important technological advances in supervision and an appreciation of how these advances might impact the supervision process. The chapters in this part are presented earlier in the second edition than in the first edition, so that students can focus on these challenges from the beginning of the course and reflect upon them as they read the rest of the book. *Reviewer highlight: Chapter 3 contains the best presentation of characteristics of groups in any available text.*

Part Three, "Functions of the Supervisor," comprises four chapters. Chapter 6, "Reaching Goals and Objectives," is a combination of the planning and control chapters in the last edition. Chapter 7, "Using Organizational Resources," focuses on organizing and delegating. Chapter 8, "The Supervisor as Leader," and Chapter 9, "Problem Solving and Decision Making," give students insights about how supervisors relate to people as leaders, the kinds of problems and decisions that supervisors face, and possible steps for solving the problems and making the decisions. *Reviewer highlight: Students always want to know about the traits of a successful leader, and so Certo is correct to point out in Chapter 8 that there is no single set of traits.*

Part Four, "Skills of the Supervisor," discusses important abilities that supervisors must have to be successful. These abilities include communication (Chapter 10), motivating employees (Chapter 11), improving productivity (Chapter 12), supervision problem employees (Chapter 13), managing time and stress (Chapter 14), and managing conflict and change (Chapter 15). These chapters focus on how supervisors share information in organizations, methods for motivating workers, workers who require special attention and how to deal with various problems they represent, understanding what stress is and how it relates to supervision, and becoming familiar with conflict and change and using them to enhance supervisory success. The material in this part stresses the practical aspects of the skills presented in the chapters and emphasizes helping students to actually build these skills. *Reviewer highlight: Throughout these chapters, the current, real-world analogies and class exercises were very enjoyable.*

The newly reorganized conclusion for this text is Part Five, "Supervision and Human Resources." Chapter 16, "Selecting Employees," focuses on the process of choosing the right person to fill an open position—the sources, methods, and legal issues that must be considered. Chapter 17, "Providing Orientation and Training," discusses the process of orienting new employees, developing skills in employees, and evaluating training methods. Chapter 18, "Appraising Performance," discusses the importance of a systematic performance appraisal and provides several appraisal methods while Chapter 19, "The Impact of the Law," emphasizes supervision and health and safety in the workplace along with a discussion of the role of unions. *Reviewer highlight: These four areas of Human Resources are ones of "highest priority emphasis" to supervisors.*

## Overview of Text Learning System

The pedagogy for each chapter of this text has been designed to make the study of supervision interesting, enjoyable, effective, and efficient.

### Chapter Quotations
The quotes that begin each chapter are drawn from business experts, historical figures, and company policies. They are designed to help frame the topics presented in the chapters. Identities and affiliations of those quoted are provided. For instance, here is the quote that opens Chapter 4 on leadership:

*Honesty is the cornerstone of all success, without which confidence and ability to perform shall cease to exist.*
**—Mary Kay Ash, founder of Mary Kay Cosmetics**

### Chapter Outlines
The chapter outlines are provided at the beginning of each chapter and are tools that students can use to preview the chapter and review the material prior to testing.

### Learning Objectives
The key points of the chapter's content form the basis for the learning objectives. This list serves as a guide for studying the material and as a means of organizing the material in Summary at the end of the chapter and in the *Instructor's Manual.*

### Opening Vignettes
The chapter openers are primarily episodes about actual supervisors on the job. For example, Chapter 8, "The Supervisor as Leader," opens with a story about Kathleen Schrank—chief of emergency medicine for a Miami Hospital; medical director for Miami Fire, Rescue and Inspection Services; and associate professor of clinical medicine at the University of Miami Medical School—who supervises more than 40 full- and part-time staff members. Her ability to make order out of chaos defines her role as a leader.

### Margin Definitions
Key terms are defined in the margin. Students can use these definitions to test their understanding of the terms and to find the places where important concepts are discussed.

### Figures and Tables
Illustrations and tables are used extensively to clarify and reinforce text concepts.

### Tips from the Firing Line
This boxed feature highlights practical guidelines that can help students be successful supervisors. The tip in Chapter 13, "The Right Way to Fire an Employee," provides guidelines for rightful termination.

### Meeting the Challenge
This new boxed feature addresses current challenges faced by supervisors as they conduct their work each day and sets forth an example of someone who has managed the challenge well. For instance, "Telecommuters Use Technology to Communicate" (in Chapter 10), discusses the issues managers and workers face to maintain effective communication in a telecommuting situation.

### Self-Quizzes

Each chapter contains short, engaging, self-assessment quizzes, which help students see the kinds of supervisors they can be. For instance, in Chapter 7, "Test Your Understanding of Delegation," is a 10-question quiz that asks students to respond to statements about delegation.

### Summary

Learning objectives are recapped at the end of each chapter with brief summaries of the chapter concepts for each learning objective.

### Key Terms

Each chapter includes a list of key terms at the end of the chapter. Reading this list can help students review by testing their comprehension of the terms. The page number where the term is first defined is included in the glossary at the end of the book. These terms also are highlighted throughout the book as margin definitions.

### Review and Discussion Questions

These questions test understanding of the chapter concepts. These questions can be used independently by students or by instructors as a method of reviewing the chapters.

### A Second Look

This is a special feature of the Review and Discussion Questions that returns to the scenario presented in the chapter opener. A Second Look asks students to respond to questions by applying the chapter's concepts to the scenario. For instance, the Chapter 8 opener about supervisor Kathleen Schrank asks the students to identify the leadership characteristics she possesses and how those characteristics make her a successful leader.

### Cases

The concluding pages of each chapter contain a short case that further applies the chapter's concepts to various supervision situations. Questions following each case provoke students' thinking and help them synthesize ideas. This feature also can be used independently by students or instructors for course assignments or classroom discussion. For instance, in Chapter 12, the case "Com-Corp Industries Keeps Productivity High," describes a successful stamping company run by a man who practices a democratic style of management.

### Exercises

There are three types of exercises at the end of chapters. Class Exercise sections suggest activities to be done during class sessions. Team-Building Exercises provide recommendations for group activities. Finally, Video Exercises summarize the videos that correspond to a particular chapter topic and ask the student to apply concepts by answering brief questions.

### End-of-Book Glossary

Terms and definitions are gathered from each chapter and provided at the end of the book. This provides ready reference for students and instructors. To encourage student review, the text pages where the terms are first defined and discussed are included.

## The Supervision *Video Series: A Special Learning Feature*

A series of videos has been developed especially for *Supervision* to help engage students in the learning process and show actual supervisors at work. These tapes have been carefully planned and scripted to illustrate key areas in the text.

### Video 1: The Role of the Supervisor

Joanne Wilson is a supervisor for Handy Andy Home Improvement Centers. The program follows Joanne through a typical day. In this predominantly male industry, Joanne demonstrates her exceptional ability to plan, organize, and lead her employees. The students viewing the video are asked to perform an evaluation of Joanne's abilities, utilizing the concepts presented in the textbooks as the evaluation criteria.

### Video 2: Quality

Not only is Aleta Holub in charge of quality at the First National Bank of Chicago, she is one of the nine members of the Malcolm Baldrige Award Committee. Quality at First Chicago starts with the chairman and is the primary responsibility of every employee at the bank. The video demonstrates how the department supervisors implement, maintain, and control quality.

### Video 3: Motivation

Motivation is the key to being competitive in the new global marketplace. In this program, J. C. Penney demonstrates how it uses nonfinancial incentives to motivate its retail sales associates, and Nucor Steel, the nation's fastest-growing and most profitable steel company, explains how its unique financial incentive system has motivated its employees to be the most productive in the world.

### Video 4: Training

Classroom and on-the-job training are two of the most common methods of training. Karen Lohss, professional trainer at LaMarsch & Associates, demonstrates how she applies both techniques when training visually impaired supervisors. The University of Michigan Hospital recently became the first medical institution to adopt the concepts of total quality management. The secret to this successful venture was the extensive training program that every individual in the hospital underwent.

### Video 5: Groups and Teamwork

Southwest Airlines is the only company ever to win the coveted Triple Crown from the Department of Transportation: for best on-time performance, best baggage handling record, and fewest customer complaints. Southwest demonstrates how their use of teamwork has won them the distinction of being one of the ten best companies to work for in America.

### Video Instructor's Manual

A *Video Instructor's Manual* accompanies the video series. Each segment includes a synopsis of the video, teaching notes on how to integrate the video with the chapters and other package components, a list of the chapter concepts covered in the video, and in-class exercises to use with each video, with accompanying handouts.

All of the videotapes are available *free* to each school using *Supervision: Quality, Diversity, and Technology.*

## Ancillaries

One of my objectives is to provide the best teaching package available. I hope you have seen evidence of this in the description of the text and video series. But there is more: Additional instructional materials are available to further enrich the supervision learning experience. Each ancillary and its highlights follow.

### Supervision Internet Study Guide

The Supervision Internet Study Guide is the first of its type to accompany a supervision text, and it represents a valuable and progressive new thrust in supervision education. The primary objective of creating the Supervision Internet Study Guide was to provide a more impactful learning instrument than a traditionally printed study guide. In addition, since the Supervision Internet Study Guide is available free for student use, it helps students to control the accelerating costs of supervision learning materials.

As its name suggests, the Supervision Internet Study Guide is an assortment of Internet-based learning activities that you can use to enhance the quality of your supervision education. Basically, the study guide contains a number of true/false, multiple choice, and short answer essay questions that students can use to test their understanding of a chapter after it is studied. After students respond to a question, they can get immediate access to the correct answer to the question by following simple directions. Through this process, students can assess their understanding of chapter content and improve this understanding as their answers are evaluated. The Supervision Internet Study Guide will evolve over time to include other types of learning activities useful for supervision students.

The Supervision Internet Study Guide is not in this book or in any bookstore. Instead, it is on the Internet. The material that you are now reading is meant only as an introduction to the Supervision Internet Study Guide. The Supervision Internet Study Guide assumes that you know how to get on and find locations on the Internet. The web site address of the Supervision Internet Study Guide is linked to the author of this text, Professor Samuel C. Certo: **http://www.samcerto.com.**

Once you have arrived at this address, you will get simple instructions about how to use the study guide. You can use the Supervision Internet Study Guide as a formal part of your study indicated by your instructor or as an informal part of your study to enhance your understanding of the concepts in this book.

In the Supervision Internet Study Guide, students are provided an e-mail feedback form that will go to the author of this text. Professor Certo always welcomes comments and suggestions for improvement from students and professors who use his learning materials.

### Test Bank and Computerized Test Bank

We all know the importance of a high-quality *Test Bank* in teaching. The development of such a *Test Bank* to accompany *Supervision* was of the utmost importance. The *Test Bank* includes more than 2,000 questions and is available in printed form, in computerized format, and through the Teletest (phone-in) service. Each chapter includes multiple-choice questions with miniature cases to allow application of the principles, true/false questions, short essay questions, matching, and crossword puzzles. Additionally, a prepared quiz is provided for each chapter; the quiz is ready for duplication or for use as a transparency. Each question includes the answer, the corresponding text page where the answer can be found, and the rationale for the answer. All questions are graded by level of difficulty and are organized according to the text learning objectives for consistency with the entire teaching package.

Questions that students can access in the Supervision Internet Study Guide are clearly marked in the test bank. Instructors can encourage students to use the Supervision Internet Study Guide by informing students that some questions from the Internet will be included on exams. Sylvia Ong of Scottsdale Community College is the author of the *Test Bank*.

### Instructor's Manual

Each chapter of the *Instructor's Manual* is organized according to the text learning objectives. Part I provides a quick summary for each chapter. Part II, "Teaching the Concepts by Learning Objectives," includes the following for each learning objective:

1. Key terms and their definitions from the text.
2. Teaching notes. These notes describe the focus of the text section where the learning objective is discussed and point out areas where the student might become confused. Suggestions for clarifying the material are provided.
3. Fresh examples not used in the text are provided and are frequently supported by supplementary transparencies or handouts.
4. A new exercise also is provided, and details on using the exercise and the anticipated results are included.

Part III, "Notes on the Boxed Features," provides a synopsis of the Meeting the Challenge, Tips from the Firing Line, and Self-Quiz features in each chapter, along with teaching tips on how to utilize these in your lectures.

Part IV, "Answers to Review and Discussion Questions," provides the answers or suggested answers for each question.

Parts V and VI provide answers and solutions to the end-of-chapter exercises and cases.

Throughout the *Instructor's Manual*, each transparency is referenced in the chapter next to the area of possible use and highlighted in the margin.

Corinne Livesay of Mississippi College is the author of the *Instructor's Manual*.

### Transparency Masters

We are all familiar with the need for supplemental overheads of exhibits not in the text that are clear, legible, and useful even in large classrooms. As a result, we designed a transparency package to meet those criteria. The package is divided into two parts:

1. All figures and tables from the text adjusted for use as transparencies to maximize readability.
2. Supplemental transparencies—10 to 12 additional transparencies for each chapter.

All the transparencies include teaching notes that describe the transparency and outline the key points for the student to notice. Corinne Livesay of Mississippi College developed the transparency package and organized it for efficient use with the *Instructor's Manual*.

### Lecture Supplements

A special feature of the *Supervision* package is the additional five complete lectures on key topics. Authored by Corinne Livesay of Mississippi College, this supplement includes lecture outlines, transparencies, and application materials for the following areas:

1. Personal organizing skills
2. Team leadership
3. Improving listening skills
4. Interviewing strategies
5. Meeting management

Experience indicates that the highest-quality supervision courses expose students to appropriate concepts, give students an opportunity to apply these concepts to solve problems, and provide an opportunity for students to learn from their experiences.

The *Supervision* learning package has been designed to allow flexibility in emphasizing any or all of these components in your supervision course. I sincerely wish you well in building your course around *Supervision: Quality, Diversity, and Technology*. Have a great class!

## Acknowledgments

I extend my sincere thanks to all the members of the *Supervision* team who helped craft this fine teaching package. Special thanks to other colleagues who have contributed to this project:

**Reviewers**

James Day
*Grambling State University*
Medhat Farooque
*Central Arizona College*
Debbie Jansky
*Milwaukee Area Technical College*

Bonnie Johnson
*Fashion Institute of New York*
Vincent Kafka
*Effective Learning Systems*
Corinne Livesay
*Mississippi College*

Lynda Massa
*Santa Barbara Business College*
James Mulvihill
*Mankato Technical Institute*
Sylvia Ong
*Scottsdale Community College*
Smita Jain Oxford
*Commonwealth College*
Carl Sonntag
*Pikes Peak Community College*
Barbara Whitney
*St. Petersburg Junior College*

**Focus Group Participants**
Dick Brigham
*Brookhaven College*
Arnold Brown
*Purdue University North Central*
Randy Busch
*Lee College*
Gloria Couch
*Texas State Technical Institute*
Richard Gordon
*Detroit College of Business*
Ruby Ivens
*Lansing Community College*
James Kennedy
*Angelina College*
Russell Kunz
*Collin County Community College—Spring Creek*
Sue Kyriazopoulous
*DeVry Institute of Technology*
Allen Levy
*Macomb Community College Center*
John Maloney
*College of DuPage*
Kim McDonald
*IPFW*
Steven Pliseth
*University of Wisconsin, Platteville*
Charles Riley
*Tarrant County Community College*
Ralph Schmitt
*Macomb Community College South*
David Way
*Galveston College*
Dan Yovich
*Purdue University North Central*

**Survey Respondents**
Raymond Ackerman
*Amber University*
Rex Adams
*Southside Virginia Community College, Daniels*
Musa Agil
*Cape Fear Community College*
Linda Alexander
*Southeast Community College, Lincoln*
Gemmy Allen
*Mountain View College*
Scott Ames
*North Lake College*
E. Walter Amundsen
*Indiana University Southeast*
Paul Andrews
*Southern Illinois University*
Solimon Appel
*College for Human Services*
Bob Ash
*Rancho Santiago College*
Glenda Aslin
*Weatherford College*
Bob Baker
*Caldwell Community College*
James Bakersfield
*North Hennepin Community College*
Robert Barefield
*Drury College, Springfield*
Laurence Barry
*Cuyamaca College*
Perry Barton
*Gwinnett Area Technical*
Becky Bechtel
*Cincinnati Technical College*
Kenneth Beckerink
*Agricultural and Technical College*
Gina Beckles
*Bethune-Cookman College*
Jim Beeler
*Indiana Vocational and Technical College, Indianapolis*
Robert Bendotti
*Paradise Valley Community College*
Jim Blackwell
*Park College*
David Bodkin
*Cumberland University*

Arthur Boisselle
*Pikes Peak Community College*
Robert Braaten
*Tidewater Community College*
James Brademas
*University of Illinois, Urbana*
Suzanne Bradford
*Angelina College*
Richard Braley
*Eastern Oklahoma State College*
Janis Brandt
*Southern Illinois University*
Stanley Braverman
*Chestnut Hill College*
Duane Brickner
*South Mountain Community College*
Eugene Buccini
*West Connecticut State University*
Gary Bumbarner
*Mountain Hope Community College*
Kick Bundons
*Johnson County Community College*
Bill Burmeister
*New Mexico State University*
Randy Busch
*Lee College*
Oscar S. Campbell
*Athens State College*
Marjorie Carte
*D. S. Lancaster Community College*
Joseph Castelli
*College of San Mateo*
James Chester
*Cameron University*
William Chester
*University of the Virgin Islands*
Jack Clarcq
*Rochester Institute of Technology*
Charles Clark
*Oklahoma City Community College*
Sharon Clark
*Lebanon Valley College*
Virgil Clark
*Sierra College*
Jerry Coddington
*Indiana Vocational and Technical College, Indianapolis*
Bruce Conners
*Kaskaskia College*

Ronald Cornelius
*University of Rio Grande*
Gloria Couch
*Texas State College Institute*
Darrell Croft
*Imperial Valley College*
Joe Czajka
*University of South Carolina*
Beatrice Davis
*Santa Fe Community College*
Irmagard Davis
*University of Hawaii, Kapiolani Community College*
Richard De Luca
*Bloomfield College*
Edwin Deshautelle, Jr.
*Louisiana State University at Eunice*
Richard Deus
*Sacramento City College*
Ruth Dixon
*Diablo Valley College*
Leroy Drew
*Central Maine Technical College*
Janet Duncan
*City College of San Francisco*
Ron Eads
*Labette Community College*
Patrick Ellsberg
*Lower Columbia College*
Earl Emery
*Baker College, Flint*
Roland Eyears
*Central Ohio Technical College*
Tom Falcone
*Indiana University*
Jim Fatina
*Triton College*
Jack Fleming
*Moorpark College*
Lee Fleming
*El Centro College*
Charles Flint
*San Jacinto College Central*
Toni Forcioni
*Montgomery College, Germantown*
Laurie Francis
*Mid State Technical College*
Cheryl Frank
*Inver Hills Community College*

Connie French
*Los Angeles City College*
Larry Fudella
*Erie Community College South*
William Fulmer
*Clarion University of Pennsylvania*
Autrey Gardner
*Industrial Technology Department,*
*Warren Air Force Base*
David Gennrich
*Waukesha County Technical College*
Sally Gillespie
*Broome Community College*
Catherine Glod
*Mohawk Valley Community College*
Tim Gocke
*Terra Technical College*
Richard Gordon
*Detroit College of Business, Dearborn*
Greg Gorniak
*Pennsylvania State University, Behrend*
Valerie Greer
*University of Maryland*
James Grunzweig
*Lakeland Community College*
James Gulli
*Citrus College*
Bill Hamlin
*Pellissippi State Technical College*
Willard Hanson
*Southwestern College*
James Harbin
*East Texas State University*
Carnella Hardin
*Glendale Community College*
Scott Harding
*Normandale Community College*
Louis Harmin
*Sullivan County Community College*
Lartee Harris
*West Los Angeles College*
Edward L. Harrison
*University of South Alabama*
Paul Hedlund
*Barton County Community College*
Kathryn Hegar
*Mountain View College*
Gene Hilton
*Brookhaven College*

Jean Hiten
*Owensboro Community College*
Roger Holland
*Cerritos College*
Larry Hollar
*Catawba Valley Community College*
Russ Holloman
*Augusta College*
Tonya Hynds
*Indiana University at Kokomo*
Robert Ironside
*North Lake College*
Ellen Jacobs
*College of St. Mary*
Bonnie Jayne
*Bryant & Stratton*
Sarkis Kavookjian
*Delaware Technical and*
*Community College*
Bernard Keller
*Pikes Peak Community College*
Robert Kemp
*Peralta Laney College*
James Kerrigan
*Stonehill College*
Scott King
*Sinclair Community College*
Edward Kingston
*Piedmont Virginia Community College*
Ronald Kiziah
*Caldwell Community College*
Mary Lou Kline
*Reading Area Community College*
Jay Knippen
*University of South Florida*
Howard Korchin
*Fashion Institute of Technology*
Sue Kyriazopoulous
*DeVry Institute of Technology*
Thomas Lloyd
*Westmoreland County Community*
*College*
Barbara Logan
*Albuquerque Technical–Vocational*
*Institute*
Rosendo Lomas
*Lawrence Technical University*
Frances Lowery
*Brewer State Junior College*

Henie Lustgarten
*University of Maryland*
Alvin Mack
*Everett Community College*
Jon Magoon
*Santa Rosa Junior College*
Marvin Mai
*Empire College*
Joseph Manno
*Montgomery College*
Edward Mautz
*El Camino College*
Ron Maxwell
*Indiana Vocational and Technical,*
*Terre Haute*
Joseph McShane
*Gateway Technical Institute, Kenosha*
Robert McDonald
*Central Wesleyan College*
William McKinney
*University of Illinois, Urbana*
Raymond Medeiros
*Southern Illinois University*
Unny Menon
*California State Polytechnic University*
Dorothy Metcalfe
*Fashion Institute of Design and*
*Merchandising, Los Angeles*
Eugene Meyers
*Western Kentucky University*
Charles Miller
*Los Angeles Southwest College*
Dominick Montileone
*Delaware Valley College*
Wayne Moorhead
*Brown Mackie College*
Peter Moran
*Wisconsin Indianhead Technical College*
Ed Mosher
*Laramie County Community College*
Donald Mossman
*Concordia College*
John Mudge
*Community College of Vermont, Rutland*
James Mulvihill
*South Central Technical College*
Hershel Nelson
*Polk Community College*
John Nugent
*Montana Technical College*

Randy Nutter
*Geneva College*
Cruz Ortolaza
*Catholic University of Puerto Rico*
Joseph Papenfuss
*Westminster College, Salt Lake City*
Mary Papenthien
*Milwaukee Area Technical College*
John Parker
*Manchester Community College*
James Peele
*Carl Sandburg College, Galesburg*
Joe Petta
*Regis College*
Bonnie Phillips
*Casper College*
Martha Pickett
*University of Arkansas at Little Rock*
Barbara Pratt
*Community College of Vermont*
Robert Priester
*Madison Area Technical College*
Barbara Prince
*Cambridge Community College Center*
John Pryor
*Northern Nevada Community College*
Marcia Ann Pulich
*University of Wisconsin–Whitewater*
Peter Repcogle
*Orange County Community College*
Margaret Rdzak
*Cardinal Stritch College*
William Redmon
*Western Michigan University*
Arnon Reichers
*Ohio State University*
Charles Reott
*Western Wisconsin Technical Institute*
Richard Rettig
*University of Central Oklahoma*
Harriett Rice
*Los Angeles City College*
Robert Richardson
*Iona College*
Charles Riley
*Tarrant County Junior College*
Richard Riley
*National College*
Michael Rogers
*Albany State College*

Robert Roth
*City University, Bellvue*
Larry Runions
*North Carolina Vocational Textile*
Henry Ryder
*Gloucester County College*
Larry Ryland
*Lurleen B. Wallace Junior College*
Duane Schecter
*Muskegon Community College*
S. Schmidt
*Diablo Valley College*
Irving Schnayer
*Peralta Laney College*
Greg Schneider
*Waukesha County Technical College*
Arthur Shanley
*Milwaukee School of Engineering*
Margie Shaw
*Lake City Community College*
Allen Shub
*Northwestern Illinois University*
Pravin Shukla
*Nash Community College*
Clay Sink
*University of Rhode Island*
Ron Smith
*DeKalb Institute of Technology*
Steve Smith
*Mid State Technical College*
Wanda Smith
*Ferris State University*
Carl Sonntag
*Pikes Peak Community College*
Marti Sopher
*Cardinal Stritch College*
Jerry Sparks
*Cannon International Business College*
David Spitler
*Central Michigan University*
Richard Squire
*Northwest Technical College*
Dick Stanish
*Tulsa Junior College*
Gene Stewart
*Brookhaven College*
John Stout
*University of Scranton*
Art Sweeney
*Troy State University*

Sally Terman
*Scottsdale Community College*
Sherman Timmons
*University of Toledo*
Don Tomal
*Purdue University*
Donna Treadwell
*Johnson County Community College*
Ron Tremmel
*Rend Lake College*
Guy Trepanier
*Iona College*
John Tucker
*Purdue University*
Bill Tyer
*Tarrant County Junior College*
Robert Ulbrich
*Parkland College*
Diann Valentini
*Fashion Institute of Technology*
Steven Vekich
*Washington State Community College*
Michael Vijuk
*William Rainey Harper College*
Charles Wall
*Bakersfield College*
Kathy Walton
*Salt Lake City Community College*
Robert Way
*Milwaukee Area Technical College*
Rick Webb
*Johnson County Community College*
Ronald Webb
*Messiah College Grantham*
Alan Weinstein
*Canisius College*
Bill Weisgerber
*Saddleback College*
Julia Welch
*University of Arkansas Medical School*
Floyd Wente
*St Louis Community College at
Florissant Valley*
Ron Weston
*Contra Costa College*
Charles Wetmore
*California State University, Fresno*
Jerry Wheaton
*North Arkansas Community College*

Luther White
*Central Carolina Community College*
Michael White
*University of Northern Iowa*
Sara White
*University of Kansas Medical Center*
Barbara Whitney
*St. Petersburg Junior College*
Tim Wiedman
*Thomas Nelson Community College*
Stephen Winter
*Orange County Community College*
Arthur Wolf
*Chestnut Hill College*
Barry Woodcock
*Tennessee Technological University*
Michael Wukitsch
*American Marketing Association*
Catalina Yang
*Normandale Community College*
Charles Yauger
*Arkansas State University*
Morrie Yohai
*New York Institute of Technology*
Teresa Yohon
*Hutchinson Community College*
James Yoshida
*University of Hawaii, Hawaii
Community College*
Allan Young
*Bessemer State Technical College*
Marilyn Young
*Waukesha County Technical College*
Richard Young
*Pennsylvania State University*

Fred Ziolhowski
*Purdue University*
Karen Zwissler
*Milwaukee Area Technical College*

## Application Exercises Contributors

E. Walter Amundsen
*Indiana University Southeast*
Stanley A. Braverman
*Chestnut Hill College*
Bruce L. Conners
*Kaskaskia College*
James E. Fatina
*Triton College*
Peter J. Gummere
*Community College of Vermont*
Bernard Keller
*Pikes Peak Community College*
Edward A. Kingston
*Piedmont Virginia Community College*
Joseph R. Manno
*Montgomery College*
Arnon E. Reichers
*Ohio State University*
John P. Wanous
*Ohio State University*
Charles Wetmore
*California State University*
Michael R. White
*University of Northern Iowa*
Timothy G. Wiedman
*Thomas Nelson Community College*
Stephen I. Winter
*Orange County Community College*
Fred Ziolkowski
*Purdue University*

*Samuel C. Certo*
August 1996

# *About the Author*

Dr. Samuel C. Certo is professor of management and former dean at the Roy E. Crummer Graduate School of Business at Rollins College. He has been a professor of management for over 20 years and has received prestigious awards, including the Award for Innovative Teaching from the Southern Business Association, the Instructional Innovation Award granted by the Decision Sciences Institute, and the Charles A. Welsh Memorial Award for outstanding teaching at the Crummer School. Dr. Certo's numerous publications include articles in journals such as *Academy of Management Review*, the *Journal of Experiential Learning and Simulation*, and *Training*. He also has written several successful textbooks, including *Modern Management: Diversity, Quality, Ethics, and the Global Environment; Strategic Management: Concepts and Applications;* and *Supervision: Quality, Diversity, and Technology*. A past chairman of the Management Education and Development Division of the Academy of Management, he has been honored by that group's Excellence of Leadership Award. Dr. Certo also has served as president of the Association for Business Simulation and Experiential Learning, as associate editor for *Simulation & Games*, and as a review board member of the *Academy of Management Review*. His consulting experience has been extensive, with notable experience on boards of directors. Recent clients include Red Lobster Restaurants, State Farm Insurance, and Harcourt Brace.

# Contents

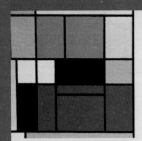

# PART ONE

## *What Is a Supervisor?*

# 1

*People and how we manage them are becoming more important because many other sources of competitive success are less powerful than they once were.*
—**Jeffrey Pfeffer, business author**

# The Role of the Supervisor

## LEARNING OBJECTIVES

After you have studied this chapter, you should be able to:

1.1 Define what a supervisor is.

1.2 Describe the basic types of supervisory skills.

1.3 Describe how the growing diversity of the workforce affects the supervisor's role.

1.4 Identify the general functions of a supervisor.

1.5 Explain how supervisors are responsible to higher management, employees, and co-workers.

1.6 Describe the typical background of someone who is promoted to supervisor.

1.7 Identify characteristics of a successful supervisor.

© John Barr/Gamma Liaison.

## SUPERVISORS' ROLES CHANGE AS THE TIGHT SHIP LOOSENS UP

Long after the ad campaign "We run the tightest ship in the shipping business" ended, the image lingered. In exchange for job security and other benefits, UPS reserved the right to dictate to its employees their every move, including how drivers should hold their keys, how many steps to take to reach a customer's door, and which packages to deliver first. Supervisors monitored these activities closely as part of their jobs.

Much of this is changing. In a reengineering effort intended to tighten purse strings and boost efficiency, UPS management is loosening its grip on employees. Instead of supervisors and computers designing daily routes, the drivers now do so themselves.

Thus, several layers of management are being eliminated. In addition, UPS plans to outsource 65 call centers. With the old system, if a package is lost, a customer must call a service rep, who calls an operating center, which contacts another office, which phones the driver, who then must try to locate the package and send an answer all the way back through the same channels. Under the new plan for outside call centers, service reps would have the authority to contact drivers directly. Supervisors would not be directly involved on a routine basis.

What do these changes mean for supervisors? Their responsibilities, once completely clear, have become somewhat ambiguous, especially since drivers and service reps have more authority to make decisions. No longer responsible for timing drivers at stoplights and producing huge daily efficiency reports, supervisors have to define their jobs other ways.

The change may be difficult, but UPS executives hope that the new way supervisors and their employees approach their jobs will drive the company toward continued prosperity. "We just hope [employees] will come on board and help this company remain successful," notes chief operating officer James P. Kelly.

Source: Robert Frank, "Efficient UPS Tries to Increase Efficiency," *The Wall Street Journal*, May 24, 1995, pp. B1, B4.

Despite the difference in titles, the supervisors at UPS and all of the following people can be considered "supervisors": a foreman in a Rollerblade skate factory, the head teller at a branch of Wells Fargo Bank, the principal of a neighborhood elementary school, the patient care coordinator (head nurse) in the orthopedics unit of a hospital, the manager of a Burger King restaurant, a sergeant on a police force or in the army. To define the term, a **supervisor** is a manager at the first level of management, which means that the employees reporting to the supervisor are not managers. From this definition and the examples opening this chapter, you can see that many different kinds of organizations need supervisors. Figure 1.1 reprints actual want ads for a variety of supervisory jobs.

The basic job of a manager is to see that an organization is meeting its goals, yet there are distinctions. For the top executives of an organization, managing entails making sure that the organization's vision and business strategy will allow it to meet its goals through the years ahead. Managing at the supervisory level means ensuring that the employees in a particular department are performing their jobs such that the department will make its contribution to the organization's goals. Usually, supervisors focus on day-to-day problems and on goals to be achieved in one year or less. This chapter introduces what supervisors do and what skills and characteristics they need to be effective.

**supervisor**
A manager at the first level of management.

## Types of Supervisory Skills

Although a supervisor in a Pizza Hut restaurant and a supervisor in a Bethlehem Steel factory work in very different environments, the skills they need to be successful fall into the same basic categories. The categories of skills are used by all levels of managers in all kinds of organizations. If these skills are developed during a beginning, supervisory job, they will prove useful in every job held throughout a management career. The basic categories of skills are technical, human relations, conceptual, and decision-making skills.

### Categorizing the Skills

**technical skills**
The specialized knowledge and expertise used to carry out particular techniques or procedures.

**Technical skills** are the specialized knowledge and expertise used to carry out particular techniques or procedures. A United Way fund-raiser's ability to persuade executives to write big checks is a technical skill. A Goodyear mechanic's ability to bring any automobile's engine back to life involves technical skills. And selling ability is the technical skill of an insurance salesperson who earns big commissions. As you can see from these examples, skills do not have to be mechanical or scientific in order to be "technical"; they can involve any work-related technique or procedure.

**human relations skills**
The ability to work effectively with other people.

Supervisors also have to be able to work effectively with other people, or possess **human relations skills.** Human relations skills include the ability to communicate with, motivate, and understand other people. Supervisors use their human relations skills to impress their superiors, to inspire employees to work efficiently, to defuse conflicts, to get along with co-workers in other departments, and in many other ways.

**conceptual skills**
The ability to see the relation of the parts to the whole and to one another.

In addition, supervisors need **conceptual skills,** or the ability to see the relation of the parts to the whole and to one another. For a supervisor, conceptual skills include recognizing how the department's work helps the entire organization achieve its goals and how the work of the various employees affects the performance of the department as a whole. For example, the supervisor of a manufacturing department

## FIGURE 1.1

### A Sampling of Supervisory Positions to Be Filled

> **Advertising**
> **PRODUCTION MANAGER**
> Electronic desktop production agency seeks self-starting, problem-solving Production Manager to supervise catalogue/retail page construction in Mac platform. Minimum 5-7 yrs. experience in managing production and personnel required. Service bureau background a plus. Send resume and salary requirements to:
> Dept. A-7
> P.O. Box 200
> Ski Springs, CO 80300

> **AUTOMATIC SCREW MACHINE**
> **SECOND SHIFT SUPERVISOR**
> Established growing suburban manufacturer looking for qualified individual to supervise second shift of manufacturing operations. Must have knowledge and experience on multiple/single spindle machines. Enjoy excellent working conditions in a new plant. Very good salary and full benefit package. Submit resume to:
> P.O. Box 1234
> Industrious, IN 46000

> **Health Care**
> **CHIEF PHYSICAL THERAPIST**
> Rural health care consortium has an immediate opening for a licensed physical therapist to develop a progressive, sophisticated therapy delivery system. The ideal candidate should understand sound management principles and possess strong assessment and clinical skills. Candidate must also be willing to assume department leadership. Competitive salary and benefit package. Send resume to:
> Director of Human Resources
> Quality Care Health Services
> Minuscule, NM 87000

> **SECRETARIAL SUPERVISOR**
> Large law firm seeks Secretarial Supervisor to join our secretarial management team. Responsibilities include orienting, coordinating, and evaluating a secretarial staff of approximately 200. Previous law firm experience (supervisory or secretarial) preferred. Ideal candidate will be able to work well with a variety of personalities in a demanding, fast-paced environment. We offer state-of-the-art technology, an excellent benefits package and salary commensurate with experience. For immediate, confidential consideration send resume and salary history to:
> Personnel
> P.O. Box 987
> City Center, TN 38000

> **SALES MANAGEMENT**
> Our growing organization is seeking an experienced Sales Management candidate to lead our expanding Color Copier Department. The successful candidate will have 3-5 years sales management experience in planning, organizing, hiring, and motivating a team of sales professionals. Previous sales experience, account development techniques, and vertical market success are required. Familiarity with printing, graphic arts, office equipment or other related industry experience helpful. To be considered for this exceptional career opportunity, please send your resume with salary requirements to:
> Dept. 001
> Suburbanite, NJ 07000

> **ASSISTANT DIRECTOR OF HOUSEKEEPING**
> Large luxury hotel is accepting resumes for an Assistant Director of Housekeeping. College degree and 4-5 years of Housekeeping Management experience required. Preferred applicants will have experience as a Director of Housekeeping for a small to medium size hotel or Assistant Director at a large hotel. Must have excellent administrative and supervisory skills. Interested candidates should send resume in confidence to:
> Luxurious Suites
> 1000 Upscale Blvd.
> Villa Grande, CA 90000

---

at General Motors should be able to see that the company's reputation depends on the department's making high-quality products. The supervisor also should realize that for the company's salespeople to be able to keep their promises, the manufacturing department must meet its production quotas.

**decision-making skills**
The ability to analyze information and reach good decisions.

Finally, supervisors must have **decision-making skills,** or the ability to analyze information and reach good decisions. For example, a supervisor might have to decide which of three candidates for a job will work out best or which of two conflicting deadlines has a higher priority. Someone who has strong decision-making skills can think objectively and creatively. (Chapter 9 provides a more detailed look at how to make decisions effectively.)

The relative importance of each type of skill depends on the level of management. As shown in Figure 1.2, human relations skills are important at every level of management. However, supervisors rely more on technical skills than do higher-level managers because employees who have a problem doing their job go to the supervisor and expect help.

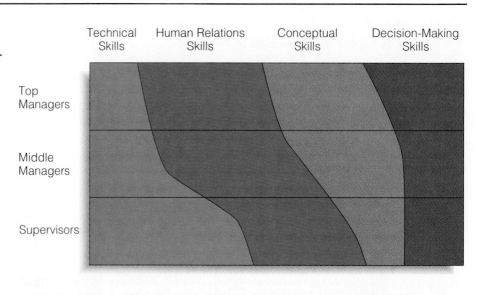

What is the purpose of learning why management skills can be categorized in this way? Supervisors can use this information to recognize the different kinds of skills needed. For example, a salesperson can see that being able to sell successfully does not in itself make him or her a good sales manager. This person will also have to develop skills in working with others and making decisions.

To develop the variety of skills needed to be good supervisor, learn and practice the concepts discussed in this book. Get to know good supervisors and managers and observe how they handle situations. Supervisors who continually develop their skills in each area are the ones most likely to be promoted to higher levels of management.

### Supervising a Diverse Workforce

Good human relations skills are especially important in today's environment because of the increasing diversity of the U.S. workforce. Whereas almost half (49 percent) of the workforce in 1976 consisted of white males, this category is expected to make up only 12 percent of net new hires (total hired minus total leaving the workforce) by the year 2000.[1] Therefore, white males' share of the workforce is expected to fall to 39 percent by the year 2000.[2] While the share of white males in the workforce declines, the share of black, Hispanic, and Asian workers is expected to rise.[3] Women are entering the workforce at about the same rate as men, but men are retiring at a faster rate; therefore, women, like racial and ethnic minorities, will have a greater role.[4] In addition, the over-65 segment of the U.S. population is growing faster than younger age groups.[5]

***Opportunities and Challenges***   Together, these changes mean that supervisors can expect to have more employees who are female, nonwhite, and more experienced—perhaps senior citizens holding a retirement job. As described in later chapters, these trends enable supervisors to draw on a greater variety of talent and gain insights into a greater variety of perspectives than ever before.

Supervisors must possess technical, human relations, conceptual, and decision-making skills. All four skills are used daily: Jenean Lord, administrative supervisor at Humana Hospital, reviews the morning report with an LPN.

Source: Courtesy of Humana Inc.

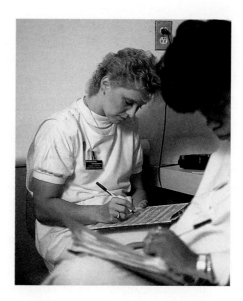

Diversity is not an entirely new issue. Management professor William P. Anthony describes how his grandfather, Alberto Spina, addressed similar needs during his career with American Manganese Steel Company in Chicago Heights, Illinois, from 1907 to 1944.[6] Most of the immigrant workers Spina supervised were white males, but they came from different cultural and linguistic backgrounds that reflected their countries of origin: England, Germany, Italy, Ireland, and the Slavic-speaking nations. Sometimes Spina had to use a translator to communicate with his employees.

Although diversity is not a new issue, the even greater diversity expected in the U.S. workforce of the future—coupled with laws and policies intended to ensure fair treatment of the various groups—requires supervisors to work successfully with a much wider variety of people.

***Subtle Discrimination***    Today hardly anyone would say that it is all right to discriminate or that a manager should be allowed to give preference to employees of the manager's race or sex. However, management professor Mary Rowe says that subtle forms of discrimination persist in every workplace and that everybody holds some stereotypes that consciously or unconsciously influence their behavior.[7] The subtle discrimination that results may include ignoring the input from the only woman at a meeting or mistaking an African-American professional for someone with a less prestigious job such as receptionist or janitor.

Rowe recommends several tactics that supervisors and other managers can use to improve attitudes:

- Have employees work with someone who is different. This gives the employees a chance to educate themselves about the customs and values others hold.
- Use the kind of behavior they expect their employees to exhibit, including demonstrations of respect for others.
- Pay attention to negative stereotypes and question them. When an employee makes an offensive comment, point out the damage it does and ask the employee to avoid such remarks in the future.

Unfortunately, many supervisors still work for organizations that fail to see the advantages of hiring and developing a diverse workforce. Even in an organization where management is not committed to these goals, supervisors can provide advice and coaching to female and nonwhite employees, helping them get along in the organization. Supervisors also can make a point of learning about the various employees in the department, such as what motivates them and what their career goals are.[8] Throughout this book, you will find more specific ideas for meeting the diversity challenge as it relates to the chapter topics.

## General Functions of the Supervisor

Jennifer Plotnick is a supervisor at her city's board of education. Her responsibilities include ensuring that the employees in her department are doing a good job, preparing a budget for her department, making sure not to spend more than the budgeted amounts, explaining to employees what they are expected to do, and justifying to her manager why she needs to add people to her department next year. In contrast, supervisors in other settings may spend most of their time enabling employees to do their jobs and may handle fewer responsibilities than Jennifer.

Although the settings and degrees of responsibility may differ, supervisors and other managers carry out the same types of functions. To describe these common activities, management experts categorize them as planning, organizing, staffing, leading, and controlling. The management functions are illustrated in Figure 1.3. The figure shows that all of the activities should be directed toward enabling employees to deliver high-quality goods and services, whether to customers of the organization or to colleagues in another department.

### Planning

**planning**
Setting goals and determining how to meet them.

Common sense tells us that we do our best work when we know what we are trying to accomplish. Thus, the supervisor's job includes determining the department's goals and the ways to meet them. This is the function of **planning.** Sometimes a supervisor has a substantial say in determining the goals themselves, while another supervisor must focus his or her efforts on how to achieve goals set by higher-level managers.

As mentioned earlier, the supervisor's job is to help the organization meet its goals. Organizational goals are the result of planning by top managers. The purpose of planning by supervisors, then, is to determine how the department can contribute to achieving the organization's goals. This includes planning how much money to spend—and, for a retailer or sales department, how much money to bring in—what level of output to achieve, and how many employees will be needed. (Chapter 6 discusses planning in greater detail.)

### Organizing

**organizing**
Setting up the group, allocating resources, and assigning work to achieve goals.

Once the supervisor figures out what needs to get done, the next step is to determine how to set up the group, allocate resources, and assign work to achieve the goals efficiently. This is the function of **organizing.**

Somebody has to decide how to set up the overall organization, creating departments and levels of management. Of course, few supervisors have much of a

**FIGURE 1.3**

**Functions of Supervisors and Other Managers**

say in those kinds of decisions. At the supervisory level, organizing usually involves activities such as scheduling projects and assigning duties to employees (or, as will be discussed later, enabling employees to carry out these organizing tasks). In addition, modern supervisors are increasingly responsible for setting up and leading teams of workers to handle special projects or day-to-day operations. (Chapter 7 discusses organizing in greater detail, Chapter 3 addresses leading a team, and the case at the end of Chapter 1 illustrates how teamwork affects the supervisor's job.)

## Staffing

The supervisor needs qualified employees to carry out the tasks that he or she has planned and organized. The activities involved in identifying, hiring, and developing the necessary number and quality of employees are known as the function of **staffing.** While an operative (nonmanagement) employee's performance is usually judged on the basis of the results that the employee has achieved as an individual, a supervisor's performance depends on the quality of results that the supervisor achieves through his or her employees. Therefore, staffing is crucial to the supervisor's success. (The various activities of the staffing function are addressed in Chapters 16 through 18.)

## Leading

Even if the supervisor has the clearest and most inspired vision of how the department and its employees should work, this vision will not become a reality unless employees know and want to do their part. The supervisor is responsible for letting employees know what is expected of them and for inspiring employees to do good work. Influencing employees to act (or not act) in a certain way is the function of **leading.**

**staffing**
Identifying, hiring, and developing the necessary number and quality of employees.

**leading**
Influencing people to act (or not act) in a certain way.

Whereas organizing draws heavily on the supervisor's conceptual skills, leading requires good human relations skills. The supervisor needs to be aware of and use behaviors that employees respond to as he or she desires. [Chapter 8 includes a more detailed discussion of leading. Other chapters discuss the ways in which supervisors influence employees to act, such as by communicating (Chapter 10), motivating (Chapter 11), and disciplining (Chapter 13).]

## Controlling

The supervisor needs to know what is happening in the department. When something goes wrong, the supervisor must find a way to fix the problem or enable employees to do so. Monitoring performance and making needed corrections is the management function of **controlling.**

**controlling**
Monitoring performance and making needed corrections.

In an increasing number of organizations, the supervisor is not supposed to control by dictating solutions. Rather, the supervisor is expected to provide employees with the resources and motivation to identify and correct problems themselves. In these organizations, the supervisor is still responsible for controlling, but he or she works with others to carry out this function. (Chapter 6 discusses these and more traditional principles of controlling in more detail.)

## Relationships among the Functions

Notice that Figure 1.3 shows the management functions as a process in which planning comes first, followed by organizing, then staffing, then leading, and, finally, controlling. This order occurs because each function depends on the preceding function(s). Once the supervisor has planned what the department will do, he or she can figure out the best way to organize work and people to accomplish those objectives. Then the supervisor needs to get the people in place and doing their jobs. At that point, the supervisor can direct their work and inspire their efforts. The results are then evaluated by the supervisor to ensure that the work is getting done properly. During the controlling function, the supervisor may wish to revise some goals, at which point the whole process begins again.

Of course, real-life supervisors do not spend one week planning, then one week organizing, and so on. Instead, they often carry out all of the management functions during the course of a day. For example, a patient care coordinator in a hospital might start the day by checking the nurses' performance (controlling), then attend a meeting to discuss the needs of the patients (planning), then help resolve a dispute between a nurse and a physical therapist (leading). Thus, Figure 1.3 is a very general model of managing that shows how the functions depend on each other, not how the supervisor structures his or her work.

Typically, supervisors spend most of their time leading and controlling. That is because supervisors work directly with the employees who are producing or selling a product or providing support services. Planning, staffing, and organizing take up less of a supervisor's time. In contrast, because higher-level managers are responsible for setting the overall direction for the organization, they spend more time on planning and organizing.

| | |
|---|---|
| ■ **TABLE 1.1**<br><br>**"Rights" That Employees Lose When They Become Supervisors** | The right to lose their temper.<br><br>The right to hobnob and be "one of the crowd."<br><br>The right to shut the door.<br><br>The right to bring personal problems to work.<br><br>The right to speak freely.<br><br>The right to be against change.<br><br>The right to pass the buck.<br><br>The right to get even.<br><br>The right to choose favorites.<br><br>The right to think of themselves first.<br><br>The right to ask an employee to do something they would not do.<br><br>The right to expect immediate reward for their work. |

Reprinted by permission of publisher, from *Supervisory Management*, July 1990. ©1990. American Management Association, New York. All rights reserved.

## Responsibilities of the Supervisor

"I wish I were the manager," grumbled Hal O'Donnell, a cook at a pizza restaurant. "Then I'd be in charge and wouldn't get bossed around all the time." Perhaps Hal has not considered that a promotion to supervisor (or any level of management) would not lessen a person's burdens. Indeed, an employee who becomes a supervisor gives up all the "rights" listed in Table 1.1. In other words, supervisors have more power than nonmanagers but also many responsibilities—to higher management, to employees, and to co-workers.

### Types of Responsibilities

Supervisors are responsible for carrying out the duties assigned to them by higher-level managers. This includes giving managers timely and accurate information for planning. They also must keep their managers informed about the department's performance. Supervisors are expected to serve as a kind of "linking pin" between employees and management. Thus, their responsibilities include building employee morale and carrying employee concerns to the relevant managers.

Some supervisors may question the notion that they have a responsibility to their employees. After all, the employees are responsible for doing what the supervisors say. Nevertheless, because supervisors link management to the employees, the way they treat employees is crucial. Supervisors are responsible for giving their employees clear instructions and making sure they understand their jobs. They must look for problems and correct them before employees' performance deteriorates further. They also need to treat their employees fairly

At the Walgreens store in Colorado Springs, store manager Dick Enders (right) supervises employees such as camera clerk Bob Parker (left), and he must also handle much of the planning and organizing for the store.

Source: Courtesy of Walgreen Co.

and to speak up for their interests to top management. William Bottom, a supervisory carpenter at the Lazarus department store in Lexington, Kentucky, has this advice for supervisors:

> You shouldn't give your crew an assignment that you'd hesitate to take on yourself. Don't allow top bosses to push more work on your crew than they can reasonably be expected to do. Employees will work smarter and harder for a supervisor who puts their welfare first.[9]

Finally, supervisors are responsible for cooperating with their co-workers in other departments. They should respond promptly when a co-worker in another department requests information. They should share ideas that will help the organization's departments work together to accomplish common goals. And supervisors should listen with an open mind when co-workers in other departments make suggestions about improving the way things are done. When supervisors learn from each other's ideas, the whole organization benefits and the supervisors have the satisfaction of working together as members of a team.

### Responsibilities after Restructuring or Reengineering

In recent years, many organizations have attempted to cut costs by reducing the number of levels of management. In this process, many middle managers, who rank between supervisors and the top executives, usually are eliminated. (By one account, middle-management positions accounted for about one-fifth of jobs eliminated in the United States since 1988.[10]) The Diner's Club unit of Citicorp was reduced from eight layers of management between the president and first-line supervisors to four layers. Other companies that have cut out layers of management include Corning, Inc., and Eastman Kodak Company.[11] (See "Meeting the Challenge.")

## MEETING THE CHALLENGE

### New Roles for Supervisors

With more and more companies adopting the team-based strategy for getting things done and computers providing employees and upper-level managers with all the information they seem to need, some management theorists have predicted that supervisors will become extinct. After all, team members don't need to be told what to do; they tell themselves. And if a major function of a supervisor is to communicate information up and down the hierarchy, why is a supervisor needed when a simple computerized function can do the job? Furthermore, as companies streamline costs and processes by eliminating layers of management, those in the "middle" have been the first to go. Indeed, 20 percent of all job losses in the United States since the late 1980s have been in that gray area between top executive and wage earner.

How can supervisors survive? Some management experts are more optimistic about the future of supervisors than those who predict their extinction. They believe that supervisors bring to the organization an important "midlevel perspective"; they understand the company's goals and know enough about the front-line jobs (and their company's customers) to see how those goals can be met. Japan's Honda once gave its younger managers some broad guidelines for a new car: "Make it youth-friendly and fuel-efficient." The managers came up with the Civic.

As team members, supervisors may become facilitators, occupying a quasi-leadership role that can include assisting members with decision making and communicating to upper management about the progress of the team. They may form collegial relationships with their counterparts at other companies, sharing information that is valuable to both parties—without the aid of a computer. They also can be instrumental in motivating workers, even giving workers career goals to aspire to. A computer cannot accomplish this type of communication.

By being resourceful and flexible a supervisor reduces the chances that his or her job will fade away. In addition, top managers in many companies are beginning to place renewed value on the supervisory position. The functions may expand or change, but it is likely that the job will be part of U.S. business for years to come.

Source: "The Salaryman Rides Again," *The Economist*, Feb. 4, 1995, p. 64.

When organizations eliminate layers of management—whether they call this process restructuring, reengineering, or something else—they generally push responsibility lower in the organization's hierarchy. Today's supervisors often have responsibilities that only a decade ago would have been the province of middle management. Supervisors not only must continue to work closely with employees but also must handle much of the planning and organizing once done by middle managers.

Furthermore, the organization may expect that operative employees will play an active role in traditional management tasks such as setting goals, allocating work, and monitoring and improving quality. An old-fashioned "command-and-control" approach to supervision in this setting would not be effective. It stifles the very creativity and empowerment that this kind of reorganization seeks to foster.

Rather, the supervisor's role in such situations is to make it easier for employees to carry out their broad responsibilities. This role assumes that employees are able and willing to contribute if only they have the information and other resources they need. Lawrence A. Bossidy, Allied Signal's CEO, refers to this new role of enabler and empowerer when he says, "We need people who are better at persuading than at barking orders, who know how to coach and build consensus."[12]

Consultant Frank Quisenberry has summarized three basic ways in which a supervisor can carry out this redefined role:[13]

1.  The supervisor *empowers* employees, making sure they understand the organization's goals and have enough freedom to make decisions in support of those goals.
2.  The supervisor *communicates* with employees and higher-level managers, sharing information extensively. He or she communicates the needs and concerns of management to employees and the needs and concerns of employees to management. (This can require skill in negotiating.)
3.  The supervisor *develops* the skills of his or her team or of individual team members by recognizing the importance of developing problem-solving and teamwork skills in addition to technical skills.

All of these activities rely heavily on interpersonal skills. Thus, the changes occurring in the modern workplace require managers to rely much less than before on their technical expertise and more on their ability to understand, inspire, and enhance cooperation among people.

For some supervisors who view their job as telling others what to do and then checking that the work gets done, this new style of supervision can feel awkward. However, many supervisors discover that their employees can, and do, contribute ideas and commitment that improve performance and the satisfaction of customers and employees alike.

### Responsibilities and Accountability

**accountability**
The practice of imposing penalties for failing to adequately carry out responsibilities and of providing rewards for meeting responsibilities.

Whatever the responsibilities of a particular supervisor, the organization holds the supervisor accountable for carrying them out. **Accountability** refers to the practice of imposing penalties for failing to adequately carry out responsibilities, and it usually includes giving rewards for meeting responsibilities. Thus, if customer service supervisor Lydia Papadopoulos effectively teaches the telephone representatives on her staff to listen carefully to customers, the company might reward her with a raise. In contrast, a higher-level manager who gets frustrated with a supervisor who fails to provide information about what is happening in the department might eventually fire the supervisor for not carrying out this responsibility.

# Becoming a Supervisor

Most supervisors started out working in the department they now supervise. Because technical skills are relatively important for first-level managers, the person selected to be supervisor is often an employee with a superior grasp of the technical skills needed to perform well in the department. The person also might have more seniority than many of the other employees in the department. Good work habits and leadership skills are also reasons for selecting an employee to be a supervisor. Sometimes a company will hire a recent college graduate to be a supervisor, perhaps because the person has demonstrated leadership potential or a specialized skill that will help in the position.

Unfortunately, none of these bases for promotion or hiring guarantee that a person knows how to supervise. When salesperson Rick Horn was promoted to inside sales manager, he was unprepared for some aspects of supervising a sales force. Instead of receiving formal training in supervision, Horn says, "I was just kind of dropped off the end of the pier." He was especially challenged by the task of figuring out how to lead his former colleagues. Recalling an early effort at handling a salesperson's poor performance, Horn says, "She screwed up, and I yelled at her. She started crying, I didn't know what to do, and my boss just looked at me and shook his head." Fortunately, Horn learned to refine his human relations skills, and he now heads Iowa Mold Tool Corporation of Garner, Iowa.[14]

As Horn discovered, becoming a supervisor marks a big change in a person's work life. The new supervisor suddenly must use more human relations and conceptual skills and devote more time to planning ahead and keeping an eye on the department's activities. Also, a change takes place in the supervisor's relationships with the employees in the department. Instead of being one of the crowd, the supervisor becomes a part of management—even the target of blame or anger when employees resent company policies. All these changes are bound to lead to some anxiety. It is natural to wonder whether you are qualified or how you will handle the problems that surely will arise.

## *Preparing for the Job*

One way to combat the anxiety is to prepare for the job. A new supervisor can learn about management and supervision through books and observation. He or she can think about ways to carry out the role of supervisor. More important than friendliness are traits such as fairness and a focus on achieving goals. A supervisor can also strive to learn as much as possible about the organization, the department, and the job.

Once on the job, a supervisor needs to continue the learning process. More important than understanding the layout of the workplace is knowing about the employees in the department or work group.[15] Who are the quiet but productive workers, for example, and who are the unofficial leaders? To get to know employees, a supervisor can talk to his or her own manager and read performance appraisals, but the most reliable sources of information are the employees themselves. Particularly in the early days on the job, a supervisor should take time to discuss goals with employees and observe their work habits.

A supervisor may learn that one or more employees had been candidates for the supervisor's job and therefore may be jealous. One constructive approach that a supervisor might take to this problem is to acknowledge the other person's feelings, to ask for the employee's support, and to discuss his or her long-term goals. Marie Davis of IDS Financial Services did this with a staff member who had applied for the same job for which Davis was chosen. The staff member said that her goal was to "break into management." Davis says, "I told her, without making false promises, that I would do what I could to help her." Until this employee moved into a management job six months later, she was one of the top performers among Davis's employees.[16] An important aspect of this approach is that the supervisor is helping employees to meet or exceed their own goals. For example, a sales supervisor can help a potentially jealous salesperson increase sales. Hugh Allen, a sales executive with Lawson Products, says that "you shouldn't be surprised that employees regard you as a much better manager when you help them make more money."[17]

## Obtaining and Using Power and Authority

To carry out his or her job, a supervisor needs not only knowledge but also power (the ability to do certain things) and authority (the right to do certain things). To acquire power upon assuming the job of supervisor, it may help to have the new supervisor's boss make an official announcement of the promotion.[18] When accepting the job, a supervisor can ask his or her boss to announce the promotion at a meeting of the employees. There the supervisor can take the opportunity to state his or her expectations, desire to work as a team, and interest in hearing about work-related problems.

A new supervisor should not rush to make changes in the department, but should first understand how the department works and what employees expect. Making changes quickly and without seeking their input can alienate employees and put them on the defensive. The supervisor can build support for change by introducing it gradually after inviting suggestions where appropriate.

(Chapter 7 discusses the delegation of authority. Chapter 15 covers sources and types of power along with more information about managing change.)

## Characteristics of a Successful Supervisor

Unfortunately, many of us have worked for someone who seemed to stifle our best efforts or to anger us with unfair decisions. Many of us also have worked for a supervisor who taught us new skills, inspired us to do better than we thought possible, or made us look forward to going to work each day. What is behind the success of this second category of supervisors? Figure 1.4 illustrates some characteristics of successful supervisors. Take the Self-Quiz on page 23 to see whether supervising is a good fit with your current traits and interests. (See also "Tips from the Firing Line.")

A successful supervisor has a *positive attitude*. Employees tend to reflect the attitudes of the people in charge. When the supervisor's attitude toward work and the organization is positive, employees are more likely to be satisfied with and interested in their work. Furthermore, managers and co-workers alike prefer working with someone who has a positive attitude.

Successful supervisors are *loyal*. As a part of the management team, they must take actions that are best for the organization. This may include making decisions that are unpopular with employees. In such situations, supervisors must recognize that taking on a supervisory job means they cannot always be "one of the gang."

Successful supervisors are *fair*. Supervisors who play favorites or behave inconsistently will lose the support and respect of their employees, and thus not be able to lead effectively. Furthermore, when supervisors make assignments and decisions based on those they like best, they will not necessarily make the assignments and decisions best suited to the organization. Another aspect of being fair is to follow the rules yourself. The supervisor can set a good example, for example, by being on time and refraining from doing personal work on the job or taking supplies home.

Supervisors also need to be *good communicators*.[19] Employees and bosses alike depend on the supervisor to keep them informed of what is going on. Employees who receive clear guidance about what is expected of them will not only perform better but also will be more satisfied with their jobs. Good communication also includes making contact with employees each day and listening to what they have to say. (Chapter 10 takes an in-depth look at the communications skills that supervisors need to develop.)

**FIGURE 1.4**

**Characteristics of a Successful Supervisor**

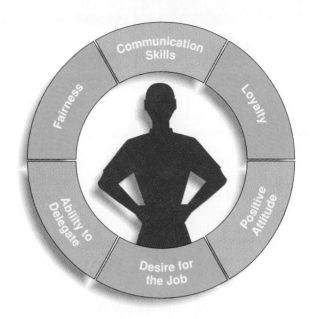

To be successful, supervisors must be *able to delegate;* that is, to give their employees authority and responsibility to carry out activities. As supervisors tend to have excellent technical skills, delegating may be a challenge. They may resist giving an assignment to an employee who may not carry it out as easily or as well as they, the supervisors, could do. Nevertheless, supervisors cannot do the work of the whole department. Therefore, they must assign work to employees. Equally important, a supervisor should give employees credit for their accomplishments. This, in turn, makes the supervisor look good; the employees' successes show that the supervisor is able to select and motivate employees as well as delegate effectively. (Chapter 7 discusses delegation in greater detail.)

Finally, a successful supervisor must *want the job.* Some people are happier carrying out the technical skills of their field, whether it is carpentry, respiratory therapy, or financial management. People who prefer this type of work to the functions of managing will probably be happier if they turn down an opportunity to become a supervisor. In contrast, people who enjoy the challenge of making plans and inspiring others to achieve goals are more likely to be effective supervisors.

## About This Book

This book introduces the many kinds of activities supervisors must carry out to accomplish their overall objective of seeing that employees contribute toward achieving the organization's goals. Part One is devoted to a broad view of the supervisor's role. Chapter 1 serves as an introduction to the general activities and responsibilities of supervisors.

## TIPS FROM THE FIRING LINE

### The Manager of the Future

What will the business owner or manager who is successful at leading a diverse workforce look like in the year 2000 and beyond? *Nation's Business* put that question to diversity experts and to businesspeople who are already managing diverse employee pools.

The successful managers of tomorrow, they said, will:

Be multilingual. Even if they are not fluent in other languages, they will understand enough of another language or two to feel comfortable around people who do not speak English.

Be well-traveled. "They have interacted with world cultures by going to other countries," says George Henderson, chairman of the Department of Human Relations at the University of Oklahoma, in Norman.

Be well-read. "They will have read not only the great literature of the dominant culture but also will be conversant with and familiar with the great literatures of a wide range of ethnic minority cultures," says Henderson.

Feel comfortable crossing cultural lines. They will establish relationships and friendships with individuals outside their own culture that go beyond business relationships.

Be open-minded. That means "being willing to break from the past, being willing to do things that have never been done before, and to see people like you've never seen them before," says Ann M. Morrison, president of the New Leaders Institute, a consulting and research firm in Del Mar, California.

Demonstrate commitment and fairness to employees. They must be able to see that opportunities for advancement are open to all employees and that standards and expectations will be applied equally to all.

Source: Reprinted by permissions, "The Manager of the Future," *Nation's Business*, June 1995, p. 27. Copyright 1995, U.S. Chamber of Commerce.

Part Two describes the challenges modern supervisors face in meeting their responsibilities. Ever-higher expectations of customers, business owners, and the general public have made high quality a necessary concern of employees at all levels, including the supervisory level. Therefore, Chapter 2 addresses how supervisors can understand and carry out their role in maintaining and constantly improving quality. Chapter 3 covers groups and teamwork, reflecting the increasingly common role of the supervisor as a team leader. Supervisors (and others in the organization) also must consider the ethical implications of their decisions, the topic of Chapter 4. Technological change also is transforming the workplace and the supervisor's role at an ever-faster pace. The nature of recent developments and their implications for supervisors are the topic of Chapter 5.

Part Three takes a deeper look at the supervisory functions introduced earlier in this chapter. Chapter 6 discusses how supervisors use planning and controlling to enable their work groups to reach goals and objectives. Chapter 7 covers the function of organizing, including supervisors' use of delegation to share authority and responsibility. Chapter 8 examines the supervisor's role in carrying out the management function of leading. Chapter 9 explains how supervisors can be effective at solving problems and making decisions.

Part Four describes skills needed by supervisors in all kinds of organizations. Individual chapters cover ways supervisors can communicate, motivate

To be a successful supervisor, you must want the job. A Roper poll found that only 27 percent of Americans were highly satisfied with their jobs. Brenda Casabona (*photo*) left a high-paying job as an international economist for the Commerce Department in Washington, D.C., to supervise her own chocolate shop: DeFluri's Decadent Desserts and Chocolates. Casabona reports that she works 65 hours or more per week, but "A lot of times I'll look up and think . . . five hours couldn't have passed."

Source: © Mark Tucker

their employees, improve productivity, supervise "problem" employees, manage time and stress, and manage conflict and change. These skills are important at all levels of management and in all types of organizations.

The last part of this book addresses activities related to managing the organization's human resources: its employees. Chapter 16 covers the supervisor's role in selecting new employees. Chapter 17 discusses the process of training new and current employees. Chapter 18 describes how supervisors appraise employees' performance. Finally, Chapter 19 introduces some of the many government laws and regulations that guide supervisors' roles and decisions with regard to human resources.

Throughout the book, the chapters include special features designed to help you apply the principles of supervision to the practice of supervising real people in a real organization. These features include "Tips from the Firing Line" and "Meeting the Challenge," which discuss actual examples of modern supervisory challenges—quality, teamwork, ethics, and technology—as well as provide practical tips on effective supervision. Chapter-opening stories and end-of-chapter cases show how real supervisors and organizations have approached the issues covered in the chapter.

An end-of-book notes section, divided by chapter, provides source and additional reading material for various topics covered within the chapters. The glossary at the end of this text provides a quick reference for all key terms. For review, each definition is followed by the number of the page where the boldfaced key term is defined.

The Applications Modules at the end of each chapter contain self-assessments, skill-building exercises, role-playing exercises, information applications, and miniature case studies. These allow you to use text concepts and develop leadership abilities.

At the end of this text, a reference guide discusses issues related to building and managing your career. The reference guide describes some basics of planning a career and includes exercises to help you plan your own career and write a résumé.

# Summary

**1.1 Define what a supervisor is.**
A supervisor is a manager at the first level of management. That is, the employees reporting to the supervisor are not themselves managers.

**1.2 Describe the basic types of supervisory skills.**
The basic supervisory skills are technical, human relations, conceptual, and decision-making skills. Technical skills are the specialized knowledge and experience used to carry out particular techniques or procedures. Human relations skills enable the supervisor to work effectively with other people. Conceptual skills enable the supervisor to see the relation of the parts to the whole and to one another. Decision-making skills are needed to analyze information and reach good decisions.

**1.3 Describe how the growing diversity of the workforce affects the supervisor's role.**
Compared with the current makeup of the U.S. workforce, an increasingly large share of employees will be female, nonwhite, and older. As a result, supervisors in the future will typically manage a more diverse group of employees. This means that supervisors can benefit from a greater variety of talents and viewpoints, but it also requires them to draw on more sophisticated human relations skills than in the past.

**1.4 Identify the general functions of a supervisor.**
The general functions of a supervisor are planning, organizing, staffing, leading, and controlling. Planning involves setting goals and determining how to meet them. Organizing is determining how to set up the group, allocate resources, and assign work to achieve goals. Staffing consists of identifying, hiring, and developing the necessary number and quality of employees. Leading is the function of getting employees to do what is expected of them. Controlling consists of monitoring performance and making needed corrections.

**1.5 Explain how supervisors are responsible to higher management, employees, and co-workers.**
Supervisors are responsible for doing the work assigned to them by higher management and for keeping management informed of the department's progress. They link higher management to the employees. Supervisors are responsible for treating employees fairly, making instructions clear, and bringing employee concerns to higher management. Organizations that have undergone restructuring or reengineering often make supervisors responsible for empowering and enabling employees instead of focusing on command and control. Supervisors are responsible for cooperating with co-workers in other departments. Organizations hold supervisors accountable for meeting these various responsibilities.

**1.6 Describe the typical background of someone who is promoted to supervisor.**
Most supervisors begin as employees in the department they now supervise. They usually have superior technical skills and may have seniority or demonstrate leadership potential.

**1.7 Identify characteristics of a successful supervisor.**
A successful supervisor is usually someone who has a positive attitude, is loyal, is fair, communicates well, can delegate, and wants the job.

## Key Terms

| | | |
|---|---|---|
| supervisor | decision-making skills | leading |
| technical skills | planning | controlling |
| human relations skills | organizing | accountability |
| conceptual skills | staffing | |

## Review and Discussion Questions

1. What are some ways that a supervisor's job is similar to that of managers at other levels? How does a supervisor's job differ from that of other managers?

2. Identify whether each of the following skills is a technical skill, a human relations skill, a conceptual skill, or a decision-making skill.

   a. The ability to communicate well with one's manager.
   b. The ability to create advertisements that grab people's attention.
   c. The ability to select the most appropriate safety training program for the housekeeping staff.
   d. The ability to see the big picture in order to understand a situation fully.
   e. Knowledge of how to machine a part without unnecessary changes in the setup of equipment.

3. Imagine that you have just been promoted to supervisor of the cashiers in a supermarket. List specific technical, human relations, conceptual, and decision-making skills you think you might need to succeed at this job. How might you develop them continually to achieve the job of store manager?

4. Population trends suggest that the workforce will become increasingly diverse. What are some advantages of greater diversity? What challenges does it pose to the supervisor?

5. What are the basic functions of a supervisor? On which functions do supervisors spend most of their time?

6. As the controlling function changes in many organizations, supervisors should no longer control by dictating solutions. How do they carry out the controlling function?

7. What responsibilities do supervisors have to each of these groups?

   a. Higher management
   b. The employees they supervise
   c. Co-workers in other departments

8. Emma has just been promoted to office manager in a small real estate office. Some of the people she will supervise are her former peers; she is aware that one of them also applied for the office manager's job. How can Emma prepare for her new position? What might be the best way to approach the co-worker who did not get the manager's job?

9. What are some ways a new supervisor can use power and authority effectively?

10. List the characteristics of a good supervisor. Besides the characteristics mentioned in the chapter, add any others you believe are important. Draw on your own experiences as an employee and/or supervisor.

### A SECOND LOOK

What steps might UPS take to prepare supervisors for their new responsibilities as a result of reengineering?

# APPLICATIONS MODULE

## CASE

### Two Supervisors' Tales

Joyce Gurtatowski and John David are both supervisors, but their jobs look quite different on the surface. Gurtatowski is an assistant vice-president with La Salle Bank Matteson in Calumet City, Illinois. She supervises six personal bankers. David is a senior property manager for Standard Parking. He supervises 30 employees in several parking garages in Chicago.

On a typical day, Gurtatowski arrives at the bank at about 7:30 A.M. She begins her day with paperwork such as auditing department accounts. When the bank is open for business, she spends much of her time answering questions from personal bankers and tellers about nonroutine customer problems and questions. According to Gurtatowski, "Every customer is a new situation," and that variety is what poses challenges to her employees—and what makes her own job interesting. From the time the bank lobby closes (at 3:00 P.M. on most days) until she leaves at about 5:30 P.M., Gurtatowski returns phone calls from customers and prepares her department schedule for the next day. In addition, she trains staff members at weekly meetings and conducts performance appraisals.

David spends about 60 percent of his day with people, both customers and employees. He devotes most of his time with employees to follow-up: to see that they are carrying out instructions. Most of the remainder of David's day is taken up with paperwork, including monthly parking accounts, market analyses, and efforts related to marketing the garages. David finds working with employees particularly interesting and challenging because they come from many countries, including Ethiopia, Kuwait, Ghana, Pakistan, and Nigeria, as well as the United States. Sometimes, the cultural differences of the employees mandates special training for serving American customers. For example, an employee from Ethiopia would speak in a monotone, a tone of voice that shows respect in his culture. David had to train this employee to speak more enthusiastically to American customers.

1. Which supervisory skills seem to be most important to Gurtatowski's and David's jobs? Why?
2. What types of responsibilities does each undertake?
3. Do you think Gurtatowski and David are examples of successful supervisors? Why or why not?

## SELF-QUIZ

### *Is Supervising Right for You?*

Answer each of the following questions Yes or No.

|  | Yes | No |
|---|---|---|
| 1. Do you consider yourself a highly ambitious person? | _____ | _____ |
| 2. Do you sincerely like people and have patience with them? | _____ | _____ |
| 3. Could you assume the responsibility of decision making? | _____ | _____ |
| 4. Is making more money very important to you? | _____ | _____ |
| 5. Would recognition from others be more important to you than taking pride in doing a detailed job well? | _____ | _____ |
| 6. Would you enjoy learning about psychology and human behavior? | _____ | _____ |
| 7. Would you be happier with more responsibility? | _____ | _____ |
| 8. Would you rather work with problems involving human relationships than with mechanical, computational, creative, clerical, or similar problems? | _____ | _____ |
| 9. Do you desire an opportunity to demonstrate your leadership ability? | _____ | _____ |
| 10. Do you desire the freedom to do your own planning rather than being told what to do? | _____ | _____ |
| **Total** | _____ | _____ |

Give yourself one point for each Yes answer. If your score is 6 or more, you might be happy as a supervisor. If your score was 5 or less, you should think hard about your preferences and strengths before jumping into a supervisory job.

Source: *Supervisor's Survival Kit: Your First Step Into Management*, p.5, by Elwood N. Chapman.© 1993. Reprinted by permissions of Prentice-Hall, Inc., Upper Saddle River, NJ.

### *Class Exercise*

Create a customized panel discussion for your class. Use one of these options:

1. List the different kinds of organizations and departments in which class members work. Select a few, and have students volunteer to ask their supervisor to visit the class to participate.
2. Class members who are supervisors may volunteer to be on the panel. If possible, use class members from a variety of types of organizations or departments.
3. The instructor may select and invite people to be on a panel.

Have the members of the panel sit in the front of the classroom. Invite each panel member to give a brief description of his or her job. Then students may ask questions of the panel members. Here are some ideas for questions:

- What do you do in the course of a typical day?
- How much of your time is spent working with people?
- What is the hardest part of your job?
- What is the most satisfying part of your job?
- Do you participate in each of the management functions (planning, organizing, staffing, leading, controlling)?

## *Team-Building Exercise**

## Performing Supervisory Functions

### *Instructions*

1. Imagine you are the supervisor in each scenario described and you have to decide which supervisory function(s) you would use in each.
2. Many of the scenarios require more than one function. The "Answer" column lists the number of functions your answer should include. Mark your answers using the following codes:

| Code | Supervisory Function | Brief Description |
|---|---|---|
| **P** | Planning | Setting goals and determining how to meet them |
| **O** | Organizing | Determining how to set up the group, allocate resources, and assign work to achieve goals |
| **S** | Staffing | Identifying, hiring, and developing the necessary number and quality of employees |
| **L** | Leading | Getting employees to do what is expected of them |
| **C** | Controlling | Monitoring performance and making needed corrections |

3. As a class, compare and discuss your answers and the reasoning you used in determining them.

### *Scenarios*

Your group's work is centered on a project that is due in two months. Although everyone is working on the project, you believe that your subordinates are involved in excessive socializing and other time-consuming behaviors. You decide to meet with the group to have the members help you break down the project into smaller subprojects with minideadlines. You believe that this will help keep the group members focused on the project and that the quality of the finished project will then reflect the true capabilities of your group.

### *Answer(s)*
(four functions)

1. _____

Your first impression of the new group you will be supervising is not too great. You tell your friend at dinner after your first day on the job: "Looks like I got a babysitting job instead of a supervisory job."

(three functions)

2. _____

Your boss asks your opinion about promoting Andy to a supervisory position. Andy is one of your most competent and efficient workers. Knowing that Andy lacks leadership skills in many key areas, you decide not to recommend him at this time. Instead you tell your boss you will work with Andy to help him develop his leadership skills so that the next time an opportunity for promotion occurs, Andy will be prepared to consider it.

(one function)

3. _____

You begin a meeting of your work group by letting the members know that a major procedure the group has been using for the past two years is being significantly revamped. Your department will have to phase in the change during the

(three functions)

4. _____

* This team-building exercises was prepared by Corinne Livesay, Belhaven College, Jackson, Mississippi.

next six weeks. You proceed by explaining the reasoning management gave you for this change. You then say, "Take the next five to ten minutes to voice your reactions to this change." The majority of comments are critical of the change. You say, "I appreciate each of you sharing your reactions; I, too, recognize that *all* change creates problems. However, either we can spend the remaining 45 minutes of our meeting focusing on why we don't want the change and why we don't think it's necessary, or we can work together to come up with viable solutions to solve the problems that implementing this change will most likely create." After five more minutes of an exchange of comments, the consensus of the group is that they should spend the remainder of the meeting focusing on how to deal with the potential problems that may arise from implementing the new procedure.

(one function)

5. _____

You are preparing the annual budget allocation meetings to be held in the plant manager's office next week. You decide to present a strong case to support your department's getting money for some high-tech equipment that will help your employees do their jobs better. You will stand firm against any suggestions of budget cuts in your area.

(two functions)

6. _____

Early in your career you learned an important lesson about employee selection. One of the nurses on your floor unexpectedly quit. The other nurses pressured you to fill the position quickly because they were overworked even before the nurse left. After a hasty recruitment effort, you made a decision based on insufficient information. You regretted your quick decision during the three months of problems that followed, until you finally had to discharge the new hire. Since that time, you have never let anybody pressure you into making a quick hiring decision.

## *Team-Building Exercise*

## Building Teams with Supervisory Skills

In Chapter 1 ("The Role of the Supervisor"), you learned to categorize the different skills that supervisors use in order to decide which skills apply to any given situation. Here you will apply your knowledge of these skill categories to several team-building situations.

### *Instructions*

Imagine that you are the supervisor in each of the following situations. On the line provided at the end of each situation, write which of the following skills will best help you to build a team: technical, human relations, conceptual, decision making. Each situation requires more than one skill.

1. As the supervisor of a group of production workers in a plant that manufactures parts for telephones, you have been asked by upper management to join a team of supervisors from different departments. Your objective will be to investigate ways to improve the time required to fill large orders from major customers. Which two skills do you think will be most important to you on this team?

_____

2.  You supervise 20 telephone operators on the night shift at a mail-order catalog company. You used to be an operator yourself, so you know a great deal about the job. Management has been pressing you and other supervisors to reduce the amount of time operators spend on the telephone with each order. You believe that a potentially negative situation for your employees can be solved in a friendly competition between two teams of operators. There are no punishments for the team that comes in second, but there is a reward for the team that wins. Team members are encouraged to find new ways to reduce telephone time without reducing customer satisfaction. Which two skills do you think would be most important as you get your teams up and running?

    _____

3.  You are a supervisor in the engineering department and a member of a team that includes people from production, finance, marketing, and engineering. After conducting marketing research, your team must determine whether to recommend that your company expand its operations overseas. Which three skills do you think would be most important in your contribution to the team?

    _____

# Video Exercise 1: *The Role of the Supervisor*

### Video Summary

This video program follows Joann Wilson, assistant store manager at the Handy Andy Home Improvement Centers, throughout a typical day. You can observe how Joann fulfills her supervisory role by applying her technical, human relations, conceptual, and decision-making skills to accomplish the supervisory functions of planning, organizing, staffing, leading, and controlling.

### Application

After viewing the video, identify the primary skill being utilized by checking the appropriate column next to each Video Item listed in the left-hand column.

| Video Item | Human Relations Skill | Conceptual Skill | Technical Skill | Decision-Making Skill |
|---|---|---|---|---|
| 1. Joann is responsible for translating into action the goals and objectives set by top management. | | | | |
| 2. Joann hires qualified employees to fill open positions. | | | | |
| 3. Shorlanda Green, senior cashier: "She's always there for little pep talks." | | | | |
| 4. Handy Andy customers want someone to be there to answer questions they have. | | | | |
| 5. Joann gives her employees on-the-job training on everything from how to receive merchandise into the store to how to move it out the door after its sale to a customer. | | | | |
| 6. Casey Griffin, locksmith: "Joann's style is unique. She has a kind of playful style, but when it's time to get serious, then it's time to get serious. . ." She makes it very fun to come in and work. | | | | |
| 7. When a problem arises, Joann uses the feedback she gets from her control system to determine the adjustments she needs to make to ensure success. | | | | |
| 8. Joann Wilson: "I've learned that giving responsibility [to my employees] . . . gives those who work for me an opportunity to know that I trust them to make decisions. It builds up their level of confidence so they can perhaps become a manager sometime in the future." | | | | |
| 9. Joann determines which duties and tasks to assign to which staff members. | | | | |
| 10. Joann provides the information and instruction that workers require to accomplish performance goals. | | | | |

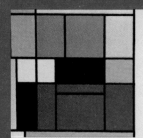

**PART TWO**

*Modern Supervision Challenges*

# 2

*Quality is never an accident; it is always the result of intelligent effort.*
   **—John Ruskin, 19th-century English essayist and proponent of quality craftsmanship**

# Ensuring High Quality

### LEARNING OBJECTIVES

After you have studied this chapter, you should be able to:

2.1  Describe consequences suffered by organizations as a result of poor-quality work.

2.2  Compare product quality control and process control.

2.3  Identify techniques for quality control.

2.4  Explain how employee involvement teams work and what makes them successful.

2.5  Describe principles for successfully using total quality management.

2.6  Identify ways organizations measure their success in continuous quality improvement.

2.7  Discuss guidelines for quality control.

Source: © George Mayernik

## BETTER—NOT BIGGER—MEANS QUALITY AT HIGHLAND PARK MARKETS

Customers who walk into each of the two Highland Park Markets in Connecticut are treated to gently curving deli shelves jammed with sliced meats and cheeses, rotisserie chicken, bulging sandwiches, and artichoke salad. At the meat counter, premium meats are wrapped to order. In the bakery, pastries, cookies, and breads rest in their own black-and-gold cardboard boxes with the Highland Park Markets logo. The small Highland Park Markets don't try to compete with warehouse supermarkets on price; instead, they offer quality in both products and service. "We try to get to a level higher than our competition," says Tim DeVanney, co-owner of Highland Park. This strategy not only helped the stores survive through a recession, but has actually helped the business grow.

DeVanney pays close attention to his staff and its interaction with customers. He believes that the success of his stores hinges on the way the staff serves customers. "Most people aren't loyal anymore," he admits. "But they are if you give them a reason to be. We feel as though we give them a reason to be." For instance, the meat, seafood, and poultry department has no self-service; each order is individually wrapped for a customer. "Our staff is phenomenal," boasts DeVanney. "They feel real comfortable and they love dealing with customers." DeVanney also puts his money where his mouth is, paying his staff higher wages than what might be considered customary at a supermarket.

Each of the two Highland Park Markets has its own kitchen and chef—for baking, creating fresh, packaged entrees, and the like—but DeVanney hopes to create a central kitchen so that his in-store staff can spend even *more* time serving customers. He also believes that customers look for consistency in his food products; a central kitchen would help achieve that.

As a supervisor, Tim DeVanney knows that his greatest resource is a staff that is motivated to wrap each steak with a smile. "You know, the biggest isn't always the best," he muses. "We feel as though we're the best, but we're by no means the biggest. Not even close." Staying small may actually help Highland Park Markets succeed.

Source: Kevin Coupe, "Not Bigger . . . But Better," *Progressive Grocer*, Aug. 1994, pp. 131–32.

At Highland Park Markets, the entire staff works hard to deliver high-quality products and customer service. A logical way to understand the meaning of *high quality* is to think of it as work that meets or exceeds customers' expectations. Table 2.1 describes eight dimensions that can be used to measure the quality of goods or services.

Many of the supervisor's activities, including planning, leading, and controlling, are directed toward improving the quality of the organization's goods and services. This chapter considers the supervisor's role in maintaining and improving quality. The chapter begins with a description of the consequences of poor quality. Then the types of quality-control efforts and several techniques for quality control are introduced, followed by an explanation of how managers at all levels can measure whether they are improving quality and meeting high-quality standards. Finally, some general guidelines for maintaining and improving quality are discussed.

# Consequences of Poor Quality

Like employees at all levels, supervisors must care about quality. They must care because poor quality limits the organization's access to resources and raises its costs.

## Limited Resources

When the quality of an organization's goods or services is poor, the whole organization suffers. As word spreads about problems with the product, customers look for alternatives. The organization develops a negative image, which drives away customers and clients. The organization loses business and therefore revenues, and it also has more difficulty attracting other important resources. An organization with a poor reputation has a harder time recruiting superior employees and borrowing money at favorable terms.

The potential for lost business has become a major competitive challenge for the cable TV industry. Cable companies have suffered from a reputation for shoddy service, including late or missed appointments for installation or repairs. Furthermore, customer surveys have shown greater consumer satisfaction with telephone service than with cable service at a time when the regional phone companies are expected to become direct competitors with cable operators. Troubled by these developments, the cable industry has begun offering service guarantees and has launched an advertising campaign.[1]

## Higher Costs

Poor-quality work can also lead to higher costs. Some managers might think it expensive to ensure that things are done right the first time. But the reality is that businesses spend billions of dollars each year on inspections, errors, rework, repairs, customer refunds, and other costs to find and correct mistakes.[2] Attracting new customers costs several times more per customer than keeping customers satisfied, so marketing costs are higher, too. Thus, poor quality often results in much wasted time and materials, besides requiring that unacceptable items be fixed or discarded. If the problems remain undetected until after the goods have been sold, the manufacturer may have to recall its products for repair or replacement. In addition, poor goods and services may result in lawsuits by disgruntled or injured customers.

**TABLE 2.1**
**Dimensions of Quality**

| Dimension | Explanation |
|---|---|
| Performance | The product's primary operating characteristic, such as an automobile's acceleration or the picture clarity of a television set |
| Features | Supplements to the product's basic operating characteristics—for example, power windows on a car or the ceremony with which a bottle of wine is opened in a restaurant |
| Reliability | The probability that the product will function properly and not break down during a specified period—a manufacturer's warranty is often seen as an indicator of this |
| Conformance | The degree to which the product's design and operating characteristics meet established standards, such as safety standards for a baby's crib |
| Durability | The length of the product's life—for example, whether a stereo lasts for 5 years or 25 years. |
| Serviceability | The speed and ease of repairing the product—for example, whether a computer store will send out a repairperson, service the computer in the store, or provide no maintenance service at all |
| Aesthetics | The way the product looks, feels, tastes, and smells, such as the styling and smell of a new car |
| Perceived quality | The customer's impression of the product's quality, such as a buyer's belief that an Audi is a safe and reliable car |

Source: Adapted from David A. Garvin, "Competing on the Eight Dimensions of Quality," *Harvard Business Review,* Nov.–Dec. 1987.

A pair of examples illustrate the high costs of poor quality.[3] First, Harper's Index reported that among patients admitted to a hospital, 1 in 25 will leave with a disabling injury that directly results from treatment. Second, congressional investigators reported that the Pentagon stores hospital supplies and perishable items for such a long time that many must be discarded. At the Pentagon's hospitals and clinics, $18 million a year is wasted on drugs alone.

These kinds of issues extend to the services that one department in the organization provides to the other departments. For example, if the maintenance crew or the payroll department does a poor job, the overall work of the organization suffers. Morale may decline. Employees may find that they spend a lot of time making up for the lapses of others.

## Types of Quality Control

**quality control**
An organization's efforts to prevent or correct defects in its goods or services or to improve them in some way.

Because of the negative consequences of poor quality, organizations try to prevent and correct such problems through various approaches to quality control. (See "Meeting the Challenge.") Broadly speaking, **quality control** refers to an organization's efforts to prevent or correct defects in its goods or services or to improve them in some way. Some organizations use the term *quality control* to refer only to error detection, while *quality assurance* refers to both the prevention and the detection of quality problems. However, *quality control* in the broader sense will be used in this chapter because it is the more common term.

## Technology and Quality Control

How can a computer decide whether a chocolate chip cookie tastes as good as it should? Debbi Fields, founder of Mrs. Fields Cookies, found a way to use a computer to ensure product quality even in the Mrs. Fields Cookies stores in locations farther away than she could visit regularly. In 1980, Fields visited the Hawaii store and found that the cookies tasted nothing like her original recipe. "They looked like little cakes," she recalls. The store's baker had allowed the recipe to shift slightly each day until the cookies had become an entirely different product that did not conform to the company's quality standards. Customers who develop loyalty to foods such as Mrs. Fields Cookies, McDonald's cheeseburgers, and Ben & Jerry's ice cream expect consistency in the products wherever they shop; Debbi Fields had to find a way to give her customers the value they wanted in the form of product quality. She ultimately discovered computer software that tells managers everything they need to know about their products' quality—at a low cost.

Other businesses have used this type of software to maintain both product and process quality. At a national chain of pizza restaurants, employees clock in and out of work on a computer instead of a manual punch clock. The computer compiles and transmits this data daily to the company's headquarters, relieving individual restaurant managers from having to tabulate the data themselves. How does this improve quality? The managers no longer waste valuable time doing unnecessary paperwork; instead, they spend more time supervising employees.

A retailer learned that its employees (usually store managers) had to fill out and wade through 260 forms companywide to keep the business running. The same information might appear on several forms, sometimes sent to the same people, sometimes not. Thus, there was not only overlap in information received, but also a gap in information received—and plenty of wasted time filling out forms. When the information concerned sales, the confusion and time lag could prove disastrous for a company trying to create value for its customers. So the company automated its reporting process, cutting the number of forms to 50. Reports were distributed electronically, and information was accessible to everyone. After automation, store managers were able to increase the time they spent on activities that directly affected customers.

Technology can help supervisors do the job they were hired to do: supervise employees and processes in a way that boosts quality and creates greater value for customers. It can even tell if a cookie contains enough chocolate chips.

Source: Randall Fields and Nicholas Imparato, "Cost, Competition & Cookies," *Management Review,* Apr. 1995, pp. 57–61.

---

Whichever term is used, many organizations—especially large ones—have a department or employee devoted to identifying defects and promoting high quality. In these cases, the supervisor can benefit from the expertise of quality-control personnel. Ultimately, however, the organization expects its supervisors to take responsibility for the quality of work in their department.

In general, when supervisors look for high-quality performance to reinforce or improvements to make, they can focus on two areas: the product itself or the process of making and delivering the product. These two orientations are illustrated in Figure 2.1.

## Product Quality Control

**product quality control** Quality control that focuses on ways to improve the product itself.

An organization that focuses on ways to improve the product itself is using **product quality control.** For example, employees in a print shop might examine a sample of newsletters or envelopes to look for smudges and other defects. A city's park district might consider ways to upgrade its playground equipment or to improve the programs it offers senior citizens.

**FIGURE 2.1**

**Types of Quality Control**

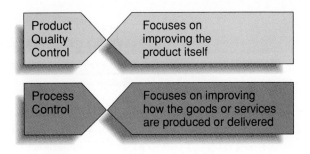

### Process Control

**process control**
Quality control that emphasizes how to do things in a way that leads to better quality.

An organization might also consider how to do things in a way that leads to better quality. This focus is called **process control.** The print shop, for example, might conduct periodic checks to make sure its employees understand good techniques for setting up the presses. The park district might ask the maintenance crew to suggest ways to keep the parks cleaner and more attractive. In this way, the park district can improve the process by which the crew members do their job.

A broad approach to process control involves creating an organizational climate that encourages quality. From the day they are hired, employees at all levels should understand that quality is important and that they have a role in delivering high quality. In our city park district example, managers and employees might consider ways to be more responsive to citizens' input. The greater responsiveness, in turn, could enable park district employees to recognize ways to better serve the community.

## Techniques for Quality Control

Within this broad framework, managers, researchers, and consultants have identified several quality-control techniques, including statistical quality control, the zero-defects approach, employee involvement teams, and total quality management. Figure 2.2 summarizes these techniques.

In choosing a technique—or, more commonly, applying the techniques selected by higher-level management—supervisors need to remember that a technique alone does not guarantee high quality. Rather, these techniques work when the people who use them are well motivated, understand how to use them, and exercise creativity in solving problems. In the words of Boston Consulting Group's Jeanie Duck, "These [techniques] are all tools, like a computer. But a computer is not the answer, it is the tool we use to create the answer."[4]

### Statistical Quality Control

It rarely makes economic sense to examine every part, finished good, or service to make sure it meets quality standards. For one thing, that approach to quality control is expensive. Furthermore, examining some products, such as packages of cheese or boxes of tissues, can destroy them. Therefore, unless the costs of

FIGURE 2.2

**Quality-Control Techniques**

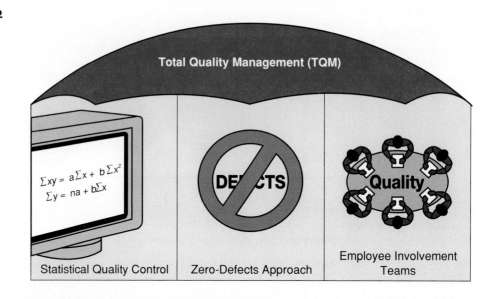

Total Quality Management (TQM)

$$\Sigma xy = a\Sigma x + b\Sigma x^2$$
$$\Sigma y = na + b\Sigma x$$

DEFECTS

Quality

Statistical Quality Control  |  Zero-Defects Approach  |  Employee Involvement Teams

**statistical quality control**

Looking for defects in parts or finished products selected through a sampling technique.

**statistical process control (SPC)**

A statistical quality-control technique using statistics to monitor production quality on an ongoing basis and making corrections whenever the results show the process is out of control.

poor quality are so great that every product must be examined, most organizations inspect only a sample. Looking for defects in parts, finished goods, or other outcomes selected through a sampling technique is known as **statistical quality control.**

The most accurate way to apply statistical quality control is to use a random sample. This means selecting outcomes (such as parts or customer contacts) in a way that each has an equal chance of being selected. The assumption is that the quality of the sample describes the quality of the entire lot. Thus, if 2 percent of the salad dressing bottles in a sample have leaks, presumably 2 percent of all the bottles coming off the assembly line have leaks. Or if 65 percent of customers surveyed report they were treated courteously, presumably about 65 percent of all customers feel that way.

Rather than wait until a process is complete to take a random sample, the operators of a process can use statistics to monitor production quality on an ongoing basis. This quality-control technique is known as **statistical process control (SPC).** The operator periodically measures some aspect of what he or she is producing—say, the diameter of a hole drilled or the correctness of an account number entered into a computer—then plots the results on a control chart such as the simplified one shown in Figure 2.3. The middle line in the chart shows the value that represents the standard—in this case, the mean (average). Above and below the mean value are lines representing the acceptable upper and lower limits. When a measured value falls between these limits, the operator may assume the process is working normally. When a value falls outside these limits, the operator is supposed to correct the process.

Thus, if a machine operator is supposed to make a part 0.0375 inch in diameter (the mean value in this case), the lower and upper limits might be 0.0370 inch and 0.0380 inch, respectively. If the operator measures a part and finds that its diameter is 0.0383 inch, the operator would adjust the machine or modify his or her

**FIGURE 2.3**

**Chart Used for Statistical Process Control**

Source: *Industrial Supervision In the Age of High Technology*, p.466, by David L. Goetsch, © 1992. Reprinted by permission of Prentice-Hall, Inc., Upper Saddle River, NJ.

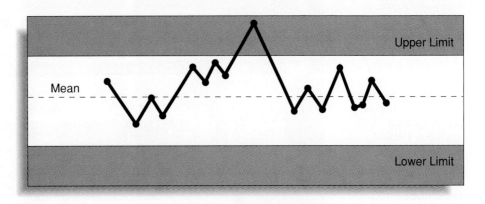

Upper Limit

Mean

Lower Limit

actions to keep such errors from recurring. The measurements in Figure 2.3 indicate that the operator made some needed adjustments after one measurement exceeded the upper limit. After that point, the measurements are clustered much closer to the mean; the process is again under control. Clearly, SPC gives the operator a great deal of control in maintaining quality, so the task does not need to be assigned to specialized personnel. That is one reason SPC is increasingly popular today, especially in manufacturing firms.

The idea of using SPC or other statistical methods makes some supervisors nervous. They worry that they or their employees will be unable to handle the statistics. However, the process requires only a basic knowledge of statistics, coupled with an understanding of what level of quality is desirable and achievable. The supervisor should see that employees get the training they need in using the SPC technique and in adjusting the processes for which they are responsible. (Chapter 17 describes the supervisor's role in employee training.)

## Zero-Defects Approach

**zero-defects approach** A quality-control technique based on the view that everyone in the organization should work toward the goal of delivering such high quality that all aspects of the organization's goods and services are free of problems.

A broad view of process quality control is that everyone in the organization should work toward the goal of delivering such a high degree of quality that all aspects of the organization's goods and services are free of problems. The quality-control technique based on this view is known as the **zero-defects approach.** An organization that uses the zero-defects approach would have products of excellent quality not only because the people who produce them are seeking ways to avoid defects, but also because the purchasing department is ensuring a timely supply of well-crafted parts or supplies, the accounting department is seeing that bills get paid on time, the human resources department is helping to find and train highly qualified personnel, and so on.

Thus, in implementing a zero-defects approach, managers and employees at all levels seek to build quality into every aspect of their work. To do so, employees work with supervisors and other managers in setting goals for quality and in identifying areas where improvement is needed. Management is responsible for communicating the importance of quality to the whole organization and for rewarding high-quality performance.

Ford Motor Company's goal, as stated in a recent annual report, is to be a low-cost producer of the highest quality products. Ford uses product quality control to achieve this goal. James Spencer examines a newly produced windshield at the quality inspection station at the Rouge Glass plant.

Source: Courtesy of Ford Motor Company.

### Employee Involvement Teams

**employee involvement teams**
Teams of employees who plan ways to improve quality in their area of the organization.

Teams of employees who plan ways to improve quality in their segment of the organization became popular in the United States during the 1970s. These **employee involvement teams** may take slightly different forms, depending on their specific functions: quality circles, problem-solving teams, process improvement teams, or self-managed work groups. The concept of employee involvement teams was created in the 1920s by Walter Shewhart of Bell Laboratories and later expanded by American statistician W. Edwards Deming, whose ideas are described later in this chapter.

The typical employee involvement team consists of up to 10 employees and their supervisor, who serves as the team leader. In this role, the supervisor schedules meetings, prepares agendas, and promotes the participation and cooperation of team members. (The next chapter describes general principles of teams, including the role of the team leader.)

***How Employee Involvement Teams Work*** Each employee involvement team in an organization holds periodic meetings, which usually take place at least once or twice a month for an hour or two during the workday. At these meetings, participants examine areas where quality needs improvement, and they develop solutions. The problems discussed may be identified by management or by operative employees. In either case, the problems should be related to the employees' everyday work because this is where they have the greatest expertise.

**FIGURE 2.4**

**Typical Procedure
for an Employee
Involvement Team**

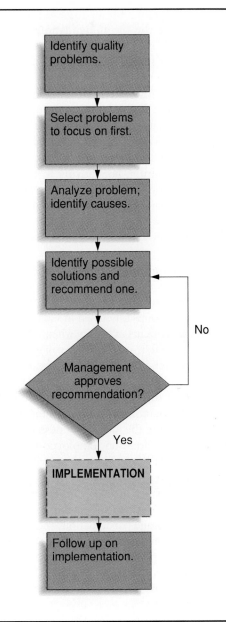

In a typical process, the members of the team might take the following steps (see Figure 2.4):

1. Identify quality problems related to the employees' areas of responsibility.
2. Select the problems to focus on first. A newly formed group may find it helpful to focus on simple problems, so that the group can build on its successes.
3. Analyze the problem to identify its causes.
4. Identify possible solutions and select one to recommend to management.

Depending on the organization's policies, one or more managers usually must approve the recommendations of the employee involvement team. Once a recommendation is approved, the appropriate people in the organization must implement it. The team should follow up on the implementation to ensure that the problem actually was solved.

University Microfilms used this approach to respond to customer complaints that orders were not getting filled on time. The Ann Arbor, Michigan, publisher of doctoral dissertations set up quality teams to investigate. The teams learned that while it took 150 days to publish an average dissertation, only about two hours were spent working on the manuscript. The rest of the time, the manuscript sat waiting, not moving to the next stage until some action took place, such as a written response from the author. The teams developed more flexible editing standards and arranged for manuscripts to move to the next stage of the process even when awaiting corrections. The time required to process the manuscripts fell by half within six months, and eventually to 60 days.[5]

***Characteristics of Successful Employee Involvement Teams***   A number of things help a supervisor to make employee involvement teams a success. These include the principles of problem solving (described in Chapter 9) and the guidelines for supervising groups (discussed in Chapter 3). In addition, teams are most likely to achieve improvements in quality when they have certain characteristics (see Figure 2.5).

First, employee involvement teams must have support from supervisors and higher-level managers. The teams are most likely to succeed when the organization's top management supports them. (Of course, supervisors have little control over top managers' attitudes, but they must be enthusiastic themselves.) Managers can demonstrate support for employee involvement teams by acting on and rewarding the ideas that these groups produce.

In addition, employee involvement teams work best when participants have the skills necessary to contribute. To get the group off to a good start, the organization should provide training at the first meeting(s). Participants may need training in problem-solving techniques and approaches to quality improvement. The group's leader may need assistance in learning to lead a group discussion and to encourage participation.

Employee involvement teams will be more successful when all group members are eager to participate. For that reason, it is a good idea to make membership in the team voluntary. Employees who are interested in problem solving will make the most valuable contributions.

### Total Quality Management

**total quality management (TQM)**
An organizationwide focus on satisfying customers by continuously improving every business process for delivering goods or services.

Bringing together aspects of other quality-control techniques, many organizations have embraced the practice of **total quality management (TQM),** an organizationwide focus on satisfying customers by continuously improving every business process for delivering goods or services. Some of the leading users of TQM are Federal Express, Hewlett-Packard, Motorola, 3M, Westinghouse, and Xerox Business Products and Systems. The Joint Commission on Accreditation of Healthcare Organizations, which accredits over 80 percent of U.S. hospitals, is revising its standards to include some TQM-style criteria.[6]

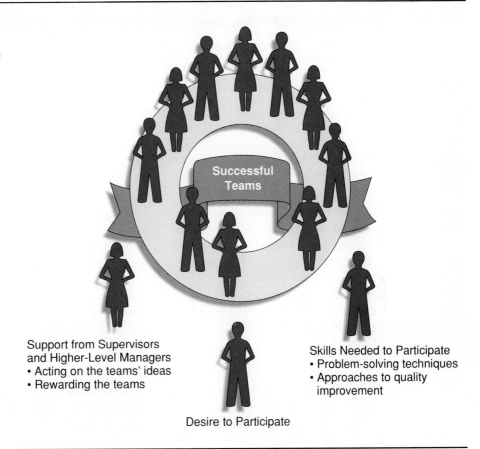

**FIGURE 2.5**

Characteristics of
Successful Employee
Involvement Teams

Successful
Teams

Support from Supervisors
and Higher-Level Managers
• Acting on the teams' ideas
• Rewarding the teams

Skills Needed to Participate
• Problem-solving techniques
• Approaches to quality
  improvement

Desire to Participate

The objective of TQM is to meet or exceed customer expectations. Thus, it is not a final outcome but, in the words of quality consultant Roy Duff, "a philosophical approach to running a business."[7] As such, it requires commitment at all levels and time for results to become evident. (See "Tips from the Firing Line.") Mike Weaver, president of the Weaver Popcorn Company in Van Buren, Indiana, puts it simply: "Quality only happens when people start caring. And they don't start caring all at once."[8]

The evidence seems to support the benefits of a TQM approach when it is fully implemented with top-level commitment. A General Accounting Office study, conducted in part to measure the impact of TQM on performance, found that errors and defects fell by 10.3 percent, sales per employee increased 8.6 percent, and customer satisfaction increased at all companies using TQM.[9] At many companies using TQM, the cost of poor quality, as determined by such measures as scrap and rework, has fallen by half or even more.[10] Motorola, a leader in the application of TQM, claims that the company's commitment to quality improvement saved $6.5 billion in manufacturing costs over seven years.[11]

**TIPS FROM THE FIRING LINE**

### Practicing TQM at Your Organization

Total quality management is a philosophy that people must put into practice every day for it to work. According to Roy Duff, vice-president of Creative Quality Enterprises Inc., companies that plan thoroughly for the change to TQM can avoid the three top barriers to success: poor internal communication, lackluster support from upper management, and no clear vision. Supervisors can help the process along.

- Practice two-way communication between supervisors and employees, and encourage employees to ask questions and offer opinions.
- Inform employees of any major change, explaining why the change is being made and what its benefits will be.
- Practice TQM principles in everyday activities. For instance, meetings should reflect TQM emphasis.

- If you have access to or decision-making authority about funding, make sure it goes toward training.
- Empower workers to manage themselves as much as possible.
- Do not ignore your own authority or accountability; provide guidelines for workers wherever necessary.
- If you have the opportunity, provide input to the company's vision for TQM.
- Have patience with employees as they adapt to the change.

Source: Roy Duff, "Why TQM Fails—and What Companies Can Do about It," *Quality Digest,* Feb. 1995, pp. 51–52.

***Advocates for Quality***    The popularity of TQM has been due largely to the compelling case that management experts have made for an organizationwide focus on quality. The three experts most frequently associated with TQM are Philip B. Crosby, W. Edwards Deming, and Joseph M. Juran.

Crosby, known worldwide as a quality expert, pioneered the quality movement in the United States. To achieve product quality, Crosby maintains, the organization must be "injected" with certain ingredients, much as a vaccination serum is intended to keep a person healthy. An organization needs to add five types of ingredients:

1. *Integrity*—Managers and employees at all levels must be dedicated to their role in providing quality to customers.
2. *Systems*—The organization needs various kinds of systems to indicate whether quality is acceptable and customers are satisfied.
3. *Communications*—Employees must be aware of their progress, and the organization must recognize employee achievements.
4. *Operations*—The organization must educate suppliers, train employees, and examine and improve its procedures, all in support of high quality.
5. *Policies*—The organization needs clear policies on quality.

Deming taught statistical quality control in Japan shortly after World War II and became an important contributor to quality improvement efforts in that country. Deming so impressed the Japanese with his lectures on quality that they named a prize after him. The Deming Prize is Japan's prestigious international quality award. Not until decades later was Deming's emphasis on total quality widely discussed in the United States. Deming's approach is this: to achieve product quality, the organization must continually improve not only the product's design but also the process of producing it.

Juran also taught quality concepts to the Japanese. He emphasizes the view that management should seek to maintain and improve quality through efforts on two levels: (1) the mission of the organization as a whole to achieve and maintain high quality and (2) the mission of individual departments in the organization to achieve and maintain high quality. In pursuing these missions, Juran says that managers must be involved in studying the symptoms of quality problems, identifying the underlying problems, and carrying out solutions.

***Successfully Using TQM*** An organization that wants to use total quality management begins by deciding what strategies to use, who will do what to carry out the strategies, and when these steps will take place. A basic strategy for implementing TQM is to use groups, such as employee involvement teams, to identify and solve problems. Another is to review criteria for improving quality (such as the categories for the Baldrige Award, to be described later), then seek to meet those criteria. The organization also may focus on improving the processes used for delivering goods and services, rather than on the products themselves. Finally, it may form self-managing work teams (see Chapter 3), groups of employees with broad responsibility for producing particular goods, services, or parts.

Some of these strategies were used at LaGrange Memorial Hospital in Illinois, where a group of employees from various departments met to discuss their work. The employees discovered that when patients visited more than one of the hospital's outpatient centers, they had to answer the same questions about their medical history at each center. To improve services to these customers (the patients), the hospital now has an employee enter the information once on a computer, where it is available to all departments.[12]

Because these strategies call for the involvement of employees at all levels, the organization needs to educate employees about why quality improvement is needed and how the TQM process will work. The Self-Quiz on page 55 consists of questions that identify whether a person has the kind of quality awareness that can make TQM work. Try taking it yourself to see where you stand.

According to a study by the General Accounting Office, the organizations that have used TQM most successfully have six characteristics in common:[13]

1. The company's attention is focused on meeting customers' requirements for quality.
2. Management leads in spreading TQM values throughout the organization.
3. Management asks and empowers employees to continuously improve all key business processes.
4. Management fosters a corporate culture that is flexible and responsive.
5. The organization's management systems support decision making based on facts.
6. The organization uses partnerships with suppliers to improve the delivery of the goods or services it buys.

In addition, the Quality and Productivity Management Association has identified four principles held in common by successful TQM users. These organizations believe it is important to focus on customer satisfaction, emphasize quality, improve continuously, and involve and empower employees. Furthermore, the executives and managers at these organizations spend 25 to 50 percent of their time on activities related to quality improvement.[14] The types of activities are listed in Table 2.2.

| **TABLE 2.2** Management Activities Related to Quality Improvement | Category of Activities | Specific Activities |
|---|---|---|
| | Infusing values | Valuing customer focus<br>Valuing quality<br>Valuing continuous improvement<br>Valuing employee involvement and empowerment |
| | Institutionalizing total quality management (TQM) | Developing a mission and vision<br>Following guiding principles<br>Organizing and planning for quality<br>Aligning policies and practices |
| | Keeping everyone informed about TQM | Assessing quality and gathering facts<br>Providing quality education and training<br>Communicating quality<br>Partnering with suppliers |
| | Managing improvement | Removing problems and barriers<br>Improving processes<br>Leading teams<br>Recognizing and rewarding |

Source: Adapted from "The 'Heart' of TQM," *Commitment Plus* (Quality & Productivity Management Association), Oct. 1991, pp. 1, 4.

An important way supervisors and other managers can build an organization with these characteristics is to behave as if quality is important. Among TQM users, this commonly is called "walking the talk." For example, if everyone is to receive training in quality improvement, supervisors who walk the talk will not look for ways to get out of the training sessions, even if they do have a lot of urgent matters to attend to.

***Customer Satisfaction***    One of the key values of total quality management is the focus by employees at all levels on meeting or exceeding the expectations of their customers. This principle assumes that everyone has a customer to serve. It is clear whom a salesclerk or a nurse serves, but even the back-office personnel at a manufacturer are delivering services to someone. Thus, part of satisfying customers is knowing who they are. They may be the people who buy the company's products, the taxpayers who support the government agency, or the other employees in the organization who use the reports, advice, or other support prepared in a given department.

Knowing the customer was the approach taken by Chuck Wise, the head of Corning's tax department. The 19 people who report to Wise spend about half their time preparing federal tax returns, so Wise identified his department's major client as the Internal Revenue Service (IRS). Wise asked the IRS to evaluate Corning's returns, which included a summary of thousands of accounts itemizing each department's expenses. The IRS replied that it did not want the summary, yet found it necessary to spend hundreds of hours interpreting it. Wise's department stopped doing the summary and saved over 400 work hours a year.[15]

If Wise had not made the effort to identify and learn about his department's biggest customer, his attempts to improve quality might have been much less effective. He probably would have tried to find ways to do the account summary faster; instead, he learned that it was unnecessary to do it at all. This principle applies to any supervisor and work group looking for ways to improve quality. Identifying customers and their needs can lead to the improvements that are most meaningful.

A supervisor can help employees focus on customers by having employees ask themselves whether they would buy the goods or services. Would they be satisfied with the work? If they can put themselves in their customers' shoes and honestly say they would be satisfied, it is a good indicator that their work is up to quality standards.[16]

# Measurement of Quality

Quality-control techniques such as statistical process control provide information about when defects occur in processes and products. But when an organization is engaged in a long-term process such as TQM, how can supervisors and others in the organization know whether they are satisfying their internal or external customers? How can they tell whether they are using practices likely to foster high quality? Guidelines for answering such questions come from the Baldrige Award, the standards known as ISO 9000, a practice called benchmarking, and a focus on customer value.

## *The Baldrige Award*

**Malcolm Baldrige National Quality Award**
An annual award administered by the U.S. Department of Commerce and given to the company that shows the highest-quality performance in seven categories.

Organizations using a TQM approach often measure their progress in terms of the criteria used to judge applicants for the **Malcolm Baldrige National Quality Award.** This is an annual award administered by the U.S. Department of Commerce and given to the company that shows the highest-quality performance as measured by seven categories:

1. Leadership
2. Information and analysis
3. Strategic quality planning
4. Human resource development and management
5. Management of process quality
6. Quality and operational results
7. Customer focus and satisfaction

The number of organizations applying for the Baldrige Award has been declining since 1991,[17] but many others use the evaluation categories as a basis for assessing their own performance. In effect, organizations use the guidelines for the award as a kind of textbook for what needs to be done to improve quality. Baxter International, the world's largest supplier of health care products and services, has established a quality program called Quality Leadership Process. This program includes competition among the company's units for the Baxter Quality Award. Winners receive trophies, plaques, and other recognition based on the same quality criteria used for the Baldrige Award.[18]

In 1992, the Ritz-Carlton Hotel became the first hotel company to win the Malcolm Baldrige National Quality Award by going to great lengths to keep employees as well as customers happy.

Source: Courtesy of the Ritz-Carlton Hotel Company.

The risk of focusing on award criteria is that an organization or department can get caught up in winning an award or meeting certain criteria instead of focusing on the intended goal of delivering quality to the customer. Competing for a challenging award such as the Baldrige can be costly in terms of dollars and managers' time. Many organizations find that the key is to proceed with moderation. For example, at the insurance unit of Cigna Corporation, the Baldrige Award is simply an inspiration. In the words of senior vice-president David Williams, "The attention it takes to go for the award over and above the effort of creating a total quality management process would take us off track."[19]

## ISO 9000

**ISO 9000**
A series of standards adopted by the International Organization of Standardization to spell out acceptable criteria for quality systems.

Another measure of success in quality management is ISO 9000 certification.[20] **ISO 9000** is a series of standards adopted in 1987 by the International Organization of Standardization to spell out acceptable criteria for quality systems. To be certified, an organization is visited by independent audit teams; if the auditors determine that the key elements of the standard are in place, they issue certification of compliance. (Note that they are evaluating quality processes, not product quality.) Organizations seek ISO 9000 certification for a number of reasons. For example, a customer may require it as a condition of doing business, or a nation's government may require it of organizations selling in that nation. As more businesses become certified, those that want to remain competitive will have to be certified as well.

## Benchmarking

**benchmarking**
Identifying the top performer of a process, then learning and carrying out the top performer's practices.

Managers at all levels can evaluate their success in improving quality by comparing their processes and results with those at other departments and organizations. This practice is known popularly as **benchmarking**: identifying, learning,

Xerox first began benchmarking when it discovered Japanese manufacturers were able to sell midsize copiers in the United States for considerably less then Xerox's production cost. A team of line managers was sent to Japan to study Xerox's own joint venture, Fuji-Xerox. Facing facts marked the beginning of the Xerox recovery, and benchmarking has served the company as a key tool ever since.

Source: Courtesy of Xerox Corporation.

and carrying out the practices of top performers. In this sense, the term first referred to the practice of comparing the products and processes at one's own company with those that are the best in the world. For example, Xerox has benchmarked the highly successful distribution system of L. L. Bean. While this might seem to be an activity for higher-level managers, supervisors can certainly apply the technique to their own department's operations or even to their own career and management style. For those who want to use benchmarking, one source of information is the business-supported International Benchmarking Clearinghouse of the American Productivity and Quality Center, based in Houston, Texas.[21]

### Customer Value

While quality improvement practices can make the organization very efficient at whatever it does, they carry the risk of never ensuring that it is doing what customers *want*. For example, an accounting department might use the zero-defects approach so well that it produces a year's worth of reports without a single error. But if the reports do not contain information useful to the recipients, has the department done high-quality work? Or suppose a maintenance group reduces its response time to requests for repair of an office's photocopiers. The office staff might benefit more from training in the prevention and correction of the most common causes of malfunctions.

Recognizing this principle, an increasing number of organizations have concluded that they need to provide a context for their efforts at quality improvement.[22] In other words, quality improvement should be directed at a larger goal, and that goal should be to deliver greater customer value. In this sense, **value** refers to the worth the customer places on what he or she gets (the total package of goods and services) relative to the cost of acquiring it.

**value**
The worth a customer places on a total package of goods and services relative to its cost.

Quality improvement directed toward value begins when the organization's employees communicate with customers to determine their needs and wants. This step defines what the organization should focus on doing. The organization is then prepared to consider ways to make those processes more efficient.

A study by the Boston Consulting Group found that insurance companies take, on average, 22 days to process a customer's application, yet the work done to carry out that task takes only 17 minutes.[23] Value-directed quality improvement would question whether these organizations are delivering value to their customers during the remainder of that time. This approach would seek process improvements that lower customers' costs and frustration by reducing cycle time without reducing the worth of what customers get from insurers. A value orientation thus does not replace the tactics described in this chapter, but directs them and detects whether they are delivering useful results.

# Guidelines for Quality Control

As with the other responsibilities of supervisors, success in quality control requires more than just picking the right technique. The supervisor needs a general approach that leads everyone involved to support the effort at improving quality. To develop such an approach, the supervisor can start by following the guidelines illustrated in Figure 2.6.

## Prevention versus Detection

It is almost always cheaper to prevent problems from occurring than it is to solve them after they happen; designing and building quality into a product is more efficient than trying to improve the product later. Therefore, quality-control programs should not be limited to the detection of defects. Quality control also should include a prevention program to keep defects from occurring.

One way to prevent problems is to pay special attention to the production of new goods and services. In a manufacturing setting, the supervisor should see that the first piece of a new product is tested with special care, rather than wait for problems to occur down the line. In the delivery of services, the supervisor should spend extra time evaluating the work carried out by new employees or employees performing a new procedure. In these situations, particularly, the supervisor might seek out feedback on customer satisfaction, rather than wait for complaints to come in. Furthermore, when prevention efforts show that employees are doing good work, the supervisor should praise their performance. Employees who are confident and satisfied are less likely to allow defects in goods or services.

## Standard Setting and Enforcement

If employees and others are to support the quality-control effort, they must know exactly what is expected of them. This calls for quality standards. At Corning, the chief executive officer decided that every employee would spend 5 percent of his or her time in job-related training, that errors would be cut by 90 percent, and that all new goods and services would meet customer requirements and equal the quality produced by competitors.[24]

In many cases, the supervisor is responsible for setting quality standards as well as for communicating and enforcing them. These standards should have the

**FIGURE 2.6**

**Guidelines for Quality Control**

characteristics of effective objectives: they should be written, measurable, clear, specific, and challenging but achievable. (For more on setting objectives, see Chapter 6.) Furthermore, those standards should reflect what is important to the client. Employees or the supervisor may benefit from asking customers how they measure the quality of the goods or services. TeleTech, a firm that handles customer service phone calls for a variety of clients, customizes its quality measurements by asking each client what measures, such as the number of calls answered or the cost per call, it considers most important.[25]

In communicating standards, a supervisor should make sure that employees know why quality is important. Specific information about the costs of poor quality and the benefits of excellent quality needs to be provided. For example, if employees know how much it costs to make a component, they can understand the costs of remaking one that is defective.[26] Similarly, a Taco Bell manager could tell employees that a typical repeat customer accounts for about $11,000 worth of lifetime total sales.[27] Therefore, providing the quality of food and service that makes a customer want to come back is more valuable than the price of a single meal might suggest.

In addition, employees must understand the difference between poor quality and excellent quality. One way to do this is through the use of examples. In teaching a new employee how to manufacture a part, a supervisor could show a sample of a part that meets specifications and one that does not. Katherine Nicastro, customer service manager for Whittaker, Clark and Daniels (a distributor of minerals, colors, and chemicals to manufacturers), provides her staff with detailed instructions and feedback. Nicastro and her employees developed a sourcebook that explains how to deliver high-quality service. Furthermore, she not only provides feedback herself but has established a practice of sending customer service reps on occasional sales calls so they can talk with customers and learn about their needs.[28]

To enforce the standards, a supervisor must participate in inspecting the quality of goods and services that employees produce. This may entail examining a random sample of parts, accompanying a salesperson on sales calls, or visiting the workplace where employees interact with customers. The timing of these inspections should be unpredictable enough that employees cannot adjust their performance with the knowledge that the supervisor will be checking up on them that day.

When an inspection uncovers a quality problem, the supervisor should inform the responsible employees immediately. Then they should get to work on solving the problem. The appropriate response may include apologizing to customers as well as fixing a problem within the organization. Requiring a quick response demonstrates the importance of quality to the organization.

For enforcement of standards to be effective, the employees must know that management is serious about quality. A catchy slogan posted on bulletin boards, inscribed on buttons, or taped to cash registers is meaningless unless supervisors and higher-level managers pay attention to these principles, reward employees for following them, and live up to them themselves.

## The Impact of Diversity

Organizations that effectively draw on the variety of talents available from a diverse workforce are in the best position to deliver high-quality goods and services.[29] Likewise, a supervisor who values diversity is in a position to help all his or her employees develop their full potential. This supervisor appreciates the various strengths of different kinds of people, which boosts employees' morale. In such a climate, working relationships among people are positive.

The supervisor who values diversity also helps to make the organization a desirable place to work, which gives the organization the largest possible pool of available talent from which to recruit. In addition, employee turnover in such an organization is likely to be low.

An organization that recruits employees who represent the various kinds of people in its markets will be most attractive to customers. A business that sells to people of various races will appeal to more customers if its sales force consists of people of those races. Customers and clients of various national and ethnic backgrounds appreciate a company where employees speak their language and know their customs. Not only is this kind of diverse organization more attractive to current and prospective customers, it is in a better position to understand and identify needs, giving the organization an edge in developing new goods and services.

Finally, many of the quality-control techniques described in this chapter rely on the creativity of managers and employees. An organization that attracts and draws on the talents of a diverse group of employees will have the widest pool of creative thinking that it can hire. In such an organization, thinking and problem solving tend to be more flexible.

## The Role of Suppliers

Organizations depend on suppliers in a variety of ways. An automaker relies on manufacturers of many types of components, and a law office relies on a printer to provide elegant stationery. Many businesses depend on outside suppliers of advice in areas such as accounting, investments, and the law.

The organization's performance is only as good as its suppliers' inputs. Digital Equipment Corporation, for example, limited the success of its TQM program in the way it conducted its relationships with some vendors. Employees complained that the company did not send defective parts back to the vendors but simply scrapped the parts. Because the company was not involving the vendors in solving the problem, employees found it harder to produce quality goods.[30] Weaver Popcorn Company employees became frustrated when the company repeatedly accepted corn with a moisture level of up to 23 percent, even though specifications called for a maximum 17 percent moisture level. Production worker Marty Hall complained, "It makes my job three times harder."[31]

To avoid or correct such problems, the quality-control effort should include setting and enforcing standards for acceptable work from suppliers. For example, the supervisor should make sure that employees have tools, materials, and supplies of acceptable quality. When choosing suppliers, the organization needs to stick to those that will be able to live up to the standards. A team from the processing plant at Weaver Popcorn developed what it called the Preferred Supplier Program. The program gives farmers generous bonuses for meeting strict standards.[32]

### Rewards for Quality

As with any area of performance that the supervisor wants to encourage, employees need valued rewards. Thus, a supervisor's job includes making sure that employees receive rewards for high-quality work. Performance measures must include an evaluation of the quality of the goods or services produced by the employees. Teams that meet or exceed the quality standards would then receive appropriate rewards (see Chapter 11). Dennis Sowards, supervisor of quality and productivity consulting for the Salt River Project, cautions that these rewards should be for doing the job right the first time, not for doing a good job of fixing a mistake. Says Sowards, "Quality is not rework with a smile."[33] (Of course, when employees make improvements, the supervisor should praise and reward their accomplishments.)

If the organization's strategy for maintaining and improving quality is TQM or some other approach that emphasizes process control, then the rewards should reflect that emphasis. In other words, supervisors should look at improvements in the process as well as the final results achieved. At Yaskawa Electric America, for example, performance appraisals and promotions are based in part on participation in the improvement process.[34]

Motorola annually holds a Total Customer Satisfaction Team Competition. In a recent year, over 3,000 teams participated worldwide. Then 22 finalist teams met in Chicago to give 15-minute presentations on how they achieved the goal of total customer satisfaction. Presenters, often in costume, used a blend of comedy, statistics, graphs, and maps. Eight of the finalist teams won gold medals, but Motorola's Gene Simpson emphasizes that "there are no losers in this kind of competition."[35]

# Summary

**2.1   Describe consequences suffered by organizations as a result of poor-quality work.**
Poor-quality work gives an organization a negative image, which drives away customers and makes it harder to recruit superior employees and borrow money. Poor-quality work can also lead to higher costs to attract customers, inspect for and correct defects, replace defective products, and defend against lawsuits.

**2.2   Compare product quality control and process control.**
Both types of quality control involve preventing and detecting quality-related problems. Product quality control focuses on ways to improve the product. Process control focuses on how to do things in a way that results in higher quality.

**2.3   Identify techniques for quality control.**
Statistical quality control involves looking for defects in parts or finished products selected through a sampling technique. In statistical process control, the operator takes samples during the process, plots the results on a chart, and makes corrections when the chart indicates the process is out of control. The zero-defects approach holds that everyone in the organization should work toward the goal of delivering such high quality that all aspects of the organization's goods and services are free of problems. Employee involvement teams plan ways to improve quality in their area of the organization. Total quality management is an organization-wide focus on satisfying customers by continuously improving every business process involved in delivering goods or services.

**2.4   Explain how employee involvement teams work and what makes them successful.**
Each employee involvement team holds periodic meetings during which participants examine needs for improvement and develop solutions. When management has approved suggested solutions, the team follows up to make sure that the problem is solved. These teams are most likely to achieve improvements in quality when they have management support, when participants have the skills necessary to contribute, and when all group members want to participate.

**2.5   Describe principles for successfully using total quality management.**
TQM must be seen as a continuous process that unfolds gradually as employees find more and more ways to improve quality. The organization should start by deciding what strategies to use and how to carry them out. Employees must play an active role in carrying out TQM, so they must be educated about the need for quality improvement and the way the TQM process will work. The organization must focus on satisfying customers and operate in a flexible, responsive manner.

**2.6   Identify ways organizations measure their success in continuous quality improvement.**
Organizations compare their practices and performance with various sets of guidelines. They may compete for the Malcolm Baldrige National Quality Award or assess their performance using its evaluation categories. They may seek certification for meeting the standards of ISO 9000. Also, they may compare their performance with that of organizations that excel in particular areas—a practice known as benchmarking.

**2.7   Describe guidelines for quality control.**
The organization should focus on preventing quality problems, which is cheaper than detecting them. Supervisors and other managers should set, communicate, and enforce standards for quality control. The organization should insist upon high quality from its suppliers inside and outside the organization. Supervisors and higher-level managers should provide valued rewards for high-quality work.

# Key Terms

quality control

product quality control

process control

statistical quality control

statistical process control (SPC)

zero-defects approach

employee involvement teams

total quality management (TQM)

Malcolm Baldrige National

Quality Award

ISO 9000

benchmarking

value

# Review and Discussion Questions

1. Brand X Corporation seeks to be the lowest-cost maker of lawn chairs and toboggans. To keep costs down, management tells the production department, "Keep that assembly line moving. We have an inspector on staff to catch the mistakes later." What are the consequences Brand X Corporation is likely to experience as a result of this approach to manufacturing?

2. What is the difference between product quality control and process control? Is balancing a checkbook a type of product quality control or process control? Explain.

3. The manager of a restaurant wants to make sure that her staff is delivering good customer service, but she does not have time to investigate the service given to every customer. So every evening at 5:30, the manager stops at customers' tables to ask if they are satisfied with their service. In effect, this is a form of statistical quality control because she is talking to a sample of the customers.
   How can the manager improve the accuracy of the information she gets from this quality-control technique?

4. Define the zero-defects approach to quality control. Do you think zero defects is attainable? Why or why not?

5. Michelle LeVerrier supervises a group of tellers at a bank located in a city. The bank manager has asked her to lead an employee involvement team designed to improve the processes of serving individual customers at the teller windows. The four steps the team must take are (1) to identify quality problems in the specific area of responsibility, (2) to select one problem to focus on, (3) to analyze the problem, and (4) to identify solutions and select one to present to management. How might Michelle use this four-step procedure to conduct her first team meeting?

6. What is total quality management (TQM)?

7. Louise Ho supervises a group of editorial assistants who read book manuscripts and write reports evaluating the manuscripts for editors at a book publishing company. How might Louise determine whether her group is providing the best value to her customers—the editors?

8. Describe how organizations can use the Malcolm Baldrige National Quality Award as a tool for measuring their success at continuous quality improvement.

9. Imagine that you are the supervisor responsible for a pharmacy. You have received a few complaints about mistakes in customers' prescriptions. To improve the quality of service delivered by the pharmacists, you can concentrate on (a) doing a better job of catching errors in the future or (b) doing a better job of avoiding errors. Which approach would you choose? Explain.

10. Sean Riley supervises the produce department at a supermarket. How can he set and enforce standards from his suppliers? What impact will his decisions have on the sales of products in his department?

11. Why is it important for employees to receive rewards for high-quality work?

## A SECOND LOOK

How does the story of Highland Park Markets illustrate both product quality control and process control?

# APPLICATIONS MODULE

## CASE

### *Quality at First National Bank of Chicago*

Process control can really boost an organization's sales. Managers at First National Bank of Chicago learned of a problem faced by customers for the bank's letters of credit. (Letters of credit are documents that are issued by a bank and used for financing exports.) Customers who called the bank about letters of credit frequently were transferred from one bank employee to another before they found a person who could help them. Neither the bank nor the customers considered this an acceptable quality of service.

First Chicago turned over the problem to one of its dozens of quality teams, each composed of a supervisor and several employees. The team analyzed the problem and found that its source was the bank's practice of having nine different employees handle each request for a letter of credit. This assembly-line process took four days.

Next, the quality team devised a solution. Employees who issued letters of credit were trained to handle all steps in the process. Thus, one employee handled each request alone. Every time a customer requested a letter of credit, that customer was assigned to the same employee. With the new process, issuing letters of credit takes only a single day.

First Chicago has benefited in several ways from the effort to improve the quality of service. First, in five years the bank more than doubled the number of letters of credit it issued annually. In addition, it operates more efficiently, handling the higher volume with fewer employees. And the bank has developed a reputation for high quality in this area. Robert J. Haider, an international credit manager for Motorola, says, "When a customer needs a letter of credit to place an order with us, we tell them to use First Chicago if they can."

1. If First National Bank of Chicago had ignored its quality problem and not taken steps to correct it, what might have been some specific consequences?
2. Why is it so important to maintain process control in a service institution like a bank?
3. How did the bank's solution to its quality problem create better customer value?

Source: Aaron Bernstein, "Quality Is Becoming Job One in the Office, Too," *Business Week,* Apr. 29, 1991, pp. 52–53, 56.

## SELF-QUIZ

### *Your Level of Quality Awareness*

Answer each question by checking Yes or No.                                          **Yes**        **No**

1. Do you trust your co-workers? Is there a feeling of cooperation rather than competition?
2. Are you truly interested in the welfare of those with whom you work?
3. Can you communicate openly and honestly with the people in your department?
4. Do you understand your department's quality performance goals?
5. Are you committed to the attainment of those goals?
6. When you need special help, do you try to tap the resources of others?
7. Can you resolve conflict successfully?
8. When your department has a meeting, do you participate by preparing and providing your own input?
9. Whether you agree or not, do you respect individual differences?
10. Do you really like your job and your fellow workers?

    **Total**

Score yourself: If you had 8 to 10 Yes answers, you're a quality-oriented person and well suited for being part of a work effort aimed at quality awareness. A lower score, however, indicates that you may have good reason for self-doubt. But don't give up. We are not born with an appreciation for quality performance or even with a grasp of what constitutes a quality lifestyle. Rather, we learn these. Seek help from the members of your department. If a commitment to quality is your mutual goal, they will support you—and everyone will benefit.

Source: Reprinted with the permission of Dartnell, 4660 N. Ravenswood Ave., Chicago, IL. 60640, (800) 621–5463.

## Class Exercise

Divide the class into groups of four to six people. Each group receives the following materials: 20 index cards, a roll of tape, a pair of scissors, and a felt-tipped pen. To complete the exercise, the groups may use these supplies and no others.

The instructor specifies how much time the groups will have to complete the project (10 or 15 minutes). When the instructor gives the signal to begin, each group is to use the materials provided to construct a house. The teams may use the materials in any way they see fit, but they may not use additional materials of their own.

When time is up, someone from each group brings the group's house to a table or other designated location in the classroom. The instructor appoints five class members to serve on a panel of judges. They rate each house on a scale of 1 to 5 (with 5 representing the highest quality). The judges' scores are totaled, and the house with the highest score is deemed the winner of this quality contest.

Finally, the class discusses the following questions:

- On what basis did the judges rate the quality of the houses? How many of the criteria in Table 2.1 did they use?
- How did your group decide on a way to make its house? How well did your group work together to produce the house?
- Given your group's experience and the information about how the judges arrived at their scores, how would you want to improve the quality of your house if you could repeat the exercise? Are your changes process improvements or product improvements?

## Team-Building Exercise

## Applying Control/Quality Principles to Customer Service

Because nearly 8 out of every 10 jobs in this country are in the service sector, it is important to understand the significance of providing quality customer service. This exercise is designed to help you apply what you learned in this chapter ("Ensuring High Quality") to a service-sector job.

### Instructions

1. Form groups of 2 or 3 people. Identify a work setting where customer service is critical. The place should be one that all of you are familiar with. It might be a workplace where one of you has worked or at least has been a customer (some examples: retail store, post office, bank, hospital, university, resort, restaurant).
2. Identify a specific job title for the work setting (e.g., waiter/waitress, nurse, clerk at the university bookstore, shoe salesperson at a store).
3. Review some of the principles covered in this chapter (see Figure A). Select those that are appropriate to the job you have identified, and develop specific customer service guidelines for the employees.
4. Now select principles appropriate for a supervisor of employees in the job you have identified, and develop some supervisory guidelines that focus on customer service. For example, how should the supervisor monitor performance to determine that employees are practicing the quality service standards you have established?
5. Share your group's efforts with the class by presenting a written statement that includes work setting, job title, principles from Figure A and how your group applied them to the job, and principles from Figure A on the next page and how your group applied them to the supervisor.

**FIGURE A**

**Quality Principles from Chapter 2**

- Process control
- Zero-defects approach
- Employee involvement teams
- Philip Crosby's five ingredients for quality (integrity, systems, communications, operations, and policies)
- Benchmarking
- Prevention versus detection
- Standard setting and enforcement
- The role of suppliers
- Rewards for quality
- Dimensions of quality (performance, features, reliability, conformance, durability, serviceability, aesthetics, and perceived quality from Table 2.1)

Team-Building exercise was prepared by Corinne Livesay, Belhaven College, Jackson, Mississippi.

# Video Exercise 2: *Ensuring High Quality*

## *Video Summary*

First National Bank of Chicago, one of the nation's largest financial institutions, is the featured company for a detailed look at total quality management (TQM). The program begins by defining quality and distinguishing a "zero-defects" approach to quality from the more encompassing TM approach. Techniques such as statistical process control (SPC), employee empowerment, customer surveys, employee teams, ISO 9000, and the Malcolm Baldrige National Quality Award criteria are also introduced and demonstrated.

## *Application*

This video program discussed the Malcolm Baldrige National Quality Award, and you also read in this chapter about the seven quality criteria of the award. This exercise will give you a chance to learn more about the *criteria* on which U.S. companies compete to win this award. Remember that this national quality award is a means (1) to recognize quality improvement efforts by U.S. companies and (2) to foster greater competitiveness in excellence and high standards.

## Quality Criteria

To help you learn more about the quality criteria, match the items listed below with the items left blank under the examination categories.

 a. Management of supplier performance
 b. Competitive comparisons and benchmarking
 c. Leadership system and organization
 d. Customer relationship management
 e. Employee education, training, and development
 f. Product and service quality results
 g. Strategy deployment

| 1996 Examination Categories/Items | | | Point Values |
|---|---|---|---|
| 1.0 | Leadership | | 90 |
| | 1.1 | Senior executive leadership | 45 |
| | 1.2 | _____ | 25 |
| | 1.3 | Public responsibility and corporate citizenship | 20 |
| 2.0 | Information and analysis | | 75 |
| | 2.1 | Management of information and data | 20 |
| | 2.2 | _____ | 15 |
| | 2.3 | Analysis and use of company-level data | 40 |

| 3.0 | Strategic planning | | 55 |
|---|---|---|---|
| | 3.1 | Strategy development | 35 |
| | 3.2 | _____ | 20 |
| 4.0 | Human resource development and management | | 140 |
| | 4.1 | Human resource planning and evaluation | 20 |
| | 4.2 | High-performance work systems | 45 |
| | 4.3 | _____ | 50 |
| | 4.4 | Employee well-being and satisfaction | 25 |
| 5.0 | Process management | | 140 |
| | 5.1 | Design and introduction of products and services | 40 |
| | 5.2 | Process management: product and service production and delivery | 40 |
| | 5.3 | Process management: support services | 30 |
| | 5.4 | _____ | 30 |
| 6.0 | Business results | | 250 |
| | 6.1 | _____ | 75 |
| | 6.2 | Company operational and financial results | 110 |
| | 6.3 | Human resource results | 35 |
| | 6.3 | Supplier performance results | 30 |
| 7.0 | Customer focus and satisfaction | | 250 |
| | 7.1 | Customer and market knowledge | 30 |
| | 7.2 | _____ | 30 |
| | 7.3 | Customer satisfaction determination | 30 |
| | 7.4 | Customer satisfaction results | 160 |
| Total Points | | | 1,000 |

Where to find out more: *The Malcolm Baldrige National Quality Award Criteria* describes in detail the award criteria. You can obtain individual copies of this document free of charge from:

Malcolm Baldrige National Quality Award
National Institute of Standards and Technology
Route 270 and Quince Orchard Road
Administration Building, Room A537
Gaithersburg, MD  20899–0001
Telephone: 301–975–2036

# 3

*None of us is as smart as all of us.*
　　—**Company slogan of Stanley Bostitch, Inc., staple manufacturer**

# Working with Teams

## LEARNING OBJECTIVES

After you have studied this chapter, you should be able to:

3.1 Explain why people join groups.

3.2 Distinguish types of groups that exist in the workplace.

3.3 Discuss how supervisors can get groups to cooperate with them.

3.4 Describe characteristics of groups in the workplace.

3.5 Identify the stages in the development of groups.

3.6 Explain why teamwork is important.

3.7 Describe how the supervisor can lead a team so that it is productive.

3.8 Discuss how to plan for effective meetings.

3.9 Provide guidelines for conducting effective meetings.

Source: © 1993, Comstock, Inc.

## TEAMWORK AT BOSTITCH IS A STAPLE ACTIVITY

At its factory in West Greenwich, Rhode Island, Stanley Bostitch, Inc., makes specialty staples and nails. At one time excess coating was being applied to these products, costing the company $180 per drum to dispose of the excess. A supervisor tried and failed to find a way to reduce the waste.

Then Bostitch assigned a group of employees—five coating machine operators and their foreman—to solve the problem. The group met one hour per week for 12 weeks. Group members collected data on every machine and identified which machines experienced problems most often. Upon examining those machines, the group determined that a particular valve was causing the excess coating. The group contacted the manufacturer of the valves and had an engineer from that firm help them redesign the valve.

Finally, the group tested the redesigned valve and found that it solved the problem.

The solution cost $1,085 to buy and install the new valves in addition to the cost of 60 worker-hours spent in meetings. The total savings amounts to over $380,000 per year. Bostitch's manufacturing manager, Deborah Pannullo, believes that, in general, groups outperform individuals in finding solutions to waste problems, especially when groups have been trained in techniques for improving quality or other areas of operations.

Source: "Recapture Lost Energy—Reuse Waste," *Maintenance Supervisor's Bulletin*, Mar. 10, 1992 Supplement, pp. 1–3.

**group**
Two or more people who interact with one another, are aware of one another, and think of themselves as a group.

Much of the work that involves supervisors takes place in groups. To define that term formally, a **group** is two or more people who interact with one another, are aware of one another, and think of themselves as a group. The supervisor must see that groups of employees work together to accomplish objectives. An increasing number of organizations are expanding group efforts by forming teams. As leader or member of a team, supervisors help plan and carry out a variety of activities. Many group and team efforts take place in meetings.

How the supervisor can work effectively as a leader and member of a team or other group is covered in this chapter. Some general characteristics of groups— why people join them, what kinds of groups operate in the workplace, how groups can be described, and how they develop—are described. Then efforts to build employee participation through the use of teamwork are discussed, and basic benefits of teamwork and ways supervisors can lead teams effectively are outlined. Finally, the chapter provides guidelines for holding meetings.

## Reasons for Joining Groups

When Felicia Watt accepted a position as math teacher at West Junior High School, she became a member of two groups: the teaching staff at the school and the teachers' union representing her district. She also joined a citywide organization of black education professionals to receive moral support and to participate in service projects sponsored by the organization. In addition, the principal of West Junior High asked Felicia to serve on a committee to plan an innovative math and science curriculum. Upon learning that Felicia likes to eat sushi, one teacher invited her to join a group of four teachers who visit a local Japanese restaurant about once a month.

This example shows that people belong to groups for many reasons. Sometimes group membership simply goes along with being an employee. In particular, all employees are members of the organization that employs them, most are part of a division or department, and some also join a union when they go to work for a particular company. At other times, employees join a group because their supervisor or some other manager asks them to. In such cases, an employee may join the group to advance his or her career or simply to avoid going against the manager's wishes. Finally, an employee may join a group because being a member satisfies personal needs. The most common personal reasons for joining a group include the following:

- *Closeness*—Being members of the same group builds ties among people. Friendships generally result from the shared experiences that come from membership in some kind of group—for example, a class at school or a bowling team.
- *Strength in numbers*—Having ties to others gives people confidence they may lack when they act alone. Their sense of confidence is well founded. In an organization, a group of people tends to be more influential than one person acting alone.
- *Common goals*—When people have a goal to meet, they can get moral and practical support by working with or alongside others who have similar goals.
- *Achievement of personal objectives*—Membership in a group can help people achieve personal objectives in a variety of ways. The time spent with group members can be enjoyable. Membership in certain groups can enhance a person's prestige. In a related vein, group membership can satisfy people's desire to feel important.

# Groups in the Workplace

As mentioned earlier, all the employees of an organization form a group. On a practical level, however, most organizations are too large for all their members to interact with one another. Therefore, except at very small organizations, most employees cluster into smaller groups. Some examples are departments, task forces, and groups that meet for lunch to play cards, do needlework, or talk about baseball. References to groups in this chapter generally mean these small groups; that is, groups small enough that all members interact with one another.

To fully benefit from the various groups in an organization, the supervisor needs to be able to identify them. The first step is to recognize the various categories of an organization's groups. Then the supervisor can apply several principles for building cooperation on the part of the groups.

## Functional and Task Groups

**functional groups**
Groups that fulfill ongoing needs in the organization by carrying out a particular function.

**task groups**
Groups that are set up to carry out a specific activity and then disband when the activity is completed.

Some groups fulfill ongoing needs in the organization by carrying out a particular function, such as producing goods, selling products, or investing funds. These are called **functional groups.** For example, a hospital's accounting department has the ongoing responsibility for keeping accurate records of the flow of money into and out of the organization. In most cases, a functional group is one that appears on a company's organization chart.

Other groups, called **task groups,** are set up to carry out a specific activity, and they disband when that activity is completed. For example, at Master Industries, Inc., of Ansonia, Ohio, a task group was responsible for buying the company's brooms and dustpans and for finding places to hang them.[1] Presumably, such a task could be completed in a matter of weeks. Another example of a task group is a committee formed by a supervisor to identify ways to promote safety in the workplace. This kind of task could go on for years with no definite end date, because the job of promoting safety is never likely to be finished.

## Formal and Informal Groups

**formal groups**
Groups set up by management to meet organizational objectives.

**informal groups**
Groups that form when individuals in the organization develop relationships to meet personal needs.

The examples of functional and task groups are also types of **formal groups.** These are groups set up by management to meet organizational objectives. Thus, these groups result from the management function of organizing (introduced in Chapter 1). A customer service department and a committee charged with planning the company picnic are formal groups.

Other groups result when individuals in the organization develop relationships to meet personal needs. These are **informal groups.** Figure 3.1 shows two informal groups in a small store. Perhaps the china department manager and three clerks like to jog after work; they might find themselves jogging together. Eventually they could build friendships around this shared activity. Most employees welcome the opportunity to be part of informal groups because these groups help satisfy social needs. The friendships established within the group can make work more enjoyable.

Informal subgroups can develop among members of a formal group when the formal group fails to meet some personal needs.[2] For example, when some group members feel angry at the group's leader or uncertain about whether they really belong, they may form a subgroup. Subgroups may also form when some group

**FIGURE 3.1**
Informal Group Structures

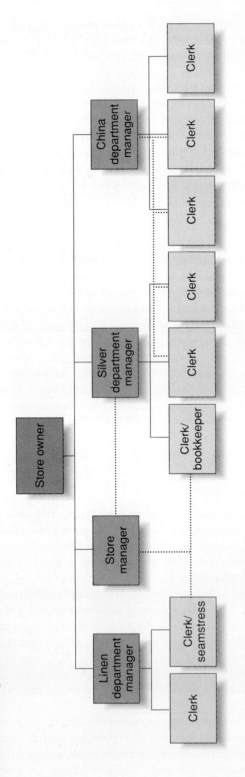

Source: Samuel C. Certo, *Human Relations Today: Concepts and Skills*, Austen Press. © 1995, Richard D. Irwin, Inc., p. 259.

This design team at SBE, Inc., is an example of a formal group. The company designs higher-performance computer products for equipment manufacturers.

Source: Courtesy of SBE, Inc.

members feel uncomfortable with the way they are expected to behave; for example, they might be expected not to express their feelings. In such a situation, the people who form a subgroup may feel more comfortable with the other members of the subgroup.

### Getting the Group to Work with You

The opening example of Bostitch shows that groups have a lot to offer with regard to decision making and problem solving. A group can generate a creative solution that a single person might not think of, and the group process can build support by letting people make decisions about what affects them. To make the most of the potential benefits of working with groups, supervisors can use several tactics.

An important step is for the supervisor to make sure all members of a formal group know what they can and should be doing. This includes setting effective group objectives (described in Chapter 6) and clearly communicating those objectives. Group members also need to understand their authority, including the limits on what they can do. For example, a group assembled to solve a problem should know whether it is to implement the solution or simply to suggest solutions, leaving to the supervisor the task of choosing an alternative and implementing it.

Besides communicating expectations, the supervisor should keep groups informed about what is happening in the organization and what changes are planned for the future. Making the effort to communicate with groups is a way of demonstrating that they are important to the organization. It also tends to create a climate in which group members will readily let the supervisor know about what is happening in the group.

The supervisor should support the group when it wants to bring legitimate concerns to higher management. For example, if some problem is keeping employees from getting their work done on time or up to standards, the supervisor should do what is possible to get the problem corrected. However, this does not mean adopting an "us versus them" attitude toward management. The supervisor is a part of management and must act accordingly.

A nurturing climate is demonstrated by the formation of this JCPenney cross-functional team, which was created to enhance diversity and foster a multicultural environment. Such participative management encourages free expression of ideas and provides optimal communication.

Source: Courtesy of JCPenney.

A supervisor who is responsible for setting up a group can help it function well by making good choices about whom to assign to the group. In many cases, the group can benefit from a combination of people with a variety of strengths or backgrounds. At the same time, the supervisor needs to be careful about splitting up informal groups when creating a formal one; doing so could hurt morale within the formal group. In addition, the number of group members can be important. Although including all employees is sometimes important, for many tasks a group will work best with only 5 to 10 members.

Some of the guidelines for supervision discussed in other chapters also will help get the group's cooperation. Supervisors should treat all employees fairly and impartially, respect the position of the group's informal leader, and find ways to give rewards to the group as a whole, rather than to individual employees only. Finally, supervisors should encourage the group to participate in solving problems. As a result of following these practices, the supervisor can benefit by receiving the group's support.

## Characteristics of Groups

You can readily conclude from this discussion and from personal experience that working with a group is not like working alone. Social scientists have summarized a number of group characteristics, including ways to describe them, how effective they are, and what pressures they place on individuals. Supervisors who are aware of this theoretical information can use it to understand what is happening in a group situation. They can decide whether the group is effectively supporting the achievement of organizational objectives or whether they need to step in and make changes.

When looking at how groups are the same or different, it helps to consider some basic ways of describing them. Some of the most useful characteristics include roles, norms, status, cohesiveness, size, homogeneity, and effectiveness (see Figure 3.2).

■ **FIGURE 3.2**

**Ways to Describe Groups**

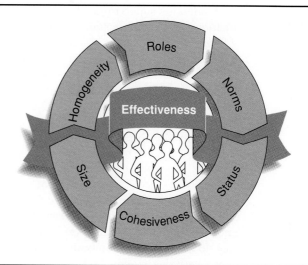

## *Roles*

**roles**
Patterns of behavior
related to employees'
positions in a group.

The character taken on by each actor in a play is the actor's role. In an organization's groups, the various group members also take on **roles,** or patterns of behavior related to their position in the group. Some common roles that you may have encountered or even held include the (formal or informal) leader of a group, the scapegoat, the class clown, and the person to whom others take their problems.

What leads a person to take on a role? Sometimes a person's formal position in an organization dictates a certain role. For example, as described in Chapter 1, certain kinds of behavior are expected of a supervisor. Another source of a person's role is a combination of the person's beliefs about how he or she ought to behave and other people's expectations about how that person will act. For example, if Anne displays empathy toward a colleague who is going through a divorce, Anne may eventually find that everyone in the department wants to cry on her shoulder when a problem arises. If she continues to respond with sympathy and concern, she may take on a role in which she hears other people's troubles but is expected not to complain herself. Similarly, if Stuart makes wisecracks during a couple of meetings, group members may start expecting to hear jokes and funny remarks from him on a regular basis.

The kinds of roles people select serve different purposes. People may take on a role, such as leader or organizer, that helps the group get its work done. Or they may take on a role that holds the group together—the person who can be counted on to smooth ruffled feathers whenever conflicts arise among group members. Finally, group members may take on roles that help them meet personal needs. Thus, Stuart may be making jokes to cover up his own discomfort with being a group participant.

Awareness of roles is important because recognizing them can help the supervisor encourage desirable behavior or bring about a change in undesirable behavior. The supervisor would probably want to include an informal group's leader in planning how to carry out a change in policy. Or a supervisor who finds an employee's wisecracks to be a distraction during meetings needs to understand that other people may be encouraging this employee's behavior. Thus, to get the employee to stop, the supervisor will have to end the encouragement of the wisecracks as well as the wisecracks themselves.

**role conflicts**
Situations in which a person has two different roles that call for conflicting types of behavior.

Sometimes supervisors also have to resolve problems involving **role conflicts,** situations in which a person has two different roles that call for conflicting types of behavior. Suppose, for example, that several employees have been members of a volleyball team for a number of years. At work, one of them is promoted to be supervisor of the others, with the expectation that he will end the goofing off that has been common in the department. The supervisor's role as teammate conflicts with his role as strict supervisor. The way the supervisor resolves this conflict—which role he chooses—will influence his performance as a supervisor as well as his relationship with the employees.

## Norms

**norms**
Group standards for appropriate or acceptable behavior.

Groups typically have standards for appropriate or acceptable behavior. These are called the group's **norms.** For instance, in some work settings the employees have a norm of doing only what is expected of them and no more. They may fear that if they do an exceptional amount of work, management will expect that much from them every day. A new employee eager to develop a strong work record could anger the others if he or she violates the norm by doing "too much." Other norms may be stated rather than implied; for example, an organization has an expectation that everyone will arrive at work on time.

When a member of the group violates a norm, the group responds by pressuring the person to conform. Formal groups have procedures for handling violations of norms that are group policies, such as arriving at work on time. With unofficial norms, a typical first step would be for someone to point out to the violator how he or she is expected to behave. If that does not work, the group may resort to shutting the person out, ridiculing the person, or even threatening him or her with physical harm.

Employees whose norm is doing no more than is required have a norm that hurts the organization. When a supervisor finds that a group of employees seems to be behaving in a way that works against the achievement of organizational objectives, the supervisor could investigate whether these employees are following some norm of an informal group. This might be the case if half a dozen employees in the department regularly leave work 15 minutes early. One way to change this kind of norm is to look at the way the organization treats the behavior. Perhaps the organization or supervisor does not properly reward those who do follow the rules. In trying to persuade employees to change or ignore an informal group's norm, the supervisor must remember that violating norms carries negative consequences for group members.

## Status

**status**
A group member's position in relation to others in the group.

A group member's **status** is his or her position relative to others in the group. Status depends on a variety of factors, including the person's role in the group, title, pay, education level, age, race, and sex. Thus, in one group, the person with the highest status might be a male who is the tallest and owns a cottage by a lake. The others find this person's presence impressive and hope for invitations to the cottage, so his status is high.

Status is important to supervisors because group members with the highest status have the most effect on the development of group norms. Group members

These employees at Timken, a roller-bearing manufacturer with plants in Virginia and North Carolina, are members of a self-managed team that has cut the time it takes to manufacture and ship orders for high-tech bearings from two days to three hours. Cohesiveness in such groups promotes hard work and helps to accomplish productivity goals.

Source: © James Schnepf

with lower status tend to pattern their behavior after that of high-status members. A supervisor who wants to reinforce or change group norms will have the greatest success by focusing on the high-status members of the group.

### Cohesiveness

**cohesiveness**
The degree to which group members stick together.

The degree to which group members stick together is known as **cohesiveness.** In other words, cohesiveness refers to the "glue" that holds the group together. A cohesive group has members who want to stay with the group even during periods of stress on the group. They abide by group norms even when under pressure to follow other norms.

Groups that are cohesive work harder than others and are more likely to accomplish their objectives. Thus, when a group's objectives support those of the organization, the supervisor will want the group to be cohesive. The supervisor can foster cohesiveness in several ways:

- By emphasizing to group members their common characteristics and goals. A supervisor of a research department might point out proudly that this is a select group of talented individuals working on an important project.
- By emphasizing areas in which the group has succeeded in achieving its goals. A history of successes, such as accomplishing a task or increasing the status of members, tends to improve cohesiveness.
- By keeping the group sufficiently small—ideally no more than eight members—so that everyone feels comfortable participating. When a larger number of employees report to a single supervisor, he or she might want to support the formation of more than one group.
- By encouraging competition with other groups. In contrast, cohesiveness diminishes when group members are competing with one another.
- By encouraging less active members to participate in group activities. Groups tend to be more cohesive when everyone participates equally.

## Size

An organization's groups may vary widely in size. As few as two people can form a group. Up to 15 or 16 group members can get to know and communicate well with one another. Beyond 20 members, however, informal subgroups tend to form.

Big groups typically operate differently than small ones. Small groups tend to reach decisions faster and to rely less on formal rules and procedures. Also, quiet group members are more likely to participate in a small group. If group processes seem overly cumbersome—for example, if the group tends to take too long in reaching decisions—the supervisor might consider dividing the group into subgroups of about 8 to 12 members. A bigger group might make sense when a lot of work needs to get done and the individual group members can work independently most of the time.

## Homogeneity

**homogeneity**
The degree to which the members of a group are the same.

The degree to which the members of a group are the same is known as **homogeneity.** Thus, a *homogeneous* group is one in which group members have a lot in common. When group members have many differences, the group is said to be *heterogeneous.* Group members can be alike or different according to age, sex, race, work experience, education level, social class, personality, interests, and other characteristics.

The members of a homogeneous group enjoy a number of benefits. Perhaps most significant is that people feel most comfortable being around others who are like themselves. This may be the reason that homogeneous groups offer better cooperation among members, greater satisfaction, and higher productivity, at least for simple tasks.

Considering the benefits of homogeneity, it might seem a shame that the U.S. workforce is becoming more diverse. But for complex, creative tasks, a heterogeneous group can perform better than a homogeneous one because group members offer a variety of skills, experience, and viewpoints. The hetergeneous group as a whole has broader skills and knowledge, and it can examine problems from different points of view. Studies show that groups with diverse membership perform complex tasks better than homogeneous groups.

Robert Hayles, vice-president of cultural diversity for Minneapolis-based Grand Metropolitan Food Sector, uses an exercise that demonstrates the effect of diversity on group performance.[3] He divides workshop participants into three kinds of groups: same sex, same race, and mixed. He asks each group to come up with a way to use $300 to benefit everyone in the workshop. Then the class evaluates each group's idea. Nine times out of 10, says Hayles, the mixed groups score highest on creativity. He attributes these results to the different viewpoints of various types of people. The more diverse the group's membership, the more points of view group members bring to a problem.

## Effectiveness

The preceding characteristics of groups can affect whether a particular group is effective—that is, whether it achieves what it set out to do. To the supervisor, a group's effectiveness is one of its most important characteristics. In general, the organization's formal groups should be as effective as possible. The supervisor

**FIGURE 3.3**

**Stages of Group
Development**

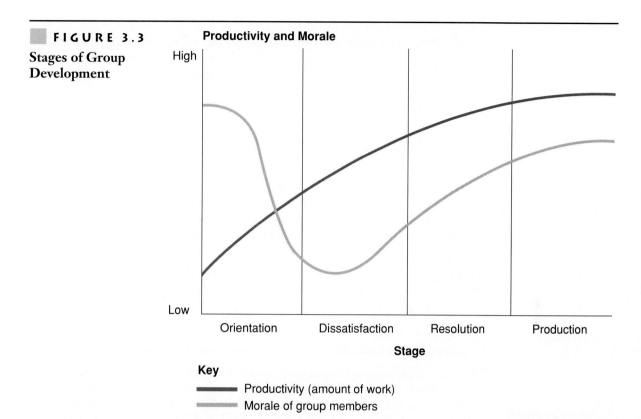

**Productivity and Morale**

Key
━━━━ Productivity (amount of work)
━━━━ Morale of group members

wants informal groups to be effective only to the extent that this supports organizational goals. For example, a company softball team that builds morale and improves working relations is properly effective. A clique that hurts morale among the employees who feel left out is not supporting organizational objectives.

## The Development of Groups

In a sense, groups are living organisms with life stages. They grow, are subjected to stresses, and either mature or die as a result. Figure 3.3 shows one view of group development, that of groups passing through the following stages:[4]

- *Orientation*—When a group first forms, its members tend to be highly committed to the group, but they do not yet have the experience and skills to work together efficiently. Group members tend to be concerned about what the group is supposed to do and how they will fit in. The supervisor's role is primarily to clarify objectives and provide direction.
- *Dissatisfaction*—If group members are able to learn their roles and the group's objectives, the group moves to the dissatisfaction stage. Although group members are more competent at working together, their initial enthusiasm has given way to disappointment with the day-to-day reality of being part of the group. While continuing to help group members develop competence, the supervisor must focus more on encouraging and motivating them.

- *Resolution*—If group members are able to reconcile the differences between their initial expectations and the realities they experience, the group moves to the resolution stage. During this stage, group members continue to be more productive and their morale also improves. The supervisor should focus on helping with conflict resolution and encourage group members to participate in planning and decision making.
- *Production*—If group members continue to resolve conflicts and develop a workable structure for the group, their output and morale will continue to increase. The group is effectively working as a team. When group structure must change or other issues arise, the group resolves them quickly. The supervisor should give group members as much autonomy as possible.
- *Termination*—At some point, many groups must come to an end. If the group had reached the production stage, group members may be sad. If the group ends before that stage, members are more likely to be relieved.

Getting a group to the resolution and production stages is challenging for supervisors who are most comfortable telling employees what to do. Instead, this process requires skill in resolving conflicts and fostering employee development (topics of Chapters 15 and 17).

# Teamwork

**team**
A group of people who must collaborate to some degree to achieve common goals.

Organizations today are increasingly looking for ways to involve employees in decision making and problem solving. For a growing number of organizations, teamwork is the means to employee involvement. A **team** is a group of people who must collaborate to some degree to achieve common goals.[5] When most organizations form a team, someone is appointed to be team leader. Often the team leader is a supervisor, and the team consists of operative employees.

Being an effective team leader draws on many of the same skills required of an effective supervisor.[6] The team leader needs excellent communication skills, patience, fairness, and good rapport with team members. In addition, because the purpose of the team is to draw on the expertise of all team members, the team leader will need to rely most on a leadership style that encourages involvement. (For more on this type of leadership, see Chapter 8.)

**self-managing work teams**
Groups of 5 to 15 members who work together to produce an entire product.

In the 1970s, it became popular to form teams in which employees suggest ways to improve the quality of their work. More recently, organizations have expanded their use of teams by creating **self-managing work teams.** These are groups of 5 to 15 members who work together to produce an entire product. The team members rotate jobs, schedule work and vacations, and make other decisions affecting their area of responsibility. Companies using self-managing work teams include Toyota, General Electric, and Xerox.[7] At GM's Saturn plant in Spring Hill, Tennessee, over 150 work teams interview and approve new team members, decide how to run their own area, and accept budget responsibility. One Saturn team rejected some assembly equipment and turned to another supplier whose equipment seemed safer.[8]

## Benefits of Teamwork

A basic benefit of using work teams is that the organization can draw more fully upon the insights and expertise of all its employees. At the beginning of this chapter, the story about Bostitch showed how a team of employees solved a problem that a supervisor was unable to solve alone. In the marketing arena, some companies are setting up sales teams combining technical and sales experts to better address the needs of their major customers. For example, the big producers of computer hardware, including IBM, Digital Equipment Corporation, and Tandem, combine experts in hardware, software, and technical support to help customers fully use the computers they buy.[9]

Teams can also serve as motivators. Employees who participate in planning and decision making are more likely to take responsibility for the quality of what they do. They also tend to be more enthusiastic about their work. Responsible, enthusiastic employees are more likely to work hard and deliver high quality. Such motivation occurred when the Tactical Electronics Division of Motorola's Government Electronics Group in Scottsdale, Arizona, began letting employees redesign production processes. As a result, says employee Doug Boone, "There was a great change around here. People were very relaxed, motivated, and happy." Joe Beard, another employee in the division, adds, "Most people, if you tell them what to do, they'll work at that pace. But if you let them decide how to do things, they'll surprise you."[10]

Ultimately, motivating employees and drawing on their strengths should enhance the performance of the organizations that use self-managing work teams. A recent survey of Fortune 1000 companies suggests that this is the case; about two-thirds of the companies that used employee involvement programs reported improvements in productivity, customer service, and the quality of their goods or services.[11]

The story at many small businesses also is positive. Growing Green, a St. Louis–based company that supplies and maintains plants for corporate clients, adopted the use of teamwork, charging its teams of employees with making decisions in their areas of responsibility. Co-owners Joel and Teri Pesapane credit employee empowerment for the company's steady revenue growth. Furthermore, notes Teri Pesapane, "We have a reputation in St. Louis for finishing a job on time and on budget, and that's because of team management."[12]

## *Leading the Team*

Many teams fall short of their potential.[13] Whether an organization's teams achieve the benefits of teamwork depends in part on the teams' leaders. Broadly speaking, the goal of a team leader is to develop a productive team. Experts in teamwork have linked team productivity to the team characteristics described in Table 3.1. In general, these characteristics describe a team whose members want to participate, to share ideas freely, and to know what they are supposed to accomplish. (See "Tips from the Firing Line" for more on leading a team.)

Westinghouse used a multidisciplinary team having these characteristics to redesign an electronic chassis (an electronically wired framework into which subassemblies can be plugged). The team's goals were to reduce the complexity and time required to manufacture the chassis. The team brainstormed new approaches to design and manufacturing. Team leader F. Suzanne Jenniches instructed the engineers on her team to look for the reasons behind the way things were done: "Their answer could not be 'because that's the way we've always done it,' " said Jenniches. Ultimately, the team reduced the number of solder joints and wire connections in the chassis from 1,700 to 0—the new chassis could be produced using only electronic data. Assembly time shrank from six weeks to four hours.[14]

**TABLE 3.1**

**Management Activities Related to Quality Improvement**

| Characteristic | Significance |
|---|---|
| Openness and honesty | These are signs that group members trust one another. Tact and timing also are important. |
| Leadership that does not dominate | The leader is flexible, changing with conditions and circumstances. |
| Decisions made by consensus | The leader will sometimes have to make a decision alone or reject suggestions, but all team members should have a voice in making many decisions, not simply a vote without a full opportunity to be heard. |
| Acceptance of assignments | Team members should willingly take on the tasks that must be done, then do them correctly and on time. Team members should view work as a cooperative effort, helping each other out as needed. |
| Goals that are understood and accepted | Goals give the team purpose and direction. Team members should view accomplishing them as the team's primary purpose. |
| Assessment of progress and results | Team members should focus on results. |
| Comfortable atmosphere | Some conflict can stimulate desirable action and change, but there should be a basic level of cooperation. |
| Involvement and participation | Team members should be involved in the work of the group. When a team member is reluctant to speak up at meetings, the leader should seek his or her input during or outside the meeting. |
| Debate and discussion | If everyone agrees all the time, it may signify that team members are unable or unwilling to contribute. |
| Atmosphere of listening | Team members should listen to each other, even when they disagree. |
| Access to information | All team members need to know what is happening. |
| Win-win approach to conflict | Team members should work to resolve conflicts in ways that let everyone be a winner. |
| Relatively low turnover | Members of a team must have a close relationship, which is impossible when the team's membership keeps changing. |

Sources: Adapted from Edward Glassman, "Self-Directed Team Building without a Consultant," *Supervisory Management*, Mar. 1992, p. 6; Louis V. Imundo, "Blueprint for a Successful Team," *Supervisory Management*, May 1992, pp. 2–3.

***Coaching the Team*** The team leader who can stimulate this high-quality performance is one who focuses on enabling team members to do their best. *Enabling* in this context means providing employees with the resources they need to do their job and removing obstacles that interfere with their work (such as procedures that slow employees down without adding value from the customer's perspective). Providing resources includes making sure employees have the training they need to be effective team members. Typically, employees are not used to working on a team and can benefit from training in decision making, conflict resolution, meeting

## TIPS FROM THE FIRING LINE

### *The Supervisor as Team Leader*

As a supervisor, you may be called upon to lead a team. With a few guidelines, you can build an effective, successful team. Here are a few hints from the experts:

- Understand what your team is supposed to accomplish.
- Select your members carefully, focusing on those who work well with others. Make sure you have a solid reason for choosing each person.
- Set clear goals and define success as achieving those goals.
- Determine a life span for your team. How long will it take to achieve the team's goals?
- Clearly establish which members will carry out particular tasks.
- Establish accountability. Do all team members report to you or to someone else?

- Set an agenda not only for meetings, but also for the life of the team. Have the team plan exactly how it will carry out the tasks that must be completed to achieve its goals.
- Have a reason for every meeting.
- Make sure team members have access to any necessary training.
- Focus on collaborative work and shared rewards.
- Deal with any conflicts among team members.

Sources: Ed Hopkins, "Effective Teams: Camels of a Different Color?" *Training & Development*, Dec. 1994, pp. 35–37; Glenn M. Parker, "Cross-Functional Collaboration," *Training and Development*, Oct. 1994, pp. 49–53; Glenn M. Parker, "Cross-Functional Teams," *Small Business Reports*, Oct. 1994, pp. 58–60.

management, interpersonal skills, problem solving, negotiation, and dealing with customers.[15] When a new member joins a team, the team leader can enable that person's full participation by making an experienced team member responsible for showing him or her the ropes and by ensuring that the team gives the new member an assignment as soon as possible.[16]

This kind of leader coaches employees—asking them questions that help them decide how to handle a situation instead of simply telling them what to do. The team leader encourages team members by expressing understanding and appreciation of their ideas and feelings, and limits his or her advice and criticism because these can interfere with members' creativity and stifle their motivation to find solutions.[17] The team leader knows when it is time to help the group stay on track and when to promote balanced participation from team members.

This style of leading may seem to leave a supervisor with less power than one who gives directions and checks up on performance. However, coaching enables the supervisor to build on the strengths and expertise of the whole group. The likely result is a stronger position for everyone, including the supervisor.

***Selection of Team Members***   A team leader may be charged either with selecting candidates for jobs that involve teamwork or with selecting existing employees to participate in a team devoted to a particular task. In either case, the supervisor should look for people who work well with others. If the team is to include people from several departments, the team leader should talk to other supervisors and employees to learn which employees would do best on the team. The employees of the new Toyota auto manufacturing plant in Georgetown, Kentucky, were expected to participate in self-managing work teams. In hiring, the company used a test in which applicants worked together to perform tasks. Experts watched the applicants to see how well they got along with one another, how much they listened to one another, and whether they seemed concerned about others.[18]

**team building**
Developing the ability of team members to work together to achieve common objectives.

*Team Building*    Once the team leader knows who will be on the team, he or she must develop the group's ability to work together to achieve common objectives. This process is known as **team building.** Team building includes several activities: setting goals, analyzing what needs to be done and allocating work, examining how well the group is working, and examining the relationships among the team members.[19]

At some organizations, a consultant with expertise in team building carries out this process. However, hiring someone often can be too expensive, especially at small organizations. Consultant Edward Glassman describes a three-step approach by which a supervisor can conduct team building:[20]

1. Set aside time at the end of team meetings to discuss the quality of the interactions during the meeting as well as the creativity of the results. Ask what went well and what needs to be improved.
2. Ask each team member to rate, on a scale of 1 to 10, how well the meeting went in terms of (*a*) whether everyone participated equally, (*b*) whether the team member influenced the outcome, and (*c*) whether the outcome was creative. Prepare a written summary of the ratings and discuss them at the next team meeting.
3. Use a questionnaire to ask team members how effective the team and team leader were in accomplishing goals. Such questionnaires are readily available from consultants in training, management, and human resources development.

Supervisors and other team leaders can embellish on this approach by drawing on the resources and talents they have available. However, supervisors need not go to the extreme that Harvey Kinzelberg did—the CEO of the Meridian Group, a computer leasing firm, took his management team on scuba-diving expeditions to stretch their creative thinking and make them aware of how much they depend on one another.[21]

*Communication in Teams*    The way the team leader communicates with the other team members will influence the success of the team. In general, the team leader should create a climate of trust and openness, and encourage team members to collaborate. The team leader also should acknowledge disagreement, not squelch it. To see whether you already have a communication style that would make you an effective team leader, or whether you need to make some changes to fill that role, take the Self-Quiz at the end of this chapter, on page 86.

Team leaders need this kind of communication style because successful teamwork requires open and positive communication among team members. Feeling able to express one's viewpoint and knowing how to do so constructively are essential for reaping the benefits of diverse viewpoints. Otherwise, peer pressure can lead to a uniformity that stifles creative thinking.[22]

Building effective communication was among the key challenges faced by Brian Wilson, charged with leading three of the production teams at GE Fanuc Automation North America. Before the company instituted teamwork, explains Wilson, "We had a situation where some people had been working together side by side for 10 or 15 years and hadn't had to speak to each other." Furthermore, the employees were used to taking orders instead of planning and making decisions. GE Fanuc helped with the change to teamwork by providing training in these skills, along with feedback on the organization's performance. Wilson (whose job under the old structure was that of a supervisor) and his team learned together that they were responsible for implementing decisions and for discussing and solving any problems that resulted. The change to teamwork has been good for GE Fanuc's business performance, but, Wilson admits, "I'm still learning to let go of the reins."[23] (See "Meeting the Challenge" for more on discussion within teams.)

## MEETING THE CHALLENGE

### *Making the Virtual Team Work*

At some point in your career, you might find yourself alone at home facing your computer screen tackling a day's work. Believe it or not, you might be doing this as part of a team. Computer technology, mostly in the form of faxes, E-mail, and software known as groupware, allows workers to communicate with each other electronically, whether they are in the same building or scattered across the globe. This means that "virtual" teams—"groups of people working closely together even though they may be separated by miles, even continents"—can tackle almost any task together, anywhere in the world.

But as technology gives organizations tremendous flexibility by allowing them to create virtual teams, it also provokes some problems. "Sometimes you just feel really lonely and disconnected," says virtual team member Barbara Recchia, communications program manager of Hewlett-Packard in California. Furthermore, how can team members who only communicate on-line read body language or silences?

Most supervisors who lead virtual teams advocate making sure that team members meet each other at least once, preferably more often. (They disagree on how much face-to-face interaction is necessary for the team to make its best effort at the task or function.) According to Chris Newell of Lotus Development Corporation, "It's important to develop some level of trust and relationship before you can move into electronic communication." John Spencer of Eastman Kodak Company agrees. "The most important part of the project is the up-front time." He believes personal contact is vital to the success of any project a virtual team tackles; recently, he brought two German engineers to the United States for six months so they and their American counterparts could get to know each other.

Sheldon Laube, national director of information and technology for Price Waterhouse, disagrees. Because some teams work together for only a week or two, it doesn't make sense to try to bring all members together. Instead, he emphasizes that Price Waterhouse's set methodology helps smooth collaboration.

Barbara Recchia relieves her own isolation by making more trips to the office. When she first started work on the team, she visited only about once a month. "It was a very odd feeling walking in and knowing you weren't exactly connected," she recalls. Once while talking with her supervisor at the office, Recchia observed her boss's body language and tone of voice as the boss told her she need not attend a certain meeting. Recchia realized that her supervisor really *did* want her to attend. She did so, then went to lunch with some of her team members, and remembers that day as one of her best with the team. Now she stops by the office once a week.

Virtual teams face many of the same issues that "tangible" teams face: selecting the right members, establishing roles, adhering to norms, and developing cohesiveness. Sharing information among team members is vital to the effectiveness of all of these team characteristics. And taking the time to add the human touch to electronic teamwork can be like adding a virtual water cooler around which people can gather to talk.

Source: Beverly Geber, "Virtual Teams," *Training*, Apr. 1995, pp. 36–40.

---

***Rewards***    For teams to remain productive, members must be rewarded appropriately. The organization should reward the entire team for its accomplishments instead of emphasizing individual rewards. The 1,100 employees of Behlen Manufacturing in Columbus, Nebraska, are organized into 32 teams. Employees are paid an hourly wage in addition to rewards based on group performance. Bonuses based on the amount a team produces free of defects can boost the pay of the team's employees by up to $1 an hour. In addition, Behlen divides 20 percent of its profits among its employees. Since Behlen has been using this compensation plan, employees have made thousands of suggestions for improvement that have saved the company almost $5 million and helped it exceed its profit goals.[24] (For more on group incentives, see Chapter 11.)

Team members also are likely to value different rewards; therefore, the rewards should be varied enough so that everyone will feel motivated. For example, the typical salesperson is motivated by money, whereas technical people might be more interested in recognition and promotion. Thus, one approach might be to use the company's basic incentive plan and also to ask the team members to reach a consensus on what additional reward they would enjoy receiving for a specific accomplishment.[25]

### Labor Law and Teamwork

An important issue concerning teamwork is whether employee teams violate federal labor law. Specifically, the National Labor Relations Act of 1935 forbids employers from dominating or interfering with the formation of any "labor organization," defined as "any organization of any kind, or any employee representation committee which exists for the purpose of dealing with employers concerning grievances, wages, hours of employment, or conditions of work." This provision—designed to prevent employers from interfering with organizing efforts by setting up "fake unions"—seems to prohibit teams that address the issues identified.[26]

In practical terms, teamwork probably need not lead to government sanctions. First, a ruling by the National Labor Relations Board suggests that while this government agency will set limits, it will not seek to prohibit most teams.[27] Furthermore, unions are unlikely to challenge unionized companies in this area, because most have approved of teams. However, during an organizing drive at a non-unionized company, the union could challenge the use of teams.

Supervisors and other managers should take some precautions to avoid violating the law. Managers who participate in team meetings should make sure they do not criticize the union at those meetings. Some legal experts recommend that supervisors avoid any discussion of topics that could become a matter for union bargaining, such as working conditions or pay, and focus instead on specific work-related projects or problems.[28] Teams also should *not* be set up to represent the company's employees. Teams should have power to solve problems, not to deal with management to seek a resolution.[29] Perhaps most important, a supervisor or other manager who wants to form a team should get legal advice on how to form and operate it without violating the law.[30]

## Meetings

Much of the work of teams and other groups takes place in meetings. When groups plan, solve problems, and reward successes, they usually do so in a meeting. Although the supervisor's role may be as participant or as leader of the meeting, this chapter emphasizes the latter. The principles described here apply to other situations as well, but supervisors will have less ability to make improvements when someone else is conducting the meeting.

### Reasons for Meetings

Meetings should take place when they serve a purpose. As obvious as this sounds, many supervisors and other managers hold meetings at a regularly scheduled time, whether or not they have something particular to accomplish. Thus, when the supervisor is thinking of calling a meeting, he or she should consider specifically what the meeting is intended to accomplish. If the supervisor wants to call a meeting as a way to make small matters seem important, to prove he or she is being democratic, or to rescue a lost cause (such as building a groundswell of support for an idea the boss has vetoed), the supervisor should not call the meeting.[31]

There are several valid reasons for holding a meeting. One is to convey news to a group of people. Doing this in a meeting gives the supervisor a chance to see and respond to people's reactions to the news. A meeting is also appropriate when the supervisor wants the group to participate in decision making. (Chapter 9 describes the pros and cons of decision making in a group.) Finally, the supervisor may use meetings to prepare group members for a change and to build support for the change. (Chapter 15 describes this process.)

As much as possible, a meeting should be scheduled at a time that is convenient for all participants. Times that tend to cause problems are peak working hours and the last few hours before a weekend or holiday. However, if a meeting is supposed to be brief, it makes sense to schedule the meeting for a half-hour before lunch or quitting time.

## Preparing for a Meeting

To prepare for a meeting, the supervisor should decide who is to attend and where to meet. When the purpose of a meeting is to convey information to the whole department, naturally the whole department should be invited. In many cases, however, the participants are to provide or evaluate information. In these cases, the supervisor should invite only those who have the needed information or expertise.

The location of the meeting usually depends on the available facilities. For a very small meeting, the participants might be able to meet in the supervisor's office. Larger meetings can take place in a conference room. When the whole department is called, finding a big enough space can be a challenge. In general, it is more comfortable to meet casually in the work area than to squeeze a big group into a stuffy conference room.

**agenda**
A list of the topics to be covered at a meeting.

One of the most basic preparation tasks is to draw up an **agenda.** This is a list of the topics to be covered at the meeting. A practical approach is to put the most important topics first, to be sure they will be covered before time runs out. To keep the focus on important topics, it is helpful to recall the purpose of the meeting. Figure 3.4 is an agenda that was used at a meeting called by an editor to discuss progress on a book. Notice that in addition to the topics to be covered, the agenda states the name of the group that is meeting, the location, the date, and the starting and ending times of the meeting.

The agenda should be distributed to all participants before the meeting is to take place. Participants should receive the agenda in time to review it before the meeting and make any necessary preparations. In addition, the person calling the meeting should make sure that participants have received any other documents they might need, so that they are prepared to contribute.

## Conducting a Meeting

Meetings should begin promptly at the scheduled starting time. This demonstrates respect for all participants' schedules and it encourages people to be on time. It helps to announce an ending time and to end the meeting promptly at that time. When critical issues come up near the end of a meeting, the group can reach an agreement to extend the meeting or continue the discussion at another time.

To make sure that meetings are as fruitful as possible, the supervisor can facilitate the discussion in several ways. One is to rephrase ideas that participants express. For example, if an employee on a printing company's health and safety

**FIGURE 3.4**

**Sample Agenda**

Team for *Supervision* Text

Sheraton O'Hare

June 24, 1996

8:30 AM – 3:00 PM

1.  Workbook (8:30–10:00)

    a.  Components and process

    b.  Possible sources of material

    c.  Tentative schedule

2.  Remaining manuscript work (10:00–12:00)

    a.  Examples in text

    b.  Opening vignettes

    c.  End-of-chapter material

    d.  Changes based upon reviewer feedback

3.  Working lunch (12:00–1:00)

4.  Videos (1:00–2:00)

5.  Ancillaries (2:00–3:00)

    a.  Components

    b.  Process

committee says, "We've got to do something about the fumes in the shop," the supervisor might comment, "You're recommending that we improve ventilation." This type of response helps to ensure that the supervisor and other participants understand what has been said. Of course, the supervisor has to use this technique with care; participants might become annoyed if the supervisor sounds like their echo. Also, the supervisor should summarize key points often enough to make sure everyone is following the discussion. Times to summarize include at the conclusion of each agenda item, the end of the meeting, and those times when people have trouble following the discussion.

**FIGURE 3.5**

Guidelines for
Conducting a Meeting

The supervisor should be careful not to dominate the discussion; instead, he or she should make sure that everyone has a chance to participate. Having everyone sit around a table or in a circle makes people feel more involved.[32] Some people find it easier than others to speak up during a meeting. The person leading the meeting is responsible for encouraging everyone to contribute, a task that can be as simple as saying, "Mary, what do you think about the suggestions that have been proposed so far?"

Quieting participants who are monopolizing a discussion can be a more delicate matter. One approach is to begin with someone other than the talkative person, then go around the table and hear each person's views on some topic. Also, the supervisor could have a one-on-one talk with the person monopolizing discussions, letting the person know his or her contributions are important but that the lengthy discourse is unnecessary.[33]

Throughout the meeting, the supervisor should take notes on what is being decided. This helps the supervisor summarize key points for participants. In addition, it helps the supervisor recall what actions are to be taken later and by whom.

When it is time for the meeting to end, the supervisor should help bring it to a close. A direct way to do this is to summarize what has been covered, state what needs to happen next, and thank everyone for coming. For example, at the end of a meeting called to decide how to make the company's purchasing decisions more efficient, the supervisor might say, "We've selected three interesting possibilities to explore. Max will research the costs of each, then we'll meet back here in two weeks to select one." Then the supervisor's job becomes one of following up to make sure that plans are carried out. As in the example, following up may include planning another meeting.

Figure 3.5 summarizes these guidelines for conducting a meeting.

### Overcoming Problems with Meetings

A frequent complaint about meetings is that they waste time because participants stray from the main topic and go off on tangents. Thus, an important job for the supervisor is to keep the discussion linked to the agenda items. When a participant begins discussing an unrelated topic, the supervisor can restate the purpose of the meeting and suggest that if the topic seems important, it could be covered in another meeting.

In steering the discussion back on course, it is important to avoid ridiculing the participants and to respect their efforts to contribute. The supervisor can do this by focusing on the effects of particular kinds of behavior instead of on the personalities of the participants. For example, if a participant tends to interrupt when others are speaking, the supervisor should not say, "Don't be so inconsiderate." A more helpful comment might be, "It's important that everyone in our group have a chance to state his or her ideas completely. Interruptions discourage people from participating."

Other problems arise because the meeting leader and participants have failed to prepare for the meeting. If there is no agenda, the discussion may ramble aimlessly. If someone failed to bring necessary background information, the participants may be unable to make plans or reach decisions, and the meeting will be unproductive. These kinds of problems lead to frustration and anger among participants who feel they are wasting precious time. The solution is to follow the guidelines described earlier, including creation and distribution of an agenda well before the meeting. When the supervisor is prepared to lead the meeting but others are unprepared to participate, the supervisor should probably consider rescheduling the meeting.

# Summary

**3.1  Explain why people join groups.**
People may join a group because membership in that group goes along with being an employee. (All employees are members of the organization that employs them.) Employers may ask employees to join particular groups such as committees or task forces. An employee also may join a group because doing so satisfies personal needs such as closeness, common goals, and achievement of personal objectives.

**3.2  Distinguish types of groups that exist in the workplace.**
Functional groups fulfill ongoing needs in the organization by carrying out a particular function. Task groups are set up to carry out a specific activity, disbanding when the activity is completed. Formal groups are set up by management to meet organizational objectives. Informal groups result when individuals in the organization develop relationships to meet personal needs.

**3.3  Discuss how supervisors can get groups to cooperate with them.**
The supervisor should make sure all members of a formal group know what they can and should be doing. The supervisor also should keep groups informed about what is happening in the organization and what changes are planned. The supervisor should support the group when members want to bring legitimate concerns to higher management. When the supervisor is responsible for setting up a group, he or she should combine people with a variety of strengths and backgrounds while avoiding separation of members of informal groups. Finally, general principles of effective supervision apply to supervising groups as well as individuals.

**3.4  Describe characteristics of groups in the workplace.**
Group members have various roles, or patterns of behavior related to their position in the group. Group

members are expected to follow norms, or the group's standards, for appropriate or acceptable behavior. The status of each group member depends on a variety of factors, which may include his or her role in the group, title, pay, education level, age, race, and sex. Some groups are more cohesive than others; that is, the members of some groups are more likely to stick together in the face of problems. Groups may vary widely in terms of size, with subgroups likely to form in groups of more than 20 members. Homogeneity refers to the extent to which group members are the same. All of these characteristics can influence the effectiveness of a group. In general, a supervisor wants a group to be effective when its goals support the achievement of organizational goals.

### 3.5 Identify the stages in the development of groups.

In the orientation stage, the group forms, and its members are highly committed to the group but lack the experience and skills to work together efficiently. In the dissatisfaction stage, group members are more competent at working together but their initial enthusiasm has given way to disappointment with the day-to-day reality of being in the group. During the resolution phase, group members become more productive and their morale improves as group members begin to resolve their conflicts. By the production phase, the group is working effectively as a team with still higher morale and productivity. At some point, many groups pass through a termination phase, during which group activity ends.

### 3.6 Explain why teamwork is important.

Teams bring employees together to collaborate on solving problems and making decisions. By using teams, the organization can more fully draw upon the insights and expertise of all its employees. Teams also can motivate employees by giving them a say in how things are done. As a result, organizations that use teams can benefit from improved performance, which is measured by higher quality and greater productivity and profits.

### 3.7 Describe how the supervisor can lead a team so that it is productive.

If building the team includes selecting team members, the supervisor should include people who work well with others. The supervisor should adopt a coaching role, enabling employees by providing them with the resources they need and removing any obstacles in their way. Then the supervisor builds the team by helping it set goals, analyze what needs to be done and allocate the work, examine how well the group is working, and examine the relationships among team members. The supervisor can increase the success of the team through effective communication that creates a climate of trust and encourages collaboration. The supervisor should see that teams receive group rewards valued by team members.

### 3.8 Discuss how to plan for effective meetings.

The supervisor should hold a meeting only when there is a valid reason for doing so. He or she should schedule the meeting at a convenient time and should plan who is to attend and where the meeting will take place. The supervisor should create an agenda, which lists the topics to be covered at the meeting. The agenda should be distributed to all participants far enough in advance so that they can be prepared to contribute at the meeting.

### 3.9 Provide guidelines for conducting effective meetings.

Meetings should start and end promptly. The supervisor should facilitate the discussion through such means as rephrasing what participants say and summarizing key points, without dominating the discussion. The supervisor should make sure that everyone participates in the discussion, take notes of what is being decided, and keep the discussion on track by reminding participants of the topic under consideration. After the meeting, the supervisor should follow up to make sure plans are carried out.

## Key Terms

| | | |
|---|---|---|
| group | roles | homogeneity |
| functional groups | role conflicts | team |
| task groups | norms | self-managing work teams |
| formal groups | status | team building |
| informal groups | cohesiveness | agenda |

# Review and Discussion Questions

1. Think of your current job or the most recent job you have held. (If you have never been employed, consider your role as a student.)
   a. What groups are you a member of? For example, what organization employs you? In which division or department do you work? Are you a member of any informal groups?
   b. Why did you join each of these groups?

2. State whether each of the following groups is formal or informal. Then state whether it is a functional group or a task group.
   a. Six employees who have decided on their own to research the possibility of establishing an on-site day care facility.
   b. The board of directors of a major corporation.
   c. Three employees who decide to plan a birthday celebration for a co-worker.
   d. Software developers at an educational publisher.

3. Joseph Dittrick is a supervisor in the marketing department of a toy manufacturer. He is responsible for leading a group of employees in finding ways to improve a problematic product. In what ways can Joseph encourage the group to be as effective as possible?

4. Why do supervisors need to know about each of the following characteristics of groups?
   a. Roles of group members.
   b. Status of group members.

5. Yolanda Gibbs supervises employees in the reference department of a public library. Her team meets once a month to discuss ways to improve the quality of services delivered at the library. Yolanda wants the team to be cohesive, so that its members will work hard. How can she encourage the cohesiveness of this group?

6. A supervisor observes that the members of a committee are not as enthusiastic about their work as they initially were. How can the supervisor help the committee move into the resolution stage of group development?

7. Describe briefly Edward Glassman's three-step approach to team building.

8. Peter Wilson is a supervisor who also leads a team that has been working on revamping an old product—snow saucers—to make them seem new and more attractive to a new generation of customers. The team includes both design people and salespeople. What type(s) of rewards might Peter consider for his team members if the project is successful?

9. How can a supervisor at an organization with self-managing work teams help the organization avoid violations of federal labor law?

10. Bonnie First supervises respiratory therapists at a large community hospital. One day her manager said, "Your department used too much overtime again last week. I want you to propose a solution to this problem, and I think you need to involve the employees in finding the solution. Get back to me in a week with your ideas." To prepare for the next meeting with her manager, Bonnie decided she needed to hold a department meeting at 1:00 the next afternoon. She askedsd two therapists to spread the word about this meeting.

    At the meeting, Bonnie described the problem. To her disappointment, no one seemed to have any suggestions. She said, "Unless someone has a better idea, you're just going to have to help each other out more when someone is having trouble keeping up. And don't hesitate to ask me to pitch in, too."

    How could the supervisor have better planned this meeting?

11. As a supervisor, you have done everything you can to prepare for a meeting, including writing up and distributing an agenda. At the meeting, you have problems with two of the participants. Ken dominates the conversation, drifting off to subjects that are not on the agenda. Sheryl refuses to talk at all, even though you know she has read the agenda and probably has something insightful to contribute. What steps might you take to elicit more positive participation from Ken and Sheryl?

## A SECOND LOOK

Recall the group that solved the problem of excess coating of staples and nails at Stanley Bostitch, Inc. Was this a functional group or a task group? A formal group or an informal group? Explain.

# APPLICATIONS MODULE

## CASE

### *Behlen Manufacturing*

One of the ways a supervisor can help ensure continued success of a team is to figure out what type of reward team members value, and provide it if possible. For organizations that use financial rewards, the issue can be particularly complex: Does everyone on the team deserve the same monetary reward? If not, how should the amount of reward be determined? Who decides which team members get what? Behlen Manufacturing in Columbus, Nebraska, has found a way to solve this problem.

Rewards for team achievement at Behlen are folded into each team member's total compensation package: A combination of base pay, bonuses, profit sharing, and employee stock ownership reflect company goals and individual as well as team performance. One reason for establishing such a plan is that Behlen's teams are permanent. Rather than forming task groups to solve a particular problem and then disband, Behlen uses teamwork to manufacture and sell its products. Behlen's teams vary in size: One team might have up to 60 people, another only 6.

"We are getting an increasing amount of cross-training all the time," notes CEO Tony Raimondo, "and productivity is rising." Increased productivity has solidified Behlen's commitment to teamwork. That is how the organization can work certain reward programs into its pay system. For instance, workers can receive bonuses of up to $1 per hour when their groups meet productivity goals. This amount may not sound like much at the outset, but the time can add up if the team has been working on a project for more than a month.

(These bonuses also are tied to quality: Defects are subtracted from the total produced by the group.) One of the best parts of the bonus system is that it is simple: Both workers and supervisors understand it, and anyone can calculate it.

Actual profit sharing is another part of the Behlen reward system: Employees receive 20 percent of profits. As teams improve their performance and increase productivity, profits rise and so do members' paychecks.

What about team members who slack off, do less work than their co-workers, or pay less attention to quality? That doesn't seem to be a problem at Behlen. According to Raimondo, "Performance has exceeded plan and expectations." Since the beginning of the team compensation program, workers have submitted 5,000 ideas for improving safety, quality, and efficiency; those ideas have saved the company $5 million. Indirectly, those savings drop right into employees' pockets.

1. Team members at Behlen seem to value the reward system that is in place. What steps might the company take to add less tangible rewards for employees who value them?
2. Do you think that rewarding an entire team for its overall performance is fair? Why or why not?
3. The Behlen teams are considered permanent. How might this affect their development?

Source: Donald J. McNerney, "Team Compensation," *American Management Association*, Feb. 1995, p. 16.

### S E L F - Q U I Z

## *How Do You Communicate as a Team Leader?*

In response to each item, circle the answer that reflects what you think you always do (SA), often do (A), rarely do (D), and never do (SD). Your answer should reflect your own perceptions of the way you communicate. Be honest with yourself; you are the only one who will see the results.

|  | SA | A | D | SD |
|---|---|---|---|---|
| 1. When people talk, I listen attentively; that is, I do not think of other things, such as my response or a deadline, or read while someone is talking to me. | SA | A | D | SD |
| 2. I provide the information the group needs, even if someone else is its source. | SA | A | D | SD |
| 3. I get impatient when people disagree with me. | SA | A | D | SD |
| 4. I ask for and carefully consider advice from other people. | SA | A | D | SD |
| 5. I cut off other people when they are talking. | SA | A | D | SD |
| 6. I tell people what I want, speaking rapidly in short, clipped sentences. | SA | A | D | SD |
| 7. When people disagree with me, I listen to what they have to say and do not respond immediately. | SA | A | D | SD |
| 8. I speak candidly and openly, identifying when I am expressing opinions or feelings rather than reporting facts. | SA | A | D | SD |
| 9. I finish other people's sentences. | SA | A | D | SD |
| 10. I find it difficult to express my feelings, except when stresses build up and I become angry. | SA | A | D | SD |
| 11. I am conscious of how I express myself: facial expressions, body language, tone of voice, and gestures. | SA | A | D | SD |
| 12. When people disagree with me, I avoid arguments by not responding. | SA | A | D | SD |
| 13. During meetings, I prefer to listen rather than to talk. | SA | A | D | SD |
| 14. When I talk, I am concise and to the point. | SA | A | D | SD |
| 15. I prevent arguments during team meetings. | | | | |

Source: Reprinted by permission of publisher from *Supervisory Management*, May 1992, © 1992. American Management Association, New York. All rights reserved.

Agreeing (SA or A) with items 1, 4, 8, 11, and 14 and disagreeing (D or SD) with the rest suggests that you encourage openness and candor; you create a climate of trust by involving the team in important decisions that affect their lives. You communicate clearly and concisely and balance task and process dynamics.

Agreeing with items 2, 3, 5, 6, and 9 suggests you tend to be task oriented and dominate the team. You are frequently intolerant of disagreement and may squelch involvement and discussion. Disagreeing with these items does not necessarily indicate that you encourage collaboration; it could be blocked by passive communication.

Agreeing with items 7, 10, 12, 13, and 15 suggests you squelch disagreement by avoiding it and therefore undermine the team's task and process dynamics. A lack of leadership will more likely destroy a team than tyrannical leadership. At least people know what to expect from a tyrant.

---

## Class Exercise

The class divides into teams of three to five people. Each team seeks to determine the best location for a new fine arts theater, student center, career placement center, or library on campus (the team or the instructor may decide which building).

With 15 minutes remaining of class time, each team should appoint a spokesperson to report to the class on the following issues: Was a consensus reached on the best location for the building? How many team members participated in the discussion and the decision making? How well did group members work together? What roles did they take on (e.g., did a leader emerge)? How did the group handle any problems?

If any further time remains, the class should discuss the experience as a whole, focusing on how task groups work, promote cohesiveness, deal with role conflicts, and so forth.

## Team-Building Exercise
## Understanding the Benefits of Working in Teams

This chapter, "Working with Teams" begins with the Stanley Bostitch, Inc., company slogan "None of us is as smart as all of us." Let's see if that statement holds true for this exercise.

### Instructions

1. Perform this part of the exercise on your own. When your instructor starts the clock, you will have two minutes to fill in the U.S. state names on Chart 1. The first letter of each of the 50 states is provided. Write the state name out in full; do not use abbreviations. Do not talk among yourselves during this step.

2. Form teams of three to five students to work on Chart 2. Your team should select someone to record your group's list. Without looking back at the first chart you completed, your group will have two minutes to fill in the second chart. Speak quietly among yourselves so that other teams will not overhear your answers.

The Team-Building exercise was prepared by Corinne Livesay, Belhaven College, Jackson, Mississippi.

3. Your instructor will read the 50 state names so that you may check your answers. Then fill in the information about your team's performance.

Chart 1: Working alone

Number of correct answers for each team member:

_____  _____  _____  _____

What is the average of these scores?  _____

Chart 2: Working in teams

Number of correct answers your team completed:  _____

How many in your team got the same or a better score on Chart 1 than the group got on Chart 2? _____

### Questions for Discussion

1. How many individual students, working alone, did as well or better than students working in one of the teams?
2. Benefiting from the collective knowledge of a group to help solve a problem is but one advantage to working in groups. Name some other advantages of working in an effective group or team that normally cannot be realized when individuals work alone.

## CHART 1: Working Alone

| | |
|---|---|
| 1. A | 26. M |
| 2. A | 27. N |
| 3. A | 28. N |
| 4. A | 29. N |
| 5. C | 30. N |
| 6. C | 31. N |
| 7. C | 32. N |
| 8. D | 33. N |
| 9. F | 34. N |
| 10. G | 35. O |
| 11. H | 36. O |
| 12. I | 37. O |
| 13. I | 38. P |
| 14. I | 39. R |
| 15. I | 40. S |
| 16. K | 41. S |
| 17. K | 42. T |
| 18. L | 43. T |
| 19. M | 44. U |
| 20. M | 45. V |
| 21. M | 46. V |
| 22. M | 47. W |
| 23. M | 48. W |
| 24. M | 49. W |
| 25. M | 50. W |

**CHART 2:** **Working in Teams**

| 1. A | 26. M |
|------|-------|
| 2. A | 27. N |
| 3. A | 28. N |
| 4. A | 29. N |
| 5. C | 30. N |
| 6. C | 31. N |
| 7. C | 32. N |
| 8. D | 33. N |
| 9. F | 34. N |
| 10. G | 35. O |
| 11. H | 36. O |
| 12. I | 37. O |
| 13. I | 38. P |
| 14. I | 39. R |
| 15. I | 40. S |
| 16. K | 41. S |
| 17. K | 42. T |
| 18. L | 43. T |
| 19. M | 44. U |
| 20. M | 45. V |
| 21. M | 46. V |
| 22. M | 47. W |
| 23. M | 48. W |
| 24. M | 49. W |
| 25. M | 50. W |

# Video Exercise 3: *Working with Teams*

## Video Summary

Southwest Airlines is the only company ever to win the coveted Triple Crown from the Department of Transportation for best on-time performance, best baggage handling record, and fewest customer complaints. You will see in this video program how Southwest Airlines' use of teamwork has helped them win the distinction of being one of the 100 best companies to work for in the United States.

## Application

1. Think about all the different kinds of groups and teams in which you've been a member or been involved. The checklist will help you to remember them, with "Other" spaces to fill in those not listed. Check all that apply.

School Groups/Teams

| | | |
|---|---|---|
| ❏ Sports teams<br>❏ Cheerleading squad<br>❏ Drama troupe<br>❏ Musical groups<br>❏ Hobby clubs<br>❏ Language clubs<br>❏ Study groups<br>❏ Parent-teacher groups<br>❏ School committees<br>❏ Other _____ | Community and Religious Groups/Teams<br><br>❏ Fund-raising groups<br>❏ Church committees<br>❏ Church groups<br>❏ Sports teams<br>❏ Chambers of Commerce<br>❏ Fraternal orders<br>❏ Political groups<br>❏ Boy/Girl Scout troops<br>❏ Volunteer organizations<br>❏ Special-interest groups<br>❏ Other _____ | Employment Groups/Teams<br><br>❏ Management teams<br>❏ Cross-functional teams<br>❏ Problem-solving teams<br>❏ Quality circles<br>❏ Boards of directors<br>❏ Work committees<br>❏ Work-unit teams<br>❏ Project teams<br>❏ Employee committees<br>❏ Labor union groups<br>❏ Work crews<br>❏ Other _____ |

2. Go back over all the checked items and circle those that you would define—any way you like—as a "really great" team.
3. Think about the "really great" ones and see if you can capture on paper what was different about these teams that you couldn't say about the teams you didn't circle. What was it that made you feel truly special about being on that "really great" team?
4. Examine the following table and circle those characteristics from columns 2 and 3 that were represented in your "really great" team experiences.
5. What can you take with you from your positive team experiences and apply to a work-related group or team situation in which you might be involved?

| Indicator | Good Team Experience | Not-So-Good Team Experience |
|---|---|---|
| Members arrived on time? | Members were prompt because they knew others would be | Members drifted in sporadically; some left early |
| Members prepared? | Members were prepared and knew what to expect | Members were unclear about agenda |
| Meeting organized? | Members follow planned agenda | Agenda was tossed aside; freewheeling discussion ensued |
| Members contributed equally? | Members gave each other a chance to speak; quiet members encouraged | Some members always dominated discussion; others were reluctant to speak their minds |
| Discussions helped members make decisions? | Members learned from others' points of view, new facts were discussed, creative ideas evolved, and alternatives emerged | Members reinforced belief in their own points of view, or their decisions were made long before the meeting |
| Any disagreement? | Members followed a conflict-resolution process established as part of team policies | Conflict turned to argument, angry words, emotion, blaming |
| More cooperation or more conflict? | Cooperation was clearly an important ingredient | Conflict flared openly as well as simmered below surface |
| Commitment to decisions? outcome | Members reached consensus before leaving | Compromise was the best possible; some members didn't care about result |
| Members feelings after team decision? | Members satisfied, valued for their ideas | Members glad it was over, not sure of results or outcome |
| Members support decision afterward? | Members committed to implementation | Some members second-guessed or undermined team decision |

Source: Michael D. Maginn, *Effective Teamwork* (Burr Ridge, IL: Business One Irwin/Mirror Press, 1994), p. 10.

# 4

*Honesty is the cornerstone of all success, without which confidence and ability to perform shall cease to exist.*
   **—Mary Kay Ash, founder of Mary Kay Cosmetics**

# Meeting High Ethical Standards

## CHAPTER OUTLINE

Ethics in the Workplace
*Benefits of Ethical Behavior*
*Challenges to Ethical Behavior*
*Differing Measures of Ethical Behavior*

Ethical Behavior of Supervisors
*Making Ethical Decisions*
*Supervising Unethical Employees*

Treatment of Whistleblowers

## LEARNING OBJECTIVES

After you have studied this chapter, you should be able to:

4.1 Define ethics, and explain how organizations specify standards for ethical behavior.

4.2 Identify benefits of ethical behavior and challenges that make ethical behavior more difficult in the modern workplace.

4.3 Discuss the impact of cultural differences on ethical issues.

4.4 Describe major types of ethical behavior that supervisors should practice.

4.5 Outline ways to make ethical decisions.

4.6 Provide guidelines for supervising unethical employees.

4.7 Define whistleblowers, and describe how the supervisor should treat such employees.

Source: © Rick Rusing/Tony Stone Images

## UNETHICAL, ILLEGAL ROAD LEADS TO JAIL

At P&H Plating Company, a Chicago industrial firm where 100 employees handle the plating of a variety of metals, owner and president Jeffrey Pytlarz directed the illegal dumping of toxic waste. The toxic material was a 4,000-gallon tank of cadmium cyanide, a solution the company had once used to plate materials for an electronics manufacturer. When that line of work ended, Pytlarz had to decide what to do with the cadmium solution. Processing it through the company's state-of-the-art pollution-control system would have generated so much heat that the system would have blown up. Having the waste treated off-site would have cost $40,000 to $100,000. Hard-pressed to handle the problem legally at a time when his company was losing money and had already heavily invested in pollution-control equipment, Pytlarz advised his wife, Cheryl Emrich, the company's environmental manager, to have the waste emptied into a drain at P&H's plant.

Pytlarz's plan, he says, was "to open the valve slightly and bleed out this solution a little at a time through our sanitary sewer." Emrich assigned a supervisor to carry out this order. The supervisor evidently misinterpreted the instructions, however, and opened the tank's drain fully and dumped the 4,000 gallons of solution into the sewer in a single night. After passing through the sewer system and a water reclamation plant, the polluted water emptied into the North Branch of the Chicago River. About 20,000 fish died as a result.

When Emrich and he discovered the empty tank, says Pytlarz, "we agonized over the decision." However, they did not report the violation to the authorities. Two days later, they learned about the dying fish. "At that point," says Pytlarz, "it was a little late to report the incident." A tip from an undisclosed citizen eventually led authorities to the P&H Plating Company.

Following his trial, Pytlarz was sentenced to 15 months in a federal prison. In addition, the former supervisor accused of actually dumping the waste was expected to plead guilty.

Sources: Matt O'Connor, "Couple Plead Guilty to Dumping Firm's Pollutants," *Chicago Tribune*, Dec. 5, 1991, sec. 3, p. 18; and Jerry Poll, "P&H Plating: How Could That Happen?" *Products Finishing*, Nov. 1992, pp. 72–83.

As discussed in Chapter 1, a supervisor is expected to be loyal and to follow the boss's directions. But other standards of behavior apply as well. Because he followed the boss's orders, a supervisor at P&H Plating harmed the environment and was accused of violating the law. To understand such situations and how to behave in them, supervisors need to be familiar with concepts of ethics.

This chapter covers the role of ethics in the workplace. Ethical behavior is distinguished from unethical behavior and supervisors are told how they can behave ethically. Suggestions are provided for handling the challenge of supervising unethical employees and employees who report unethical or illegal behavior in the organization.

# Ethics in the Workplace

**ethics**
The principles by which people distinguish what is morally right.

In general, **ethics** refers to the principles by which people distinguish what is morally right. For example, most people would agree that cheating is wrong, or at least they would agree that it is unethical to cheat an elderly widow out of her life savings. Many decisions about ethics are more difficult. For example, is it cheating or just clever to pad an expense report or to take advantage of a supplier's mistake in totaling a bill? The Self-Quiz on page 110 is a chance for you to examine your own standards of ethical behavior. To get an accurate score, be honest with yourself!

Some people say that "business ethics" is an oxymoron—that is, a contradiction in terms. Can businesspeople behave ethically, and if so, should they? One view is that profitability should be the overriding concern of business. This view makes it easy to behave ethically unless an ethical choice is also costly to the organization. Another view is that organizations and their employees have an obligation to behave ethically, even if doing so cuts into short-term economic advantages. The implication is that we are all better off if organizations and individuals consider the common good. A. Thomas Young, Martin Marietta Corporation's president and chief operating officer, describes ethical people this way: "[They] honor their word, follow the law, act honestly, respect other people's property, are loyal, and they work hard."[1] Presumably, as a supervisor, you are looking for just this kind of behavior in your employees.

Ethical issues are of particular concern in today's workplace. The toxic waste example at the beginning of this chapter illustrates how modern technology has made the potential consequences of unethical decisions enormous. Consider an even more shocking example: When journalist Rushworth M. Kidder toured the Chernobyl nuclear power plant during the cleanup that followed the 1986 explosion, he learned that two electrical engineers had been conducting an "unauthorized experiment" on the night of the accident. To see how long a turbine would keep turning when they removed the power, the engineers shut down the reactor, overriding six computer-operated alarm systems, and even padlocked valves open so they would not interrupt the experiment by shutting down automatically.[2]

**code of ethics**
An organization's written statement of its values and its rules for ethical behavior.

Recognizing the importance of preventing such lapses, many organizations have adopted a **code of ethics.** This is an organization's written statement of its values and its rules for ethical behavior. According to a recent survey, 60 percent of U.S. companies have codes of ethics.[3] (Furthermore, to help people resolve ethical dilemmas, one-third of the companies surveyed have an office or ombudsman charged with ethics.) To help U.S. organizations address ethical issues, the Clinton administration has drafted a code of ethics that is a voluntary code for

**FIGURE 4.1**

The Johnson &
Johnson Code
of Ethics

We believe our first responsibility is to the doctors, nurses, and patients, to mothers and all others who use our products and services.

In meeting their needs everything we do must be of high quality.

We must constantly strive to reduce our costs in order to maintain reasonable prices.

Customers' orders must be serviced promptly and accurately.

Our suppliers and distributors must have an opportunity to make a fair profit.

We are responsible to our employees, the men and women who work with us throughout the world.

Everyone must be considered as an individual.

We must respect their dignity and recognize their merit.

They must have a sense of security in their jobs.

Compensation must be fair and adequate, and working conditions clean, orderly and safe.

Employees must feel free to make suggestions and complaints.

There must be equal opportunity for employment, development, and advancement for those qualified.

We must provide competent management, and their actions must be just and ethical.

We are responsible to the communities in which we live and work and to the world community as well.

We must be good citizens—support good works and charities and bear our fair share of taxes.

We must encourage civic improvements and better health and education.

We must maintain in good order the property we are privileged to use, protecting the environment and natural resources.

Our final responsibility is to our stockholders.

Business must make a sound profit.

We must experiment with new ideas.

Research must be carried on, innovative programs developed and mistakes paid for.

New equipment must be purchased, new facilities provided, and new products launched.

Reserves must be created to provide for adverse times.

When we operate according to thee principles, the stockholder should realize a fair return.

conducting international business in a way that is fair and respects workers' rights. Figure 4.1 shows the code of ethics for Johnson & Johnson Corporation.

Codes of ethics provide guidelines for behavior and, perhaps more importantly, support top management's assertion that they care about ethical behavior. However, a code of ethics cannot ensure ethical behavior.

## Benefits of Ethical Behavior

Besides being morally right, ethical behavior offers some potential advantages to the organization. To be known as an ethical individual or organization is a satisfying way of maintaining a reputation for high standards. St. Louis–based Bi-State Development Agency sent the following letter to its suppliers to help them handle the ethics of giving holiday gifts to the organization's employees:

> We have chosen to buy your product or service over the year solely because of its quality, price, and service, and we confidently hope to do so in the future. Product excellence is the best gift we can receive at any time. Hence, at this time of the year, we know you will refrain from presenting seasonal gifts of a more personal nature to those of our organization you meet and work with. Actually, it's a policy based on our own feeling—which we know you share—that the best thing an organization like ours can do for the public is to deliver high quality service with the utmost efficiency and courtesy.[4]

Not only does this letter set high ethical standards, it spotlights the agency's commitment to quality.

When customers, clients, and suppliers see that they are treated ethically, they are more likely to want to work cooperatively with the organization and to do their best for it. For example, Curtis Rocca III, the head of Bio-Dental Technologies Corporation in Rancho Cordova, California, recalls that a salesperson offered him big discounts in exchange for sending Bio-Dental's check to the salesperson's home. Instead of snapping up the low prices, Rocca called the supplier's president and told him about the offer. Rocca says, "My call created so much goodwill we now receive preferential treatment and rock-bottom pricing."[5]

Ethical behavior can also improve the organization's relations with the community, which tends to attract customers and top-notch employees. In addition, ethical behavior tends to reduce public pressure for government regulation—a situation that most managers would view as beneficial.

In contrast, the costs of unethical behavior can be high. Organizations whose employees are unethical may lose respect, customers, and qualified employees who are uncomfortable working in an environment that compromises their moral standards. Following the disclosure of a fraud and embezzlement scheme at Phar-Mor, a discount drugstore chain, top management was fired and the company entered bankruptcy. Rebuilding Phar-Mor has involved slashing the number of employees by two-thirds and closing one-third of the stores.[6]

Unethical behavior has personal consequences as well. We have seen that the owners of P&H Plating went to jail. Phar-Mor's former president was convicted of over 100 felony counts related to the embezzlement and fraud scheme; he was expected to spend years in prison and be fined millions of dollars.[7] On a more mundane level, a supervisor may simply find that tolerating lapses of ethics leads employees to behave in increasingly unacceptable ways. For example, if the supervisor looks the other way when employees take home small items like pencils or screws, employees may eventually start "borrowing" bigger items.

## Challenges to Ethical Behavior

In spite of these implications, the restructurings, cutbacks, and layoffs of recent years have made ethical behavior harder to encourage. With greater responsibilities, supervisors and other managers in restructured or downsized organizations cannot monitor employees' day-to-day behavior.[8] At the same time, the

John Trent worked for 23 years for Digital Equipment Corporation. In May 1992, he took an early retirement package rather than be forced out of the company. With four children, Trent now works as a car-service driver for 10 hours a day for minimum wage plus tips, and his wife Joan is a waitress. Is It ethically correct for workers like John Trent to be removed from their jobs for the economic benefit of the company?

Source: © Steve Lewis.

uncertainty of the work environment has made many employees afraid of being ethical when doing so conflicts with other goals. Fudging numbers on performance records or producing shoddy merchandise to keep costs down is tempting, given the alternatives. In the words of Kirk Hanson, president of the Business Enterprise Trust, an ethics research group, "Quite simply, the individual who isn't perceived as a top achiever is a candidate for a layoff."[9]

Fear of being laid off also may lead employees to cooperate with unethical activities sponsored by others. For example, a Japanese company operating in the United States reportedly had its employees unpack machine tools when they arrived from Japan and relabel them "Manufactured in the U.S." so that they could be sold to the U.S. military, which required domestic products. An employee who objected to this task was told that if he did not like it, he could look for another job.[10] The fear of losing one's job makes it all the more important for supervisors to consciously consider the ethics of their decisions and to actively foster a climate that encourages ethical behavior. (See "Meeting the Challenge.")

## Differing Measures of Ethical Behavior

Meeting high ethical standards is especially challenging for those who work with people from more than one culture because ethical standards and behavior can vary from one culture to another. A survey of expatriate managers (managers from other countries) ranked the levels of corruption in business in several Asian countries (see Figure 4.2). According to the survey, the biggest risk of operating in the most corrupt countries is shifts in the political winds. An organization that has dealt with a bureaucrat or government-controlled enterprise in an Asian country may become the object of suspicion if that person or organization falls out of favor. The risks are greatest if the organization is relatively small or the matters handled are routine and require contact with lower-level officials.[11]

One reason for perceived differences in corruption levels is that gift giving in the workplace can have different meanings from one culture to another. In the United States, the giving of gifts often is interpreted as bribery, an attempt to buy influence. However, in many parts of the world, giving a gift is the proper way to

## Is It Too Hard to Be Good?

American businesses struggle with ethics at home and abroad. Two researchers, Joseph Badaracco of the Harvard Business School and Allen Webb of the McKinsey consulting agency, conducted interviews with young businesspeople to learn about their attitudes toward ethics in business. The results were published in the *California Management Review*.

Many of the people interviewed believed that the companies they worked for interpreted "ethics" as turning in a good performance and remaining loyal to the company. Unethical behavior by managers was often overlooked in these companies, as long as the managers were successful. Two-thirds of the interviewees believed their organizations would not respect an employee who disclosed unethical behavior. "The ethical climate of an organization is extremely fragile," note Badaracco and Webb.

Does a clear code of ethics help? Not necessarily. Even some of the best-known and most respected organizations have fought some battles over ethics. Johnson & Johnson, whose code of ethics pledges that managers' actions "must be just and ethical," was lauded for its level-headed, responsible behavior during the crises caused when criminals laced bottles of the company's Tylenol pills with cyanide. But recently, Johnson & Johnson admitted that the company had shredded documents related to a federal probe of its marketing strategy for the drug Retin-A. The company will pay $7.5 million in fines and other costs. Prudential, which has a strict code of ethics directing employees "to strive to be the best at helping each of our customers achieve financial security and peace of mind," must now settle claims for its subsidiary, Pru-

dential Securities, because of the subsidiary's improper sale of $8 billion of limited partnerships.

Another difficulty is the reality that supervisors are often caught in the middle. Young, idealistic employees may be able to afford blowing the whistle or quitting a job. Top managers may insulate themselves from these problems. But supervisors, who are partway up the career ladder and often have mortgages to pay and families to support, are more apt to remain loyal to the company's business purposes.

Finally, doing business abroad has its own set of challenges. Cheap labor in developing countries, along with differing sets of ethical standards in different countries, tend to cloud the issue.

But some American companies have begun to turn the trend around, even capitalizing on their reputations for ethical practices. Levi Strauss, Nike, and Cannondale are well known for their business ethics. In addition to adopting formal codes of ethics, some companies have ethics offices or ombudsmen that operate like watchdogs over procedures. Many business schools now require M.B.A. candidates to take courses in business ethics, and the federal government recently announced the establishment of a voluntary code of business ethics and workers' rights for U.S. companies that conduct business overseas. The code is supposed to designate "a worldwide standard for the conduct of American business."

Wrestling the ethics beast to the ground is not an easy task, but American businesses should try on a continual basis. Eventually, maybe they can tame it.

Source: "Good Grief," *The Economist*, Apr. 8, 1995, p. 57.

indicate one's gratitude toward and respect for the receiver.[12] Furthermore, although bribery is a violation of U.S. law, it may not be in other countries, which have different legal standards. For example, bribes paid by Danish companies to foreign companies are tax-deductible business expenses.[13]

What can a supervisor do if refusing a gift might insult the giver? Most important, the supervisor must follow company policy, and in many cases that means turning down the gift. At the same time, however, the supervisor should explain carefully and politely the reason for not accepting the gift. If a supervisor has immigrant employees who might not understand U.S. views about gift giving, this might be an area about which to educate all the employees before such a problem arises.

A company that prospered as a result of adhering to its ethical standards is Empire Southwest, a Phoenix-based distributor of Caterpillar equipment. Empire was shut out of the market in Mexico for years because the company refused to make payoffs known as *mordita* (meaning "little bite"). However, potential

**FIGURE 4.2**

**Ratings of Corruption Levels in 11 Asian Countries**

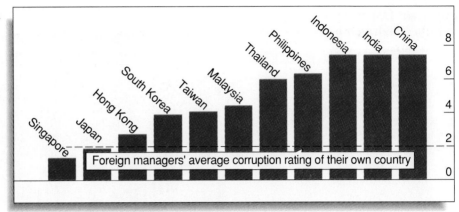

Source: "Hard Graft in Asia," *The Economist*, May 27, 1995, p. 61, with data from Political & Economic Risk Consultancy. © 1995, The Economist, Ltd.

customers—mining companies, farmers, and contractors—learned about Empire's determination to stick by its ethical standards. They were impressed and wanted to buy from the company. The potential customers lobbied the Mexican government and eventually got Empire the approvals necessary to open two dealerships in Mexico. Empire's chief executive, Jack Whiteman, says, "There is no doubt in my mind that ethical behavior pays off at the bottom line." When all things are equal in competing for business, he explains, "customers frequently give us the benefit of a doubt."[14]

Likewise, John Tu and David Sun found that importing the best of their cultures' values to the United States has helped their company prosper. Tu (from Shanghai) and Sun (from Taiwan) decided that their company, Kingston Technology, would demonstrate traditional Asian values—trust, loyalty, and mutual support—toward its customers and employees. The company never pressures suppliers for price concessions, has never canceled an order, and pays its employees generously. Far from cutting into profits, these standards have helped to create an organization that boasts soaring revenue growth, exceptionally high revenues per employee, and employee turnover of only 2 percent. Furthermore, despite recurrent shortages of the components used in Kingston's products (memory modules for personal computers), suppliers like working with Kingston so much that they always fill the company's orders.[15]

## Ethical Behavior of Supervisors

If supervisors wish to see a high standard of ethical behavior in the workplace, they must behave ethically themselves. Supervisors in particular must exhibit important dimensions of ethical behavior including loyalty, fairness, and honesty (see Figure 4.3.

As a leader, a supervisor is expected to be loyal to the organization, to his or her manager, and to his or her subordinates (see Chapter 8). When these loyalties

**FIGURE 4.3**

**Important Dimensions of Ethical Behavior by Supervisors**

**nepotism**
The hiring of one's relatives.

conflict, ethical dilemmas result. These loyalties also may at times come into conflict with the supervisor's self-interests. If supervisors are seen by others in the organization to put their own interests first, they will have difficulty earning the loyalty, trust, and respect of others.

Fairness is another important trait of a supervisor. Employees expect to be treated evenhandedly. They resent it if the supervisor plays favorites or passes the blame for mistakes on to them. Supervisors may find it harder to be fair—or to convince others that they are fair—when they supervise their own relatives. Therefore, supervisors may find it wise to avoid **nepotism,** the hiring of one's own relatives. A related problem can arise when supervisors accept a gift from a supplier or someone else who may wish to influence their judgment. Even if a supervisor is sure about remaining objective in the acceptance of cash, lavish entertainment, or other gifts, other people may question whether the supervisor can be fair. When supervisors place themselves in such a position, management tends to doubt their ability to exercise good judgment.

Honesty includes several types of behavior by the supervisor. First, when employees make a suggestion or accomplish impressive results, the supervisor should be sure that the employees get the credit. Pretending that other people's accomplishments are your own is a type of dishonesty. So is using the company's resources for personal matters. For example, a supervisor who spends work time chatting with friends on the phone or who takes supplies home for personal use in effect is stealing what belongs to the organization. Furthermore, the supervisor is demonstrating that such behavior will be overlooked, thus encouraging employees to be equally dishonest. Finally, supervisors should be honest about what the organization can offer employees (see "Tips from the Firing Line").

## Supervisors Should Ask for Commitment

The workplace is constantly changing. With restructuring, downsizing, and cutbacks, employees are afraid of losing their jobs. This fear can create challenges to ethical behavior, but supervisors can alleviate some of that fear through a new way of looking at things.

Daniel A. Skoch, vice-president of human resources at Brush-Wellman Inc., in Cleveland, says that his organization asks for "commitment—not loyalty—in exchange for employability." In turn, Brush-Wellman makes a commitment to its employees:

> We will help you grow and develop. We will provide you opportunities to learn, to be involved, to practice new skills, to have responsibility, to be respected and valued, and to be rewarded and recognized for your contributions. In return, we seek your commitment to our company's mission. We cannot guarantee what is going to happen in the future, but if it doesn't

work out, you will leave here a more talented, responsible, self-confident, and employable person.

Here are a few tips for supervisors who want to adopt the philosophy of commitment:

- Encourage employees to take advantage of training and educational opportunities.
- Encourage employees to "live the values of the organization, to be change agents, to be role models."
- Be honest and direct with employees with regard to employment security (or lack of it).
- Encourage employees to take responsibility for their own actions and careers.

Source: Adapted from Daniel A. Skoch, "Ask for Commitment, Not Loyalty," Reprinted with permission from *Industry Week*, Nov. 21, 1994, p. 38. Copyright 1994 Penton Publishing, Inc., Cleveland, Ohio.

## Making Ethical Decisions

Assuming that it is desirable to choose ethical behavior and to help employees do so, the challenge is to decide what action is ethical in a particular situation and then determine how to carry it out. There are no hard-and-fast rules for making ethical decisions. In some cases, two possibilities might seem equally ethical or unethical. Perhaps someone will get hurt no matter what the supervisor decides. Furthermore, as discussed earlier, people from different cultures may have different measures of ethical or unethical behavior.

When an ethical decision is hard to make, the following questions can help the supervisor think it through:[16]

- Have you defined the problem accurately?
- How would you define the problem if you stood on the other side of the fence?
- How did this situation occur in the first place?
- To whom and to what do you owe your loyalty as an individual and as a member of the organization?
- What is your intention in making this decision?
- How does your intention compare with the probable results?
- Who could your decision or action hurt?
- Can you discuss the problem with the affected parties before making your decision?
- Are you confident that your position will be as valid over the long term as it seems now?

Cargo-related crimes for all modes of transport in the United States cost at least $10 billion, according to the National Cargo Security Council. Computer-components importer Ron Collins (*photo*) of Miami says he has "seen palletloads of hard-disk drives worth maybe half a million dollars just disappear." Yet, many cargo crimes go unreported by company supervisors, who ignore the crime to avoid the risks of bad publicity and higher insurance rates.

Source: © Frank Zagarino, Black Star

- Could you comfortably disclose your decision or action to your manager, the head of your organization, your family, and society as a whole?
- What is the symbolic potential of your action if it is understood? misunderstood?
- Under what conditions would you allow exceptions to the stand you have taken?

As implied by some of these questions, the supervisor can promote ethical decision making by involving others in the process. When the group discusses the issue, group members can discuss their perspective of the situation and the underlying values. Discussing the ethical implications of the decision can help the supervisor see consequences and options that he or she might not have thought of alone. (Chapter 9 provides further guidelines for group decision making.)

Deciding what behavior is ethical does not always end an ethical dilemma. Employees are sometimes afraid that doing what is morally right will cause their performance to suffer and may even cost them a job. Andrew S. Grove, president of Intel Corporation, says, "The nub of ethical dilemmas is not whether we understand what's right—most of us instinctively do. What we are not so sure about is whether we want to deal with the risk and hassle involved in challenging something we know is wrong."[17] Grove recommends acting only when willing to accept these risks. However, he cautions against trying to rationalize a decision not to choose the ethical course of action; doing so can erode your ethical standards.

### Supervising Unethical Employees

It is tempting to ignore the unethical behavior of others, hoping they will change on their own. However, the problem usually gets worse as the unethical employee sees that he or she can get away with the behavior. Consequently, when the supervisor suspects that an employee is behaving unethically, the supervisor needs to take prompt action. The steps to take are summarized in Figure 4.4.

The first step is to gather and record evidence. The supervisor needs to be sure that unethical behavior is actually occurring. For example, if the supervisor

**FIGURE 4.4**

**Steps to Take When an Employee Is Suspected of Unethical Behavior**

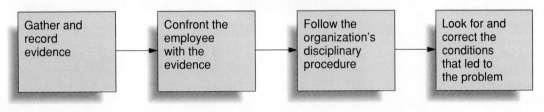

suspects that one or more employees are padding their expense accounts, the supervisor regularly should review expense reports. As soon as the supervisor sees something that looks odd, he or she should ask the employee about it.[18] After confronting the employee with the evidence, the supervisor should follow the organization's disciplinary procedure. (Discipline is discussed in Chapter 13.)

After dealing with the specific problem, the supervisor should try to understand what conditions contributed to this problem. That can help the supervisor avoid similar ethical lapses in the future. In analyzing why an employee has behaved unethically, consider whether you have created a climate for ethical behavior in the department. Have you set a good example through your own ethical behavior? Are the rewards for productivity so great that they tempt employees to cut ethical corners? Do the employees hear messages that say the organization cares only about achievements, such as, "I don't care how you get it done, just do it"? Martin Marietta's A. Thomas Young says, "If you expect honesty, you get honesty. If you don't, you get what you probably deserve."[19]

## Treatment of Whistleblowers

**whistleblower**
Someone who exposes a violation of ethics or law.

Someone who exposes a violation of ethics or law is known as a **whistleblower.** Typically, a whistleblower brings the problem first to a manager in the organization. If management seems unresponsive, he or she then contacts a government agency, the media, or a private organization. For example, as an unnamed company increased the number of personal computers it used from 2 to 200, employees often made copies of software programs rather than buying new ones. (Legally, this is somewhat like an instructor making photocopies of a textbook rather than requiring each student to buy a copy.) Someone called the toll-free hotline of the Software Publishers Association, which took the company to court. As a result, the company had to buy legitimate copies of the software and also pay a fine equal to the retail price of the additional software.[20]

A whistleblower's report may be embarrassing as well as costly to the organization. Nevertheless, whistleblowers are protected by federal laws, the laws of several states, and some recent court decisions.[21] For example, federal laws protect employees who make complaints pertaining to violations of antidiscrimination laws, environmental laws, and occupational health and safety standards. Thus, in general, employers may not retaliate against someone for reporting a violation. Suppose an employee files a complaint of sexual harassment; the organization may not react by firing the employee who complained.

To promote safety and eliminate the need for employee whistleblowing, Micro Metallics, a San Jose, California, firm that determines the recycling value of scrap metal used in manufacturing and electronic equipment, employs Mark TenBrink as an environmental manager. TenBrink conducts safety training (*photo*) and uses participation to avoid any language or literacy problems. For example, he gives the workers outlines of the facility and asks them to identify the location of fire and poison hazards. This promotes communication and allows the company to identify problems.

Source: © Linda Sue Scott.

In spite of these protections, whistleblowers often do suffer for going public with their complaints. Typically, the whistleblower is resented and rejected by co-workers, and the whistleblower may be demoted or terminated. Even when the courts agree that the whistleblower was treated unlawfully, it can take years for that person to be compensated by the organization or even appreciated by the public. Engineer Thomas D. Talcott quit Dow Corning in 1976 to protest what he saw as safety problems with the company's silicone breast implants.[22] Not until 15 years later did that issue receive widespread publicity. Talcott at least had the credentials to start a successful consulting business when he left his job, whereas many people would have a much harder time finding work. Because of these consequences—and out of fairness to one's employer—a would-be whistleblower should try to resolve problems within the organization before blowing the whistle.

The supervisor's general attitude toward whistleblowing should be to discourage reports of wrongdoing when these are motivated simply by pettiness or a desire to get back at someone. Nevertheless, when someone does complain, the supervisor should investigate the complaint quickly and report what will be done. This lets employees know that their complaints are taken seriously and that the supervisor wants to handle them fairly and appropriately. The supervisor should bear in mind that the typical whistleblower is not simply a troublemaker but a person with high ideals and competence.[23] Keeping communication flowing and responding to problems will allow the organization to find solutions without the costs and embarrassment of public disclosure. Finally, engaging in ethical behavior can eliminate the need for whistleblowing—and the other negative fallout of misconduct—in the first place.

# Summary

## 4.1 Define ethics, and explain how organizations specify standards for ethical behavior.

Ethics refers to the principles by which people distinguish what is morally right. Organizations are particularly concerned about ethical behavior because modern technology has made the potential consequences of unethical behavior enormous. Recognizing the importance of preventing ethical lapses, many organizations have adopted a code of ethics. Codes of ethics provide guidelines for behavior and support top management's assertion that they care about ethical behavior.

## 4.2 Identify benefits of ethical behavior and challenges that make ethical behavior more difficult in the modern workplace.

To be known as an ethical organization is a satisfying way of maintaining a reputation for high standards. When customers, clients, and suppliers see that they are treated ethically, they are more likely to want to work cooperatively with the organization and to do their best for it. Ethical behavior can also improve community relations, attracting customers and qualified employees. Unethical behavior, on the other hand, can cause an organization to lose both respect and the best employees (who may be uncomfortable working for an unethical organization). Unethical behavior may even land employees and managers in jail, if they break the law.

An uncertain work environment can make ethical behavior harder to encourage. Fear of losing one's job can lead employees to cooperate with unethical activities sponsored by others, so it is important for supervisors to foster a climate that encourages ethical behavior.

## 4.3 Discuss the impact of cultural differences on ethical issues.

In some cases, ethical standards and behavior vary among cultures. The biggest risk of operating in the most corrupt countries is shifts in the political winds. One reason for perceived differences in levels of corruption is that gift giving in the workplace is interpreted differently from country to country. The supervisor should always follow company policy, but should do so carefully and politely in order not to offend members of another culture.

## 4.4 Describe major types of ethical behavior that supervisors should practice.

Supervisors should be loyal to the organization, their manager, and their subordinates. Supervisors should treat others, especially employees, fairly. Ways to dispel any doubts about one's fairness are to avoid nepotism and to decline gifts from suppliers and others seeking influence. Finally, supervisors should be honest, which includes giving subordinates credit for their accomplishments and avoiding personal use of the company's resources.

## 4.5 Outline ways to make ethical decisions.

There are no hard-and-fast rules for making ethical decisions, but asking some essential questions can help. The supervisor can promote ethical decision making by involving others in the thought process. Discussing the ethical implications of the decision can help the supervisor see consequences and options that he or she might not have thought of alone.

## 4.6 Provide guidelines for supervising unethical employees.

When the supervisor believes an employee is doing something unethical, the supervisor should take immediate action. First, the supervisor should gather and record evidence. Then the supervisor confronts the employee with the evidence and follows the organization's disciplinary procedure. After dealing with a specific problem, the supervisor should try to understand what conditions contributed to the problem and then seek to correct those conditions.

## 4.7 Define whistleblowers, and describe how the supervisor should treat such employees.

Whistleblowers are people who expose a violation of ethics or law. They are protected from retaliation by federal and state laws as well as recent court decisions. The supervisor should discourage reports of wrongdoing when they are motivated simply by pettiness or a desire for revenge. However, when someone does complain, the supervisor should quickly investigate the complaint and report what will be done. This lets employees know that their complaints are taken seriously. Keeping communication flowing and responding to problems ultimately allows the organization to find its own solutions.

## Key Terms

ethics

code of ethics

nepotism

whistleblower

## Review and Discussion Questions

1. What are some of the benefits of ethical behavior? What are some of the challenges to ethical behavior?
2. Gift giving in the workplace is interpreted differently from culture to culture. What can a supervisor do if his or her company prohibits accepting gifts but a customer from another culture insists on offering one?
3. In what ways can loyalty create conflict for a supervisor?
4. In what ways should a supervisor practice honesty in the workplace?
5. In each of the following situations, what would have been the ethical thing for the employee or supervisor to do? What criteria did you use to decide? What would you have done in that situation? Why?

    a. Upon being hired, a new employee offers his supervisor confidential information about his former employer's marketing plan for a new product. The two companies have competing product lines.

    b. The associate editor of a magazine learns that a particularly newsworthy individual wants to be paid to grant an interview with the magazine. The magazine's policy is never to pay for interviews, but the editor knows she could "bury" the expense elsewhere in her budget. She desperately wants the story; she knows it will be good for both the magazine and her career.

6. Devon Price supervises a crew of maintenance workers. One day a secretary at the company took him aside and asked, "Do you know that Pete [a member of the crew] has been taking home supplies like nails and tape to work on personal projects?" What should Devon do?

7. Assume that Pete, the maintenance worker in question 6, was discovered pilfering supplies and was disciplined. Upset, he decides to act on some safety problems he has observed and complained about, and he reports them to the local office of the Occupational Safety and Health Administration (OSHA). When Devon, Pete's supervisor, finds out that the department will be investigated by OSHA, he is furious. It seems as though Pete is nothing but a troublemaker. What should Devon do?

### A SECOND LOOK

In the story of P&H Plating at the beginning of this chapter, a supervisor had to choose between obeying his boss and obeying environmental laws. What would you have advised the supervisor to do when faced with that choice?

# APPLICATIONS MODULE

## CASE

### *DuPont Sweeps Test Results under the Rug*

When a few small nursery growers noticed that their trees were a bit stunted, no one seemed worried. Then larger growers in Florida and Hawaii began to complain that their plants had a yellowish hue, the leaves were rotting, and the roots were dying. Fruit and vegetable growers reported entire acres of dead or deformed vegetation. The growers believed that the culprit was Benlate, a DuPont product used to deter fungus growth. DuPont actually pulled the product off the market because the organization believed that Benlate had been contaminated by a common, relatively harmless herbicide. The company's aim seemed to be to work with its customers, not against them.

But as the company began to research the problem, it stumbled into a nightmare. Researchers discovered that Benlate had been contaminated by one of DuPont's hottest new products—a superpotent weed killer. The weed killer and Benlate were manufactured at the same plant, and company records showed that quality-control measures were substandard.

Thus began the cover-up, in which employees involved in research or other aspects of the problem received strict instructions on how to behave. DuPont told researchers not to share findings or other information with their supervisors and not to have hallway conversations about their work. They were warned not to "draw conclusions" or "speculate" about the results of their experiments. A company lawyer suggested that no document containing research findings contain the word "Benlate," and that any meetings pertaining to the situation be called "Luncheon Update Meetings."

When research findings at an outside laboratory showed evidence of contamination, one of the principal scientists now admits that he simply "doubled the threshold for a positive finding."

All of this activity was designed to prepare for the massive court cases that were getting under way. In the end, data were so skillfully manipulated or withheld that several settlements were made out of court, to DuPont's benefit. DuPont's chairman called one major settlement "a victory for DuPont, our employees, and our science." But the nightmare is returning. Several plaintiffs have asked for retrials on the grounds of withheld evidence, and new claims have emerged. Everyone's ethics have been challenged—DuPont's top executives, its lawyers, its scientists, its consultants. In the end, the company's reputation may pay the highest price of all.

1. What circumstances made ethical behavior difficult for DuPont's research scientists in the Benlate situation?
2. If there had been a whistleblower early on in the situation, do you think that the problem would have grown as large as it did? Why or why not?
3. What do you think will be the ultimate costs in terms of ethical or unethical behavior to DuPont when the Benlate situation is finally resolved?

Source: Milo Geyelin, "DuPont Draws Fire for Stonewall Defense of a Suspect Fungicide," *The Wall Street Journal*, May 3, 1994, pp. A1, A6.

### SELF-QUIZ

## *Your Ethical Standards*

Ethics have different degrees of importance to the career prospects of different people. To determine if ethics are likely to play an important role in your career, take the following quiz:

1. If my boss asked me to lie to cover one of his or her mistakes, I would:
   a. Quit.
   b. Lie.
   c. Say it made me uncomfortable.
   d. Do it this time but refuse if it became a pattern.
2. If I discovered that I unintentionally had violated an important regulation, I would:
   a. File a report acknowledging my mistake.
   b. Wait and see if it was as important a violation as it seemed.
   c. Discuss the situation with my supervisor.
   d. Try to straighten out the error and talk to my supervisor if I could not.
3. If I observed a fellow employee stealing from the company, I would:
   a. Report the employee.
   b. Keep an eye on the employee.
   c. Ask the employee why he or she did it and then decide what to do.
   d. Try to make the employee return what he or she stole.
4. If I knew my boss and a co-worker were having an affair, I would:
   a. Transfer to another department.
   b. Ignore it.
   c. Wait and see if I was affected.
   d. Talk to my supervisor to clear the air.
5. If a headhunter approached me with an attractive offer, I would:
   a. Talk it over with my supervisor before proceeding.
   b. Ask my current employer to make a better counteroffer.
   c. Meet the representatives of the outside firm and talk to my supervisor if I was serious about leaving.
   d. Ask my employer to make his or her best offer and then take the highest offer.
6. If I thought one of my employees had a drug problem, I would:
   a. Exercise my right to ask the employee to take a drug test.
   b. Wait and see if the employee's performance declines.
   c. Talk it over with the employee.
   d. Seek guidance from the personnel department.

7. If a fellow employee was having trouble keeping up with his or her work because of family problems, I would:
    *a.* Try to help by taking up the slack.
    *b.* Advise him or her to talk to our supervisor.
    *c.* Help out for a short while.
    *d.* Try to talk to a member of the family.

8. If a fellow employee was a victim of racial discrimination, I would:
    *a.* Create a file documenting the problem.
    *b.* Offer the employee my support if he or she complained.
    *c.* Complain to a superior likely to be sympathetic.
    *d.* Advise the person that he or she might be happier elsewhere.

9. If I took a job with a competing company, I would:
    *a.* Never use information from my current job.
    *b.* Use information to support my new employer.
    *c.* Use only general information.
    *d.* Seek legal counsel before using information.

If you answered (*a*) most often, you have a strong sense of ethics but tend to be rigid. You will run into ethical conflicts in your career unless you find a very like-minded company.

If you answered (*b*) most often, you are too willing to compromise on ethics. You will run into trouble if your job requires you to exercise judgment without clear guidelines.

If you answered (*c*) most often, you have a strong sense of ethics balanced with flexibility. You can act ethically and succeed in most organizations but will leave those that are wholly unethical.

If you answered (*d*) most often, you are unwilling to deal with ethical conflicts. You will run into trouble when others sense that you avoid hard issues.

Source: Copyright Mark Pastin, 1993, P.O. Box 24838, Tempe, AZ 85285, (602) 831–6920.

## *Class Exercise*

Each student completes the survey in Figure 4.5 anonymously, circling all the answers that apply. The instructor tabulates the results and distributes them for discussion at the next class session.

For each item in the survey, the class discusses the following questions:

- Which answer(s) were selected by most students?
- What is the justification for the answers selected?

- If you were the supervisor of an employee who acted in this way, how would you respond (assuming that you observed the behavior)?
- If your supervisor learned that you had acted in the way indicated by the survey response, how do you think your career would be affected?

Source: This exercise is based on a suggestion submitted by James Mulvihill, Mankato, MN.

### FIGURE 4.5

**Survey for Class**

### Exercise

Which of the following actions would you take?

Circle the letters of as many choices as apply to you.

1.  Put false information in your résumé:

    *a.* If necessary to get a job.
    *b.* Only about minor details.
    *c.* If most people are doing it.
    *d.* Never.

2.  Tell a competing company secrets about your employer's product or procedures:

    *a.* To land a job with the competitor.
    *b.* In exchange for $100.
    *c.* In exchange for $1 million.
    *d.* Never.

3.  Cheat on a test used as the basis for promotion:

    *a.* If you have a family to support.
    *b.* If you think the test is unfair.
    *c.* If your co-workers are doing it.
    *d.* Never.

4.  Use the office copier:

    *a.* To make a copy of your dentist's bill.
    *b.* To make six copies of a report that is related to charitable work you do.
    *c.* To make 50 copies of your résumé.
    *d.* Never.

5.  Pad your expense account for a business trip:

    *a.* If you believe you are underpaid.
    *b.* Only for small amounts that the employer won't miss.
    *c.* Only when you are experiencing financial problems.
    *d.* Never.

6.  Call in sick when you aren't sick:

    *a.* If you're worn out from working on a big project.
    *b.* If your child is sick.
    *c.* If you need to recover from the weekend.
    *d.* Never.

7.  Lie about your supervisor's whereabouts when he or she takes a long, liquid lunch:

    *a.* Only if specifically instructed to do so.
    *b.* If the supervisor gives you a generous raise in return.
    *c.* Only when the person asking is your supervisor's superior.
    *d.* Never.

## Team-Building Exercise

## Making Tough Choices in the World of Work

This exercise provides you with an opportunity to practice what you learned in this chapter, "Meeting High Ethical Standards."

### Instructions

1. You and the rest of the class are supervisors at Martin Marietta Corporation in Orlando, Florida. You are getting ready to do the group exercise in an ethics training session. The training instructor announces you will be playing *Gray Matters: The Ethics Game. Gray Matters,* which was prepared for Martin Marietta employees, also is played at 41 universities, including Harvard, and at 65 other companies. Although there are 55 scenarios in *Gray Matters,* you will have time during this session to complete only five scenarios.[1]

2. The training instructor asks you to form into groups of four to six supervisors and to appoint a group leader who will read the case to the group, conduct a discussion of the case, obtain a consensus answer to the case, and then report the group's answers to the training instructor. You will have five minutes to reach each decision, after which all groups will discuss their answers and the instructor will give the point values and rationale for each choice. Then you will have five minutes for the next case, until all five cases have been completed. Keep track of your group's score for each case; the group scoring the most points will be the winning team.

3. You may believe some cases lack clarity or that some of the choices are not as precise as you would have liked. Also, some cases have only one solution, whereas others have more than one solution. In still others there is no ideal solution, and you must choose the answer that is the best of those presented. Each choice is assessed points to reflect which answer is the most correct. Your group's task is to select only *one* option in each case.

**Case 1.** Two of your subordinates routinely provide their children with school supplies from the office. How do you handle this situation?

   *a.* Lock up the supplies and issue them only as needed and signed for.
   *b.* Tell these two subordinates that supplies are for office use only.
   *c.* Report the theft of supplies to the head of security.
   *d.* Send a notice to all employees that office supplies are for office use only and that disregard will result in disciplinary action.

**Case 2.** Your operation is being relocated. The personnel regulations are complex and might influence your employee's decisions about staying on the "team." Relocating with no experienced staff would be very difficult for you. What do you tell your employees about their options?

   *a.* State that the relocation regulations are complex; you won't go into them right now. However, you tell them that everything probably will come out all right in the end.
   *b.* Suggest that they relocate with you, stating that a job in hand is worth an unknown in the bush.
   *c.* Present them with your simplified version of the regulations and encourage them to come along.
   *d.* Tell them only that you'd like them to relocate with you and conserve the team, which has worked so well together.

---

[1]Permission granted by the author of *Gray Matters* (George Sammet, Jr., Vice-President, Office of Corporate Ethics, Martin Marietta Corporation, Orlando, FL) to use these portions of *Gray Matters: The Ethics Game* © 1992. If you would like more information about the complete game, call 1–800–3ETHICS.

**Case 3.** A friend of yours wants to transfer to your division, but he may not be the best qualified for the job. You do have an opening for which one other person, whom you do not know, has applied. What do you do?

   *a.* Select the friend you know and in whom you have confidence.
   *b.* Select the other person, who you are told is qualified.
   *c.* Request a qualifications comparison of the two from the human resources department.
   *d.* Request the human resources department to extend the search for additional candidates before making the selection.

**Case 4.** Your new employee is the niece of the vice-president of finance. Her performance is poor, and she has caused trouble with her co-workers. What do you do?

   *a.* Call her in and talk to her about her inadequacies.
   *b.* Ask the human resources department to counsel her and put her on a performance improvement plan.
   *c.* Go see her uncle.
   *d.* Maybe her problems are caused by the newness of the job; give her some time to come around.

**Case 5.** After three months you discover that a recently hired employee who appears to be very competent falsified her employment application by claiming to have a college degree when she did not. As her supervisor, what do you do?

   *a.* You are happy with the new employee, so you do nothing.
   *b.* Discuss the matter with the human resources department to determine company policy.
   *c.* Recommend that she be fired for lying.
   *d.* Consider her performance, length of service, and potential benefit to the organization before making any recommendation to anyone.

# Video Exercise 4: *Meeting High Ethical Standards*

## *Video Summary*

This video program produced by Arthur Andersen contains five vignettes that raise ethical issues faced by many supervisors and their employees in today's business world. They deal with choosing a supplier based on friendship, handling perceived wage discrimination based on race, responding to sexual harassment in the office, resorting to rumors to gain an edge over the competition, and "ballparking" on an expense report.

## *Application*

1. Form groups of three to five students to discuss each vignette after viewing it on the videotape.
2. The two questions posed after each vignette are:
   What is the ethical dilemma?
   What would you do?
3. The information in the table below answers the first question for you. After your group has generated some alternatives and decided what is the best way to handle the ethical dilemma, fill in the answer to the second question.

| Case 1 | **Scenario:** In this vignette, a project manager has been instructed to award a contract to the lowest bidder on a job, assuming all other things, such as quality and delivery, are fairly equal. After making his selection, the project manager is reminded by his boss that one of the boss's fraternity brothers, who is also a good friend, heads another company bidding on the contract. |
|---|---|
| | **Ethical Dilemma:** Should the project manager award the job to the lowest bidder or go with the company owned by the boss's fraternity brother and friend? |
| | **Your Group's Decision:** |

| Case 2 | **Scenario:** Two secretaries discuss their pay and discover that one makes 30 cents per hour more than the other. The lesser-paid secretary is openly hostile and plans to file a lawsuit against her employer for discrimination. |
|---|---|
| | **Ethical Dilemma:** Should the lawsuit be filed? What could be some extenuating factors? |
| | **Your Group's Decision:** |

| Case 3 | **Scenario:** This self-proclaimed office playboy can't seem to keep his comments, or his hands, to himself. |
| --- | --- |
| | **Ethical Dilemma:** When does "just kidding around" become sexual harassment? |
| | **Your Group's Decision:** |

| Case 4 | **Scenario:** An employee was fired from his job and immediately went into business for himself, soliciting his former employer's clients by underbidding them on jobs. Management at the former company is discussing beginning a "smear campaign" to spread the word how Jack was fired for incompetency. |
| --- | --- |
| | **Ethical Dilemma:** Do two wrongs make a right? What action, if any, should the former employer take? |
| | **Your Group's Decision:** |

| Case 5 | **Scenario:** Two salesmen are preparing their expense reports for a recent trip to New York City. One has misplaced several receipts and is "ballparking" what his expenses must have been. |
| --- | --- |
| | **Ethical Dilemma:** When does "ballparking" on an expense report become outright lying and theft from one's employer? |
| | **Your Group's Decision:** |

# 5

*One machine can do the work of 50 ordinary men. No machine can do the work of one extraordinary man.*

**—Elbert Hubbard, late-19th-century writer**

# Using Modern Technology

## LEARNING OBJECTIVES

After you have studied this chapter, you should be able to:

5.1 Define *technology* and *modern technology*.

5.2 Describe the impact of automation and information technology on the modern workplace.

5.3 Explain how modern technology helps supervisors carry out the basic management functions.

5.4 Discuss how modern technology has affected the supervisor's role by enabling the restructuring of organizations and work processes.

5.5 Describe the supervisor's role in identifying needs for new technology and selecting the appropriate technologies to meet those needs.

5.6 Identify common reactions to new technology and ways supervisors should handle those reactions.

## YOGURT GOES HIGH-TECH

Chocolate yogurt? Thousands of cups of Stonyfield Farm Inc.'s new flavor hit store shelves because consumers asked for it. But without technology, the company wouldn't have known what its customers wanted.

Christine Ahearn, supervisor and coordinator for Stonyfield's consumer relations, used to answer every customer call. Some people phoned to rave about a new flavor. Others called to complain that a certain flavor or container size was not available in their region. For nearly every call, Ahearn had to make a trip to the filing cabinet—to check the name of a distributor or to find the address of a grocery store. There was no system for tracking and analyzing the comments. Thus, when Ahearn became aware that some customers wanted chocolate yogurt and went to her boss, she couldn't tell him how many people had requested the new flavor. "I was doing the same thing over and over," Ahearn recalls. It was time to introduce computer technology to customer service.

Source: © 1996 Seth Resnick.

New Hampshire–based Stonyfield hired a local computer company, Cocci Computers Inc., to help decide what kind of technology was best for the company. Ahearn met with one of Cocci's engineers to answer as many questions as she could about Stonyfield's business and needs. In the end, Cocci came up with easy-to-use software that records pertinent customer information and stores it in a database that Ahearn and other Stonyfield managers can retrieve to help them solve problems or make decisions about products.

When the system was in operation, one of the first things that Ahearn's boss, CEO and president Gary Hirshberg, did was to retrieve a report on customers' preference for flavors. The report told him that 11 people in one week had phoned to request chocolate yogurt. The new flavor is now in grocery stores.

Source: Jennifer deJong, "Turbocharging Customer Service," *Inc. Technology*, no. 2, 1995, pp. 35–37.

**FIGURE 5.1**

**Elements of
Technology**

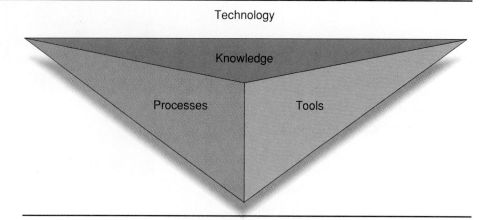

At Stonyfield Farm Inc., modern technology has transformed the jobs of supervisors, including consumer-relations coordinator Christine Ahearn. Like Ahearn, supervisors can expect technology to influence the techniques and scope of their work. Broadly defined, **technology** consists of the knowledge, tools, and processes that people use to carry out their work (see Figure 5.1). It encompasses technologies as old as the tools of a blacksmith and as innovative as virtual reality. However, when we think about the impact of technology, we usually mean *modern technology* (also called *high technology*); that is, the forms of technology that have been developed recently.

This chapter covers the supervisor's challenge to use modern technology in the ways that most benefit his or her organization. The chapter begins with an overview of the kinds of modern technology affecting supervisors today. Then the ways in which these forms of technology have changed the way supervisors work are discussed. Finally, the supervisor's role in introducing new technology to the workplace is investigated.

**technology**
The knowledge, tools, and processes that people use to carry out their work.

## Modern Technology in the Workplace

Whether using a satellite hookup to participate in a conference with people in other time zones or using a computer to look up current data on production status or inventory levels, today's supervisors operate in a workplace dramatically different from that of even a decade ago. To understand how technological advances have shaped the workplace and the supervisor's job, it is helpful to begin by recognizing areas in which technology has changed most significantly. In general, modern technology automates work processes or provides greater and easier access to information.

### Automation Technology

Since prehistoric times, people have been using tools to get their work done. But hand tools—whether the hammer of a carpenter, the whisk of a chef, or the pen of a writer—rely on the energy and skill of people to operate them. With the coming of the Industrial Revolution, organizations increasingly began to use electric or diesel energy to power machinery. Thus began the major drive to automate work.

About 45,000 robots work on U.S. assembly lines, and Japan has over 400,000 robots at work according to a recent estimate by the Robotic Industries Association. At Engineering Concepts in Fishers, Indiana, CEO Adam Suchko (*photo*) says four robots and three employees operate a business with about $1 million in sales.

Source: © Shawn Spence

**automation**
Use of equipment to perform work that once was done by human beings.

**voice mail**
A telephone messaging system that records messages, plays them back, and distributes them to others in the organization.

**Automation** means using equipment to perform work that once was done by human beings. One example is to use robots instead of human welders to assemble cars. Another is to answer telephone calls with **voice mail** (a telephone messaging system that records messages, plays them back, and distributes them to others in the organization) instead of a receptionist. Either way, cars get assembled and telephones get answered; automation lessens the amount of human labor needed to carry out these processes. Today, computers and electronically controlled machines are automating a growing range of activities, from the simple to the sophisticated.

Organizations automate processes because doing so can save money and reduce errors. Even highly complex and expensive computer systems can cost less than the pay and benefits for the employees who formerly carried out a process. Furthermore, machines do not get tired or distracted, so they may produce more consistent results than people. When the organization uses automation in place of work that was boring, exhausting, or dangerous, employees may be grateful to be relieved of these tasks. They then have more time for challenges such as improving the ways they work individually and with others. A national pizza chain once used a manual system to gather and report data about employee attendance; every week its store managers phoned headquarters to recite the attendance report. After the company automated this procedure, employees entered their arrival and departure times on a computer, which transmitted the data to headquarters. This freed store managers to spend more time coaching employees and focusing on customer needs.[1]

Of course, automation isn't perfect. A computer program may contain "bugs" (programming errors that cause the computer to make mistakes), and machinery may be installed improperly. Any machine will need maintenance and eventually wear out or become obsolete. And—not yet, at any rate—computers and other machines cannot suggest improvements or solve problems beyond those they were designed to solve. Therefore, organizations still need people to operate the machines, detect and correct problems with them, and look for ways to improve the organization's processes. Organizations also must have supervisors to direct or coach those employees.

Some kinds of automation, including sewing machines (to automate hand-stitching) and vending machines (to automate selling), have become so common that we take them for granted. This section focuses instead on major high-tech applications of automation: computer-aided design and manufacturing, flexible manufacturing, and expert systems.

### Computer-Aided Design and Manufacturing

**computer-aided design and manufacturing (CAD/CAM)**
Computer programs that automate tasks related to designing goods and the processes for producing them.

Organizations that produce and sell tangible goods need to design those products and decide how to make them. Today, most of these organizations use some form of **computer-aided design and manufacturing (CAD/CAM),** computer programs that automate tasks related to designing goods and the processes for producing them. Typically, a CAD program automates design by displaying two- and three-dimensional models of the product from any angle and automatically reflecting the impact of any change to the design. The program also analyzes the product design, such as the correct alignment of parts or the strength of the materials used. A CAM program uses the design information to direct the manufacturing of the product.

Organizations that use CAD/CAM may be able to develop new products faster and more frequently than in the past. Also, these organizations may use the CAD/CAM system to support closer links between the design and manufacturing functions. Therefore, supervisors whose employees perform these functions must be able to keep up with rapid and frequent product changes as well as communicate and cooperate with co-workers who handle other functions.

### Flexible Manufacturing

**flexible manufacturing**
A manufacturing process that is modified frequently and efficiently in light of changing market needs.

Another area of automation that is primarily relevant to manufacturers of tangible goods is **flexible manufacturing**—a manufacturing process that is modified frequently and efficiently in light of changing market needs. In practice, a flexible manufacturing system often consists of microcomputers stationed at machine tools or robots and linked to a mainframe computer. The mainframe transmits messages related to specifications for the product being manufactured. Those specifications might include which components to use and directions for how parts are to be machined. Switching from one product to another requires using a different set of instructions, rather than retooling the plant and retraining workers. Thus, an organization using flexible manufacturing can afford to adapt its goods to the specific needs of its customers.

The details of a flexible manufacturing system vary from one organization to another and are constantly changing to reflect new technological developments. However, a modern flexible manufacturing system typically includes links to a CAD/CAM system and to software that tracks inventories and determines what parts or components to order. It also generally uses robots and machine tools that can be electronically reconfigured according to the product specifications for a particular order.

Flexible manufacturing requires that employees be able to use the computers, computer-driven machine tools, and other components of the system. The organization also needs people who are motivated and able to meet specific customer needs. For the supervisor, these conditions require selecting people who have these characteristics and enabling them—through training, motivation, and adequate resources—to be flexible. Because the use of flexible manufacturing is typically part of a broader strategy to deliver high value (through products tailored to individual customers' needs), these requirements apply to all supervisors in the organization, not only to those in production. For example, supervisors in every function need to encourage their employees to listen to customers and adapt their responses to the needs they hear.

### Expert Systems

**artificial intelligence**
The use of software to mimic human thought processes.

Automating manual tasks is nothing new, but computers also have begun to automate mental tasks, particularly with **artificial intelligence,** or the use of software to mimic human thought processes. Computer programmers have applied the principles of artificial intelligence to create software that makes certain categories of decisions or solves certain types of problems. This software, called an **expert system,** follows the decision rules used by one or more persons thought to possess great skill in the decisions to be handled by the software. Examples are programs that diagnose certain illnesses and screen job applicants.

**expert system**
Software that makes certain categories of decisions or solves certain types of problems by using the decision rules of one or more skilled persons.

Artificial intelligence may reduce the need for people to make routine decisions, but it does not eliminate an organization's need for human intelligence. Instead, supervisors and other employees who use expert systems must have skills in using the software and evaluating the reasonableness and usefulness of what the software produces.

## Information Technology

Besides automating work processes, technology has been changing the workplace by making information more readily available to employees at all levels of the organization. (See "Meeting the Challenge.") Computers and other electronics have given employees widespread access to the knowledge of others inside and outside the organization. Major developments in **information technology**—electronic hardware and software for communicating and processing information—have occurred in the areas of computer networks, management information systems, and communication systems.

**information technology**
Electronic hardware and software for communicating and processing information.

### Computer Networks

**network**
The combination of hardware and software that allows computers to communicate with one another.

The early computers were set apart from most people in the workplace. They were housed in air-conditioned rooms and operated by specialists. Today, however, most workplaces contain many computers, and many (if not most) employees use them at least occasionally. Often, the computers in the modern workplace are personal computers in a **network,** the combination of hardware and software that allows them to communicate with one another. As networks of personal computers become more sophisticated and economical, they have become a major means for increasing productivity in offices and other service settings.[2]

Besides linking together its own computers, the organization may also connect them to outside networks. In many industries, on-line databases are an important source of information. For instance, a law office would likely have computers with access to the LEXIS service, which allows users to look up court cases and laws electronically. Real estate offices usually belong to a multiple listing service (MLS), which provides information about the properties for sale in a particular area; increasingly, brokers are signing up for electronic links to the MLS.

## MEETING THE CHALLENGE

### Information Technology: Is It an Invasion of Privacy?

Suppose you bought a sweater at a clothing shop that just opened in your town. Two weeks later, you receive a postcard addressed to you as a "preferred customer," inviting you to a special sale at the shop. How did the store get your address? You didn't sign a mailing list or write a check; you used your credit card to pay for the sweater. The store apparently is creating its database of new customers by typing names and addresses from credit card slips into the computer. Is this illegal? No, but some customers may think it is unethical. And no business wants to lose customers because of a mistake like this.

As marketing goes high-tech through the use of information technology, issues of privacy come up. Even though credit card companies are prohibited from releasing data about their customers, organizations can easily get all kinds of information about consumers through surveys, access to electronic databases provided by marketing organizations, and the like. Whether this is right is another question, and whether customers are flattered or offended may be a tough call.

Organizations may use technology to compile information in other ways as well. Suppose, when you bought your sweater, the salesperson asked you a few casual questions—your size, your occupation, what kind of clothes you like to wear. After you left the store, the salesperson typed your personal information into a computer. A few months later, you return to the shop a few pounds heavier (and a size larger). When you enter, a salesperson punches up your information on the computer and heads straight to the rack for a jacket in your smaller size. Annoyed, you explain that you now wear a larger size, and you weren't in the market for a jacket anyway.

How can supervisors use information technology to enhance their marketing techniques without offending potential customers? A store manager can train salespeople to ask customers' permission before entering any kind of personal information into a computer database. In recording information, it also makes sense to note which customers do *not* want to be questioned. Organizations that operate on-line "stores" usually attract customers who are more comfortable with technology and who are less wary of providing information that is helpful to marketing efforts. Still, these companies should be open about their information-gathering techniques.

This is old-fashioned, good business sense. If a customer fears an invasion of privacy through technology, he or she may just put that sweater back on the store shelf.

Source: Stephen M. Silverman, "Information Backlash," *Inc. Technology*, June 13, 1995 (No. 2), p. 27.

---

**Internet**
A network linking together about 1 million smaller networks worldwide.

The network that is expected to have the greatest impact on organizations in the near future is the **Internet,** a network linking together about 1 million smaller networks worldwide.[3] Originally designed to link the federal government, contractors, and scientists for military purposes, the Internet today provides electronic connections to roughly 30 million users, no matter what type of computer they operate. By the year 2000, according to some estimates, the Internet will have 100 million servers (computers that contain information available to clients of the Internet). As of this writing, experts were predicting that most PC software packages within a few years would be compatible with the World Wide Web (an Internet system that provides users with text, graphics, video, and sound).[4]

Dell Computer uses the Internet as a means of promoting quality by catching and correcting problems. A team of Dell employees cruises the Internet full time, looking for messages that refer to Dell. When someone uncovers a mention of a problem, a member of the technical support team quickly transmits a response to help the sender of that message, usually within 24 hours. Dell has often learned of problems in this way before its own staff uncovers them. Steve Smith, Dell's director of technical customer support, admits that he also scans the Internet for mention of problems with competitors' goods and services.[5]

**FIGURE 5.2**

**Growth in the Use of Electronic Data Interchange (EDI)**

Source: Thomas A. Stewart, "The Information Age in Charts," *Fortune*, Apr. 4, 1994, p. 78, with data from EDI Yellow Pages. © 1994 Time, Inc. All rights reserved.

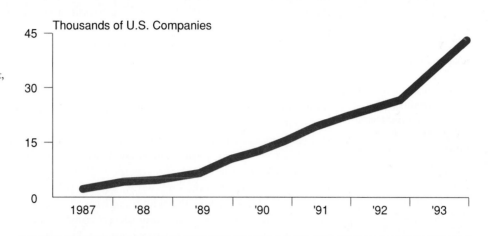

**management information system (MIS)**
A formal system for gathering and sorting data and disseminating information needed by the organization, its suppliers, or customers.

**electronic data interchange (EDI)**
The sharing of current data among organizations by means of computer links; a system that makes an organization's MIS accessible to customers or suppliers.

### Management Information Systems

In many cases, computer networks are the means by which supervisors and other managers gain access to a **management information system (MIS).** An MIS is a formal system for gathering and sorting data and disseminating information needed by the organization, its suppliers, or customers. (The term *data* refers to facts and figures; *information* refers to data organized in a meaningful way.) In practice, MISs generally are computerized, and they take many forms. They may be as simple as a system for providing monthly sales or inventory data, or they may support decision making by enabling managers to test the impact of their assumptions and predictions.

When an organization's MIS is accessible by employees of suppliers or customers, the system is known as **electronic data interchange (EDI)**—that is, the sharing of current data among organizations by means of computer links. The use of EDI in the United States has grown rapidly (see Figure 5.2). Federal Express Corporation offers clients EDI capability; they can use the Internet to contact FedEx's mainframe computer and learn the status of their shipments.[6] United Parcel Service offers customers a similar capability.[7] Many U.S. companies that want to sell to the federal government do so through EDI. They list their goods and services on the government's EDI system, then interested agencies send requests for bids electronically to the companies' electronic mailboxes. Acceptances and payments also are sent through this network.[8]

In an organization where supervisors have access to a management information system, they may be able to make more informed decisions. Such an organization is likely to expect its supervisors to be knowledgeable about the conditions influencing their decisions and the impact of those decisions. These supervisors must ensure that they understand how to use the MIS effectively. That understanding requires not only computer skills, but also the ability to interpret information and decide what is important.

### Communication Systems

Thanks to modern technology, today's supervisors and other employees have more ways to communicate than ever before. Besides meeting with other people, phoning them, or writing letters, the modern supervisor can send and receive messages by fax (short for *facsimile*), electronic mail, cellular phones, and video-conferencing.

Fax machines and electronic mail (E-mail) both transmit written messages electronically. A **fax machine** reads a document fed into it and then transmits the message to a receiver's fax machine, where it is printed out in the same format as the original. **E-mail** is a system in which a message is sent by typing it into a computer, which transmits the message to a file that the receiver can retrieve at his or her own computer. Both communications systems offer the advantages of speed and convenience (for anyone with the necessary equipment).

Other communication technology enables people to interact directly. **Cellular phones** provide telephone service with messages transmitted by means of radio signals instead of through wires. Thus, a person can travel throughout a service area without leaving the telephone behind. For a supervisor who travels frequently—say, someone supervising several construction projects or managing several apartment buildings—this capability can keep him or her in closer touch with callers than a beeper (or frequent trips to the office for messages). Thus, cellular phones can support an effort to be responsive to customers. However, supervisors who must keep their messages private should limit their use of cellular phones because messages transmitted in this way are easy to intercept.

A more sophisticated way to communicate electronically is with **videoconferencing.** This technology involves sending images and sound messages between computers via satellite or network links. The most advanced systems use satellite links and are expensive (but often less costly than assembling a team of people from widely scattered locations). PC-based systems that send videoconferencing signals through wires are still somewhat primitive, but as the technology develops they will likely become more common. If so, the role of supervisors may increasingly include interactions with peers from other cities, states, and even countries. This would undoubtedly expand the need for communication skills, including the ability to interact constructively with people from other cultures.

For more on communication, including the selection of ways to transmit a message, see Chapter 10.

**fax machine**
Equipment that reads a document fed into it and then transmits the message to a receiver's fax machine, where it is printed out in the same format as the original.

**E-mail**
A system in which a message is sent by typing it into a computer, which transmits the message to a file that the receiver can retrieve at his or her own computer.

**cellular phones**
Telephones that transmit and receive messages by means of radio signals instead of through wires.

**videoconferencing**
Electronic communication that involves sending images and sound messages between computers via satellite or network links.

# How Technology Affects the Job of a Supervisor

A supervisor who is familiar with the kinds of technology is able to ascertain the actual and potential impact of technology on his or her work. In general, modern technology affects the job of a supervisor by providing ways to perform his or her functions more efficiently and effectively. Also, as organizations apply technology, they often restructure the way work gets done, and these organizational changes can affect the nature of supervisors' jobs. (Other chapters discuss the impact of technology in particular areas, including productivity (Chapter 12) and the safety and health of employees (Chapter 19).)

## Help with the Management Functions

Modern technology, when appropriately selected and used, can help supervisors carry out the various management functions. (These were introduced in Chapter 1 and will be covered in greater detail in Part Three.) A supervisor with access to modern technology—and the ability to use it—therefore may be able to do his or her job better.

### Reaching Goals and Objectives

By carrying out the functions of planning and controlling, supervisors enable themselves and their employees to reach goals and objectives. Management information systems (MISs) can provide supervisors with useful information for planning. Most organizations use spreadsheets or more specialized software for preparing budgets (discussed in the next chapter).

An MIS may also help supervisors and employees to prevent problems and to make corrections when their outcomes are less than desirable. AMP Inc., a major producer of electrical and electronic connectors, learned that a recurring source of dissatisfaction was late shipments and missed delivery dates. The company arranged for its computerized order-processing system to alert the customer service department and production schedulers automatically whenever it detects a problem that might interfere with on-time delivery (such as low inventory of needed parts). Production schedulers then have four hours within which to inform customer service either that the problem was handled, or the reason it persists and the date the product will ship. Customer service employees then contact the customer with an explanation. By using this system, AMP has improved its on-time delivery rate from 67 percent to 95 percent.[9]

When supervisors or employees do not work in the same location, modern communication technology helps them keep in touch. Faxes, E-mail, cellular phones, and the like help supervisors ensure that employees know what is expected of them. They also enable supervisors to know whether employees have all the resources and information they need.

### Using Organizational Resources

Through the practice of organizing and delegating, the supervisor decides how to use the organization's resources, particularly its human resources (employees). Sparkling Spring Water Company, based in Highland Park, Illinois, uses a type of management information system to schedule deliveries of spring water to be dispensed from a company-supplied cooler. Whenever a customer calls to arrange for the service, the Sparkling Spring Water employee asks when the customer would like to receive the cooler, then adds that date to the database. When a supervisor is ready to build the next day's delivery routes, he or she transfers the data into the system and enters the number of hours the drivers are to work; the computer draws the day's routes. Based on the number of routes the program draws, the supervisor can either adjust the number of drivers to be scheduled or have the computer redraw the routes with a longer or shorter workday.[10]

In the past, managers, including supervisors, have emphasized tight control. That emphasis requires a strict chain of command so that managers can keep close tabs on the progress of everyone who reports to them. However, when information and decisions must make their way up and down through these chains of command, the organization moves slowly and does not always benefit as much as it can from the insights and abilities of operative employees.

Information technology is changing this style of using organizational resources. Computer networks, management information systems, and communication systems make it easy to share information. Therefore, supervisors can distribute responsibility more widely throughout their work group without losing their ability to keep track of what is going on and intervene if necessary. Electronic access to detailed information about clients has helped sales representatives at Pfizer's International Pharmaceuticals Group use their time more effectively and

ACT! is a contact management software program that can store a salesperson's contact history with conversation details, schedule meetings, dial the telephone, connect to E-mail, and print out letters and memos. Craig Phillips, a sales and marketing specialist at CAP Marketing Services in Belmont, California (*shown at right with a customer*), begins his day by checking his schedule on the program, which "has all my contacts, my activity plan, and other information, so I don't have to worry about it, remember it, or put it on paper."

Source: © George Olson.

efficiently without specific directives from their managers to do so. For instance, they spend a larger share of their time with high-potential clients.[11]

### Leading Employees

As we will discuss in Chapter 8, the function of leading employees comprises two broad kinds of activities. First, the supervisor must ensure that employees are clear about what they are supposed to do. Second, the supervisor needs to use interpersonal skills to inspire employees. Modern technology can help with both aspects of leadership.

Information technology can be useful in supporting the efforts of supervisors to communicate instructions and other information employees need to do their jobs well. As noted earlier, supervisors and employees can keep in touch even when they are away from the organization's facilities.

Modern technology also helps with leadership when it enables supervisors to work efficiently and delegate extensively. When supervisors do not spend as much time on routine tasks or tasks that operative employees can handle, they have more time for a variety of interpersonal issues. They can learn what motivates their employees, who the informal leaders are in their work group, and what resources—training, information, and additional technology—would help their group perform even better. A supervisor who devotes time to such leadership issues has the potential to build a high-performance work group.

### Problem Solving and Decision Making

As supervisors carry out all of these functions, they encounter a variety of problems and other situations calling for decisions. Supervisors sometimes can use modern technology to help make better decisions or to arrive at a solution more efficiently.

Solving a problem or making a decision requires gathering information. A management information system or on-line database may provide ready access to the information needed for many of the supervisor's problems or decision-making situations. The supervisor also may need to communicate with experts or with the people involved in a problem. When a face-to-face meeting is impossible or impractical, the supervisor benefits from the use of communication technologies such as those described in this chapter.

Some technologies have been developed specifically to help with problem solving and decision making. Expert systems automate the decision-making process, enabling a person to make decisions faster and more easily. Furthermore, since the system typically is based on how a highly skilled person makes the type of decision, using an expert system can improve the quality of decisions.

A wide variety of software and databases are available to automate or support particular kinds of decisions. The organization might use a program for interviewing job candidates, calculating price quotes, or diagnosing problems with machinery. Performance appraisal software leads the user through the steps of conducting an appraisal of an employee's performance (see Chapter 18).

In Cambridge, Massachusetts, Boomer Kennedy subscribes to a program called ALLDATA to help her run her repair shop, Chicago Auto. Every 90 days, ALLDATA provides Kennedy with a set of compact discs (CDs) containing labor manuals, manufacturers' technical service bulletins, and guides for estimating labor costs. Kennedy can pop a CD into her computer; enter the make, model, engine size, and year of a car; then retrieve a wealth of information that has dramatically cut the time the shop spends diagnosing problems and estimating labor costs.[12]

When group decision making is useful, the group can benefit from using a kind of software called **groupware.** This software enables the users of personal computers to simultaneously view and comment on the same text and images. It can enhance decision making when group members are in different locations, and it can encourage contributions from everyone in the group.

**groupware**
Software that enables the users of personal computers to simultaneously view and comment on the same text and images.

## Role Change Resulting from Structural Change

Besides directly affecting how supervisors perform their functions, technology can indirectly affect the supervisor's role by enabling management to reshape part or all of the organization. When the organization has been restructured, supervisors' responsibilities often change.

### Downsizing

**downsizing**
Reducing the number of employees in order to operate more efficiently.

When technology allows the organization to do as much or more work with fewer people, it may engage in **downsizing.** This means reducing the number of employees in order to operate more efficiently. Groups may be reconfigured so that supervisors are responsible for the work of more employees. The organization may eliminate layers of management and push authority downward. In other words, supervisors must handle some of the responsibilities that middle managers used to handle, and they must give operative employees responsibilities formerly considered the supervisors' domain. Both changes require supervisors to place more emphasis on interpersonal concerns such as delegating work, assessing training needs, and enhancing motivation. Supervisors have less time for telling employees what to do and checking up on their progress.

### Reengineering

**reengineering**
Complete review of the organization's critical work processes and redesign of those processes as needed to make them more efficient and able to deliver higher quality.

Another kind of structural change that can result from technology is **reengineering,** or complete review of the organization's critical work processes and redesign of those processes as needed to make them more efficient and able to deliver higher quality. A major reason organizations began using reengineering some years ago was that they were disappointed that modern technology did not seem to be helping service productivity. By reviewing their work processes, they realized that often they were simply automating existing processes, even if those processes were inefficient. You don't benefit from doing something faster if that is not what you should be doing in the first place.

Reengineering can affect the supervisor's role in various ways. First, it should shift the supervisor's focus away from a "this-is-the-way-we-do-things" attitude toward a concern for improving processes. Besides having a general awareness of the processes in which he or she is involved, the supervisor must encourage operative employees to generate ideas. These employees are most acquainted with the processes they carry out, and they often know precisely where inefficiencies lie. Furthermore, as organizations conduct reengineering, they often determine that employees working together can prevent many problems or solve them as they arise. Thus, reengineering may result in the use of teamwork, requiring that supervisors take on the role of team leader (see Chapter 3).

## Introducing New Technology

An organization may introduce technology to meet the needs of employees at any level, but at least some of the organization's operative employees implement most technologies. Therefore, supervisors are affected by and are involved in introducing new technology. Whether their role is to direct employees in using the technology or to empower them by seeing that they have the needed resources to use it, supervisors help ensure the successful use of the technology.

### Identifying Needs for New Technology

Organizations adopt new technology because someone has perceived a need for it. In practice, people sometimes see a "need" simply because a form of technology has worked elsewhere or they like to have the newest gadgets. From the organization's perspective, these are poor reasons for making a change. Rather, supervisors and others in the organization should look for ways that the organization can get better results, such as happier customers, safer employees, lower costs, or higher profits.

At Garland Heating and Air Conditioning Company in Garland, Texas, service coordinator Rick Kelley saw a need for new technology because customers were unhappy. When customers called to request repair service, they had to wait while Kelley sifted through files to find a record of their repair history, then reviewed a handwritten schedule to find the availability of the repairperson who had last served them. Recognizing that customers were impatient with the process, Kelley arranged for the company to acquire a database that allows him to quickly retrieve information on repair history and repairperson availability.[13]

Controlling costs motivated the U.S. Postal Service to adopt new technology. It plans to spend $1 billion on 3,200 machines that read bar codes and sort letters. Sorting 1,000 letters costs $40 if postal workers do it by hand and only $4 when done by one of these machines.

Source: © 1995 *Nation's Business*/T. Michael Keza.

### Selecting Appropriate Technologies

In selecting uses of technology, supervisors and others in the organization should consider the effects of the new technology on employees, customers, and the organization as a whole. Will the new technology make work easier, safer, more or less interesting? Will customers get faster service, more (or less) personal attention, higher-quality or cheaper products? Will the organization save money, attract new customers, earn more? (See "Tips from the Firing Line.")

Sometimes the organization has to balance a combination of positive and negative effects. For instance, the organization might conclude that voice mail would save money by automating tasks related to handling phone calls. Employees might appreciate getting more accurate phone messages than those written down by a human operator. Regular customers might appreciate the convenience of reaching employees immediately by pressing their extension numbers. But many other callers may dislike listening to a recorded message, especially if it is long and contains many instructions. The people selecting the voice mail system might make it easy for callers into the system to connect with a human operator should they wish to do so.

To identify and balance the various consequences of new technology, supervisors may find it helpful to involve their employees and their peers in other departments when they make selection decisions. Bringing together people with different areas of expertise and direct experience in performing the affected work processes can uncover concerns that might be overlooked. These areas of impact could range from productivity (see Chapter 12) to employee safety and health (see Chapter 19).

Decisions about what technologies to use should also take into consideration the relationship between the technology and the work processes. In particular, people making decisions about new technology should be careful not to simply automate

## TIPS FROM THE FIRING LINE

### Choosing the Right Technology

Choosing the best information technology for your organization involves more than signing up for all the bells and whistles your company can afford to buy. It means asking the right questions and getting the right answers. Suppose you have determined that your company would benefit by setting up a customer service database. Here's how to decide what your company needs:

- Consider the human elements first. Do you have enough staff to answer telephones when customers call? Is your staff trained and equipped with the information they will need to help customers who call?
- Be clear about what kind of support you plan to offer customers. Will you be troubleshooting certain technical problems or simply handling complaints?
- Where and how will the information the telephone staff needs to complete calls be stored?

- As you investigate the technology you are thinking of buying, be sure that it will be compatible with the computers and databases you already have in use.
- Think through your long-range plan. Although your immediate goal may be to help customers with problems, ultimately you may hope to use your database to generate new business, point your company in a new direction, or analyze the competition.
- Make whatever technology you choose easy for customers to use. They should feel comfortable dialing your company's line and secure in the knowledge that they will get the help they need.

Source: Jennifer deJong, "Turbocharging Customer Service," *Inc. Technology*, no. 2, 1995, p. 39.

an existing process without considering whether there is a better way to carry out that process. For instance, if a management information system gives everyone in the organization access to order information, the order department may no longer have to carry out tasks that require making multiple copies of order information or reporting it on a variety of different forms. Selecting technologies for getting the order information into the MIS would be more appropriate than automating the process of printing and distributing forms.

### Employee Reactions to New Technology

The selection of new forms of technology by the supervisor or others in the organization marks only the beginning of the job of introducing that technology. Applying new technology requires change in the organization and, as with any change process, the affected employees must be willing to make a change and have the knowledge and skills to do so. The supervisor of these employees plays a key role in introducing new technology (no matter who has selected it) because he or she is responsible for ensuring that employees have the necessary motivation and abilities. Chapter 15 will explore the supervisor's role in implementing changes, but for now let's consider how employees tend to react when the change involves new technology.

**alienation**
A state characterized by feelings of powerlessness and isolation, a belief that one's work is meaningless, and an attitude of dissatisfaction.

### Alienation

Depending on the type of technology and the way it is implemented, new technology can contribute to the **alienation** of employees. This is a state characterized by feelings of powerlessness and isolation, a belief that one's work is meaningless, and an attitude of dissatisfaction.[14] The supervisor should consider the possibility of alienation if technology cuts off contact among employees or limits job scope so much that employees cannot see how they make a difference to anyone.

If employees seem to be alienated, the supervisor should try to improve the situation. The supervisor may be able to rearrange work assignments so that employees work in teams. Better communication and leadership by the supervisor may help employees appreciate how they *do* make a difference. If the benefits of using the technology outweigh the potential disadvantages of alienation, the supervisor should try to boost employee motivation in other ways (described in Chapter 11).

### Fear of New Technology

For some employees, new technology is threatening. They may fear that they cannot learn to use the new technology or that learning it will be difficult. Just a decade ago, a study determined that subjects reacted to computers with real physical symptoms, including nausea, dizziness, and elevated blood pressure.[15] More recently, a survey found that 93 percent of respondents were *not* intimidated by computers;[16] however, this probably means that computers aren't such a new development anymore.

Furthermore, employees may be afraid that new technology will cost them their jobs. This fear is widespread. In the past, new technology typically involved automating production processes, and layoffs mainly affected blue-collar production workers. Today, computer technology allows many organizations to do as much or more with fewer employees in all departments at all levels of the organization's hierarchy. The view that technology creates more new jobs than it eliminates is supported by a great deal of evidence. However, those jobs often require different skills than employees already have, and the prospect of new jobs being created in the future offers little comfort to people being laid off today.[17]

To address employee fears, the supervisor should actively communicate with employees. Honesty is important; if the workforce will be reduced, the supervisor should not pretend that this is unlikely. The supervisor should encourage and answer questions, being sure to tell employees what resources the organization will provide, including training, experts to contact for help in using the new technology, and outplacement services if the change will bring about layoffs. (Figure 5.3 illustrates what employees report they need to keep up with modern technology.) Perhaps most important, the supervisor should learn and communicate the technology's expected benefits—be they a reduction in injuries, work that is more interesting, or a chance to win a big contract (and perhaps enhance job security).

### Positive Reactions to New Technology

Fortunately for the supervisor, not everyone has negative feelings about new technology. Some people derive great satisfaction from learning to use a new machine or computer system. Some people find change exciting rather than threatening. Others are aware that using technology can improve their lives. For instance, VeriFone's software testing facility is located in rural Hawaii partly because its employees enjoy the lifestyle there. (That location is possible because computer networking enables VeriFone's employees to send and receive the software to be tested and the test results.[18]) Finally—especially when the supervisor helps create a climate of teamwork and cooperation—some employees simply are pleased when technology enables them to do their work better.

**What People Need
to Keep Up with
Technology**

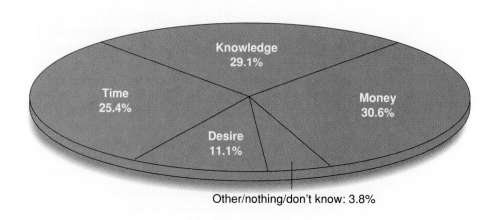

Source: Dennis Kneale, "Unleashing the Power," *The Wall Street Journal*, June 27, 1994, p. R6, with data from ICR Survey Research Group. Reprinted by permission of *The Wall Street Journal*, © 1994 Dow Jones and Company, Inc. All Rights Reserved Worldwide.

The positive reactions of these employees to new technology can help the supervisor introduce it. The supervisor should make a point of knowing which employees view the change favorably and select employees from this group to learn the technology first, then teach it to others or be available to support their co-workers as they become familiar with it. Ultimately, the successful use of new technology requires not only technical skills (such as a familiarity with computers), but the ability to create a positive climate in which the supervisor has employee support.

# Summary

**5.1    Define *technology* and *modern technology*.**
Technology consists of the knowledge, tools, and processes people use to carry out their work. Modern technology (also called high technology) refers to the forms of technology that have been developed recently.

**5.2    Describe the impact of automation and information technology on the modern workplace.**
Automation means using equipment to perform work that once was done by human beings; thus, automation lessens the amount of human labor to carry out certain processes. Computers and electronically controlled machines now automate a growing range of activities. Automation can save money and reduce errors; it also gives employees

more time for such challenges as improving the ways they work individually and with others. Organizations may use CAD/CAM, flexible manufacturing, or expert systems to achieve automation.

Major developments in information technology have occurred in computer networks, management information systems, and communication systems. Networks of personal computers have become a major means for increasing productivity in offices and other service settings. Organizations may link themselves with outside networks, including the Internet, which gives employees access to about 1 million networks worldwide. Management information systems and communication systems (e.g., fax, E-mail, cellular phones, and videoconferencing) offer speed and convenience for people interacting over great distances.

**5.3    Explain how modern technology helps supervisors carry out the basic management functions.**

Modern technology affects the job of a supervisor by providing ways to perform the supervisory functions more efficiently and effectively. Also, as organizations apply technology, they often restructure the way work gets done, which affects the nature of supervisors' jobs. Management information systems can provide supervisors with useful information for planning. When supervisors or employees do not work in the same location, modern communication technology such as faxes, E-mail, cellular phones, and so forth help them stay in touch. Information technology makes it easy for supervisors to share information, distributing responsibility more widely throughout the work group without losing track of what is happening. Modern technology helps with leadership when it enables supervisors to work efficiently and delegate extensively. It also can help them make better or more efficient decisions.

**5.4    Discuss how modern technology has affected the supervisor's role by enabling the restructuring of organizations and work processes.**

As a result of restructuring, supervisors may have to handle more responsibilities and more employees. In reengineering, supervisors focus on improving processes, often introducing the use of teamwork.

**5.5    Describe the supervisor's role in identifying needs for new technology and selecting the appropriate technologies to meet those needs.**

Supervisors should look for ways the organization can get better results through technology. In selecting new technology, supervisors should consider its effects on employees, customers, and the organization as a whole. If necessary, the organization will have to balance a combination of positive and negative effects. To identify and balance the consequences of new technology, supervisors can involve employees and colleagues in the selection decision. The decision also should take into consideration the relationship between the technology and the work processes it will change.

**5.6    Identify common reactions to new technology and ways supervisors should handle those reactions.**

New technology can contribute to the alienation of employees. Supervisors can improve this situation by having employees work in teams. Technology also may cause employees to feel threatened or to worry that they will lose their jobs. Supervisors should communicate with employees about their fears and try to convey the expected benefits of the technology. If certain employees react positively to the new technology, supervisors can call on them to teach it to other employees or to be supportive in other ways. These employees can help create a positive climate for the new technology.

# Key Terms

| | | |
|---|---|---|
| technology | information technology | videoconferencing |
| automation | network | groupware |
| voice mail | Internet | downsizing |
| computer-aided design and manufacturing (CAD/CAM) | management information system (MIS) | reengineering |
| flexible manufacturing | electronic data interchange (EDI) | alienation |
| artificial intelligence | fax machine | |
| expert system | E-mail | |
| | cellular phones | |

# Review and Discussion Questions

1. Make a list of the technological innovations that have affected you in the last three years (e.g., did you subscribe to an on-line computer network so you could communicate with friends by E-mail?). Note whether these innovations have had a positive or a negative impact on your life.

2. What are the benefits of automation? What are some of the drawbacks?

3. Define CAD/CAM and flexible manufacturing, and explain how each works.

4. Will artificial intelligence replace human beings in the workforce? Why or why not?

5. Reggie supervises the paralegals who do background research for law cases in a large law firm. He believes that the installation of a management information system would improve his efficiency as a supervisor as well as the overall efficiency of the group. In what ways could Reggie and his group make good use of an MIS?

6. How might a regional sales manager for a sporting goods manufacturer use communication technology to supervise the sales reps who are on the road?

7. How does information technology change a supervisor's leadership role?

8. Caitlin is the office manager for a small construction company. She supervises a secretary, a bookkeeper, and a receptionist. Recently, she has begun to believe that the office could respond better to customers by installing some type of communication technology. How should she determine what type of technology would be best for the office?

9. Ron supervises a group of production workers in a plant that manufactures automobile parts. The company has decided to introduce technology that will automate certain segments of the work process. Several of Ron's employees have expressed fear and alienation about the coming change. How should Ron respond to their feelings?

10. Two of Ron's employees (see question 9) have expressed a positive attitude toward the upcoming automation. How might he engage their positive attitude so that it benefits the entire group?

## A SECOND LOOK

Why was Christine Ahearn's role important in the successful introduction of new technology to the consumer relations department at Stonyfield Farm Inc.?

# APPLICATIONS MODULE

## CASE

### Data General Transforms Data into Information

Downsizing and other structural changes often leave organizations with a dilemma: How will they produce more with fewer people? Faced with this problem after radical downsizing at Data General (where the number of employees dropped from 18,000 to 6,000), vice-president of sales and service Angelo Guadagno decided that technology was the answer. In particular, he wanted to automate as much of the sales process as possible.

"We wanted to reduce the time [salespeople] spent on nonrevenue-producing jobs," he explains. "But also, we wanted them to focus on new market areas. We felt automation could help us analyze whether or not they were do this." After identifying this need, Guadagno assigned a team to investigate and determine which computers and software would serve the sales force best. Because Data General manufactures laptops, that decision was easy: The team settled on an account management program (SNAP) from Sales Technologies Inc.

Response to the new technology was positive. The automation process reduced the amount of time reps had to spend on administrative tasks. They were able to collect tremendous amounts of data and keep their accounts organized. "We received a 15 percent increase in productivity," notes Guadagno.

But there was one problem. The new technology opened the floodgates. So much data poured into the main office at Data General that managers couldn't make sense of it. They couldn't successfully track their reps because they had no mechanism for analyzing what their reps were doing. "We wanted our reps to focus on new accounts," says Guadagno. "Yet, we didn't know whether they were or not. They may have been increasing their quotas, but it wasn't easy for us to tell whether they were meeting the targets we wanted them to."

So Guadagno went back to the drawing board. He tried a new software program called CrossTarget (from Dimensional Insight), which not only allows salespeople to send business and forecasting information, but also allows managers to analyze the data, turning it into useful information that is updated every day. When Guadagno passed CrossTarget along to his managers, they had it up and running within a week. "CrossTarget is different from other . . . software," explains product manager Bernard Seban, "because it mimics a user's frame of mind."

In addition, CrossTarget allows managers to communicate with and supervise their reps while the reps are traveling. "In a few seconds, by punching a key, now I can easily find out where my reps are spending their time and how much time they are spending with a customer," notes Guadagno. This helps the whole sales group feel less isolated and more like a team. Everyone has access to important sales information, and everyone can communicate about it.

1. Do you think that Guadagno's initial decision to automate the sales process was good or bad? Why?
2. How did the new technology affect the sales force? Consider the demands of their jobs after downsizing, as well as managers' greater ability to keep tabs on the sales reps.
3. Guadagno successfully combined automation technology and information technology at Data General. What steps might he and other managers take to ensure that the sales group continues to get optimum benefit from technology?

Source: Melissa Campbell, "Turning Data into Information," *Sales and Marketing Management,* Jan. 1995, pp. 51–52.

**SELF-QUIZ**

## *What Is Your Reaction to New Technology?*

Whether you are an entry-level employee or a supervisor, you are likely to be introduced to some kind of new technology in the near future. Answer each of the following questions with yes or no. (There are no "right" or "wrong" answers.)

1. Are you comfortable using some type of computer? _____
2. Does the idea of communicating with co-workers by means of electronic mail make you feel isolated? _____
3. Are you put off if you encounter voice mail before talking with a human being when you make a phone call? _____
4. Do you believe that the proliferation of computers in the workplace will cause more people to lose their jobs? _____
5. Do you enjoy buying and using new gadgets? _____
6. Would you like the idea of being freed from routine tasks by some degree of automation? _____
7. Do you believe that access to information through technology is a threat to people's privacy? _____
8. Do you believe that information technology will increase business competition in a positive way? _____
9. Are you afraid that artificial intelligence will ultimately replace human intelligence in the workplace? _____
10. If you had access to a management information system, would you use it? _____

Scoring: Responding Yes to questions 1, 5, 6, 8, and 10 and No to the other questions indicates that you are currently comfortable with using or being introduced to technology.

## Class Exercise

This exercise can be done individually or in groups. Consider a process in your workplace, school, or home that could benefit from automation. Describe why you think automation would make the process more efficient. Then create a diagram showing the steps of the new automated process and provide brief written descriptions of each step. Finally, explain how automation would change the role of workers or others involved.

## Team-Building Exercise

### Bringing Technology to an Office Setting

Divide the class into groups. Each group should choose a type of business, such as real estate, a retail store, a bank, or the like. Then design an office space for that business, including in the space as many technological innovations as you can think of; use examples from the chapter as well as others you may know of. Don't be afraid to shift things around as you develop your space. Discuss the pros and cons of each type of technology, and delete those that might slow down work processes or obstruct contact with customers. Finally, present your design to the class.

# Video Exercise 5: *Using Modern Technology*

### *Video Summary*

This video program illustrates how companies use modern technology to increase productivity, improve communication, sell products, and train employees.

### *Application*

1. As you read the following information, answer these two questions:

   - What percentage of companies now require their managers and supervisors to be computer literate? _____
   - How much more do computer-literate employees earn compared with employees who are not computer literate? _____

   > A nationwide survey of 1,481 management information systems executives conducted by the Olsten Corp., in Westbury, New York, found that 71 percent of companies now require their managers and supervisors to be computer literate—up 36 percent from only three years ago. In addition, computer-literate employees generally earn 15 to 20 percent more than those without such experience.[1]

2. From computer novice to computer expert, all supervisors should have a lifelong goal of improving their level of computer literacy. Computer novices will need to take the initiative to enroll in a basic introductory computer course. Those with moderate to expert levels of computer literacy cannot rest on their laurels very long. In a world where the cost of computing power drops roughly 30 percent every year and microchips double in performance power every 18 months, it is very easy to lose your literacy status in a short period of time.

3. As a class, discuss some ideas to help you keep pace with the rapid changes in computer technology. Write the ideas on the lines below.

   ❑ _____

   ❑ _____

   ❑ _____

   ❑ _____

   ❑ _____

   ❑ _____

[1] "Tech Watch," *Black Enterprise*, May 1993, p. 45.

4. Look at your responses to question 3. Place check marks next to the one or two ideas on which you determine to take action within the next two to four weeks.

5. Remember, computer literacy shows employers that you have knowledge and skills that can keep pace with changing computer technology. Therefore, computer literacy can improve your ability to get hired, to make more money once you are employed, and to maintain and improve your employment status.

6. Do something today to enhance your computer literacy.

**PART THREE**

# *Functions of the Supervisor*

**6**

*Achieving good performance is a journey, not a destination.*
—**Kenneth H. Blanchard, management consultant**

# Reaching Goals and Objectives

**LEARNING OBJECTIVES**

After you have studied this chapter, you should be able to:

6.1 Describe types of planning that take place in organizations.

6.2 Identify characteristics of effective objectives.

6.3 Define *management by objectives (MBO)* and discuss its use.

6.4 Discuss the supervisor's role in the planning process.

6.5 Explain the purpose of using controls.

6.6 Identify the steps in the control process.

6.7 Describe types of control and tools for controlling.

6.8 List characteristics of effective controls.

Source: © Comstock, Inc./Bob Pizaro.

## PLANNING FOR EFFICIENCY

When crew members from One Call Does It All Maintenance Company, based in Stamford, Connecticut, went to a home or business to make repairs, they often had to interrupt their work to make trips back to the shop. It occurred to the company's operating manager, Tom Kipphut, that the company would operate more efficiently if crew members did not have to do all that traveling. When he began to keep track of why workers were coming back to the shop, he discovered that it almost always happened because they did not have all the tools and supplies they needed.

Kipphut decided that the solution was to plan for what crew members would need. He determined that most repair jobs required only a few basic tools: two sizes of Phillips and flathead screwdrivers, a crescent wrench, duct tape and electrical tape, and a tape measure.

Next, Kipphut ascertained the kinds of tools that were needed for specific kinds of jobs and added them to the basic tools to create job-specific tool kits. For example, to answer a call about a blocked or overflowing toilet, the crew member would take a kit containing a plumber's snake, a plunger, and a wax seal (in case the worker had to reinstall the toilet). The toilet repair kit also contained the parts for the flush assembly; if the worker found another common problem with the toilet, he or she could offer to repair that on the spot.

Kipphut assembled each set of tools in a plastic carrying case. He cut a block of Styrofoam to fit inside the case and carved out compartments to hold each piece of equipment. That made it easy to replace any parts used on a job. Besides the plumbing kits, the company now has kits for general appliance repair and general electronics.

Providing workers with parts in advance is less costly than having workers go to the nearest store and pay full retail price. The company also avoids paying for the time and cost of the extra traveling by its crew members. Furthermore, employees find their work less frustrating when they are prepared for an assignment and know where the tools are. Perhaps most important, customers are so pleased by the fast service that referrals have caused the business to grow substantially.

Source: "Planning: Job-Specific Tool Kits," *Maintenance Supervisor's Bulletin* (Bureau of Business Practice), Jan. 25, 1992, pp. 1–3.

Like Tom Kipphut, supervisors are expected to ensure that they and the members of their work group reach goals and objectives. Doing this requires knowledge of what the group is supposed to accomplish and whether the group is actually accomplishing it. Supervisors acquire that important knowledge by carrying out the functions of planning and controlling.

This chapter describes how supervisors can and should carry out those functions. The chapter begins with a description of how planning takes place in organizations, including the types of objectives and planning that are common. Next, the chapter discusses the supervisor's role as planner: setting and updating objectives and including employees in these processes. The second half of the chapter addresses the management function of controlling. It describes the process supervisors follow and some of the tools they use in controlling, as well as the characteristics of effective controls.

# Planning in Organizations

**planning**
The management function of setting goals and determining how to meet them.

As you learned in Chapter 1, **planning** is the management function of setting goals and determining how to meet them. For supervisors, this includes figuring out what tasks the department needs to carry out to achieve its goals, as well as how and when to perform those tasks. For action-oriented people, planning can seem time-consuming and tedious. But the need for planning is obvious, especially if you consider what would happen in an organization where no one plans. For example, if a store did not implement planning, customers would not know when the store would be open, and employees would not know what inventory to order or when to order it. The location of the store might be an accident, with no marketing research to determine where business would be good enough to generate a profit. The managers would not know how many employees to hire, because they would have no idea how many customers they would be serving. Clearly, this business would fail in the mission of providing its customers with high-quality service and merchandise.

Supervisors and other managers plan for several reasons. Knowing what the organization is trying to accomplish helps them set priorities and make decisions aimed at accomplishing their goals. Planning forces managers to spend time focusing on the future and establishes a fair way for evaluating performance. It helps managers use resources efficiently, thus minimizing wasted time and money. Japanese managers, for example, spend more of their time planning than U.S. managers do, but they spend less time correcting problems.[1] Time spent in planning a project can reduce the time required to carry it out. The total time for planning and execution can actually be shorter for a thoroughly planned project than for one started in haste.

Finally, the other functions that managers perform—organizing, staffing, leading, and controlling—all depend on good planning. Before supervisors and other managers can allocate resources and inspire employees to achieve their objectives, or before they can determine whether employees are meeting those objectives, they need to know what they are trying to accomplish.

Supervisors rarely have much input into the way an organization does its planning. Rather, they participate in whatever process already exists. To participate constructively, supervisors should understand the process.

TIPS FROM THE FIRING LINE

## Fundamental Questions for Planners

Creating any type of plan, whether it is overall strategic planning for the organization or some aspect of operational planning, requires asking the right questions. Oren Harari, professor of management at the University of San Francisco, suggests some questions that can help an organization's planners pin down the right objectives.

First, focus on the purpose of the organization:

- Why does the organization exist?
- What is the purpose of the organization?
- What business is the organization in? What business does the organization expect to be in three years from now?
- Who are the organization's customers? Who will the customers be three years from now?
- Who are the organization's competitors?
- What changes in the environment must the organization respond to?
- How does the organization define "success"?
- What controls will help the organization know whether it is succeeding or failing to meet its goals?
- What are the potential barriers to success?

Next, planners in the organization should focus on what makes the organization unique:

- What makes the organization different from others?
- What unique value does the organization offer its customers?
- What does the organization do better than anyone else?
- What steps is the organization taking currently to make sure it stays "the best" in the future?

Finally, planners should review an organization's standards for behavior:

- What is the organization's overall philosophy?
- What do managers and employees really care about?
- How do employees and managers behave toward each other and toward customers?
- How can employees and managers rally to achieve a common goal?

Source: Adapted from Oren Harari, "Good/Bad News About Strategy." Reprinted by permission of the publisher, from *Management Review*, July 1995, pp. 30–31. © 1995 American Management Association, New York, all rights reserved.

## Objectives

**objectives**
The desired accomplishments of the organization as a whole or of part of the organization.

**goals**
Objectives, often those with a broad focus.

Planning centers on the setting of goals and objectives. (See "Tips from the Firing Line.") **Objectives** specify the desired accomplishments of the organization as a whole or of a part of it. According to one school of thought, **goals** are objectives with a broad focus. For example, an organization seeks to be the number one supplier of nursing home care by the end of next year. That would be considered a goal. In contrast, the accounting department seeks to have all invoices mailed within two weeks of a patient's departure; this is more specific and is therefore an objective. This text uses the term *objectives* in most cases and treats the two terms synonymously.

### Strategic Objectives

**strategic planning**
The creation of long-term goals for the organization as a whole.

Planning should begin at the top, with a plan for the organization as a whole. **Strategic planning** is the creation of long-term goals for the organization. These typically include the type and quality of goods or services the organization is to provide and, for a business, the level of profits it is to earn. When Wal-Mart readied itself to move into the urban markets once dominated by Kmart, it concentrated on its skill in discount retailing and adopted a strategy of building superior

| | Strategic Planning | Operational Planning |
|---|---|---|
| **Planners** | Top managers, possibly with a planning department | Middle managers and supervisors |
| **Scope** | Objectives for the organization as a whole | Objectives for a division, department, or work group |
| **Time Frame** | Long range (more than one year) | Short range (one year or less) |

■ **TABLE 6.1**

**Characteristics of Strategic and Operational Planning**

operations: its order and distribution systems. Kmart, in contrast, emphasized marketing to boost its image, and the company diversified by acquiring specialty retailers, including the Sports Authority.[2]

Usually it is the top managers who engage in strategic planning; in other cases, a planning department prepares objectives for approval by top management. Either way, the managers at the top decide where the organization should be going.

### Operational Objectives

**operational planning**
The development of objectives that specify how divisions, departments, and work groups will support organizational goals.

The objectives for divisions, departments, and work groups support the goals developed in strategic planning. These objectives, developed through **operational planning,** specify how the group will help the organization achieve its goals. Operational planning is done by middle managers and supervisors. Table 6.1 summarizes the characteristics of strategic and operational planning.

Middle managers set objectives that will enable their division or department to contribute to the goals set for the organization. Supervisors set objectives that will enable their department or work group to contribute to divisional or departmental goals. For example, if the organizational objective for a bank is to increase profits by 8 percent next year, the goal of a branch located in a high-growth area might be to increase its own profits by 9 percent. At this branch, the vice-president (supervisor) in charge of lending operations might have the objective of increasing loans to businesses by 15 percent. The head teller might have the objective of keeping customer waits to five minutes or less. (The good service is designed to support organizational objectives by attracting new customers to the bank.)

Notice in the example that the objectives become more specific at lower levels of the organization, and planning tends to focus on shorter time spans. This is the usual pattern for planning in an organization. Thus, top managers spend a lot of their time thinking broadly over several years, whereas much of the supervisor's planning may involve what actions to take in the current week or month.

### Personal Objectives

Besides planning for the department as a whole, each supervisor should apply good planning practices to his or her individual efforts. This includes determining how to help the department meet its objectives, as well as how to meet the supervisor's own career objectives. Another important application of planning is effectively managing one's use of time. (Chapter 14 discusses time management, and Appendix A presents ideas for career management.)

FIGURE 6.1

**Characteristics of Effective Objectives**

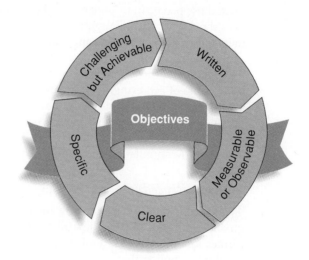

### Characteristics of Effective Objectives

For objectives to be effective—that is, clearly understood and practical—they should have certain characteristics. They should be written, measurable or observable, clear, specific, and challenging but achievable (see Figure 6.1).

Putting objectives *in writing* might seem like a nuisance, but doing so gives them importance; employees can see they are something to which managers have devoted time and thought. The people required to carry out the objectives can then look them up as a reminder of what they are supposed to be accomplishing, and they can take time to make sure they understand them. Finally, writing down objectives forces the supervisor to think through what the objectives say.

Making objectives *measurable* or at least observable provides the supervisor with a way to tell whether people are actually accomplishing them. Measurable objectives might specify a dollar amount, a time frame, or a quantity to be produced. Examples are number of sales calls made, parts manufactured, VCRs repaired, and customers served. The words *maximize* and *minimize* are tip-offs that the objectives are not measurable. If the objective is to "maximize quality," how will anyone be able to know whether maximum quality has been obtained? Rather, the objective might call for a defect rate of no more than 2 percent or for no customer complaints during the month. Other objectives that are difficult to measure are those that simply call for something to "improve" or get "better." The person writing the objective should specify a way to measure or observe the improvement.

Making objectives *specific* means spelling out who is to do what and by what time to accomplish the objective. Specific objectives describe the actions people are to take and what is supposed to result from those actions. For example, instead of saying, "Computer files will be backed up regularly," a specific objective might say, "Each word-processing operator will back up his or her files at the end of each workday." Being specific simplifies the job of ensuring that the objectives are accomplished; the supervisor knows just what to look for. Also, specific objectives help the employees understand what they are supposed to be doing.

When the supervisor needs other people to play a part in accomplishing objectives, those people must understand the objectives. Thus, it is easy to see why objectives should be clear. The supervisor makes sure the objectives are clear by spelling them out in simple language and asking employees whether they understand them.

Objectives that are challenging are more likely to stimulate employees to do their best than those that are not. However, the employees have to believe they are capable of achieving the objectives. Otherwise, they will become frustrated or angry at what seem to be unreasonable expectations. Most of us have had the experience of tackling a challenging job and enjoying the sense of pride and accomplishment that comes with finishing it. In setting goals, the supervisor should remember how stimulating and confidence-building such experiences can be.

## Policies, Procedures, and Rules

To meet his objective of staffing his information systems department with top-quality employees, Bruce Frazzoli hired some people he used to work with at his former job. He was later embarrassed to be called on the carpet for violating his employer's policy that managers must work with the personnel department in making all hiring decisions. Bruce learned that supervisors and other managers must consider the organization's policies, procedures, and rules when setting objectives. The content of the objectives and the way they are carried out must be consistent with all three.

**policies**
Broad guidelines for how to act.

**Policies** are broad guidelines for how to act; they do not spell out the details of how to handle a specific situation. Monsanto Company, a chemical and drug manufacturer based in St. Louis, has a policy of increasing the number of women and minorities in its workforce. This policy is designed to meet federal requirements, as well as what management sees as its moral duty.[3] The policy does not dictate whom to hire or when; it merely states a general expectation.

**procedures**
The steps that must be completed to achieve a specific purpose.

**Procedures** are the steps that must be completed to achieve a specific purpose. An organization might specify procedures for hiring employees, purchasing equipment, filing paperwork, or many other activities. Publishing company Richard D. Irwin's management guidelines include suggested procedures for how to conduct performance appraisals and employment interviews. A supervisor may be responsible for developing the procedures for activities carried out in his or her own department. For example, a restaurant manager might spell out a cleanup procedure or a maintenance supervisor might detail the shutdown procedure for a piece of machinery. Procedures free managers and employees from making decisions about activities they carry out repeatedly.

**rules**
Specific statements of what to do or not do in a given situation.

**Rules** are specific statements of what to do or not do in a given situation. Unlike policies, they are neither flexible nor open to interpretation. For example, one rule at G & W Electric Company states that safety glasses and safety shoes (shoes with steel toes or leather uppers) must be worn in the factory. Restaurants have rules stating that employees must wash their hands before working. Rules of this kind are often imposed by law.

## Action Plans

**action plan**
The plan for how to achieve an objective.

Objectives serve as the basis for action plans and contingency plans (see Figure 6.2). An **action plan** is the plan for how to achieve an objective. If you think of objectives as statements of where you want to go, then an action plan is a map that tells you how to get there. For a successful trip, you need to have both kinds of information.

**FIGURE 6.2**

**Areas of Planning**

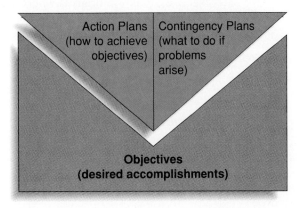

Action Plans (how to achieve objectives)

Contingency Plans (what to do if problems arise)

**Objectives (desired accomplishments)**

The supervisor creates an action plan by answering the questions *what, who, when, where,* and *how:*

- *What* actions need to be taken? Do sales calls need to be made, customers served in a certain way, goods produced? The supervisor should outline the specific steps involved.

- *Who* will take the necessary steps? The supervisor may perform some tasks, but many activities will be assigned to specific employees or groups of employees.

- *When* must each step be completed? With many types of processes, certain steps will determine when the whole project is completed. The supervisor should be particularly careful in scheduling those activities.

- *Where* will the work take place? Sometimes this question is easy to answer, but a growing operation may require that the supervisor plan for additional space. Some activities may require that the supervisor consider the arrangement of work on the shop floor or the arrangement of items in a warehouse or supply room.

- *How* will the work be done? Are the usual procedures and equipment adequate, or does the supervisor need to innovate? Thinking about how the work will be done may alert the supervisor to a need for more training.

## *Contingency Planning*

A lot of people believe in Murphy's law: "If anything can go wrong, it will." Even those who are less pessimistic recognize that things don't always go as planned. A delivery may be delayed by a strike or a blizzard, a key employee may take another job, a "foolproof" computer system may crash. The sign of a good supervisor is not so much never having these nasty surprises, but being prepared with ideas about how to respond.

**contingency planning**
Planning what to do if the original plans don't work out.

Planning what to do if the original plans don't work out is known as **contingency planning.** The wise supervisor has contingency plans to go with every original plan. One useful technique for contingency planning is to review all objectives, looking for areas where something might go wrong. Then the supervisor determines how to respond if those problems do arise.

Contingency planning is not always formal. It would be too time-consuming to create a written contingency plan for every detail of operations. Instead, the supervisor simply has to keep in mind how to respond if some details of the operation do not go as planned.

## Management by Objectives

**management by objectives (MBO)**
A formal system for planning in which managers and employees at all levels set objectives for what they are to accomplish; their performance is then measured against those objectives.

Many organizations use a formal system for planning known as **management by objectives (MBO)**. This is a process in which managers and employees at all levels set objectives for what they are to accomplish. Their performance is then measured against those objectives. Basically, MBO involves three steps:

1. All individuals in the organization work with their managers to set objectives, specifying what they are to do in the next operating period (such as a year).
2. Each individual's manager periodically reviews the individual's performance to see whether he or she is meeting the objectives. Typically, these reviews take place two to four times a year. The reviews help the individual and the manager decide what corrective actions are needed, and they provide information for setting future objectives.
3. The organization rewards the individuals based on how close they come to fulfilling the objectives.

Figure 6.3 shows examples of objectives for employees at several levels of an organization using MBO. Notice that the sample objective for the nonmanagement employee supports the achievement of the supervisor's objective, which in turn supports the achievement of his or her manager's objective, and so on up the hierarchy. (In practice, of course, each person in the organization would have several objectives to meet.)

For effective use of MBO, the managers at all levels (especially top management) must be committed to the system. Also, the objectives they set must meet the criteria for effective objectives described earlier. For example, a salesperson would not be expected merely to "sell more," but to help to develop specific objectives, such as "make 40 sales calls a month" and "sell 50 copiers by December 31." Finally, managers and employees must be able to cooperate in the objective-setting process.

Some people dislike MBO because setting and monitoring the achievement of objectives can be time-consuming and requires a lot of paperwork. However, the organization can benefit from involving employees in setting goals, which may lead to greater commitment in achieving them. Furthermore, the employees can benefit from a system of rewards that is rational and based on performance rather than personality. In light of these advantages, a supervisor may want to use the principles of management by objectives with the employees in his or her own department even if the organization as a whole has not adopted a formal MBO system.

**FIGURE 6.3**

**Sample Objectives in an Organization Using MBO**

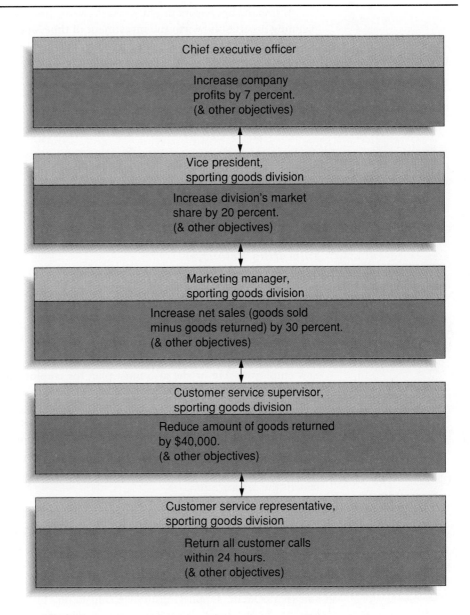

The Supervisor as Planner

In most organizations, supervisors are responsible for the creation of plans that specify goals, tasks, resources, and responsibilities for the supervisor's own department.[4] Thus, at the supervisor's level, objectives can range from the tasks he or she intends to accomplish on a certain day to the level of production the department is to achieve for the year. To be an effective planner, the supervisor should be familiar with how to set good objectives in these and other areas.

Although supervisors might resist doing the necessary paperwork, thoughtful planning is certainly worth the investment of time and effort. In carrying out their planning responsibilities, supervisors may engage in a variety of activities, from providing information to allocating resources, involving employees, coaching a team's planning effort, and updating objectives. (Take the "Self-Quiz" on page 175 to see if you are a planner.)

## Providing Information and Estimates

As the manager closest to day-to-day operations, the supervisor is in the best position to keep higher-level managers informed about the needs, abilities, and progress of his or her department or work group. For that reason, higher management relies on supervisors to provide estimates of the personnel and other resources they will need to accomplish their work.

## Allocating Resources

The department for which the supervisor is responsible has a limited number of resources—people, equipment, and money. The supervisor's job includes deciding how to allocate resources to the jobs that will need to be done.

The process of allocating human resources includes determining how many and what kind of employees the department will need to meet its objectives. If the department's workload is expanding, the supervisor may need to plan for hiring new employees. He or she also must plan for employee vacations and other time off, as well as for employee turnover.

The process of allocating equipment resources includes determining how much equipment is needed to get the job done. For example, does every bookkeeper need a personal computer, or will adding machines be enough? The supervisor may find that the department needs to acquire more equipment. In that case, the supervisor must justify the request to buy or rent it by showing how it will benefit the organization.

### Developing a Budget

**budget**
A plan for spending money.

The process of allocating money resources is called budgeting. A **budget** is a plan for spending money. Many households use budgets for deciding how much of each paycheck should go for housing, car payments, food, savings, and so on. Businesses use budgets to break down how much to spend on items such as wages and salaries, rent, supplies, insurance, and so on. These items would be part of an *operating budget;* big-ticket items such as machinery or a new building would more likely be accounted for separately as part of a *capital budget.*

Some organizations expect their supervisors to prepare a budget showing what they think they will need to spend in the next year to meet departmental goals or carry out a specific project. Table 6.2 illustrates a sample budget for a machine shop project. The line items show different categories of expenses. The first column of figures contains the amounts budgeted for expenses in each category. The right-hand columns have the actual amounts spent each month in each category. The supervisor uses the actual amounts in controlling, which is described later in this chapter.

**TABLE 6.2**

**Sample Budget for a Machine Shop Project**

**BUDGET MONITORING REPORT**

Organizational unit  Machine shop  Job number  1763  Period  January–June

Total parts needed  6,000  Parts produced to date  2,700  Remaining work  3,300

Parts per month projection  1,000  Current production per month  900  Difference  (–100)

**ACTUAL EXPENDITURES**

| Line item | Budgeted Amount | January | February | March | April | May | June |
|---|---|---|---|---|---|---|---|
| Direct labor | $60,000 | $10,000 | $10,000 | $10,000 | | | |
| Indirect labor | $5,400 | 900 | 900 | 900 | | | |
| Material | 13,200 | 2,195 | 3,156 | 1,032 | | | |
| Operating supplies | 3,000 | 1,200 | 0 | 296 | | | |
| Equipment repair | 5,400 | 0 | 0 | 3,600 | | | |
| **Total** | **$87,000** | **$14,295** | **$14,056** | **$15,828** | | | |

Source: *Industrial Supervision in the Age of High Technology*, p.281, by David L. Goetsch, © 1992. Reprinted by permissions of Prentice-Hall, Inc., Upper Saddle River, NJ.

In preparing a budget, the supervisor typically has rules and guidelines to follow. For example, one company may say that pay increases for the department as a whole must be no more than 5 percent of the previous year's budget for salaries. Another organization may specify a total amount that the department may spend, or it may give the supervisor a formula for computing the department's overhead expenses. Based on these guidelines, the supervisor then recommends how much to spend in each area. In most cases, the supervisor and his or her manager review the budget. The supervisor must be willing to modify it when higher-level managers require a change.

**scheduling**
Setting a precise timetable for the work to be completed.

**Gantt chart**
Scheduling tool that lists the activities to be completed and uses horizontal bars to graph how long each activity will take, including its starting and ending dates.

### Scheduling

The supervisor continually needs to think about how much work the department needs to accomplish in a given time period and how it can meet its deadlines. Setting a precise timetable for the work to be done is known as **scheduling.** This includes deciding which activities will take priority over others and deciding who will do what tasks and when.

Many organizations expect supervisors to use one or more of the techniques and tools that have been developed to help with scheduling. Two of the most widely used techniques are Gantt charts and PERT networks. A **Gantt chart** is a scheduling tool that lists the activities to be completed and uses horizontal bars to graph how long each activity will take, including its starting and ending dates (see Figure 6.4).

**FIGURE 6.4**

**Sample Gantt Chart for Building a Church**

| Activities | Mar '97 | | | | | Apr '97 | | | | | May '97 | | | | | Jun '97 | | | | Jul '97 | | | | |
|---|---|---|---|---|---|---|---|---|---|---|---|---|---|---|---|---|---|---|---|---|---|---|---|---|
| | 25 | 4 | 11 | 18 | 25 | 1 | 8 | 15 | 22 | 29 | 6 | 13 | 20 | 27 | 3 | 10 | 17 | 24 | 1 | 8 | 15 | 22 | 29 | |
| 1. Elev. shaft wall system | | ▬ | | | | | | | | | | | | | | | | | | | | | | |
| 2. Interior framing | | ▬▬▬ | | | | | | | | | | | | | | | | | | | | | | |
| 3. Rough fire protection | | ▬▬▬ | | | | | | | | | | | | | | | | | | | | | | |
| 4. Rough plumbing | | ▬▬▬▬ | | | | | | | | | | | | | | | | | | | | | | |
| 5. Rough HVAC | | ▬▬▬▬ | | | | | | | | | | | | | | | | | | | | | | |
| 6. Hydraulic elevator | | ▬▬▬▬▬ | | | | | | | | | | | | | | | | | | | | | | |
| 7. Rough electrical | | ▬▬▬▬▬▬ | | | | | | | | | | | | | | | | | | | | | | |
| 8. Gypsum drywall | | | ▬▬▬ | | | | | | | | | | | | | | | | | | | | | |
| 9. Slate roofing | | | ▬▬ | | | | | | | | | | | | | | | | | | | | | |
| 10. Misc. metals | | | ▬ | | | | | | ▬ | | ▬ | | ▬ | ▬ | ▬ | ▬ | | | | | | | | |
| 11. Waterproofing | | | | ▬ | | | | | | | | | | | | | | | | | | | | |
| 12. Stair following lift | | | | ▬ | | | | | | | | | | | | | | | | | | | | |
| 13. Exterior masonry (West elev.) | | | | | ▬▬▬ | | | | | | | | | | | | | | | | | | | |
| 14. Interior taping & painting | | | | | ▬▬▬▬▬▬▬▬▬▬ | | | | | | | | | | | | | | | | | | |
| 15. Exterior stucco (West elev.) | | | | | | | ▬▬▬ | | | | | | | | | | | | | | | | | |
| 16. Exterior masonry (South elev.) | | | | | | | ▬▬▬ | | | | | | | | | | | | | | | | | |
| 17. Exterior stucco (Northeast elev.) | | | | | | | | | ▬▬ | | | | | | | | | | | | | | | |
| 18. Exterior stucco (South elev.) | | | | | | | | | | ▬▬▬ | | | | | | | | | | | | | | |
| 19. Exterior masonry (Northeast elev.) | | | | | | | | | ▬ | | | | | | | | | | | | | | | |
| 20. Exterior alum windows | | | | | | | ▬ | | ▬ | | ▬ | | | | | | | | | | | | | |
| 21. Joint Sealers | | | | | | | | | | | | | | | | | | | | | | | | |

Source: Thomas C. Belanger, DMSI, "How to Plan Any Project: A Self-Teaching Guide." Nashua, NH 03060, 1991, p. 98.

**program evaluation and review technique (PERT)**
Scheduling tool that identifies the relationships among tasks as well as the amount of time each task will take.

The **program evaluation and review technique (PERT)** is a scheduling tool that identifies the relationships among tasks and the amount of time each task will take. To use this tool, the planner creates a PERT network. For example, in Figure 6.5, the circles represent the tasks that must be completed in order to change a tire. The lines with arrows between the circles represent the sequence of activities needed to carry out each task. The numbers in the circles represent the order of tasks, in this case, counting by fives. The numbers in parentheses next to the arrows represent the time (number of minutes) required to complete each task. An important piece of information in a PERT network is the *critical path*—the sequence of tasks that will require the greatest amount of time. A delay that occurs in the critical path will cause the entire project to fall behind.

Besides these tools, supervisors may use a computer to help with scheduling. Many project management software packages have been developed for this application. Programs such as *Superproject for Windows*, *Project Scheduler 5*, and *Time Line* make it easier for a planner to create and update Gantt charts, look at graphs relating cost to time, and even schedule multiple projects, specifying the priorities of each.[5]

**PERT Network for Changing a Flat Tire**

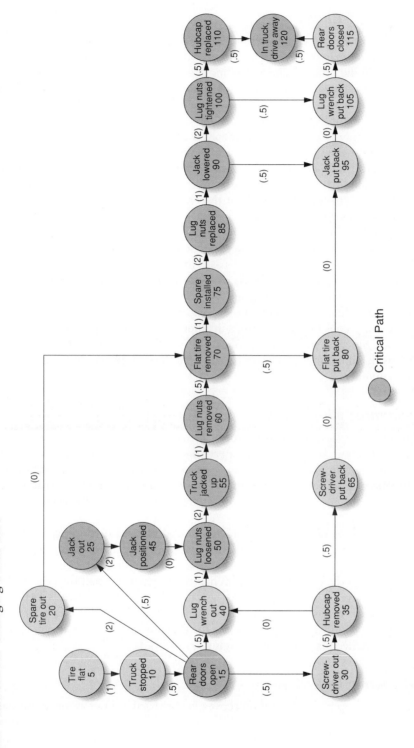

Source: Samuel C. Certo and Lee A. Graf, *Experiencing Modern Management*, 5th ed. (Boston: Allyn and Bacon, 1992), p. 133. Reprinted with permission of Prentice-Hall, Inc., Upper Saddle River, NJ.

## Involving Employees

To make sure that employees understand objectives and consider them achievable, supervisors may involve them in the goal-setting process. Employees who are involved in the process tend to feel more committed to the objectives, and they may be able to introduce ideas that the supervisor has not considered. In many cases, employees who help set objectives agree to take on greater challenges than the supervisor might have guessed.

One way to get employees involved in setting objectives is to have them write down what they think they can accomplish in the coming year (or month or appropriate time period). Then the supervisor discusses the ideas with each employee, modifying the objectives to meet the department's overall needs. Another approach is to hold a meeting of the entire work group at which the employees and supervisor develop objectives as a group. (Chapter 3 provides ideas for holding successful meetings.)

To set objectives for salespeople at Davis & Geck (a medical supply company), sales manager Dave Jacobs asks the salespeople and their regional supervisors to come up with sales levels they can guarantee. The supervisors are expected to discuss each salesperson's figures with him or her to assess how realistic they are. Jacobs then may modify those numbers in light of broad industry trends. The first year Jacobs used this bottom-up approach, some projections were overly optimistic. Since then, supervisors have begun asking salespeople to prepare action plans detailing how they expect to achieve their numbers. The result: more accurate numbers.[6]

## Planning with a Team

In many applications of teamwork, teams, not individual managers, are charged with planning. In these cases, supervisors are expected not only to seek employee involvement in planning, but also to coach their team in carrying out the planning function. This requires knowing and communicating a clear sense of what the plan should encompass and encouraging team members to cooperate and share ideas freely.

When teams draw on the many viewpoints and diverse experience of team members, they can come up with creative plans that dramatically exceed past performance. At one time, Toshiba had the objective of producing a VCR with half the parts of the previous model, in half the time, and at half the cost. It assigned a team to develop an action plan for accomplishing that objective. The team cut the number of necessary parts by more than half and had the VCR in production in one year (compared with two years for previous models).[7] (Chapter 3 provides a more detailed discussion of managing teamwork.)

## Updating Objectives

Once the supervisor has set objectives, he or she should monitor performance and compare it with the objectives. The control process will be described later in this chapter. Sometimes the supervisor determines that objectives need to be modified.

When should supervisors update the objectives for their department or work group? They will need to do so whenever top management updates organizational objectives. Also, organizations with a regular procedure for planning will specify when supervisors must review and update their objectives.

# The Supervisor as Controller

**controlling**
The management function of ensuring that work goes according to plan.

As you learned in Chapter 1, **controlling** is the management function of making sure that work goes according to plan. Supervisors carry out this process in many ways. Consider the following fictional examples:

- Bud Cavanaugh told his crew, "I expect the work area to be clean when you leave each day. That means the floors are swept and all the tools are put away."
- Once or twice each day, Maria Lopez took time to check the documents produced by the word-processing operators she supervised. Maria would look over a few pages each employee had produced that day. If one of the employees seemed to be having trouble with some task—for example, deciphering handwriting or preparing neat tables—Maria would discuss the problem with that employee.
- Sonja Friedman learned that citizens calling her housing department complained of spending an excessive amount of time on hold. She scheduled a meeting at which the employees discussed ways they could handle calls faster.

As shown in these examples, supervisors need to know what is going on in the area they supervise. Do employees understand what they are supposed to do and can they do it? Is all machinery and equipment (whether a computer-operated milling machine or a touch-tone telephone) operating properly? Is work getting out correctly and on time?

To answer such questions, a supervisor could theoretically sit back and wait for disaster to strike. No disaster, no need for correction. More realistically, the supervisor has a responsibility to correct problems as soon as possible, which means that some way to *detect* problems quickly must be found. Detection of problems is at the heart of the control function.

By controlling, the supervisor can take steps to ensure quality and manage costs. Visiting the work area and checking up on performance, as Maria Lopez did, allows the supervisor to make sure that employees are producing satisfactory work. By setting standards for a clean workplace, Bud Cavanaugh reduced costs related to spending time looking for tools or to slipping on a messy floor. Sonja Friedman engaged her employees in improving work processes. In many such ways, supervisors can benefit the organization through the process of control.

## The Process of Controlling

While the specific ways in which supervisors control vary according to the type of organization and the employees being supervised, the basic process involves three steps. First, the supervisor establishes performance **standards,** which are measures of what is expected. Then the supervisor monitors actual performance and compares it with the standards. Finally, the supervisor responds, either by reinforcing success or by making some adjustment to bring performance and the standards into line. Figure 6.6 illustrates this process.

**standards**
Measures of what is expected.

If the control system is working properly, the supervisor should be uncovering problems before customers and management discover them. This gives the supervisor the best opportunity to fix the problem in time to minimize damage.

### Establish Performance Standards

Performance standards are a natural outgrowth of the planning process. Once the supervisor knows the objectives employees are to achieve, he or she can determine

**FIGURE 6.6**

**The Control Process**

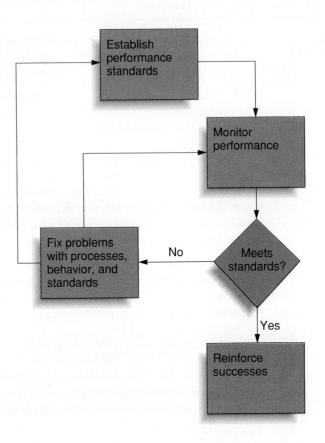

what employees must do to meet those objectives. Assume that the objective of an eight-person telephone sales (telemarketing) office is to make 320 calls an evening, resulting in 64 sales. To achieve this objective, each salesperson should average 10 calls an hour, with 2 in 10 calls resulting in a sale. Those numbers could be two of the office's performance standards.

Standards define the acceptable quantity and quality of work. (The measure of quantity in the example is the number of telephone calls made; the number of sales measures the quality of selling; that is, turning a telephone call into a sale.) Other standards can spell out expectations for level of service, amount of money spent, amount of inventory on hand, level of pollution in the workplace, and other concerns. Ultimately, all these standards measure how well the department contributes to meeting the organization's objectives for serving its customers and—for a business—earning a profit.

The way supervisors set standards depends on their experience, their employer's expectations, and the nature of the work being monitored. Often, supervisors use their technical expertise to estimate reasonable standards. Past performance also is a useful guide for what can be expected. However, the supervisor must avoid being a slave to the past. In creating a budget, some supervisors assume that because they have spent a given sum in a given category in the past, that expense will be appropriate in the future. Sometimes there are better alternatives. Supervisors may have additional sources of information in setting performance standards. Equipment

Bottlenecks in producing rubber parts were lowering the performance standards set by supervisors at the Tralee Park, Delaware, site of E. I. DuPont de Nemours and Company. This employee team increased the performance standards by solving the bottlenecks and reduced the average cycle time from 70 to 16 days, resulting in a 100 percent on-time delivery record to customers.

Source: Courtesy of DuPont, Inc.

manufacturers and systems designers can provide information about how fast a machine or computer system will perform. Some companies arrange for time-and-motion studies to analyze how quickly and efficiently employees can reasonably work.

To be effective, performance standards should meet the criteria of effective objectives; that is, they should be written, measurable, clear, specific, and challenging but achievable. Standards also should measure dimensions of the goods or services that customers care about. Finally, because standards serve as the basis for deciding whether to make changes, they should measure things the group, supervisor, or organization has the ability to act on.[8]

Not only should the supervisor have standards in mind, but the employees should be aware of and understand those standards. In communicating performance standards, the supervisor should put them in writing so that employees can remember and refer to them as necessary. (Chapter 10 provides more detailed suggestions for communicating effectively.)

The supervisor should also be sure that the employees understand the rationale for the standards. It is human nature to resist when someone lays down restrictive rules, but the rules seem less of a burden when they serve a purpose we can understand. Thus, if a law office's word-processing department is to produce error-free documents, the department's supervisor can explain that it is part of the firm's plan to build a prestigious clientele by delivering an excellent product. With such an explanation, the word processors are less likely to feel overwhelmed by the stringent quality standard and more likely to feel proud that they are part of an excellent law firm.

### Monitor Performance and Compare with Standards

Once performance standards are in place, the supervisor can begin the core of the control process: monitoring performance. (See "Meeting the Challenge.") In the example of the telephone sales force, the supervisor would want to keep track of how many calls each salesperson made and how many of those calls resulted in sales.

One way to monitor performance is simply to record information on paper or enter it into a computer, a task that can be done by the supervisor, the employees, or both. The telephone salespeople in the example might provide the supervisor with information to enter into a log such as the one shown in Table 6.3. Some

## MEETING THE CHALLENGE

### Planning and Controlling in the Post-Reengineering World

Have we reached the end of an era? Two top executives at Gemini Consulting, a wildly successful high-tech venture that established 19 offices worldwide within the first four years of operation, believe that we have. Francis Gouillart and James Kelly have even written a book about it: *Transforming the Organization*. The authors believe that very soon companies will have to face concerns raised by a post-reengineering business environment. Forcing people to do more with less can only last for a short period of time; ultimately, organizations must address broader strategic questions.

Gouillart and Kelly break down the problem—which boils down to planning and controlling—into four phases: reframing, restructuring, revitalizing, and renewing. First, the authors say that organizations must reframe their vision; they must establish new strategic goals and operational objectives. Organizations must then integrate the goals and objectives with a measurement system—control—that can monitor whether they are met. Second, organizations must restructure if necessary to meet the goals and

objectives. Third, they must revitalize: adopt the customer's point of view and use their core technology to branch into new areas. This requires planning so that an organization remains unified instead of splintering into a group of tiny, uncontrolled businesses. Finally, Gouillart and Kelly propose that organizations engage in renewal, extending their performance systems to suppliers and other partners, and making sure they reward workers for increased involvement such as acquiring new skills.

Gemini relies on the philosophy of its executives to enter new markets, combining seemingly different types of companies to achieve new goals in serving customers in the world of high technology. Gemini understands the opportunities that lie in the hands of those who can take radically different visions, technologies, and markets and meld them into one. Gouillart and Kelly understand that the only way to achieve this is through plans and controls.

Source: "A Brief Theory of Everything," *The Economist*, May 6, 1995, p. 63.

---

types of machinery and equipment have electronic or mechanical counting systems that provide an unbiased way to measure performance. For instance, the electronic scanners at store checkout stations can keep track of how fast cashiers are ringing up merchandise.

From a quality perspective, monitoring performance should include assessing whether customers are satisfied. Supervisors of groups that provide services to other employees in the organization should ask those internal customers whether they are getting what they need, when they need it. They may find it helpful to conduct a survey assessing whether the customers are happy with the group's reports, response times, ideas, repairs, or other services.[9]

When monitoring performance, the supervisor should focus on how actual performance compares with the standards he or she has set. Are employees meeting standards, exceeding them, or falling short? Two concepts useful for maintaining this focus are variance and the exception principle.

**variance**
The size of the difference between actual performance and a performance standard.

In a control system, **variance** refers to the size of the difference between actual performance and the standard to be met. When setting standards, the supervisor should decide how much variance is meaningful for control purposes. It can be helpful to think in terms of percentages. For example, if a hospital's performance standard is to register outpatients for lab tests in 10 minutes or less, the supervisor might decide to allow for a variance of 50 percent (5 minutes). (In a manufacturing setting, a variance of 5 to 10 percent might be more appropriate for most standards.) As described in the Chapter 2, some organizations strive for a standard of accepting zero defects.

**TABLE 6.3**

**Sample Performance Record**

Week of _____

Performance Standard: __40__ calls, __8__ sales

| Name | Number of Calls Completed | Number of Sales Made | Action |
|---|---|---|---|
| Forrest | 32 | 6 | Discuss slow pace of work |
| French | 41 | 8 | Praise performance |
| Johnson | 39 | 7 | None |
| Munoz | 47 | 9 | Praise performance |
| Peterson | 38 | 8 | Praise performance |
| Spagnoli | 50 | 7 | Praise hard work; discuss how to turn more calls into sales |
| Steinmetz | 29 | 5 | Discuss poor performance; discipline if necessary |
| Wang | 43 | 9 | Praise performance |
| **Total** | **319** | **59** | |

**exception principle**
The control principle stating that a supervisor should take action only when a variance is meaningful.

According to the **exception principle,** the supervisor should take action only when a variance is meaningful. Thus, when monitoring performance in the previous example, the supervisor would need to take action only if outpatients spent more than 15 or fewer than 5 minutes registering for lab tests.

The exception principle is beneficial when it helps the supervisor to manage his or her time wisely and to motivate employees. A supervisor who did not tolerate reasonable variances might try to solve the "problem" every time an employee made one component too few or went over the budget for office supplies by the cost of a box of paper clips. In such a case, employees might become frustrated by the control system, and morale would deteriorate. At the same time, the supervisor would be too busy with trifles to focus on more significant issues.

### Reinforce Successes and Fix Problems

The information gained from the control process is beneficial only if the supervisor uses it as the basis for reinforcing or changing behavior. If performance is satisfactory or better, the supervisor needs to encourage this. If performance is unacceptable, the supervisor needs to make changes that either improve performance or adjust the standard. The right-hand column in Table 6.3 lists some ways the telemarketing supervisor plans to respond to performance data.

**reinforcement**
Encouragement of a behavior by associating it with a reward.

When employees are doing excellent work, customers are happy, and costs are within budget, the supervisor needs to reinforce these successes. **Reinforcement** means encouraging the behavior by associating it with a reward. Praise from the supervisor for performance that meets standards not only gives the employee a good feeling, but also clarifies what is expected. For exceptionally high performance, the supervisor also may reward the employee with a monetary bonus. The supervisor's actions will depend on company and union rules regarding superior performance.

**problem**
A factor in the organization that is a barrier to improvement.

When performance significantly falls short of standards, the supervisor should investigate. Below-standard performance is the sign of a **problem**—some factor in the organization that is a barrier to improvement. The supervisor's task is to identify the underlying problem. For example, if the supervisor in the telephone sales company learns that the group is not meeting its sales objectives, the supervisor could find out who is falling short of the sales goals: everyone or only one or two employees. If everyone is performing below standard, the problem may be that the sales force needs better training or motivation. Or the problem may lie outside the supervisor's direct control; the product may be defective or customers may lack interest for some other reason, such as poor economic conditions. If only one employee is failing to make sales, the supervisor needs to search for the problem underlying that employee's poor performance. Does the employee understand how to close a sale? Does the employee have personal problems that affect performance?

**symptom**
An indication of an underlying problem.

Poor performance itself is rarely a problem, but a **symptom**—an indication of an underlying problem. To make effective use of information gained through controlling, the supervisor needs to distinguish problems from symptoms. No one did this at a business that had trouble paying its bills on time and therefore set up a hotline, a telephone number its vendors could call to find out when they would be paid. This company was treating the symptom of late payments by setting up a system to handle mistakes (the late payments). The company should have addressed the problem by figuring out how it could make payments on time in the first place.[10]

Sometimes a problem underlying a significant variance is that the standard is too low or too high. For example, if no employees on the telephone sales force are achieving the desired number of sales, the standards may be too high, given current economic or market conditions. In other cases, what the manager learns about performance may indicate that a standard is not measuring the right thing. In response to Monsanto's policy of increasing the number of women and minorities in its workforce, the percentage of new hires in both categories rose. However, the percentages of women and minorities *leaving* Monsanto also were high.[11] Apparently, hiring practices were not the only barrier to achieving a diverse workforce at Monsanto.

Fixing the problem may entail adjusting a process, the behavior of an individual employee, or the standard itself. For process and behavioral problems, supervisors can choose from among a number of possible actions:

- Develop new rewards for good performance.
- Train employees.
- Improve communications with employees.
- Counsel and/or discipline poor performers.
- Ask employees what barriers are interfering with their performance, then remove those barriers. (Common barriers include insufficient supplies or information, poorly maintained equipment, and inefficient work procedures.)

The best response to problems related to standards is to make the performance standard more appropriate. The supervisor may need to make the standard less stringent or more challenging. At Monsanto, the key to increasing diversity

On-time delivery for Burlington Northern Railroad Company was only 60 percent in 1994. To meet its goal of improving performance, the company built this $120 million state-of-the-art communications center in Fort Worth, Texas. Dispatchers and their supervisors can view up-to-the-minute status reports of the entire rail system and national weather maps on massive 18-foot screens. This information allows them to use concurrent control to improve the handling of immediate problems and to use precontrols to avoid future problems. The new goal for on-time delivery is 90 percent.

Source: © Doug Milner.

has been to broaden control efforts to encompass the retention as well as the hiring of minorities. The company has sought to create an atmosphere in which many kinds of people can feel comfortable and able to contribute.[12]

Whatever actions the supervisor selects, it is important to give employees feedback soon after observing a deviation from the standard. This enables the employees to make changes before performance deteriorates further. A problem that has been allowed to continue is often harder to correct. For example, an employee may get into the habit of doing a task the wrong way or may fall so far behind that it is impossible to catch up.

Modifying standards brings the control process full circle. With new standards in place, the supervisor is again ready to monitor performance.

## Types of Control

From the description of the control process, it might sound as though controlling begins when employees' work is complete. The employees finish their job, then the supervisor checks whether it was done well. However, this is only one type of controlling. There are three types of control in terms of when it takes place: feedback control, concurrent control, and precontrol.

**Feedback control** is the type just described; that is, control that focuses on past performance. A supervisor reviewing customer comments about service is practicing feedback control. The customers provide information about the quality of service; the supervisor reacts by reinforcing or trying to change employee behavior.

The word *concurrent* describes things that are happening at the same time. Thus, **concurrent control** refers to controlling work while that work is taking place. A restaurant manager who greets customers at their tables and visits the kitchen to see how work is progressing is practicing concurrent control. This supervisor is gathering information about what is going smoothly and what problems may be developing. The supervisor can act on any problems before customers or employees become upset. Another technique for concurrent control is statistical process control, described in Chapter 2.

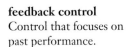

**feedback control**
Control that focuses on past performance.

**concurrent control**
Control that occurs while the work takes place.

## TABLE 6.4

**Budget Report for a Manufacturing Project**

Organizational Unit  Machine Shop          Job Number 1763   Date March 31, 19xx

| Line Item | Six-Month Budget | Budgeted Year to Date (Jan.–Mar.) | Actual Year to Date (Jan.–Mar.) | Variance |
|---|---|---|---|---|
| Direct labor | $60,000 | $30,000 | $30,000 | $  0 |
| Indirect labor | 5,400 | 2,700 | 2,700 | 0 |
| Material | 13,200 | 6,600 | 6,383 | 217 |
| Operating supplies | 3,000 | 1,500 | 1,496 | 4 |
| Equipment repair | 5,400 | 2,700 | 3,600 | −900 |
| Total | $87,000 | $43,500 | $44,179 | −$679 |

Source: *Industrial Supervision in the Age of High Technology* by David L. Goetsch, © 1992. Reprinted by permission of Prentice-Hall, Inc., Upper Saddle River, NJ.

**precontrol**
Efforts aimed at preventing behavior that may lead to undesirable results.

**Precontrol** refers to efforts aimed at preventing behavior that may lead to undesirable results. Such efforts may include setting rules, policies, and procedures. A production supervisor might provide employees with guidelines about the detection of improperly functioning machinery. The employees can then request repairs before they waste time and materials on the machinery. Precontrol is one of the functions of the management philosophy known as total quality management (see Chapter 2).

## Tools for Control

When considering how to monitor performance, the supervisor can start with some of the basic tools used by most managers. Budgets and reports are common in most organizations. In addition, supervisors can benefit from personally observing the work taking place.

### Budgets

Creating a budget—a plan for spending money—is part of the planning process. In controlling, a budget is useful as a kind of performance standard. The supervisor compares actual expenses with the amounts in the budget.

Table 6.4 is a sample budget report based on the example in Table 6.2. The left-hand column shows each category of expenses for the machine shop project, which was scheduled to last for six months, from January through June. Thus, the six-month budget represents the total the supervisor expected to spend in each category for the project. This report was prepared on March 31 (halfway through the project), so the next column shows what would be budgeted for half of the project. The next column shows the amounts that actually were spent during the first three months. In the right-hand column appears the variance between the actual and budgeted amounts. In this case, the machine shop has a negative total variance because the project is $679 over budget for the first three months.

**FIGURE 6.7**

**FIGURE 6.7**

**Graph of Variances Determined from Table 6.4**

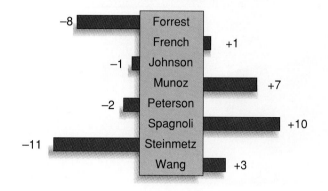

Calls Completed—Variances from a Standard of 40

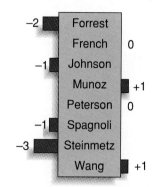

Sales Made—Variances from a Standard of 8

When using such a budget report for controlling purposes, the supervisor focuses on the variance column, looking for meaningful variances. In Table 6.4, the supervisor would note that the total unfavorable variance is due entirely to a large expense for equipment repair. The machine shop is otherwise under budget or exactly meeting the budget standards. Following the exception principle, the supervisor takes action when a meaningful variance occurs. Typically, this involves looking for ways to cut costs when the department goes over budget. The supervisor in the example will want to focus on avoiding further equipment breakdowns. Sometimes the supervisor can change the budget when a variance indicates that the budgeted figures were unrealistic.

### Performance Reports

**performance report**
A summary of performance and comparison with performance standards.

A well-structured report can be an important source of information. **Performance reports** summarize performance and compare it with performance standards. They can simply summarize facts, such as the number of calls made by sales representatives or the number of deliveries completed by delivery personnel, or they can be analytical; that is, they may interpret the facts.

Most supervisors both prepare and request performance reports. Typically, the organization requires that the supervisor do a particular type of reporting of the department's performance. The supervisor's role is to prepare this report. Supervisors also may request that employees prepare reports for them. In that case, the supervisor can influence the type of reporting.

As much as possible, supervisors should see that reports are simple and to the point. A table or log may be more useful than an essay-style report. Graphs can sometimes uncover a trend better than numbers in columns. Figure 6.7 shows how the data from Table 6.4 can be converted into a graph. In this case, variances were first computed of the difference between each employee's performance and the performance standards. Notice how easy it is to tell from the graph the wide variation in the number of calls made by each employee. Does this mean some

At Hershey Chocolate U.S.A.'s H. B. Reese plant, supervisor Sandra Wolfersberger (*left*) uses "management by walking around" while discussing operational improvements with employees Mary Cope (*center*) and Veronica Purdy (*right*).

Source: Courtesy of Hershey Foods Corp.

employees are working harder than others? Maybe, but remember the process of searching for a problem. It is also possible that some employees are better at keeping calls short and to the point.

Perhaps even more important is the supervisor's role in creating a climate that fosters full and accurate reporting. The example of Wal-Mart and Kmart early in this chapter described two very different strategies for the retailers. After several years of pursuing those strategies, Wal-Mart surged past Kmart in several measures, including sales, income, and stock price. However, the strategy difference may have been less important than the behavior of managers. At Wal-Mart, executives routinely visited stores and sought suggestions for improvement. In contrast, Kmart's CEO, Joseph Antonini, reportedly discouraged criticism.[13] Although this example describes the behavior of top management, supervisors also can shape a favorable climate by actively seeking ideas from employees and being willing to listen to reports that something may be wrong.

The supervisor also should determine whether every report he or she is receiving still is useful. Many reports continue to be generated long after they have lost their usefulness. In deciding whether to continue using a report, the supervisor can consider whether it has the characteristics of effective controls, described at the end of this chapter.

### Personal Observation

A supervisor who spends the entire day behind a desk reading budgets and reports is out of touch. An important part of controlling involves spending time with employees and observing what is going on. Management consultant Tom Peters has popularized this approach, which he calls "management by walking around." While engaged in this approach, the supervisor can listen to employees, help them discover better ways of doing their jobs, and make the changes necessary to help employees carry them out. For example, a nursing supervisor might observe that the nurses frequently spend time debating which demands to respond to first. The supervisor could discuss this with the nurses and help them develop criteria for setting priorities.

Personal observation can help the supervisor understand the activities behind the numbers in reports. However, the supervisor must be careful in interpreting what he or she sees. Often the presence of a supervisor causes workers to alter their behavior. Also, the supervisor must visit work areas often enough to be sure of witnessing routine situations, not just an unusual crisis or break in the action. At the same time, the supervisor must not spend so much time among employees that they feel the visits interfere with their work. How much time is the right amount to spend in management by walking around? The supervisor probably will have to rely on trial and error, weighing employee reactions and the amount of information obtained.

The inability to control through personal observation is a challenge of supervising employees who work at home. This issue is growing in importance as communications technology makes telecommuting possible for people with disabilities, working parents, and others who simply prefer not to dress up. How can a supervisor make sure employees are not devoting their time to raiding the refrigerator and catching up on the latest soap operas?

Evidence suggests that employees who choose to work at home tend to be self-motivated. If anything, they have trouble taking a break. One telecommuter reportedly became so wrapped up in his computer programming that he gave himself headaches by working for hours without interruption. He eventually had to set a clock radio to go off every two hours, reminding him to take a break. Dramatic examples aside, supervisors and employees alike can benefit from training in handling the long-distance relationship. According to Jack Nilles, a consultant on the subject, "We tell the managers they have to change from being administrators to being leaders. We tell them your job isn't to act as a cop but as a goal setter and motivator."[14]

# Characteristics of Effective Controls

No supervisor can keep track of every detail of every employee's work. An effective control system is one that helps the supervisor direct his or her efforts toward spotting significant problems. Normally, a supervisor has to use whatever control system higher-level managers have established. However, when making recommendations about controls or setting up controls to use within the department, the supervisor can strive for the following characteristics of effective controls.

### Timeliness

The controls should be *timely*, enabling the supervisor to correct problems in time to improve results. For example, an annual budget report does not let the supervisor adjust spending in time to meet the budget's goals. In contrast, monthly budget reports give the supervisor time to identify spending patterns that will pose a problem. If the supervisor's annual budget includes $500 to spend on overnight couriers but the department has already spent $200 by the end of February, the supervisor knows that work must be planned far enough ahead that materials can be sent by other, less expensive means.

## Cost-Effectiveness

The controls should be *economical*. In general, this means that the cost of using the controls should be less than the benefit derived from using them. In a supermarket, for example, an elaborate system designed to ensure that not a single item of inventory gets lost or stolen may not save the store enough money to justify the cost of the system.

## Acceptability

The controls should be *acceptable to supervisors and employees*. Supervisors want controls that give them enough information about performance so that they can understand what is going on in the workplace. Employees want controls that do not unduly infringe on their privacy. One area of controversy has been electronic monitoring of employee performance. For example, computers can keep track of how many telephone calls operators handle and how much time they spend on each call. Electronic monitoring gives the supervisor a lot of information, including how much time operators spend going to the bathroom. Does this close scrutiny enhance performance by encouraging employees to work hard, or does it merely lower morale and remove the incentive to take time to greet customers in a friendly way? The answer lies partly in the way supervisors use this information.

Employees also appreciate controls that focus on areas over which they themselves have some control. For example, a control that measures the number of units produced by an employee would be acceptable only if the employee always has the parts needed to produce those units. An employee whose performance looks poor because of an inventory shortage would feel frustrated by the control.

## Flexibility

Finally, the controls should be *flexible*. This means that the supervisor should be able to ignore a variance if doing so is in the best interests of the organization. For example, in comparing expenditures to a budget, a supervisor should be aware of occasions when spending a little more than was budgeted actually will benefit the company. That might be the case when employees have to put in overtime to fill an order for an important customer. In the future, better planning might make it possible to avoid the overtime, but the immediate goal is to satisfy the customer.

One reason flexibility is important is that performance measures might be incompatible. For instance, employees may find it impossible to cut costs and improve quality at the same time. In that case, the supervisor may have to set priorities or adjust the control measures. Such actions are in effect a type of planning, an example of how controlling and planning work together to help the organization reach its goals.

# Summary

### 6.1 Describe types of planning that take place in organizations.

At the top level of an organization, managers engage in strategic planning, which is the creation of long-term goals for the organization. The plans for divisions, departments, and work groups are known as operational plans and are set by middle managers and supervisors. Operational plans support the strategic plan; they are more specific and focus on a shorter time frame. Supervisors also must apply good planning practices to their individual efforts.

### 6.2 Identify characteristics of effective objectives.

Effective objectives are written, measurable or observable, clear, specific, and challenging but achievable.

### 6.3 Define *management by objectives (MBO)* and discuss its use.

Management by objectives is a process in which managers and employees at all levels set objectives for what they are to accomplish, after which their performance is measured against those objectives. In MBO, all individuals in the organization work to set objectives; each employee's manager periodically reviews the employee's performance against the objectives, and the organization rewards individuals based on how close they come to fulfilling the objectives. To use MBO effectively, managers at all levels of an organization must be committed to the system.

### 6.4 Discuss the supervisor's role in the planning process.

Supervisors are responsible for the creation of plans that specify goals, tasks, resources and responsibilities for their own departments. Supervisors keep higher-level managers informed about the needs, abilities, and progress of their groups. They decide how to allocate resources to the jobs that need to be done, including creating budgets. Supervisors also engage in scheduling. Where possible, they should involve employees in the planning process.

### 6.5 Explain the purpose of using controls.

By identifying problems in time for them to be corrected, controlling enables supervisors to ensure high-quality work and to keep costs under control.

### 6.6 Identify the steps in the control process.

First, the supervisor sets and communicates performance standards in writing. The supervisor then monitors performance and compares it with the standards. Depending on whether performance is above, at, or below the standards, the supervisor reinforces successes or fixes problems. Fixing a problem may entail adjusting a process, the behavior of an employee, or the standard itself.

### 6.7 Identify types of control and tools for controlling.

Feedback control focuses on past performance. Concurrent control occurs while the work is taking place. Precontrol is aimed at preventing behavior that may lead to undesirable results. Budgets, performance reports, and personal observation are all tools for controlling.

### 6.8 List characteristics of effective controls.

Effective controls are timely, economical, acceptable to both supervisor and employee, and flexible.

# Key Terms

| | | |
|---|---|---|
| planning | action plan | variance |
| objectives | contingency planning | exception principle |
| goals | management by objectives (MBO) | reinforcement |
| strategic planning | budget | problem |
| operational planning | scheduling | symptom |
| policies | Gantt chart | feedback control |
| procedures | program evaluation and review technique (PERT) | concurrent control |
| rules | controlling | precontrol |
| | standards | performance report |

# Review and Discussion Questions

1. Why is it important for supervisors and other managers to spend time planning?
2. Define policies, procedures, and goals. How does each relate to an organization's objective?
3. Jill Donahue is the supervisor of the telephone operators who handle emergency calls from citizens and dispatch police, fire fighters, and ambulances. One of her objectives for the coming year is to reduce the average time it takes for calls to be answered from one minute to 30 seconds. How can Jill go about creating an action plan to achieve this objective? What questions must she answer? Suggest a possible answer for each question.
4. Assume you are the supervisor of the machine shop whose budget appears in Table 6.2.

   a. Modify the budgeted amounts to create a budget for a new project of the same size and type. Use the following assumptions and guidelines:

   - The organization says that direct labor costs may increase by no more than 6 percent.
   - You have been instructed to cut expenses for equipment repair by 10 percent.
   - You expect that materials costs will increase about 5 percent.

   b. What additional assumptions did you make to create the budget?

5. What is wrong with each of the following objectives? Rewrite each so that it has the characteristics of an effective objective.

   a. Improve the procedure for responding to customer complaints.
   b. Meet or exceed last year's sales quotas.
   c. Minimize the number of parts that are defective.
   d. Communicate clearly with patients.

6. What are some advantages of involving employees in the process of developing objectives? How can supervisors do this?
7. Your best friend just got promoted to a position as a supervisor and feels uncomfortable about "checking up on people." How can you explain to your friend why controlling plays an important role in helping the organization meet its goals?
8. What are the steps in the process of controlling?
9. How is the control process related to the management function of planning?

10. Bonnie Goode supervises telephone operators in the customer service department of a software company. The operators are expected to handle 50 phone calls per day (250 in a five-day workweek). Every Monday, Bonnie receives a report of each operator's weekly performance relative to this standard. Her most recent report contained the following information:

| Operator | Mon. | Tues. | Wed. | Thurs. | Fri. | Total | Variance |
|----------|------|-------|------|--------|------|-------|----------|
| Brown | 10 | 28 | 39 | 42 | 16 | 135 | −115 |
| Lee | 48 | 51 | 58 | 43 | 49 | 249 | −1 |
| Mendoza | 65 | 72 | 56 | 83 | 61 | 337 | 87 |
| Smith | 53 | 48 | 47 | 40 | 45 | 233 | −17 |

   a. As supervisor, how should Bonnie respond to each operator's performance?
   b. Is this control system an effective one for ensuring quality performance? Explain.

11. If failure to meet a performance standard indicates some type of underlying problem, how might the supervisor attempt to solve the problem?

12. Mildred Pirelli supervises salespeople in a department store. One day she walked around her department to observe the salespeople in action. She saw a salesperson approve a charge card purchase without following the company's policy of verifying the signature on the card.

   a. How should Mildred respond to this variance from company policy?
   b. Should the way Mildred obtained the information (personal observation) influence her choice of how to act? Explain.

10. Why do controls need to be timely and economical?

### A SECOND LOOK

In the story of One Call Does It All Maintenance Company at the beginning of this chapter, how might Tom Kipphut have included his employees in the planning task? Do you think involving the employees would have resulted in better planning? Why or why not?

# APPLICATIONS MODULE

## CASE

### *Planning and Controlling Drive the Great Game of Business*

Jack Stack probably didn't plan to become a business guru. But when he found himself one of the new owners and CEO of a former division of International Harvester, he realized he had a great deal to learn. As plant manager at International Harvester, Stack knew his own job well, but he knew nothing about planning and running an entire business. "I was economically so illiterate and stupid it was unbelievable," he recalls. Although he had studied business, attended seminars, and supervised people, Stack says, "I knew only pieces." He didn't know how to put the whole business picture together.

Thus, the first year of the new company, Springfield Remanufacturing Corp (SRC), ended in near disaster. Stack realized that without a plan, the company was doomed, so he and other executives began to create a ritual of strategic and operational planning. Now considered a pioneer of planning, Stack added a radical element: He involved every SRC employee in the planning process and even established a bonus system tied to achieving the plan's objectives. Every SRC worker has access to the company's financial data and can monitor the progress of the plan. The employee stock ownership program gives workers an added stake in the success of the plan.

Each October, the yearly planning process begins. Sales figures, growth targets, and other data are studied. In one division, called Heavy Duty, the national sales manager, Bob Bigos, interviews supervisors and workers at every level. He asks questions: What impact will the proposed plan have on inventory levels? Should SRC be discounting? Can workers meet proposed schedules and levels of productivity? Bigos also talks to customers and studies market information. "We take everyone's ideas," he says. "Then we blend them down to what we think is realistic."

In addition to the main plan, Bigos develops a contingency plan, ensuring that Heavy Duty will reach its objective of 15 percent growth even if Plan A fails. "We spend a tremendous amount of time on the what-ifs," CEO Stack comments. "So we don't just want a plan, we want a trap door."

Once the yearly plan goes into effect, controls play an important part in the way it unfolds. Precontrol has already been in effect, and concurrent control receives a great deal of attention. "Jack Stack feels that if you're off more than 5 percent up or down, you're out of control," notes one manager. "Nobody gets mad if you bring in extra profits, but the point is, you should have known you were going to do that."

Because information flows so freely at every level in SRC, deviations from the plan are caught quickly. Weekly divisional performance reports, biweekly manager meetings, and staff meetings with supervisors and workers keep everyone informed. "We all have different jobs, but we're all pulling for the same goals," observes Kevin Dotson, a worker in the Heavy Duty warehouse.

Stack's method of planning and controlling ultimately proved so successful that he formalized his management system under the name, the Great Game of Business, which became a book and then a seminar. Without intent, Stack had become a guru. But he is not a philosopher removed from the daily business of doing business, and therein lies his success. "Everything we've learned here was through failures," he observes modestly. Planning and controlling turned those failures into profits.

1. In what ways does SRC's involvement of employees at every level help create a superior yearly plan?
2. Conducting concurrent control requires being flexible. Why might SRC's practice of concurrent control be more effective than a system of feedback control?
3. In addition to publishing performance reports and holding regular meetings, what further steps might SRC take to ensure that the flow of information and ideas results in the best possible planning and controlling?

Source: Jay Finegan, "Everything According to Plan," *Inc.*, Mar. 1995, pp. 78–85.

■ **SELF-QUIZ**

## Are You a Planner?

Answer each of the following questions with a yes or no.

1. Do you decide the night before what to wear each day? _____

2. Do you buy birthday gifts at the last minute? _____

3. Do you divide up household chores with your roommates or family members? _____

4. When you receive a paycheck, do you designate certain portions of it for specific expenses? _____

5. At the beginning of the workday or school day, do you make a list of what you must accomplish? _____

6. Do you buy a big-ticket item because a friend has the same item and raves about it? _____

7. Do you start studying for final exams before the last week of classes? _____

8. When you purchase a new piece of electronic equipment, such as a computer or CD player, do you read the instructions about how to use it? _____

9. Before taking a trip, do you study a map? _____

10. When you have several projects to handle at once, do you first tackle the one that appeals to you most? _____

Scoring: Answering Yes to questions 1, 3, 4, 5, 7, 8, and 9 and No to questions 2, 6, and 10 indicates that you are a planner.

## Class Exercise

This exercise provides you with an opportunity to practice what you learned in this chapter ("Reaching Goals and Objectives"). You will practice setting personal goals (objectives) that are written, measurable, specific, clear, and challenging.

### Instructions

1. In the space provided on the next page, write four goals that are important for you to achieve during the remainder of this semester.

2. Some of the goals should be short term (maybe something you need to finish by the end of this week); others should have a longer time frame (maybe by the end of the semester).

3. Write your goal statement so you can check all four boxes (measurable, specific, clear, and challenging) as being represented. Provided here is a brief summary of each term:

   - *Measurable:* Provide a tangible way (dollar amount, time frame, or quantity) to determine if you have reached your goal—avoid *maximize, improve,* and other terms that cannot be measured.

   - *Specific:* Describe the actions you will need to take to achieve your goal.
   - *Clear:* Use simple language.
   - *Challenging* (yet realistic and obtainable): Choose motivating and stimulating goals that when achieved will give you a sense of pride and build your confidence.

4. Your four goals should represent several different areas; for example, academic, job, career, spiritual, family, financial, social, or physical goals. An example of a financial goal that meets all four criteria is "I will save 20 percent of every paycheck starting this Friday so I'll have enough to pay for my auto insurance when it comes due the last week of the semester." If you are having trouble meeting any of the four criteria in your personal goals, discuss your goal with a classmate or your professor to see if one of them can help you define your goal more clearly.

5. After successfully achieving each goal, write the date in the "Follow-up" column next to the goal.

This Class Exercise was written by Corinne Livesay, Belhaven College, Jackson, Mississippi.

| **Goal:** | **Follow-up**<br><br>**(When you've achieved this goal, write the date here.)** |
|---|---|
| ✓ if statement is:      Measurable ☐    Specific ☐    Clear ☐ | Challenging ☐ |

| **Goal:** | **Follow-up**<br><br>**(When you've achieved this goal, write the date here.)** |
|---|---|
| ✓ if statement is:      Measurable ☐    Specific ☐    Clear ☐ | Challenging ☐ |

| **Goal:** | **Follow-up**<br><br>**(When you've achieved this goal, write the date here.)** |
|---|---|
| ✓ if statement is:      Measurable ☐    Specific ☐    Clear ☐ | Challenging ☐ |

| **Goal:** | **Follow-up**<br><br>**(When you've achieved this goal, write the date here.)** |
|---|---|
| ✓ if statement is:      Measurable ☐    Specific ☐    Clear ☐ | Challenging ☐ |

### FIGURE 6.8

**Instructions for Origami Yachts**

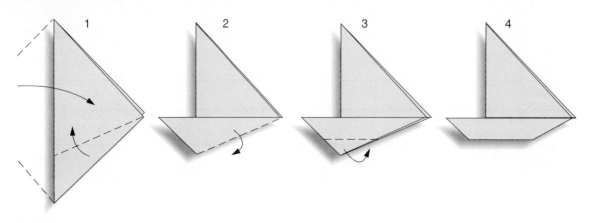

*Team-Building Exercise*

## Controlling a Yacht-Making Operation

Divide the class into groups of five or six members. One member of each group will act as the supervisor; the rest are employees. Since few real-life work groups get to choose their supervisor, the instructor might arbitrarily designate the supervisor in each group. The instructor provides each group with square sheets of paper; 5⅞″ × 5⅞″ is a good size.

1. Each person reviews instructions for making origami yachts (see Figure 6.8).
2. The supervisor in each group sets performance standards for making the yachts in 10 minutes. These should include quality as well as quantity standards. In setting the standards, the supervisor may use whatever information he or she can obtain; it is up to the supervisor whether to seek input from the group.

   At the same time, each employee estimates how many yachts he or she can make correctly in 10 minutes. The employee writes down this estimate but does not reveal it to the supervisor at this time.
3. For 10 minutes, the employees make as many yachts as they can according to the instructions. During that time, the supervisor tries to monitor their performance in whatever way seems helpful. If employees seem to be falling short of the performance standard, the supervisor should try to find ways to improve performance. (This may include simply waiting patiently for skills to improve, if that seems most beneficial.)

4. After the 10 minutes have ended, determine how many yachts each group made and assess the quality of the work. As a class, discuss the groups' performance. Did each group meet its supervisor's performance standards? If not, was any variance significant? Based on their own estimates of how much they could do, do employees think their supervisor's standards were reasonable?
5. The class should also consider supervisors' efforts to take corrective action. Did supervisors intervene too much, or not enough? How did supervisors' attempts help or hurt employees' efforts? What does this experience reveal about the way supervisors should behave in the workplace?

Corinne Livesay of Belhaven College, Jackson, Mississippi, supplied the origami instructions.

# Video Exercise 6: *Reaching Goals and Objectives*

### *Video Summary*

This video program shows how Marshall Industries believes that customer satisfaction is not a fixed goal, but a continuous refining process with quality of service to the customer as the ultimate measuring stick. To achieve this end, good planning and controlling systems must be in place within the organization. Marshall made a move away from a traditional command-and-control system to a more competitive team approach of planning and controlling for desired results.

### *Application*

While the video focused on organizational planning, this application focuses on your personal attitude toward planning by allowing you to gain a greater understanding of your attitude toward goal setting.

## Instructions:

1. Complete the evaluation that follows by placing a check mark in the box next to each statement that indicates the extent to which the following statements are true about you.
2. Determine your total points from the information provided on the last four lines of the chart.
3. See if you agree with the "Indications from Your Score" comments.

| No. | Statement | Very True | True | Somewhat True | Not True | Not True At All |
|-----|-----------|-----------|------|---------------|----------|-----------------|
| 1 | I feel I have a more positive approach to life when I am reaching for a goal than when I am not. | | | | | |
| 2 | A day goes better for me when I start the day working toward achieving a goal. | | | | | |
| 3 | I think it is a good idea to write out daily and weekly goals. | | | | | |
| 4 | I believe each goal should have a reward attached to it. | | | | | |
| 5 | I feel better at the end of the day when I have accomplished something I set out to do compared with days when I have accomplished nothing of substance. | | | | | |
| 6 | I feel that goals are beneficial whether or not they are reached. | | | | | |

| No. | Statement | Very True | True | Somewhat True | Not True | Not True At All |
|---|---|---|---|---|---|---|
| 7 | My friends and family would identify me as a goal-oriented person. | | | | | |
| 8 | I believe that goal-oriented people are more positive than people who are not. | | | | | |
| 9 | Goal setting is the most important tool to help me live up to my potential. | | | | | |
| 10 | Goals are worth having, even if they might cause frustration and disappointment if not reached on time. | | | | | |
| | Total number of checkmarks in each column | | | | | |
| | Multiply by: | 4 | 3 | 2 | 1 | 0 |
| | Total points for each column | | | | | |
| | **Grand total** | | | | | |

### Indications from Your Score

More than 30:   You see goal setting as a major contributor to achieving your potential and are enthusiastic about using this skill.

15–30:   You recognize the importance of goals and feel they make a contribution to achieving your potential.

Less than 15:   It appears that you prefer to live with few, if any, goals and achieve your potential in other ways.

| Questions for You to Consider: | Yes | No | Unsure |
|---|---|---|---|
| Are you satisfied with your attitude toward goals? | | | |
| Are you satisfied that you're using goal setting at the level where you should be? | | | |
| Do you believe that your goal-setting skills are developed enough for effective use in leadership positions? | | | |

If you haven't done so already, complete the class exercise, Practicing Personal Goal Setting, in this chapter.

Source: Corinne R. Livesay, *Strengthen Your Skills: A Skills-Building Manual*, Austen Press, © 1995, Richard D. Irwin, Inc.

# 7

*The best executive is the one who has sense enough to pick good men to do what he wants done, and self-restraint enough to keep from meddling with them while they do it.*
—**Theodore Roosevelt, 26th President of the United States**

# Using Organizational Resources

## LEARNING OBJECTIVES

After you have studied this chapter, you should be able to:

7.1 Describe organization charts.

7.2 Identify basic ways in which organizations are structured.

7.3 Distinguish between line and staff authority and between centralized and decentralized authority.

7.4 Compare and contrast *authority, power, responsibility,* and *accountability.*

7.5 Identify the steps in the process of organizing.

7.6 Describe four principles of organizing.

7.7 Discuss why and how supervisors delegate.

7.8 Identify causes of reluctance to delegate.

Source: © Imke Lass.

## THE NEW XEROX: NOT A PHOTOCOPY OF ITS OLD SELF

It's a fact of business life: Big companies are slimming down. They also are rethinking and reorganizing the way they operate. Xerox is no exception. Once an enormous, lumbering bureaucracy traditionally organized by functional areas—marketing, engineering, production, finance, and the like—the new Xerox is smaller, and much more limber.

Xerox is now organized into business teams led by managers whose key attribute is flexibility. Supervisors and other managers have the authority to make many more decisions than they did under the old structure; they also have more responsibility. Their own career success is clearly tied to the success of the team.

Once such manager is Ursula Burns, an employee who started out with the company as one of its few African-American females. When Xerox changed its structure, Burns went from an engineering position into a management position. First, she became a member of the committee that made structural decisions about the whole organization. Then she was assigned the job of systems engineering manager for the design team for a new office copier, which ultimately became one of Xerox's most successful products. Then she leaped up the ladder to head the unit that creates all digital equipment. As Burns's responsibilities grew, so did the number of employees she supervised. The first group she supervised had about 20 people; now her staff is about 300.

Burns has been able to tough out the many changes at Xerox because she understands the organization's objectives, and trusts and supports her employees in making decisions. She is also flexible. "She has an ability to work up, down, and across the organization," observes former executive vice-president Wayland Hicks. "She has the courage to change things that need to be changed. And she has a great sense of urgency." In short, Burns knows how to operate the new Xerox machine.

Source: Andrea Gabor, "The Making of a New-Age Manager," *Working Woman*, Dec. 1994, pp. 18, 20, 27.

**organizing**
The management function of setting up the group, allocating resources, and assigning work to achieve goals.

In the opening story, a change in the structure of an organization brought about a change in the way managers worked. As you read in Chapter 1, **organizing** is the management function of setting up the group, allocating resources, and assigning work to achieve goals. By organizing, supervisors and other managers put their plans into action. When done well, organizing helps to ensure that the organization is using its resources—especially human resources—efficiently. For this reason, a business that is well organized is in a better position to be profitable.

Managers in even the simplest organizations need to organize. If you were to set up a softball team, you would have to collect equipment, arrange for a place to play, find players, decide what position each is to play, and create a batting lineup. If you were operating a one-person business, you would have to decide where you would work, what activities you would need to accomplish, and whether you should contract with vendors to provide some services.

This chapter describes the ways organizations are structured and the way supervisors organize. The process of organizing includes sharing authority and responsibility. The chapter explains how supervisors share both of these with the people who report to them.

# The Structure of the Organization

Some of the most fundamental and far-reaching organizational decisions involve the structure of the organization as a whole. For example, top management could assign managers authority for a particular product, a particular geographic region served by the organization, or a particular specialty such as sales or finance. Supervisors have little, if any, input into this type of decision. However, supervisors need to understand how they and their department fit into the big picture, and that includes understanding the structure of the organization.

## Organization Charts

Businesspeople have come up with a standard way to draw the structure of an organization: the organization chart. These charts use boxes to represent the various positions or departments in an organization (usually just at management levels). Lines connecting the boxes indicate who reports to whom. Figure 7.1 is an organization chart showing the structure of an international company. Note, for example, that someone is in charge of all North American operations, and someone is in charge of all international operations. These two managers report to the person who serves as president and chief operating officer of the entire company.

The positions at the top of an organization chart are those with the most authority and responsibility. Logically, the people in these positions are referred to as the top managers. By following the lines from the top managers down the chart to the lower levels, you can see which middle managers report to these top managers. In other words, the top managers are authorized to direct the work of the middle managers who report to them and are responsible for the performance of those middle managers. The bottom of the chart may show the first-level managers (or sometimes the operative employees). Supervisors are not shown on the chart in Figure 7.1.

Organization charts sometimes show only a portion of an organization. Like Figure 7.1, a chart may show only the top levels of management or it may show a single division in a large company. Reading the titles of the people associated with each box gives an indication of the scope of a particular organization chart.

**FIGURE 7.1**

**Organization Chart: An International Company**

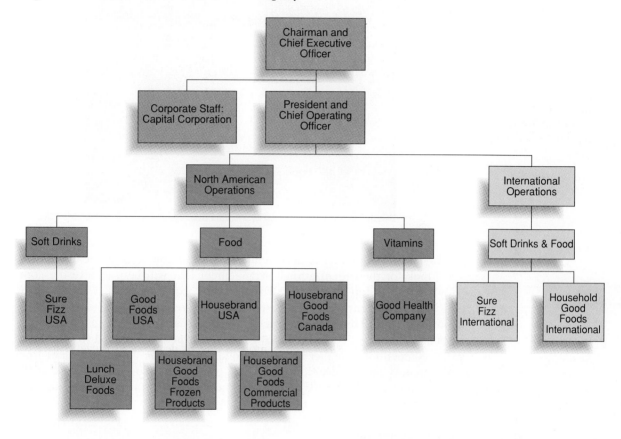

Being able to understand organization charts enables supervisors to figure out where they fit in the organization and where opportunities might lie for future promotions. Supervisors can see the variety of responsibilities held by others at their level in the organization. Knowing where they fit in helps supervisors see how their department or group contributes to achieving the goals of the organization.

## Types of Structures

**department**
A unique group of resources that management has assigned to carry out a particular task.
**departmentalization**
Setting up departments in an organization.

An organization with more than a handful of people works most efficiently when it is grouped into departments. A **department** is a unique group of resources that management has assigned to carry out a particular task, such as selling the company's products to customers in the Midwest, treating patients with cancer, or teaching mathematics. The way management sets up the departments—an activity called **departmentalization**—determines the type of structure the organization has.

Over the years, organizations have been structured in a limited number of ways. Traditionally, organization charts have indicated structures that fall into four categories: functional structure, product structure, geographic structure, and customer structure. More recently, organizations have sought other structures that achieve greater flexibility and responsiveness to customer needs.

Cindy Muñoz is a pipeline foreman for UP Liquid Pipeline, Inc., in Corpus Christi, Texas. The Union Pacific subsidiary ships feedstocks into five refineries in the area, and its pipeline department is an example of departmentalization according to functional structure.

Source: Courtesy of Union Pacific Corporation.

In deciding which types of structure to use and how to combine them, managers look for the organizational arrangement that will best achieve the company's goals. As top managers learn from their experiences or as the company and its environment change, the structure may require minor adjustments or major overhauls. Thus, the "restructuring" that has occurred at many organizations in recent years consists of changes in the structure designed to respond to stiffer competition, tougher economic conditions, or the desire to benefit from new practices such as decision making by teams of employees. The case at the end of this chapter (page 205) illustrates an occasion when restructuring does not appear to have worked smoothly.

### Functional Structure

A functional structure groups personnel and other resources according to the types of work they carry out. For example, a business might have vice-presidents of finance, production, sales, and human resources. Assigned to each vice-president is the staff needed to carry out these activities. Figure 7.2 provides an example of a company with a functional structure. Wiss, Janney, Elstner Associates is an architectural firm where one vice-president is responsible for operations (i.e., the work of all the architects and engineers who provide services to customers), and the other is responsible for administration (i.e., support services). Under the vice-president of administration, the organization is divided into such functions as marketing and personnel.

### Product Structure

In an organization with a product structure, work and resources are assigned to departments responsible for all the activities related to producing and delivering a particular product (good or service). In an automobile business, there might be one department for each make of automobile. Colleges and universities are often departmentalized according to the subject matter taught. At the company shown in Figure 7.1, North American operations are departmentalized according to

## FIGURE 7.2

**Functional Structure**

Partial organization chart for Wiss, Janney, Elstner Associates

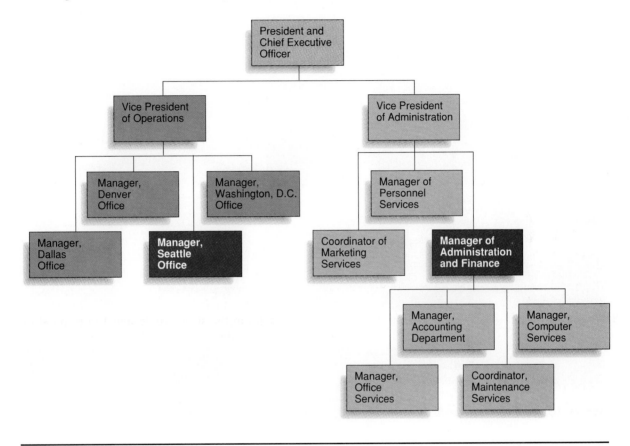

three product categories: soft drinks, food, and vitamins. Figure 7.3 illustrates a product structure at a division of the Evangelical Lutheran Church in America (ELCA). One director is concerned with disaster relief, another is responsible for health care programs, and so on.

### Geographic Structure

A geographic structure results when an organization is departmentalized according to the location of the customers served or the goods or services produced. A manufacturing company might have a department for each of its factories scattered around the world. An insurance company might have a department for each of its 12 sales territories. The manager of each department would be responsible for producing and/or selling all the company's goods or services in that geographic region. At the architectural firm in Figure 7.2, operations are departmentalized on the basis of the cities where the offices are located: Dallas, Denver, Seattle, Washington, D.C., and other cities not shown.

## FIGURE 7.3

**Product Structure**

Partial organization chart for ELCA Division for Social Ministry

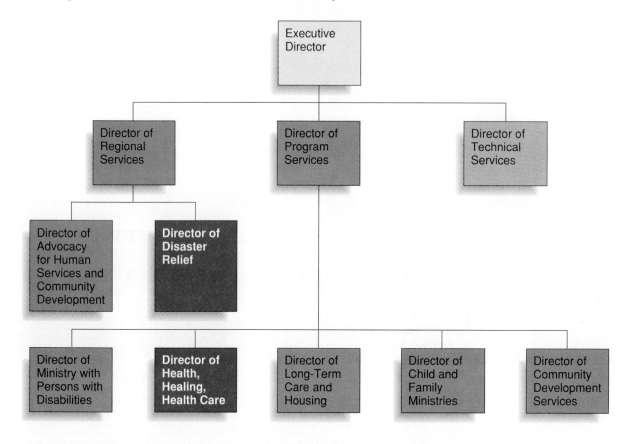

### Customer Structure

A customer structure departmentalizes the organization according to the type of customer served. For example, an aerospace company might have different departments serving business, the military, and the space program. Digital Equipment Corporation recently reorganized its sales force so that each account manager is responsible for all locations of each of his or her accounts (e.g., all factories or branch offices of a single business client) rather than a single geographic location.[1]

### Combinations

As you can see from the figures, organizations often combine the basic types of structures. Thus, Figure 7.1 combines geographic and product structures, while Figure 7.2 combines functional and geographic structures. A typical arrangement would be a large corporation with divisions for each of its product lines. Within each division, managers are assigned responsibility for carrying out a particular function, including sales and operations (i.e., making goods or delivering services). Each sales department in turn is structured geographically.

Various combinations of structures occur when the organization forms teams of employees to meet objectives such as improving quality, developing products, or applying new technology. These teams may require diverse kinds of expertise, so the organization brings together people who perform different functions or work in different geographical areas. Often these teams of employees are grouped according to product or customer. For example, a team formed to develop a new kind of stereo speaker might combine people from sales, engineering, and production functions under the umbrella of that new product. For a more in-depth discussion of forming and leading teams, see Chapter 3.

### New Organizational Structures

The managers of many organizations consider the basic forms of departmentalization too rigid for a turbulent, highly competitive environment. Grouping people according to function or geographic area can create barriers that interfere with coordinating activities and sharing ideas. A rigid structure is rarely suitable for a very small organization. Such organizations typically have a highly **organic structure,** one in which the boundaries between jobs continually shift and people pitch in wherever their contributions are needed.

**organic structure**
Organizational structure in which the boundaries between jobs continually shift and people pitch in wherever their contributions are needed.

Larger organizations, too, are seeking the flexibility of organic structures. They may do so by organizing around teams and *processes* (series of activities that deliver value to customers) or *projects* (groups of tasks with defined scope and ending). The customer service division of Sun Life of Canada (U.S.), based in Wellesley, Massachusetts, reorganized from functional groups, such as sales and product development, to process-related teams. The former functional managers became coaches for those teams. The teams are responsible for meeting performance standards, and the coaches are accountable to the teams for guiding them to high performance.[2]

Ford Motor Company has reorganized from geographic departmentalization to a structure in which product development takes place in teams called vehicle-platform centers (VPCs). Each VPC brings together stylists, design engineers, and production experts—but not necessarily at a single site. Thanks to modern communications technology, including videoconferencing, team members can collaborate, even if some are in Michigan and others in Germany.[3]

**network organizations**
Organizations that maintain flexibility by staying small and contracting with other individuals and organizations as needed to complete projects.

A growing number of organizations are trying to stay flexible by staying small. Rather than adding employees to meet customer demands, these organizations, called **network organizations,** contract with other individuals and organizations as needed to complete specific projects.[4] In practice, this structure may involve *outsourcing*, or paying another organization to carry out a function. Woodspirits Limited, based in St. Paris, Ohio, has only three employees but makes arrangements with three contractors to produce the company's old-fashioned soaps.[5] Other organizations arrange *alliances*, or relationships based on partnership, including joint ventures, minority investments linked to contractual agreements, agreements to jointly fund research, and other, less formal arrangements. At the extreme is a *virtual organization*, in which a small core organization (maybe a single person) arranges alliances as needed to carry out particular projects. In Hollywood, Free Willy Two Inc.—a temporary corporation responsible for making the film *Free Willy II*—was at the hub of a virtual organization. Its scores of contractors, handling everything from payroll to special effects, included Cinnabar, the group that made the miniature seascapes and robotic whale props used in the sequence where an oil tanker is wrecked during a storm.[6]

**TABLE 7.1**

**Everyday Meaning of Terms Related to Organizing**

| Term | Everyday Meaning |
|---|---|
| Departmentalization | "Let's divide up the work." |
| Authority | "I (or you) get to decide how this is going to get done." |
| Responsibility | "I (or you) own this job; you can hold me accountable for it." |
| Accountability | "The buck stops here." |
| Unity of command | "No matter with whom else you work, you are accountable to only one person." |
| Span of control | "There are limits to how many people a manager can effectively manage." |
| Delegation | "You have the responsibility and authority to accomplish this assignment." |
| Empowerment | "I trust you to perform these functions and accomplish these results; this means much more than just delegating a task to you." |

Source: Adapted from Brad Lee Thompson, *The New Manager's Handbook* (Burr Ridge, IL: Richard D. Irwin, Inc., 1995), p. 49.

Like the organizations themselves, supervisors in these new structures must be flexible. They have to contribute wherever the organization currently needs their talents—a requirement that calls for continually knowing, updating, and communicating one's skills. They may have to identify how they can contribute to a particular project, then be ready to move to a new assignment when they no longer add value to the current one. In addition, supervisors in the new structures must rely more on human relations skills than on technical skills. Coaching a team or project group requires the ability to motivate, lead, and communicate as the team handles many project- or process-related decisions. This is especially true for coaching teams that bring together people from a variety of functions.

# Authority

**authority**
The right to perform a task or give orders to someone else.

When a supervisor assigns duties, he or she gives employees the authority to carry them out. **Authority** is the right to perform a task or give orders to someone else (see Table 7.1). The supervisor in turn has authority in certain areas, and his or her manager has even broader authority. (See "Tips from the Firing Line.")

## Line, Staff, and Functional Authority

**line authority**
The right to carry out tasks and give orders related to the organization's primary purpose.

The basic type of authority in organizations is **line authority,** or the right to carry out tasks and give orders related to the organization's primary purpose. Line

## *How* Not *to Abuse the Responsibility of Authority*

"Authority must be seen as a responsibility with the right to make certain well-defined decisions," writes Michael J. O'Connor, special retailing consultant to Arthur Andersen & Company. "Authority can be a dangerous thing. It can cause real damage if it is seen as a right or a privilege. When seen as a responsibility, authority can be a positive force in any organization."

Learning to use authority with skill takes practice. O'Connor offers the following suggestions for supervisors and other managers:

- Understand what authority is.
- Understand your organization's philosophy, mission, goals, and progress.
- Know where authority begins and ends.
- Obtain training in the use of authority, however possible.

- Learn how to delegate authority to appropriate employees.
- Be accountable for your actions.
- Gain as much information as you can in order to make informed decisions.
- Involve employees in teams or other groups even if their authority is limited.
- Use suggestion systems in which employees can participate; then follow through with them.
- Listen to your employees.

Source: Michael J. O'Connor, "Authority," *Supermarket Business*, Apr. 1994, pp. 38ff.

authority gives a production supervisor at Deere & Company the right to direct a worker to operate a machine; it gives the head chef in a restaurant the right to direct the salad chef to prepare a spinach salad using certain ingredients. At the architectural firm represented in Figure 7.2, the manager of the Seattle office has line authority.

**staff authority**
The right to advise or assist those with line authority.

In contrast, **staff authority** is the right to advise or assist those with line authority. For example, the employees in the human resource department help the other departments by ensuring that they have qualified workers. The quality-control manager at a manufacturing company helps the production manager see that the goods produced are of acceptable quality. In Figure 7.2, the manager of administration and finance has staff authority.

One way to appreciate the difference between line authority and staff authority is to think of a lawyer's job. In a law firm, the lawyer has line authority (he or she delivers the services the firm is selling). But in the legal department of a manufacturing company, the lawyer has staff authority (supporting the firm by offering legal advice in matters related to producing and selling goods).

Conflicts often arise between line and staff personnel. Line personnel may feel that staff workers are meddling and don't understand their work or how important it is. Staff personnel may conclude that line personnel are resisting new ideas and don't appreciate the valuable assistance they are getting. Whether the supervisor has line or staff authority, he or she can benefit from being aware that these kinds of conflicts are common and trying to appreciate the other person's point of view.

**functional authority**
The right given by higher management to specific staff personnel to give orders concerning an area in which the staff personnel have expertise.

Supervisors and other personnel with staff authority may also have **functional authority.** This is the right given by higher management to specific staff personnel to give orders concerning an area in which the staff personnel have expertise. For example, members of the accounting department might have authority to request the information they need to prepare reports. Or the human resource manager might have authority to ensure that all departments are complying with the laws pertaining to fair employment practices.

### Centralized and Decentralized Authority

In some organizations, the managers at the top retain a great deal of authority; in others, management grants much authority to middle managers, supervisors, and operative employees. Organizations that share relatively little authority are said to be centralized; organizations that share a lot of authority are said to be decentralized.

These terms are relative. In other words, no organization is completely centralized or decentralized, but organizations fall along a range of possibilities from one extreme to another. An example of a decentralized organization is steelmaker Nucor Corporation, which has only four levels of management. Supervisors (foremen) report to department heads (such as a manager of rolling, or melting and casting). They in turn report to a general manager of the facility, who reports to top management. With 22 factories, Nucor has only 17 employees at its headquarters, including secretaries and the company's chairman—the smallest headquarters of any Fortune 500 company. This structure gives each general manager relatively greater independence and control in operating a particular facility.[7]

In contrast, a reporter recently determined that General Motors (admittedly a larger company) had 36 vice-presidents and more than 20 layers of management.[8] In this more centralized organization, supervisors can expect to have much less decision-making authority.

Supervisors who know whether their employer has a centralized or decentralized structure understand how much authority they can expect to have. Suppose that a supervisor wants to expand the authority of her position so she can make improvements in the department. This ambition probably will be viewed less favorably in a centralized organization than in a decentralized one.

### Power, Responsibility, and Accountability

**power**
The ability to get others to act in a certain way.

It is easy to confuse authority with power, accountability, or responsibility. However, when used precisely, these terms do not mean the same thing. **Power** is the ability (as opposed to the right) to get others to act in a certain way. The supervisor's authority usually confers a degree of power; employees usually do what their supervisor asks them to do. However, some people have power that comes from sources other than their position in the organization. Also, some people with authority have trouble getting others to act in the desired way. (Chapter 15 discusses power in greater detail.)

**responsibility**
The obligation to perform assigned activities.

**Responsibility** is the obligation to perform assigned activities. People who accept responsibility commit themselves to completing an assignment to the best of their ability. Of course, doing a good job is easier when you have authority to control the necessary resources, including personnel. An important aspect of the supervisor's job, therefore, is to ensure that people have accepted responsibility for each of the tasks that the work group must complete—and that they clearly

At Motor Technology, Inc., a company that repairs electric motors in York, Pennsylvania, employee training is seen as the key to developing employees who accept responsibility. Through apprenticeship training, followed by continuing education and cross-training to understand the tasks of other employees, the Motor Technology worker learns to accept responsibility. This has resulted in excellent customer service and pride in craftsmanship, which have helped the company to achieve revenues of almost $9 million.

Source: © Blair Seitz

understand what those responsibilities are. The supervisor also must ensure that people have enough authority to carry out their responsibilities.

Employees who accept responsibility may be rewarded for doing a good job, and those who do not may be punished. This practice is called *accountability* (see Chapter 1). Assume an organization makes a supervisor responsible for communicating policies to his or her employees. Accountability means the supervisor can expect consequences related to whether that responsibility is met. Thus, accountability is a way of encouraging people to fulfill their responsibilities.

The authority to transfer (delegate) responsibility to employees and hold them accountable adds to a supervisor's power. At the same time, even when a supervisor delegates, the supervisor remains accountable for employees' performance.

# The Process of Organizing

For a supervisor, organizing efforts are generally focused on allocating responsibilities and resources in a way that makes the department or work group operate effectively and efficiently. In addition, supervisors may want or need to set up teams (see Chapter 3). Whether the organizing job involves setting up a whole new company, restructuring an existing one, or deciding how to organize a department or team, the process should be basically the same. The supervisor or other manager should define the objective, determine what resources are needed, and then group activities and assign duties. This three-step approach leads to a structure that supports the goals of the organization (see Figure 7.4).

## Define the Objective

Management activities should support the objectives developed during the planning process. In the case of organizing, the supervisor or other manager should begin by defining what objective the department or work group is supposed to be achieving. If the supervisor does not know, then he or she has not finished planning and should complete that job before trying to organize work. Long-range

**FIGURE 7.4**

**The Process of Organizing**

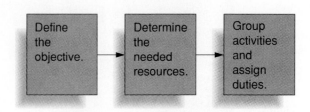

objectives at the Ritz-Carlton Hotel Company are 100 percent guest satisfaction, 100 percent customer retention, and zero defects in customer transactions.[9] Organizing decisions support these companywide objectives.

## Determine the Needed Resources

The planning process also should give the supervisor an idea of what resources—including personnel, equipment, and money—are needed to achieve goals. The supervisor should review the plans and identify which resources are needed for the particular areas being organized.

To achieve Ritz-Carlton's lofty quality goals, its managers have determined that they need employees committed to ensuring high quality. They also realize that every employee must be empowered to contribute to customer satisfaction. This in turn requires that employees have access to information about what customers want and how well the company's processes are working. Modern information systems help fulfill that need.

## Group Activities and Assign Duties

The final step in the process is what most people think about when they consider organizing. The supervisor groups the necessary activities and assigns work to the appropriate employees. To ensure that all the necessary responsibilities are assigned, the supervisor also can foster a climate that encourages all the employees working on a project to raise the question, "Who is taking care of this?"[10]

At the Ritz-Carlton in New York, this step has included creating the position of director of quality. Paul Roa, who holds that job, says technology and training help keep the hotel's staff knowledgeable about what customers want. The hotel's employees receive training in how to actively notice guest preferences (e.g., feather rather than polyester pillows or more oranges than apples in fruit baskets). Employee observations are entered into the company's national database. Each day, the hotel prints a report highlighting the preferences of the guests scheduled to arrive the next day. A full-time guest history coordinator analyzes the report so that the hotel can cater to those preferences. Furthermore, all employees are empowered to resolve guest complaints and rebate up to $2,000 a day per guest without management approval. They also are expected to analyze the problem and prepare an action plan for solving it. If defects recur, the company forms a team to engage in a formal problem-solving process to eliminate future occurrences.[11] In sum, staffing decisions and highly decentralized authority contribute to achieving the Ritz-Carlton's quality objectives.

## MEETING THE CHALLENGE

### *Astra/Merck Organizes with Information Technology*

In a streamlined economy, newly streamlined organizations must find innovative ways to do more with less people. Astra/Merck, a joint venture between Astra of Sweden and the U.S. company Merck Pharmaceuticals, has found a way to use technology to keep its trimmed-down sales force competitive. (Instead of sending out upwards of 2,000 reps as its competitors do, Astra/Merck does the job with 500.)

First, the company defined its new objective: to provide information (competitors still focus on selling pharmaceutical products). Next, it decentralized authority. The Astra/Merck sales force is grouped into 31 regional units that function as semi-independent businesses covering large territories. Astra/Merck reps have the authority to offer physicians customized marketing materials such as brochures that teach patients about certain illnesses and their care. For instance, if most of a physician's patients speak Spanish, the rep can have a brochure translated and produced in Spanish. If a physician wants to market his or her practice with a steady presence, the Astra/Merck rep can order newsletters, personalized by the physician, to be sent to the patients.

Following the objective, Astra/Merck reps talk to physicians more about their practices than about specific pharmaceutical products. Instead of asking, "What pills do you need to buy?" they ask, "What are your biggest information needs?" Amy Farris,

director of human resources, comments, "We are trying to become partners with doctors and medical institutions. We want to be looked at as a resource."

How does the Astra/Merck sales force provide its customers with so much information? Each rep has a Compaq DeskPro color 486XE laptop with several different types of information and networking software. Since Astra/Merck structures its markets by *what types of information customers need* (instead of by the type of customer), customized databases furnish salespeople (and customers) with everything from data about costs to up-to-date research in a physician's particular field.

Using this approach, Astra/Merck raked in first-year revenues of around $1 billion. Enjoying success, company president Wayne Yetter views the new structure this way: "One Astra/Merck rep, leveraged with information technology organized in a different way, and trained and supported in a different way, would equal two or three people at another [company]." Proof, perhaps, that downsizing doesn't have to spell disaster, and that a clear objective supported by decentralized authority and the necessary resources (technology) can magnify the power of a good sales force.

Source: "Technology Magnifies the Force of a Streamlined Sales Group," *Total Quality*, Dec. 1994, p. 5.

The remainder of this chapter discusses how to carry out the third step of the organizing process. (For another example of the process, see "Meeting the Challenge.")

## Principles of Organizing

Supervisors, especially those who are new to the job, may be unsure how to group activities and assign duties. The task seems so abstract. Fortunately, management experts have developed some principles that can guide the supervisor: the parity principle, unity of command, chain of command, and span of control.

### *Parity Principle*

**parity principle**
The principle that personnel who are given responsibility must also be given enough authority to carry out that responsibility.

Parity is the quality of being equal or equivalent. Thus, according to the **parity principle,** personnel must have equal amounts of authority and responsibility. In other words, when someone accepts a responsibility, he or she also needs enough authority to be able to carry out that responsibility. If a head teller at a Citicorp branch is responsible for providing high-quality customer service but does not have the authority to fire a surly teller, the head teller will find it difficult or impossible to carry out this responsibility.

## Unity of Command

Meredith Buckle handled the maintenance jobs for a small office building. When building occupants experienced a problem, such as a leaky faucet or a cold office, they would call Meredith. Often, to get a faster response, they would call her repeatedly, complaining about how the problem was interfering with work. As a result, Meredith felt she could never keep everyone satisfied, and she had trouble deciding which jobs to do first.

**unity of command**
The principle that each employee should have only one supervisor.

According to the principle of **unity of command,** each employee should have only one supervisor. Employees who receive orders from several people tend to get confused and aggravated. As a result, they tend to do poor work. The example of Meredith is a case in point. It would have helped her if the building manager had collected messages from the occupants and assigned the jobs to Meredith along with a schedule for completing them.

Sometimes a supervisor's manager violates this principle by directing the employees who report to the supervisor. This puts the employees in the awkward position of receiving directions from two people, and it puts the supervisor in the awkward position of needing to correct his or her manager's behavior. Norma Jean Schmieding, a professor who advises nurses on management issues, recommends that a supervisor tell his or her manager, "I find my staff gets confused when both you and I give them directions. I'd prefer that you discuss with me what you want, and I'll relate it to the staff. Do you have any objections to doing it this way?"[12] Of course, the supervisor also should refrain from directing employees who report to someone else.

## Chain of Command

**chain of command**
The flow of authority in an organization from one level of management to the next.

In a chain, each link is connected to no more than two links, one on either side. In an organization, authority progresses like the links on a chain. Along this **chain of command,** authority flows from one level of management to the next, from the top of the organization to the bottom. The case in the Applications Module for this chapter (page 205) describes a chain of command to be used for reporting damage to the freight tunnel under downtown Chicago.

When someone skips a level, the principle of chain of command is violated. For example, suppose that Fred Paretsky wants to take Friday off, but he suspects that the division manager will be more sympathetic to his request than his supervisor. So Fred goes directly to the division manager, who grants permission. Unfortunately, the division manager does not know it, but Fred's group now will be understaffed on Friday because two other workers also will be absent. By violating the chain of command, Fred and the division manager have created a staffing problem that the supervisor could have avoided with a little planning. Similarly, in the earlier example of a supervisor's manager directing the supervisor's employees, the boss is violating both the principles of chain of command and unity of command.

Of course, taking every decision through every level of the organization can be time-consuming and difficult, especially in an organization with many layers of management. The solution is to use common sense. For example, a request for information probably does not have to travel through every layer of management. In contrast, a decision that will affect the group's operations should probably pass through the chain of command.

## Span of Control

**span of control**
The number of people a manager supervises.

Clearly, keeping track of and developing the talents of one employee is easier than supervising 100 employees, but hiring a supervisor for every employee would be tremendously expensive. The number of people a manager supervises is known as the manager's **span of control.** The more people the manager supervises, the greater the span of control.

In organizing, managers must be aware of how many people they can supervise effectively. Ideally, managers supervise as many people as they can effectively guide toward meeting their goals. That number depends in part on several factors that describe the work situation:[13]

- *Similarity of functions*—The more similar the functions performed by employees, the greater the span of control can be.
- *Geographic closeness*—The closer subordinates are physically, the greater the span of control can be.
- *Complexity of functions*—The simpler the functions performed by subordinates, the greater the span of control can be.
- *Coordination*—This refers to how much time managers must spend coordinating the work of their subordinates with that of other employees. The less time they need to spend on coordination, the greater the span of control can be.
- *Planning*—The less time a manager needs to spend on planning, the greater the span of control can be.
- *Availability of staff support*—The more staff specialists available to provide support in a variety of areas, the larger the span of control can be.
- *Performance standards*—If there are clear, objective standards for performance, and employees are familiar with them, the span of control can be larger than in a situation where the supervisor continually must clarify what is expected of employees.

Characteristics of the managers and employees also are important. Managers may find that as their experience grows, so does the number of people they can supervise effectively. Managers with strong skills in time management and decision making also are likely to be able to supervise more employees. As to employees, the more able they are to work independently, the greater the span of control can be.

# Delegating Authority and Responsibility

**delegating**
Giving another person the authority and responsibility to carry out a task.

The concept of organizing implies that one person cannot do all the work of an organization. Even a one-person business usually contracts with outside people to provide some services. For example, a hairdresser who sets up shop might arrange for experts to prepare tax returns, design and print stationery, and provide legal advice. Giving someone else the authority and responsibility to carry out a task is known as **delegating.** You can test your awareness of delegation principles by taking the Self-Quiz on page 207.

## Benefits of Delegating

Whereas the performance of most nonmanagement employees is evaluated in terms of their individual accomplishments, a supervisor's performance is evaluated

The concept of organizing implies that one person cannot do all the work of an organization. Jim Henson Productions, the organization behind the Muppets, was founded by Jim Henson, a charismatic, larger-than-life leader who died suddenly in 1990. Today the success continues, and the company employs about 200 people. It is widely judged to be better run than ever because, according to Brian Henson, Jim Henson's son and company CEO, employees "are respected and counted on . . . [and their] ideas are needed and encouraged. They are used to inventing things; they are used to making decisions." The photo shows Kermit the Frog, one of Jim Henson Productions' most famous "employees."

Source: © Gamma Liaison

according to the achievements of the whole department. Thus, the department's output will be of the highest quality and the supervisor looks best when he or she draws on the expertise of employees. Consultant DeAnne Rosenberg writes that supervisors who delegate are not "limited by what they can do but . . . by what they can assign."[14] For example, a production supervisor might establish a team of employees to devise ways to make the workplace safer. Those employees are likely to come up with more ideas than the supervisor could identify alone. Some employees might have backgrounds or areas of expertise that lead them to notice where improvements are needed—improvements that the supervisor might never have considered.

A supervisor who delegates also has more time for the jobs only a supervisor can do, such as planning and counseling. Kelly Hancock, who supervises the order takers for classified ads at the *Toronto Sun*, says, "Delegating gives me more opportunity to do tasks of a more pressing, creative nature. I can work on special projects . . . such as sales contests for the staff." One way to think of this benefit of delegating is that it is an important tool for time management (discussed in Chapter 14). If the production supervisor in the example handled all aspects of safety, it could take weeks simply to identify and describe safety problems and solutions. That time might be better spent in scheduling and arranging for employees to receive various types of training.

Delegating also has a beneficial effect on employees. Delegation of work gives employees a chance to develop their skills and their value to the organization. Depending on the kinds of tasks delegated, this can enhance their career and their earning potential. It also can make employees' work more interesting. It is reasonable to expect that employees who are more interested in their work and more involved in meeting the organization's objectives are likely to do higher-quality work and remain with the organization longer. (This topic will be discussed in Chapter 11.) Thus, the production employees who serve on the safety team might find that this added responsibility leads them to care more about the quality of their day-to-day work.

**FIGURE 7.5**

The Process of
Delegating

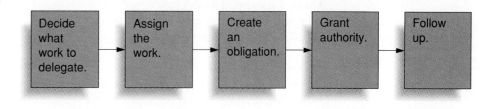

**Empowerment**

These benefits of delegating explain why many organizations use employee involvement to improve the quality of their goods and services (see Chapter 2). In other words, they delegate decision-making authority and responsibility in a variety of areas to employees. This practice—called **empowerment**—is based on the expectation that employees will provide more insight and expertise than managers can provide alone, and that this participation will make employees more committed to doing their best.

BriskHeat Corporation, a manufacturer of electric heating elements based in Columbus, Ohio, uses empowerment extensively. BriskHeat charges employees at all levels to make whatever decisions are necessary to further the organization's best interests. Operative employees organize their work—setting work hours, scheduling shifts, and even deciding how tools should be laid out. They also recommend and vote on capital expenses and order their own materials. The company enables skilled decision making by providing training and feedback about organizational performance. CEO Richard E. Jacob reported that after the employees learned the company's needs and priorities from experience, they began making decisions that helped to fuel substantial sales growth in a mature industry.[15]

**empowerment**
Delegation of broad
decision-making
authority and
responsibility.

**The Process of Delegating**

When delegating effectively, the supervisor is not merely handing out jobs at random, but should be following a logical process: deciding what work to delegate, assigning the work, creating an obligation, granting authority, and following up (see Figure 7.5).

**Decide What Work to Delegate**

There are several ways to select which tasks to delegate. When an employee knows how to do a particular task better than the supervisor, delegation certainly makes sense. Another approach is to delegate simple tasks that employees clearly can handle. For example, Kelly Hancock of the *Toronto Sun* has her employees handle administrative duties such as counting the lines for birth and death notices. The supervisor also can delegate the tasks that he or she finds most boring. This approach can backfire, however, if employees perceive they always are chosen to do the dirty work. Tasks performed regularly are good candidates for delegation because it may be worth the effort to train employees to do them.

Of course, there are some tasks a supervisor should *not* delegate, including personnel matters and activities assigned specifically to the supervisor. Thus, the supervisor should not assign duties such as appraising performance and resolving conflicts. Likewise, if a sales supervisor's boss has asked her to fly to Vancouver to resolve a customer complaint, it would be inappropriate for the supervisor to delegate this assignment to someone else.

### Assign the Work

The supervisor continues the delegation process by selecting employees to carry out the work. In delegating a particular task, the supervisor considers who is available and asks questions such as the following:[16]

- Who can do the job best?
- Who can do it least expensively?
- Who can save the most time?
- Who would gain the most growth from the assignment?

The supervisor also weighs the personalities involved, safety considerations, and any company policies or union rules that may apply. Supervisors can be most effective in carrying out this step when they know their employees well.

A manager who makes a point of knowing his employees is Rick Hess, a general manager at Massachusetts-based M/A Com, a microwave electronics firm. Hess goes out of his way to learn about employees in an effort to support their development. For instance, one of the engineers reporting to Hess told him she felt pigeonholed and frustrated. He responded by giving the engineer new assignments where her accomplishments would be noticed, a move that increased her motivation.[17] As in this example, matching assignments to employee desires as well as their skills can help the organization reap the full potential of its human resources.

When two jobs must be done at the same time and the same person is best qualified to do both, the process of selecting an employee to do the work becomes complex. In such cases, the supervisor must set priorities. The supervisor must consider how important the particular task is to achieving the department's goals and serving customers. If priorities among jobs are unclear, the supervisor should check with his or her manager.

To finish the step of assigning work, the supervisor tells the designated employees what they are supposed to do. The supervisor must be sure that the employees understand what they are supposed to be doing and have the necessary knowledge and skills. (Employees should be able to exercise some freedom in deciding exactly how to carry out the assignment, however.) Employees also need to know which jobs have the greatest priority. To communicate this information clearly, it helps to be specific and to ask employees to restate the assignment in their own words. (Chapter 10 provides more information on how to communicate clearly.)

### Create an Obligation

When the supervisor makes an assignment, he or she needs to be sure that the employee accepts responsibility for carrying it out. A supervisor can encourage employees to accept responsibility by involving them in making decisions and by listening to their ideas. Workers who feel involved are more apt to feel responsible. Supervisors cannot force employees to feel responsible, but fortunately many employees willingly take on responsibility as a matter of course. In addition, by making employees accountable for their actions, supervisors lead them to accept responsibility.

Although the employee should accept responsibility for carrying out a task, this does not mean that the supervisor gives up the responsibility for its proper completion. The organization still holds the supervisor accountable. Therefore, following delegation, both parties have responsibility for the work. The supervisor's job becomes one of ensuring that the employee has the necessary resources and that the task is completed and meets quality standards. The supervisor does so through the management function of controlling, described in the previous chapter.

Failure to understand the principle of delegation can cause major problems. According to professor and consultant Peter F. Drucker, one of the reasons the Reagan administration's "Irangate" policies became a scandal was that the administration confused delegation of authority with abdication of responsibility. Therefore, it failed to exercise tight control over those who carried out the policy, allowing them to "protect" the President by keeping secrets from him.[18]

### Grant Authority

Along with responsibility, supervisors must give employees the authority they need to carry out their jobs. This is how supervisors follow the parity principle, discussed earlier in this chapter. Thus, if a supervisor at Abbott Laboratories gives a researcher responsibility to carry out a particular procedure, the researcher must also be given the authority to obtain the materials and equipment needed to do the job.

### Follow Up

After assigning duties and the authority to carry them out, the supervisor needs to give the employees some freedom to act independently and creatively. This does not mean that the supervisor should abandon employees to succeed or fail on their own; after all, the supervisor is equally responsible for the success of the work. Therefore, it should be made clear to employees that the supervisor is available for guidance. The supervisor also should set forth a plan for periodically checking on the progress of the work. The supervisor may find that employees need additional information or help in removing obstacles to success, or perhaps they simply need praise for the work they have done so far.

If an employee's performance of an unfamiliar task is less than perfect, the supervisor should not be discouraged from delegating in the future. Everyone needs time to learn, and disappointing performances may offer a chance for the supervisor to learn what is needed to strengthen an employee's skills. In addition, poor performance may have resulted from the way the work was delegated, not from a problem with the employee. The supervisor can check whether the dos and don'ts of delegation listed in Table 7.2 have been observed.

## Reluctance to Delegate

Ruby Singh works late every night, reviewing all her employees' work and preparing detailed instructions for them to carry out the next day. Her own manager has suggested that she give the workers more freedom, which would save her a lot of time and probably increase their job satisfaction. However, Ruby is afraid that if she does not keep close tabs on her employees, the department's performance will suffer.

Ruby is hardly alone in her reluctance to delegate authority and responsibility to employees. In a recent study, economics professor Peter Sassone found that

**TABLE 7.2**

**Some Dos and Don'ts of Delegating**

| Do | Don't |
|---|---|
| Establish goals and performance standards for the tasks. | Delegate responsibilities without the necessary authority and training. |
| Tell employees what to do, not how to do it. | Sit back and wait for employees to sink or swim. |
| Be familiar with employees' strengths and interests. | Delegate personnel problems, most planning activities, and tasks specifically assigned to the supervisor, such as taking a trip, attending a meeting or seminar, and serving on a committee. |
| Delegate on the basis of employee interests when possible. | |
| Delegate authority as well as responsibility. | Be afraid of delegating too much. |
| Assign entire projects when possible, rather than portions of a project. | Expect perfection the first time. |
| Practice and encourage good communication. | |
| Give employees time to try before offering assistance. | |

managers spent only 30 percent of their time doing work that could not be delegated to lower-level employees. Assuming that this means organizations are paying too much to get the rest of the work done, Sassone estimates that the failure to delegate costs the average corporation an extra 15 percent in payroll costs.[19]

Many supervisors are convinced that they are able to do a better job than their employees. They might even say, "If you want something done right, you have to do it yourself." Often they may be correct, particularly if their own promotion to a supervisory post resulted from high performance. Observing an employee making mistakes can be difficult, especially if the supervisor will look bad for allowing the mistake to occur.

AES Corporation experiences its share of mistakes by operative employees. AES, a power producer that sells electricity to public utilities and steam to industrial customers, uses delegation extensively throughout the organization. As its employees shoulder responsibilities more typical of managers, they are bound to make mistakes until they learn the ropes. For instance, when chemical engineer Ann Murtlow took on the task of buying air pollution credits (which industrial companies trade to gain flexibility in meeting emissions regulations), she first spent $10,000 for an option on a type of credit that turned out to be worthless for the AES plant.[20]

Overall, however, a department's long-term performance requires that its supervisor let employees work up to their potential. This means the supervisor must overcome reluctance, delegate work, and let employees learn from their experiences. Ann Murtlow's mistake inspired her to educate herself, and she became the company's expert on air pollution permits. AES's top management credits such fruits of delegation for its low employee turnover and growing profits.

In some cases, employees may really be unable to carry out jobs that they have been delegated. If so, the supervisor must consider ways to bring the workforce's talents into line with the department's needs. Perhaps employees need training or the department's hiring practices need improvement. (For more on selecting and training employees, see Chapters 16 and 17.)

As mentioned earlier, delegating frees supervisors to concentrate on the tasks that they do best or that only they can do. Sometimes a supervisor is more comfortable being an expert at employees' work than struggling with supervisory responsibilities such as motivating employees and resolving conflicts. However, the supervisor must overcome that discomfort or fear, because the organization needs supervisors who supervise.

# Summary

### 7.1 Describe organization charts.
Organization charts are a standard way to draw the structure of an organization. Boxes represent the departments or positions, and connecting lines indicate reporting relationships. The positions at the top of the organization chart have the most authority and responsibility.

### 7.2 Identify basic ways in which organizations are structured.
Unless they are very small, organizations are grouped into departments. An organization with a functional structure groups personnel and other resources according to the types of work they carry out. A product structure groups work and resources according to the product produced and delivered. In a geographic structure, the departments are set up according to the location of the customers served or the goods or services produced. A customer structure departmentalizes the organization according to the category of customer served.

Organizations now often combine the basic types of structures, particularly where teams of employees are formed to meet objectives such as improving quality or applying new technology. Those seeking flexibility often favor an organic structure—one in which boundaries between jobs continually shift and people pitch in wherever their contributions are needed. They may form network organizations, which contract with other individuals and organizations to complete specific projects (instead of adding permanent employees).

### 7.3 Distinguish between line and staff authority and between centralized and decentralized authority.
Authority is the right to perform a task or give orders to someone else. Line authority is the right to carry out tasks and give orders related to the organization's primary purpose. Staff authority is the right to advise or assist those with line authority. When authority is centralized, it is shared by a few top managers; when authority is decentralized, it is spread among a greater number of people.

### 7.4 Compare and contrast *authority, power, responsibility,* and *accountability.*
Authority is the right to perform a task or give orders. Power is the ability (as opposed to the right) to get others to act in a certain way. Responsibility is the obligation to perform certain tasks. Accountability is the practice of imposing penalties for failure to adequately carry out responsibilities and giving rewards for success in meeting responsibilities. The authority to transfer responsibility to employees and hold them accountable adds to a supervisor's power. (However, a supervisor always is held accountable for his or her employees' performance.)

### 7.5 Identify the steps in the process of organizing.
To organize a department or work group, the supervisor should first define the objective of the department or work group, then determine what resources are needed. Finally, the supervisor groups activities and assigns duties to appropriate employees.

### 7.6 Describe four principles of organizing.
According to the parity principle, personnel with responsibility must also be given enough authority to carry out that responsibility. The principle of unity of command states that each employee should have only one supervisor. A chain of command is the flow of authority from one level of the organization to the next; most decisions and information should flow along the chain of command. Finally, supervisors and other managers should have an appropriate span of control; the best number of employees for a specific situation depends on a variety of factors.

### 7.7 Discuss why and how supervisors delegate.
Supervisors delegate to enhance the quality of the department's and supervisor's performance by

drawing on the expertise of employees. Delegation also frees time for supervisory tasks. It may improve employee morale and performance by empowering them to make decisions in a variety of areas. To delegate, supervisors follow a five-step process: Decide what work to delegate, assign the work, create an obligation, grant authority, and follow up. When delegating, supervisors must make sure employees understand and are able to do the work, and they retain the responsibility to see that the work is done properly.

**7.8 Identify causes of reluctance to delegate.**

Many supervisors are reluctant to delegate because they believe no one else can do the job as well. They may not want to give up activities they enjoy. Some supervisors are more comfortable doing what their employees should be doing than in carrying out supervisory responsibilities.

## Key Terms

| | | |
|---|---|---|
| organizing | line authority | unity of command |
| department | staff authority | chain of command |
| departmentalization | functional authority | span of control |
| organic structure | power | delegating |
| network organizations | responsibility | empowerment |
| authority | parity principle | |

## Review and Discussion Questions

1. Emily Sanford has just been promoted to supervisor of the salespeople in the gift department at a department store. Which of the following organizing activities is she likely to carry out?
   a. Scheduling her employees' work hours.
   b. Forming a team of her employees to work on a promotional event within the department.
   c. Helping decide the best location for a new branch of the department store.
   d. Assigning an employee to sit at the bridal registry desk.
   e. Determining whether the department store should launch its own line of products.

2. What might be the best structure for each of the following organizations?
   a. A three-person company that sells complete, prepackaged gourmet dinners to specialty grocery stores.
   b. A small organization that supplies antique cars to movie studios.
   c. A manufacturer of windows, with offices in Toronto, Seattle, Miami, and Chicago.

3. What special attributes must supervisors have to be successful in some of the new types of organizational structures?

4. Which of the following supervisors have primarily line authority? Which have staff authority?
   a. The production supervisor at a publishing company, who is responsible for getting books typeset and printed.
   b. The housekeeping supervisor at a hospital.
   c. The word-processing supervisor at a law firm.
   d. The payroll department supervisor for a fire department.

5. In recent years, many organizations have become more decentralized. Typically this change involves eliminating middle-management jobs and sharing more control with those at lower levels of the organization. How do you think this affects the role of supervisors in those organizations?

6. Does someone with authority always have power? Does a person who accepts responsibility necessarily have authority? Explain.

7. What are the steps in the process of organizing? How would they apply to the manager of an Olive Garden restaurant who needs to schedule employees? Explain in general how this supervisor could follow each step.

8. Describe each of the following principles of organizing.
   a. Parity principle.
   b. Unity of command.
   c. Chain of command.
   d. Span of control.

9. A production supervisor at a company that makes furniture learns about the factors that should influence the span of control. The supervisor believes that his own span of control is too large for him to supervise effectively. Is there anything a person in his position can do? If not, explain why. If so, suggest what he can try.

10. Harry Jamison, CPA, is planning to set up a business to prepare tax returns. Harry is the only person in the business, at least for now. Can he delegate any work? Should he? Explain.

11. What steps do you think a supervisor who is reluctant to delegate could take to overcome this discomfort?

---

### A SECOND LOOK

The story at the beginning of this chapter describes some changes in the structure of a large corporation, Xerox. How do you think the chain of command at Xerox has changed? Give two examples.

---

# APPLICATIONS MODULE

---

## CASE

### Whose Responsibility Is It?

On April 13, 1992, in a disaster that came to be called the Great Chicago Flood, water from the Chicago River poured into a freight tunnel under downtown Chicago streets, flooding basements and shutting businesses and government offices. According to one estimate, 350 million gallons of water had to be pumped out. How could the tunnel walls have been so neglected as to permit a leak that caused millions of dollars' worth of damage?

One view came from the city's general services commissioner, Benjamin Reyes. In an interview with the *Chicago Tribune*, Reyes denied any responsibility, instead holding his employees accountable for not taking quick action when they learned of structural problems with the aging tunnel. Of his own role, Reyes said, "I didn't do anything wrong. I didn't know anything about it."

A cable television company working in the tunnel had informed Reyes's staff of the leak in February 1992, but the department didn't inspect it until March 16. The cable company told an inspector named James McTigue that the tunnel was cracked. In the department's chain of command, McTigue should have informed the department's chief construction engineer, who should have notified a deputy commissioner.

McTigue's version was that the day he learned of the damage from the cable company, he reported it to his supervisor. He researched the cable company's report, found the leak, and again reported it to his supervisors. McTigue added that he told another superior about the problem on March 17, and that this manager said he told Reyes.

McTigue and other critics attributed management's inaction in part to a recent reorganization in city departments. In an attempt to make the public works department more efficient, it was split in two: transportation and general services. Due to layoffs accompanying the reorganization, no city employees were available to repair the tunnel. Also, several commissioners complained that the reorganization had led to "mass confusion" in early 1992.

Reyes claimed that he was not responsible for the crisis because of his newness to the department. With 350 other employees, he had been transferred to general services on January 1, 1992. Said Reyes, "The first contact I had with Jim McTigue was when the water started rushing through the tunnels."

Chicago mayor Richard Daley fired acting transportation commissioner John LaPlante, who had failed to act in spite of receiving a memo on April 2 warning of possible disaster. Daley did not hold Reyes accountable for his lack of knowledge. The mayor reasoned that employees in Reyes's department had informed the transportation department, which should have repaired the damage. Although Reyes was in charge of tunnel inspections, the job of freight tunnel inspector had been cut in 1987. Daley sought to fire McTigue, who appealed, claiming he was a scapegoat.

1. Do you think Commissioner Reyes should have been held accountable for the disaster? Why or why not?
2. Do you think that a more centralized authority, in the wake of the reorganization, would have helped avert the disaster? Why or why not?
3. If James McTigue had followed the official chain of command when he learned of the leak, could the disaster have been averted? Why or why not? Do you think McTigue was treated fairly? Why or why not?
4. What effect did the reorganization of the public works department apparently have on resources? on line, staff, and functional authority? on parity?

Sources: John Kass, "Daley Aide Reyes Denies Tunnel Responsibility," *Chicago Tribune*, Apr. 17, 1992, sec. 2, pp. 1, 8; *Chicago Tribune*, Apr. 20, 1992, sec. 1, pp. 1, 12; John Kass, "City Worker Hits Back at Daley Flood Bashing," *Chicago Tribune*, May 7, 1992, sec. 2, pp. 1, 6.

### SELF-QUIZ

## *Test Your Understanding of Delegation*

Circle the correct answer.

1. There are some tasks a supervisor should never delegate.

    True        False

2. If you want something done right, it is best to do it yourself.

    True        False

3. Delegation is an important motivational tool.

    True        False

4. Effective delegation involves transferring responsibility to another person.

    True        False

5. The degree to which a supervisor can delegate is defined by the competence of his or her subordinates.

    True        False

6. The biggest problem with delegating is the increased possibility of mistakes.

    True        False

7. Controls and feedback are necessary parts of every delegated task.

    True        False

8. In delegating to an employee, supervisors can choose from a range of degrees of responsibility and authority.

    True        False

9. Not every supervisor has a need to delegate.

    True        False

10. Some tasks should not be delegated because it takes more time to delegate them than to do them.

    True        False

Items 1, 3, 5, 7, 8, and 10 are true statements about delegation; the others are false. If you answered at least 7 correctly, you have a good understanding of delegation. If at least 9 answers were correct, your understanding is excellent.

Source: Adapted from David Engler, *Delegating Effectively* (Omaha, NE: Vital Learning Corp., 1986), pp. 5–7.

## Class Exercise

Divide the class into groups of five or six students. Each group is to prepare a one- to three-minute presentation on any of the following topics:

- A summary of the material in Chapter 7.
- An example of how an actual company is organized.
- A real or fictional anecdote about delegating, such as a summary of a real supervisor's experience or a skit showing how not to delegate.

The instructor will decide whether the presentations are to take place after a designated preparation time during class or during another class session.

1. Decide what you are trying to accomplish. Which topic will you cover? How do you want to present it? Will you need to do research?
2. Determine the needed resources. Will you have audiovisual aids? Costumes or props? What activities will need to be done?

3. Group activities and assign duties. Who will do the various activities? What is your basis for delegating these tasks? How will you get your presentation ready on time and keep it within the required time limit?

After each group has made its presentation, the class should discuss the process of organizing the presentations. Which presentations were most interesting? What made them work? Were responsibilities shared fairly within your group? Why or why not? What different skills did you see in group members? Did this affect which tasks each group member took on? How would you have handled this project differently if you had been the supervisor of the group instead of a member of the group?

## Team-Building Exercise

### Organizing a Fund-Raising Team

Divide the class into teams of four to six members. Appoint a leader to act as supervisor for each team. Each team will hold the initial meeting to organize a fund-raising event for a cause of their choice. The teams should define their objectives, determine the needed resources, group activities, and assign duties. The supervisor should delegate whatever responsibilities he or she can, including asking for a volunteer to take notes at the meeting itself.

Before the end of class, a spokesperson for each team may report to the class on the effectiveness of the meeting: How quickly were objectives defined? How evenly were duties assigned? What was each member's responsibility? How efficient was the supervisor at delegating? Did some members seem to have more power than others?

# Video Exercise 7: *Using Organizational Resources*

## *Video Summary*

Managing a diverse multinational corporation successfully requires unique organizational skills. The chairman at Brunswick discusses the company's organizational structure and the layers of management used for controlling everything from bowling balls to defense equipment.

## *Application*

While the video focused on organizing from a corporate perspective, this application asks you to focus on organizing skills from a personal perspective.

1. Analyze your level of personal organizing skills by answering the following questions. Put a check mark in the appropriate column after each question.

| Organizing Guideline | Already Do Well | Need to Improve | Need to Start |
|---|---|---|---|
| ***Select what should be organized.*** Have you identified the areas of your life that you use the most and organized them to get the greatest value from your organizing time? | | | |
| ***Unclutter your life.*** Do you set a limit on the number of items you will keep (e.g., pens, ties, back issues of magazines) to cut down on clutter? <br><br> Do you analyze usage, so that items that have outlived their usefulness no longer clutter your life? | | | |
| ***Break organizing tasks into specific steps.*** Do you break down your organizing tasks into manageable steps, so you don't become frustrated? | | | |
| ***Establish a simple system.*** Have you established a workable flow for the organizational systems you have in place? <br><br> Are the things you use most often in locations that are easy to get at? <br><br> Have you grouped together the supplies and materials you need to perform common tasks? <br><br> Have you taken advantage of store-purchased "organizers" to get multiple items in an organized system? | | | |
| ***Develop organizing habits.*** Do you practice "place habits" for items you use daily? <br><br> Do you practice "time habits" for necessary routine tasks? | | | |

| Organizing Guideline | Already Do Well | Need to Improve | Need to Start |
|---|---|---|---|
| Do you wait to see whether you really need more storage space until after you discard or give away items you will no longer use from the current storage space? | | | |
| Do you use "to do" lists to help focus on the most important tasks you need to do each day? | | | |
| Do you use some kind of planner for coordinating your schedule and other important information? | | | |
| Do you use a budget to avoid wasting your money on impulse purchases? | | | |
| *Strive to maintain a balance that is best for you.* Do you regularly assess whether the most important areas of your life are well organized? | | | |

2. Circle at least one area in the chart above for which you checked the "Need to Start" or "Need to Improve" column. If you have several from which to choose, your main criterion should be to select the one that you think would give you the most value if you improved your organization of it. Develop an action plan to improve the area you selected.

3. State in one sentence exactly what your goal is. What specifically do you want to do? When do you expect to achieve your goal?

_____

_____

4. Your action plan should include:

a. The specific steps you need to take:

_____

_____

b. Why this is important for you to do:

c. What benefits you expect to realize after improving your organizational skills in this area:

_____

_____

Sources for further help in developing your organizing skills include Corinne R. Livesay, *Getting and Staying Organized* (Burr Ridge, IL: Irwin Professional Publishing, 1994); Susan Silver, *Organized to Be the Best! New Timesaving Ways to Simplify and Improve How You Work* (Los Angeles: Adams-Hall Publishing, 1991); Stephanie Winston, *The Organized Executive: New Ways to Manage Time, Paper, and People* (New York: Norton, 1983); Stephanie Winston, *Getting Organized: The Easy Way to Put Your Life in Order* (New York: Warner Books, 1978).

# 8

*To lead in the 21st century—to take soldiers, sailors, and airmen into battle—you will be required to have both character and competence.*
**—General H. Norman Schwarzkopf, ret., U.S. Army**

# The Supervisor as Leader

## ■ CHAPTER OUTLINE

## ■ LEARNING OBJECTIVES

After you have studied this chapter, you should be able to:

8.1 Discuss the possible link between personal traits and leadership ability.

8.2 Compare leadership styles that a supervisor might adopt.

8.3 Explain contingency theories of leadership.

8.4 Identify criteria for choosing a leadership style.

8.5 Describe guidelines for giving directions to employees.

8.6 Tell why supervisors need to understand and improve their views of themselves.

8.7 Explain how supervisors can develop and maintain good relations with their employees, managers, and peers.

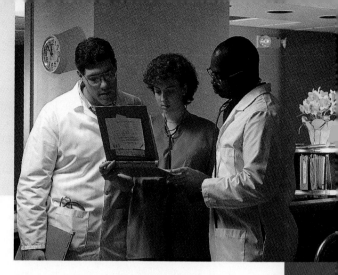

Source: © Chip Henderson/Tony Stone Images

## A LEADER IN EMERGENCIES

Kathleen Schrank knows all about emergencies. She is chief of emergency medicine for Jackson Memorial Hospital in Miami, one of the largest and busiest hospitals in the United States. She also holds two other posts: medical director for Miami Fire, Rescue and Inspection Services; and associate professor of clinical medicine at the University of Miami Medical School. Schrank is not an absent administrator; she's a hands-on supervisor who is also an effective leader.

Schrank doesn't spend a lot of time in her office. Instead, she spends most of her long workday developing her relationships with people. She supervises 20 full-time and 20 part-time physicians, who in turn treat nearly 100,000 patients each year. On a rotating basis, she supervises a team of residents, interns, and students, accompanying them on hospital rounds, showing them how to improve the way they practice medicine. She keeps in constant communication with her staff, listening to their concerns and complaints. "I want to know something about the people who work here," she says. "We don't socialize a lot on the outside, but it keeps it more on a personal level to know about children, pets, and hobbies."

Schrank also must maintain a relationship with her peers, such as the director of nursing. Schrank and the nursing director agree to disagree on many issues, but they put aside their differences to advocate for their patients and staff to upper management. "Our needs are so great, it takes all of us working together to plead our case," Schrank notes. Schrank knows how to communicate well with her own superiors, another quality of a good leader. "We've developed a credibility that we'll tell the executives what we really need," she explains.

Last, but not least, Schrank deals with patients and their families in a brisk but sympathetic personal style. These are, after all, her customers (as are the insurers with whom she must maintain communication); and she wants to make sure they get the service they need and deserve.

Leadership for Kathleen Schrank boils down to results and people. "I'm always optimistic about what I can get done," she muses. She chose this job—one that many doctors would avoid—because she likes the challenge. "We thrive on chaos," she says about her colleagues in emergency care. "Most doctors and nurses in this specialty can make a difference in a hurry—they make decisions very quickly and see results very quickly as well." A person who can bring people together to make order out of chaos— perhaps that's the definition of a leader. It certainly is one definition of Kathleen Schrank.

Source: Catherine Romano, "A Day in the Life: Managing for the Emergencies," *Management Review*, July 1995, pp. 15–20.

**leading**
The management function of influencing people to act or not act in a certain way.

When the supervisor knows what the department should be doing and who should be doing it, the job becomes one of creating the circumstances in which employees will do what is required of them. In other words, supervisors must be leaders. As you learned in Chapter 1, **leading** is the management function of influencing people to act or not act in a certain way.

What makes leadership work is examined in this chapter. A variety of leadership styles are described and criteria for matching a style to a situation are provided. Next, the chapter discusses how to carry out an important activity related to leadership: giving directions. Because leading requires mainly human relations skills, a discussion of how supervisors can relate effectively to the various people in an organization concludes the chapter.

## Characteristics of a Successful Leader

According to business professor Paul B. Malone III, an important distinction between managers and leaders is that a manager focuses only on getting a task done whereas a leader focuses on getting it done in a way that gives employees a feeling of accomplishment and willingness to follow the leader again.[1] A leader gives employees such feelings by instilling in them a sense of common purpose, a belief that together they can achieve something worthwhile. Are some people better equipped to do this than others? Figure 8.1 shows the results of a survey that asked over 5,200 top-level managers to identify the traits they most admire and look for in a leader. Most managers reported that they seek leaders who are honest, competent, forward-looking, and inspiring.

To find out whether people are natural leaders, social scientists have studied the personalities of effective leaders, looking for traits they hold in common. Presumably, such traits would be predictors of good leadership. Some traits that might be considered significant are the following:

- *Sense of responsibility*—A person who is promoted to a supervisory position is given responsibility for the work of others as well as for his or her own performance. Supervisors must be willing to take this responsibility seriously.
- *Self-confidence*—A supervisor who believes in his or her ability to get the job done will convey confidence to employees.
- *High energy level*—Many organizations expect supervisors to put in long hours willingly to handle the variety of duties that come with the job. Some supervisory positions also are physically challenging, requiring that the supervisor actively observe and participate in what is happening in the workplace.
- *Empathy*—In settling disputes, answering questions, and understanding needs, supervisors should be sensitive to the feelings of employees and higher management. Supervisors who have difficulty understanding what makes people tick will be at a disadvantage.

**internal locus of control**
The belief that you are the primary cause of what happens to yourself.

- *Internal locus of control*—An **internal locus of control** is the belief that you are the primary cause of what happens to yourself. People with an external locus of control tend to blame others or events beyond their control when something goes wrong. Those with an internal locus of control are thought to be better leaders because they try harder to take charge of events.

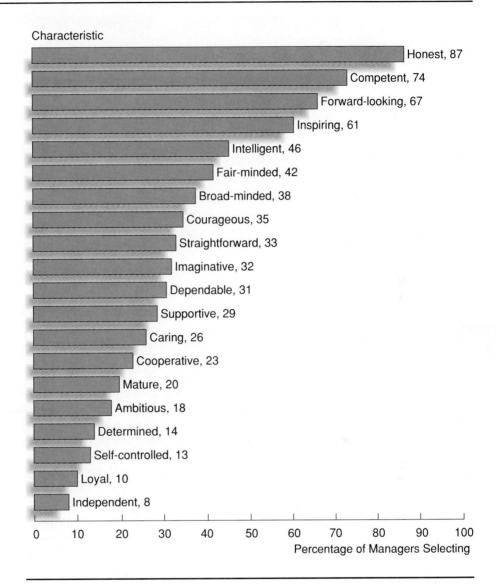

**FIGURE 8.1**

**What Managers Admire and Look For in a Leader**

Characteristic

- Honest, 87
- Competent, 74
- Forward-looking, 67
- Inspiring, 61
- Intelligent, 46
- Fair-minded, 42
- Broad-minded, 38
- Courageous, 35
- Straightforward, 33
- Imaginative, 32
- Dependable, 31
- Supportive, 29
- Caring, 26
- Cooperative, 23
- Mature, 20
- Ambitious, 18
- Determined, 14
- Self-controlled, 13
- Loyal, 10
- Independent, 8

Percentage of Managers Selecting

Source: Data from James M. Kouzes and Barry Z. Posner, "The Credibility Factor: What Followers Expect from Their Leaders," *Management Review*, Jan. 1990, p. 33.

- *Sense of humor*—People with a good sense of humor are more fun to work with and to work for (assuming they use appropriate humor—not racist or sexist anecdotes—and do not overuse rehearsed jokes that are unrelated to work). Communications consultant Roger Ailes reports that among people who lose their jobs, the most common cause is personality conflicts, and the most common reason for disliking someone is that the person takes himself or herself too seriously—the person lacks a sense of humor.[2]

The U.S. Air Force claims to know the traits necessary for good leadership and recognizes one such leader in this advertisement, hoping to attract others with similar qualities.

Source: Painted by SSGT. Ruben Armenta, U.S. Air Force.

Focusing on traits such as these, ask yourself whether you have leadership qualities.

While these traits sound plausible as characteristics of a successful leader, results of the various studies of leadership traits have been inconsistent. Some studies have found one set of traits to be significant, while others have identified a completely different set of traits. As a result, research has not established a clear link between personality traits and leadership success. Thus, if you have most of the traits described here, you may be a successful leader, but your success is not guaranteed. Also, if you have only a few of these traits, you need not be discouraged; you can still develop the skills that effective leaders use.

# Leadership Styles

Anita O'Donnell runs a tight ship; she lays down the rules and tolerates no deviation from them. Greg Petersen focuses on what he perceives to be the needs of his employees; they in turn do good work out of loyalty to him. George Liang is an easygoing supervisor when the work is routine, but when a big order comes in, he turns tough.

If you have worked for more than one boss, chances are you have experienced more than one leadership style. Anita, Greg, and George illustrate only some of the possibilities. Some supervisors instinctively lead in a way they are comfortable with; others adopt their style of leadership consciously. However, a supervisor who is aware of basic types of leadership styles is probably in the best position to use the style (or styles) that will get the desired results.

## Degree of Authority Retained

One way to describe leadership styles is in terms of how much authority the leader retains. Do employees get to make choices and control their own work? Or does the supervisor make all the decisions? To describe the possibilities, management theorists refer to authoritarian, democratic, and laissez-faire leadership.

### FIGURE 8.2

**Possibilities for Retaining Authority**

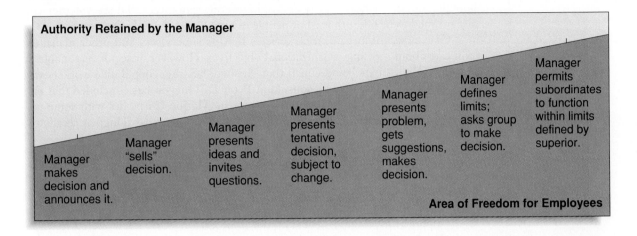

**Authority Retained by the Manager**

Manager makes decision and announces it.

Manager "sells" decision.

Manager presents ideas and invites questions.

Manager presents tentative decision, subject to change.

Manager presents problem, gets suggestions, makes decision.

Manager defines limits; asks group to make decision.

Manager permits subordinates to function within limits defined by superior.

**Area of Freedom for Employees**

Source: Robert Tannebaum and Warren H. Schmidt, "How to Choose a Leadership Pattern," *Harvard Business Review*, May–June 1973. Adapted and reprinted by permission of *Harvard Business Review*. Copyright © by the President and Fellows of Harvard College; all rights reserved.

**authoritarian leadership**
A leadership style in which the leader retains a great deal of authority.

**democratic leadership**
A leadership style in which the leader allows subordinates to participate in decision making and problem solving.

**laissez-faire leadership**
A leadership style in which the leader is uninvolved and lets subordinates direct themselves.

In **authoritarian leadership,** the leader retains a great deal of authority, making decisions and dictating instructions to employees. An example would be a military commander who expects unquestioning obedience.

Some supervisors share more authority than authoritarian supervisors. With **democratic leadership,** the supervisor allows employees to participate in decision making and problem solving. A supervisor with a democratic style of leadership might have the staff meet weekly to discuss how to improve client relations. When a conflict arises, this supervisor asks the group to discuss possible solutions and to select one.

At the opposite extreme from authoritarian leadership is **laissez-faire leadership.** A laissez-faire manager is uninvolved and lets employees do what they want. Supervisors are rarely, if ever, able to practice this style of leadership because the nature of the supervisor's job requires close involvement with employees.

Nor are many supervisors totally authoritarian or totally democratic. Most supervisors give employees some degree of freedom to do their jobs but they still make some of the decisions for the department. Years ago, Robert Tannenbaum and Warren H. Schmidt drew a graph showing the continuum, or range of possibilities, for the degree of authority a manager can retain. This continuum is still popular today as a way to picture the possibilities (see Figure 8.2).

### Task Oriented versus People Oriented

Another way to look at differences in leadership styles is to consider what supervisors focus on in making decisions and evaluating accomplishments. In general terms, leaders may be task oriented or people oriented. A task-oriented leader is one who focuses on the jobs to be done and the goals to be accomplished. When the work gets done correctly and on time, a task-oriented leader is satisfied. On the other hand, a people-oriented leader is concerned primarily with the well-being of the people he or she manages. This type of leader emphasizes issues such as morale, job satisfaction, and relationships among employees. To see whether you are inclined to be task oriented or people oriented, take the Self-Quiz on page 237.

Of course, the organization expects that its supervisors and other managers will care about meeting organizational objectives. However, it seems reasonable to assume (other things being equal) that satisfied, healthy, cooperative workers will perform best. In that regard, consultant Peter L. Thigpen has concluded that one source of the high level of commitment in the Marine Corps lies with some unwritten rules of behavior for the officers. The four rules that Thigpen recalls reflect deep concern for the troops:[3]

1. Never eat before your troops eat.
2. Never bed down until your guards are posted and your troops are bedded down.
3. Your job, up to and including the commandant of the Marine Corps, is to support the private rifleman on the front line.
4. Never ask your troops to do something you wouldn't do.

These rules incorporate a people-oriented view of leadership in an organization where leaders are committed to getting the job done.

Most organizations expect that their supervisors can combine some degree of task orientation with some degree of people orientation. A supervisor who tends to focus on getting out the work should remember to check sometimes how employees are feeling and getting along. A supervisor who regularly sticks up for employees' welfare should make sure that he or she also remembers to promote the organization's goals.

Researchers Robert R. Blake and Jane S. Mouton recommend that supervisors and other managers be strong in both leadership orientations. They developed a Managerial Grid® (see Figure 8.3) that identifies seven styles of leadership by managers. Along one axis is the manager's concern for people and along the other is the manager's concern for production. Blake and Mouton's research led them to conclude that productivity, job satisfaction, and creativity are highest with a (9,9), or team management, style of leadership. To apply this model of leadership, supervisors identify where their current style of leadership falls on the managerial grid, then determine the kinds of changes they must make to adopt the (9,9) style, which is high in concern for both people and production.

## Leader Attitudes

**Theory X**
A set of management attitudes based on the view that people dislike work and must be coerced to perform.

In observing the behavior of managers, Douglas McGregor noted that many tended to have a group of attitudes that reflected their beliefs about workers and the workplace. He termed this set of attitudes **Theory X.** To summarize, a Theory X manager assumes that people dislike work and try to avoid it, that they therefore must be coerced to perform, that they wish to avoid responsibility and would prefer to be directed, and that their primary need is for security. Not surprisingly, these beliefs influence how supervisors and other managers behave. A Theory X supervisor would adopt an autocratic role, keeping a close eye on employees and looking for occasions when they need to be disciplined to keep them performing adequately.

### FIGURE 8.3

## The Managerial Grid

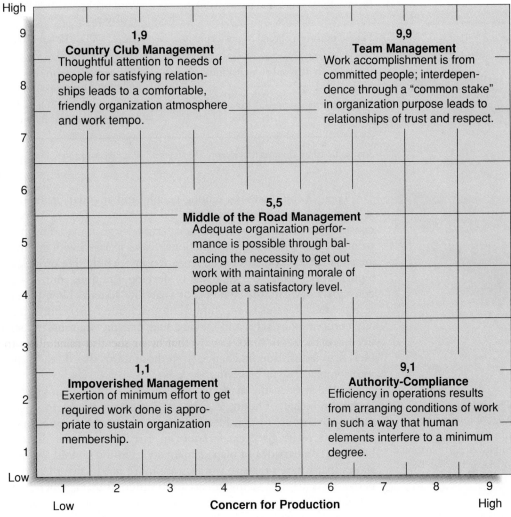

**Concern for People**

High

9 — **1,9**
**Country Club Management**
Thoughtful attention to needs of people for satisfying relationships leads to a comfortable, friendly organization atmosphere and work tempo.

**9,9**
**Team Management**
Work accomplishment is from committed people; interdependence through a "common stake" in organization purpose leads to relationships of trust and respect.

**5,5**
**Middle of the Road Management**
Adequate organization performance is possible through balancing the necessity to get out work with maintaining morale of people at a satisfactory level.

**1,1**
**Impoverished Management**
Exertion of minimum effort to get required work done is appropriate to sustain organization membership.

**9,1**
**Authority-Compliance**
Efficiency in operations results from arranging conditions of work in such a way that human elements interfere to a minimum degree.

Low

1  2  3  4  5  6  7  8  9

Low    **Concern for Production**    High

Source: The Leadership Grid® Figure for *Leadership Dilemmas—Grid Solutions,* by Robert R. Blake and Ann Adams McCanse (formerly the Managerial Grid® figure by Robert R. Blake and Jane S. Mouton). (Houston: Gulf Publishing Company), p. 29. Copyright 1991 by Scientific Methods, Inc. Reproduced by permission of the owners.

**Theory Y**
A set of management attitudes based on the view that work is a natural activity and that people will work hard and creatively to achieve objectives they are committed to.

McGregor advises that managers can benefit from adopting a much different set of attitudes, which he terms **Theory Y.** According to Theory Y, working is as natural an activity as resting or playing, and people will work hard to achieve objectives they are committed to. They can learn to seek responsibility and to be creative in solving organizational problems. Supervisors and other managers who adhere to Theory Y focus on developing the potential of their employees. Their style of leadership tends to be democratic. Table 8.1 summarizes these two sets of assumptions.

### TABLE 8.1

**Contrasting Leader Attitudes**

| Theory X | Theory Y |
|---|---|
| People dislike work and try to avoid it. | Working is as natural an activity as resting or playing. |
| People must be coerced to perform. | People will work hard to achieve objectives they are committed to. |
| People wish to avoid responsibility. | People can learn to seek responsibility and prefer to be directed. |
| People's primary need is for security. | Many people are able to be creative in solving organizational problems. |

Source: Based on Douglas McGregor, *The Human Side of Enterprise* (New York: McGraw-Hill, 1960).

Today a common view among people studying management is that Theory Y is appropriate for many situations. To see what a Theory Y manager looks like, consider Louis Lenzi, general manager of design for Thomson Consumer Electronics. Lenzi coaches cross-functional teams charged with ensuring that the Indianapolis-based company's products are user-friendly. He provides each team with a goal; in one case, the team was to develop a remote-control device for helping consumers navigate the channels of a satellite system. Then he lets each team determine how it wants to accomplish its goal while Lenzi concentrates on removing any corporate obstacles and making sure that the team has whatever resources it needs. At the same time, Lenzi requires frequent updates on team progress, and he is firm in insisting on change from those teams that don't keep up or that lapse into complacency or bickering.[4]

**Theory Z**
A set of management attitudes that emphasizes employee participation in all aspects of decision making.

In the last decade, management experts extended their view of managing and leading to include **Theory Z**. Theory Z supervisors seek to involve employees in making decisions, to consider long-term goals when making plans, and to give employees relatively great freedom in carrying out their duties. This theory is based on comparisons of management styles in the United States and Japan; it assumes that where Japanese workers are more productive than their U.S. counterparts, the difference stems in part from different management styles. Thus, Theory Z was developed in an attempt to adapt some Japanese management practices to the U.S. workplace. The Japanese practices include employee involvement and lifetime employment.

## Contingency Theories of Leadership

With all of these possibilities, is there one best approach to leading employees? Should the supervisor consciously cultivate one leadership style? A common view is that the best style of leadership depends on the circumstances.

### Fiedler's Contingency Model

One of the first researchers to develop such a theory—called a contingency theory—was Fred Fiedler. According to Fiedler, each leader has a preferred leadership style, which may be relationship oriented (i.e., people oriented) or task oriented. Whether relationship-oriented or task-oriented leaders perform better

## FIGURE 8.4

**Fiedler's Contingency Model of Leadership**

| Leader–Member Relations | Good | Good | Good | Good | Poor | Poor | Poor | Poor |
|---|---|---|---|---|---|---|---|---|
| **Task Structure** | Structured | Structured | Unstructured | Unstructured | Structured | Structured | Unstructured | Unstructured |
| **Leader Position Power** | Strong | Weak | Strong | Weak | Strong | Weak | Strong | Weak |
| **Which Leader Performs Better?** | Task-Oriented Leader | Task-Oriented Leader | Task-Oriented Leader | Relationship-Oriented Leader | Relationship-Oriented Leader | Relationship-Oriented Leader | Task- or Relationship-Oriented Leader | Task-Oriented Leader |

Characteristics of the situation        Optimal leadership style for situation

Source: Fred E. Fiedler, "Engineer the Job to Fit the Manager," *Harvard Business Review,* Sept.–Oct. 1965. Adapted and reprinted by permission of *Harvard Business Review.* Copyright © 1965 by the President and Fellows of Harvard College; all rights reserved.

depends on three characteristics of the situation: leader–member relations, task structure, and the position power of the leader (see Figure 8.4). Leader–member relations refers to the extent to which the leader has the support and loyalty of group members. Task structure describes any specified procedures that employees should follow in carrying out the task. Position power refers to the formal authority granted to the leader by the organization.

Fiedler recommends that a leader determine whether his or her preferred leadership style fits the situation. For instance, if a situation involves good leader–member relations, a structured task, and strong position power, the situation calls for a leader who is task oriented. If the leader's preferred style does not fit, Fiedler says, the leader should try to change the characteristics of the situation. In the preceding example, a relationship-oriented leader might try to make the task less structured; the result would be a situation in which the leader is likely to be more effective.

### Hersey-Blanchard Theory

Fiedler's work led others to develop their own contingency theories of leadership. For example, Paul Hersey and Ken Blanchard developed a model called the life cycle theory. This model, like Fiedler's, considers degrees to which managers focus on relationships and tasks. Unlike Fiedler's model, however, the Hersey-Blanchard theory assumes that the leader's behavior should adapt to the situation. Specifically, the leadership style should reflect the maturity of the followers as measured by traits such as ability to work independently.

According to the Hersey-Blanchard life cycle theory, leaders should adjust the degree of task and relationship behavior in response to the growing maturity of their followers. As followers mature, leaders should move through the following combinations of task and relationship behavior:

1. High task and low relationship behavior.
2. High task and high relationship behavior.
3. Low task and high relationship behavior.
4. Low task and low relationship behavior.

Under special conditions, such as short-term deadlines, the leader may have to adjust the leadership style temporarily. However, Hersey and Blanchard maintain that this pattern of choosing a leadership style will bring about the most effective long-term working relationship between leader and followers.[5]

## Choosing a Leadership Style

Viewing contingency theories as a whole provides some general guidelines for choosing a leadership style. To identify the most effective style, the supervisor should consider the characteristics of the leader, of the subordinates, and of the situation itself. Figure 8.5 shows some key characteristics to weigh. (For more ideas on leading see "Tips from the Firing Line.")

### Characteristics of the Leader

Thanks to sources of variation such as personality type and cultural values, different leaders prefer different styles of leading. Whereas one supervisor might feel more comfortable backed up by a clear system of rules, regulations, and schedules, another might prefer to come up with creative approaches on the spur of the moment. One supervisor may like the results of involving employees in decision making, whereas another cannot get used to the time and effort this requires.

To some extent at least, a supervisor gets the best results using a leadership style with which he or she feels comfortable. That comfort level depends on characteristics such as the following:

- *The manager's values*—What is most important to the supervisor in carrying out his or her job? Is it the department's contribution to company profits? The employees' or the manager's own growth and development? A manager concerned about developing employees is most likely to involve them in making decisions.
- *Level of confidence in employees*—The more confidence the supervisor has in employees, the more he or she will involve them in planning and decision making.
- *Personal leadership strengths*—Some supervisors have a talent for leading group discussions; others are better at quietly analyzing information and reaching a decision. Some are good at detecting employee wants and needs; others excel at keeping their focus on the numbers. Effective leaders capitalize on their strengths.
- *Tolerance for ambiguity*—When the supervisor involves employees in solving problems or making decisions, he or she cannot always be sure of the outcomes. Supervisors differ in their level of comfort with this uncertainty, which is called ambiguity.

## FIGURE 8.5

**Characteristics Affecting Choice of Leadership Style**

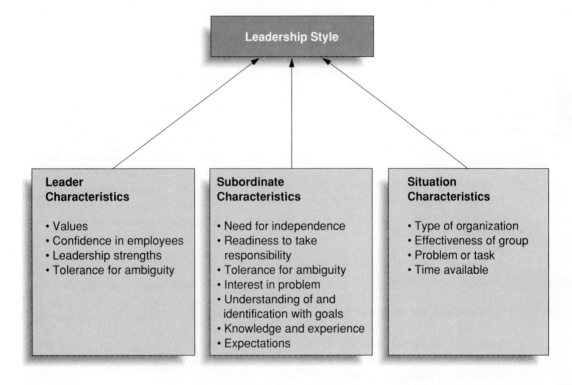

Logically, greater diversity in the workplace would generate greater diversity in some of these characteristics, such as values and leadership strengths. Particularly noteworthy is the possibility that women bring a different set of values and experiences to the workplace than men do. UCLA professor Helen Astin, who conducted a study of well-known women leaders, believes that there is a "feminine way of leadership." She claims that women tend to focus on interpersonal issues and to emphasize collective leadership, which involves empowering one's followers. The women leaders Astin studied tended to describe accomplishments as being accomplishments of the whole group, not just the leader.

Similarly, Alice H. Eagly, a social psychology professor at Purdue University, reviewed more than 360 studies on gender and leadership. She found that the only significant difference between men and women in these studies was that women tend to be more democratic in their leadership style. In many cases, this leadership style is supported by a view that the people in an organization are interdependent. A leader with this belief is more likely to respond to a problem by saying to employees, "Let's work out a solution together."

Of course, women are not the only leaders who adopt a democratic leadership style based on interdependence. Anne Hyde says:

## Managing Like a Leader

A leader and a supervisor are not necessarily the same thing. According to *Guide Lines for Managing*, a management newsletter, a leader is thought to be "visionary, empathetic, and flexible." A supervisor, on the other hand, is "practical, reasonable, and decisive." But supervisors often are called on to be leaders, and it is important for them to learn to combine roles. Craig R. Hickman, author of *Mind of a Manager, Soul of a Leader*, offers some suggestions for a successful blend of the two:

- **Blend strategy with culture.** Consider *what* you are going to do, as well as *why* you are going to do it.
- **Pay attention to risks as well as opportunities.** Supervisors are usually aware of risks involved in their actions; leaders are always looking for opportunities. If you are a cautious supervisor, seek the opinion or help of a co-worker who is more opportunistic.
- **Combine versions with visions.** A supervisor usually concentrates on specific versions, or scenarios, of a situation. A leader is more apt to emphasize an abstract vision or long-term goal. If you tend to

focus on the scenario, make sure it reflects a vision; if you operate according to vision, back it up with a concrete plan.
- **Include details in your big picture.** A supervisor is apt to focus on details; a leader usually sees the big picture. Combine these tendencies by identifying the details, then seeing how they fit the whole problem or situation. That way your solutions are more likely to be practical, but with a broad influence.
- **Try to anticipate future problems and implement current solutions.** Supervisors tend to focus on immediate situations and problems; leaders gaze at the horizon. You can use both to increase your effectiveness: Pay attention to both long-term and short-term concerns. You may find that solving an immediate problem will alter the long-term outlook, or that viewing a situation from a long-term perspective will help you find an immediate solution.

Source: "Manager—Or Leader?" *Guide Lines for Managing*, Texas Professional Training Associates, Inc., 1994, pp. 1–2.

Women value humanistic qualities and place an emphasis on the individual, not just the goal, because they have been rewarded in society for doing so. That is not to say men don't share humanistic values, or that men never use this new management paradigm. It is just that society has not encouraged men to manage in this way.

Some people think emphasis on teamwork is compelling more men to adopt aspects of the leadership style that has characterized women.[6]

### Characteristics of the Subordinates

In selecting a leadership style, smart supervisors consider their employees as well as themselves. Employees who are at their most creative and productive when they have a lot of freedom will dig in their heels if their supervisor is autocratic with them, even if that is the supervisor's natural leadership style. At the other extreme, employees who expect and rely on structure and direction will tend to drift and even become paralyzed if their leader has a laissez-faire or even democratic style.

What should the supervisor look for in deciding on the kind of supervision employees want? Here are some characteristics that should influence the choice:

- *Need for independence*—People who want a lot of direction will welcome autocratic leadership.

Occupation make a difference in how a leader deals with employees or team members at work. Doug Morris, chairman of Time Warner Inc.'s Atlantic Music Group, leads a team that manages musical artists such as Pete Townshend, Stevie Nicks, En Vogue, Stone Temple Pilots, and All-4-One (*photo*). The music field requires employees to be more independent, but Morris still speaks of "empowerment" and "decentralization" to describe his role as leader.

Source: © Alan Levenson

- *Readiness to assume responsibility*—Employees who are eager to assume responsibility will appreciate a democratic or laissez-faire style of leadership.
- *Tolerance for ambiguity*—Employees who are tolerant of ambiguity will accept a leadership style that gives them more say in solving problems.
- *Interest in the problem to be solved*—Employees who are interested in a problem and think it is important will want to help solve it.
- *Understanding of and identification with goals*—Employees who understand and identify with organizational or departmental goals will want to play an active role in deciding how to meet those goals. Furthermore, the supervisor will find that such employees are reliable in carrying out their responsibilities. Employees who don't identify with goals may need more active direction and control from the supervisor.
- *Knowledge and experience*—Employees with the knowledge necessary to solve a problem are more apt to want to help find a solution. Furthermore, their input will be more valuable to the supervisor. Thus, someone who is new on the job will probably need a supervisor who engages in both task-oriented and relationship-oriented behavior, but the supervisor can become less involved as the employee gains experience.
- *Expectations*—Some employees expect to participate in making decisions and solving problems. Others think that a supervisor who does not tell them what to do is not doing a good job. Cultural standards can also influence employee expectations. For example, Arthur Edwards supervises Vietnamese immigrants at a computer company in California's Silicon Valley. To build more friendly relations with his employees, he worked alongside them and joined them for lunch in the employees' cafeteria. However, the Vietnamese culture expects managers to be more formal, and the employees distanced themselves from Edwards.[7]

Organizations that use self-managing work teams (see Chapter 3) generally encourage a variety of employee characteristics that are associated with successful use of democratic leadership and a low degree of task-oriented behavior. They tend to train employees to assume extensive responsibility (or to select such employees). They generally provide the team with information about issues to be handled and about the performances of the organization and the team. This information should produce knowledgeable employees with an understanding of the problems faced by the team. Finally, the members of a self-managing work team expect to be involved in making a wide variety of decisions. What is left for a leader to do? Much of importance: communicating a vision of the team's mission and fostering a climate in which team members contribute to and care about the success of the team and the organization.

### Characteristics of the Situation

Besides the personalities and preferences of supervisor and subordinates, the situation itself helps to determine what leadership style will be most effective. Several characteristics are important:

- *Type of organization*—Organizations often lend themselves to one leadership style or another. If the organization expects supervisors to manage large numbers of employees, a democratic leadership style may be time-consuming and relatively challenging to use. If higher-level managers clearly value one style of leadership, the supervisor may find it difficult to use a different style and still be considered effective. At Federal Express Corporation, a high degree of empowerment in addition to annual surveys asking employees about management (including whether their supervisor is open to their ideas) requires a relatively democratic leadership style.[8]
- *Effectiveness of the group*—Regardless of the characteristics of individual employees, some groups are more successful in handling decisions than others. If a department, team, or other work group has little experience in making its own decisions, the supervisor may find that an authoritarian approach is easier to use. Supervisors should delegate decisions to groups that can handle the responsibility.
- *The problem or task*—The work group or individual employees can easily reach a solution to relatively simple problems, but the supervisor should retain greater control of complex or difficult problems. This is the case for leading in crisis situations, says consultant Hap Klopp, citing the example of a Himalayan mountain-climbing expedition that fell apart because the leader asked the group to choose a route to the top and the group members could not agree. "Democracy doesn't work at 20,000 feet," says Klopp.[9] Besides difficulty, the supervisor should consider how structured a task is. A structured task—that is, one with a set procedure to follow—is best managed by an autocratic leader. However, some tasks, such as generating ideas to improve customer service or planning the department picnic, are relatively unstructured. These tasks benefit from the employee involvement sought by a democratic, people-oriented leader.
- *Time available*—An autocratic leader is in a position to make decisions quickly. Group decision making usually requires more time for discussion and the sharing of ideas. Thus, the manager should use a relatively democratic leadership style only when time allows for it.

When employees and managers work in teams, a democratic leadership style based on Theory Y, which emphasizes people, is appropriate. Some management experts think that a coach is a good analogy for this leadership style.[10] Coaches delegate responsibility to carry out operations, and they are willing to share authority. They focus on picking qualified people, helping them learn to do their jobs well, and inspiring peak performance. Joseph Lipsey, who manages training and development for a major insurance company, credits this leadership style with transforming his department from one with little impact to one that works effectively:

> By driving out fear, hiring top-notch people . . . , implementing a team structure, making decisions by consensus, and unleashing the tremendous creativity and desire to contribute and to find meaning in work that is innate to everyone, we have created a real "force" within this organization.[11]

## Giving Directions

Supervisors can practice leadership by giving directions. In the workplace, giving directions can range from issuing detailed formal procedures for a particular task to inspiring the work group with a mission that unites them in a common cause. The supervisor can give directions simply by stating what an employee is to do in a particular situation. Or, if the supervisor leads a group that is expected to make many of its own decisions, the supervisor's directions may emphasize broad principles: "In our group, we don't waste time blaming; we figure out how to convert this angry customer into a happy one." In all cases, the way the supervisor gives directions can influence how willingly and how well employees respond.

The supervisor should make sure that the employee understands the directions. If the supervisor says, "I need those figures today," can the employee leave a note on the supervisor's desk at 6:00 P.M., half an hour after the supervisor has left? Or does the supervisor need time to review the numbers, so that he actually needs them by a specific time, say, 3:00 P.M.? Thus, the supervisor should state directions in specific, clear terms. Another way to make sure employees understand is to ask them to restate what they are supposed to do and to check on their progress before they are finished. (Chapter 10 provides further guidelines for effective communication.)

Supervisors may benefit from regularly asking their employees for feedback about their ability to give directions. The most useful feedback comes from specific questions: "Are my directions usually clear, or do you depend on co-workers to help you figure out what I want?" and "Do I often change my mind about what you should do after you've already started an assignment?"[12] When the supervisor emphasizes conveying broad goals and letting employees work out the details, the supervisor will need to seek evidence that employees know what those broad goals are.

The supervisor should make sure that employees also see the reason for the directions. In a crisis, people are willing to pitch in; they easily can see a need. Thus, if a hospital patient has a cardiac arrest, the staff members do not object to someone barking orders in an effort to revive the patient. But sometimes the

Employee feedback is very important to Jim Wong, a lumber wholesaler from Oak Brook, Illinois. Born in Shanghai, China, Wong understands how to do business in Hong Kong, the destination for much of his lumber, but he must make sure that cultural differences do not cause communication problems for employees such as Marilyn Nuter (*shown in the photo with Wong*).

Source: © Ralf-Finn Hestoff.

supervisor has to identify the crisis or explain the need. The supervisor on a loading dock could say, "This order is for our biggest customer, who's getting fed up with late shipments. If we don't get the order on the truck today, we'll be in deep trouble." That approach is more likely to get results than giving no reason and shouting, "Get moving!"

The most effective way to give instructions is to do so confidently and politely, but without apologies. If a supervisor says, "I'm sorry—I know you're busy, but I'd appreciate seeing those lab results by noon," the employee may think that he or she has been given an option, not instructions. The employee also may be unclear about who is in charge of the department. Instead, the supervisor can say, "Please have those lab results ready by noon." Of course, it is never appropriate to be rude.

If employees are not complying with a supervisor's directions, the supervisor can examine whether the directions follow these guidelines. Perhaps employees do not understand what is expected of them, or perhaps they do not realize that the supervisor is giving them directions, not a suggestion.

# Human Relations

Leading is clearly an application of human relations skills and is perhaps the most important measure of whether the supervisor excels at relations with his or her employees. Of course, supervisors need good human relations skills for other relationships as well. They need to work effectively with their manager and peers, and to be positive about themselves. In his book *Your Attitude Is Showing*, Elwood Chapman describes the skilled use of human relations as doing "everything you can to build strong, friendly, and honest working relationships with *all* the people you work with."[13]

Most books about business focus on the technical skills of managing. How can a supervisor develop human relations skills? Ways to get along with almost anyone include projecting a positive attitude, taking an interest in other people, and helping out. In addition, the supervisor can take some steps to work on each of the categories of relationships that are important to his or her success.

## Supervisors' Self-Images

Order-processing supervisor Eleanor Chakonas thinks of herself as a risk taker and a person who makes things happen. When she was asked to plan the expansion of her department, she attacked the job with a gusto that inspired her employees to contribute to the effort. The result was a plan that called for extra efforts by employees but would result in the department performing beyond management expectations. A supervisor who considers him- or herself more cautious or prone to error than Eleanor would have approached the planning job differently.

**self-concept**
A person's self-image.

The self-image a supervisor has—that is, the supervisor's **self-concept**—influences the supervisor's behavior. Someone who believes that he or she has power will act powerfully; someone who thinks of him- or herself as intelligent is apt to make careful decisions. It is worthwhile for supervisors to be aware of the thoughts they have of themselves.

Doing this can also help supervisors cultivate positive thoughts, which will help them act in positive ways. When you find yourself thinking "I'm so stupid" or "I wouldn't lose my cool the way he did," notice what you are thinking, and consider what it says about your self-concept. Take time to consider what your strengths and goals are. When you do something well, give yourself credit. When someone compliments you, smile and say thank you. Making the effort to behave this way will not only allow you to understand yourself better, but also to discover that your beliefs about yourself are more positive.

## Supervisors' Relations with Their Employees

A supervisor who is liked and respected by employees will inspire them to work harder and better. (See "Meeting the Challenge.") This does not mean that the supervisor should be friends with employees. Rather, the supervisor should consistently treat them in a way that reflects his or her role as a part of management. The modern supervisor empowers rather than commands employees, seeking consensus and spending time with employees to learn what they need for job success and career development.[14]

### Supervisors as Role Models

For employees, the supervisor is the person who most directly represents management and the organization. Thus, when employees evaluate the organization, they look at the supervisor's behavior. They also use the supervisor's behavior as a guide for how they should act. If a supervisor takes long lunch breaks, employees either will think that the use of their time is unimportant or will believe that the company unfairly lets managers get away with violating rules.

To set a good example for employees, the supervisor should follow all the rules and regulations that cover employees. The supervisor should be impartial in the treatment of employees—for example, assigning unpopular tasks to everyone, not just to certain employees. Supervisors also should be ethical, that is, honest and fair. (Chapter 4 discussed ethics in greater detail.)

## MEETING THE CHALLENGE

### A Supervisor Leads Employees to Quality

An effective leader influences people to act in a certain way, making them feel good about their achievements. Katherine Nicastro, customer service manager for Whittaker, Clark and Daniels, a distributor of minerals and chemicals to a wide range of customers, not only gets employees to serve customers, she gets them to care about the *quality* of service.

Nicastro is committed to the vision of the company's former president: "We excel through our ability to understand customers' needs and to meet them with great precision." While she sticks close to her supervisory goals, she does so in a people-oriented manner.

First, Nicastro makes sure her employees know the definition of quality as it pertains to the company and their jobs. Indeed, she and her employees together wrote specific guidelines for procedures leading to excellence in their department. Thus, Nicastro's employees are clear about what is expected of them.

> I make sure all of my employees know exactly what's expected for them to be doing a good job—to earn good reviews and get increases . . . It wouldn't be fair at the end of the year to say, "You didn't do this and you didn't do that." They'd say, "But you never told me!"—and they'd be right.

Nicastro ensures that her employees see the impact of their high-quality work by having them communicate directly with customers through letters and in person. By getting to know customers, Nicastro's staff can better meet their needs, improving the overall performance of the department. "A satisfied customer is real proof of accomplishment and something to be proud of," notes Nicastro. When customers praise the company, Nicastro passes that praise along to her staff.

Nicastro's human relations skills as a leader are also evident in the good example she sets for her employees and the trust she develops among them. When her workers achieve a goal, she takes them out for a group lunch. She holds biweekly "Breakfast Club" meetings to encourage staff members to talk about their concerns, ideas, or solutions to problems. Then she acts upon the matters discussed.

Nicastro also maintains a positive climate in the office. Instead of focusing on the negative aspect of mistakes, she emphasizes finding solutions. This helps maintain trust with her staff. "I don't dwell on petty mistakes," she says. "My job is to find the root cause, fix it, and get on with things." Finally, Nicastro's high energy level is hard to ignore; her employees can't help but catch the quality wave. "In a ball game, it's possible to do everything right and still not win. But if you treat customers with quality, and treat your people right and teach them to care about what they're going, you *always* win." Spoken like a true leader.

Source: "Getting People to Care About Quality," *Practical Supervision*, Texas Professional Training Associates, Inc., 1993, p. 6.

### Developing Trust

Pat Carrigan, the first female plant manager at General Motors Corporation, says her job is to "create a climate of trust," and she evidently meets that objective. United Auto Workers official Jack Whyte says, "Pat Carrigan ain't got a phony bone in her body." Not surprisingly, Carrigan was able to obtain the union's support in making important quality improvements at GM.[15] This example illustrates how employees will work most cooperatively with a supervisor they trust.

Building trust takes time and effort, yet the supervisor can lose it with a single unreasonable act. The most important way to build trust is to engage in fair, predictable behavior. The supervisor should fulfill promises and give employees credit when they do something well. Keeping the lines of communication open also builds trust. When the supervisor listens carefully and shares information, employees will not think that he or she is hiding something from them. Training and education consultant Jim Kouzes keeps his firm's computer printer next to his desk. He considers the resulting interruptions worthwhile because of what he learns from his employees when they stop by to pick up their documents.[16]

**FIGURE 8.6**

**What Managers Expect of Supervisors**

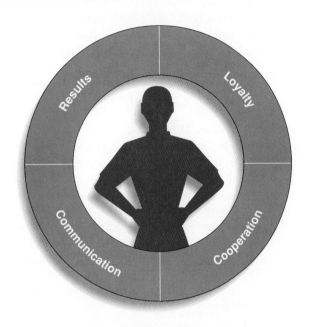

## Supervisors' Relations with Their Managers

No matter how good you are at planning, organizing, and leading, your ability to get along with your manager can determine the course of your career at a particular organization. That may not always seem fair, but your manager is the person who usually decides whether you will be promoted, get a juicy assignment or a raise, or even have a job next week. A manager who likes to work with you is more likely to take a favorable (or at least tolerant) view of your performance.

### Expectations

While every manager is different, most expect certain kinds of behavior from the people they manage. As summarized in Figure 8.6, a supervisor can reasonably assume that the manager expects loyalty, cooperation, communication, and results.

- *Loyalty* means that the supervisor says only positive things about company policies and about his or her manager. If the supervisor cannot think of anything positive to say, silence is better than criticism.
- *Cooperation* means that the supervisor works with others in the organization to achieve organizational goals. If the manager offers criticism, the supervisor should listen and try to make improvements. If the criticism seems unreasonable, the supervisor should first make sure that there was no misunderstanding and then try to find constructive aspects of the criticism.
- *Communication* means that the manager expects the supervisor to keep him or her informed about the department's performance.
- *Results* means that the supervisor should see that the department meets or exceeds its objectives. The best way to look good to the manager is to have a high-performing department.

### Learning About Your Manager

You can better meet your manager's expectations if you understand him or her as an individual. Observe how your manager handles various situations, try to determine his or her leadership style, and notice what issues are of most importance to your manager. As much as possible, adapt your own style to match your manager's when you are with this person. Also, ask what your manager's expectations are for you and how your performance will be measured.

### If You Are Dissatisfied

Despite your best efforts, you may find that you are dissatisfied with your manager. It happens to many people at some point in their career. If you are unhappy, begin by considering the source of the problem. Most interpersonal problems arise from the behavior and attitudes of two people, so determine what changes you can make to improve the situation.

If you cannot improve the situation enough by changing your own behavior, talk to your manager, stating the types of actions you are dissatisfied with and how those actions are affecting you. If you cannot resolve the problem, your best bet is probably to hunt for another job. But try to keep your present job while you look for a new one. Prospective employers look more favorably on job candidates who are already employed.

## Supervisors' Relations with Their Peers

If you get along well with your peers in the same and other departments, they will help you look good and get your job done. Their resentment or dislike for you can cause an endless stream of problems. Therefore, supervisors need to cultivate good relations with their peers.

### Competition

Sometimes your peers will be competing with you for raises, bonuses, or promotions. Remember that the more you can cooperate, the better you will all look. This means that your competition should be fair and as friendly as possible. If you try to sabotage a co-worker, you probably will be the one who ultimately ends up looking bad.

### Criticism

Because you are trying to maintain a positive attitude, you should not go looking for things to criticize about your peers or anyone else. However, if you know that a co-worker has done something that works against the organization's best interests, you should go directly to that person and point out the problem. It usually helps to be polite and diplomatic and to assume that the problem was unintended—an error or an oversight.

If the co-worker resists listening to your criticism and the problem will harm the company, its employees, or its customers, then you should go to your manager to discuss the problem. Focus on the problem and its consequences to the organization, not on the personalities involved. Gossip is not the behavior of a leader; overcoming problems is.

# Summary

**8.1 Discuss the possible link between personal traits and leadership ability.**

To find which people will succeed as leaders, researchers have looked for traits that successful leaders hold in common. Traits that may be significant include a sense of responsibility, self-confidence, high energy level, empathy, an internal locus of control, and a sense of humor. However, research results have been inconsistent, leading to the conclusion that traits alone do not predict success as a leader.

**8.2 Compare leadership styles that a supervisor might adopt.**

Depending on how much authority they retain, supervisors can be authoritarian (retaining much authority), democratic (sharing authority), or laissez-faire (giving up most authority). Supervisors may also be task oriented, people oriented, or both. They may build their leadership style on Theory X assumptions that employees must be coerced to work, on Theory Y assumptions that employees can be motivated to seek responsibility and achieve objectives creatively, or on Theory Z values such as employee involvement and focus on long-term goals.

**8.3 Explain contingency theories of leadership.**

These theories hold that leaders can be most effective by matching different leadership styles to varying circumstances. For example, Fiedler's contingency model says that whether people- or task-oriented leaders perform better depends on leader–member relations, task structure, and the leader's position power. Fiedler recommends that, if the leader's preferred leadership style does not fit the situation, the characteristics of the situation should be changed. In contrast, Hersey and Blanchard's life cycle theory maintains that the leader should modify his or her behavior to fit the situation. As followers mature, leaders should use varying levels of task and relationship behavior.

**8.4 Identify criteria for choosing a leadership style.**

The supervisor should select a leadership style that suits his or her own characteristics, as well as those of the employees and the situation. Criteria for evaluating the characteristics of the leader are his or her values, level of confidence in employees, leadership strengths, and tolerance for ambiguity. Criteria for evaluating the characteristics of employees include their need for independence, readiness to assume responsibility, tolerance for ambiguity, interest in the problem, expectations, understanding of and identification with goals, and knowledge and experience. Criteria for evaluating the characteristics of the situation include the type of organization, effectiveness of the group, the nature of the problem or task, and the time available.

**8.5 Describe guidelines for giving directions to employees.**

The supervisor should make sure that employees understand the directions and the reasons behind them. The supervisor should give the instructions confidently and politely, but without being apologetic.

**8.6 Tell why supervisors need to understand and improve their views of themselves.**

The supervisor's self-concept influences how he or she behaves. People who believe they are capable tend to act capably. The supervisor needs to cultivate the self-concept of an effective leader.

**8.7 Explain how supervisors can develop and maintain good relations with their employees, managers, and peers.**

The supervisor should project a positive attitude, take an interest in others, and help out as needed. With employees, the supervisor should set a good example, be ethical, and develop trust. The supervisor should give his or her manager loyalty, cooperation, communication, results, and adapt to the manager's style. The supervisor should keep competition with peers as fair and friendly as possible and should offer any necessary criticism in a constructive way.

## Key Terms

| | | |
|---|---|---|
| leading | democratic leadership | Theory Y |
| internal locus of control | laissez-faire leadership | Theory Z |
| authoritarian leadership | Theory X | self-concept |

## Review and Discussion Questions

1. Describe the six traits that researchers believe may indicate a good leader. However, research has *not* established a clear link between personality traits and leadership success. What other factors do you think might contribute to success or failure?

2. Claire Callahan supervises the camping department of a large outdoor-equipment store. The store manager (Claire's boss) has given her the objective of increasing sales by 10 percent during the next quarter. Choose one of the three leadership styles for Claire (authoritarian, democratic, or laissez-faire). Then state three or more steps that she might take to influence her employees to meet the new sales objective.

3. Ann Wong is the accounts payable supervisor at an insurance company. During a time of layoffs, she decides to adopt a more people-oriented leadership style than the style she normally uses. What does this change mean?

4. Pete Polito supervises a cross-functional team whose task is to evaluate whether the in-line skates his company manufactures are safe and up to date in design and style. Using Theory Y, what steps might Pete take to lead his team to its goal?

5. Do you think it is more realistic to expect supervisors to adjust the situation to meet their preferred leadership style, as suggested by Fiedler's contingency model of leadership, or to adjust their leadership style to fit the situation, as suggested by Hersey and Blanchard? Explain your reasoning.

6. In which of the following situations would you recommend that the supervisor use an authoritarian style of leadership? In which situation would you recommend a democratic style? Explain your choices.

    a. The supervisor's manager says, "Top management wants us to start getting employees to suggest ways to improve quality in all areas of operations." Each department is given wide latitude in how to accomplish this.

    b. A supervisor is uncomfortable in meetings and likes to be left alone to figure out solutions to problems. The supervisor's employees believe that a good supervisor is able to tell them exactly what to do.

    c. A shipment of hazardous materials is on its way to a warehouse. The supervisor is responsible for instructing employees how to handle the materials when they arrive later that day.

7. Prakash Singh prefers a very democratic style of leadership and is uncomfortable telling someone what to do. His solution is to make his instructions as general as possible, so that employees will feel they have more control. He also tends to apologize for being authoritarian. Do you think this method of giving directions is effective? Why or why not?

8. Why should supervisors have a positive view of themselves? What are some ways a supervisor can be aware of and improve his or her self-concept?

9. Identify the human relations error in each of the following situations. Suggest a better way to handle each.

   a. Carole Fields's boss compliments her on the report she submitted yesterday. She says, "It was no big deal."

   b. When Rich Peaslee was promoted to supervisor, he told the other employees, "Now, remember, I was one of the gang before this promotion, and I'll still be one of the gang."

   c. The second-shift supervisor observes that the first-shift employees have not left their work areas clean for the last three days. He complains to his manager about the lax supervision on the first shift.

10. Carla Santos doesn't get along with her new manager; the two have disliked each other since the first day they met. Carla was transferred to a new department when the previous supervisor left the company, so neither Carla nor her manager actually chose to work together. Carla doesn't want her job as a supervisor to be jeopardized by an unpleasant relationship. What steps might she take to improve the situation?

## A SECOND LOOK

Which characteristics of a successful leader does Kathleen Schrank of Jackson Memorial Hospital exhibit? Does she exhibit any other qualities that you think contribute to her success but that are not discussed in the chapter or listed in Figure 8.1?

# APPLICATIONS MODULE

## CASE

### Leadership with Style

After years as a successful professional football coach and a commentator for NBC, Bill Walsh accepted a position as head coach at Stanford University in California. The move surprised many observers: The move from professional to college football involved a pay cut and looked like a step down. Walsh had a notable track record as coach of the San Francisco 49ers, including three Super Bowl victories, and his reputation as a mentor for quarterbacks is legendary.

What made this leader turn "amateur"? Walsh explains that coaching at Stanford provides an opportunity to return to the kind of work he loves. A people-oriented leader who never loses sight of the goal, Walsh develops not only the players but also the assistant coaches, some of whom are former 49ers with coaching experience.

Walsh exhibits many of the characteristics that people look for in a leader. Informal with his players (he asks them to use his first name), he has self-confidence and a sense of humor that surprises those who do not know him well. In his early days on the job, he baffled players by disguising himself as a bellhop and trying to get tips from players exiting the team bus at the hotel. Observes junior quarterback Steve Stenstrom, "In the beginning he would say something funny, but we weren't sure we should laugh. Now we laugh at his jokes every day. He keeps us loose."

At the same time, Walsh insists on high quality. For example, he did not hesitate to teach the Stanford players the offense he used as coach of the 49ers. "The whole network of terms had to be learned and applied," he explains, "with really no room for mistakes." Some of his actions have been unpopular with individual players, but necessary for the team's overall performance.

Some people have interpreted certain of Walsh's actions as evidence that he is unfeeling. For example, when he left the 49ers, he never called the players together to announce his retirement. But Walsh behaved this way because he *did* care about his players: "You want to get up and make an emotional speech, and you can't because you know your nerve endings are exposed. You know you'll never be able to finish."

One person who gives high marks to Walsh's leadership style is James Stockdale, who was Ross Perot's running mate in the 1992 presidential election. Says Stockdale, "He is absolutely straight with his men. No matter what pressure he was under, he never lashed out at anybody . . . No one can top Bill for compassionate, clean effectiveness."

1. Would you characterize Bill Walsh as an authoritarian, democratic, or laissez-faire leader? Which leadership style would be most effective for a football team? Why?
2. Do you think Walsh has a Theory X, Theory Y, or Theory Z attitude? Explain your answer.
3. State some specific characteristics of the situation that could determine adjustments in Walsh's leadership style, including the type of organization, effectiveness of the group, the problem or task, and time available.
4. Describe what you think Bill Walsh's self-concept is.

Sources: Kenny Moore, "Back to School," *Sports Illustrated*, Nov. 2, 1992, pp. 42–44ff; and Paul Witteman, "The Second Coming," *Time*, Nov. 2, 1992, pp. 62–64.

■ **SELF-QUIZ**

*Assessing Your Leadership Style*

This is the T-P (task-oriented/people-oriented) Leadership Questionnaire. The following items describe aspects of leadership behavior. Respond to each item according to the way you would act if you were the leader of a work group. Circle whether you would most likely behave in the described way: always (A), frequently (F), occasionally (O), seldom (S), or never (N).

| | | |
|---|---|---|
| A F O S N | 1. | I would most likely act as the spokesperson of the group. |
| A F O S N | 2. | I would encourage overtime work. |
| A F O S N | 3. | I would allow members complete freedom in their work. |
| A F O S N | 4. | I would encourage the use of uniform procedures. |
| A F O S N | 5. | I would permit members to use their own judgment in solving problems. |
| A F O S N | 6. | I would stress being ahead of competing groups. |
| A F O S N | 7. | I would speak as a representative of the group. |
| A F O S N | 8. | I would needle members for greater effort. |
| A F O S N | 9. | I would try out my ideas in the group. |
| A F O S N | 10. | I would let members do their work the way they think best. |
| A F O S N | 11. | I would be working hard for a promotion. |
| A F O S N | 12. | I would tolerate postponement and uncertainty. |
| A F O S N | 13. | I would speak for the group if visitors were present. |
| A F O S N | 14. | I would keep the work moving at a rapid pace. |
| A F O S N | 15. | I would turn the members loose on a job and let them go to it. |
| A F O S N | 16. | I would settle conflicts when they occur in the group. |
| A F O S N | 17. | I would get swamped by details. |
| A F O S N | 18. | I would represent the group at outside meetings. |
| A F O S N | 19. | I would be reluctant to allow the members any freedom of action. |
| A F O S N | 20. | I would decide what should be done and how it should be done. |
| A F O S N | 21. | I would push for increased production. |
| A F O S N | 22. | I would let some members have authority, which I could keep. |
| A F O S N | 23. | Things would usually turn out as I had predicted. |
| A F O S N | 24. | I would allow the group a high degree of initiative. |
| A F O S N | 25. | I would assign group members to particular tasks. |
| A F O S N | 26. | I would be willing to make changes. |
| A F O S N | 27. | I would ask the members to work harder. |
| A F O S N | 28. | I would trust the group members to exercise good judgment. |
| A F O S N | 29. | I would schedule the work to be done. |
| A F O S N | 30. | I would refuse to explain my actions. |

A F O S N    31.    I would persuade others that my ideas are to their advantage.

A F O S N    32.    I would permit the group to set its own pace.

A F O S N    33.    I would urge the group to beat its previous record.

A F O S N    34.    I would act without consulting the group.

A F O S N    35.    I would ask that group members follow standard rules and regulations.

T _____                                                P _____

Score the T-P Leadership Questionnaire as follows:

*a.* Circle the item number for items 8, 12, 17, 18, 19, 30, 34, and 35.

*b.* In front of each *circled item number*, write the number 1 if you responded S (seldom) or N (never) to that item.

*c.* In front of *item numbers not circled*, write a 1 if you responded A (always) or F (frequently).

*d.* Circle the 1s that you have written in front of the following items: 3, 5, 8, 10, 15, 18, 19, 22, 24, 26, 28, 30, 32, 34, and 35.

*e.* *Count the circled 1s.* This is your score for concern for people. Record the score in the blank following the letter P at the end of the questionnaire.

*f.* *Count the uncircled 1s.* This is your score for concern for task. Record this number in the blank following the letter T.

---

Source: The T-P Leadership Questionnaire was adapted by J. B. Ritchie and P. Thompson in *Organization and People* (New York: West, 1984). Copyright 1969 by the American Educational Research Association. W. Pfeiffer and John Jones, *American Educational Research Journal*, 1969, pp.62–79. Adapted by permission of the publisher.

## Class Exercise

Divide the class into groups of four or five students. Each group is assigned one of the four sections in Figure A, which is a checklist of ways that employees, including supervisors, can demonstrate competence in human relations.

Each group discusses the principles in its section of the checklist. Based on jobs they have held or situations they have observed, group members describe good or bad human relations practices. In particular, consider how you have seen supervisors practice or fail to practice these principles.

After the groups have discussed these principles among themselves, they take turns making presentations. Each group selects one principle to present to the class. One representative (or more) from the group gives a brief illustration of that principle.

This exercise was suggested by Corinne R. Livesay, Belhaven College, Jackson, Mississippi.

## FIGURE A
## Human Relations Competencies Checklist

**1. Consistently communicate the following attitudes to co-workers, superiors, customers, or patients:**

❑ Send out positive verbal and nonverbal signals in all contacts, including telephone.
❑ Remain positive while working with those who are negative.
❑ Be positive and sensitive when those you are dealing with are not.
❑ Deal with all people in an honest, ethical, and moral way.
❑ Avoid ethnic or sexual remarks that could be misinterpreted.
❑ Maintain a sense of humor.
❑ Recognize when you begin to become negative, and start an attitude renewal project.
❑ Develop and maintain a good service attitude.

**2. Demonstrate the following human-relations skills in dealing with co-workers:**

❑ Build and maintain equally effective horizontal working relationships with everyone in your department. Refuse to play favorites.
❑ Build a productive, no-conflict relationship with those who may have a different set of personal values.
❑ Build relationships based on mutual rewards.
❑ Develop productive, healthy relationships with those who may be substantially older or younger.
❑ Maintain a productive relationship even with individuals who irritate you at times.
❑ Treat everyone, regardless of ethnic or socioeconomic differences, with respect.
❑ Work effectively with others regardless of their sexual orientation.
❑ Do not take human-relations slights or mistakes from others personally; do not become defensive or attempt to retaliate in kind.
❑ Repair an injured relationship as soon as possible.
❑ Even if you are not responsible for the damage to a working relationship, protect your career by taking the initiative to restore it.
❑ Permit others to restore a relationship with you.
❑ Release your frustrations harmlessly without damaging relationships.
❑ Handle teasing and testing without becoming upset.

**3. Demonstrate the following human-relations skills in dealing with your superiors:**

❑ Build a strong vertical relationship with your supervisor without alienating co-workers.
❑ Be a high producer yourself and contribute to the productivity of co-workers.
❑ Survive, with a positive attitude, under a difficult supervisor until changes occur.
❑ Establish relationships that are mutually rewarding.
❑ Show you can live up to your productivity potential without alienating co-workers who do not live up to theirs.
❑ Live close to your productivity potential without extreme highs or lows regardless of difficult changes in the work environment.
❑ Do not underestimate or overestimate a superior.
❑ Report mistakes or misjudgments rather than trying to hide them.
❑ Show that you can turn any change into an opportunity, including accepting a new supervisor with a different style.
❑ Refuse to nurse small gripes into major upsets.

**4. Demonstrate the following professional attitudes and human-relations skills:**

❑ Be an excellent listener.
❑ Establish a good attendance record.
❑ Keep a good balance between home and career so neither suffers.
❑ Demonstrate that you are self-motivated.
❑ Communicate freely and thoroughly.
❑ Prepare yourself for a promotion in such a manner that others will be happy when you succeed.
❑ Share only positive, nonconfidential data about your organization with outsiders.
❑ Pass only reliable data on to others.
❑ Keep your business and personal relationships sufficiently separated.
❑ Concentrate on the positive aspects of your job while trying to improve the negative.
❑ Make only positive comments about a third party not present.
❑ Leave a job or company in a positive manner; train your replacement so that productivity is not disturbed.
❑ If you prefer to be a stabilizer, develop patience; if you prefer to be a zig zagger, don't stomp on other people's feet, hands, or heads while climbing the success ladder.
❑ Always have a Plan B (a contingency plan for your career).
❑ Avoid self-victimization.

Source: *Your Attitude Is Showing:* by Elwood N. Chapman. © 1995. Reprinted by permission of Prentice-Hall, Inc. Upper Saddle River, NJ.

## *Team-Building Exercise*

### Trying on a Team Leadership Style

Divide the class into teams of four to six. Either appoint a supervisor for each team, or ask for volunteers. The teams have the following objective: to determine whether the campus library is as user-friendly as it could be, and to come up with suggestions for improvement if necessary.

Each supervisor should privately choose a leadership style (task oriented or people oriented) and an attitude (following Theory X or Theory Y)

and practice these during the exercise. Team members should decide on their own characteristics, such as a need for independence, readiness to assume responsibility, and so forth.

At the end of the exercise, each team should discuss with the rest of the class how effective its leader and team members were. Also, they should present their results: Did they come up with some good suggestions for the library?

# Video Exercise 8: *The Supervisor as Leader*

## *Video Summary*

In this video program, you will see how effective leadership at every level of the organization was instrumental in orchestrating Marshall Industries' phenomenal restructuring and turnaround. You will meet Gordon Marshall, the company's founder: Robert Rodin, president; and Mike Lelo, warehouse manager.

## *Application*

In an eight-year series of executive seminars, over 15,000 managers have completed James M. Kouzes and Barry Z. Posner's checklist of admired leadership characteristics. Respondents were asked to select from a list of 20 qualities the 7 that they "most looked for and admired in a leader, someone whose direction they would willingly follow."[1]

1.  Place a check mark next to the seven qualities that you most look for and admire in a leader, someone whose direction you would willingly follow.

| Check Seven Only | Leadership Characteristics |
|:---:|:---|
| ❏ | Ambitious |
| ❏ | Broad-minded |
| ❏ | Caring |
| ❏ | Competent |
| ❏ | Cooperative |
| ❏ | Courageous |
| ❏ | Dependable |
| ❏ | Determined |
| ❏ | Fair-minded |
| ❏ | Forward looking |
| ❏ | Honest |
| ❏ | Imaginative |
| ❏ | Independent |
| ❏ | Inspiring |
| ❏ | Intelligent |
| ❏ | Loyal |
| ❏ | Mature |
| ❏ | Self-controlled |
| ❏ | Straightforward |
| ❏ | Supportive |

[1]James M. Kouzes and Barry Z. Posner, *Credibility: How Leaders Gain and Lose It, Why People Demand It* (San Francisco: Jossey-Bass, 1993), p. 14.

2. Compare your selections with the findings from the Kouzes and Posner survey, which your instructor will give to you.
3. Discuss the survey findings from the Kouzes and Posner study:

   a. By a show of hands, determine how many students selected each of the characteristics.
   b. How closely did the choices made by the class parallel those in the Kouzes and Posner study?
   c. Did any of the rankings surprise you? Discuss as a class.
   d. Do you agree or disagree with the following statement?

   Followers do attribute distinguishing characteristics to leaders, and these perceptions are important in their own right. Social-cognitive theory holds that people use idealized personal traits to distinguish leaders from nonleaders.[2]

[2]Robert E. Coffey, Curtis W. Cook, Phillip L. Hunsaker, *Management and Organizational Behavior* (Homewood, IL: Austen Press, 1994), p. 293.

**9**

*In every affair consider what precedes and what follows, and then undertake it.*
**—Epictetus, Greek Stoic philosopher, first century A.D.**

# Problem Solving and Decision Making

## LEARNING OBJECTIVES

After you have studied this chapter, you should be able to:

9.1 Identify the steps in the rational model of decision making.

9.2 Discuss ways people make compromises in following the decision-making model.

9.3 Describe guidelines for making decisions.

9.4 Explain how probability theory, decision trees, and computer software can help in making decisions.

9.5 Discuss advantages and disadvantages of making decisions in groups.

9.6 Describe guidelines for group decision making.

9.7 Describe guidelines for thinking creatively.

9.8 Discuss how supervisors can establish and maintain a creative work climate.

9.9 Identify ways to overcome barriers to creativity.

## MAKING DECISIONS AT MINOLTA

Source: © Frank White/Gamma Liaison

Everyone, at every job, must make decisions. Supervisors who are effective know not only how to make good decisions, but also when to let their employees make their decisions. Mike Rakosnik, national program manager for Minolta Corporation in New Jersey, is one such supervisor. "I work with smart and motivated people," remarks Rakosnik. "I give them a lot of freedom, and I expect, and get, results."

When Rakosnik holds a meeting for the sales trainers he supervises, he may assign projects to the trainers. Then it's up to group members to decide how the projects will be completed, and when. Rakosnik follows up on the trainers' progress, but he says, "My style isn't to look over people's shoulders."

Rakosnik spends much of his time on the road with his trainers so that he has a basis on which to make decisions. "Many executives get afflicted with an ivory tower mentality," he explains. "They make decisions based on their view from the home office, not from what's actually going on in the field."

Being the kind of supervisor who not only makes his own decisions but also empowers employees to do so did not come naturally to Rakosnik; he had to work at it. "I used to be more intimidating," he admits. "I would bark orders and expect people to hop to, no questions asked. But over time, as I've gotten more secure with myself, I've learned that people want to be treated like partners, and don't want their creativity restricted." Maintaining a creative work climate has paid off for Rakosnik in sales figures: Minolta has experienced a 50 percent increase in the sales of its high-volume copiers in areas that also have had a 50 percent increase in sales training.

Source: Geoffrey Brewer, "The New Managers," *Sales & Marketing Management—Performance*, Mar. 1995, pp. 33–34.

No matter how carefully a supervisor plans or how effectively a supervisor leads, he or she is bound to encounter problems. Human imperfections, new challenges from the environment in which the department operates, and the desire to achieve higher quality are only three sources of problems for a supervisor to solve. Therefore, according to management consultant Clark Wigley, "Success does not equal no problems (as in 'If I were a good manager, I would have no problems'). Success is having and solving the right problems."[1] Wigley means that the best managers, including supervisors, are those who know what issues to focus on and who respond to problems in a positive way. By solving the right problems—the ones that can improve the quality of work—effective supervisors improve their department's activities and the service they deliver to their customers.

**decision**
A choice from among available alternatives.

A **decision** is a choice from among available alternatives. Solving problems involves making a series of decisions: deciding that something is wrong, deciding what the problem is, deciding how to solve it. Successful problem solving depends on good decisions. This chapter describes how supervisors make decisions and offers some guidelines for doing so effectively. The chapter includes a discussion of decision making in groups and suggestions for thinking creatively.

# The Process of Decision Making

Much of a supervisor's job is making decisions, which cover all the functions of management. What should the supervisor or the department accomplish today or this week? Who should handle a particular project or machine? What should a supervisor tell his or her manager about the customer who complained yesterday? Do employees need better training or just more inspiration? How can a supervisor end the ongoing dispute between two staff members? These are only a few of the issues a typical supervisor has to act on.

In many cases, supervisors make decisions like these without giving any thought to the process of deciding. A supervisor automatically does something because it feels right or because he or she always has handled that problem that way. When a decision seems more complex, a supervisor is more likely to give thought to the decision-making process. For example, in deciding whether to purchase an expensive piece of machinery or to fire an employee, a supervisor might make a careful list of pluses and minuses, trying to include all the relevant economic, practical, or ethical concerns. (Making ethical decisions is discussed in Chapter 4.) Even though making many decisions seems to be automatic, supervisors can improve the way they make them by understanding how the decision-making process works in theory and in practice.

## The Rational Model

If you could know everything, you could make perfect decisions. How would an all-knowing person go about making a decision? This person would probably follow the rational model of decision making, illustrated in Figure 9.1.

### Identify the Problem
According to this model, a decision maker first identifies the problem. Recall from Chapter 6 that it is important to distinguish the symptoms of a problem from the problem itself. Usually a supervisor notices the symptoms first, so that he or she has to look for the underlying problem.

### FIGURE 9.1

**The Rational Model of Decision Making**

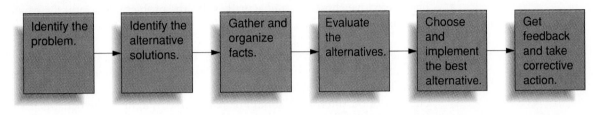

For example, Dave Frantz finds that he has to work 60 hours a week to do his job as supervisor of a group of janitorial service workers. Dave works hard and spends little time socializing, so his effort is not the problem. He observes that he spends approximately half his time doing paperwork required by higher-level management. He decides that the major problem is that too much of his time is spent on paperwork. (Along the way, Dave also may find and resolve minor problems.)

### *Identify Alternative Solutions*
The next step is to identify the alternative solutions. In our example, Dave thinks of several possibilities. He might delegate the paperwork to other employees, hire a secretary, buy a personal computer and software that will automate some of the work, or persuade management to eliminate the required paperwork.

### *Gather and Organize Facts*
Next, a decision maker gathers and organizes facts. Dave asks his manager if he really has to do all the paperwork; the manager says yes. From the human resources office, Dave gets information on the pay scale for secretaries. He evaluates which aspects of his work could be delegated, and he collects advertisements and magazine articles about various personal computers and software.

### *Evaluate Alternatives*
A supervisor evaluates the alternatives from the information gathered. Dave determines that he cannot eliminate or delegate the paperwork. He calculates that a personal computer would cost much less than a secretary, though a secretary would save more of his time. He predicts that his manager will be more open to buying a computer than to hiring a secretary.

### *Choose and Implement the Best Alternative*
A supervisor next chooses and implements the best alternative. In our example, Dave decides to buy a personal computer and prepares a report showing the costs and benefits of doing so. He emphasizes how the company will benefit when he is more efficient and can devote more time to leading and controlling. He selects the brand and model of computer that he thinks will best meet his needs at a reasonable cost.

When evaluating and selecting alternatives, how can a supervisor decide which is best? Sometimes the choice is obvious, but at other times a supervisor needs formal criteria for making decisions, such as these:

- The alternative chosen should actually solve the problem. Ignoring the paperwork might enable Dave to leave work on time, but it would not solve the problem of how to get the job done.
- An acceptable alternative must be feasible. In other words, a supervisor should be able to implement it. For example, Dave learned that requesting less paperwork was not a feasible solution.
- The cost of the alternative should be reasonable in light of the benefits it will deliver. Dave's employer might consider a personal computer to be a reasonable expense, but the cost of a full-time secretary is high compared with the benefits of making Dave's job easier.

### Get Feedback

The last step is to get feedback and take corrective action. In the example, Dave takes his proposal to his manager, who suggests some additions and changes. Dave orders the computer. When it arrives, it automates some of his work, using his experiences to improve on his original ideas.

When a decision will affect the course of someone's career or the expenditure of a lot of money, a supervisor will want to make the best decision possible. One way of doing so is to try to complete each of the steps in the rational model. In general, supervisors can benefit from using this model when they are making complex, formal decisions or when the consequences of a decision are great.

## Human Compromises

The example of the rational model of decision making may appear to be far removed from the daily experiences of most supervisors. Often supervisors have neither the time nor the desire to follow all these steps to a decision. Even when supervisors try to follow these steps, they often have trouble thinking of all the alternatives or gathering all the facts they need. Sometimes no alternative emerges as being clearly the best.

Given these human and organizational limitations, supervisors—like all decision makers—make compromises most of the time (see Figure 9.2). The resulting decision may be less than perfect, but it is typically one the decision maker is willing to live with. A supervisor who is aware of the kinds of compromises people make is more apt to be aware of when he or she is using them. In addition, a supervisor may find that although some kinds of compromises are useful in some situations, others are to be avoided as much as possible.

### Simplicity

Although we often think we have approached a problem with a fresh perspective and have analyzed all the options, most people take a simpler approach. Usually what we are doing is simply mulling over our experiences and considering ways

## FIGURE 9.2

**Human Compromises in Decision Making**

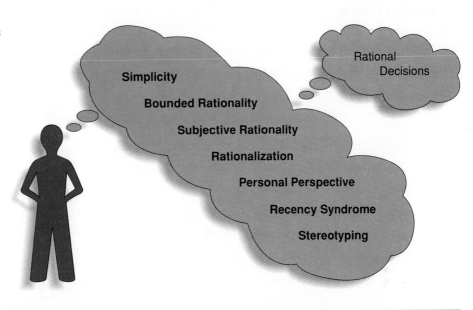

we have handled similar problems in the past. If we consider a few possibilities, we conclude that we have covered them all. People tend to select an alternative that they have tried before and that has delivered acceptable results. The downside of this kind of attempt at simplicity is that it tends to bypass innovative solutions, even though they sometimes deliver the best results.

### Bounded Rationality

When time, cost, or other limitations, such as the tendency to simplify, make finding the best alternative impossible or unreasonable, decision makers settle for an alternative they consider good enough. Choosing an alternative that meets minimum standards of acceptability is a form of **bounded rationality;** that is, a decision maker places limits, or *bounds*, on the *rational* model of decision making. (Figure 9.3 shows how bounded rationality works.) The decision maker considers alternatives only until one is found that meets his or her minimum criteria for acceptability.

For example, a supervisor who is fed up with tardiness might first be inclined to fire everyone who was late in a particular week. But she knows that will be demoralizing, will create a sudden and large need for hiring and training, and will probably not impress her manager. She rejects that alternative. Then she remembers that she gave "timeliness awards" last year, but that did not stop tardiness, so she rejects that alternative. Finally, she remembers reading an article that recommends spelling out the consequences of the undesirable behavior and then letting the employee experience those consequences. She decides to try that approach. There probably are other ways to solve the problem—maybe even better ways—but the supervisor does not spend any more time trying to think of them.

**bounded rationality** Choosing an alternative that meets minimum standards of acceptability.

**FIGURE 9.3**

**The Process of
Bounded Rationality**

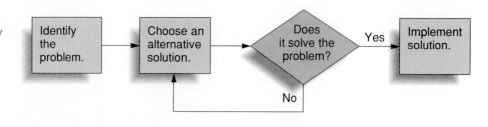

### Subjective Rationality

When people analyze alternatives, they tend to rely on their intuition and gut instincts instead of on collecting impartial data. For example, a sales supervisor might estimate, "I think orders will be up next year, but just slightly, say, 2 percent." The sales supervisor did not arrive at that figure through marketing research or an analysis of industry data but relied on his experience with trends in demand for the product. Thus, even when the process for arriving at the decision is otherwise rational, the numbers used in the process may be subjective and thus not completely accurate.

### Rationalization

People tend to favor solutions that they believe they can justify to others. For example, production supervisor Renata King knows that her manager focuses on containing costs. When Renata is considering alternative ways to approach a problem, she tends to favor the low-cost alternative. Another alternative might be more successful, but Renata feels that whatever the outcome, her manager is likely to appreciate her effort to keep costs down.

A version of this pattern of behavior was evident at AlliedSignal when Lawrence A. Bossidy became CEO. Bossidy met with customers and learned they were dissatisfied with the manufacturing firm's rate of filling orders as promised. Customers complained that this "order-fill rate" was just 60 percent, but AlliedSignal employees argued it was really 98 percent. The employees' problem-solving efforts focused on justifying why AlliedSignal's numbers were more correct. However, when employees realized that Bossidy was more interested in how to make customers happy than in arguing about statistics, they adopted the customers' measurements and began to tackle the underlying problems.[2] Like Bossidy, supervisors can benefit from rationalization by communicating what they consider important; employees will tend to make decisions that reflect those priorities.

### Personal Perspective

In supervising computer programmers, Abraham Wassad has to review their documentation and the instructions they write for using their programs. Abraham pointed out to one programmer that some portions of his instructions needed clarification. "It's OK the way it is," insisted the programmer. "*I* understand it."

Stereotyping interferes with rational decision making. Ambulance service founder Victoria Rosellini had to overcome stereotypes about women to make her company a success. Among other things, it was said that she would not have the mechanical knowledge to keep her vehicles on the road. She proved that stereotyping wrong, and today her Absolute-Care Ambulance Service Inc. and Absolute Life support companies employ more than 70 workers and have earned nearly $3 million in annual sales.

Source: © 1995 *Nation's Business*/T. Michael Keza

**recency syndrome**
The tendency to more easily remember events that have occurred recently.

People often make this programmer's mistake: assuming everyone sees things the way he does. The programmer thinks the instructions must be clear to any (reasonable) person. Such assumptions can lead to incorrect decisions in many areas, including how much information to convey, what working conditions are most important to employees, or what product characteristics customers want. To avoid this problem, decision makers must find out what other people are thinking, then take those views into account. (See "Meeting the Challenge.")

### Recency Syndrome

People more readily remember events that have occurred recently than those that took place sometime in the past. This tendency is known as the **recency syndrome.** For example, a supervisor might remember that the last time she gave a negative performance appraisal the employee became hostile, but will not recall that a negative appraisal two years earlier led an employee to improve his performance. Clearly, in most situations, an event should not carry more weight simply because it is more recent. This is one reason that decision makers need to consider the alternatives as fully as is reasonable.

### Stereotyping

**stereotypes**
Rigid opinions about categories of people.

Rigid opinions about categories of people are called **stereotypes.** Stereotyping interferes with rational decision making because it limits a decision maker's understanding of the people involved.[3] Stereotypes distort the truth that people offer a rich variety of individual strengths and viewpoints. For example, the stereotype that black people are athletic may seem flattering at face value but it is insulting and misleading when applied to a particular black employee whose strengths are reliability and a gift for public speaking. No doubt, this employee would prefer to be recognized on the basis of her unique talents than some stereotypical ones, and a supervisor who can do that will be best able to lead her.

## MEETING THE CHALLENGE

### *Be Decisive—Not Offensive*

Decision-making traps can snare almost anyone. It might seem ironic that decisiveness could actually render a supervisor ineffective as a manager, but critics believe this is the case of John P. DeVillars, the regional administrator for the New England office of the U.S. Environmental Protection Agency. "Given his ego and abrasive style, people in the region have generally given up trying to reason with him," observes one staffer.

Charged with a huge job—updating and rejuvenating a government agency that many believed had grown stagnant—DeVillars came to the post with a vision: He wanted to "reinvent" his agency's government. The problem was that he didn't communicate this vision to his employees. He made sweeping decisions, issued orders, and expected them to be carried out, but he was met with resistance and resentment. "Perhaps people are taking my impatience as arrogance and bullheadedness, but I'm impatient because we're dealing with some very big problems and we need to move fast to more effectively deal with those problems," explains DeVillars. Whereas it's true that responding quickly in a crisis can be considered a virtue in a supervisor, alienating everyone in the process will have its consequences, particularly when the changes are for the long term.

Without consulting managers and other staff who work in the field, DeVillars announced a reorganization that, according to Matt Schweisberg, senior wetlands ecologist at EPA, will actually impair efforts to protect wetlands because the new organization spreads too few specialists over too great an area. "To split [the work] up between six supervisors all trying to apply the same law, that's a recipe for disaster," he warns. Although staff meetings were held in which employees made recommendations about how to improve the agency, DeVillars implemented none of their suggestions, further reducing morale.

DeVillars has a reputation for taking a firm stand on tough issues. He scuttled a major highway project in New Hampshire despite its political support, and initiated a crackdown on some pollutants in the Charles River, which flows through Boston. But his lack of communication with his employees and his apparent unwillingness to consider their input in decisions may reduce his effectiveness as a supervisor over the long haul. It takes more than one person to protect New England's environment—and more than one supervisor to run the agency that does the protecting. DeVillars can't do it all by himself.

Source: Scott Allen, "Staff Polls Blast EPA's Leadership, Action Plan," *Boston Globe*, July 26, 1995, p. 22.

The cure for stereotyping is *not* to assume that everyone is alike. Not only does this assumption oversimplify the situation, but it is, in effect, an insult to other people. It ignores the strengths and values people receive from their culture. Rather, a supervisor should make a conscious, ongoing effort to learn about the various groups of people represented in the workplace. The purpose is to acquire information that serves as a starting point for understanding others while recognizing that individuals within any group are unique.

In addition, a supervisor needs to be aware of his or her own stereotypes about people and situations. In making a decision, a supervisor should consider whether those stereotypes truly describe the situation at hand.

## Guidelines for Decision Making

Should a supervisor always avoid human compromises in making decisions? Not necessarily. In some situations, seeking to match the rational model would be too costly and time-consuming. However, a supervisor has a variety of ways to make decisions more rationally. The following paragraphs provide further guidelines for making decisions in the workplace.

To train firefighting supervisors and their employees to make quick and accurate decisions in a crisis, AAI/MICROFLITE Simulation International has developed the AAI's Fire Trainer™.

Source: © Michael Melford

## Consider the Consequences

A supervisor should be aware of the possible consequences of a decision. For example, hiring and firing decisions can have great consequences for the performance of the department. Purchases of inexpensive items are less critical than purchases of major equipment and computer systems. Some decisions affect the safety of workers while others make only a slight difference in their comfort.

When the consequences of a decision are great, a supervisor should spend more time on the decision, following the rational model of decision making and seeking to include as many alternatives as possible. When the consequences of the decision are slight, a supervisor should limit the time and money spent in identifying and evaluating alternatives. A supervisor may choose to accept some of the human compromises described earlier.

## Respond Quickly in a Crisis

When a nuclear reactor is overheating, the supervisor has no time to weigh each employee's qualifications and to select the best employee for each task in handling the crisis. When a store's customer is shouting about poor service, the supervisor has no time to list all the possible responses. Both cases require fast action.

In a crisis, a supervisor should quickly select the course of action that seems best. This is an application of bounded rationality. Instead of waiting to evaluate other alternatives, the supervisor should begin implementing the solution and interpreting feedback to see whether the solution is working. Based on the feedback, the supervisor may modify the choice of a solution.

## Inform the Manager

A supervisor's manager does not want to hear about every minor decision the supervisor makes each day. However, the manager does need to know what is happening in the department, so the supervisor should inform the manager about

Source: Gary Blake, "Do You Use Weasel Words?" *Supervisory Management*, May 1995, p. 3.

## TIPS FROM THE FIRING LINE

### Use Decisive Words to Communicate Your Decision

You may not always be 100 percent certain about the decisions you make. But if you want people to take your decisions seriously, you need to communicate them in a decisive manner. Gary Blake, a writing consultant and author of several business books, recommends avoiding what he calls "weasel words"—phrases that hedge a decision and make the speaker seem unsure. Here are a few weasel words that can undermine a decision:

- "In my opinion" and "I think." Usually, a listener will know that you are giving your opinion, but your argument will be stronger if you omit the phrase.

- "To the best of my recollection." This suggests that you can't be blamed if you fail to remember something correctly.
- "As I understand it." If you are repeating information, just state it. Someone will correct you if you are wrong.
- "Probably." Use this word sparingly so that it doesn't lose its meaning.
- "I'll try." Another phrase that gets you off the hook if you don't succeed. It could easily be translated, "Don't count on me."

major decisions, including those that affect meeting departmental objectives, responses to a crisis, and any controversial decision.

When the manager needs to know about a decision, it is usually smart for a supervisor to discuss the problem before reaching and announcing the decision. The manager may see an aspect of the problem that has escaped the supervisor's attention or may have different priorities leading to a veto or modification of the supervisor's solution. For example, when a supervisor wanted to create a new position for a valued employee, her director gave approval on condition that the supervisor not increase her total budget (see the case in the Applications Module at the end of this chapter). Knowing and adjusting for such information while weighing the alternatives is less embarrassing to the supervisor and avoids annoying the manager. Of course, in a crisis, the supervisor may not have time to consult with the manager and will have to settle for discussing the decision as soon as possible afterward.

### Be Decisive Yet Flexible

Sometimes it is difficult to say which alternative solution is most likely to succeed or will bring the best results. Two alternatives may look equally good, or perhaps none of the choices look good enough. In such cases, a supervisor may find it hard to move beyond studying the alternatives to selecting and implementing one of them. However, avoiding a decision is merely another way of deciding to do nothing, and doing nothing is usually not the best choice. Furthermore, employees and peers find it frustrating to work with someone who never seems to make up his or her mind or get back to them with answers to their questions. Therefore, supervisors need to be decisive. (See "Tips from the Firing Line.")

Being decisive means reaching a decision within a reasonable amount of time. What is reasonable depends on the nature of the decision. For example, a supervisor should not spend hours deciding what assignments to give technicians each morning, but he or she would probably spend several days selecting a candidate to fill a job opening because this decision is more complex and its consequences are greater. The supervisor should pick the alternative that looks best (or at least acceptable) within the appropriate time frame for the decision, and then focus on implementing it.

Certain kinds of behavior are typical of a decisive supervisor.[4] A decisive supervisor quickly clears his or her desk of routine matters, promptly referring them to the proper people, and keeps work moving. A decisive supervisor assumes complete responsibility for getting the facts needed when he or she must solve a problem. Finally, a decisive supervisor keeps his or her employees informed of what they are expected to do and how they are progressing relative to their objectives.

Being decisive does not mean a supervisor is blind to signs that he or she has made a mistake. When implementing a solution, a supervisor needs to seek feedback that indicates whether the solution is working. If the first attempt at solving a problem fails, a supervisor must be flexible and try another approach.

## Avoid Decision-Making Traps

Some supervisors seem to delight in emergency deadlines and crisis situations, and they act as though each decision is a life-or-death issue. But good planning can avert many crises; life-or-death issues are not the usual stuff of a supervisor's job. Making a major issue out of each decision does not make the supervisor more important, but it does interfere with clear thinking. A supervisor must be able to put each issue into perspective so that he or she can calmly evaluate the alternatives and devote an appropriate amount of time to finding a solution.

Another trap for decision makers is responding inappropriately to failure. When a supervisor makes a wrong decision, the supervisor will look best if he or she acknowledges the mistake. Finding someone to blame only makes the supervisor seem irresponsible. At the same time, supervisors need not agonize over their mistakes. The constructive approach is to learn whatever lesson the mistake can teach and then to move on.

By trying to save time or work independently, some supervisors fail to draw on easily available information. One important source of information is precedent. Have some of the alternatives been tried before? If so, what was the outcome? Answering these questions can help a supervisor evaluate alternatives more realistically. For problems and decisions that are likely to recur, supervisors can set up a system for collecting information to use in future decisions. Ronald Mendell, a legal investigator in Austin, Texas, evaluates product failures by keeping records on a form that asks questions such as How did the product fail? What activities and processes were going on when the product failed? Where else is this product used? Answers that show a pattern help Mendell diagnose the underlying problem.[5] Similarly, by consulting with other members of the organization or with outside experts, a supervisor often can find readily available data that will improve his or her decision.

Sometimes supervisors are tempted to promise too much. This mistake traps many supervisors because the promises keep people happy—at least until they are broken. For example, a supervisor may promise an angry employee a raise before being sure the budget can handle it. This promise may solve the immediate problem of the employee's anger, but it will backfire if the supervisor cannot deliver the raise. Similarly, a supervisor may tell her manager that she can continue meeting existing deadlines even while a new computer system is being installed. She is not sure of this, but making the promise is a way of avoiding a confrontation with her manager (until the department does miss a deadline). Ultimately, everyone will be more pleased if supervisors make realistic promises. Then it is possible to arrive at solutions that will work as expected.

# Tools for Decision Making

In preparing a budget for next year, LaTanya Jones, manager of a store's appliance department, needed to determine how many sales associates should work each day of the week. At a factory that produces air conditioners, production supervisor Pete Yakimoto had to determine why the rate of defects was rising and what to do to correct the problem. Pete's employees complained that they were making mistakes because they had to work too fast, and Pete wondered if hiring more workers could be justified economically.

Problems such as these are difficult to solve mentally. Usually a supervisor facing such complex decisions needs tools and techniques for analyzing the alternatives. Some widely used tools are probability theory, decision trees, and computer software.

## Probability Theory

Sometimes a supervisor needs to choose which course of action will have the greatest benefit (or least cost), but a supervisor cannot completely control the outcome. Therefore, a supervisor cannot be 100 percent sure what the outcome will be. For example, a sales supervisor can tell salespeople whom to call on but cannot control the behavior of the customers. Pete Yakimoto in the previous example can recommend that new workers be hired, but he has only limited control over how the workers will perform. In statistical terms, situations with uncertain outcomes involve risk.

**probability theory**
A body of techniques for comparing the consequences of possible decisions in a risk situation.

To make decisions about risk situations, a supervisor can compare the consequences of several decisions by using **probability theory.** To use this theory, a supervisor needs to know or be able to estimate the value of each possible outcome and the likelihood (probability) that this outcome will occur. For example, a production supervisor is comparing two stamping presses. The supervisor wants to use a press to produce $1 million in parts per year. Press A costs $900,000, and Press B costs $800,000. Based on the suppliers' claims and track record, the supervisor believes there is a 90 percent chance that Press A will last 10 years (thus producing $10 million in parts) and only a 10 percent chance that it will fail after 5 years (thus producing $5 million in parts). The supervisor believes there is a 30 percent chance that Press B will fail after five years.

To use probability theory to make decisions about risk situations, the supervisor can begin by putting the possible outcomes into table format. Table 9.1 shows the possible outcomes for the stamping presses. In this case, the supervisor subtracted the cost of the press from the value of what the press could produce in 5 or 10 years. Notice that because Press B is cheaper, the possible outcomes for that press are greater. Remember, however, that Press B is also more likely to fail after five years. To find the *expected* value (*EV*) of each possible outcome, multiply the

## TABLE 9.1

**Possible Outcomes for a Risk Situation**

|  | Five Years of Production | Ten Years of Production |
|---|---|---|
| Press A | \$5 million − \$900,000 = \$4.1 million | \$10 million − \$900,000 = \$9.1 million |
| Press B | \$5 million − \$800,000 = \$4.2 million | \$10 million − \$800,000 = \$9.2 million |

Note: Outcomes are computed as value of production minus cost of press.

## TABLE 9.2

**Expected Value of Possibilities**

|  | Five Years of Production | Ten Years of Production |
|---|---|---|
| Press A | \$4.1 million × .10 = \$410,000 | \$9.1 million × .90 = \$8.2 million |
| Press B | \$4.2 million × .30 = \$1.3 million | \$9.2 million × .70 = \$6.4 million |

Note: Values are computed as possible outcomes (from Table 9.1) times probability of outcome.

possible outcome ($O$) by the probability of that outcome ($P$). Stated as a formula, $EV = O \times P$. Table 9.2 shows the results of this computation. The supervisor should select the press with the highest expected value, in this case, Press A.

### Decision Trees

In the real world, most decisions involving probability are at least as complex as the example of purchasing machinery. Sorting out the relative value of the choices can be easier with the use of a graph. Thus, a supervisor may find it helpful to use a decision tree for making decisions in risk situations. A **decision tree** is a graph that helps in decision making by showing the expected values of decisions under varying circumstances.

**decision tree**
A graph that helps decision makers use probability theory by showing the expected values of decisions under varying circumstances.

As depicted in Figure 9.4, a decision tree shows the available alternatives, which stem from decision points. For each alternative, one of several chance events may occur. As before, the decision maker estimates the probability of each chance event occurring. To find the expected value of each outcome, the decision maker multiplies the probability by the value of the outcome ($EV = O \times P$). The decision maker should select the alternative for which the expected value is greatest.

For example (see Figure 9.4), a sales supervisor is trying to decide whether to hire a new salesperson at a salary of \$40,000. The supervisor estimates that with the new salesperson on board, there is a 60 percent chance that the department's sales will increase from \$200,000 to \$250,000. Without the new salesperson, the chance for the sales increase is only 50 percent. The supervisor assumes that, at worst, the department will hold steady in either case. The dollar value of each possible outcome is the amount of sales minus the cost of the choice (hiring or not hiring). To find the expected value of each choice, the supervisor multiplies the probability of each outcome by the value of that outcome. Assuming there is a 60 percent chance of sales increasing if the supervisor hires that salesperson (and a 40

**FIGURE 9.4**
A Simple Decision Tree

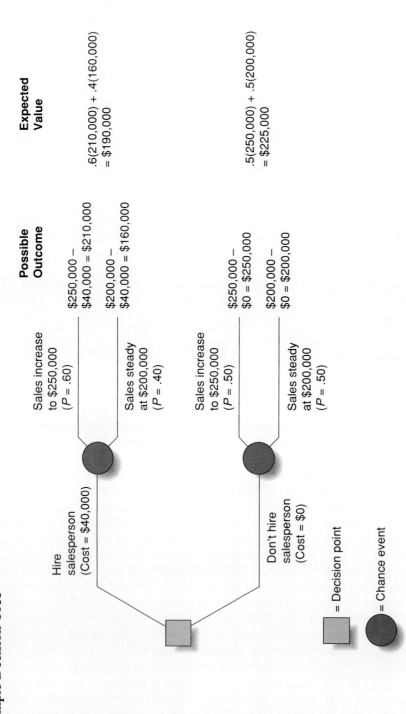

percent chance of sales remaining steady), the expected value of hiring is .60($210,000) + .40($160,000), or $190,000. The expected value of not hiring is $225,000. Based on the greater expected value for not hiring, the supervisor would decide that it makes more economic sense not to hire a salesperson at this time.

### Computer Software

**decision-making software**
A computer program that leads the user through the steps of the formal decision-making process.

Some computer programs have been developed to help people make decisions. This **decision-making software** leads the user through the steps of the formal decision-making process (see Figure 9.1). Besides having the user identify alternatives, the programs ask the user about his or her values and priorities.

For help in sorting out information, a supervisor might also use spreadsheet or database management software. Spreadsheet software, such as Lotus 1-2-3, Excel, and SuperCalc, helps the user organize numbers into rows and columns; it can automatically perform computations such as adding a column of numbers. A database management program, such as Access or Paradox, systematically stores large amounts of data and makes it easy for the user to request and retrieve specific categories of data. A computerized index of periodicals at your library is an example of this kind of software. In addition, software companies are continually developing new ways to help users find and manipulate information. For example, a program called MailBag lets users retrieve E-mail messages containing a specified word, phrase, or number.[6]

These kinds of computer software do not make decisions for supervisors, but they can make it easier for supervisors to organize their thoughts and gather information. A supervisor still must creatively identify alternatives and use his or her judgment in selecting the best solution.

## Group Decision Making

Some organizations allow or expect supervisors to work with a team or other group in arriving at a decision. For example, a supervisor might seek input from a team of employees in deciding how to meet production targets or encourage them to come up with a solution among themselves. The supervisor also might call on peers in other departments to share their expertise. In the Applications Module at the end of this chapter, a supervisor relies on her staff's input in deciding how to improve the quality of care at the hospital where they work.

### Advantages and Disadvantages

Group decision making has some advantages over going it alone. Group members can contribute more ideas for alternatives than an individual could think of alone. Since people tend to draw on their own experiences when generating and evaluating alternatives, a group will look at a problem from a broader perspective. This is important because, as Clark Wigley notes, problems are like beach balls: There is no one place you can stand on the ball and see the whole ball. Likewise, he explains:

> No matter where you stand in an organization, regardless of how much you get paid, how many degrees you have, or how many years of experience, there is no place where you can stand and see the whole problem.[7]

**FIGURE 9.5**

**A Potential Drawback of Group Decision Making**

Source: DILBERT reprinted by permission of United Feature Syndicate, Inc.

Also, people who are involved in coming up with a solution are more likely to support the implementation of that solution. They will better understand why the solution was selected and how it is supposed to work, and they will tend to think of it as *their* solution. (Chapter 3 elaborates on ways organizations are enjoying these benefits by establishing self-managing work teams and transforming the supervisor's role from commander to coach.)

Of course, group decision making also has disadvantages. First, an individual usually can settle on a decision faster than a group. Figure 9.5 illustrates this disadvantage humorously. Second, there is a cost to the organization when employees spend their time in meetings instead of producing or selling. A third drawback is that the group can reach an inferior decision by letting one person or a small subgroup dominate the process. Finally, groups sometimes fall victim to **groupthink,** or the failure to think independently and realistically that results when group members prefer to enjoy consensus and closeness.[8] Here are some symptoms of groupthink:

**groupthink**
The failure to think independently and realistically as a group because of the desire to enjoy consensus and closeness.

- An illusion of being invulnerable.
- Defending the group's position against any objections.
- A view that the group is clearly moral, "the good guys."
- Stereotyped views of opponents.
- Pressure against group members who disagree.
- Self-censorship, that is, not allowing oneself to disagree.
- An illusion that everyone agrees (because no one states an opposing view).
- Self-appointed "mindguards," or people who urge other group members to go along with the group.

During the making of the movie *The Bonfire of the Vanities*, many of the people involved had doubts about casting decisions and changes in the story line, but they did not tell the director, Brian DePalma. DePalma wondered about the wisdom of some of the decisions, but because no one objected, he convinced himself that his decisions were correct. Perhaps that is why the $50 million movie was a flop at the box office.[9]

When a supervisor notices that his or her group is showing the symptoms of groupthink, it is time to question whether the group is really looking for solutions. A supervisor who also is the group leader should draw forth a variety of viewpoints by inviting suggestions and encouraging group members to listen with an open mind. Another way to overcome groupthink is to appoint one group member to act as devil's advocate, challenging the position of the majority. When the group has reached a decision, the leader also can suggest that everyone sleep on it and settle on a final decision at a follow-up meeting.

## Using Group Decision Making

Given the advantages and disadvantages of group decision making, a supervisor would be wise to involve employees in some but not all decisions. When a decision must be made quickly, as in an emergency, a supervisor should make it alone. Individual decisions also are appropriate when the potential benefit of a decision is so small that the cost of working as a group to make the decision is not justified. But when a supervisor needs to build support for a solution, such as measures to cut costs or improve productivity, the group process is useful. Group decision making also can be beneficial when the consequences of a poor decision are great; the benefits of a group's collective wisdom are worth the time and expense of gathering the input.

A supervisor can have a group actually make the decision, or a group may simply provide input, leaving more decision-making responsibility to the supervisor. For example, a supervisor might ask a group only to generate alternatives. If a group is to make the decision, a supervisor may let group members select any alternative, or a supervisor may give the group a few alternatives from which to choose. Whenever supervisors ask for input, they should be sure they intend to use the information. Employees are quickly wise to—and offended by—a supervisor who only pretends to be interested in their ideas.

### Encouraging Participation

Since a main benefit of making decisions as a group is the variety of opinions and expertise available, a supervisor leading a decision-making meeting should be sure that everyone is participating. One basic way of encouraging participation is for a supervisor to avoid monopolizing the discussion. The supervisor should focus on hearing participants' opinions. Also, some group members will find it easier than others to speak up. The supervisor should notice which participants are quiet and should ask their opinions about specific topics being discussed. Finally, a supervisor can encourage participation by reacting positively when people contribute ideas. A barrage of criticism or ridicule will quickly discourage group members from speaking.

Andrew S. Grove, the chief executive of Intel Corporation, recommends an interesting approach to group decision making. First, the supervisor assembles the group and spends plenty of time describing the problem to be solved. The supervisor should not assume that employees understand the problem as well as he or she does, but should allow enough time for employees to ask questions. Then the supervisor divides the employees into groups with a variety of levels and specialties represented in each group. The supervisor assigns each group a task and a

## FIGURE 9.6

**The Brainstorming Process**

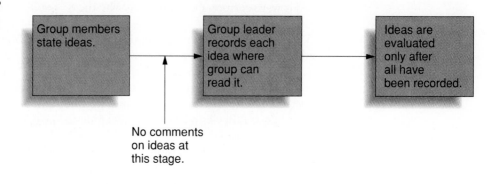

Group members state ideas. → Group leader records each idea where group can read it. → Ideas are evaluated only after all have been recorded.

No comments on ideas at this stage.

deadline and asks the groups to report on their progress at the next meeting. In this way, the supervisor stimulates the employees by delegating responsibility and giving them all a chance to excel in front of their peers.[10]

### Brainstorming

**brainstorming**

An idea-generating process in which group members state their ideas, a member of the group records them, and no one may comment on the ideas until the process is complete.

Another way to generate ideas in a group is to use brainstorming. **Brainstorming** is an idea-generating process (see Figure 9.6) in which group members state their ideas, no matter how far-fetched these may seem. A member of the group records all the ideas, and no one may criticize or even comment on them until the end of the process. To enforce this rule, the supervisor might try the tactic used by Armstrong International's David M. Armstrong. At a meeting called to generate new-product ideas, Armstrong handed each employee an M&M candy and said, "You are allowed one negative comment during the meeting. Once you make that comment, you must eat your M&M. If you don't have an M&M in front of you, you can't say anything negative." As a result, the group members willingly collaborated on an idea.[11]

Hearing other people's ideas often stimulates the thinking of group members. The supervisor can further open people's thought processes through such mind-expanding tactics as meeting in the work area rather than the usual conference room, asking people outside the group to identify problems, or asking employees to prepare for the meeting by individually listing problems to name at the meeting.[12] Once all the ideas are listed, the group can evaluate those that hold the most promise.

## Creativity

Rebecca Liss, a branch operations manager with Kemper Securities, had to be creative when she hired Gail as a new employee. With Gail on board, Liss's group was larger than it ever had been, but there was no money in the budget for additional office space or a computer terminal for Gail. That meant two employees would somehow have to share a terminal. Working with her staff, Liss developed the idea to arrange the desks into an island formation with a computer terminal between the two employees who were to share it.

Creative thinking helped Wendy Wigtil develop her product: cloth designs for children to color. It also helped her company, Barnyard Babies, Inc., based in Annapolis, Maryland, to survive. During slow domestic growth, she explored the global marketplace. Exporting to Japan, France, and Canada has increased the profit margin and put her company in the black.

Source: © Ken Touchton

**creativity**
The ability to bring about something imaginative or new.

This example shows how creative thinking can lead to excellent solutions. **Creativity** is the ability to bring about something imaginative or new. With decision making, it means being able to generate innovative or different alternatives from those used in the past. When a problem seems unsolvable, the supervisor especially needs creativity to find a fresh approach.

A common notion is that some people are creative, whereas the rest of us are stuck with following routine and ordinary courses of action. Taking the Self-Quiz on page 270 will provide you with a measure of the state of your own creative skills. If you do not score as high as you would like, take heart—the evidence suggests that people can develop their ability to be creative.

### Thinking More Creatively

A fundamental way to become more creative is to be open to your own ideas. When trying to solve a problem, think of as many alternatives as you can. Jot them all down without rejecting any; evaluate them only when you are done. This is like the group process of brainstorming. When you can, brainstorming with a group can help stimulate the creativity of the other participants as well as your own. Whether you are alone or in a group, practice should help your ideas flow more easily.

Years ago, advertising executive James Webb Young described a five-step technique for generating creative ideas:[13]

1. Gather the raw materials by learning about the problem and developing your general knowledge. Young says, "Constantly expanding your experience, both personally and vicariously, [matters] tremendously in an idea-producing job."[14]
2. Work over those materials in your mind. As you think of partial ideas, jot them down so you can refer to them later.

3. Incubate; let your unconscious mind do the work. Instead of thinking about the problem, do whatever stimulates your imagination and emotions, such as listening to music.
4. Identify an idea. It will probably pop into your head unexpectedly.
5. Shape and develop the idea to make it practical. Seek out constructive criticism.

Two decades after Young developed this technique, it still remains practical.

Young points out that creative thinking is not always a conscious process. Sometimes creative ideas come from dreaming or daydreaming, or they will come to you while you are doing something else. If you are stuck on a problem, leave it for a while. Walk the dog, take a shower, work on a different task. Above all, do not neglect time for resting and daydreaming. If you are trying to solve the problem as a group, and the discussion is not going anywhere, adjourn or at least take a break, and then continue the discussion later.

Some people find it worthwhile to call in an expert who can provide training in thinking more creatively. More than half of the Fortune 500 companies have provided employees with training programs in creativity.[15] Other experts provide consulting services. Consultant William J. J. Gordon once advised a small company that had to tackle the problem of potato chips: They take up too much shelf space but packing them more tightly causes them to crumble. Gordon asked, "What in nature reminds you of potato chips?" Someone compared chips to dried leaves; both crumble when pressed together. That thought led someone else to observe that *wet* leaves will pack together without crumbling. With that inspiration, the group came up with the idea of shaping potato slices before they dry—a process the group later sold to Procter & Gamble for use in making Pringles potato chips.[16] The creative tactic this group used—looking for analogies—could be used by any group in creative problem solving.

### Establishing and Maintaining a Creative Work Climate

A supervisor can benefit from the entire work group's creativity by establishing a work climate that encourages creative thinking. The most important step a supervisor can take in this regard is to show that he or she values creativity. When employees offer suggestions, a supervisor should listen attentively and look for the positive aspects of the suggestions. A supervisor should attempt to implement employees' ideas and should give them credit.

When ideas fail, a supervisor should acknowledge that failure is a sign that people are trying. A supervisor should help employees see what can be learned from the failure. The aim is to avoid discouraging employees from making more suggestions in the future.

### Overcoming Barriers to Creativity

Often supervisors and employees have difficulty being creative because they are afraid their ideas will fail. A supervisor can overcome this barrier by accepting that failures by employees will occur. Overcoming your own fear of failure is more challenging; indeed, the organization may not always reward creativity. The best the supervisor can do is to keep in mind that a lack of creativity will probably prevent big successes as well as big failures.

If an idea does fail, a supervisor should acknowledge the problem and not try to pass the blame on to someone else. The emphasis should be on finding a solution, not on placing blame. Most managers admire supervisors who try ideas after careful thought and who focus on learning from mistakes rather than passing blame. A supervisor who prepares contingency plans (see Chapter 6) and is prepared to focus on solutions is likely to impress his or her superiors, even when the specific idea does not work out as hoped.

Another barrier to creativity is being overly busy. As described earlier, creative thinking requires time for quiet and rest. If a supervisor cannot get these at the workplace, he or she needs to allow time for thinking elsewhere—at home, while walking in the woods, while driving. For example, the supervisor can turn off the television for a while each evening. Besides reflection, another good substitute for TV watching is reading. (The imagination required to read a book actually helps people develop their ability to think, but the average American adult reads only 24 minutes a day.[17])

Isolation also interferes with creativity. Supervisors need to talk to co-workers in other departments of the organization. They need to talk and listen to their employees. Colleagues in other organizations can be a good source of ideas, as can friends and family members. However, the supervisor must be careful about spending a great deal of time with the same few people. They are less likely to be sources of fresh ideas than are new or less familiar acquaintances.

# Summary

### 9.1 Identify the steps in the rational model of decision making.

According to the rational model, the decision maker first identifies the problem and then identifies the alternative solutions. Next, he or she gathers and organizes facts. The decision maker evaluates the alternatives and then chooses and implements the best alternative. Finally, he or she gets feedback and takes corrective action.

### 9.2 Discuss ways people make compromises in following the decision-making model.

People usually simplify the rational approach to decision making, selecting an alternative that they have tried before and has delivered acceptable results. Choosing an alternative that meets minimum standards of acceptability is a form of bounded rationality. People tend to analyze alternatives subjectively, relying on intuition and instinct, and they tend to favor solutions they can justify. People's analyses also tend to be clouded by adoption of a personal perspective, the tendency to remember recent events best, and the use of stereotypes.

### 9.3 Describe guidelines for making decisions.

Supervisors should be aware of the possible consequences of their decisions. In a crisis, a supervisor should respond quickly. With regard to crises and other situations that influence the department's performance, a supervisor should inform his or her manager about the decision, if possible, before making it. Supervisors should be decisive but flexible. They should avoid decision-making traps such as treating all problems as crises, responding inappropriately to failure, failing to draw on available information, and promising too much.

### 9.4 Explain how probability theory, decision trees, and computer software can help in making decisions.

Probability theory defines the expected value of an outcome in a risk situation as the value of the possible outcome times the probability of that outcome. The decision maker using this theory selects the outcome with the greatest expected value. A decision tree is a graph that shows the expected values of decisions under varying circumstances. Thus, it helps the decision maker use probability theory. Decision-making software leads the user through the rational decision-making process, and spreadsheet and database management software helps users organize their information. The software does not make the decision, but it helps the user think through the problem more logically.

### 9.5 Discuss advantages and disadvantages of making decisions in groups.

Group members can contribute more ideas for alternatives than an individual could alone. Also, people who are involved in coming up with a solution are more likely to support its implementation. Disadvantages are that groups make decisions more slowly than individuals, the process is more costly, and groups may fall victim to groupthink, actually suppressing different viewpoints.

### 9.6 Describe guidelines for group decision making.

A supervisor can benefit from group decision making when time permits and when the consequences of a poor decision justify the cost of group decision making. Group decision making is also useful when a supervisor needs to build support for the alternative selected. The group may actually make the decision, or it may provide input such as suggested alternatives, letting the supervisor make the final decision. A supervisor leading a decision-making meeting should make sure that everyone is participating and should react positively when they do so.

Brainstorming, in which members state their ideas no matter how far-fetched they may seem, often helps stimulate the thinking of group members.

### 9.7 Describe guidelines for thinking creatively.

A fundamental way to become more creative is to be open to your own ideas. When trying to solve a problem, think of as many alternatives as you can, without rejecting any. Some people use the five-step technique: gathering raw materials, thinking about the materials, incubating, identifying an idea, and shaping and developing the idea. Creative thinking is not always conscious; dreaming, daydreaming, and engaging in distracting activities actually can help generate ideas.

### 9.8 Discuss how supervisors can establish and maintain a creative work climate.

Supervisors should show that they value creativity. They should listen to and encourage suggestions. When ideas fail, supervisors should acknowledge that failure is a sign that people are trying. Instead of focusing on blaming, the supervisor should see what lessons can be learned from the failure.

### 9.9 Identify ways to overcome barriers to creativity.

Some barriers to creativity are fear of failure, excessive busyness, and isolation. To overcome these barriers, supervisors need to remember that failing inevitably accompanies trying, to set aside time for thinking and resting, and to communicate with co-workers and peers in other organizations.

## Key Terms

| | | |
|---|---|---|
| decision | stereotypes | groupthink |
| bounded rationality | probability theory | brainstorming |
| recency syndrome | decision tree | creativity |
| | decision-making software | |

# Review and Discussion Questions

1. Andrea is in charge of scheduling the work for the service department of a car dealership. Lately, people in the sales department have been taking telephone calls from customers and promising that service work could be completed on a certain day or by a certain time. Consequently, everyone is unhappy—mechanics, salespeople, customers, and Andrea—because the work schedule is disrupted and the service department can't keep up with the promises made to customers. Using the rational model of decision making, what steps might Andrea take to correct the situation?

2. Define *bounded rationality*. Describe a situation in which you resorted to bounded rationality as a method of decision making. What were the results of your decision? Do you think this was the best way to make a decision under the circumstances? Why or why not?

3. Franklin Jones, a supervisor in the buying department for a department store, says, "I think these men's jackets are going to be hot this fall. Let's place a big order." What kind of compromises to rational decision making is he using in making his decision? Using the decision-making model, what would be a more rational approach?

4. In each of the following situations, what is interfering with the supervisor's ability to make the best decision? Suggest how the supervisors can improve their decision making.

   a. "I think this new answering machine model should be blue," said the design supervisor. "I like blue."
   b. "Let's conduct training at three o'clock on Fridays," said the customer service supervisor. "After all, it's been slow the last couple of Friday afternoons."
   c. "I'll bet we could boost sales by attracting more women," said the sales manager at an auto dealership. "To generate some traffic, we could hold a little fashion show or a makeup demonstration or something like that every week or so."

5. This chapter presents several guidelines for decision making: Consider the consequences, respond quickly in a crisis, inform the manager, be decisive but not inflexible, and avoid decision-making traps. How would such guidelines influence the way a nursing supervisor handles the following two situations?

   a. The supervisor is scheduling nurses for the next month.
   b. One of the nurses calls on Friday afternoon to say her father just died, so she will be out next week.

6. Philip is a supervisor who likes to work independently. Whenever he faces a new situation, he prefers to analyze it and make his decision without consulting other sources. How might this method of decision making impact the results of his decision? What might be a better way for Philip to proceed?

7. Rita McCormick is the supervisor of the state office that processes sales tax payments. She has noticed that workers are falling behind and wants to get authorization either to hire two more employees or to schedule overtime until the work gets caught up. Rita estimates that there is an 80 percent chance the workload will continue to be this high and a 20 percent chance that work will fall back to previous levels, which the current employees can handle during regular working hours. (She assumes there is no chance of less work

in the future.) Because she will have to pay time and a half for overtime, she assumes that the annual cost of overtime will be $150,000, whereas a workforce with two more employees will cost only $140,000.

    *a.* Construct a decision tree for this problem.
    *b.* Which alternative should the supervisor choose?

8. What are some advantages of making decisions as a group? What are some disadvantages?

9. What are the symptoms of groupthink? What can a supervisor do to overcome groupthink in a team meeting?

10. Roberto Gonzalez wants to make his solutions more creative. When he has a problem to solve, he sits down at his desk and tries to generate as many alternative solutions as he can. Unfortunately, he usually gets frustrated before he comes up with an alternative that satisfies him, so he just picks an acceptable solution and tries to implement it. How can Roberto modify his decision-making process to come up with more creative ideas?

11. How can supervisors foster creativity in their department or work group?

## A SECOND LOOK

In the story at the beginning of the chapter, Mike Rakosnik maintains a creative work climate. Does this mean that he lets his employees do whatever they want? What clues in the story might give you the answer?

# APPLICATIONS MODULE

## CASE

### *The Satisfaction of Solving Problems*

Marilyn Bowie is a nurse manager for obstetrical care at St. Joseph's Hospital and Medical Center in Phoenix, Arizona. She supervises 80 employees, including nurses, nursing assistants, student assistants, and unit secretaries. As a supervisor, Bowie has to solve different kinds of problems than those she faced as a nurse. As a nurse, she made life-and-death decisions pertaining to individual patients. As a supervisor, Bowie solves problems involving the support of the people who now make those life-and-death decisions. She considers problem solving to be the most satisfying part of her job.

One problem that Bowie solved concerned staffing her unit. One of Bowie's employees had attended school for a while and eventually received her degree. At that time, the employee wanted a new job. Bowie considered the consequences of losing a valued employee and informed her own director of the situation. Bowie and her director valued the employee's strengths, such as courtesy and willingness to work, so Bowie was able to persuade her director to create a new position for the valued employee. The employee now handles secretarial duties and also teaches the nurses and managers how to use the hospital's computers. Bowie says creating the job for this employee "has been paid back tenfold," thanks to the employee's talents.

Bowie then had to make some decisions involving the entire structure of her unit. She observed that the staff were not educating new mothers at the hospital as well as they should and that they were sometimes not discharging mothers and babies properly. Bowie met with her staff as a group to discuss her observations. They concluded that the problem lay with having separate nurses for the mothers and their new babies. The group developed the idea of "couplet nursing" at St. Joseph's, that is, a system in which each mother and her baby are cared for by the same nurse. Bowie formed a task force of staff members that meets regularly to continue discussing ideas to make the new system work better. According to Bowie, "group consensus was very important" in making the new system work.

1. What are some decision-making traps that Bowie avoided by proceeding the way she did in each of the situations described above?
2. If Bowie had chosen to make decisions on her own about the new mothers and their infants, do you think she would have come up with as creative a solution? Why or why not?
3. Would you want to work for a supervisor like Marilyn Bowie? Why or why not?

**S E L F - Q U I Z**

### How Creative Is Your Thinking?

Circle a number next to each statement to indicate whether that statement is true of you always, often, seldom, or never.

|  | Always | Often | Seldom | Never |
|---|---|---|---|---|
| 1. You are stimulated by complex problems and situations that tax your thinking. | 4 | 3 | 2 | 1 |
| 2. You dislike the sort of rigid problem solving that attacks every single problem with a similar, mechanical approach. | 4 | 3 | 2 | 1 |
| 3. You encourage open discussion and disagreement among your people. | 4 | 3 | 2 | 1 |
| 4. You read voraciously to expand your experience. | 4 | 3 | 2 | 1 |
| 5. You entertain new ideas with enthusiasm rather than skepticism. | 4 | 3 | 2 | 1 |
| 6. You ask numerous questions, never worrying about whether they reveal your ignorance. | 4 | 3 | 2 | 1 |
| 7. You look at things from a variety of viewpoints before making a decision. | 4 | 3 | 2 | 1 |
| 8. You surround yourself with people who promote distinctly different points of view. | 4 | 3 | 2 | 1 |
| 9. You make decisions that others call "innovative." | 4 | 3 | 2 | 1 |
| 10. You search for new and better ways of approaching work within your organizations. | 4 | 3 | 2 | 1 |

The more each statement describes you, the higher your creative abilities.

Source: Craig R. Hickman and Michael A. Silva, "What's Your Creativity Quotient?" *Working Woman*, Sept. 1985, p. 30.

## *Class Exercise*

You learned in this chapter ("Problem Solving and Decision Making") that a major challenge in the problem-solving process is generating creative solutions. As supervisors work to get their teams involved in this process, it helps to understand the various working styles that each member prefers. Wilson Learning Corporation, a worldwide training firm, has developed a comprehensive training program titled "The Innovation Series" that examines strategic innovation management and its role in quality improvement and employee empowerment.*

The four *Innovation Styles* (trademark of Global Creativity Corporation) that Wilson Learning identifies are as follows:

| Style | Approach | Contribution to Team |
|---|---|---|
| **Modifying** | "Modifiers" are stimulated by facts and make decisions based on them. They prefer to move forward one step at a time, building on what is known and proven. | Modifiers add stability and thoroughness to a team's creative process. |
| **Exploring** | "Explorers" are stimulated by insights and use them to gather more information. They thrive on the unknown and the unpredictable and are comfortable challenging assumptions and using analogies to approach problems from new angles. | Explorers contribute to teams by questioning basic assumptions and models. |
| **Visioning** | "Visioners" are stimulated by insights and make decisions based on those insights. They focus on ideal results and let those images guide them. | Visioners provide teams with long-term direction and momentum. |
| **Experimenting** | "Experimenters" are stimulated by facts and use them to gather more information. They generate new ideas by combining established processes. | Experimenters contribute to teams by combining input from everyone to ensure workable, consensus-based solutions. |

Wilson Learning Corporation has developed a quick quiz† (see page 272) to help you determine your style.

---

*Permission granted by Wilson Learning Corporation, Eden Prairie, MN (800–328–7937), to provide this brief introduction to The Innovation Series.

†The quiz is an adaptation of a fully validated instrument and has no research compiled as to its validity. For information on the fully validated instrument that is adapted here, please call the number above.

## *Instructions*

1. For each of the following eight statements, divide a total of five points between the two possible responses. Assign the most points to the statement that you identify with the most. If you give five points to one option, give zero points to the other. If you give four points to one option, give one point to the other, and so on.

2. As you consider each statement, keep this question in mind: "How do I handle challenges most successfully in my current job?" If you are a full-time student not currently employed, ask yourself, "How do I handle most successfully the challenges I face as I pursue my education?"

---

1. I like solving problems best when
   _____ *a.* there are some standard ways to go about solving them.
   _____ *b.* there needs to be a new way to go about solving them.
2. One of my strengths is
   _____ *c.* seeing how different ideas and viewpoints can be related.
   _____ *d.* being highly committed to making things work.
3. I can help innovation by making sure there is
   _____ *a.* steadiness and thoroughness when developing new ideas.
   _____ *b.* open-mindedness to a wide range of assumptions and ideas.
4. Sometimes, I might hinder constructive change by
   _____ *c.* "leaving others behind" when I focus on future goals.
   _____ *d.* getting lost in the details of implementation and forgetting the goal.
5. I am best at solving problems that
   _____ *a.* are specific and have a single, best answer.
   _____ *b.* need many perspectives and alternatives to be considered.
6. I am most successful when I deal with
   _____ *c.* insights and connections among ideas.
   _____ *d.* detailed, factual information.
7. I like to find solutions by
   _____ *a.* applying expert ideas in new ways.
   _____ *b.* using metaphors and analogies for new insights.
8. I like to find solutions by
   _____ *c.* imagining the best possible outcome for everyone.
   _____ *d.* combining the most practical ideas of many people.

---

Source: Adapted from Craig Steinburg, "Computing Your Innovation Style," *Training & Development*, Dec. 1992, p. 11.

3. Transfer your points to the following chart:

| Statement | a | b | c | d |
|---|---|---|---|---|
| 1 | | | | |
| 2 | | | | |
| 3 | | | | |
| 4 | | | | |
| 5 | | | | |
| 6 | | | | |
| 7 | | | | |
| 8 | | | | |
| Total points | | | | |
| Style | Modifying | Exploring | Visioning | Experimenting |

You probably use a combination of the four Innovation Styles; however, your highest score identifies your preferred style. Supervisors must learn to appreciate and encourage the use of all four styles in the problem-solving process.

## Team-Building Exercise

### Brainstorming a Cost-Control Solution

Divide the class into groups of five or six people. Each group will brainstorm solutions for the following problem: The head librarian for an art museum has been directed to cut library expenses by 15 percent. The library currently operates during the same hours as the museum (10:00 A.M. to 5:00 P.M. every day except Wednesday, when the museum is open until 9:00 P.M.). Half of the library's budget goes for the salaries of the head librarian, two reference librarians, and a clerk. One-quarter of the budget goes to purchase books and periodicals, and another one-quarter goes to operating expenses such as the library's share of heat and lighting. Given this information, how can the library cut expenses with a minimal impact on the quality of its service?

1. Each group picks a facilitator to record its ideas.
2. Group members suggest ideas, and the facilitator writes them down where everyone can see them. No one is to comment on the ideas at this point.

3. When group members feel they are out of ideas, the group discusses the ideas listed and picks the most promising one(s). The facilitator should try to make sure that all group members contribute to this discussion.
4. As a class, discuss the following questions:

   a. Did hearing other people's ideas help you come up with more ideas?
   b. How did it feel to hear ideas without commenting on them? How did it feel to express ideas, knowing that no one was allowed to criticize them?
   c. How well did your group carry out this assignment? What could it have done better? Was it difficult to get everyone to participate?
   d. Is brainstorming an appropriate technique for solving a problem such as this? Why or why not?

# Video Exercise 9: *Problem Solving and Decision Making*

## *Video Summary*

Managers at all levels of an organization continually engage in decision making. Because approximately 50 percent of a supervisor's time is spent dealing with the consequences of bad decisions, the quality of the decisions the supervisor makes is very important. This video examines six steps in the decision-making process: (1) identify the problem, (2) generate alternative courses of action, (3) evaluate the alternatives, (4) select the best alternative, (5) implement the decision, and (6) evaluate the decision. Intuition, emotion and stress, framing, escalation of commitment, and confidence and risk propensity also influence the decision-making process. You will see how the managers and supervisors at the Heavenly Ski Resort and Second City Theater have made decisions affecting their respective organizations.

## *Application*

After completing the Self-Quiz, "How Creative Is Your Thinking?" at the end of this chapter, you may decide that you need to work to enhance your creative abilities. Here are some mental aerobic exercises that you can try.

1. Between now and the next class session, select three items from the list of mental aerobic exercises presented below.
2. At the next class session, use one of the following formats to report the results of your creativity conditioning.
   a. Write a two- to three-paragraph paper for your instructor in which you highlight some positive/negative results of your "mental workouts."
   b. Take a few minutes at the beginning of class to have several students describe the results of their participation in these mental conditioning exercises.
   c. Break into groups of three or four students and share some outcomes of your participation in this exercise.

## Mental Aerobic Exercises

❑ If you're right-handed, try using your left hand to do things. If you're left-handed, switch to your right hand for awhile.
❑ Do a jigsaw or crossword puzzle.
❑ Try a new way of expressing your creativity; for example, cook something you've never made before, paint a picture, write a poem, or give a party with an interesting theme.
❑ Guess at measurements instead of using a ruler, tape measure, or measuring cup. Then measure and see how close you were.
❑ Watch three-quarters of a movie on video, stop the tape, and think of your own ending.
❑ Stretch your thinking beyond what might be your typical approach to solving problems. Try to solve one of these brainteasers (your instructor has the answers):

1. Arrange the letters below into one word:

    NEW DOOR

2. Change the roman numeral that represents the number 9

    IX

    into a 6 by using only one line.

3. Determine in what order the numbers below are arranged.

    8, 5, 4, 9, 1, 7, 6, 3, 2, 0

❑ Go to the library and look up an article or find a biography about a famous creative person (e.g., Thomas Edison, Walt Disney, Steven Spielberg) and spend 20 minutes skimming the material, looking for insights into the creative process. For example, Thomas Edison is considered to be the most prolific inventor the world has ever known. Among his inventions are the incandescent light, the phonograph, and the motion-picture projector. Edison is reported to have said, "[Creative] genius is 99 percent perspiration and 1 percent inspiration."

❑ Go to a day care center and spend a half hour observing two-, three-, and four-year-olds at play. Jot down any "creative" things you observe the children doing. ("Tests show that a child's creativity plummets 90 percent between ages five and seven. By the age of 40 most adults are about 2 percent as creative as they were at 5."[1])

Source: Corinne R. Livesay, *Strengthen Your Skills: A Skills-Building Manual* (Burr Ridge, IL: Austen Press/Irwin, 1995), pp. 135–6.

### Resources for Further Information

Albrecht, Karl. *Brain Power: Learn to Improve Your Thinking Skills*. Englewood Cliffs, NJ: Prentice Hall, 1980.

De Bono, Edward. *Six Action Shoes*. New York: HarperBusiness, 1991.

———. *Six Thinking Hats*. New York: Little, Brown, 1985.

Drucker, Peter F. *Innovation and Entrepreneurship: Practices and Principles*. New York: Harper & Row, 1985.

Fritz, Robert. *Creating*. New York: Fawcett-Columbine, 1989.

———. *The Path of Least Resistance*. New York: Fawcett-Columbine, 1991.

Ray, Michael, and Rochelle Myers. *Creativity in Business*. New York: Doubleday, 1986.

Von Oech, Roger. *A Kick in the Seat of the Pants*. Harper & Row, 1986.

———. *A Whack on the Side of the Head*. Stamford, CT: U.S. Games Systems, 1990.

Williams, Robert H., and John Stockmyer. *Unleashing the Right Side of the Brain*. The Stephen Green Press, 1987.

[1]Emily T. Smith, "Are You Creative?" *Business Week*, Sept. 30, 1985, p. 81.

**PART FOUR**

## *Skills of the Supervisor*

# 10

*The reason why we have two ears and only one mouth is that we may listen the more and talk the less.*

**—Zeno of Citium, Greek Stoic philosopher, third century B.C.**

# Communication

■ **LEARNING OBJECTIVES**

After you have studied this chapter, you should be able to:

10.1 Describe the process of communication.

10.2 Distinguish between hearing and listening.

10.3 Describe techniques for communicating effectively.

10.4 Identify barriers to communication and suggest ways to avoid them.

10.5 Distinguish between verbal and nonverbal messages, and name types of verbal messages.

10.6 Identify the directions in which communication can flow in an organization.

10.7 Distinguish between formal and informal communication in an organization.

10.8 Discuss the role of the grapevine in organizations.

Source: © Ted Lacey

## GETTING THE MESSAGE ACROSS

Loretta M. Flanagan is executive director of West Side Future, a community organization sponsored by the YMCA. The organization's objectives are to reduce infant mortality and address related problems in the local community. Thus, most of West Side Future's clients are pregnant women and mothers of children under the age of one. Flanagan supervises 22 employees.

Most of Flanagan's workday is devoted to writing to or talking with people. She must communicate with employees, clients, and representatives of other community organizations, the government, and key funding agencies. These communications include policy statements and strategies as well as meetings and discussions with employees.

While Flanagan particularly enjoys the challenges and rewards of talking with others face-to-face, she finds that written words are important in some situations. For example, her staff once had 35 days in which to computerize their client data, a deadline that put employees under a great deal of pressure. Compounding the problem, employees also were involved in the important but time-consuming process of having West Side Future recertified. In Flanagan's experience, this kind of pressure makes it hard for employees to set priorities, so clear, brief, written directions can help them. Flanagan worked with staff members to develop and write a brief procedure for handling client data, freeing some employees to move on to other tasks.

**communication**
The process by which people send and receive information.

Whether employees are in a community-based nonprofit organization such as West Side Future or an international corporation such as IBM, they must be able to communicate with one another to perform high-quality work. **Communication** is the process by which people send and receive information. The information may be about opinions, facts, or feelings. Even hard-nosed businesspeople need information about feelings; for example, a supervisor should know when his or her boss is angry or when employees are discouraged.

Communication is at the heart of the supervisor's job. To work with their manager, their employees, and supervisors in other departments, supervisors send and receive ideas, instructions, progress reports, and many other kinds of information. These and other communications occupy three-quarters of a supervisor's workday.[1] Thus, supervisors need to know how to communicate and how to do so effectively. This chapter describes basic communication skills and the types of communication that commonly occur in organizations.

# How Communication Works

Robert Rodriguez, an agent for the U.S. Bureau of Alcohol, Tobacco and Firearms (ATF), testified before Congress about a tragic failure in communication. Rodriguez said that in 1993 he was an undercover agent posing as a college student at the Branch Davidian compound in Waco, Texas, investigating whether the Davidians had illegal firearms. While Rodriguez was talking to leader David Koresh, Koresh left the room to take a telephone call. He returned trembling and saying, "They're coming . . . The time has come."

Concluding that Koresh had been tipped off, Rodriguez called his supervisor, Chuck Sarabyn, and said, "They know, Chuck. They know—they know we're coming!" Nevertheless, the ATF raid on the compound proceeded as planned, during which four ATF officers and six Davidians were killed. A standoff followed, resulting in the deaths of another 80 Davidians, including Koresh. Sarabyn later claimed that he had interpreted Rodriguez's message as referring to just another of Koresh's many claims that law enforcement agents would someday try to arrest him.[2]

At times all of us, like agent Rodriguez, have found that simply talking or writing does not guarantee effective communication. Rather, our intended audience should be receiving and understanding the message.

## The Communication Process

To describe and explain issues such as these, social scientists have attempted to diagram the communication process. As a result, we have a widely accepted model of how communication works. Figure 10.1 illustrates one version of this model.

Communication begins when the sender of a message encodes the message. This means the sender translates his or her thoughts and feelings into words, gestures, facial expressions, and so on. The sender then transmits the encoded message by writing, speaking, and other personal contact. If communication is working properly, the intended audience receives the message and is able to decode, or interpret, it correctly. Of course, mistakes do occur. Communication breakdowns may occur because of **noise**, that is, anything that can distort a message by interfering with the communication process. Examples of noise are distractions, ambiguous words, and worn equipment used to transmit the message.

**noise**
Anything that can distort a message by interfering with the communication process.

FIGURE 10.1

**The Communication Process**

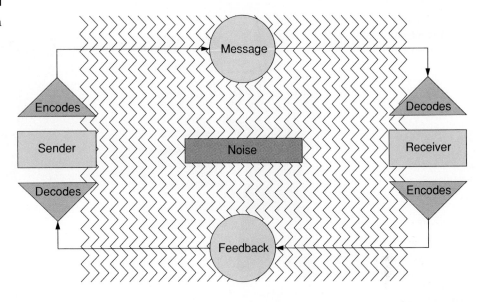

**feedback**
The way the receiver of a message responds or fails to respond to the message.

The sender of the message can recognize and resolve communication problems by paying attention to feedback. **Feedback,** in this sense, is the way the receiver responds—or fails to respond—to the message. Feedback may take the form of words or behavior. For example, employee behavior was feedback to one executive that the employees were paying attention to the company's financial reports. Besides running a pool to bet on football scores, the employees began using the financial data they received from the company to bet on the size of their monthly profit-sharing bonus.[3] In the earlier example of ATF agent Robert Rodriguez, the raid on the Branch Davidian compound was feedback telling Rodriguez that his supervisor either misunderstood his message or chose to disregard it.

## Hearing versus Listening

Notice in Figure 10.1 that the receiver must decode the message, meaning that the receiver as well as the sender has an active role to play in communication. If the receiver is not playing that role, communication is not occurring.

In many cases, this means the receiver of a message must *listen* to it rather than just *hear* it. Hearing means the brain is registering sounds. Most of us have at some point heard a parent nagging at us to clean our room or a co-worker complaining about working conditions, but we may not be listening. Listening means paying attention to what is being said and trying to understand the full message. This is the meaning of "decoding" a message. When parents nag or when co-workers complain, we often choose not to listen to them.

Thus, as the model of the communication process shows, when we want communication to work, we need to make sure that people are decoding messages as well as sending them. Because communication is an essential part of a supervisor's job, a supervisor must practice good listening skills as well as good writing and speaking skills. The next section discusses listening in greater detail.

**■ FIGURE 10.2**

**Techniques for Effective Communication**

Communicate from the receiver's viewpoint.

Learn from feedback.

Use strategies for effective listening.

Overcome barriers to communication.

# Communicating Effectively

Supervisors need to understand the requests that cross their desks and the questions that employees raise. They need to know when the boss is angry or impressed. They need to ensure that employees understand their instructions. When supervisors succeed in these responsibilities, they are communicating effectively. Figure 10.2 demonstrates that effective communication is most likely to occur when the parties communicate from the receiver's viewpoint, learn from feedback, use strategies for effective listening, and overcome barriers to communication.

### Communicate from the Receiver's Viewpoint

Even though we know that other people do not share all our experiences, views, priorities, and interests, we find it is easy to forget this when we are communicating. But such differences make the intended audience more likely to ignore or misunderstand the messages we send. For example, a business owner may find it fascinating and noteworthy that his company has been in the family for four generations. Skilled sales personnel, on the other hand, know that customers would rather hear how the company's services will benefit them. The salespeople therefore communicate with the audience's viewpoint in mind; they focus on what the company can offer customers.

This sales principle applies to all kinds of communication. Simply put, if you want the receiver's attention, interest, and understanding, you must communicate from his or her viewpoint. Applying this principle includes tactics such as using understandable vocabulary, referring to shared experiences, and addressing the receiver's interests. Thus, in explaining to employees that the department will be reorganized, a supervisor should focus on topics such as job security and job design, not on how the changes will make the company more profitable or more like its nearest competitor. After all, employees naturally are most concerned about their own jobs.

## Learn from Feedback

Feedback can help supervisors communicate effectively. When a supervisor sends a message, he or she generally expects a certain kind of response. Suppose a supervisor explains a policy requiring that all employees take their lunch break at some time between 11:00 A.M. and 1:00 P.M. One type of feedback would be the expressions on employees' faces—do they seem to understand or do they look confused? Employees also might respond verbally; one might ask whether employees are to take a two-hour lunch break. Another type of response comes from the employees' later behavior. If the employees understood the message, no one will be having lunch after 1:00 P.M. By evaluating the words, facial expressions, and behavior of the people who received the message, the supervisor can determine whether they understood it.

When feedback indicates that a message was not received fully and correctly, the supervisor can try modifying it, so that it is better adapted to the receiver. The supervisor may have to eliminate sources of noise; for example, by talking in a location with fewer distractions or choosing clearer words.

Image National, a sign manufacturer based in Boise, Idaho, holds monthly meetings at which managers discuss the company's financial statements with employees. Feedback indicated that employees failed to understand the basics of the reports, so Ron Eardley, Image National's president, used a visual aid to clarify the message. He displayed a giant replica of a dollar bill to represent the company's total sales; as the chief financial officer read off the costs of sales, Eardley cut off portions of the dollar bill representing their proportion of total sales. Watching the dollar being "eaten away" brought home to employees that the company's sales dollars do not go straight to its owner's pockets.[4]

A supervisor also can use feedback when he or she is receiving a message. In particular, when a supervisor is uncertain about the meaning of a message, he or she can ask the sender to clarify it. Asking questions is usually a smarter tactic than guessing.

## Use Strategies for Effective Listening

"Things just aren't done like they used to be," grumbled Tom Wiggins to Allen Pincham, his supervisor at the construction site. "Oh, boy," thought Allen, "here we go again with the complaining." Allen began studying some blueprints, ignoring Tom until he blew off some steam and returned to work. Later that week, the general contractor confronted Allen with a report he had received from Tom that some work was not being done according to code. Tom had complained that he had tried to inform Allen, but that his attempts were ignored.

Better listening could have saved the construction project much expense and could have saved Allen Pincham considerable embarrassment. Listening is a key part of communication, and most supervisors could be better listeners. (Test your own listening skills by taking the Self-Quiz on page 307.) Table 10.1 lists 10 rules for being a good listener.

| **TABLE 10.1** | |
|---|---|
| **Ten Rules for Good Listening** | 1. Remove distractions and give the speaker your full attention. |
| | 2. Look at the speaker most of the time. |
| | 3. When the speaker hesitates, give a sign of encouragement such as a smile or nod. |
| | 4. Try to hear the main point and supporting points. |
| | 5. Distinguish between opinions and facts. |
| | 6. Control your emotions. |
| | 7. Be patient; do not interrupt. |
| | 8. Take notes. |
| | 9. At appropriate times, ask questions to clarify your understanding. |
| | 10. Restate what you think the speaker's point is, and ask if you heard correctly. |

Effective listening begins with a commitment to listen carefully. A supervisor should not assume that a message will be boring or irrelevant and should instead decide to listen carefully and to try to identify important information. For example, when an employee complains frequently about seemingly petty matters, the complaints may hide a broader concern that the employee is not stating directly. If a supervisor does not have time to listen when someone wants to talk, he or she should schedule another time to continue the conversation.

A supervisor also should concentrate on the message and tune out distractions. A major type of distraction is planning one's own responses; another is assuming that the listener has nothing interesting to say. When tuning out distractions proves difficult, it may help to take brief notes of what the person is saying, focusing on the key points.

If the speaker uses words or phrases that evoke an emotional reaction, a supervisor must try to control those emotions so that they do not interfere with understanding. One way to respond is to consider whether the speaker is merely trying to vent emotions. In that case, the best response is to listen and acknowledge the emotions without agreeing or disagreeing. Wait until the employee is calm before trying to solve a problem. Then ask questions that seek out the facts underlying an emotional statement: "Stan, you say you are treated unfairly. Would you give me some examples?"

**active listening**
Hearing what the speaker is saying, seeking to understand the facts and feelings the speaker is trying to convey, and stating what you understand that message to be.

In many situations, a supervisor can benefit from using a technique called active listening, pioneered by psychologist Carl R. Rogers. **Active listening** is not only hearing what the speaker is saying but also seeking to understand the facts and feelings the speaker is trying to convey and then stating what you understand the message to be. The sample dialogues in Table 10.2 illustrate two types of listening. In Example 1, the supervisor is simply hearing the employee's words; in Example 2, the supervisor is using active listening. According to Rogers, active listening is a way that supervisors can help employees understand their situation, take responsibility, and cooperate. However, active listening is only used effectively when a supervisor demonstrates a genuine respect for employees and a belief in their ability to direct their own activities.[5]

**TABLE 10.2**

**Hearing versus Active Listening**

| | |
|---|---|
| **Example 1: Hearing** | **Word-Processing Operator:** Hey, Wanda, is Finchburg kidding? He wants the whole report ready by the end of the day? That's impossible! |
| | **Supervisor:** But that's the job. You'll have to work as fast as you can. We're under tremendous pressure this week. |
| | **Operator:** Doesn't he realize we're behind schedule already because of the quarterly reports? |
| | **Supervisor:** Look, Don, I don't decide what the managers want. I just have to see that the work gets done, and that's what I'm trying to do. |
| | **Operator:** How can I tell my wife I'll be working late *again?* |
| | **Supervisor:** You'll have to handle that with her, not me. |
| **Example 2: Active Listening** | **Word-Processing Operator:** Hey, Wanda, is Finchburg kidding? He wants the whole report ready by the end of the day? That's impossible! |
| | **Supervisor:** Sounds like you're pretty upset about it, Phyllis. |
| | **Operator:** I sure am. I was just about caught up after doing all these quarterly reports. And now this! |
| | **Supervisor:** As if you didn't have enough work to do, huh? |
| | **Operator:** Yeah. I don't know how I'm gonna meet this deadline. |
| | **Supervisor:** Hate to work late again, is that it? |
| | **Operator:** That's for sure. I made other plans two weeks ago. Seems like everything we do around here is a big rush. |
| | **Supervisor:** I guess you feel like your work cuts into your personal time. |
| | **Operator:** Well, yeah. I know Finchburg needs this report to land a big customer. I guess that means that this job really *is* important. Maybe if Joel will help me by doing the tables, I can get out of here at a reasonable hour. |

Source: Based on "Active Listening" by Carl R. Rogers and Richard E. Farson.

## *Be Prepared for Cultural Differences*

Supervisors today, more often than in the past, have employees or customers from cultures other than their own. Preparation for cultural differences can help supervisors communicate clearly with these people. To be prepared, supervisors can acquaint themselves with basic guidelines for cross-cultural communication:[6]

Stick to simple, basic words: "use," not "utilize," and "before," not "prior to." Every culture has its own slang and idioms, such as "over the hill" and "in the ballpark." People from other cultures, especially those who speak another language, may be unfamiliar with these terms. In addition, avoid using the jargon of your industry. If you have time to prepare the message in advance, as in the case of a letter or speech, ask a third person to read or listen to the message to make sure it is clear.

When speaking, talk slowly and pronounce words carefully. You do not need to speak loudly; a common error is to assume that a loud tone of voice is the only way to get the message across. Seek feedback by asking your listener what he or she has heard, but do not ask, "Do you understand?" Many people are too embarrassed to respond that they do not understand the message. The following clues also may indicate a lack of understanding:

- Nodding and smiling in a way that is not directly connected to what you are saying.
- A complete lack of interruptions.
- Efforts to change the subject.
- A complete lack of questions.
- Inappropriate laughter.

Give your listener plenty of time to come up with questions. If you still are not sure that an employee has understood instructions, check on the progress of his or her work, allowing ample time to make any needed corrections or clarify what you meant.

Make sure you understand what the other person is saying. Ask for clarification when you need it. Help the speaker to relax, and invite him or her to speak more slowly. If you are having trouble understanding a word pronounced by a nonnative speaker of English, try asking the person to spell it. Most important, assume you can understand, and then try.

Learn about the communication styles used by people from different cultures, and try to match them when appropriate. For example, in some Far Eastern cultures, it is considered extremely rude to interrupt someone during a conversation whereas people from Arabic cultures tend to tolerate interruptions as a sign of enthusiasm. Asians are likely to view loudness as rude, but a Middle Easterner is more often comfortable with it. In any case, a wise supervisor will avoid jumping to conclusions about an individual's character on the basis of cultural preferences.

Supervisors also can help their employees communicate by stressing the importance of keeping communication simple. Share what you learn about communication styles. Compliment employees as they make progress in cross-cultural communication.

# Barriers to Communication

The model of the communication process suggests where barriers to communication can arise. In general, the sender may fail to encode the message clearly, the message may be lost in transmission, or the receiver may misinterpret the message. In practice, these categories of problems often overlap. The resulting barriers may take the form of information overload, misunderstandings, and biases related to perception.

## Information Overload

Today's world is often called the information age. People are bombarded with information daily. On the way to work, radio ads and billboards proclaim which brand of automobile or soft drink to buy. At the workplace, memos, magazines, and managers report on trends, policies, and responsibilities. During the course of a day, many employees get information from colleagues, computer screens, printed pages, and telephone calls. In the evening, family members and the television recount the day's news. People cope with this barrage of information by tuning out a lot of what they see and hear.

How can a supervisor respond to this barrier to communication? An important way is to give employees only information that will be useful to them. For example, when employees need instructions, a supervisor should think them through carefully, so that new instructions don't have to be provided later. Also, a supervisor should be sure that employees are paying attention. The way to do this is to observe the people receiving the information and to look for feedback. A supervisor can say to an employee, "Do you understand what I want you to do? Try putting it in your own words." To his or her manager, a supervisor might say, "Do you think this idea supports your goals for the department?"

## Misunderstandings

In decoding a message, the receiver of a message may make errors that lead to misunderstandings. This barrier can arise when a message is needlessly complicated. Imagine a supervisor's memo that reads, "The deterioration of maintenance practices will inevitably lead to conditions that will be injurious to our heretofore admirable safety record." The person who receives this memo is likely to misunderstand it because so much effort is required to figure out what the words mean. Instead, the supervisor could write, "Because the maintenance workers are no longer tuning up the machines each month, the machines are going to wear out and cause injuries."

When the supervisor is the receiver of a message, he or she needs to be careful to understand its true meaning. The supervisor should not hesitate to ask questions about unclear points. It is also helpful to check on the meaning with such responses as "So you'd like me to . . ." or "Are you saying that . . . ?"

Sometimes the sender prefers that the receiver not understand the message. William V. Haney recounts the story of a congressman running for reelection who responded to questions following a speech. A constituent asked the congressman for his views on Social Security. The congressman replied with a wink, a smile, and the words, "Don't worry about that subject, my friend—I'm all right on that one!" In this way, the politician pleased all of the audience members even though they were evenly divided on the issue.[7] In similar situations, a supervisor needs to recognize when people are intentionally vague or misleading. On those occasions, the supervisor should interpret messages with particular care.

### Word Choices

To avoid misunderstandings, a supervisor should be careful to make appropriate word choices when encoding the message. Besides choosing simple words, this means avoiding ambiguous words. If an employee asks, "Should I use the solvent in the bottle on the left?" the supervisor should not say, "Right."

Problems also can arise from using words that attribute characteristics to another person. Saying "You're so irresponsible!" leads an employee to tune out a message. Instead, a supervisor could describe specific behaviors and his or her own feelings: "That's the second time this week you've made that mistake. I get annoyed when I have to explain the same procedure more than once or twice." This approach is called using "I statements" instead of "you statements." Table 10.3 gives examples of the difference between the two types.

### ▓ TABLE 10.3
## Two Ways to Address Comments to Others

|  | You Statements | I Statements |
|---|---|---|
| **Examples** | "You're so irresponsible!" | "I'm upset that you've missed the deadline for the third time. When someone in the department misses a deadline, the whole department looks bad. What can we do?" |
|  | "At the next department meeting, you'd better be prepared and be on time, or you're going to be sorry when we review your salary." | "I was not pleased that you were late to the meeting and unprepared. I expect a higher standard of performance." |
|  | "You're bugging the women with those dirty jokes, so just knock it off before we get in trouble." | "I have received complaints from two of the employees in the department that you are embarrassing them by telling dirty jokes. Our company policy and the law both forbid that type of behavior." |
| **Likely Response** | Defensiveness, ignoring speaker. | Listening, collaborating on a solution. |

Choosing words carefully is especially important when addressing others. A careful supervisor uses the name of a co-worker or customer instead of "dear" or "honey" unless the supervisor is completely certain that the receiver in a business setting likes being called by such endearments. New Orleans lawyer Harry Mc-Call, Jr., learned the hard way about the importance of how people are addressed. While representing the state of Louisiana in a prison rights case before the U.S. Supreme Court, McCall said, "I would like to remind you gentlemen" of a legal point. When he finished, Justice Sandra Day O'Connor asked, "Would you like to remind me, too?" Amid nervous laughter, McCall apologized. Only moments later, McCall referred to the court as "Justice O'Connor and gentlemen." Justice Byron White broke in, "Just 'Justices' would be fine."[8]

### *Cultural Differences*
Another concern involves misunderstandings that result from cultural differences. For example, the mainstream culture in the United States places relatively great emphasis on expressing one's personal opinion. A supervisor from this culture thus could expect that employees would feel free to share ideas and express disagreements. In contrast, people from a culture that places a high value on harmony (e.g., Japan) might agree with the speaker out of politeness rather than a shared opinion. People from a culture that values demonstrating respect according to one's place in the hierarchy (e.g., Mexico or the Middle East) might be reluctant to express disagreement to a manager or other high-ranking person. A U.S. manager who was unfamiliar with such values might assume mistakenly that employees from these cultures were unable or unwilling to contribute their ideas.

To avoid misinterpreting the words and behavior of others, a supervisor must be familiar with the communication styles of the various cultures of people with

## TABLE 10.4
**Cultural Differences in Communication**

| Aspect of Communication | Example |
| --- | --- |
| Language | Even within the United States, employees may speak many different languages. |
| Word choices | In the United States, a direct refusal is considered clear and honest; in Japan, it is considered rude and immature. |
| Gestures | In the United States, nodding means *yes* and shaking the head means *no;* the reverse is true in Bulgaria, parts of Greece, Turkey, and Iran. |
| Facial expressions | In mainstream American culture, people smile relatively often and view smiling as a way to convey goodwill. Someone from the Middle East might smile as a way to avoid conflict, and someone from Asia might smile to cover up anger or embarrassment. |
| Eye contact | Arabs often look intently into the other person's eyes as a way to know and work well with the other person; in England, blinking one's eyes is a sign that the other person was heard and understood. |
| Distance between speaker and listener | Middle Easterners may interpret standing a foot apart as an indication of involvement in a conversation; an American may interpret the relative closeness as a sign of aggression. |
| Context (situation in which message is sent and received) | Holding a business conversation during the evening meal is acceptable in the United States but rude in France. |
| Conversational rituals (phrases and behaviors that are customs, not meant to be interpreted literally) | In the United States, people often greet one another with "How are you?" not expecting an answer; in the Philippines, they ask, "Where are you going?" Men make more use of jokes and friendly put-downs; women more often use equalizers such as saying, "I'm sorry" and making requests indirectly. |

Sources: Roger E. Axtell, *Gestures: The Do's and Taboos of Body Language around the World* (New York: Wiley, 1991); Philip R. Harris and Robert T. Moran, *Managing Cultural Differences,* 3rd ed. (Houston: Gulf Publishing, 1991); Deborah Tannen, *Talking from 9 to 5* (New York: William Morrow, 1994); Sondra Thiederman, *Bridging Cultural Barriers for Corporate Success: How to Manage the Multicultural Work Force* (New York: Lexington Books, 1991).

whom he or she works. Table 10.4 identifies some aspects of communication affected by culture and provides examples of cultural differences. Information about the values and customs of different cultures, of course, does not apply to every member of any culture, but it can sensitize a supervisor to areas where extra care may be needed to promote understanding.

When interpreting communication styles, it can be useful to recognize women as a different cultural group from men in the United States. (See "Tips from the Firing Line.") In other words, although there are many sources of individual differences, men and women tend to communicate in gender-specific ways. For example, assertiveness in women is often viewed as being pushy or aggressive, so women tend to use a less assertive style of communication than men. Women also tend to value modesty and to describe their accomplishments as group rather than personal achievements. Supervisors who want to benefit fully from the talent of their women employees may have to take an active role in asking for their ideas and identifying their accomplishments.[9]

### TIPS FROM THE FIRING LINE

## Communication Between Men and Women

Perhaps nowhere is there more opportunity for miscommunication in the workplace than in exchanges between men and women; entire books have been written on the subject, and serious legal cases have gone to court. Most men and women genuinely want to find a way to communicate effectively and professionally with each other, without misunderstanding. Andrea P. Baridon and David R. Eyler, authors of *Working Together: The New Rules and Realities for Managing Men and Women at Work*, propose a new "workplace etiquette" in which they offer some "practical business-etiquette guidelines to live by."

- Workplace etiquette requires that men and women adapt their normal social behavior to the job setting, taking a more restrained approach.
- Be quick to understand when a co-worker is telling you no to a social relationship outside the workplace. Persistence could

embarrass both parties and damage the working relationship.

- Be quick to say no if you do not want a social relationship. It is more difficult to say so later on.
- Control your actions and words. Impulsive behavior in the workplace is inappropriate.
- Beware of biases based on stereotypes of members of the opposite sex. Don't assume that you can predict another person's behavior based on gender.
- If you think you are being left out of the communication loop (or a project or meeting) because of your gender, speak up with confidence, not stridency.

Source: Andrea P. Baridon and David R. Eyler, "Workplace Etiquette for Men and Women," *Training*, Dec. 1994, pp. 31–34.

### Inferences versus Facts

**inference**
A conclusion drawn from the facts available.

Misunderstandings also can arise when the listener confuses inferences with facts. An **inference** is a conclusion drawn from the facts available. A supervisor may observe that an employee is not meeting performance standards. That would be a fact. If a supervisor says, "You're lazy!" he or she is making an inference based on the fact of the below-par performance. The inference may or may not be true.

Statements using the words *never* and *always* are inferences. A supervisor may claim, "You're always late"—knowing for certain that the employee has been late to work six days straight. However, the supervisor cannot know for certain what the employee *always* does.

To overcome mistakes caused by treating inferences as facts, a supervisor should be aware of them. When sending a message, a supervisor should avoid statements that phrase inferences as facts. When listening to a message, a supervisor should be explicit with his or her inferences. For example, a supervisor in a bakery could say, "When you tell me the test of the recipe was a failure, I assume you mean the quality of the bread is poor. Is that correct?"

### Biases in Perception

**perceptions**
The ways people see and interpret reality.

Based on their experiences and values, the sender and receiver of a message make assumptions about each other and about the message. The ways people see and interpret reality are known as **perceptions.** Look at the picture in Figure 10.3. What do you see? You may perceive either an old woman or a young woman.

When perceptions about others are false, messages might get distorted. Imagine that supervisor Al Trejo has decided his employees would like him to pay

### ■ FIGURE 10.3

**A Drawing That May Be Perceived in More than One Way**

Source: Edwin G. Boring, "A New Ambiguous Figure," *American Journal of Psychology*, July 1930, p. 444. Also see Robert Leeper, "A Study of a Neglected Portion of the Field of Learning—The Development of Sensory Organization," *Journal of Genetic Psychology*, Mar. 1935, p. 62. Originally drawn by cartoonist W. E. Hill and published in *Puck*, Nov. 8, 1915.

more attention to their day-to-day problems and successes. So Al stops by the desk of one of his employees, Kim Coleman, and asks, "What are you doing?" Based on her experiences, Kim believes that supervisors are quick to criticize, so she perceives that Al's question is intended to determine whether she is goofing off. Feeling defensive, Kim snaps, "My work, of course." Al then perceives that Kim does not want to discuss her work with him.

#### Prejudices

**prejudices**
Negative conclusions about a category of people based on stereotypes.

Broad generalizations about a category of people—stereotypes—can lead to negative conclusions about them. These negative conclusions are called **prejudices,** and they can distort perceptions. In our culture, it is common to attribute certain characteristics to women, African Americans, Asians, blue-collar workers, and many other groups. Of course, these characteristics often do not apply to a particular person. Imagine that a male manager assumes women are irrational and highly emotional, and that a female supervisor who reports to him discusses her desire for a raise. Even if she outlines a series of logical points supporting her request, he may perceive her request as irrational and respond by telling her to "take it easy, things will work out OK." If such poor communication continues, the supervisor might eventually quit in frustration.

Downcast eyes in the United States are seen as submissive, even lacking in self-confidence. In Japan, downcast eyes are seen as a sign of attentiveness and agreement.

Source: © Dan Bosler/Tony Stone Images.

The way to overcome communication barriers resulting from prejudices is to be aware of the assumptions we make. Are we responding to what a person is saying or to what he or she is wearing? Are we responding to the message or to the speaker's accent? To the words or to our beliefs about the person's race? Awareness enables the sender and the receiver of a message to focus on understanding rather than assuming.

### Biases in Paying Attention

Perception begins when people pay attention to a message or other stimulus. However, biases occur even at this early stage of the perception process. People tend to pay more attention to a message that seems to serve their own self-interest. They also are more apt to hear messages that fit their existing viewpoints and to discount messages that contradict those viewpoints. Imagine that an employee suggests a new procedure, to which the supervisor responds, "Your idea will never work." The employee is more likely to think the supervisor is opposed to change than that the idea is unworkable.

The supervisor can combat biases in attention by phrasing messages carefully to appeal to the receiver. In the case of the new idea from an employee, the supervisor might say, "Thank you for your suggestion. I estimate that it will save us about $50 a month. Can you think of a way we can modify it so that implementing it will cost less than $1,500?" This response shows the supervisor was paying attention to the suggestion and recognized at least some of its merit.

## Types of Messages

When Sandy walked into her cubicle at the insurance company where she worked, a note signed by her supervisor was on her desk: "See me," it read. "Uh-oh," thought Sandy nervously, "what did I do?"

Sandy walked into her supervisor's office and saw that he was smiling. "Congratulations," he said, "you got the raise we requested."

**■ FIGURE 10.4**

**The Etiquette of
Proper Distance:
Some Cross-
Cultural Examples**

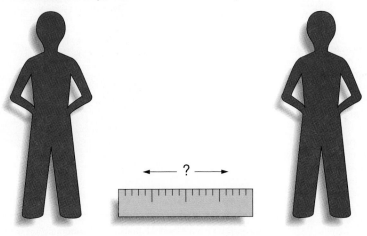

- Americans, on average, stand 2 feet apart when conducting business.
- Middle Eastern males typically stand up to 18 inches apart.
- Asians and many African cultures leave a space of 3 feet or more.

Source: Based on Sondra Thiederman, *Bridging Cultural Barriers for Corporate Success: How to Manage
the Multicultural Work Force* (New York: Lexington Books, 1991), p. 132.

**verbal message**
A message that consists
of words.

**nonverbal message**
A message conveyed
without using words.

In this example, Sandy's supervisor communicated with her through a note, a
facial expression, and spoken words. Two of the messages were **verbal messages;**
that is, they consisted of words. The third—the smiling face—was a **nonverbal
message;** that is, it was conveyed without words.

### Nonverbal Messages

How can anyone get a point across without using words? While the idea of nonverbal messages might seem surprising or unimportant at first, we continuously
send and receive messages through our facial expressions, posture, and other nonverbal cues. In the example of Sandy, the message conveyed by the supervisor's facial expression was as important as the verbal message, "See me." The smile, unlike the note, conveyed to Sandy that her supervisor had good news.

Major types of nonverbal messages are gestures, posture, tone of voice, facial
expression, and even silence. We learn the meaning of many such messages simply
by participating in our culture. From experience, we can recognize a friendly
handshake, a cool silence in response to something we say, and the "proper" distance to stand from the person with whom we are talking, part of a concept known
as personal space (see Figure 10.4). Imagine that a supervisor and an employee are
discussing a problem concerning the employee's work. The employee drops her
eyes, looking away from the supervisor. Based on the usual assumptions in American culture, a supervisor is apt to conclude that the employee is dishonest, unin-
terested, or guilty of something.

Because we learn the meaning of nonverbal messages from our culture, people
from different cultures have different nonverbal vocabularies. In the previous example, if the employee is a Cambodian woman, she may be trying to communicate

### FIGURE 10.5

**Relative Contributions of Several Factors to Total Impact of a Message**

When a message is both verbal and nonverbal, the nonverbal message may have more impact on the receiver than the words themselves. This pie chart shows the relative impact, expressed as a percent, of words, vocal tones (tone of voice), and facial expressions.

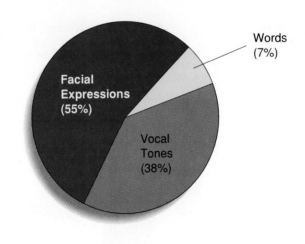

Words (7%)

Facial Expressions (55%)

Vocal Tones (38%)

Source: Data from Albert Mehrabian, "Communication without Words," *Psychology Today*, Sept. 1968, pp. 53–55.

respect; according to Cambodian custom, looking her supervisor in the eye would be rude. The meanings of nonverbal cues may vary even among different groups of people born in the United States. For instance, people of European backgrounds tend to maintain eye contact when listening but allow their eyes to wander somewhat when they are speaking, while African Americans are more apt to follow the opposite pattern, maintaining steadier eye contact when they are speaking.[11] Failure to recognize different interpretations of nonverbal signals can be misleading, as in the case of a European American speaker who concludes, on the basis of eye contact, that an African American listener is not interested in what he or she is saying.

A supervisor needs to send nonverbal signals communicating that he or she is businesslike and professional.[12] Some ways supervisors can send these signals are to sit or stand straight, use open hand gestures, and sit with their hands resting comfortably in their lap. Dressing conservatively signals that a supervisor commands respect and has self-control. Smiling when appropriate and shaking hands readily indicate enthusiasm and interest. Finally, a pleasing, moderate tone of voice gets respect from others. A supervisor can develop such a voice by practicing with a tape recorder or friend.

When a person is sending both verbal and nonverbal messages, the nonverbal message may have more influence on the receiver. A *Chicago Tribune* reporter found that it was common at city hall to send memos stating that needed repairs were emergencies, but the word *emergency* carried less weight than whether the memo was hand delivered or sent through the office mail system.[13] Figure 10.5 shows the weight that different components of a message may carry. If the relative importance of nonverbal communication seems surprising, imagine that someone is saying, "You're in trouble!" in an angry tone of voice. Now imagine the same person saying that while laughing. Are the messages identical?

## Verbal Messages

Most nonverbal communication supplements verbal messages. People send verbal messages by speaking (oral communication) or writing (written communication). In the example at the beginning of this chapter, Loretta Flanagan effectively combined the two types of verbal communication. She talked with staff members in order to develop procedures, then put the procedures in writing.

### Oral Communication

To communicate with employees, supervisors usually depend on oral communication. Every day they talk to employees to explain work duties, answer questions, assign tasks, check progress, and solve problems. This type of communication gives the supervisor an opportunity to send and receive many nonverbal cues along with the verbal ones. Thus, a supervisor can benefit from applying nonverbal communication skills when talking to employees. For example, the supervisor should use a well-moderated tone of voice and allow plenty of time for questions.

Most oral communication occurs face-to-face—in conversations, interviews, meetings, and formal presentations. (Meetings were discussed in Chapter 3.) Technology offers an increasing selection of oral communication channels for people in different locations. We take telephone calls for granted; newer technologies include voice mail, teleconferencing, and videoconferencing.

Speaking before a group makes many supervisors nervous, but nervousness can be positive if it inspires supervisors to be well prepared.[14] Following these steps can help you prepare to give a presentation:

1. Start by learning about the audience. What are the listeners' values and interests, and what do they already know about the topic? Continuing to focus on the audience instead of your fears can help to minimize those fears.
2. Spell out the main point of the presentation and the three or four supporting points. For example, the main point might be that the department needs a full-time secretary, and the supporting points would describe the benefits. Or, the main point might be that employees can benefit from managing their time better, and the supporting points would be some ideas for doing so.
3. When you have a clear plan for what to say, write notes on index cards. It is important to speak naturally, which usually requires speaking from notes rather than reading a script.
4. Practice the speech until it is easy to deliver. For useful feedback, practice with a video camera, a tape recorder, or a friend.
5. Think positively. This requires setting realistic, achievable goals that emphasize what you have control over (e.g., delivering your message enthusiastically) rather than what is under someone else's control (e.g., convincing someone of your argument).

If you want more formal, in-depth help with speaking before a group, the organization may be willing to send you to one of the many training seminars available or to a speech class at a community college. Many people have benefited from participating in meetings of the Toastmasters organization. Practice not only can improve your public speaking skills but also diminish your anxiety.

Full wireless communication—voice, video, fax, computer data, and things not yet invented—is the present and future for communications. Large urban areas such as Los Angeles and New York already have so many cellular phone users that the base-station infrastructure is strained.

Source: Courtesy of Harris Corporation.

### Written Communication

Many situations call for a record of what people tell one another. Therefore, much of the verbal communication that occurs in organizations is in writing. Common forms of written communication include memos, letters, reports, bulletin board notices, posters, and electronic messages.

Memos (short for *memoranda*) are an informal way to send a written message. At the top of the page, the sender types the date, receiver's name, sender's name, and subject matter. Because of their informality memos lend themselves to communication within an organization.

People writing to someone outside the organization usually send a letter, which is more formal than a memo but has basically the same advantages and disadvantages. Both provide a written document for the receiver to review, and both take a relatively long time to prepare and deliver.

An analysis of how to meet a need or solve a problem takes the form of a report. A report describes the need or problem, then proposes a solution. Many reports contain charts and graphs to make the message easy to understand. Another helpful technique for a long report (more than two pages) is to start off with a paragraph that summarizes the contents. Busy managers can review what the report is about, even if they cannot read the full report right away.

Written messages also can be sent electronically by fax machine or E-mail (see Chapter 5). Software for E-mail makes communication easier in many ways. For example, a program called BeyondMail allows the user to set rules for how the system will sort and forward mail, signals the user when an urgent message has been received, and routes messages to someone else if the user is away from the workplace.[15]

To communicate a single message to many people, the organization may use posters and electronic or printed bulletin board notices. These are efficient but impersonal ways to send messages, so they usually supplement more personal types of communication. For example, if a factory's managers want to promote quality, they can use posters that say "Quality First." For the message

## Telecommuters Use Technology to Communicate

Telecommuting—a term that refers to workers who "commute" by means of technology such as cellular phone, fax, E-mail, and modem—has become a solution to some of the challenges of today's business world. With companies cutting costs by downsizing, revisions in the Clean Air Act (requiring employers of more than 100 workers to reduce employee trips to work in certain polluted cities), and the Americans with Disabilities Act (requiring that the workplace be accessible to disabled workers), managers have had to find ways to accommodate these changes. Telecommuting, which essentially allows employees to work at home while remaining in contact with the office or plant, can address each of these changes.

But telecommuting raises its own problem for workers and managers: Can communication be effective? Some supervisors resist the idea of allowing their employees to telecommute because they are afraid they will lose touch with them and thus be unable to monitor their performance.

One consultant recommends that telecommuters receive training in how to structure their work and communicate with their supervisors. Supervisors and telecommuters must agree on how and when they will communicate with one another. Will they use phone or E-mail? Will they touch base every hour or every day?

AT&T addresses these issues at the outset by providing formal training for employees who plan to telecommute. They take eight classes, which cover topics such as the impact technology has on the workplace and how to work in their "virtual office." Telecommuters also learn how to use the technology that is supposed to free them up.

Managers who are experienced with telecommuters insist on meetings. Greg Hopkins, general manager for AT&T's Global Business Services in Phoenix, holds monthly meetings scheduled a year in advance for his entire staff, half of whom are telecommuters. Both his telecommuters and office-based employees serve on committees. These activities maintain the flow of communication in all directions.

Telecommuting has its doubters, among them Labor Secretary Robert Reich, who calls it a "minor trend," and *Los Angeles Times* columnist Jonathan Gold, who fears that it represents further "white flight" from the cities. Still, others such as Robert Moskowitz, president of the American Telecommuting Association, predict that it is the "first phase of a new era of work." More than seven million workers now telecommute, and the number is growing by 15 percent each year. Olsten Corporation, a human resources provider, says that 86 percent of the companies it has surveyed have had increased productivity with telecommuting programs. As technology provides us with more modes of workplace communication, businesses probably will find more ways to use it.

Sources: Marc Hequet, "How Telecommuting Transforms Work," *Training,* Nov. 1994, pp. 57–61; Eileen Davis, "Have Modem, Won't Travel," *Management Review,* Apr. 1995, p. 7.

to be effective, however, managers and supervisors also should praise individuals for doing quality work, discuss quality when evaluating performance, and set an example in the quality of their own work.

### Technology and Message Types

Developments in technology have provided an increasing number of ways to deliver messages. (See "Meeting the Challenge.") Among the more recent developments are E-mail, fax machines, teleconferencing, cellular phones, and videoconferencing.

These message types provide exciting options but make selecting a communications channel more difficult. Furthermore, the ability to send and receive information not only in the workplace but also in one's home, car, and airplane seat can contribute to the information overload described earlier in the chapter. Some employees may feel as if they are never able to fully leave their workplace because they can be reached by fax or cellular phone wherever they are.

## Choosing the Most Effective Message Type

With so many ways to send a message, which is the best for a supervisor to use? While face-to-face communication conveys the most information (words plus tone of voice plus body language plus immediate feedback), the most effective and efficient method for a message depends on the situation. Therefore, when deciding whether to call, meet with, or fax a message to someone, the supervisor should consider time and cost limits, the complexity and sensitivity of the issue, the need for a record of the communication, the need for feedback, and the capabilities of the audience.

### Time and Cost Limits

When the supervisor needs to reach someone in a hurry, a letter or memo may be too time-consuming. An employee might be easy to find at his or her desk or on the shop floor. Often, the fastest way to reach someone in the organization is to make a telephone call.

Modern technology shortens the time required to send messages. Fax, E-mail, and voice mail allow a supervisor to contact people who are away from the telephone much of the day or who are taking other calls. However, these technologies do not ensure that messages will be *received* quickly because it is the receiver who decides when to pick up the fax or retrieve messages from voice mail or E-mail.

Like time, costs place some limits on the choice of communications media. Sending a report through the mail costs less than faxing it, and the cost difference is sometimes more important than the time difference. When people who need to discuss an issue are located far apart, the costs of a videoconference may be less than the costs of bringing everyone together. For that reason, Veri-Fone, which provides credit card verification services, uses videoconferencing for initial interviews of job candidates (then flies in those who will receive follow-up interviews) and supplements visits to customers with quick updates through videoconferences.[16]

### Complexity and Sensitivity of the Issue

A complex message is clearer if written. For example, the results of a survey or the analysis of a work group's performance are easier to understand in a written report. In a meeting, an oral report will be clearer if supplemented with written handouts, slides, posters, or overhead transparencies. When speed is critical in communicating complex information to someone outside the organization, it may be cost-effective to use a fax machine or a computer modem.

For emotionally charged issues or when the state of mind of employees is at issue, communicators need the information that comes from tone of voice, gestures, and facial expressions. Such information is also essential for assessing how well employees (especially new ones) are doing. Written communications such as E-mail are thus best-suited for objective messages. In contrast, sarcasm, humor, and emotion-laden messages are likely to be misinterpreted by receivers of E-mail. To avoid such problems, technology-savvy VeriFone bans the use of arguments and sarcasm on E-mail.[17]

The more sensitive a message or situation, the more opportunity there should be for nonverbal communication. Telephone calls, voice mail, and audio E-mail messages provide information through vocal tones. Most information, of course, comes from communicating face-to-face. Holding a one-on-one or group meeting allows the message sender to defuse anger and dispel misconceptions. It gives the receivers a chance to air their feelings and ask questions. For example, a supervisor who needs to discipline an employee must ensure that the employee understands the problem and has a chance to present his or her point of view. Similarly, an announcement of layoffs or restructuring should be made in person.

### Need for a Record

As you will learn in Chapter 13, a disciplinary action calls for a written record as well as a face-to-face meeting. A supervisor needs to combine a written message with oral communication. Other actions that call for written records include placing an order and establishing goals for an employee or department.

### Need for Feedback

The easiest way to get feedback is to send an oral message. The listeners at the meeting or on the telephone can respond immediately with comments and questions. If feedback is critical, face-to-face communication is more effective than a telephone conversation because the person delivering the message can watch facial expressions as well as hear reactions. Do people look confused, excited, angry, satisfied? If a supervisor explaining a new procedure says, "Do you understand?" and the employee responds with a doubtful "I guess so," a supervisor knows that an example or some other clarification is needed.

### Capabilities of the Receiver

People will receive a message only if it comes through a channel they feel comfortable using. In many settings, for example, some employees lack reading skills. If a supervisor believes that an employee cannot read the message, he or she will need to find ways to deliver it through the spoken word, pictures, gestures, or some other means of communication. This situation arises when an employee cannot read at all or reads too poorly to understand a particular message. Some employees may read well in other languages but not in English; in such a case, the supervisor may want to make written messages available in other languages.

The issue of illiteracy is a sensitive one. Supervisors therefore must be tactful and look carefully for signs that employees have trouble reading. Employees with reading difficulties are typically embarrassed about this problem and try to hide it.

A potentially more widespread concern is the comfort and skill in using modern technology. Some people feel frustrated or angry when a voice mail system answers the telephone. Supervisors can help by recording an answering message that offers information such as when to expect a return call and how to reach an operator or secretary. Likewise, information offered on-line will seem convenient to some and inaccessible to others.

The key is to assess the receivers' expertise in using high-tech media. That expertise is relatively great among the customers of Norand Corporation, which sells handheld computers for use in tracking inventory. Norand therefore set up an electronic bulletin board where customers from around the world can post questions or problems at their convenience. Norand posts answers and also transmits files and software upgrades as needed.[18]

# Communicating in Organizations

In business, government, and other organizations, communication tends to follow certain patterns. Understanding these patterns can help the supervisor make the best use of them.

## *Direction of Communication*

**downward communication**
Organizational communication in which a message is sent to someone at a lower level.

Think back to the organization charts in Chapter 7. When someone sends a message to a person at a lower level, **downward communication** is occurring. A supervisor is receiving a downward communication when listening to instructions or an evaluation from his or her manager or when reading a memo from top management describing a new company policy. The supervisor is sending a downward communication when he or she discusses a problem with an employee or tells an employee how to perform a task. Employees expect to receive enough downward communication in order to understand how to do their jobs, and they typically like to know enough so that they understand what is going on.

**upward communication**
Organizational communication in which a message is sent to someone at a higher level.

When someone sends a message to a person at a higher level, **upward communication** is occurring. A supervisor is receiving an upward communication when an employee asks a question or reports a problem. A supervisor is sending an upward communication when he or she tells the manager how work is progressing or asks for a raise. Managers especially want to receive upward communications about controversial matters or matters affecting their own performance.

To be well informed and to benefit from employees' creativity, a supervisor should encourage upward communication. Writer and business consultant Denis Waitley advises sales managers to spend more time listening to their salespeople. Not only will sales managers get answers to their questions, but also they will help to create an organization that is continually learning and improving from the ideas of its people.[19]

A supervisor can enhance upward communication by applying the strategies for effective listening. A supervisor should respond to employees so they know their messages have been received. Another means of encouraging upward communication is to establish a formal way, such as a suggestion box, for employees to provide comments and suggestions. As part of an effort to institute total quality management, supervisors at the distribution branch of a major manufacturer of high-tech equipment began to meet once a month with each of their employees. These sessions are for sharing information, clarifying work priorities, and making supervisors aware of employee activities and abilities. A year into the program, the monthly meetings had helped to improve employee views of supervision and communications in the division.[20]

**lateral communication**
Organizational communication in which a message is sent to a person at the same level.

A message sent to a person at the same level is **lateral communication.** Supervisors send and receive lateral communications when they discuss their needs with co-workers in other departments, coordinate their group's work with that of other supervisors, and socialize with their peers at the company.

Why should a supervisor need to know about the directions of communication? One way a supervisor can use this information is to be sure that he or she is participating in communication in all directions: enough downward communication so that employees know what is expected of them and the supervisor understands what is happening in the organization, enough upward communication so

To be well informed and to benefit from employees' creativity, the supervisor should encourage upward communication. By listening to their workers, Ted Kaufman (*seated in center*) and Jim Berloti (*standing in background*), owners of Eastern Connection, a Boston-based courier service, have created a company with an open environment. Employees developed the company motto, "Driven to Deliver," and upward communication has helped the company reach $27 million in sales.

Source: © 1995 Richard Howard.

that his or her manager is aware of the supervisor's accomplishments and employees feel encouraged to offer ideas, and enough lateral communication so that the work of the supervisor's department is well coordinated with the work of other departments.

## Formal and Informal Communication

**formal communication**
Organizational communication that is work-related and follows the lines of the organization chart.

The communication that follows the lines of the organization chart is known as **formal communication,** which is directed toward accomplishing the goals of the organization. For example, when a supervisor discusses an employee's performance with that employee, the supervisor is helping the employee to perform high-quality work. When a supervisor gives the manager a report of the department's weekly activities, the supervisor is helping the manager perform his or her responsibilities for controlling.

However, much of the communication that occurs in an organization is directed toward meeting people's individual needs. For example, managers and employees alike may spend time discussing the performance of their favorite sports teams, the behavior of their children, and good places to eat lunch. This type of communication is called **informal communication.**

**informal communication**
Organizational communication that is directed toward individual needs and interests and does not necessarily follow formal lines of communication.

### Gossip and Rumors

Much informal communication takes the form of gossip and rumors. According to Allan J. Kimmel, a psychology professor at Fitchburg State College in Massachusetts, gossip is small talk about people.[21] People use gossip to indicate what behavior is acceptable. Thus, employees gossiping about who got promoted or who is dating the new supervisor in the payroll department are typically airing and refining their views about promotion policies and love affairs between co-workers.

In contrast, Kimmel says, "Rumors are what people say among themselves to try to make sense out of what's going on around them." For example, if a factory gets a visit from the company's board of directors, employees at the factory may spread rumors that the factory is to be sold or the operations moved to South Korea. When people are afraid, they spread rumors to ease their fear while trying to get at the facts. Thus, rumors tend to circulate chiefly during crises and conflicts—and they are often false.

Although rumors and gossip are a fact of life in the workplace, it does not look good for a supervisor to participate in spreading either. As a member of management, a supervisor is expected to know and report the facts about company business. When a supervisor spreads gossip or rumors, word eventually will get around that he or she is responsible for the message. The following guidelines are useful to keep rumors and gossip under control:[22]

- Do not share any personal information about other employees, including your desire or intention to criticize or discipline an employee. Discuss the matters with others only when they truly need to know, such as discussing a personnel matter with your manager or someone in the human resources department.
- When you hear company information, such as plans for expansion or cutbacks, keep it to yourself until the organization makes an official announcement. Otherwise, you could embarrass yourself and upset your manager or employees if the information is inaccurate or the plans fall through.
- If you hear a rumor, investigate it and find out the truth and the cause. The rumor may be a tip-off that employees are worried or angry about something, and it is the supervisor's job to address those concerns.

### The Grapevine

**grapevine**
The path along which informal communication travels.

The path along which informal communication travels is known as the **grapevine.** The grapevine is important to supervisors because employees use it as a source of information. Thus, a supervisor must expect that employees sometimes have information before the supervisor has delivered it. Supervisors also must realize that employees may be getting incorrect information through the grapevine, especially in times of crisis or conflict.

The grapevine springs up on its own, and managers are generally unable to control it. However, knowing about the grapevine can help the supervisor seek out and correct misinformation. The supervisor also can take some steps to see that at least some of the messages in the grapevine are positive and in line with the organization's objectives:[23]

- Regularly use the tools of formal communication to inform employees of the organization's version of events.
- Be open to discussion; be someone employees will turn to when they want a rumor confirmed or denied.
- Use performance appraisal interviews as a way to listen to employees as well as to give them information.
- Have a trusted employee act as a source of information about the messages traveling the grapevine.
- When it is necessary to clear the air, issue a formal response to a rumor.

Furthermore, if supervisors and other managers are exercising their leadership skills to create an environment in which employees can and want to make a positive contribution, both formal and informal communication are important. Supervisors will want to encourage communication among employees so that they can improve the ways they work together.

That was the goal of Lou Hoffman, who heads a San Jose, California, public relations firm. To spur more informal communication among the firm's 18 employees, Hoffman announced he would pay for the lunch of any two employees who ate together at the nearest restaurant. Furthermore, he divided the employees into two groups and offered a gift certificate to anyone who had lunch with each person in the other group. Everyone won a certificate, and Hoffman claims employees have begun solving more of their problems together, rather than expecting him to mediate every dispute.[24]

# Summary

**10.1   Describe the process of communication.**
The communication process occurs when people send and receive information. It begins when someone encodes a message by putting it into words or nonverbal cues. The sender of the message transmits it by speaking or writing. Then the receiver of the message decodes, or interprets, it. Usually the receiver gives the sender feedback.

**10.2   Distinguish between hearing and listening.**
Hearing occurs when the brain registers sounds. Listening occurs when the person who hears sounds also pays attention and tries to understand the message.

**10.3   Describe techniques for communicating effectively.**
Effective communication is most likely to occur when the parties communicate from the receiver's viewpoint, learn from feedback, use strategies for effective listening, and overcome barriers to communication. To listen effectively, the listener should make a commitment to listen, set aside time for listening, and then concentrate on the message. The listener also should try to control his or her emotions, not letting an emotional reaction interfere with understanding. Active listening involves hearing what the speaker is saying, seeking to understand the facts and feelings the speaker is trying to convey, and stating what one understands the message to be.

Supervisors also should be prepared for cultural differences in order to communicate effectively. They should stick to simple words, avoid jargon, speak slowly, give the listener time to ask questions, ask for clarification, and learn about the communication styles of different cultures.

**10.4   Identify barriers to communication and suggest ways to avoid them.**
Barriers to communication include information overload, misunderstandings, perceptions and prejudices, and biases related to perception. Ways to avoid these barriers include giving employees only the information they need, encoding messages carefully and simply, observing feedback, avoiding name-calling, being aware of inferences and prejudices, and phrasing messages to appeal to the receiver.

**10.5   Distinguish between verbal and nonverbal messages, and name types of verbal messages.**
Verbal messages consist of words. Nonverbal messages are messages encoded without words, such as facial expressions, gestures, or tone of voice. Types of verbal messages include face-to-face discussions, telephone calls, memos, letters, reports, E-mail messages, faxes, and videoconferences.

**10.6   Identify the directions in which communication can flow in an organization.**
Organizational communication may flow upward, downward, or laterally. Upward communication travels to the sender's superior. Downward communication travels from manager to employees. Lateral communication flows between people at the same level.

**10.7   Distinguish between formal and informal communication in an organization.**
Formal communication travels along the lines of the organizational chart and is related to accomplishing the goals of the organization. Informal communication may travel in any direction between any members of the organization. It tends to be aimed at achieving personal, rather than organizational, objectives.

**10.8   Describe the role of the grapevine in organizations.**

The grapevine is the path of much of the organization's informal communications. Much of the information that travels through the grapevine is gossip and rumors. The supervisor generally cannot control this flow of information but should be aware that it exists and that he or she may have to correct misinformation. In addition, by encouraging communication with his or her employees, a supervisor may be able to ensure that some of the messages in the grapevine are positive.

## Key Terms

| | | |
|---|---|---|
| communication | perceptions | upward communication |
| noise | prejudices | lateral communication |
| feedback | verbal message | formal communication |
| active listening | nonverbal message | informal communication |
| inference | downward communication | grapevine |

## Review and Discussion Questions

1. Phyllis Priestley, a supervisor, wants to tell her boss what she plans to accomplish at a leadership seminar she will be attending next week. She decides to do so in the form of a memo. Briefly describe how this communication will follow the model shown in Figure 10.1.

2. Can a person be hearing but not listening well? Can a person be listening but not hearing well? Explain.

3. Every Monday morning, Ron Yamamoto, a supervisor, must attend a divisional meeting to discuss progress and make plans. Ron finds that most people at the meetings are long-winded and that the meetings as a whole are boring. However, he needs to know what is going on in the division. How can Ron listen effectively, even though he is bored?

4. Sheila James owns her own catering business employing four workers. She just got a contract to cater a wedding reception for a Chinese couple who speak very little English. What steps can Sheila take to make sure her communication with the couple is successful? As a supervisor, what steps might Sheila take with her employees to make sure they understand the couple's wishes as well?

5. In a staff meeting held to introduce new software that will provide office employees with information about the company's financial status, sales figures, and marketing plans, you notice that one of your employees is alternately staring out the window and doodling in his notebook. You are certain he is not paying attention. What barrier to communication might be occurring here? What steps might you take as a supervisor to overcome it?

6. The following examples describe some ways to send messages. Indicate whether each is verbal or nonverbal. For each verbal message, indicate whether it is oral or written.

   a. A long silence accompanied by an icy stare.
   b. A letter delivered by fax machine.
   c. Voice mail.
   d. Laughter.

6. As mail room supervisor, you need to report to your manager that a sack of mail has been misplaced (you are not sure how it happened). Would you want to send this message through written or oral communication? Would you want to deliver it face-to-face?

   Describe the form of communication you would choose and why you would choose it.

7. Nina Goldberg has been asked by her manager to give a presentation to employees about changes the company is going to make in health care benefits. Using the five steps described in this chapter, how should Nina go about preparing her presentation?

8. Face-to-face communication conveys the most information because the people communicating can learn from each other's body language and tone of voice as well as from the words themselves. However, why shouldn't a supervisor always choose face-to-face communication over other ways?

9. Lee Hamel is a busy supervisor. He rarely hears from his employees except when there is a production snag or scheduling problem. Lee figures that as long as things run smoothly, his employees are happy. Why might Lee's attitude be counterproductive in the long run? What steps could he take to improve upward communication from his employees?

10. Which of the following organizational communications are formal? Informal?

    a. A memo providing information about the company picnic.
    b. A meeting at which employees discuss the department's goals for the month.
    c. A rumor about a new vacation policy.
    d. A discussion between a supervisor and an employee about who will win the World Series.

11. Should a supervisor participate in informal communication? If so, when? If not, why not?

## A SECOND LOOK

This chapter described various categories of communication: verbal and nonverbal, oral and written, formal and informal. Which kinds of communication can you identify in the opening example of Loretta Flanagan?

# APPLICATIONS MODULE

## CASE

### Communication: Right from the Start

Perhaps there is no more important time for a supervisor to communicate with an employee than on the employee's first day at the job. Many companies are beginning to recognize this, putting more and more emphasis on the formal communication known as orientation. Orientation involves mostly downward communication, showing the employee the "ropes" of the organization; but it also fosters upward communication.

At Great Plains Software in Fargo, North Dakota, new employees start out with an automatic three-month orientation period. They take eight classes in topics that range from E-mail to benefits to the company's overall vision. (Great Plains avoids the problem of information overload by dispensing with tedious hours of filling out forms and forcing new workers to read long policy manuals.) In addition, each new employee is teamed up with a more senior employee who acts as a designated "coach."

At the end of the program, the new hire's supervisor collects feedback from peers and the coach, then meets with the employee to discuss his or her future at Great Plains. Thus, the orientation program fosters formal and informal communication, as well as communication in all organizational directions. Lynn Dreyer, former vice-president of human resources, claims that this program of communication fosters a "solid, long-term commitment to the company," unlike the one-day orientation that employees used to receive.

Other companies also have picked up on the importance of communication right from the start. Some, such as Southwest Airlines and Rosenbluth International, foster communication in even more unconventional ways than Great Plains. At Rosenbluth (a travel-services organization), new hires attend formal presentations at the Philadelphia headquarters; then they play communication games with each other; finally, they are served high tea by the CEO and other senior executives.

"It lets [new employees] know that they really *do* come first," explains Diane McFerrin Peters, a consultant for the company.

Southwest's orientation includes scavenger hunts and the organization's own version of *Wheel of Fortune*. "People aren't just sitting around like giant sponges absorbing too much information," says vice-president Libby Sartain. Still, the needed information does travel to new hires. Underlying the party atmosphere is a highly structured program of formal communication: a history of the airline, a description of the company's vision, an outline of necessary customer care, and a listing of benefits.

After orientation, positive informal communication is encouraged through a buddy system. Each new hire is matched with an old hand in the Co-Hearts program. "It's somebody to have lunch with, to bounce ideas off of—a friend in the company," notes Sartain. Thus, good communication takes off right from the start.

1. Do you think these new approaches to communication through orientation will have a long-term effect on employees' performance at Great Plains, Rosenbluth, and Southwest? Why or why not?

2. The Co-Hearts program at Southwest encourages positive informal communication. How might it backfire?

3. What message do you think Rosenbluth's high tea service sends to employees? What steps must Rosenbluth's management take to make sure the gesture is effective?

4. "We try not to take ourselves too seriously," says Southwest vice-president Libby Sartain. What nonverbal signals might reveal the meaning of her message?

Source: Nancy K. Austin, "Giving New Employees a Better Beginning," *Working Woman*, July 1995, pp. 20–21, 74.

### SELF-QUIZ

## *Are You an Effective Listener?*

For each statement, score yourself on a scale of 1 (seldom) to 10 (usually) to indicate how often that statement is true about you. Be as truthful as you can in light of your behavior in the last few meetings or gatherings you have attended.

1. I listen to one conversation at a time.
2. I like to hear people's impressions and feelings, as well as the facts of a situation.
3. I really pay attention to people; I don't just pretend.
4. I consider myself a good judge of nonverbal communications.
5. I don't assume I know what another person is going to say before he or she says it.
6. I look for what is important in a person's message, rather than assuming it is uninteresting and ending the conversation.
7. I frequently nod, make eye contact, or whatever to let the speaker know I am listening.
8. When someone has finished talking, I consider the meaning of his or her message before responding.
9. I let the other person finish before reaching conclusions about the message.
10. I wait to formulate a response until the other person has finished talking.
11. I listen for content, regardless of the speaker's "delivery" style.
12. I usually ask people to clarify what they have said, rather than guess at the meaning.
13. I make a concerted effort to understand other people's point of view.
14. I listen for what the person really is saying, not what I expect to hear.
15. When I disagree with someone, the person feels that I have understood his or her point of view.

Add your total points. According to communication theory, if you scored 131–150 points, you strongly approve of your own listening habits, and you are on the right track to becoming an effective listener. If you scored 111–130, you have uncovered some doubts about your listening effectiveness, and your knowledge of how to listen has some gaps. If you scored 110 or less, you probably are not satisfied with the way you listen, and your friends and co-workers may not feel you are a good listener either. Work on improving your listening skills.

---

Source: Reprinted by permission of the publisher, from *Supervisory Management*, Jan. 1989, pp. 12–15. © 1989 American Management Association, New York. All rights reserved.

## *Class Exercise*

You learned many principles in this chapter to help you improve your communication skills. This exercise reviews six of those principles and gives you a chance to see how you can use them to improve supervisory communications.

### *Instructions*

1. Review the following list of communication principles:

   *a.* Use feedback to verify that your message has been received accurately.
   *b.* Practice active listening.
   *c.* Select appropriate method for sending your message.
   *d.* Be tuned in to nonverbal messages.
   *e.* Be well prepared when speaking before a group.
   *f.* Understand the important role of informal communication in the workplace, particularly rumors, gossip, and the grapevine.

2. Read the scenarios and determine which of the communication principles the supervisor violated. In each blank provided, write the letter of that principle from the list in step 1. The principle you choose should indicate the one that the supervisor could have used to achieve a more positive outcome. (Hint: Each principle will be used only once; there is one *most* correct answer for each.)

**Scenario**

On Tuesday afternoon, the plant manager gave each of the 12 supervisors throughout the plant a five-page document that spelled out some changes in the employee handbook that would be effective the following month. The plant manager instructed the supervisors to call departmental meetings sometime within the next three days to present the changes to their own staff. Jeff sent out a notice to his employees to be at a 45-minute meeting on Thursday afternoon. Several unexpected events occurred that demanded most of Jeff's time during the next two days. Jeff did manage to make it to the meeting; however, he had only a few minutes beforehand to skim the document. He ended up mostly reading aloud from the document at the meeting.

Pete went to talk to his supervisor about a personal problem. He left the meeting feeling that he hadn't gotten through to his supervisor, who seemed preoccupied and distracted throughout their entire conversation.

Sid was on his way out the door to meet a customer for a business lunch at a local restaurant. He stopped long enough to give about 90 seconds of hurried instructions on a task he needed one of his employees to do for a P.M. deadline that same day. Sid finished his instructions by glancing at his watch and saying, "I'm going to be late for my luncheon appointment. You got everything OK, didn't you?" The employee mumbled, "Yeah, I guess so," and Sid was out the door.

Krista overheard one of the employees in her department telling someone on the phone that he had heard from a reliable source that the company was going to pink-slip 10 percent of the employees on Friday. Krista shook her head in disgust and thought to herself, "Another ridiculous rumor. With all the rumors floating around this place, I could spend all my time dispelling rumors. I'll let this one die a natural death on Friday; I don't have time to deal with it right now."

**Principle**

1. _____

2. _____

3. _____

4. _____

Shannon had a long "to do" list for the day and decided to dispense with as many items as she could first thing in the morning by using the E-mail system. She had gotten rid of six tasks by sending messages to the appropriate people. She sent a seventh message that contained confidential information about one of her employees. The next day Shannon's manager spoke with her about a negative situation that had arisen as a result of her seventh message being accessed by some people who should not have seen it. He told her to consider more carefully the messages she chose to send via E-mail.

5. _____

Michael had decided to delegate an important project to Susan, his most capable employee. He called Susan to go over some of the specifics of the project—one that he saw as a great opportunity for her to show higher management what she was capable of doing. Susan, however, did not share Michael's enthusiasm about her new work assignment. Michael ignored her expressionless face, and chose to respond to her verbal responses. For example, when he asked her whether she agreed this was an exciting project, she responded after a few seconds of silence with a mere yes.

6. _____

This Class Exercise was prepared by Corinne Livesay, Belhaven College, Jackson, Mississippi.

## Team-Building Exercise

## Choosing the Right Words

Before class, or when your instructor sets aside time in class, read the following memo. The writer was an employee of the U.S. Department of Transportation:

The purpose of this PPM [Policy and Procedure Memorandum] is to ensure, to the maximum extent practicable, that highway locations and designs reflect and are consistent with Federal, State and local goals and objectives. The rules, policies and procedures established by this PPM are intended to afford full opportunity for effective public participation in the consideration of highway location and design proposals by highway departments before submission to the Federal Highway Administration for approval. They provide a medium for free and open discussion and are designed to encourage early and amicable resolution of controversial issues that may arise.*

1. Did you find this memo easy to understand? If not, why not? Did the author succeed in communicating?

2. As a class, rewrite this paragraph so that it is easier to understand. As you write, consider these questions:

    a. Are there any long sentences that you can divide into two or more sentences?

    b. Who is doing what in each sentence? Try to rephrase each sentence so that it is easy to define these items.

    c. Where did the writer use two or more words when one word would mean the same thing?

    d. Do these sentences sound natural, as if the writer were talking to you? Figure out what each sentence means, then think about how you would say it if you were talking to someone. Use a dictionary if necessary.

3. Compare the class's rewritten paragraph with the following (you may have found better solutions):

    This PPM is intended to ensure that the design and location of highways meet the goals of federal, state, and local governments. It tries to let the public participate fully when highway departments consider proposals to send to the Federal Highway Administration for approval. The policies and procedures in this memorandum provide a basis for open discussion. As a result, the people involved should be able to resolve any conflicts early on.

4. As a supervisor, how can you put into practice the techniques that worked in this class exercise?

*Reprinted from Kenneth W. Houp and Thomas E. Pearsall, *Reporting Technical Information* (New York: Macmillan, 1984), p. 187.

# Video Exercise 10: *Communication*

## *Video Summary*

In its predictions for the future, AT&T's Knowledge Network presents an exciting look at how technology will allow information to be transmitted instantly to anyone, anyplace, at anytime.  Communication is the key to successful business, and this video will open your eyes to the seemingly unlimited communications possibilities.

## *Application*

No matter how high tech our communications become, we will continue to rely on the interpretation of nonverbal cues to help us fully understand the messages we *receive* from others. We also need to be aware of the nonverbal cues that accompany the messages we *send* to others. The nonverbal communication channels through which we send and receive information are explained in the following table:

| Channel | Explanation | Example(s) |
|---------|-------------|------------|
| Actions | Body language or kinesics | Facial expressions, eye movements, posture, and gestures |
| Symbols | Pictures or characteristics that represent meaning | Corporate logos (Prudential's "piece of the rock" or the Rolex crown), computer software icons (clicking the picture of the printer sends your document to the printer to be printed), road signs and signals (red, yellow, and green lights communicate stop, caution, and go in all countries), and status symbols (the house you live in or the clothes or jewelry you wear) |
| Tactile | The use of touch to impart meaning | Patting someone on the back while congratulating him or her |
| Vocal | How things are said | Pitch, rate, rhythm, clarity, and changes in loudness |
| Use of time | Time is a continuous and irreversible scarce resource, so who we spend it with and how much we give of it communicate our feelings about who and what are important to us. | Responding quickly to a written communication conveys meanings such as respect, interest, a sense of urgency, or efficiency. |

| Channel | Explanation | Example(s) |
|---------|-------------|------------|
| Use of image | People do judge a book by its cover; through clothing and other dimensions of physical appearance, we communicate our values and expectations. | This nonverbal communication channel also impacts written communications. Some contrasting examples illustrate the use of image: Laser jet vs. dot matrix output Four-color glossy brochure vs. black and white Résumé printed on high-quality, expensive bond paper vs. 3¢ copy on inexpensive paper |
| Use of space | The way we use physical space to communicate things about us | *Territory*—Some people sit in the same area of the classroom in every class. When they can't sit in their favorite territory, they feel uncomfortable.  In an organizational context, consider a top-floor office with a view vs. a lower-floor office with no window; who's more important to the company based on territory assigned? *Things*—Office arrangement; do people have to talk to each other with a barrier between them, such as a big desk, or are the chairs arranged to convey a more open communication environment? *Personal space zones*—Few people are allowed in our intimate distance, which in the United States is 0 to 18 inches.  If someone who doesn't belong tries to get into our intimate zone, we find ourselves backing away. |

Source: Corinne R. Livesay, *Strengthen Your Skills: A Skills-Building Manual* (Burr Ridge, IL: Austen Press/Irwin, 1995), pp. 31–32.

Now you will have a chance to practice interpreting nonverbal cues.

1. Work with one or two other students to complete this exercise.
2. Read the items in the first column, "Observed Nonverbal Communication Cue."
3. In the second column, determine the most likely interpretation you would make from the cue, using the following a–j listing.

   a. Amazement or doubt
   b. Embarrassed, nervous, or hiding something
   c. Excited or angry
   d. Status and importance
   e. Honesty, interest, openness, and confidence
   f. Support, liking, or intimacy
   g. Agreement
   h. Does not care
   i. Frustration
   j. Evaluation

4. Because some interpretations may vary from culture to culture, your answers should be based on U.S. culture.

| Observed Nonverbal Communication Cue | Likely Interpretation |
|---|---|
| 1. Avoids eye contact with you | |
| 2. Large office | |
| 3. Direct eye contact | |
| 4. Hand rubbing back of neck | |
| 5. A smile and a nod | |
| 6. Raised eyebrows | |
| 7. Gentle touching such as a hand on the arm or a hug | |
| 8. Peering over glasses | |
| 9. Raising one's voice | |
| 10. Frequently late to department meetings | |

# 11

*People often ask me what I feel is my most significant insight about managing and motivating others. Without a doubt I'd have to say it's the concept of "catching people doing something right" that first appeared in* The One Minute Manager.

—**Ken Blanchard, management consultant, from the *Blanchard Management Report***

# Motivating Employees

## LEARNING OBJECTIVES

After you have studied this chapter, you should be able to:

11.1 Identify the relationship between motivation and performance.

11.2 Describe content theories of motivation.

11.3 Describe process theories of motivation.

11.4 Explain when financial incentives are likely to motivate employees.

11.5 Describe pay plans using financial incentives.

11.6 Discuss the pros and cons of keeping pay information secret.

11.7 Identify ways supervisors can motivate their employees.

## MOTIVATING THROUGH TEAM SPIRIT

James Kisson is regional sales manager for a gas products company that originally was founded to sell carbon dioxide for fountain drinks. He helps the sales representatives in his region to develop new business and to resolve problems with existing customers. An important part of his job is motivating; that is, giving the salespeople various kinds of incentives to work hard and deliver high-quality service.

According to Kisson, the most important way he motivates is by building team spirit. He holds sales meetings at which the sales reps can meet one another and share leads for new business. Kisson says, "It is critical that the reps have respect for each other and be able to work as a team."

Kisson also runs sales contests. At his company, salespeople can win awards for the most new business signed, the most renewal business, the most improved sales rep, highest

Source: © Taylor/Fabricius/Gamma Liaison

profit, and overall best sales rep. The monetary rewards are important, explains Kisson, but the employees also are motivated by the recognition for a job well done. In addition, he finds it helpful to give a humorous award to the lowest-performing sales rep as a way to motivate that individual to do better next time.

The sales representatives at the gas products company are paid a base salary plus a bonus. The bonus is paid each quarter based on how much the rep's sales grew during that time. If Kisson were able to set up the company's pay system, however, he would rather pay a yearly bonus based on how well the sales reps meet performance criteria established at the beginning of the year. He believes that such an arrangement would enable the supervisor to measure performance more fairly and to promote teamwork more effectively.

**FIGURE 11.1**

**The Effect of Motivation on Performance**

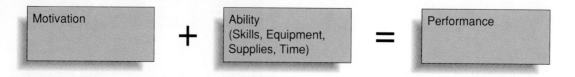

---

**motivation**
Giving people incentives that cause them to act in desired ways.

Giving people incentives that cause them to act in desired ways is known as **motivation.** Among other things, supervisors must motivate their employees to do good work, to complete assignments on time, and to have good attendance. At the gas products company, the sales contests and bonuses are intended to motivate the sales representatives.

When employees are motivated and also have the ability—the necessary skills, equipment, supplies, and time—they are able to perform well (see Figure 11.1). Thus, the objective of motivating employees is to lead them to perform in ways that meet the goals of the department and the organization. Because supervisors are evaluated largely on the basis of how well their group as a whole performs, motivation is an important skill for supervisors to acquire.

How the supervisor can make good use of the link between employees' objectives and their performance is discussed in this chapter. Theories of what motivates employees and how the motivation process works are described, legal issues are identified, and the role of money as a motivator is discussed. Finally, practical ways that supervisors can motivate employees are suggested.

## How Does Motivation Work?

"What's wrong with these people?" exclaimed Martha Wong about the sales clerks she supervises in the shoe department. "We pay them good wages, but when we hit a busy season like this, nobody's willing to put forth the extra effort we need—giving up a break once in a while or even just moving a little faster." Martha needs to figure out what to do so that employees will *want* to keep customers happy during busy periods. Perhaps they expect more money, or perhaps they want something else, such as a feeling of being part of a team.

Imagine that supervisors like Martha could know exactly what motivates employees. For example, imagine that all salespeople are motivated solely by the money they earn and that social scientists have devised an accurate formula to determine how much money the company must pay to get a given amount of selling. Suppose that all secretaries are motivated by flexible work hours and all production workers are motivated by recognition from the plant manager. A company that knew this would be in a position to devise the kinds of rewards that employees want. The supervisor could hand out the rewards and would know that if employees had the necessary skills, they would do good work.

Of course, no such simple knowledge about motivation exists. Instead, supervisors have to rely on a variety of theories that social scientists have developed.

None of the theories are perfect, proven explanations of how to get employees to behave in a certain way, but all give supervisors some guidance. Familiarity with the best-known theories can help supervisors think of ways to motivate their employees.

## Content Theories

Some theories of motivation have focused on what things motivate workers. These are called content theories because they focus on the content of the motivators. Although money is the motivator that comes most readily to mind, some people respond more to other sources of satisfaction. To help you think about what motivates *you*, try the Self-Quiz at the end of this chapter (page 338).

Three researchers whose content theories of motivation are widely used are Abraham Maslow, David McClelland, and Frederick Herzberg.

### Maslow's Hierarchy of Needs

Psychologist Abraham Maslow assumed that people are motivated by unmet needs. When a person's need for something is not met, the person feels driven, or motivated, to meet that need. To give a basic example, a person who needs food feels hungry and therefore eats something.

According to Maslow's theory, the needs that motivate people fall into five basic categories:

1.  Physiological needs are needs required for survival: food, water, sex, and shelter.
2.  Security needs keep you free from harm. In modern society, these might include insurance, medical checkups, and a home in a safe neighborhood.
3.  Social needs include the desire for love, friendship, and companionship. People seek to satisfy these needs through the time they spend with family, friends, and co-workers.
4.  Esteem needs are the needs for self-esteem and the respect of others. Acceptance and praise are two ways these needs are met.
5.  Self-actualization needs describe the desire to live up to your full potential. People on the path to meeting these needs will not only be doing their best at work and at home but also will be developing mentally, spiritually, and physically.

Maslow argues that these needs are organized into a hierarchy (see Figure 11.2). The most basic needs are at the bottom of the hierarchy. People try to satisfy these needs first. At the top of the hierarchy are the needs people try to satisfy only when they have met most of their other needs. However, people may be seeking to meet more than one category of needs at a time.

Based on this view, people tend to rely on their jobs to meet most of their physiological and security needs through paychecks and benefits such as health insurance. Needs higher on the hierarchy can be satisfied in many places. For example, people satisfy some of their social needs through their relationships with family and friends outside of work, and they may seek to meet their self-actualization needs through volunteer work or membership in a religious organization. Nevertheless, people can also satisfy higher-level needs in the workplace. An employee who is applauded for solving a difficult problem or who takes pride in skillfully performing a craft such as carpentry is meeting some higher-level needs at work.

Maslow's hierarchy is a widely cited view of motivation, but it has shortcomings. Critics (including Maslow himself) have noted that the theory is based on clinical work with neurotic patients and was not tested much for relevance to the work setting.[1] Are the needs identified by Maslow really all-inclusive? Do they describe people of many cultures, or just the majority of Americans? The lack of studies investigating the hierarchy of needs makes it impossible to answer such questions with certainty. However, the popularity of Maslow's theory implies that it can be helpful in offering suggestions about what motivates people.

Applied to a work situation, Maslow's theory means that the supervisor must be aware of the current needs of particular employees. During a serious recession, a factory supervisor may find that many employees are highly motivated just to keep their jobs so they can pay their bills. In contrast, employees who are less worried about keeping a job may respond well to spontaneous dinners such as the ones hosted by the Richard Michael Group, a Chicago placement firm. Staff members are invited to bring their spouse or a friend, and the company credits the resulting friendships with keeping employees on the payroll much longer than the industry average.[2]

In this era of an increasing number of single parents and two-income families in the workforce, a practical concern of many employees is their need for flexibility in their work hours to balance the demands of home and work. Some organizations have responded with "family-friendly" policies, which typically include flexible work arrangements such as the following:

**flextime**
A policy that grants employees some leeway in choosing which eight hours a day or which 40 hours a week to work.

- **Flextime**—This is a policy that grants employees some leeway in choosing which eight hours a day or which 40 hours a week to work.
- *Part-time work*—For employees who can afford to work less than full time, this option frees them to spend more time meeting other needs. This option is economically appealing to organizations because few offer a full range of benefits to part-time employees.

Motivation can come from developing team spirit. Ronnie Taylor (*left*), a supervisor on the day shift at Tyson Foods in Shelbyville, Tennessee, is shown enjoying the annual softball tournament, which helps develop good relationships among employees.

Source: Courtesy of Kelly/Mooney photography.

**job sharing**
An arrangement in which two part-time employees share the duties of one full-time job.

- **Job sharing**—To create part-time jobs, two employees share the duties of a single position.
- *Telecommuting*—Some employees can and want to work from home, keeping in touch by means of computer and telephone lines.

The view among many human resources experts is that family-friendly policies are an important way to get and keep the best workers. According to Robert Montgomery, vice-president of human resources at Quaker Oats, "There was a time when companies expected employees to not let their families interfere with work. Today that can't be done."[3] By a recent account, over 40 percent of employers offer flexible scheduling in some form.[4]

### McClelland's Achievement-Power-Affiliation Theory

In the 1960s, David McClelland developed a theory of motivation based on the assumption that through their life experiences, people develop various needs. His theory focuses on three such needs:

1. *The need for achievement*—the desire to do something better than it has been done before.
2. *The need for power*—the desire to control, influence, or be responsible for other people.
3. *The need for affiliation*—the desire to maintain close and friendly personal relationships.

According to McClelland, people have all these needs to some extent. However, the intensity of the needs varies from one individual to the next. The nature of a person's early life experiences may cause one of these needs to be particularly strong.

The relative strength of the needs influences what will motivate a person. A person with a strong need for achievement is more motivated by success than by money. This person tends to set challenging but achievable goals and to assess risk carefully. Someone with a strong need for power tries to influence others and

**TABLE 11.1**

Two-Factor Theory:
Hygiene Factors and
Motivating Factors

| Hygiene Factors | Motivating Factors |
| --- | --- |
| Company policy and administration | Opportunity for achievement |
| Supervision | Opportunity for recognition |
| Relationship with supervisor | Work itself |
| Relationship with peers | Responsibility |
| Working conditions | Advancement |
| Salary and benefits | Personal growth |
| Relationship with subordinates | |

seeks out advancement and responsibility. A person with a strong need for affiliation gives ambition a back seat in exchange for approval and acceptance.

This theory provides a possible explanation for some recent findings in a U.S. Department of Labor survey of women employees. According to that survey, a large proportion of low-income women reported that the best thing about going to work was being with their co-workers. As incomes rose, the importance of workplace relationships gave way to high ratings for being paid well.[5] We might guess that more of the women in low-paying positions had a high need for affiliation. Further, many of them may have developed this need through experiences that taught them they need to rely on the support of family and friends to help them in the struggle to meet work, safety, and family needs with limited resources.

McClelland's theory differs from Maslow's in that it assumes different people have different patterns of needs, whereas Maslow's theory assumes the same pattern of needs for all people. Thus, McClelland takes into account individual differences. Both theories, however, imply that supervisors must remember that employees are motivated by a variety of possibilities.

### Herzberg's Two-Factor Theory

Frederick Herzberg's research led to the conclusion that employee satisfaction and dissatisfaction stem from different sources. According to this two-factor theory, dissatisfaction results from the absence of what Herzberg calls *hygiene factors*, which include salary and relationships with others. For example, someone whose pay is poor (e.g., a physical therapist earning $5,000 less than the average for the position) is going to be dissatisfied with the job. In contrast, satisfaction results from the presence of what Herzberg calls *motivating factors*, which include opportunities offered by the job. Thus, an employee who sees a chance for promotion is likely to be more satisfied with the current job than one who does not. Table 11.1 lists the items that make up hygiene and motivating factors.

Herzberg found that employees are most productive when the organization provides a combination of desirable hygiene factors and motivating factors. Based on this theory, an organization cannot ensure that its employees will be satisfied

**FIGURE 11.3**

**FIGURE 11.3**

Vroom's Expectancy-Valence Theory

| Strength of Motivation | = | Perceived Value of Outcome (Valence) | X | Perceived Probability of Outcome Resulting (Expectancy) |

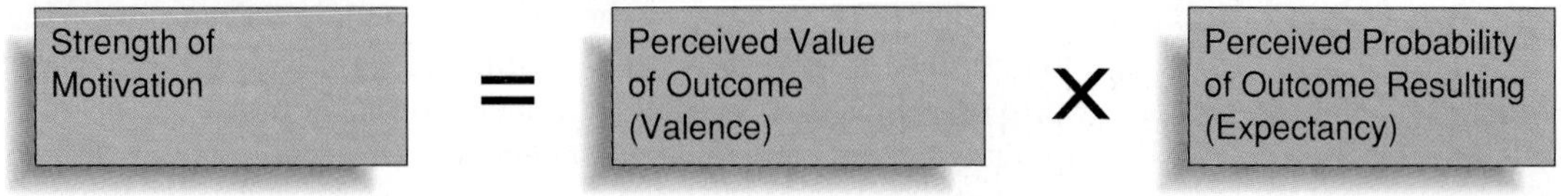

and productive simply by giving them a big pay raise every year. Employees will also need motivating factors such as the ability to learn new skills and to assume responsibility. Like the other content theories, Herzberg's theory tells supervisors that they need to consider a variety of ways to motivate employees.

## Process Theories

Another way to explain how motivation works is to look at the process of motivation instead of specific motivators. Theories that pertain to the motivation process are known as process theories. Two major process theories are Vroom's expectancy-valence theory and Skinner's reinforcement theory.

### Vroom's Expectancy-Valence Theory

Assuming that people act as they do to satisfy their needs, Victor Vroom set out to explain what determines the intensity of motivation. He decided that the degree to which people are motivated to act in a certain way depends on two things:

1. *Valence*—the value a person places on the outcome of a particular behavior. For example, a person may highly value the prestige and the bonus that result from submitting a winning suggestion in a contest for improving quality.
2. *Expectancy*—the perceived probability that the behavior will lead to the outcome. A person in the example may believe that his or her idea has a 50–50 chance of winning the quality improvement contest.

Vroom's expectancy-valence theory says that the strength of motivation equals the perceived value of the outcome times the perceived probability of the behavior resulting in the outcome (see Figure 11.3). In other words, people are most motivated to seek results they value highly and think they can achieve.

This theory is based on employees' *perceptions* of rewards and whether they are able to achieve them. Employees may place different values on rewards than a supervisor, and they may have different opinions about their abilities. If a supervisor believes that a good system of rewards is in place but that employees are not motivated, the supervisor might investigate whether employees think they are expected to do the impossible. To learn this, supervisors must be able to communicate well (see Chapter 10).

### Skinner's Reinforcement Theory

From the field of psychology comes reinforcement theory, pioneered by B. F. Skinner. Reinforcement theory maintains that people's behavior is influenced largely by the consequences of their past behavior. Generally, people keep doing things that have led to consequences they like, and people avoid doing things that have had undesirable consequences. For example, praise feels good to receive, so people tend to do things that, in their experience, result in praise.

Reinforcement theory implies that supervisors can encourage or discourage a particular kind of behavior by the way they respond to the behavior. They can administer **reinforcement,** which can involve either giving a desired consequence or ending a negative consequence in response to behavior the supervisor wants. Or the supervisor can administer **punishment,** which is an unpleasant consequence of the behavior the supervisor wants to end. As described in the story at the beginning of this chapter, when salespeople performed well, they earned bonuses or won contests—a form of reinforcement. The lowest-performing sales rep received the undesirable attention of winning a "prize" for rating at the bottom—a form of punishment. Using reinforcement theory to motivate people to behave in a certain way is known as **behavior modification.** In everyday language, we call it "using the carrot and the stick."

For long-term results, reinforcement is more effective than punishment. Psychologists have found that repeated punishment (or failure) can lead to an unhappy consequence called "learned helplessness."[6] This means that if employees are punished repeatedly for failing in some aspect of their work, these employees will eventually believe that they are unable to succeed at the job. These employees begin to approach the job passively, believing that they will fail no matter what.

Together, Vroom's and Skinner's process theories support the idea that supervisors motivate most effectively when they place less emphasis on punishing infractions and more on giving employees a desirable goal and the resources that enable them to achieve that goal. These theories are consistent with the following assertion by AlliedSignal's CEO, Lawrence A. Bossidy:

> The day when you could yell and scream and beat people into good performance is over. Today you have to appeal to them by helping them see how they can get from here to there, by establishing some credibility, and by giving them some reason and some help to get there. Do all those things, and they'll knock down doors.[7]

### Motivation Theories and the Law

Most of these motivation theories have one element in common: that supervisors must consider individual differences in designing rewards. What motivates one person may not motivate another, so supervisors need to offer a variety of rewards. At the same time, to avoid discrimination, employers must distribute benefits fairly.

Boston-based Work/Family Directions, which provides referral services, uses a formal procedure to balance these objectives with flexible scheduling. If employees want an alternative work arrangement such as flextime, telecommuting, or job sharing, they must fill out a form that details the hours and location they are requesting, the impact on the organization, and a proposal for overcoming any

**reinforcement**
A desired consequence or the ending of a negative consequence, either of which is given in response to a desirable behavior.

**punishment**
An unpleasant consequence given in response to undesirable behavior.

**behavior modification**
The use of reinforcement theory to motivate people to behave in a certain way.

At Marshall Industries, an electronics distributor in El Monte, California, commissions and every other incentive (cars, bicycles, VCRs, or trips to Hawaii) have been discontinued. Instead, the company's 600 salespeople earn salaries. Denise Stoll, one of Marshall's star salespeople, says she prefers the predictability of a salary.

Source: © Philip Saltonstall.

drawbacks of the arrangement. The company then decides whether to grant the request based on business-related concerns instead of the employee's reasons for requesting the arrangements.[8]

The types of rewards a supervisor may use are not entirely under his or her control. Not only does a supervisor have to follow the organization's policies, but a variety of laws require that employers provide certain types of benefits. For example, federal laws set requirements for overtime pay, rest breaks, health insurance for retirees, and many other areas. Most organizations have a human resources professional or department responsible for helping the organization comply with laws related to benefits. The details of these laws are beyond the scope of this book.

However, the requirements of the Family and Medical Leave Act of 1993 are worth noting because they affect the supervisor's role in scheduling work and staffing the department. Under this law, organizations with 50 or more employees within a 75-mile radius must give employees up to 12 weeks of unpaid leave to care for a newborn, adopted child, or foster child within one year of the child's arrival. These employers also must offer this time off if employees need to care for a seriously ill child, parent, or spouse or if they themselves have medical conditions that prevent them from doing their job. During the time off, the employer must continue to pay the employee's health insurance premiums. The employer also must guarantee that the employee will be able to return to his or her job or an equivalent one. If the need for the leave is foreseeable, the employee must give the organization 30 days' notice.

## Money as a Motivator

Some supervisors and other managers assume that the main thing employees want out of a job is money. Most people work to earn at least enough to get by. Though money is only one of many available ways to motivate employees, it is an important one.

## When Money Motivates

The content theories of motivation imply that money motivates people when it meets their needs. The opportunity to earn more can be very important to a college student, considering the high cost of college tuition and the potentially great impact of a college degree on the student's future lifestyle. A retired person or a married person whose spouse earns a comfortable income might work primarily for nonfinancial rewards such as a sense of accomplishment or the satisfaction derived from performing a needed service.

If money is to work as a motivator, employees must believe they are able to achieve the financial rewards the organization offers. Thus, if a theater company offers its staff a bonus for selling a given number of season-ticket subscriptions over the telephone, the bonus will motivate the employees only if they believe they can sell that many tickets. Or, if an organization pays a bonus for employee suggestions that improve quality, the bonus will motivate employees only if they believe they are capable of coming up with ideas.

## Pay Plans Using Financial Incentives

The way a pay plan is structured can influence the degree to which employees are motivated to perform well. Some pay plans offer bonuses, commissions, or other kinds of pay for meeting or exceeding objectives. For instance, a growing number of organizations tie raises and bonuses to success in retaining existing customers and meeting established quality goals.[9] Others, such as the Quaker Oats pet food plant in Topeka, Kansas, pay employees a higher rate for learning additional skills, including how to operate lift trucks and computer-controlled machinery.[10] Such pay plans are said to use **financial incentives.**

**financial incentives**
Payments for meeting or exceeding objectives.

Supervisors rarely have much say in the type of pay plan an organization uses. However, they can motivate better if they understand the kinds of pay plans that offer a financial incentive. Knowing whether the organization's pay system is designed to motivate gives a supervisor clues about the needs of employees for nonfinancial incentives. If the organization's pay plan includes financial incentives but the employees remain unmotivated, a supervisor might look for other kinds of motivators. On the other hand, if the organization's pay plan contains no financial incentives, a supervisor might seek permission to include money for bonuses in the department's budget.

### Piecework System

**piecework system**
Payment according to the quantity produced.

The **piecework system** pays people according to how much they produce. This method is often used to pay independent contractors; that is, people who are self-employed and perform work for the organization. For example, a magazine might pay a writer a fixed rate for each word, or a clothing manufacturer might pay a seamster a set amount for each shirt sewed. Farmworkers may be paid according to how much they harvest. Unlike independent contractors, however, few employees are paid by this system.

### Production Bonus System

Production department employees may receive a basic wage or salary plus a bonus that consists of a payment for each unit produced. Thus, an employee might earn $8.50 an hour plus $.20 for each unit produced. This is called a production bonus

### TABLE 11.2

**Production Bonus System at Natural Decorations**

| Factor | Formula | Number of Points |
|---|---|---|
| Starting points | | 50 |
| Tardiness | −5 × number of days = | |
| Time off | −10 × number of days = | |
| Absenteeism | −15 × number of days = | |
| Reworks | −5 × number of times = | |
| Violations of safety, maintenance, and procedural rules | −5 × number of times = | |
| Production time above average | +2 × number of days = | |
| Production time below average | −2 × number of days = | |
| **Total Bonus Points** = | | |

Source: Reprinted with permission, *Inc.* Magazine, Feb. 1992. Copyright 1992 by Goldhirsh Group, Inc., 38 Commercial Wharf, Boston, MA 02110.

system. If employees do not appear to be motivated by a production bonus system, the bonus may not be large enough to be worth the extra effort.

Employees who work faster earn more money under such a system, but the pay system does not necessarily encourage high-quality work. A production bonus system that does account for quality—as well as several other factors employees can control—is used at Natural Decorations, an Evergreen, Alabama, maker of dried-flower and artificial-flower arrangements (see Table 11.2).[11] Employees start with 50 points, then each month the company uses various factors to calculate the bonus points each employee earns for the month. The bonus points were worth $1 each when the program was initiated. At whatever the going rate, employees are paid according to the number of points they have earned (but they are not charged for a negative score).

### Commissions

**commissions**
Payment linked to the amount of sales completed.

In a sales department, employees may earn **commissions,** or payment linked to the amount of sales completed. For example, a real estate agent listed a house for her brokerage. Upon the sale of the house, the agent might receive a commission of 2 percent of the sale price. The selling agent and the brokerage also would get commissions.

Most organizations that pay commissions also pay a basic wage or salary. Otherwise, the financial uncertainty can worry employees to the point that it interferes with motivation. Some people, however, like the unlimited earnings potential of a commission-only job.

It is possible to use commissions with employees other than salespeople. De Mar Plumbing, Heating and Air-conditioning of Clovis, California, pays its plumbers and installers entirely on commission. Depending on the type of work they handle, the employees earn a 15 to 20 percent base commission on parts sold and labor billed. They earn additional commissions for calling on first-time customers and receiving compliments from customers. Some employers cannot live with this system, so they quit; but for those who stay, the potential earnings are unlimited. In an early year of this pay program, the top service employee earned $60,000, about twice the industry average. Management at De Mar is happy because revenues are rising faster than the payroll.[12]

### Payments for Suggestions

To build employee participation and communication, many companies pay employees for making suggestions on how to cut costs or improve quality. Typically, the suggestion must be adopted or save some minimum amount of money before the employee receives payment. The size of the payment may be linked to the size of the benefit to the organization. In other words, an idea with a bigger impact results in a bigger payment.

### Group Incentive Plans

**group incentive plan**
A financial incentive plan that rewards a team of workers for meeting or exceeding an objective.

Organizations today are focusing increasingly on ways to get employees and their supervisors to work together as teams. A financial incentive to get people to work this way is the **group incentive plan,** which pays a bonus when the group as a whole exceeds some objective. An organization measures the performance of a work unit against its objectives, then pays a bonus if the group exceeds the objectives. Cabletron Systems, a computer cable maker based in Rochester, New Hampshire, wants its telephone salespeople to cooperate with its outside sales force, rather than compete for leads and other information. So the company pays employees quarterly bonuses, half of which are based on how well their region meets sales goals and half on how well the entire company meets its sales goals.[13]

**profit-sharing plan**
A group incentive plan under which the company sets aside a share of its profits and divides it among employees.

A frequently used type of group incentive is the **profit-sharing plan.** Under this kind of plan, the company sets aside a share of its profits earned during a given period, such as a year, and divides these profits among the employees. The assumption is that the better the work done, the more the company will earn and, therefore, the bigger the bonuses. In the past, profit sharing was limited chiefly to executives, but more companies today are sharing profits among all employees.

Steelmaker Nucor Corporation contributes a minimum of 10 percent of annual pretax earnings to its profit-sharing plan. About 20 percent of that money is paid to the company's employees; individuals receive the remainder of their share when they leave the company.[14] In 1990 the average hourly employee earned $36,000, considered good pay in the areas where Nucor's plants are located.[15]

**gainsharing**
A group incentive plan in which the organization encourages employees to participate in making suggestions and decisions, then rewards the group with a share of improved earnings.

An increasing number of companies are adopting a **gainsharing** program, under which the company encourages employees to participate in making suggestions and decisions about improving the way the company or work group operates. As performance improves, employees receive a share of the greater earnings. Thus, gainsharing seeks to motivate not only by giving financial rewards but also by making employees feel they have an important role as part of a team.

## Secrecy of Wage and Salary Information

In our society, money is considered a private matter, and most people do not like to talk about what they earn. Thus, in private (nongovernment) organizations, employees generally do not know one another's earnings, although supervisors

**FIGURE 11.4**

Some Ways
Supervisors Can
Motivate Employees

Making Work Interesting
• Job rotation
• Job enlargement
• Job enrichment
• Customer contact
Having High Expectations
Providing Valued Rewards
Relating Rewards to Performance
Treating Employees as Individuals
Encouraging Participation
Providing Feedback

know what their subordinates earn. In contrast, government employees' earnings are public information, often published in local papers, because taxpayers ultimately pay their wages and salaries.

Does secrecy help or hurt the usefulness of money as a motivator? Certainly, it does not make sense to disclose information if it only embarrasses employees. However, surveys that ask employees to estimate their co-workers' earnings indicate that most employees overestimate what others earn.[16] This overestimation can result in dissatisfaction because employees believe they are underpaid in comparison.

To motivate employees with the possibility of a raise and a belief that pay rates are fair, the organization must let them know what they can hope to earn. A typical compromise between maintaining privacy and sharing information is for the organization to publish pay ranges. These show the lowest and highest wage or salary the organization will pay an employee in a particular position. Employees do not know how much specific individuals earn, but the ranges show what they can expect to earn if they get a raise, promotion, or transfer to another position.

## How Supervisors Can Motivate

The first part of this chapter addressed the theories of motivating. These theories suggested some practical ways supervisors can motivate. Several possibilities are summarized in Figure 11.4. In addition, "Tips from the Firing Line" suggest ways for supervisors to keep themselves motivated.

### Making Work Interesting

When employees find their work interesting, they are more likely to give it their full attention and enthusiasm. In general, work is interesting when it has variety

---

### TIPS FROM THE FIRING LINE

## *Motivating Your Employees—and Yourself*

As a supervisor, you may find that you concentrate so much on motivating your employees that you forget to motivate yourself. Zig Ziglar, chairman of his own training and development company and author of *See You at the Top*, offers some suggestions for motivating yourself, even when the chips are down.

- *Give yourself a pep talk.* If you expect your employees to believe in you, you have to believe in yourself. Write positive phrases about yourself, such as "I am honest, intelligent, and responsible," on three-by-five-inch cards. Keep them where you can read them several times a day.
- *Set goals.* Be specific about the goals you want to achieve. Even create a "wild idea sheet" that lists "everything you want to be, do, or have."
- *Think positive; get positive training.* It's important to be enthusiastic about what you are doing, but you also need to *know* what you are doing. Get the training you need to support a positive attitude.
- *If necessary, get professional counseling.* There may be times in your career when you need help. Don't be afraid to ask for it from someone who has wisdom and the necessary knowledge to assist you.

- *Control your environment.* Control as many elements of your environment as you can. Exercise and eat well so you feel your best. Listen to music with positive messages, especially in the morning.
- *Use positive words to convey your message.* Learn to phrase your communications in a positive manner. For instance, avoid saying to an employee, "This is an important account. Don't foul it up." Instead, say, "This is an important account. That's why I'm assigning it to you. I know you will handle it well."
- *Leave every encounter on a positive note.* Try to end every exchange with another person on a good note. This may be difficult sometimes, but doing so will not only make you feel upbeat, it will make the other person feel good as well. That person will remember you that way.

Source: Adapted from Zig Ziglar, "Zig Ziglar's Motivation Secrets," *Bottom Line*, Apr. 15, 1995, pp. 9–10. Used with permission of Zig Ziglar and The Zig Ziglar Corp.

---

and allows employees some control over what they do. Work can be made more interesting through job rotation, job enlargement, job enrichment, and increased customer contact.

**job rotation**
Moving employees from job to job to give them more variety.

**cross-training**
Training in the skills required to perform more than one job.

**job enlargement**
An effort to make a job more interesting by adding more duties to it.

**Job rotation** involves moving employees from job to job to give them more variety. For example, the employees in a production department may take turns operating all the machines in the factory. Job rotation requires that employees have relatively broad skills. As a result, the supervisor or company must provide for **cross-training,** or training in the skills required to perform more than one job. The opportunity to learn new skills through cross-training can in itself motivate employees. The management of Highland Park Hospital in Highland Park, Illinois, developed a cross-training plan with the initial goal of cutting costs for nursing personnel. However, the response to the program was so positive that management realized that the nurses saw cross-training as a means to make their work more interesting.[17]

**Job enlargement** is an effort to make a job more interesting by adding more duties to it. Thus, a machine operator might be responsible not only for running a particular machine, but also for performing maintenance on the machine and inspecting the quality of the parts produced with the machine. As with job rotation, this approach assumes that variety in a job makes it more satisfying, with the result that employees are more motivated.

**job enrichment**
The incorporation of motivating factors into a job—in particlular, giving the employee more responsibility and recognition.

**Job enrichment** is the incorporation of motivating factors into a job. Herzberg called the factors that enrich a job motivators (see Table 11.1). Generally, an enriched job gives employees more responsibility to make decisions and more recognition for good performance. Thus, enriched jobs are more challenging and, presumably, more rewarding. For example, instead of requiring salespeople in a department store to call a supervisor whenever a customer has a complaint, the store might authorize them to handle complaints as they see fit. They would have to call a supervisor only if solving the problem would cost the store more than some set amount, say, $500.

When modifying jobs to make them more interesting, the organization and supervisor must remember that not all employees are motivated by the same things at the same time. Thus, while some employees may eagerly accept the new variety in their jobs, others are likely to be less enthusiastic. Some workers may think jobs are being redesigned simply to get more work out of people for the same amount of money. A supervisor must be careful to emphasize the advantages of the new arrangement and to listen to employee reactions.

Work also can be made more meaningful by giving employees some contact with the people who receive and use their products (goods or services). Nurses and salespeople are routinely in contact with the people they serve, but production workers and accounting personnel have less customer contact. Sometimes a supervisor can arrange to have workers visit the users of the products. For example, a group of production workers might be sent to visit a customer who is having trouble operating a machine the company manufactures. The workers not only would be able to help the customer, but they might also get some ideas for making the machine better. Accounting personnel might meet the people in the company who use their reports to make sure they understand and are satisfied with the reports.

## Having High Expectations

Effective motivation can lead to performance beyond employees' own expectations of themselves. When someone expects a lot of us, we often find that we can do a lot. When little is expected, we tend to provide little. In either case, the expectations are self-fulfilling.

**Pygmalion effect**
The direct relationship between expectations and performance; high expectations lead to high performance.

The direct relationship between expectations and performance is known as the **Pygmalion effect.** The name comes from the Greek myth of Pygmalion, a king of Cyprus who carved a statue of a beautiful maiden and then fell in love with her. He so wished she were real that she became real.

According to the Pygmalion effect, a supervisor who says to an employee, "You're so dense, you never get the procedures right," will not motivate effectively. Instead, the employee will decide that understanding procedures is beyond his or her capacity. Therefore, a supervisor who wishes employees to set high standards for themselves must think and speak with the assumption that the employees are capable of meeting high standards. A supervisor might say, "These procedures are complicated, but I'm sure that if you study them regularly and ask questions, you can learn to follow them."

General H. Norman Schwarzkopf, who came to prominence during the Persian Gulf War, described how he put the Pygmalion effect to work earlier in his career when he was in charge of helicopter maintenance. He asked how much of the helicopter fleet could fly on any given day, and the answer was 75 percent. Schwarzkopf recalled, "People didn't come in at 74 or 76, but always at 75, because that was the standard that had been set for them. I said, 'I don't know anything about helicopter maintenance, but I'm establishing a new standard: 85 percent." Before long, 85 percent of the fleet could fly each day.[18]

### Providing Rewards That Are Valued

The content theories of motivation indicate that a variety of rewards may motivate, but that not all employees will value the same rewards at the same time. The supervisor's challenge is to determine what rewards will work for particular employees at particular times. This involves appreciating the needs people are trying to meet and the variety of ways a supervisor can provide rewards.

Of course, there are some limits to a supervisor's discretion in giving rewards. Company policy or a union contract may dictate the size of raises employees get and the degree to which raises are linked to performance as opposed to seniority or some other measure. However, supervisors can use the theories of motivation, coupled with their own experience, to identify the kinds of rewards over which they have some control. For example, a supervisor has great freedom in administering rewards such as praise and recognition. Many supervisors have some discretion in job assignments. Employees who have a high need for achievement (McClelland's theory) or are trying to meet esteem or self-actualization needs (Maslow's theory) may appreciate opportunities for additional training. Employees who have a high need for affiliation or are seeking to meet social needs may appreciate being assigned to jobs where they work with other people.

### Relating Rewards to Performance

The rewards that a supervisor uses should be linked to employee performance. Unfortunately, less than half of employees see a clear link between good job performance and higher pay, according to a survey of about 5,000 employees.[19] If there is a connection, employees should be aware of it and understand it. Linking rewards to the achievement of realistic objectives is a way to help employees believe they can attain desired rewards. As Vroom's expectancy-valence theory described, rewards are most likely to motivate employees when the employees view them as achievable.

The use of objectives is a basic way to link rewards to performance (see Chapter 6). For example, the management by objectives (MBO) system provides rewards when employees meet or exceed the objectives they have helped set for themselves. Thus, if a museum's cafeteria workers are supposed to leave their work areas spotless at the end of each shift, they know whether they have done what is necessary to receive their rewards, such as regular pay raises or extra time off.

Using clear objectives to help motivate employees is an important way to make sure that when employees try hard, they are trying to do the right things. Consultant and trainer Will Kaydos writes, "You only have to imagine a basketball court without baskets to realize that motivating someone without clear goals and measures is practically impossible."[20] In contrast, the Von Maur department

### FIGURE 11.5

**Job Characteristics Rated Important by American Workers**

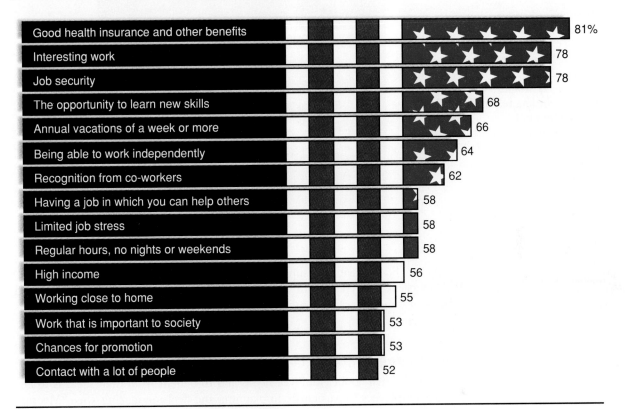

Source: Data from Gallup poll cited in Patricia Braus, "What Workers Want," *American Demographics*, Aug. 1992, pp. 30–31*ff.*

store chain has built an outstanding reputation by linking challenging goals to rewards. Employees are expected to deliver exceptional customer service "for every single customer, every single day." To reward such behavior, the stores hold weekly meetings at which thank-you notes from customers are read to employees. The subjects of those letters receive applause in addition to a prize such as movie tickets or cash.[21] (For a discussion of communicating goals and other information to employees, see Chapter 10.)

### Treating Employees as Individuals

Most of the theories of motivation emphasize that different things motivate individuals to different degrees. A supervisor who wishes to succeed at motivating has to remember that employees will respond in varying ways. A supervisor cannot expect that everyone will be excited equally about cross-training or overtime pay. Some employees might prefer an easy job or short hours, so that they have time and energy for outside activities. Figure 11.5 shows how American workers rated job characteristics in a Gallup poll.

Doug and Aleta Dent (*center*) of Modesto, California, manage a franchise of Huntington Learning Centers, which provides remedial learning by supplementing students' classroom work. According to the Dents, Huntington's management is supportive of its franchisees. The company uses team leadership, promotes open communication, and welcomes new ideas on coursework or solutions to learning problems. This management style was the deciding factor in the Dents' decision to buy a franchise.

Source: © Charles Moore/Black Star

As much as possible, a supervisor should respond to individual differences. When a particular type of motivation does not seem to work with an employee, a supervisor should try some other motivator to see if it better matches the employee's needs.

## Encouraging Employee Participation

One way to learn about employee needs and to benefit from their ideas is to encourage employees to participate in planning and decision making. (See "Meeting the Challenge.") As you read in Chapter 9, employees tend to feel more committed when they can contribute to decisions and solutions. They also are likely to cooperate better when they feel like part of a team.

Work/Family Directions established a task force of employees to develop its request form for flexible work arrangements, including which questions to use on the form. The company's founders maintain that this employee involvement contributed to a widely shared belief that the process of granting requests is fair.[22]

## Providing Feedback

People want and need to know how well they are doing. Part of a supervisor's job is to give employees feedback about their performance. When the supervisor tells employees that they are meeting or exceeding objectives, the employees know that they are doing something right. When a supervisor tells employees that they are falling short of objectives, the employees know that they need to improve. Most people will try to improve when given a chance to do so.

## MEETING THE CHALLENGE

### *Disney and Motorola Motivate Employees Toward High Quality*

The Walt Disney Company, which owns the sprawling Disney World theme park in Florida, and Motorola, leader in the telecommunications industry, may appear at first to be two entirely different types of companies. Yet, both thrive on service and both are committed to quality. To provide customers with the highest-quality service, they need to motivate employees every way possible.

Disney motivates its employees according to its own basic principles. Providing good food and good service is not enough. Visitors to Disney World must be enthralled; they must also feel that the staff genuinely cares about them. Thus, Disney hires employees who have what the organization considers the right attitude, then trains them in service skills. Disney looks for job candidates who possess "self-direction, pride, self-discipline, assertiveness, a need for physical movement, and enjoyment of role-playing."

Since the service workers who deal directly with customers are vital to the success of the business, Valerie Oberle, vice-president of Disney University, recommends that supervisors tap them for sugges-

tions concerning the improvement of how things are run. Then supervisors should follow up on those suggestions. Employees and their managers constantly are challenged to offer customers excitement, magic, and fun.

Motorola focuses on motivating employees through training. By making a commitment to training, Motorola makes a commitment to its employees; offering appropriate training shows workers that the company will provide the resources to achieve the quality for which it strives. "Don't speak about anything without talking about quality first," says president and chief operating officer Christopher Galvin.

Workers are motivated when they know that Motorola supports their efforts. In addition, Galvin insists that employees be treated with dignity and respect. In return, he expects that they perform their best—and they do.

Source: "Disney, Motorola Nurture Service Cultures," *Restaurants & Institutions*, Dec. 15, 1995, p. 47.

---

Praise is an important kind of feedback. In monitoring employees, a supervisor should look for signs of excellent performance and let the employees know, in specific terms, that the good work is appreciated and that it benefits the organization.

There are many ways to deliver praise. For example, a nursing supervisor might write a memo to a nurse, in which the supervisor comments on the nurse's courteous manner with patients and how it gives patients a good impression of the hospital. Or, a police force supervisor might remark to an officer that the officer's paperwork is always complete and legible.

At Adams & Adams Building Services of Enfield, Connecticut, managers carry cards bearing a message of congratulations. Whenever a manager sees an employee doing a high-quality job, the manager gives the employee a card. Twice a year, the employees enter their cards in a drawing for various prizes.[23]

A supervisor does not have to use a dramatic approach to praising a behavior. Praise is so easy to give and its potential rewards are so great that the supervisor can and should use it routinely, as long as it is sincere.

# Summary

### 11.1 Identify the relationship between motivation and performance.

To perform well, employees must be motivated. Motivation is giving people incentives to act in certain ways. For motivation to work, a supervisor needs to know what rewards employees value.

### 11.2 Describe content theories of motivation.

Content theories of motivation attempt to identify what motivates people. According to Maslow's theory, people are motivated by unmet needs. These needs fall into a hierarchy: physiological, security, social, esteem, and self-actualization. People attempt to satisfy lower-level needs before they focus on higher-level needs. According to McClelland, people have achievement, power, and affiliation needs. The intensity of each kind of need varies from person to person. Herzberg's two-factor theory says that employees are dissatisfied when hygiene factors are absent and satisfied when motivating factors are present.

### 11.3 Describe process theories of motivation.

Process theories explain how motivation works through its process. According to Vroom's expectancy-valence theory, the intensity of a person's motivation depends on the value the person places on the outcome of a behavior multiplied by the perceived probability that the behavior will actually lead to the outcome. People are most motivated to seek results they value highly and think they can achieve. Reinforcement theory, pioneered by B. F. Skinner, says that people behave as they do because of the kind of consequences they experience as a result of their behavior. The supervisor can therefore influence behavior by administering the consequences (in the form of reinforcement or punishment).

### 11.4 Explain when financial incentives are likely to motivate employees.

Money motivates people when it meets their needs. The employees must believe they are able to achieve the financial rewards the organization offers.

### 11.5 Describe pay plans using financial incentives.

Under a piecework system, employees are paid according to how much they produce. A production bonus system pays a basic wage or salary plus a bonus based on performance; for example, an amount per unit assembled. Commissions are payments tied to the amount of sales completed. Some organizations pay employees for making useful suggestions on cutting costs or improving quality. Group incentive plans pay a bonus when the group as a whole exceeds an objective. Profit-sharing and gainsharing plans are types of group incentives.

### 11.6 Discuss the pros and cons of keeping pay information secret.

Keeping pay secret respects employees' desire for privacy. However, to be motivated by the possibility of greater earnings and a sense that pay rates are fair, employees must know what they can hope to earn. Typically, an organization balances these needs by publishing pay ranges that show the least and most the organization will pay an employee in a particular job.

### 11.7 Identify ways supervisors can motivate their employees.

Supervisors can motivate employees by making work interesting through job rotation, job enlargement, job enrichment, and contact with users of the product or service. Other ways to motivate include having high expectations of employees, providing rewards that are valued, relating rewards to performance, treating employees as individuals, encouraging employee participation, and providing feedback, including praise.

## Key Terms

motivation

flextime

job sharing

reinforcement

punishment

behavior modification

financial incentives

piecework system

commissions

group incentive plan

profit-sharing plan

gainsharing

job rotation

cross-training

job enlargement

job enrichment

Pygmalion effect

## Review and Discussion Questions

1. Name and rank the five basic needs, from lowest to highest, that Maslow described in his hierarchy of needs. If a supervisor applies this hierarchy to his or her employees, what are some specific ways that employees' needs could be met?

2. What are some family-friendly policies that companies now have in place so that employees can balance home and work? What other family-friendly policies might help employees to meet the demands in their lives and thus motivate them at work?

3. What are the three categories of needs that McClelland identified in his theory? Which category of needs do you think is strongest for you?

4. What are the hygiene factors and motivating factors described by Herzberg? Consider your current job or one you held most recently. Which factors are (were) present at that job? How would you say they affect(ed) your level of satisfaction? Your level of motivation?

5. John Lightfoot believes he has a 75 percent chance of earning a bonus of $100. Mary Yu believes she has a 75 percent chance of qualifying for a raise of $1,000 a year. According to Vroom's expectancy-valence theory, is it correct to conclude that Mary will be more intensely motivated by her potential reward than John will be by his? Explain.

6. Andre Jones supervises computer programmers. He expects each programmer to turn in a progress report by quitting time each Friday.

    a. Name at least one way Andre can use reinforcement to motivate employees to turn in their reports on time.

    b. Name at least one way Andre can use punishment to motivate employees to turn in their reports on time.

    c. Which of these approaches do you think would be most successful? Why?

7. In which of the following situations do you think money will be an effective motivator? Explain.

    a. The economy is slow, and even though the salespeople think they are doing their best, sales are down. Sales supervisor Rita Blount tells the sales force that anyone whose weekly sales are up by 10 percent next week will receive a $5,000 bonus.

    b. A retailer such as Radio Shack announces that the top performer in the store will be a prime candidate for a management job in a store the company is opening in another state. Whoever takes the job will receive a raise of at least 9 percent.

    c. A respiratory therapist who is the parent of two high-school-age children can earn an extra $500 this month by accepting a schedule that involves working on weekends.

8. Which type(s) of pay plan (piecework, production bonus, commission, payment for suggestions, group incentive) would work best in each of the following situations? Why?

   a. A company wants to motivate employees in the manufacturing department to fulfill increased orders for wooden toys as the company tries to expand from a regional market to a national market.

   b. A car dealership wants to emphasize teamwork in its service department.

9. Antonio Delgado supervises the police officers of the fourth precinct. Name some ways that he can make their work more interesting.

10. A supervisor at a mail-order catalog company reads a report stating that 15 percent of all orders subsequently are returned, but this figure is considered better than the industry average. How can she use the Pygmalion effect to motivate employees to reduce the number of returns even further?

11. What is wrong with each of the following attempts at motivation?

    a. A sales supervisor for an insurance company believes that employees appreciate an opportunity to broaden their experience, so she rewards the top performer each year with an all-expenses-paid leadership seminar. The seminar lasts a week and is conducted at a hotel in a city 200 miles away.

    b. The supervisor of a hospital cafeteria awards one employee a $50 bonus each month. To give everyone an equal chance at receiving the bonus, the supervisor draws names written on slips of paper from a jar.

    c. A maintenance supervisor in a pickle factory believes that qualified employees should be able to tell whether they are doing a good job. Therefore, the supervisor focuses his motivation efforts on thinking up clever rewards to give out each year to the best performers.

## A SECOND LOOK

Given the information about motivating the sales force of the gas products company in the story at the beginning of this chapter, how well would you expect the company's incentives to motivate its sales representatives? Explain. What, if any, additions or improvements would you suggest to the way Kisson motivates the sales reps?

# APPLICATIONS MODULE

## CASE

### *U.S. Department of Labor Learns What Motivates Women*

Sometimes the best way to find out what motivates people is to ask them. The Women's Bureau of the U.S. Department of Labor did just that. It developed a thorough questionnaire, which it distributed to 250,000 working women around the country. Then it followed up more closely on 1,200 of the survey respondents.

Surprisingly, the researchers learned that 70 percent of the women reported that they liked their jobs. Apparently, working women have strong social or affiliation needs; half of both the white-collar and blue-collar workers said that spending time with their co-workers was "the best thing about going to work." However, these were the lower-paid workers, with wages of about $10,000 to $25,000 per year. "The fact that low-income women enjoy their co-workers more than anything else at work speaks volumes about the need women have for support systems, how much more difficult their lives are," explains Ethel Long-Scott, executive director of the Women's Economic Agenda Project in Oakland, California. "Remember, earning only $10,000 is living in poverty."

Since the jobs these women hold barely satisfy security needs and may do little to satisfy the needs higher on Maslow's hierarchy or McClelland's achievement-power needs, the women look for ways to satisfy social or affiliation needs. "It's good to be able to have someone to exchange experiences with," Long-Scott continues. "You need to be supported when you're trying to have a life of dignity. But the choice of friendships at work also is an indirect way of saying how hard life is when you don't have money."

On the other hand, women with higher salaries and higher positions within their organizations were more apt to cite money as the most important motivator. And women who were union members said that good benefits—in other words, security—were the most important thing about their jobs.

Other motivators uncovered by the survey included equal opportunity, job training, and family-friendly policies such as flexible hours. The first two are examples of needs for esteem, self-actualization, and achievement; the third is, in a sense, a security need because so many working women struggle to balance the demands of job and family.

The Department of Labor's survey can't possibly say what motivates all women, in all jobs, all the time. But its findings may help supervisors understand what is important to women in the workplace.

1. Do the findings of the survey surprise you? Why or why not?
2. Why do you think higher-paid women workers place more emphasis on money?
3. If you are unable as a supervisor to give workers higher pay, what steps might you take to motivate the women in your group?
4. What rewards are valued by higher-paid women? What rewards are valued by lower-paid women? Do you think women might value some of the same rewards? Why or why not?

Source: Carol Kleiman, "Survey Says Personal Friends Can Be Perk for Women Personnel," *Chicago Tribune*, Mar. 30, 1995, sec. 3, p. 3.

### SELF-QUIZ

## *What Motivates You?*

What makes a job appealing to you? Rank the following job factors from 1 to 12. Assign 1 to the factor you consider most important and 12 to the factor you consider least important.

_____    1. Work that is interesting and meaningful.

_____    2. Good wages or salary.

_____    3. Authority to make important decisions.

_____    4. Comfortable work environment, such as a clean, modern laboratory, fancy store, or attractive office.

_____    5. Likable co-workers.

_____    6. Good relationship with supervisor.

_____    7. Clear understanding of the department's and company's goals and performance requirements.

_____    8. Appreciation and recognition for doing a good job.

_____    9. Opportunities to learn new skills.

_____   10. Prestigious title or occupation.

_____   11. Chance for advancement.

_____   12. Job security.

## Class Exercise

If you have not already done so, answer the Self-Quiz questions. Then, by a show of hands, determine how many class members selected each response as most important and how many as least important. The instructor might tally the responses on the chalkboard or overhead projector or fill in the table below:

Discuss the following questions:

- Which response(s) did most class members choose as most important?
- Which response(s) did most class members choose as least important?
- Do you think these choices are typical of most employees today? Why or why not?
- How could a supervisor use this information to motivate employees?

| Self-Quiz Item | Number of Students Rating the Item | |
|---|---|---|
| | Most Important | Least Important |
| 1. | _____ | _____ |
| 2. | _____ | _____ |
| 3. | _____ | _____ |
| 4. | _____ | _____ |
| 5. | _____ | _____ |
| 6. | _____ | _____ |

| Self-Quiz Item | Number of Students Rating the Item | |
|---|---|---|
| | Most Important | Least Important |
| 7. | _____ | _____ |
| 8. | _____ | _____ |
| 9. | _____ | _____ |
| 10. | _____ | _____ |
| 11. | _____ | _____ |
| 12. | _____ | _____ |

## Team-Building Exercise

### Developing Motivational Methods

This chapter deals with one of the most challenging areas for supervisors: motivating employees. This exercise will help you develop a comprehensive list of motivating methods on which to draw when faced with employees whom you feel are not performing to their full potential.

#### Instructions

1. The table on page 340 shows five suggested categories of motivational methods and gives an example of each. Drawing on what you have learned about motivation in this class and elsewhere, list methods, techniques, and strategies that can serve as a source of ideas on how to motivate people.

2. For purposes of this exercise, do not be concerned about the economic impact of your ideas or a plan for carrying them out. For ex-

ample, if you suggest a bonus to reward your employees for good performance, there is no need to provide a formula for computing the bonus. At the same time, however, do not make ridiculous suggestions that would not make good business sense, such as suggesting that you reward all employees and their families with a two-week all-expenses-paid vacation to Bermuda.

3. Divide the class into groups. Then develop a group list that can be copied for each group member. There will undoubtedly be many days in your management career when you will be able to use this list to help you generate some ideas on how to motivate an unmotivated employee. Also, the list can be improved over time as you develop greater expertise as a motivational leader.

| Things I can do to be a motivational leader | Characteristics of a motivating work environment | Ways to reward my employees for good performance | Strategies I can use to improve the way work is done | Organizational policies or benefits |
|---|---|---|---|---|
| Help employees set challenging yet achievable goals | Goods and services employees believe in | Publish achievements in company newsletter | Communicate clear performance standards | Flexible work schedules to accommodate personal and family needs |
| | | | | |
| | | | | |
| | | | | |
| | | | | |
| | | | | |
| | | | | |
| | | | | |
| | | | | |
| | | | | |
| | | | | |
| | | | | |
| | | | | |
| | | | | |
| | | | | |
| | | | | |
| | | | | |
| | | | | |
| | | | | |

# Video Exercise 11: *Motivating Employees*

## *Video Summary*

Motivation is the key to being competitive in a global marketplace. In this program, J. C. Penney will demonstrate how it uses nonfinancial incentives to motivate its retail sales associates; Nucor Steel, the nation's fastest growing and most profitable steel company, will explain how its unique financial incentive system has motivated its employees to be the most productive in the world.

## *Application*

In this exercise, you will examine characteristics of PLAY to determine if you can develop any supervisory applications to WORK. This nontraditional perspective of work should provide you with some insights about motivation.

Look at the table. You will note several characteristics of "play" in column 1. Fill in column 2, "Supervisory Application to WORK," by selecting 7–10 characteristics of play from the list and thinking about how supervisors could make "work" more like "play." Include ideas you just saw demonstrated at Nucor and J. C. Penney on the video.

| Characteristics of PLAY | Supervisory Application to WORK |
|---|---|
| 1. Alternatives available | |
| 2. New games to be played on different days | |
| 3. Contact with friends and peers | |
| 4. Flexibility of choosing teammates | |
| 5. Flexible duration of play | |
| 6. Flexible time to play | |
| 7. Opportunity to be/express oneself | |
| 8. Opportunity to use one's talents | |
| 9. Skillful play brings applause, praise, and recognition from spectators | |
| 10. Existence of healthy competition, rivalry, and challenge | |
| 11. Opportunity for social interaction | |

| Characteristics of PLAY | Supervisory Application to WORK |
|---|---|
| 12. Opportunity for ongoing teams to develop | |
| 13. Availability of mechanisms for scoring one's performance (feedback) | |
| 14. Basic fairness and justice assured by rules | |
| 15. Experiences of achievement, thrill of winning, handling losing with grace, etc. | |

## Questions for Discussion

1. What prevents supervisors from making work more like play?

   _____

   _____

2. Are these forces real, or imagined?

   _____

   _____

3. What would be the likely (positive and negative) results of making work more like play?

   _____

   _____

4. Could others in the organization accept such creative behaviors?

   _____

   _____

Source: Adapted from Edward E. Scannell and John W. Newstrom, *Still More Games Trainers Play* (New York: McGraw-Hill, 1991), pp. 265–7.

# 12

*A company cannot increase its productivity. People can.*

—Robert Half, chief executive of Robert Half International, a worldwide permanent/temporary personnel agency

# Improving Productivity

## CHAPTER OUTLINE

The Productivity Challenge
*Trends in Productivity in the United States*
*Constraints on Productivity*

Measurement of Productivity

Improving Productivity by Controlling Quality

Improving Productivity by Controlling Costs
*Determining Costs*
*Cost-Control Strategies*

Employee Fears About Productivity Improvement

## LEARNING OBJECTIVES

After you have studied this chapter, you should be able to:

12.1 Define *productivity*.

12.2 Identify constraints on productivity.

12.3 Describe how productivity and productivity improvements are measured.

12.4 Identify the two basic ways in which productivity may be improved.

12.5 Describe cost-control strategies available to supervisors.

12.6 Explain why employees have fears about productivity improvement, and tell how supervisors can address those fears.

Source: Courtesy of Classic Kitchen and Baths.

## PRODUCTIVITY PAYS

As the founder and president of Classic Kitchen and Baths in Mercer Island, Washington, Jinny Bray supervises one part-time and two full-time employees. The full-time employees are a foreman and a carpenter's helper, and the part-time employee is a designer for the construction projects handled by the company. In addition, Bray oversees the work of suppliers and subcontractors.

To stay in business, Bray must be concerned with the quantity and quality of results she gets from her employees and subcontractors. She needs to be sure that when she is paying them to work, they are actually working. Thus, she takes note of which workers engage in personal conversation on the job.

When the chatting interferes with work, she schedules some of the talkative workers to come in on different days from others. She does not want to dampen the cooperative spirit among the workers, so she tries to be subtle in discouraging the personal talk.

Another challenge for Bray is satisfying all the requirements of government building codes. When Bray believes the government inspectors are being unrealistic, she must discuss and resolve the matter with them. However, because Bray's company adheres to the building codes on all projects, this problem remains a minor one.

■ **FIGURE 12.1**

**The Productivity Formula**

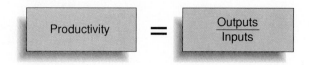

When Jinny Bray is addressing issues such as how much work subcontractors are doing or the way government regulations add to the cost and time needed for completing a project, she is concerned with productivity. **Productivity** is the amount of results (output) an organization gets for a given amount of inputs (see Figure 12.1). Thus, productivity can refer to the amount of acceptable work employees do for each dollar they earn or the number of acceptable products manufactured with a given amount of resources.

**productivity**
The amount of results (output) an organization gets for a given amount of inputs.

This chapter takes a deeper look at the meaning of productivity and how it is measured. It describes the two basic ways to increase productivity: controlling quality and controlling costs. Ways that supervisors can participate in efforts to improve productivity are suggested.

## The Productivity Challenge

Stiff competition from around the world is forcing U.S. businesses to pay attention to productivity. In addition, widespread opposition to paying higher taxes is forcing governments to make their operations more productive. To help improve productivity, supervisors must understand why it is important and what limits an organization's productivity.

### Trends in Productivity in the United States

When the productivity of organizations in a country is improving, people benefit. They can get goods and services at lower prices or with lower taxes than they otherwise could. Employers tend to pay higher wages and salaries to workers who are more productive. People also have access to more and better goods and services. Because of these benefits, statisticians keep track of productivity trends in various countries.

Overall, the performance of U.S. businesses has been mixed.[1] The amount of goods and services produced by the average U.S. worker is higher than that for any other industrialized nation. In 1990 the average U.S. worker produced $45,100 worth of goods and services, compared with $34,500 by the average Japanese worker. However, the rate of productivity growth suffered during the 1980s, igniting cries of alarm that U.S. business was no longer globally competitive. Most disturbing was productivity at service organizations, which are becoming an increasingly large part of the U.S. economy. Productivity in service organizations is difficult to measure, but accepted statistics showed that it declined during the late 1970s and remained flat during the following decade.

Happily, more recent reports show productivity rising again in both the manufacturing and service sectors of the U.S. economy.[2] In fact, a recent study identified the United States as the world's most competitive economy for the first time since 1985.[3]

Slow growth in productivity does not necessarily mean employees are reluctant to work better and faster. Rather, organizations sometimes hesitate to invest in the necessary equipment and training. Based on the current evidence, organizations achieve the greatest improvement in productivity when they couple investments in technology with better systems and management practices.

Thus, the productivity improvements of this decade have resulted from efforts to reengineer or restructure organizations and to empower employees.[4] For example, productivity may improve when organizations effectively use total quality management and teamwork (see chapters 2 and 3). At Procter & Gamble, productivity is reportedly up to 40 percent greater in factories using team-based production than in traditionally run plants.[5]

## Constraints on Productivity

When you read about ways to improve productivity, keep in mind that several constraints limit the impact of a supervisor or even of a higher-level manager. Supervisors and other managers should be aware of these constraints, so that they can either plan ways to overcome them or set realistic goals within them. Some of the most important constraints on productivity are management limitations, employee attitudes and skills, government regulations, and union rules.

### Management Limitations

Operative employees will contribute to improving productivity only if they believe management is truly committed to this objective. All too often, however, employees believe management is more interested in the next quarter's profits than in producing high-quality goods or services as efficiently as possible. Employees become frustrated, especially when managers do not seem to listen to their ideas for improvements.

The most important way supervisors can overcome this constraint is to set a good example. Supervisors should demonstrate by their actions and words that they are interested in the department's productivity. This behavior includes seeing that the job is done right the first time, as well as using resources wisely, which, on a personal level, includes being well organized. To test your own level of personal productivity, take the Self-Quiz at the end of the chapter (page 366).

Supervisors also must communicate instructions clearly and plan carefully, so that employees are able to live up to managers' expectations. Furthermore, supervisors should listen to employees' concerns and ideas about improving productivity. If the organization has a formal program for submitting ideas, supervisors can offer to help employees write down or explain their suggestions. In organizations that allow or expect employee participation in planning and decision making, supervisors should encourage, not stifle, this participation.

### Employee Attitudes and Skills

Improving productivity means making changes. People have a natural tendency to resist change because it is challenging and often frightening (see Chapter 15). Employees who have a negative attitude toward productivity improvements will not be motivated to make the changes work. Part of a supervisor's job is to identify employee attitudes and, when necessary, help employees take a more positive view. (The last section of this chapter addresses this issue in greater detail.)

These engineers designed Oracle Corporation's Video Server, a program that can deliver 100 different digitized video films to 100 houses at 100 different times, and they completed the prototype in only two months. Key to their productivity were the immediate and enthusiastic approval of Oracle management, financial support for developmental equipment, and the positive attitudes and skills of the employees. One of the uses for the Video Server is to send images to a window on desktop PCs by using high-speed integrated services digital network (ISDN) phone lines. That would make video E-mail possible.

Source: © Robert Holmgren.

The skills of employees also influence how effective productivity-building efforts will be. When an organization wants each member to contribute more to the goods or services it produces, each member must either work faster or do the job differently. Some employees are able to perform new tasks or do their jobs in a new way with little or no training. Other employees understand only one way of working. Supervisors can possibly overcome this constraint among employees who are willing to work simply by providing more training. When employees are either unwilling or unable to learn, this constraint is more difficult to overcome.

Attitudes and skills alike may require improvement when productivity suffers as a result of culture shock. According to Sondra Thiederman, president of Cross-Cultural Communications, a San Diego–based training firm, culture shock is "a state of mind that occurs when people find themselves immersed in a strange culture."[6] Immigrant employees, supervisors of people from another culture, and employees whose culture differs from that of most of their co-workers find that others do not respond to their behaviors in an expected manner. Furthermore, employees in a strange culture do not know how they are expected to behave and do not receive the credit they expect for their achievements, skills, and ideas. Common responses include depression, loneliness, aggression, short attention span, frustration, passivity, and quickness to fatigue.

How can a supervisor help prevent or correct the isolation, confusion, and aggression that can result from culture shock? The basic solution is more exposure to a variety of people. The more that people are exposed to diversity and the more they learn about it, the more comfortable they will be. Supervisors and their employees may benefit from formal training in this area. It is also helpful to be open and honest about the problem. Discussing feelings helps to diffuse culture shock and leads people to a better understanding of one another.

### Government Regulations

Businesses and other organizations in the United States are regulated in many areas, including payment of overtime wages, disability compensation, environmental pollution, minimum safety standards, and child labor. In addition, as mentioned in the story of Jinny Bray at the beginning of this chapter, construction companies must contend with extensive building codes.

Following these regulations costs money, but the laws reflect the values of the majority in our society. For example, it might be cheaper to hire children to assemble electronic components, but few people want to return to the days of children laboring long hours within factory walls. Likewise, scrubbers on smokestacks cost money, but clean air to breathe is essential. Even when government regulations seem illogical or unreasonable, an organization can face serious penalties for ignoring or disobeying them. Thus, the proper role of supervisors and other managers is to know these regulations and seek ways of improving productivity without violating the law.

### Union Rules

Union contracts typically specify rules for what tasks particular employees may do, what hours they may work, and how organizations may use employees. Sometimes an organization's managers see a way to improve productivity that violates one of these rules. For example, it might be more efficient to have two employees learn each other's jobs so they can get the work done even when one of them is away or busy. However, the union contract might contain a rule against this. Similarly, the International Brotherhood of Teamsters objected to certain aspects of UPS's restructuring. According to the Teamsters, hourly workers would be given authority over more senior employees, so the company had to negotiate these changes with the union. (UPS management maintains that the greater freedom and responsibility brought about by the changes are just what employees want.)[7]

When employers and unions collaborate on a solution, they can overcome such constraints, although the process usually takes time. If an organization explains how everyone will benefit from the changes, the union may agree to revise the contract, especially if the alternative is employee layoffs. Even though a supervisor can propose changes, it is not part of a supervisor's job to remove these constraints. Supervisors must do their best to get work done as efficiently as possible under the existing work rules.

## Measurement of Productivity

The basic way to measure productivity is to divide outputs by inputs (see Figure 12.1). In other words, productivity is the amount of output produced with the inputs used. Table 12.1 provides examples of inputs and outputs for several types of organizations. The productivity equation can compare the output and input for an individual, a department, an organization, or even an entire country's paid workforce. The remaining discussion focuses on the direct concern of supervisors with the productivity of their department and their individual employees.

By applying basic arithmetic to the formula for productivity, the supervisor can see what has to change for productivity to increase. The right side of the equation is a fraction. Remember that when the top (numerator) of a fraction gets bigger, the number becomes greater. When the bottom (denominator) of a fraction gets bigger, the number becomes smaller. For example, 3/2 is greater than 1/2, and 1/5 is less than 1/3. To increase productivity, a supervisor needs to increase outputs, reduce inputs, or both.

■ **TABLE 12.1**

**Examples of Inputs and Outputs**

| Organization | Inputs | Outputs |
|---|---|---|
| Bus line | Buses; gas, oil, and other supplies; terminals; drivers; ticket sellers; managers; tickets; schedules; funds; data | Transportation services to passengers |
| Manufacturing firm | Trucks; plants; oil, rags, and other supplies; raw materials; purchased parts; production workers; supervisors; engineers; storekeepers; bills of material; inventory records; production schedules; time records; funds; data | Goods for use by customers |
| Hospital | Ambulances; hospital rooms; beds, wheelchairs, X rays; receptionists; administrators; nurses; doctors; medicines; drugs; splints, bandages, food, and other supplies; medical charts; funds; data | Health care services to patients |
| Police force | Cars and vans; offices; police officers; forms; handcuffs, radios, guns, office supplies, and other supplies; office furniture; equipment for forensic research; uniforms; funds; data | Protection of public safety |

Source: Adapted from Samuel C. Certo, *Modern Management*, 6th ed. (Boston: Allyn and Bacon, 1994), p. 459. Reprinted by permission of Prentice-Hall, Inc., Upper Saddle River, NJ.

Consider an employee who processes 96 driver's license applications in the course of an eight-hour day at the secretary of state's office. One way to measure this employee's productivity is 96/8, or 12 applications per hour (see Figure 12.2). A supervisor might note that a more experienced employee can process 20 applications per hour, so by this measure the first employee is less experienced than desirable and might require more training, motivation, or just more experience.

But the organization is also interested in the cost of the employee. So the supervisor might measure the input as the employee's cost per day (hourly wage times number of hours). If the employee earned $6 per hour, the productivity measure would be 96/($6 × 8), or 2 (see Figure 12.2). If the employee who processes 20 applications per hour earns $8 per hour, that employee's productivity would be 160/($8 × 8), or 2.5. Thus, the more experienced employee is more productive, even taking into account his or her higher wages.

Bear in mind that the "output" measured in the productivity formula is only goods and services of acceptable quality. A rude salesclerk and a production worker making defective components are not really productive. In these cases, the productivity formula would include only the number of correctly made components or the amount of sales made courteously and accurately. The production worker in the cartoon on page 352 has evidently missed this point (see Figure 12.3).

The following anecdote illustrates the importance of quality in determining productivity. A professor of sociology specializing in management was hospitalized at Yale–New Haven Hospital. He requested a meeting with the hospital's

**FIGURE 12.2**

**Productivity Measurements**

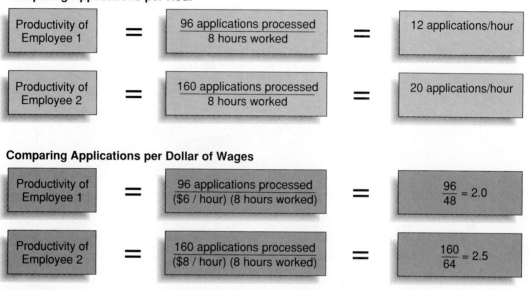

**Comparing Applications per Hour**

| Productivity of Employee 1 | = | 96 applications processed / 8 hours worked | = | 12 applications/hour |

| Productivity of Employee 2 | = | 160 applications processed / 8 hours worked | = | 20 applications/hour |

**Comparing Applications per Dollar of Wages**

| Productivity of Employee 1 | = | 96 applications processed / ($6 / hour) (8 hours worked) | = | $\frac{96}{48} = 2.0$ |

| Productivity of Employee 2 | = | 160 applications processed / ($8 / hour) (8 hours worked) | = | $\frac{160}{64} = 2.5$ |

vice-president of patient services and asked her what the hospital was doing to study the effectiveness of its nurses. The vice-president explained that the hospital evaluated nurses' work in terms of the *time* they spent on particular tasks. "No, don't count that," replied the professor. "It's not important. What you have to document is the *impact of problem solving* [italics added] on a patient's outcome." He explained that his nurse had solved two of his own problems—uncomfortable surgical dressing and constipation—by getting the right employees involved. She had done this in just a few minutes, but the professor valued that effort more than if she had spent hours in his room talking with him. Thus, he believed that the proper measure of the nurse's productivity was her success in solving his problems.[8]

## Improving Productivity by Controlling Quality

The 10-page report came back to the word-processing department so full of corrections that the department's supervisor, Molly O'Donnell, concluded it would have to be retyped entirely. When she showed it to the operator responsible, Molly said, "What happened? This isn't the first time." "It's not my fault!" exclaimed the operator. "Finkelstein's handwriting is impossible to read."

When problems like this occur, a department has to have a sufficient number of employees to fix mistakes as well as to do the initial work. That cuts into productivity. Quality analysts say that 20 to 40 percent of costs cover waste and the correction of defects.[9]

**FIGURE 12.3**

**Quantity Without Quality Does Not Boost Productivity**

"I don't get it! I turn out a record 370 units, and I don't even get a lousy 'thank you!'"

Source: *Front Line Supervisor's Bulletin*, July 10, 1992, p. 4. Copyrighted material reprinted with permission of the Bureau of Business Practice, 24 Rope Ferry Road, Waterford, CT 06386.

Part of a supervisor's job, therefore, is to think of and implement ways to get the job done right the first time. (See "Meeting the Challenge.") Molly might look for ways to help word-processing operators who are having trouble reading the handwriting on the documents they prepare. Or she might investigate other ways for people in the organization to submit their work; for example, people could tape-record their documents for the word-processing operators to transcribe.

An organization that boosted productivity by improving quality is IBM's Austin, Texas, manufacturing facility for electronic circuit cards (the "engines" that run computers). The company had failed in its effort to save money through automation (the robots it installed were not flexible enough), so it turned its attention to ways of making the production process more efficient. The workforce was divided into six "focus factories," each of which has the machines needed to make a few different products instead of having the entire factory make all the products. Employees receive training in the entire production process and in how to maintain the machines they operate. With this broad knowledge, employees understand what is going on in their area and can help spot and correct problems. Thus, when an assembly line was loaded with the wrong parts one day, employees noticed the mistake, stopped the line, and quickly corrected the problem. Automated inspection equipment would have missed this problem, and the company would have had to remake thousands of panels instead of four.[10]

### Restaurants Improve Productivity—and Service—by Reaching Out

Most of us don't judge a restaurant's service before we walk in the door, but some restaurateurs think we should. They are taking steps to boost the productivity of their employees the moment they answer the telephone to take a reservation. For these restaurateurs, quality of service begins on the telephone.

Chris Elias, owner of Eddy's in Oklahoma City, instructs employees to spend a little time on the telephone with customers in order to better meet their needs. "We ask if they want nonsmoking, separate checks, how they found out about Eddy's," Elias explains. The payback? "Since we started personalizing the reservation, we haven't had a single no-show."

No-shows—customers who make reservations and then fail to show up—can be costly for a restaurant, lowering the overall productivity for the evening. Nancy Prosser, general manager of Emil's Twenty-One Restaurant in Independence, Ohio, soft-pedals this issue with customers. She (or an employee) obtains a telephone number when the reservation is made, then calls customers to confirm their reservations. "We tell guests everything is set up for them, as a reminder. Then they feel we are expecting them and that we are planning for them."

Kevin Taylor, co-owner and general manager of Rusty Staubs on 5th in New York City, takes a similar approach. "Our managers on duty say, 'Please call us if you have any changes or need to cancel' when making a reservation. We're letting our guests know they won't be browbeaten if they have to cancel, and we really want their business, if not this time, then the next time."

Other restaurateurs deal with the cost issue more directly. "We tell people when they make a reservation we will hold their table for five minutes," remarks Sandi Carpenito, owner of Carpenito's Restaurant in Monticello, New York. Aqua, located in San Francisco, takes this policy a step or two further. "We have a strict no-show policy where we take a deposit for parties of six or more," explains business manager James Kohler. "We attempt to contact them to confirm, plus they're told they have to call us by 3:00 P.M. on the day of their reservation." If the party doesn't call or show up, the restaurant sends them a gift certificate for the value of the deposit.

Some restaurateurs have created actual reservation and confirmation scripts for the reservationist or maître d', expanding both of these jobs somewhat so that customer contact includes building a relationship by telephone. These restaurants not only control costs by minimizing no-shows, they enhance their quality of service.

Source: Jeff Weinstein, "Too Many No-Shows? Here's Some Advice," *Restaurants & Institutions*, Dec. 15, 1994, p. 76.

## Improving Productivity by Controlling Costs

When supervisors and other managers look for ways to boost productivity, they often start by looking at their costs per unit of output. Productivity improves when the department or organization can do as much work at a lower cost. It also improves when output rises without a cost increase.

### Determining Costs

Not surprisingly, before a supervisor can make intelligent decisions about how to trim costs, he or she has to know where the money is going. The most important source of such information is budget reports, described in Chapter 6. By reviewing budget reports regularly, a supervisor can see which categories of expenses are largest and identify where the department is spending more than it budgeted. Then a supervisor should spend time with workers, observing how they use the

**FIGURE 12.4**

Cost-Control Strategies

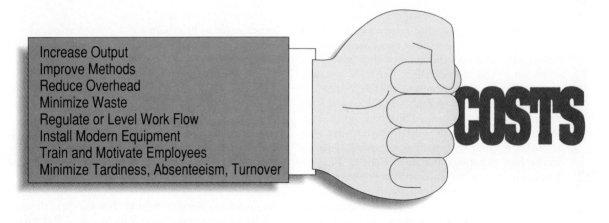

Increase Output
Improve Methods
Reduce Overhead
Minimize Waste
Regulate or Level Work Flow
Install Modern Equipment
Train and Motivate Employees
Minimize Tardiness, Absenteeism, Turnover

department's resources, including their time. The process of gathering information about costs and working with employees to identify needed improvements is part of a supervisor's control function.

### Cost-Control Strategies

To lower costs, supervisors can use a number of strategies. (See the basic alternatives summarized in Figure 12.4.) These strategies are not mutually exclusive. Supervisors can get the greatest productivity by using as many of these strategies as will work. In deciding which strategies to use, supervisors should consider which will appeal to higher-level management, which will be acceptable to employees, and which involve areas within their control.

An important part of many of these strategies is encouraging and using employees' ideas for saving money. Operating the machines, preparing the reports, and serving clients or customers gives employees a close-up view of how things are done, enabling them to see the shortcomings of the organization's way of doing things.

Examples abound. American Airlines has a program called "IdeAAs in Action" that asks for and evaluates suggestions, then rewards the employees and supervisors who provide them. The company estimates that cost-cutting ideas from employees saved $58 million in a single year.[11] A contest held by Advance Transformer Company generated several hundred cost-saving ideas. One came from Ward Huege, an employee in the company's data-processing department, who arranged for the company to switch to environmentally safe paper that will cost several thousand dollars less than the paper that was used previously.[12] At United Electric Controls Company, based in Watertown, Massachusetts, assembler Vinny Petrillo responded to a call for suggestions by asking why the company was ordering a type of switch with three unnecessary terminals. Petrillo was spending up to two hours a day removing the terminals. The company investigated and learned that switches without the terminals were available for less money; the buyer, however, did not know enough about the switches to ask.[13]

Employees often have great ideas to save their companies money. This task force consists of representatives from Best Foods' marketing, purchasing, packaging technology, engineering, manufacturing, and logistics management departments. They redesigned the Mazola corn oil bottle, which reduced packaging costs by 32 percent.

Source: Courtesy of Kelly-Mooney photography.

### Increase Output

Remember that the numerator in the productivity equation (output/input) represents what the department or organization is producing. The greater the output at a given cost, the greater the productivity. Thus, a logical way to increase productivity is to increase output without boosting costs.

What does this mean in practical terms? Sometimes, by applying themselves, people can work faster or harder. Servers in a restaurant may find they can cover more tables and factory production workers may find they can assemble more components. Of course, it is not always possible to increase output without sacrificing quality.

Needless to say, this method of improving productivity makes employees unhappy most frequently. A supervisor who wants to boost productivity by increasing output must first ensure that the new goals for output are reasonable. This could perhaps be learned by including employees in the decision-making process. A supervisor must also communicate the new goals carefully, emphasizing any positive aspects of the change. For example, a supervisor might mention that if employees are more productive, the organization has a chance to remain competitive without layoffs. In the end, improving productivity by increasing output works only when employees are motivated to do more (see Chapter 11).

### Improve Methods

According to consultant Mary Crabtree Tonges, there are only limited ways of doing the same thing better or faster. The major improvements in productivity result from taking a fresh look at what needs to get done.[15] Reviewing and revamping the way things are done is the basic principle of reengineering, which led to productivity improvements at Liberty Mutual, an insurance and financial services company. At Liberty, the time from initial customer contact to the issuance of an insurance contract was 62 days, even though the actual preparation of a contract took only 3 days. The rest of the time was spent shuffling paperwork between departments, each of which had an independent computer system requiring that data be entered by hand. After studying this process, Liberty came up with a new

These employees were part of a 12-member team that spent 18 months looking for ideas to save production costs for the Honda Motor Company. Money-saving suggestions were received from factory workers and suppliers in the United States and Japan. As a result of cost-saving strategies such as manufacturing bumpers, dashboards, and other parts with fewer pieces, the new model of Honda Civic costs some $800 less per car to build than older models.

Source: © Michael Abramson.

method: Teams comprising members from each department would handle the entire process together. Not only has the new system cut the processing time by more than half, but it has enabled the company to offer quotes to more prospects and thus generate more sales.[16]

A potentially powerful approach to improving methods is to apply the principles of job enlargement and job enrichment. Enlarging and enriching jobs makes them more interesting, which should motivate employees to deliver higher quality as well as work harder. UPS hopes to achieve that outcome by empowering its truck drivers to plan the routes they cover.[17]

Like managers at all levels, supervisors should be constantly on the lookout for ways to improve methods. Some ideas will come from supervisors themselves. (Chapter 9 provides suggestions for creative thinking.) Employees often have excellent ideas for doing the work better because they see the problems and pitfalls of their jobs. Supervisors should keep communication channels open and actively ask for ideas.

### Reduce Overhead

**overhead**
Expenses not related directly to producing goods and services; examples are rent, utilities, and staff support.

Many departments spend more than is necessary for **overhead,** which includes rent, utilities, staff support, company cafeteria, janitorial services, and other expenses not related directly to producing goods and services. (See "Tips from the Firing Line.") Typically, an organization allocates a share of the total overhead to each department based on the department's size. This means that a supervisor has limited control over a department's overhead expenses. However, a supervisor can periodically look for sources of needless expenses, such as lights left on in unoccupied areas or messy work areas that mean extra work for the janitorial staff. By reducing these costs to the company, a supervisor ultimately reduces the amount of overhead charged to his or her department.

Staff departments in particular can be guilty of contributing too much to the cost of overhead by generating unnecessary paperwork. Supervisors and their employees who produce or handle reports and forms should evaluate this paperwork to make sure it is needed. Keith Snidtker, facility services manager for GAF Cor-

---

### TIPS FROM THE FIRING LINE

## *A Company's Appearance Says Something About Its Productivity*

Would you trust your teeth to a dentist whose waiting room is a mess? Would you buy clothes in a shop with dim lighting and outdated decorating? Would you leave your car in the hands of a mechanic whose shop is littered with tools? Several experts think not. They believe that the way a business looks says a lot about how the business performs. While some of their suggestions cost more than others, and can certainly be considered as overhead, the experts believe that the following improvements can translate into improvements in overall productivity.

- Make maximum use of space. "Some people say they need more storage space," says Sandy Lucas of The Bryan Design Associates, "when they really need a reorganization."
- Take pictures of the work space; they'll show areas that are entirely empty or cluttered with debris.

- Think about how easy it is for people to enter or leave the work space. Will they bump against a table corner? Will they trip on the steps? "Pay particular attention to the entry of your business, and evaluate anything that may be a hazard," notes Lucas.
- Freshen the office or shop with paint, window treatments, or the like. "You don't want people to think your business is stagnating, just because your offices are," notes Darrel Rippeteau, an architect in Washington, D.C. "You don't want workers to stagnate in their surroundings."
- Keep straightening up. Neaten the pile of magazines, remove outdated notices and clippings, clean countertops, replace burned-out lightbulbs, and the like.

Source: Roberta Maynard, "Could Your Shop Use a Face-Lift?" *Nation's Business*, Aug. 1994, pp. 47–49.

---

poration of Wayne, New Jersey, recounts the story of a company that had one full-time employee whose entire day was spent filling out reports that no one used. Another company eliminated the sending of copies of documents and reports to transferred, retired, or dead employees—and reduced the number of documents generated per year by 22,000.[18] Another way to reduce the amount of paper is to make sure that when a procedure calls for a form with several parts, all the parts are actually used.

### *Minimize Waste*

Waste occurs in all kinds of operations. A medical office may order too many supplies and wind up throwing some away or taking up unnecessary storage space. A factory may handle materials in a way that produces a lot of scrap. A sales office may make unnecessary photocopies of needlessly long proposals, contributing more to landfills than to the company's profits.

**idle time (downtime)**
Time during which employees or machines are not producing goods or services.

A costly form of waste is **idle time,** or **downtime**—time during which employees or machines are not producing goods or services. This term is used most often in manufacturing operations, but it applies to other situations as well. In a factory, idle time occurs while a machine is shut down for repairs or while workers are waiting for parts. In an office, idle time occurs when employees are waiting for instructions, supplies, a computer printout, or a response to a question they asked the supervisor.

**detour behavior**
Tactics for postponing or avoiding work.

Another form of wasted time results from **detour behavior,** which is a tactic for postponing or avoiding work. Employees and their supervisors use a wide variety of detour behavior: A supervisor enjoys a cup of coffee and the newspaper before

### FIGURE 12.5

**The Costs of
Uneven Work Flow**

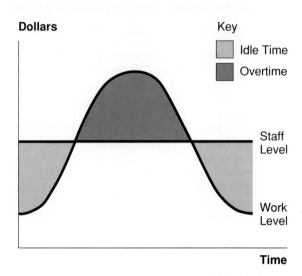

turning to the day's responsibilities or an employee stops by a colleague's desk to chat. Detour behavior may be especially tempting when a person's energy is low or when a person is facing a particularly challenging or unpleasant assignment. (The opposite of detour behavior is effective time management, discussed in Chapter 14.)

Wasted time may be a more important measure of lost productivity than wasted costs. Management consultants at the Boston Consulting Group compared the performance of their U.S. clients with that of their Japanese competitors and found that the Japanese companies were producing goods in half the time with fewer workers in smaller factories.[19] The difference was that the Japanese companies actively sought ways to manufacture products efficiently. In contrast, a U.S. manufacturer of heavy vehicles spent 45 days to prepare an order for assembly and just 16 *hours* actually assembling the product. The Boston Consulting Group concluded that companies should emphasize cutting time, not dollar costs, from operations.

Supervisors should be on the alert for wasted time and other resources in their department. They can set a good example for effective time management and can make detecting waste part of the control process (see Chapter 6). Often, employees are good sources of information on how to minimize waste. The supervisor might consider holding a contest to find the best ideas.

### Regulate or Level the Work Flow

An uneven flow of work can be costly (see Figure 12.5). When work levels are low, the result is idle time. When the department faces a surge in demand for its work, employees have to work extra hours to keep up. As a result, the department may have to pay workers overtime rates—one and a half or two times normal wages—during peak periods. In addition, people are rarely as efficient during overtime hours—they get tired—as they are during a normal workday. If a supervisor can arrange to have a more even work flow, the department can be staffed appropriately to get the job done during normal working hours, and fewer employees will be idle during slow periods.

A supervisor can take several steps to regulate departmental work flow:

1. A supervisor should first make sure that adequate planning has been done for the work required.
2. A supervisor may also find it helpful to work with his or her manager and peers or to form teams of employees to examine and solve work flow problems. Cooperation can help make the work flow more evenly or at least more predictably. For example, a manager who travels extensively may assign a great deal of work upon her return, not realizing that she is clustering deadlines instead of spreading them out for an even work flow. The sales department may be submitting orders in batches to the production department instead of submitting them as soon as they are received.
3. If the work flow must remain uneven, a supervisor may find that the best course is to use temporary employees during peak periods, an approach that can work if the temporary employees have the right skills.

### Install Modern Equipment

Work may be slowed because employees are using worn or outdated equipment. If that is the case, a supervisor may find it worthwhile to obtain modern equipment. According to Brian Papke, president of the U.S. division of Japanese toolmaker Yamazaki Mazak, modern computer-controlled tools are so far superior to the machinery they were designed to replace that an organization will be most successful if it tears out its old equipment and actually gives it away to competitors.[20] Although the strategy of installing modern equipment is obvious for manufacturing departments, many other workplaces can benefit from using modern equipment, including up-to-date computer technology.

Ingersoll Milling Machine Company, which makes customized machines for heavy industries, has a rule that any 10-year-old machine will be replaced unless someone on the staff can show why the company should keep it. Ingersoll's president, Fred S. Wilson, explains, "Some machines you're justified in keeping because technology hasn't changed much, but in most 10-year periods, you'll see a better idea coming along." With this strategy, the company reduced the number of machines it used from 154 to 81, yet it produced twice the output and made nine times the sales volume.[21]

**payback period**
The length of time it will take for the benefits generated by an investment (such as cost savings from machinery) to offset the cost of the investment.

In deciding to buy new equipment or in recommending its purchase, a supervisor needs to determine whether the expense will be worthwhile. One way to do this is to figure out how much money per year the new equipment will save, for example, in terms of lower repair costs, less downtime, and more goods produced. Then compute the number of years before the savings will offset the cost of buying the equipment, a time known as the **payback period.** A payback period is computed according to the first formula shown in Figure 12.6. Thus, if a computer system will cost $120,000 and is expected to save the office $40,000 per year, the payback period is three years ($120,000 ÷ $40,000 per year). Higher-level management or the finance department usually has an opinion on what payback period is acceptable for the organization.

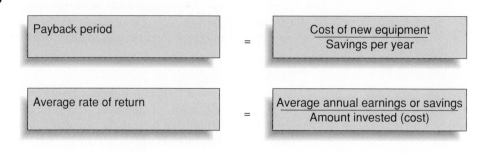

**FIGURE 12.6**

**Basic Formulas for Evaluating an Investment**

| Payback period | = | $\dfrac{\text{Cost of new equipment}}{\text{Savings per year}}$ |

| Average rate of return | = | $\dfrac{\text{Average annual earnings or savings}}{\text{Amount invested (cost)}}$ |

**average rate of return (*ARR*)**
A percentage that represents the average annual earnings for each dollar of a given investment.

Another way to evaluate whether an investment is worthwhile is to find the **average rate of return (*ARR*)** for that investment. *ARR* is a percentage that represents the organization's average annual earnings for each dollar of a given investment. An *ARR* of 15 percent means that each dollar invested yields income (or savings) of 15 cents a year. A basic formula for *ARR* is the second equation in Figure 12.6. For the computer system in the previous example, the *ARR* would be the $40,000 annual savings divided by the $120,000 cost, or .33—a 33 percent return. To determine whether this return is acceptable, a supervisor compares it with what the money spent could earn in another form of investment. Again, higher-level management or the finance department usually has established standards for this measure.

Payback period and *ARR* as described here are only two of the simplest ways to evaluate investments. Other, more complex, methods take into account factors such as the timing of payments and earnings. For a supervisor with access to a computer, software is available to compute payback period, average rate of return, and other analyses of the financial worthiness of an investment. Azure Software of Warsaw, Indiana, sells a program called Project Analysis for Capital Equipment Expenditures (PACEE), which defines the needed information, makes suggestions, calculates a variety of statistics, and then summarizes the results with graphs and numbers. PACEE takes into consideration user-defined variables such as the benefits of quality and the value of greater market share.[22]

### Train and Motivate Employees

To work efficiently, employees need a good understanding of how to do their jobs. Thus, a basic way to improve productivity is to train employees. For example, Hector Ruiz, the general manager of Motorola's Boynton Beach, Florida, plant, says that training has allowed the plant to produce three times as many pagers with only 22 percent more manufacturing employees.[23] (Chapter 17 discusses types of training and the supervisor's role in providing training.)

As you learned in Chapter 11, training alone does not lead to superior performance; employees also must be motivated to do good work. In other words, employees must want to do a good job. Motivation is a key tactic for improving productivity because employees are often in the best position to think of ways to achieve their objectives more efficiently. In China, the government hopes that a new policy mandating Saturdays off will improve productivity as workers try to get the same work done in five days instead of six. Josef Wilfling, general manager for Siemans AG in Shanghai, agrees: "People are visibly tired at the end of the day [with a six-day week]. This will help, I'm sure."[24]

### Minimize Tardiness, Absenteeism, and Turnover

Lack of motivation is often the problem underlying time lost to tardiness and absenteeism. When employees dislike their jobs or find them boring, they tend to use excuses to arrive late or not at all. Lost time is costly; in most cases, the organization is paying for someone who is not actually working. Furthermore, other employees may be unable to work efficiently without the support of the missing person. As a result, minimizing absenteeism and tardiness is an important part of the supervisor's job. (Chapter 13 provides some guidelines for this task.)

**turnover**
The rate at which employees leave an organization.

Absenteeism may be the first step to leaving the company. The employee misses more and more days, then finally quits altogether. The rate at which employees leave an organization is known as **turnover.** High turnover is expensive, because the organization must spend a lot of money to recruit and train new employees. For example, according to a recent estimate, it costs $2,500 to replace a hotel worker.[25] Therefore, an important part of controlling costs is to keep good employees by making the organization a place they want to stay.

Fel-Pro, which manufactures gaskets in the Chicago suburb of Skokie, is known nationwide for retaining employees with its program of family-oriented benefits. For example, the company provides tuition benefits to employees and their children, has an on-site day care center, gives employees a $1,000 bond at the birth of a child, and makes summer jobs available for employees' children. Turnover and absenteeism rates at Fel-Pro are lower than at comparable companies, and over one-third of its employees have been with the company for 10 years or more.[26]

Supervisors can minimize turnover by applying the principles of motivation. In general, supervisors should identify what employees want from their job and meet those needs when possible. At Pittsburgh-based G.S.I. Transcomm Data Systems, this means letting employees switch jobs within the company. For example, receptionist Kelly Gezo moved into a sales job and eventually became the company's top salesperson.[27]

## Employee Fears about Productivity Improvement

A highly productive organization is in an ideal position to thrive and grow. Thus, employees can benefit from productivity improvements. This is true especially when efforts to boost productivity focus on improving the quality of processes rather than simply cutting payroll costs. Even so, many employees react with fear when managers start talking about improving productivity.

Employees may have good reason to be fearful. Many have experienced or have heard of cost reductions leading to less overtime pay, more difficult work, and even layoffs. For example, AT&T's plan to have a computerized voice-recognition system handle information calls meant the elimination of as many as 6,000 jobs for long-distance operators.[28] When layoffs occur, the people who are left behind often have to struggle to keep up with the work that still has to be done.

Supervisors must respond to these fears. Most importantly, they must be prepared with information. A supervisor who does not understand the types of changes to be made and the reasons for them should discuss the matter with his or her manager as soon as possible. After obtaining a clear view of the organization's plans and goals, a supervisor should present this information to the employees. In doing so, a supervisor should emphasize what the benefits will be and avoid dwelling on the negatives. At AT&T, for example, supervisor Corliss Kyles doubted that customers would like the voice-recognition systems, but she decided not to share her views out of fear of further hurting morale.[29]

Sometimes it is difficult to see how individual employees will benefit, but at other times the benefits are clear. At Ingersoll, the manufacturer that updates its equipment every 10 years, the move toward automation has never been intended to reduce the workforce. Indeed, the number of employees has remained near 2,000, and their work has become more interesting. For example, machine operators now learn to do maintenance on their machines. As a result, says machinist Terry Coleman, "I understand better how the machine works, and that really helps me do my job. We keep a running list of problems that we could have with the machine and anticipate those problems with our scheduled maintenance."[30]

When a supervisor gives information about productivity improvement, employees should have an opportunity to ask questions. The supervisor who cannot answer some of the questions should promise to get answers—and then do so. Although information alone will not make employees enthusiastic about a productivity program, uninformed employees almost certainly will suffer from low morale.

In Chapter 15, we will take a closer look at how supervisors can help employees cope with the fears and related challenges that accompany productivity improvements and other types of change.

# Summary

### 12.1 Define *productivity*.

Productivity is the amount of results (output) an organization gets for a given amount of inputs such as labor and machinery. Typically, it refers to the amount of acceptable work employees do for each dollar they earn or the number of acceptable products manufactured with a given amount of resources.

### 12.2 Identify constraints on productivity.

Management limits productivity when it does not seem truly committed to improving it. Employee attitudes and skills limit productivity when employees are unable or unwilling to meet standards for performance. Government regulations impose responsibilities on organizations that limit their productivity to achieve other objectives. A union contract may contain work rules that limit productivity.

### 12.3 Describe how productivity and productivity improvements are measured.

To measure productivity, divide the amount of outputs by the amount of inputs. Outputs are the amount of work done or goods and services produced, assuming that these are of acceptable quality. Inputs may be measured as dollars, hours, or both. Productivity increases when output increases, input decreases, or both.

### 12.4 Identify the two basic ways productivity may be improved.

Two ways to improve productivity are to control quality and to control costs. Controlling quality involves minimizing defects or errors. Controlling costs involves producing the same amount of goods or services at a lower cost or producing more at the same cost.

### 12.5 Describe cost-control strategies available to supervisors.

A supervisor may increase output by having people or machines work faster or harder. A more effective approach may be to improve methods; that is, to get things done more efficiently. The supervisor may identify ways to reduce overhead and minimize waste, including idle time and wasted physical resources. Regulating or leveling the work flow can make staffing more efficient. Installing modern equipment reduces costs when the new equipment is more efficient. To cut costs related to personnel, a supervisor should see that workers receive adequate training and motivation, and he or she should take steps to minimize tardiness, absenteeism, and turnover.

### 12.6 Explain why employees have fears about productivity improvement, and tell how supervisors can address those fears.

Many employees are fearful of productivity improvements because many organizations make such changes through layoffs and extra work for the remaining employees. Supervisors can respond by keeping employees informed about the organization's plans, emphasizing the benefits, and listening to employees.

# Key Terms

| | | |
|---|---|---|
| productivity | idle time (downtime) | average rate of return (*ARR*) |
| overhead | detour behavior | turnover |
| | payback period | |

# Review and Discussion Questions

1. Frank Ouellette works at a government agency where neither managers nor employees seem to worry about how long it takes to complete an assignment. Should Frank's coworkers be concerned about productivity? Why or why not?

2. Anna Holt, a supervisor in a boot manufacturing plant, just received a memo from her manager that productivity on her shift must increase by 10 percent during the next fiscal quarter. However, when she recently approached her manager about upgrading two of the machines, she was turned down. In addition, she knows that her employees' union will balk at an increase in the number of boots her group must produce in a given shift. What constraints on productivity does Anna face? How might she attempt to resolve them?

3. At the claims-processing office for All-Folks Insurance, 25 employees process 2,500 claims a day. The claims-processing office for Purple Cross Insurance uses a state-of-the-art computer system, and its 15 employees process 3,000 claims a day.

   *a.* Which office is more productive?

   *b.* At which office would you expect employees to be paid more? Why?

4. In question 3, suppose that half the claims processed by the employees at Purple Cross contain errors and all of the claims processed at All-Folks are done correctly. Which office would you say is more productive? Why?

5. Where can supervisors get information to help them determine costs?

6. How would you expect employees to respond to each of these efforts to cut costs?

   *a.* A plan to increase output by scheduling fewer rest breaks.

   *b.* A plan to increase output by hiring someone to bring supplies to laboratory workers, rather than having them get their own supplies.

7. Sam Marshall was just promoted to manager of a fast-food restaurant. The restaurant owner has asked Sam to look for ways to reduce overhead. What might be some sources of needless expense (that are under Sam's control), and what steps might Sam take to reduce these?

8. At a telemarketing office, 36 employees make telephone calls to people's homes, trying to sell services for the company's clients. When the employees arrive at work, the supervisor hands each of them a list of the homes to call. However, the supervisor is sometimes tied up in a meeting or on the telephone, so the employees have to wait to get their lists. They use the time to discuss their family or social lives and to carry on a long-running Trivial Pursuit tournament.

   What productivity problem is occurring in this office? Suggest at least one way the supervisor can address this problem.

9. Rachel Roth supervises a shift of workers who manufacture ski clothing. Because of its seasonal nature, the work flow tends to be uneven, and Rachel feels that this hurts productivity. What steps might Rachel take to try to regulate the work flow in her department?

10. A maintenance supervisor learned that installing a type of high-efficiency light bulb in the building can save the organization $1,000 a year. Replacing the current system with the new one would cost about $2,500.

    *a.* What is the payback period for this system?

    *b.* What is the average rate of return?

    *c.* Do you think this is a worthwhile investment? Why or why not?

11. How does high turnover hurt productivity? What can a supervisor do to minimize turnover?

12. Why do employees sometimes resist productivity improvements? How can supervisors prepare for and respond to employee attitudes?

## A SECOND LOOK

In the story of Jinny Bray at the beginning of this chapter, building codes are considered a constraint on the productivity of her construction company. In what ways, if any, might Bray be able to overcome this constraint?

# APPLICATIONS MODULE

## CASE

### *Com-Corp Industries Keeps Productivity High*

It's no coincidence that Com-Corp Industries, a metal-stamping shop that manufactures headlight parts, keeps productivity high with democratic management in which employees have a say in many aspects of their jobs. That's because president John Strazzanti started out at the bottom and has learned many lessons over the years in what keeps workers working, costs down, and quality high.

At his first job as a press operator in the stamping department at a plant that made bicycle parts, Strazzanti was eager to impress his boss. "The maximum number of parts ever produced from the machine I was assigned was 40,000 in a 10-hour shift," he recalls. "I went to work trying to learn how to make the machine run faster. By the end of the week I had produced 46,000 pieces." But Strazzanti's supervisor didn't give him the praise he expected; instead, the boss said, "I really think 50,000 is attainable. That's what I want you to shoot for." Instead of hitting 50,000 pieces, Strazzanti never reached more than 32,000 after that. It was a lesson he never forgot—one in how *not* to increase productivity.

Twenty-five years later, Strazzanti's Com-Corp employees earn above-market pay increases; they make decisions about compensation rates, get tenure, enjoy profit sharing, and they have access to all kinds of company information and training. All of this and more is written in the company's Policy and Procedure Manual. Thus, employees are motivated—and they produce.

To prevent management constraints on productivity, an internal corporate auditor reviews pertinent documents generated by supervisors, such as performance appraisals, purchasing records, and so forth. To control costs, the company charges managers with "maximizing the company's return on investment" in exchange for profit sharing.

Employee compensation costs also are controlled; the policy manual stipulates that employee decisions about compensation must be based on the economic rule of thumb that the marketplace determines the worth of employees' skills and services.

Com-Corp also tracks the costly rate of turnover and has identified two types. Positive turnover occurs when employees leave Com-Corp for jobs that are more challenging than the company can offer. Negative turnover occurs when workers leave for jobs that pay more, which signals that Com-Corp's pay rates are not always competitive in the marketplace. This occurrence is rare: In a recent year, Com-Corp experienced only a 2 percent negative turnover.

If productivity is measured in the amount of outputs an organization gets for its inputs, Com-Corp can mark its productivity high on the scale. The company has grown steadily since its incorporation more than 15 years ago, and it has never lost money.

1. If Strazzanti had to face union constraints on productivity, how do you think he might handle the situation?
2. Do you think Com-Corp's employees suffer from fears about productivity improvement? Why or why not?
3. Com-Corp has several ways of controlling costs. Do you think that its democratic management system also helps control quality? Why or why not?

Source: Teri Lammers Prior, "If I Were President . . . ," *Inc.*, Apr. 1995, pp. 56–61.

**SELF-QUIZ**

## *Test Your Personal Productivity*

Answer each of the following questions by circling Y for yes or N for no.

Y    N    1. Does it often take you more than 10 minutes to find a particular letter, bill, report, or other paper in your files or in piles of paper on your desk?

Y    N    2. Do things amass in corners of closets or on the floor because you cannot decide where to put them?

Y    N    3. Are there papers on your desk, other than reference materials, through which you have not looked for a week or more?

Y    N    4. Has your electricity or another utility ever been turned off because you forgot to pay the bill?

Y    N    5. Within the last two months, have you forgotten any scheduled appointment, anniversary, or specific date you wanted to acknowledge?

Y    N    6. Do your magazines and newspapers pile up unread?

Y    N    7. Do you frequently procrastinate so long on a work assignment that it becomes an emergency or panic situation?

Y    N    8. Has anything ever been misplaced in your home or office for longer than two months?

Y    N    9. Do you often misplace keys, glasses, gloves, handbags, briefcases, or other such items?

Y    N    10. Does your definition of "working in organized space" mean fitting as many objects as you can into a limited area?

Y    N    11. Do you feel that your storage problems would be solved if you had more space?

Y    N    12. Do you want to get organized but find that everything is in such a mess that you do not know where to start?

Y    N    13. Do you regularly receive letters, comments, or calls that begin: "You haven't gotten back to me yet, so . . ."?

Y    N    14. Are you harassed by frequent interruptions—telephone calls or visitors—that affect your ability to concentrate?

Y    N    15. Are you so busy with details that you ignore opportunities for new business or promotional activities?

Y    N    16. When you get up in the morning, do you know what your two or three primary tasks are?

Y    N    17. By the end of an average day, have you accomplished at least the most important tasks you set for yourself?

For questions 1 to 15, give yourself one point for each Y you circled. For questions 16 and 17, give yourself one point for each N you circled. Here is how to interpret your total:

| | |
|---|---|
| 4 or less | Systems are under control! |
| 5–8 | Disorganization is troublesome. |
| 9–11 | Life must be very difficult. |
| 12 or more | You are disorganized to the point of chaos. |

Source: Adapted by Corinne Livesay from Stephanie Winston, *Getting Organized: The Easy Way to Put Your Life in Order* (New York: Warner Books, 1978), and Stephanie Winston, *The Organized Executive: New Ways to Manage Time, Paper, and People* (New York: W. W. Norton, 1983).

## Class Exercise

Imagine that you have been asked by the dean of students to act as host to a foreign-exchange student for a semester at your school. The student's major is identical to your own. The student speaks some English, but not as a primary language. What steps would you take to maximize the student's productivity while at your school? What constraints might you face? How would you deal with potential culture shock? Write a plan outlining your ideas.

## Team-Building Exercise

## Measuring Teams' Productivity

This class exercise requires jigsaw puzzles, one for each five or six students in the class. Puzzles with no more than 500 pieces would probably work best.

Divide the class into teams for each puzzle. Each team works on its puzzle for 15 minutes. When time is up, the class discusses the following questions:

1. Compare the productivity of the teams. How should productivity be measured? When the whole class agrees on a proper measure, each team computes its own productivity.
2. Which team was most productive? Why? Did it use methods that could have helped the other groups?
3. How could you have improved the productivity of your team?

# Video Exercise 12: *Improving Productivity*

### Video Summary

Founder Gordon Marshall, along with Robert Rodin, president and chief executive officer, attribute Marshall Industries' phenomenal success to their embracing of W. Edward Deming's quality principles. Marshall and Rodin are joined by Mike Lelo and other company employees to explain how motivation and learning contributed to their job growth and personal development, while at the same time the company was experiencing unprecedented productivity and profitability.

### Application

According to Malcolm Kushner in *The Light Touch: How to Use Humor for Business Success*:

> Humor is a powerful management tool. It can gain attention, create rapport, and make a message more memorable. It can also relieve tension, enhance relationships, and motivate people. . . . In today's competitive business environment, success requires developing your full potential. Every skill counts. And humor can provide the winning edge.[1]

In this chapter you have learned about improving productivity, so it is also appropriate to work on improving your humor skills. In an executive survey conducted by Accountemps, 96 percent of the executives believed that people with a sense of humor do better at their jobs than those who have little or no sense of humor. Studies also have shown that people who enjoy their work are more productive, more creative, and have greater job satisfaction.[2]

C. W. Metcalf, consultant and author on the role of humor in managing oneself and others, says you need to develop three humor skills:

- The ability to see the absurdity in difficult situations.
- The ability to take yourself lightly while taking your work seriously.
- A disciplined sense of joy in being alive.[3]

This exercise will help you improve the first humor skill by using "Follow-Ups to Murphy's Law." You may be familiar with the original Murphy's Law: "Whatever can go wrong, will." These laws can help you view your problems from a more humorous perspective, which can help lessen your stress and frustration and increase your productivity.

---

[1]New York: Simon and Schuster, 1990, p. 18.

[2]Karen Matthes, "Lighten Up! Humor Has Its Place at Work," *HR Focus*, Feb. 1993, p. 3.

[3]C. W. Metcalf and Roma Felible, *Lighten Up: Survival Skills for People under Pressure* (New York: Addison-Wesley, 1992), p. 17.

## Instructions

1. Break into groups of three to five students.
2. Each group member is to select one law from the list below that he or she can relate from personal experience to the rest of the group. You are not restricted to the list provided. For example, a worker at a medical clinic might relate the experiences of a particularly hectic day with his or her own follow-up to Murphy's Law: "The last patient of the day is always the sickest, especially if you're about to go on vacation."
3. You may already have a law that helps you to deal with difficult situations, or you may want to create a new one to fit a problem you commonly face.
4. When it is your turn to relate your personal experience, include a description of a work-related situation. If your work experience is limited, choose a home- or school-related situation. Conclude with a description of how you already use a follow-up to Murphy's Law to help you deal with the situation or how you will cope with the situation next time it happens by applying the law.

## Follow-Ups to Murphy's Law

1. Nothing is ever as simple as it first seems.
2. Every activity takes more time than you have.
3. It is easier to make a commitment or to get involved in something than to get out of it.
4. Every clarification breeds new questions.
5. The greater the importance of decisions to be made, the larger must be the committee assigned to make them.
6. Things get worse under pressure.
7. Opportunity always knocks at the least opportune time.
8. The number of people watching you is directly proportional to the stupidity of your action.
9. It is a mistake to allow any mechanical object to realize you are in a hurry.
10. People who snore tend to fall asleep first.
11. The estimate to repair anything will always be more than it's worth and less than what it takes to get a new one.
12. Measure twice because you can only cut once.
13. The one time in the day that you lean back and relax is the one time your supervisor walks through the office.
14. By working faithfully 8 hours a day, you may eventually get to be a manager and work 12 hours a day.
15. Every solution breeds new problems.

# 13

*The only difference between a problem and a solution is that people understand the solution.*

—**Charles Kettering, engineer and inventor**

# Supervising "Problem" Employees

## CHAPTER OUTLINE

Problems Requiring Special Action

*Absenteeism and Tardiness*
*Insubordination and Uncooperativeness*
*Alcohol and Drug Abuse*
*Theft*

Counseling

*Benefits of Counseling*
*Appropriate Times to Counsel*
*Counseling Techniques*

Discipline

*Administering Discipline*
*Positive Discipline*
*Self-Discipline*

Troubled Employees

*Detection of the Troubled Employee*
*Confrontation of the Troubled Employee*
*Aid in and Evaluation of Recovery*

Sources of Support

## LEARNING OBJECTIVES

After you have studied this chapter, you should be able to:

13.1 Identify common types of problem behavior among employees.

13.2 Explain why and when supervisors should counsel employees.

13.3 Describe counseling techniques.

13.4 Discuss effective ways of administering discipline.

13.5 Describe the principles of positive discipline and self-discipline.

13.6 Explain how supervisors can detect and confront troubled employees.

13.7 Specify how supervisors can direct troubled employees in getting help and then follow up on the recovery efforts.

13.8 Discuss the role of the supervisor's manager and the human resources department in helping the supervisor with problem employees.

Source: © 1995, Comstock, Inc.

## ARRESTING PROBLEM SITUATIONS

Tommy Hunnicutt, Jr., supervises two crews for Harris Tire Company in Lynchburg, Virginia. One crew of eight men services vehicles with brake jobs, wheel alignments, and new-tire installations. The four employees in the other crew work in the company's 64,000-square-foot warehouse.

One day a man (we will call him Sam) came to Harris Tire looking for work. He followed up persistently and told Hunnicutt that he would work for a week without pay so the company could try him out without risk. After a brief reference check, the company hired Sam to work in the warehouse for $5 per hour. Sam was very dependable and had a good attitude.

About six months later, a neighbor who lived behind Harris Tire's warehouse called the company's owner. The neighbor said that on several occasions he had witnessed somebody on the roof of the warehouse throwing tires into the empty lot behind the warehouse. Later in the evening, the neighbor would see three people arrive in a car to pick up the tires.

The owner contacted the Lynchburg Police Department. Over the next few days, police investigated the charges. They caught the people picking up the tires from the empty lot and arrested them immediately. Later that evening, the police picked up Sam. The day after Sam was released on bail, he was rearrested—this time for selling crack cocaine.

Harris Tire Company estimates that it lost 60 Bridgestone tires to this employee.

Source: Corinne R. Livesay, Belhaven College, Jackson, Mississippi.

When a supervisor does a good job of leading, problem solving, communicating, and motivating, most employees will perform well. Even so, a supervisor occasionally faces the challenge of a "problem" employee, one who persistently is unwilling or unable to follow the rules or meet performance standards. In general, problem employees fall into two categories: (1) employees *causing* problems—for example, by starting fights or leaving early—and (2) employees *with* problems, such as an employee whose money worries are a distraction from work. By handling these troubled employees appropriately, a supervisor can help resolve the problem without hurting the morale or performance of other employees.

This chapter provides guidelines for supervising problem employees. It describes some common problems requiring special action on the part of a supervisor and explains two basic courses of action to take: counseling and discipline. The chapter also discusses how to help a troubled employee. Finally, the chapter describes the kinds of support a supervisor can expect from superiors, the human resources department, and other experts.

# Problems Requiring Special Action

For the third straight Monday, Peter Dunbar had called in sick. The other employees were grumbling about having to do extra work to make up for his absences, and rumors were flying about the nature of Peter's problem. Peter's supervisor knew she would have to take action, beginning with some investigation into what the problem was.

When supervisors observe poor performance, they tend to blame the employee for lacking ability or effort. But when supervisors or employees need to explain their own poor performance, they tend to blame the organization or another person for not providing enough support.[1] This inconsistency suggests that some digging is needed to uncover the true source of a performance problem. For example, the supervisor might consider the following questions:

- Has the employee performed better in the past?
- Has the employee received proper training?
- Does the employee know and understand the objectives he or she is to accomplish?
- Is the supervisor providing enough feedback and support?
- Has the supervisor encouraged and rewarded high performance?
- Are other employees with similar abilities performing well? Or are they experiencing similar difficulties?

Although persistent failure to perform up to standards results from many problems, the problems that supervisors most commonly encounter among employees are absenteeism and tardiness, insubordination and uncooperativeness, alcohol and drug abuse, and theft.

## *Absenteeism and Tardiness*

An employee who misses work, even part of a day, is expensive for an employer. The company frequently must pay for those unproductive hours—for example, by providing sick pay to an employee who calls in sick. In addition, the other employees may be less productive when they have to cover for someone who is absent or tardy.

Poor employee performance in the restaurant industry can result from conflicts behind the scenes. Cooks can fight with servers, servers with hosts, day shifts with night shifts—all due to common causes: lack of communication and an inability to empathize. *Restaurants & Institutions* magazine advises, "Good managers resolve conflicts before they turn into all-out war" and "cross-training is the most effective way to build empathy."

Source: © David Pearlman

Of course, employees who really are sick should take time off. The company provides sick days for good reasons: to allow employees to rest and recover and to prevent them from infecting the rest of the workforce. The problem arises with absences that are unexcused or recur with suspicious regularity. In addition, missing work is often a sign of a deeper problem, such as a family crisis, anger about something at work, or plans to leave the organization.

## Insubordination and Uncooperativeness

When poor performance results from not understanding how to do a job, the solution is relatively simple. A supervisor must make sure that instructions are communicated clearly and that the employee is receiving the proper training. But sometimes an employee performs poorly or breaks rules because he or she chooses to do so. Such an employee may simply be uncooperative, or the employee may engage in **insubordination,** the deliberate refusal to do what a supervisor or other superior asks.

**insubordination**
Deliberate refusal to do what the supervisor or other superior asks.

Many kinds of negative behavior fall into these categories. An employee may have a generally poor attitude—criticizing, complaining, and showing a dislike for a supervisor and the organization. He or she might get into arguments over many kinds of issues. An employee may make an art form out of doing as little as possible. The employee might spend most of the day socializing, joking around, or just moving slowly. Another employee might regularly fail to follow rules—"forgetting" to wear safety equipment or sign out at lunchtime. In rare cases, the more common forms of insubordination may escalate into physical violence.[2]

The owner of a restaurant in Austin, Texas, relates the story of an extremely negative waitress: "She had nothing good to say about anything or anybody. Her constant complaints were affecting everyone—instead of her picking up others' upbeat attitudes, she was bringing everyone down." The last straw was when she yelled at the owner on the restaurant floor during a busy period.[3]

Kerry Connolly, a human resources manager at Wang Laboratories, points out that sarcastic, hostile, or passive behavior is actually a symptom of an underlying problem.[4] Thus, an employee who never takes the initiative and does just enough to get by may have a personal problem that is distracting that employee from focusing on work. The supervisor's job, according to Connolly, is to "get to the source" through the use of counseling, which is described later in this chapter.

### Alcohol and Drug Abuse

Unsafe practices, sloppy work, and frequent absences may be symptoms of a deeper problem. Some employees abuse alcohol or drugs on or off the job. According to a recent estimate, one out of six workers has a serious drug problem.[5] The most abused substance is alcohol, with approximately 18 million Americans having a serious drinking problem, according to the National Council on Alcoholism and Drug Dependence.[6]

These employees are expensive to the organization. According to a widely cited estimate, drug abuse costs U.S. industry about $50 billion a year. Although critics have questioned the accuracy of this figure,[7] drug abuse by employees clearly hurts organizations in many ways. Not only are substance-abusing employees less productive than they could be, they are more likely to quit, boosting costs for recruitment and training. Substance abusers are more likely to cause accidents; the National Safety Council estimates that almost half of the two million industrial accidents reported each year are related directly to alcohol or drug abuse.[8] Disabilities related to substance abuse can lead to higher use of disability and sick benefits, as well as higher insurance costs. Over a recent five-year period, employees with an alcohol or drug problem were absent from work 113 days more than the average employee and filed an average of $23,000 more in medical claims.[9] Finally, drug abusers may steal from the organization to support their habit.

The Americans with Disabilities Act (ADA), which prohibits discrimination on the basis of physical or mental disability, treats substance abuse arising from an addiction as a disability. Therefore, substance abuse may not be legal grounds for firing an employee. The supervisor should encourage the employee to get help, even if doing so requires adjusting the employee's work schedule or permitting the employee to take a disability leave to get treatment. In addition, actions taken with regard to the employee should focus on work performance, not on the substance abuse itself. For example, a supervisor might warn, "If I catch you picking fights with your co-workers again, I will have to suspend you." This warning addresses the employee's job-related behavior. (For more on the ADA and other laws against employment discrimination, see Chapter 16.)

Although a supervisor must treat each employee fairly and avoid discrimination, he or she also has responsibility for helping to ensure that the workplace is safe for employees and others.[10] If an employee's suspected substance abuse is creating a hazard, a supervisor must act. Again, the key is to address job-related behavior. (See the section on troubled employees, page 385, which provides guidelines for handling employees who abuse drugs or alcohol.)

### Theft

The story of Harris Tire at the beginning of this chapter describes an employee who was stealing from his employer. The U.S. Chamber of Commerce recently estimated that employee theft of companies' inventory, supplies, and money costs U.S. employers $40 billion a year.[11]

**FIGURE 13.1**

**Employee Theft at U.S. Supermarket Chains***

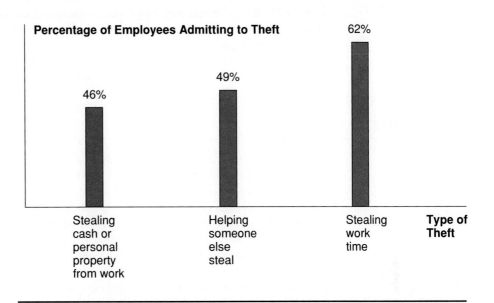

*Percentage of employees admitting to each category of theft. From an anonymous survey of employees at 26 supermarket chains nationwide.

Source: Phyllis Gillespie, "Stolen Trust: Employee Theft Costs $320 Billion," *Arizona Republic*, May 4, 1992, pp. E1, E8.

Oddly enough, an employee of the aerospace company AlliedSignal once spotted a large jet part from the company at a bar in Crown King, Arizona. Robert R. Smith, general supervisor for plant security at AlliedSignal's Fluid Systems Division, commented, "We have had some things walk out of here. Usually it's not airplane parts, because they're not worth much without the rest of the plane. More often, it's computer equipment and tools."[12] The manager of a store complains that employees "steal sandwiches, meat, potatoes, tools, equipment, and whatever else we do not nail down."[13]

Not all thefts involve money or tangible goods. Employees can also "steal time" by giving the employer less work than they are paid for, taking extra sick leave, or altering their time cards. A supervisor of a Pennsylvania health care facility once told his employer that he would need weeks to recover from a totally disabling back injury. Suspicious, the organization had the supervisor investigated; the investigator spotted him lifting a set of golf clubs from his rental car at an Arizona golf course.[14] When employee theft is viewed broadly to include the theft of time, the problem is especially great (see Figure 13.1).

The widespread nature of employee theft indicates that supervisors must be on their guard against it. Besides following the broad guidelines in this chapter for handling employee problems, supervisors should take measures to prevent and react to theft. Each organization has its own procedures, varying according to type of industry. In addition, supervisors should carefully check the background of anyone they plan to hire (part of the selection process described in Chapter 16). They should make sure that employees follow all procedures for record keeping. They should take advantage of ways to build employee morale and involvement;

employees who feel like a part of the organization are less likely to steal from it. Supervisors should make sure employees understand the costs and consequences of theft. Perhaps most important, supervisors should set a good example by following the principles of ethical behavior.

The Small Business Administration advises supervisors who suspect an employee is stealing not to investigate the crime themselves. Instead, they should report their suspicions to their manager and to the police or professional security consultants.[15]

# Counseling

**counseling**
The process of learning about an individual's personal problem and helping him or her resolve it.

If a supervisor responds to problem behavior immediately, he or she will sometimes be able to bring the problem to a quick end without complex proceedings. For example, a supervisor can respond to each complaint from an employee who constantly complains about the way things are done by calmly asking the employee to suggest some alternatives. Not only does this discourage complaining, but it may uncover some good, new ways of operating. In many cases, however, the supervisor must take further steps to demonstrate the seriousness of the problem behavior.

Often the most constructive way a supervisor can address problem behavior is through counseling. **Counseling** refers to the process of learning about an individual's personal problem and helping the employee resolve it. Employees themselves should be able to resolve a relatively simple problem, such as tardiness caused by staying up too late watching television, without the supervisor's help. For more complex problems, such as those stemming from financial difficulties or substance abuse, the solution will require getting help from an expert. Because counseling is a cooperative process between supervisor and employee, employees are likely to respond more positively to it than to a simple order that they "shape up or ship out."

## Benefits of Counseling

Counseling benefits employees in several ways. It can ease their worries or help them solve their problems. Working cooperatively with a supervisor to resolve a problem gives employees a sense that the supervisor and organization are interested in their welfare. This belief in turn can improve job satisfaction and motivation. The resulting improvements in productivity benefit the employee through performance rewards.

The organization benefits, too. Employees who receive needed counseling are well motivated and more likely to meet performance standards. The changes in an employee's attitudes also carry over to the work of other employees. When personal problems affect one employee's work, the others suffer consequences such as working harder to make up for the problem employee's lapses. Also, being around someone with a negative attitude tends to drag down the spirits of others in the group. After counseling improves the problem employee's performance and attitude, the whole group tends to do better.

## Appropriate Times to Counsel

A supervisor should counsel employees when they need help in determining how to resolve a problem that is affecting their work. Sometimes an employee will approach

**FIGURE 13.2**

Directive versus
Nondirective
Counseling

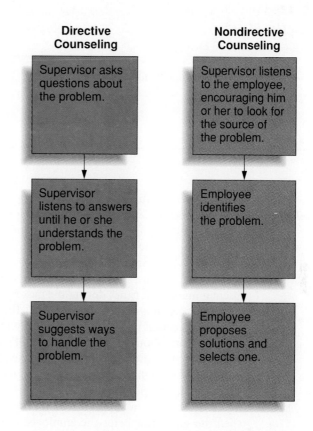

**Directive
Counseling**

Supervisor asks questions about the problem.

Supervisor listens to answers until he or she understands the problem.

Supervisor suggests ways to handle the problem.

**Nondirective
Counseling**

Supervisor listens to the employee, encouraging him or her to look for the source of the problem.

Employee identifies the problem.

Employee proposes solutions and selects one.

a supervisor with a problem, such as marriage worries or concern about doing a good job. At other times, a supervisor may observe that an employee seems to have a problem when, for example, the quality of the employee's work is declining.

It is essential for supervisors to remember that they lack training to help with many kinds of problems. They are not in a position to save a marriage, resolve an employee's financial difficulties, or handle an alcoholic family member. Only when qualified should a supervisor help an employee resolve the problem. In other cases, a supervisor should simply listen, express concern, and refer the employee to a trained professional. The human resources department may be able to suggest sources of help.

## Counseling Techniques

Counseling involves one or more discussions between the supervisor and the employee. These sessions should take place in a location where there will be privacy and freedom from interruptions. The sessions may be directive or nondirective (see Figure 13.2).

**FIGURE 13.3**

**The Counseling Interview**

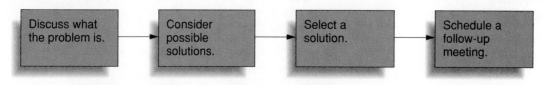

___

*Directive versus Nondirective Counseling*

**directive counseling**
An approach to counseling in which the supervisor asks the employee questions about the specific problem; when the supervisor understands the problem, he or she suggests ways to handle it.

The most focused approach to counseling is **directive counseling,** in which a supervisor asks an employee questions about a specific problem. The supervisor listens until he or she understands the source of the problem. Then the supervisor suggests ways to handle the problem.

For example, assume that Bill Wisniewski, a computer programmer, has been absent a number of times during the past month. The supervisor might ask, "Why have you been missing so many days?" Bill replies, "Because my wife has been sick, and someone needs to look after my kids." The supervisor would follow up with questions about the condition of Bill's wife (e.g., to learn whether the problem is likely to continue), the ages and needs of Bill's children, and so on. Then the supervisor might suggest finding alternative sources of care, perhaps referring Bill to a company program designed to help with such problems.

In most cases, a supervisor and employee will receive the greatest benefit when the supervisor helps the employee to develop and change instead of merely looking for a solution to a specific problem. To accomplish this, the supervisor can use **nondirective counseling.** With this approach, a supervisor should primarily listen, encouraging the employee to look for the source of the problem and to propose possible solutions. In the preceding example, a supervisor would ask open-ended questions such as "Would you tell me more about that?" Ideally, by working out his own solution, Bill would find that he has the ability to resolve many family problems without missing a lot of work.

**nondirective counseling**
An approach to counseling in which the supervisor primarily listens, encouraging the employee to look for the source of the problem and to propose possible solutions.

*The Counseling Interview*

The counseling interview starts with a discussion of what the problem is (see Figure 13.3). It then moves to consideration of possible solutions and selection of one solution to try. The interview ends with the supervisor scheduling a follow-up meeting.

The person who requested the counseling begins by describing the problem. If the employee requested help, the employee should begin. If the supervisor set up the interview because something seemed wrong, the supervisor should begin. The supervisor should focus on behavior and performance—what people do, not who they are—and encourage the employee to do the same. For example, if the employee says, "The other employees are prejudiced against me," the supervisor should ask the employee to describe what actions led to that conclusion. In addition, the supervisor should use the principles of active listening, described in Chapter 10.

Because counseling often takes place as a result of an employee's personal problems, the employee may be emotional during counseling sessions. The supervisor needs to be prepared for crying, angry outbursts, and other signs of emotion. He or she should be calm and reassure the employee that these signs of emotion are neither good nor bad. Of course, there are appropriate and inappropriate ways to express emotions. Suppose that a salesperson in a hardware store has a 10-year-old son with behavior problems. It would not be appropriate for the salesperson to express his worry and frustration by snapping at customers.

Next, the supervisor and employee should consider ways to solve the problem. Instead of simply prescribing a solution, the supervisor usually can be more helpful by asking the employee questions that will help the employee come up with ideas. Employees are more likely to cooperate in a solution they helped to develop. Asking an employee to suggest solutions can be an especially effective way to end constant whining and complaining by that employee.[16] When the supervisor and employee agree on a particular solution, the supervisor should restate it to make sure the employee understands. (Chapter 9 provides more detailed guidelines for mutual problem solving.)

Finally, the supervisor should schedule a follow-up meeting, which should take place just after the employee begins to see some results. At the follow-up meeting, employee and supervisor will review their plans and discuss whether the problem has been or is being resolved. For example, in the case of the salesperson in the hardware store, the supervisor might say, "I've noticed that we haven't received any more customer complaints about your service. In fact, one woman told me you went out of your way to help her." Notice that the supervisor is focusing on work performance, which he is qualified to discuss, rather than on the employee's family problems. If the employee replies, "Yes, I've been so much calmer ever since I started talking to that counselor about my son," the supervisor has a good indication that the employee is resolving his problem.

# Discipline

**discipline**
Action taken by the supervisor to prevent employees from breaking rules.

"I can't stand Marcia's surly attitude any longer!" fumed Don Koh, her supervisor. "If she doesn't cut it out, she's going to be sorry." This supervisor is eager for the employee to experience the consequences of her behavior. However, despite the anger and frustration that can be generated by supervising a problem employee, a supervisor needs to apply discipline in constructive ways. **Discipline** is action taken by a supervisor to prevent employees from breaking rules. In many cases, effective discipline can quickly bring about a change in an employee's behavior.

## Administering Discipline

In administering discipline, a supervisor should distinguish between discipline and punishment. (See the Self-Quiz on page 394 to help you determine the difference.) As described in Chapter 11, punishment is an unpleasant consequence given in response to undesirable behavior. Discipline, in contrast, is broader; it is a teaching process. The supervisor explains the significance and consequences of the employee's behavior, then, if necessary, lets the employee experience those consequences.

**FIGURE 13.4**

**Possible Steps in the Discipline Process**

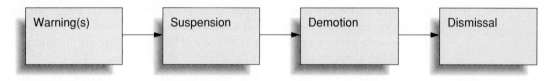

The specific ways in which a supervisor applies these steps may be dictated by company policies or the union contract, if any. Thus, a supervisor must be familiar with all applicable policies and rules. These should include respecting the rights of employees in the discipline process. Employees' rights include the following:[17]

- The right to know job expectations and the consequences of not fulfilling those expectations.
- The right to receive consistent and predictable management action in response to violations of the rules.
- The right to receive fair discipline based on facts.
- The right to question management's statement of the facts and to present a defense.
- The right to receive progressive discipline (described in the next section).
- The right to appeal a disciplinary action.

### *The Discipline Process*

Before administering discipline in response to problem behavior, supervisors need to have a clear picture of the situation. They may observe the problem themselves or someone may tell them about the problem. In either case, supervisors need to collect the facts before taking further action.

As soon as possible, a supervisor should meet with the employees involved and ask for each employee's version of what happened. For example, a supervisor believed that one of her employees was using the office telephone for personal business. The employee had a girlfriend in England, and the supervisor suspected the company was paying for the employee's long-distance calls. The solution to this problem would come not from making hasty accusations or from issuing a general memo about company policy but from asking the employee directly and privately what his telephone conversations were about.[18] In getting the employee's version of a problem, a supervisor should use good listening practices and resist the temptation to get angry.

When a supervisor observes and understands the facts behind problem behavior, disciplining an employee takes place in as many as four steps (see Figure 13.4): warnings, suspension, demotion, and dismissal. This pattern of discipline is "progressive" in the sense that the steps progress from the least to the most severe action a supervisor can take. A warning is unpleasant to hear but fulfills the important purpose of informing employees about the consequences of their behavior before more punitive measures are taken. Suspension, demotion, and discharge are more upsetting to an employee because they hurt the employee in the pocketbook.

*Warning.*    A warning may be either written or oral. Some organizations have a policy that calls for an oral warning followed by a written warning if performance does not improve. Both types of warning are designed to make sure that the employee understands the problem. A warning should contain the following information:

- What the problem behavior is.
- How the behavior affects the organization.
- How and when the employee's behavior is expected to change.
- What actions will be taken if the employee's behavior does not change.

Thus, a supervisor might say, "I have noticed that in the last two staff meetings, you have made hostile remarks. Not only have these disrupted the meetings, but they lead your co-workers to take you less seriously. I expect that you will refrain from such remarks in future meetings, or I will have to give you a suspension." As in this example, the warning should be brief and to the point.

In the case of a written warning, it is wise practice to ask the employee to sign the warning, which documents that the first step in the discipline process took place. If the employee refuses to sign the warning, even with minor changes, the supervisor should note the employee's refusal or should call in someone (such as the supervisor's manager) to witness the refusal.

**suspension**
Requirement that an employee not come to work for a set period of time; the employee is not paid for the time off.

*Suspension.*    A **suspension** is the requirement that an employee not come to work for a set period of time, during which the employee is not paid. The length of the suspension might run from one day to one month, depending on the seriousness of the problem. Suspensions are useful when the employee has been accused of something serious, such as stealing, and the supervisor needs time to investigate.

**demotion**
Transfer of an employee to a job involving less responsibility and usually lower pay.

*Demotion.*    A **demotion** is the transfer of an employee to a job having less responsibility and usually lower pay. Sometimes a demotion is actually a relief for an employee, especially if the employee has been goofing off or performing poorly because the job was more than he or she could handle. In such a case, the employee might welcome returning to a job where he or she is competent. More often, however, a demotion leads to negative feelings—a punishment that continues for as long as the employee holds the lower-level job.

**dismissal**
Relieving an employee of his or her job.

*Dismissal.*    The permanent removal of an employee from a job is called **dismissal,** or termination or discharge. The organization cannot really regard dismissal as a success because it then has to recruit, hire, and train a new employee. Nevertheless, a supervisor sometimes must dismiss an employee who commits a serious offense or who will not respond to other forms of discipline. Occasionally an employee or supervisor may decide that correcting a problem is impossible, or at least too difficult or expensive.[19] In addition to continued failure to correct problem behavior, dismissal may occur because an employee deliberately damages the organization's property, fights on the job, or engages in dangerous practices (e.g., a railroad engineer who drinks on the job).

Dismissing an employee is never easy; however, it is sometimes a necessary part of the job to ensure a positive work environment for the remaining employees. The owner in the previous example fired the difficult waitress at the Austin restaurant, and the next day the other staff members said their jobs were now much less stressful. Phil Roberts, president of the Premier Ventures restaurant group, comments: "As a manager, you are a leader. Employees depend on you to

Dismissing an employee is never easy, and supervisors and organizations must make appropriate decisions based on established guidelines and laws. One month after Robert Burch informed his supervisor that he was being treated for alcoholism, Coca-Cola Company fired him. A jury in the U.S. District Court in Dallas decided that his rights had been violated under the Americans with Disabilities Act. The reason: disabilities under the law include alcoholism.

Source: © Roger Allyn Lee/SuperStock

make decisions—even tough ones—that are for the good of the whole."[20] In addition, many organizations have policies requiring a supervisor to involve higher-level management before dismissing an employee. Supervisors should be familiar with any such policy and follow it. (See "Tips from the Firing Line" for an expert's suggestions on how to conduct a termination interview.)

In following the steps in the discipline process, a supervisor should keep in mind that the objective is to end the problem behavior. A supervisor takes only as many steps as are necessary to bring about a change in behavior: The ultimate goal is to solve the problem without dismissing the employee.

### Guidelines for Effective Discipline

When an employee is causing a problem—from tardiness to theft to lack of cooperation—the supervisor needs to act immediately. That is not always easy to do. Pointing out poor behavior and administering negative consequences are unpleasant tasks. However, by ignoring the situation, a supervisor is signaling that the problem is not serious. As a result, the problem gets worse. Seeing that the problem behavior leads to no consequences, an employee may increase it and other employees may follow this example.

In contrast, when Kathleen R. Tibbs was an in-flight supervisor with Eastern Airlines, she faced up to the unpleasant task of disciplining an employee with unacceptable attendance. Tibbs had the employee suspended for seven days. Her action inspired the employee to address the personal problems that led to her poor attendance.

When discussing the problem with an employee, a supervisor should focus on learning about and resolving the issue at hand. This meeting is no time for name-calling or for dredging up instances of past misbehavior. Nor is it generally useful for a supervisor to dwell on how patient or compassionate he or she has been. Instead, a supervisor should listen until he or she understands the problem, then begin discussing how to correct it in the future. Talking about behaviors instead of personalities helps the employee understand what is expected.

## TIPS FROM THE FIRING LINE

### *The Right Way to Fire an Employee*

Probably the worst part of any supervisor's job, the part dreaded most, is having to fire an employee. But if discipline has been administered properly, by the time both supervisor and employee reach this point, the actual termination should be no surprise. James Walsh, author of *Rightful Termination*, has a few suggestions to help the process go smoothly and productively:

- Conduct the termination in a neutral location, not the employee's or supervisor's office.
- Have a neutral witness, someone who does not have a work relationship with the employee, attend the termination interview.
- Prepare in advance a written termination notice documenting relevant problems, disciplinary action, and so forth.
- Don't argue with the employee.
- Remain calm. Listen to the employee. Refrain from getting angry.

- Be sure that you've followed company rules, procedures, and policies correctly and consistently in applying discipline and conducting the termination.
- Don't offer career advice to the employee you have just let go. However, you can offer assistance in finding a new job.
- Do not use a euphemism that does not express what you mean. For instance, *layoff* could imply that you will rehire the employee at a later date. It is better to use *termination*.
- Write an account of the interview and give a copy to the terminated employee.
- Do not terminate an employee at the end of a workday, just after a business trip, or just before a major holiday.

Source: James Walsh, *Rightful Termination* (Santa Monica, CA: Merritt Publishing, 1994.)

A supervisor should keep emotions in check. Although it is appropriate to convey sincere concern about the problem, a supervisor's other feelings are largely irrelevant and can even stand in the way of a constructive discussion. When an employee breaks the rules or seems unwilling to do a good job, it is only natural for a supervisor to feel angry. The supervisor should get control over this anger before confronting the employee in order to be objective rather than hostile. Being calm and relaxed when administering discipline tells an employee that the supervisor is confident of what he or she is doing.

Discipline should be a private matter. The supervisor should not humiliate an employee by reprimanding the employee in front of other employees. Humiliation only breeds resentment and may actually increase problem behavior in the future.

A supervisor also should be consistent in administering discipline. One way to do this is to follow the four steps of the discipline process outlined earlier. Also, a supervisor should respond to *all* instances of misbehavior rather than, for example, ignore a longstanding employee's misdeeds while punishing a newcomer. Consistency is a key part of preventing workplace violence; the most effective policy is widely thought to be one of zero tolerance. In other words, whenever *any* employee threatens or carries out *any* act of violence, the organization quickly responds with discipline in some form (whatever is most appropriate under the circumstances).[21] The guidelines for effective discipline are summarized in Figure 13.5.

**FIGURE 13.5**

Guidelines for
Effective Discipline

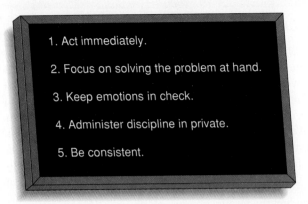

1. Act immediately.

2. Focus on solving the problem at hand.

3. Keep emotions in check.

4. Administer discipline in private.

5. Be consistent.

### Documentation of Disciplinary Action

Employees who receive discipline sometimes respond by filing a grievance or suing the employer. To be able to justify his or her actions, a supervisor must have a record of the disciplinary actions taken and the basis for the discipline. These records may be needed to show that the actions were not discriminatory or against company policy. As noted earlier, one type of disciplinary record is a signed copy of any written warning. In addition, other disciplinary actions should be recorded in the employee's personnel file, as directed by the human resources department.

Supervisors often use past performance appraisals as documentation of the need for disciplinary action. However, this often backfires because many supervisors are reluctant to give negative evaluations. A performance appraisal that has an employee's work recorded as average, adequate, or meeting only minimal standards does not support dismissal of that employee. This is why it is essential for the supervisor to give accurate performance appraisals (see Chapter 18).

Documentation is especially important when a supervisor must terminate an employee. Because the experience is so emotional, some former employees respond with a lawsuit. The employee's file should show the steps the supervisor took leading up to the termination and a record of the specific behaviors that led the supervisor to dismiss the employee.

### Positive Discipline

**positive discipline**
Discipline designed to
prevent problem
behavior from
beginning.

Ideally, discipline should not only end problem behavior, it should also prevent problems from occurring. Discipline designed to prevent problem behavior from beginning is known as **positive discipline,** or preventive discipline. An important part of positive discipline is making sure employees know and understand the rules they must follow. A supervisor also should explain the consequences of violating rules. For example, a production supervisor might explain that company policy calls for dismissal of any employee caught operating machinery while under the influence of drugs or alcohol.

A supervisor also can administer positive discipline by working to create the conditions under which employees are least likely to cause problems. Employees may engage in problem behavior when they feel frustrated. For example, if the organization sets a sales quota higher than salespeople think they can achieve, they may give up and goof off instead of trying their best. If computer operators complain that they need more frequent rest breaks to prevent health problems, and no changes are made, they may adopt a negative attitude toward the company's apparent lack of concern for their well-being. This reaction is related to another source of problem behavior: feeling as if one is not an important part of the organization. If employees conclude that they and management are at odds with one another, some may turn their energy toward seeing what they can get away with.

To combat such problems, a supervisor needs to be aware of and responsive to employees, needs and ideas. A supervisor should encourage upward communication, promote teamwork, and encourage employees to participate in decision making and problem solving. Effective use of motivation techniques also helps prevent the frustration and alienation that can lead to problem behavior. Finally, through good hiring and training practices, a supervisor can help to ensure that employee values, interests, and abilities are a good match with the job and the organization. (See "Meeting the Challenge" to learn how one small company encourages positive discipline in these ways.)

**decision-making leave**
A day off during which a problem employee is supposed to decide whether to return to work and meet standards or to stay away for good.

At some companies, positive discipline includes a day off with pay for employees who fail to respond to efforts to educate them about following the rules and meeting performance standards. During this suspension, known as a **decision-making leave,** the employees are supposed to decide whether to return to work and meet standards or to stay away for good. If the employees choose to come back, they work with a supervisor to develop objectives and action plans for improvement.

Finally, a supervisor should not only punish problem behavior but reward desirable kinds of behavior, such as contributing to the department's performance. For example, a supervisor should recognize those who make suggestions for improvements or who resolve sticky problems. (See chapter 11 for specific ideas.)

### Self-Discipline

An effective program of positive discipline results in self-discipline, in which employees voluntarily follow the rules and try to meet performance standards. Most people get satisfaction from doing a job well, so self-discipline should result when employees understand what is expected. Supervisors can help to encourage self-discipline by communicating not only the rules and performance standards, but the reasons for those rules and standards.

In addition, a supervisor who takes long lunch breaks or spends hours chatting with friends on the telephone is in no position to insist that employees put in a full workday. If supervisors expect employees to follow the rules, they must set a good example by exercising self-discipline.

## Troubled Employees

So far, this chapter has emphasized problems that can be solved by giving employees more information or helping them to change their behavior. However, some employees have problems that make them unable to respond to a simple process of discipline or counseling. These troubled employees include people who are substance abusers or have psychological problems.

## MEETING THE CHALLENGE

### *Wainwright Industries Uses Quality and Teams to Create Positive Discipline and a Nonviolent Culture*

When they set out to apply for the prestigious Malcolm Baldrige National Quality Award, owners of Missouri-based Wainwright Industries, a 275-employee shop that manufactures stamped and machined products, didn't think about violence—or the lack of it—in their workplace. But they soon discovered a correlation. After employees walked out on strike in the late 1970s, management decided they could no longer afford an adversarial relationship; certainly not if they were going to improve quality standards. "We decided it can't be we and they; it has to be us. We set about to try to develop that kind of environment," recalls David Robbins, vice-president of Wainwright.

First, Wainwright gave employees more decision-making power; then employees decertified their union, whereupon Wainwright management declared all employees salaried workers. "Everybody in our company is paid whether they come to work or not," says Robbins, "and yet consistently, since 1984, we have had in excess of 99 percent attendance." However, discipline for tardiness and absenteeism does apply. "Obviously, when people are salaried, we expect them to come to work. If people show a propensity not to come to work, we take that pretty seriously," notes Robbins. Wainwright administers progressively severe penalties to employees who are consistently late or absent.

Then there's the introduction of teams—if a worker is too often late or absent, his or her teammates take it pretty seriously, too, because they have to make up the missing employee's work. In addition, "everybody is in a profit-sharing plan, so if somebody is on salary and not coming to work, that's eating into their profit sharing," Robbins continues.

Robbins believes that team motivation is a positive form of discipline. "I would much rather have the team be self-motivating, rather than for me to be involved in discipline. If the team tells Joe that he's letting them down, that's far more effective than anything I can do."

How do the positive discipline of the quality movement and teamwork promote a nonviolent work atmosphere? Robbins believes that Wainwright has created "an environment where people take more ownership in each other and the company. When you have that ownership, a lot of problems and frustrations are easier to deal with," and less apt to deteriorate into violence. The open communication that comes with quality and teamwork also means that managers are more aware of potential problems. In this type of atmosphere, "you're going to get threats reported more readily," explains manager Garry Mathiason. "You're going to get a clearer transmission of what the company values are."

Finally, the company offers an employee assistance program (EAP) in which counselors help employees deal with problems such as alcohol and drug abuse, financial difficulties, family matters, and the like. Wainwright management believes that if these problems are faced early on, they are less likely to undermine employees' performance at work. Wainwright makes certain that all employees know about the EAP so that "problems can be addressed proactively," according to Robbins.

Perhaps it's no surprise that Wainwright Industries won the Malcolm Baldrige National Quality Award.

Source: "Creating a Violence-Free Company Culture," *Nation's Business*, Feb. 1995, pp. 22–24.

### *Detection of the Troubled Employee*

The first signs that a supervisor has a troubled employee tend to be the kinds of discipline problems described earlier in this chapter. A supervisor may notice that an employee is frequently late or that the quality of an employee's work has been slipping. If disciplinary action or counseling seems ineffective at resolving the problem, a supervisor may have a troubled employee.

In the case of substance abuse, the supervisor might notice signs that the employee has been using alcohol or drugs. The examples listed in Table 13.1 are among the most common behavioral signs. (Note that these are only hints that the employee might be using drugs or alcohol. There may be other explanations for

A crime consultant's recent poll of convicted armed robbers revealed that fast-food restaurants were becoming a prime target. Studies also have shown that up to 64 percent of armed robberies of fast-food restaurants involve current or former employees who provided information to outsiders. To try to avoid problems, supervisors and their organizations need to train employees about the importance of self-discipline in disclosing information. For example, if someone pressures them for information, they should discourage the person by providing only the facts approved by their employers such as no one can access the restaurant's safe during the day, cashiers can trip alarms outside while they take out the trash, or everything is on videotape.

Source: © B. McAllister/ Gamma Liaison

these behaviors.) Perhaps a supervisor will even find the employee has possession of drugs or alcohol. When an employee is suspected of drug use, some organizations have a policy of confirming the suspicion through the use of drug testing.

Because there may be another explanation for symptoms that look like the effects of using alcohol or illicit drugs (e.g., taking prescription medications), a supervisor should avoid making accusations about what he or she believes is going on. For example, a supervisor should not say, "I see you've been drinking on the job." Instead, the supervisor should focus on job performance: "I see something is hurting the quality of your work this week. Let's talk about what the problem is and how to solve it."

## Confrontation of the Troubled Employee

Ignoring a problem does not make it go away. Thus, hoping an alcoholic employee will seek help rarely works. It only helps the employee maintain the illusion that the substance abuse is not causing significant problems. After all, if the boss does not complain, how bad can the work be? Therefore, when a supervisor suspects a problem, he or she needs to confront the employee.

The first step is to document the problem. A supervisor should keep notes of instances in which an employee's performance is not acceptable. When collecting this information, a supervisor should be sure to keep notes on all employees whose performance is slipping, not just the one person targeted.

When a supervisor has gathered enough supporting evidence, he or she should confront the employee. The supervisor should go over the employee's performance, describing the evidence of a problem. Then the supervisor should refer the employee to a source of counseling or other help. For example, the supervisor could say, "I don't know what's wrong with you, but I want you to see an employee assistance counselor."[22] Finally, the supervisor should explain the consequences of not changing. In some cases, accepting help may be a requirement for keeping the job. Thus, the supervisor might say, "There's no shame in getting

## TABLE 13.1

**Possible Signs of Alcohol or Drug Use**

Slurred speech.

Clumsy movements and increased accidents.

Personality changes.

Decreased ability to work as part of a team.

Smell of alcohol on the employee's breath.

Growing carelessness toward personal appearance and the details of the job.

Increase in absenteeism or tardiness along with unbelievable excuses.

Daydreaming.

Leaving the work area; making frequent visits to the rest room.

Violence in the workplace.

help, and we'll keep it private. But you are responsible for doing your job safely and up to standards. If you don't, I'll have to follow our disciplinary procedures for unacceptable performance."

Experts agree that this type of warning from a supervisor can be one of the most effective ways to motivate a substance-abusing employee to get help. Carol Cepress of the Hazelden treatment center in Center City, Minnesota, says, "The reality that your job is on the line is usually quite an eye-opener."[23]

During the confrontation, the employee may become angry or defensive. This reaction is common in such situations, so the supervisor should not take it personally or overreact. The employee also may come up with excuses that sound particularly sad and compelling. In any case, the supervisor must continue to focus on the employee's behavior on the job and the way the employee's behavior affects the organization. No matter how outraged the employee or how impressive or creative the excuse, the employee's behavior must improve.

### Aid in and Evaluation of Recovery

Most organizations have developed procedures for providing help to troubled employees. When a supervisor believes that problems are occurring because an employee is troubled, the organization's procedures need to be investigated. In most cases, the place to start is with the human resources department.

The type of treatment program tends to depend on the size of the organization. Many small organizations refer troubled employees to a counseling service. Another policy is simply to tell the employee to get help or lose the job. A supervisor should be careful in pursuing the latter approach. If possible, the ultimate objective should be the employee's rehabilitation, not dismissal. Rehabilitation is not only more compassionate, it tends to be less costly than hiring and training a new employee, and it is less likely to violate laws prohibiting employment discrimination.

**employee assistance program (EAP)**
A company-based program for providing counseling and related help to employees whose personal problems are affecting their performance.

Other organizations, especially large ones, offer an **employee assistance program (EAP).** An EAP is a company-based program for providing counseling and related help to employees whose personal problems affect their performance. It may be simply a referral service or it may be fully staffed with social workers, psychologists, nurses, career counselors, financial advisers, and other professionals. These programs are voluntary (employees do not have to participate unless they want to) and confidential (participation is a private matter).

As the diversity of the U.S. workforce has increased, employers have broadened their concept of the kinds of help troubled employees will need, and EAPs have expanded their services accordingly. Originally, EAPs focused on helping employees recover from substance abuse. Some of the relatively new services include financial or career counseling, referrals for child care and elder care, AIDS education and counseling, and "cultural adjustment counseling," which is directed toward helping employees work with others of a different cultural background. At Personal Performance Consultants, an EAP based in St. Louis, one of the most common requests is for help in balancing family and work responsibilities.[24]

The reason for providing EAPs and other sources of counseling is to improve the employee's performance. It is up to the supervisor to see that the treatment plan is producing the desired results at the workplace. Any signs of improvement not related to performance (e.g., abstinence from alcohol) are irrelevant from the supervisor's point of view.

## Sources of Support

Supervising problem employees is a delicate matter. Supervisors must be careful to motivate and correct rather than to generate hostility and resentment. At the same time, supervisors must be careful to follow organizational procedures, union requirements, and laws regarding fair employment practices. Fortunately, supervisors can get support from their superiors, the organization's human resources department, and outside experts.

When an employee fails to respond to initial attempts at counseling, a supervisor should try discussing the problem with his or her manager. The manager may be able to offer insights into how to handle the problem. In addition, some steps, such as suspension or dismissal, may require that the supervisor get authorization from a higher-level manager.

It is also wise to consult with the human resources department, which has information about company policies on discipline and how to document it. Human resources personnel can advise a supervisor on how to proceed without breaking laws, violating a contract with the union, or putting the organization at risk in case of a lawsuit. In addition, personnel specialists have expertise that can make them good sources of ideas on what to say or what corrective measures to propose. Sometimes just talking about a strategy helps a supervisor to think of new ways to approach the problem.

In small organizations with no human resources staff, a supervisor and his or her manager may agree that the problem requires the help of outside experts. They may contract with a consultant, a labor attorney, or a human relations specialist who provides services on a temporary basis. The fee paid to such an expert may seem high but can be far less than the cost of defending a wrongful-termination lawsuit. The local office of the Small Business Administration (SBA) also may be able to provide help. SBA assistance may include a referral to an executive in one of its programs for providing small businesses with free advice.

In sum, when an employee's problems or problem behavior threaten to disrupt the workplace, a supervisor should not despair. The effective use of counseling and discipline can solve many of these problems. When they do not, a variety of people inside and outside the organization stand ready to help.

# Summary

### 13.1 Identify common types of problem behavior among employees.

The problems that supervisors most often encounter are absenteeism and tardiness, insubordination and uncooperativeness, alcohol and drug abuse, and employee theft.

### 13.2 Explain why and when supervisors should counsel employees.

Counseling helps employees solve their problems, which enables them to perform better at work. It therefore improves productivity as well as the attitudes and job satisfaction of employees. Supervisors should counsel employees when they need help in determining how to resolve a problem that is affecting their work. When an employee has a problem with which the supervisor is unqualified to help, the supervisor should refer the employee to a professional.

### 13.3 Describe counseling techniques.

Counseling consists of one or more discussions between the supervisor and the employee. These discussions may involve directive counseling, in which the supervisor asks the employee questions to identify the problem and then suggests solutions. Or the discussions may be nondirective, with the supervisor primarily listening and encouraging the employee to look for the source of the problem and identify possible solutions. At the beginning of the interview, the person who identified the problem describes it, focusing on behavior and performance. Next, the supervisor and employee consider ways to solve the problem. Finally, the supervisor schedules a follow-up meeting to review the planned solution and determine whether the problem is being resolved.

### 13.4 Discuss effective ways of administering discipline.

After collecting the facts of the situation, the supervisor should meet with the employee(s) involved and ask for their version of what has happened. The supervisor should use good listening techniques. Then the supervisor issues a warning. If necessary, the supervisor lets the employee experience the consequences of unsatisfactory behavior through suspension, demotion, and ultimately dismissal. The supervisor takes as many steps as are necessary to resolve the problem behavior. The supervisor should administer discipline promptly, privately, impartially, and unemotionally. The supervisor should document all disciplinary actions.

### 13.5 Describe the principles of positive discipline and self-discipline.

Positive discipline focuses on preventing problem behavior from ever beginning. It can include making sure employees know and understand the rules, creating conditions under which employees are least likely to cause problems, using decision-making leaves when problems occur, and rewarding desirable behavior. Effective positive discipline results in self-discipline among employees; that is, employees voluntarily follow the rules and try to meet performance standards. Supervisors who expect self-discipline from their employees must practice it themselves.

### 13.6 Explain how supervisors can detect and confront troubled employees.

The supervisor can look for discipline problems and investigate whether these are symptoms of personal problems. With substance abuse, the supervisor might notice signs that the employee is using alcohol or drugs. When the supervisor suspects that an employee is troubled, he or she should document the problem and then meet with the employee and describe the evidence of a problem, focusing on the employee's performance at work. The supervisor should refer the employee to a source of help and explain the consequences of not getting help. The supervisor should be careful not to overreact to an employee's emotional response or creative excuses.

### 13.7 Specify how supervisors can direct troubled employees in getting help and then follow up on the recovery efforts.

Supervisors should learn their organization's procedures for helping troubled employees and then follow those procedures. This may involve referring employees to help outside the organization or to the organization's employee assistance program. The supervisor is responsible for seeing that the employee's performance is improving, not for evaluating evidence of improvement unrelated to work.

**13.8 Discuss the role of the supervisor's manager and the human resources department in helping the supervisor with problem employees.**

The supervisor's manager and the human resources department can help the supervisor handle problem employees in ways that follow organizational guidelines, legal requirements, or union contracts. A supervisor should discuss the problem with his or her manager and the human resources department to get information about the organization's policies for handling problem employees and suggestions for handling the specific problem. The organization may offer an employee assistance program whose ultimate goal is the employee's rehabilitation.

## Key Terms

| | | |
|---|---|---|
| insubordination | discipline | positive discipline |
| counseling | suspension | decision-making leave |
| directive counseling | demotion | employee assistance program (EAP) |
| nondirective counseling | dismissal | |

## Review and Discussion Questions

1. Dennis McCutcheon supervises the employees who work in the building supplies department of a large discount hardware store. One of his employees, Kelly Sims, has been late to work every Tuesday and Thursday for the last three weeks. Sometimes she disappears for more than an hour at lunch. Although Kelly had a positive attitude when she started the job, recently Dennis has overheard her complaining to co-workers and being less than friendly to customers. Using the questions listed in the section "Problems Requiring Special Action" (page 372), how might Dennis go about uncovering the true source of Kelly's performance problem?

2. What is the difference between directive and nondirective counseling? Give an example of each in the form of a brief dialogue.

3. An employee explains to her supervisor that her performance has been slipping because she has been distracted and frightened by threats from her former husband.

   a. Should the supervisor counsel the employee about her job performance? Explain.
   b. Should the supervisor counsel the employee about the threats from her former husband? Explain.

4. While counseling an employee, a supervisor made the following statements. What is wrong with each statement? What would be a better alternative for each?

   a. "Your laziness is becoming a real problem."
   b. "Knock off the shouting! The way your performance has been lately, you have no right to be angry."
   c. "What you need to do is to take this job more seriously. Just focus on getting your work done, and then we won't have a problem."

5. What are the steps in the discipline process? In what kinds of situations would a supervisor take all these steps?

6. What additional type of information should be included in the following warning to an employee?

   "I noticed that you returned late from lunch yesterday and three days last week. This upsets the other employees because they get back promptly in order to give others a chance to take their breaks. Beginning tomorrow, I expect you to be back on time."

7. Describe four guidelines for disciplining employees effectively.

8. Jackie Weissman supervises a group of technicians in a laboratory that conducts medical tests. It is extremely important that the technicians follow lab procedures to obtain accurate test results. What steps can Jackie take to apply positive discipline with her group?

9. *a.* What are some signs that an employee has been abusing alcohol or drugs?

   *b.* Why should a supervisor avoid making a statement such as "You've been coming to work high lately"?

10. What steps should a supervisor take in confronting an apparently troubled employee?

11. Rick Mayhew's nine-year-old son was recently diagnosed with a chronic illness that is difficult and expensive to treat. In addition, Rick's elderly mother-in-law is going to be moving in to live with his family. Rick's supervisor has noticed that his performance has been suffering lately; he is often late to work, leaves early, and has trouble concentrating on his work. The supervisor does not want to lose Rick as an employee. Would an employee assistance program help Rick? Why or why not?

12. Tom Chandra has a problem with one of the production workers he supervises. The worker has been ignoring Tom's instructions about the new procedures for operating a lathe, preferring instead to follow the old procedures. What kind of help can Tom get from his manager and the human resources department in handling this problem?

## A SECOND LOOK

In the story of Harris Tire Company at the beginning of this chapter, what kind of problem behavior did Sam exhibit? If you were Tommy Hunnicutt, how would you have handled this situation?

# APPLICATIONS MODULE

## CASE

### General Electric: Is Insubordination Really a Disability?

Insubordination is the deliberate refusal to do what a supervisor asks. So how can it be called a disability? One former employee of General Electric tried to do just that, claiming that under the Americans with Disabilities Act (ADA), an employee with a disability must receive a reasonable accommodation from his or her employer.

Donald, the GE employee, claimed that he was unable to follow his supervisor's orders (this went on for more than 20 years). Further, he claimed that the source of his incapacity to follow orders was actually his supervisor, Gary. Gary continuously exacerbated Donald's "disability" to the point that Donald simply walked out of the plant one day. Instead of firing Donald, GE put him on decision-making leave; if he was insubordinate again, he *would* be fired.

Donald claimed that Gary did not treat him with respect, and when Gary made a request that Donald did not agree with, Donald argued. Gary threatened to fire him. Another manager encouraged Donald to obey the request, which he did. But when Gary later reminded Donald that he was still facing disciplinary action for previous insubordination, Donald lost his temper. Gary fired him.

Donald retaliated, taking his case to court under the ADA. He claimed that he had two disabilities. First, he stated that he suffered from "an emotional condition that is characterized by feelings of inferiority and unacceptability." This disability rendered him incapable of following orders. In a sideline, he claimed a related disability: tardiness. Thus, he claimed, GE must make a "reasonable accommodation" for his condition. Second, Donald stated that he was unable to get along with his supervisor (he considered this to be a handicap), and that GE should accommodate him on this as well. Then Donald made a final claim: that GE had intentionally inflicted emotional distress on him by firing him.

The judge didn't see things Donald's way. The court refused to view insubordination, tardiness, or an inability to get along with one's supervisor as legal disabilities. His termination was ruled legal as well. Donald was stuck looking for another job.

1. Do you think that Donald could be classified as a troubled employee? Why or why not?
2. What steps might Gary have taken in administering discipline to prevent Donald's eventual firing and the subsequent lawsuit? (Or do you think *anything* could have been done?)
3. Would counseling have helped Donald? Why or why not?

Source: Milton Bordwin, "Is Insubordination a New Disability?" *Management Review*, Oct. 1994, pp. 33–35*ff*.

**SELF-QUIZ**

## *Can You Distinguish Between Discipline and Punishment?*

Write True or False on the line before each of the following statements.

_____    1. If an employee failed to do something I requested, I would immediately dock his or her pay.

_____    2. If I noticed that an employee were leaving work early on a regular basis, I would revoke his or her lunch privileges.

_____    3. If I saw two employees arguing, I would ask each separately for his or her version of the story.

_____    4. If I had to issue a warning to an employee, I would make certain that he or she understood exactly what behavior the warning referred to.

_____    5. If an employee insults me personally, I will insult the employee in return, so that he or she understands how I feel.

_____    6. No matter how angry I feel inside at an employee, I will not act hostilely.

_____    7. If an employee is doing poorly, I will note that in the performance appraisal.

_____    8. If an employee were late to work the day of the company picnic, I would force him or her to stay on the job rather than leave early with everyone else to attend the picnic.

_____    9. If I smelled alcohol on the breath of an employee after lunch, I would immediately fire the person.

_____    10. If I caught an employee violating a company policy, I would immediately discuss the behavior and its consequences with the person.

Scoring: True responses to statements 1, 2, 5, 8, and 9 illustrate punishment; true responses to statements 3, 4, 6, 7, and 10 illustrate discipline.

## Class Exercise

Think about discipline in your own life. As an adult, in what ways do you exhibit self-discipline? If you do not, give examples of ways in which you do not. What reasons do you think contribute to your self-disciplined or unself-disciplined behavior? After writing down the answers to these questions, discuss and compare them with those of your classmates.

## Team-Building Exercise

### Handling Performance Problems

This is a role-playing exercise. One class member volunteers to take on the role of supervisor. Another classmate volunteers to be the problem employee. The scenario:

> Chris Johnson has a been teller in the main branch of a bank for five years. Lately, Chris has been making a lot of mistakes. Chris often counts out money wrong and has had to redo many receipts that contain errors. Customers have begun complaining about the mistakes Chris makes and the detached, distracted manner in which Chris provides service. But at Chris's most recent performance appraisal, just two months ago, Chris's overall rating was excellent, leading to a generous wage increase. Chris's supervisor, Pat Smith, must decide how to respond to the decline in Chris's performance.

Before the role play begins, the class discusses what the supervisor should do. Based on the information given, should Pat use counseling, discipline, both, or neither? Once the class agrees on a general strategy, the two volunteers act it out.

Then the class discusses what happened:

- Did the supervisor do a good job of applying the techniques selected? What did the supervisor do well? What could the supervisor have done better?
- Did the employee and supervisor arrive at a workable solution? Explain.
- How can the supervisor follow up to see if the employee is improving?

# Video Exercise 13: *Supervising "Problem" Employees*

## Video Summary

This video program presents information about the nature and scope of alcohol and other drug problems in the workplace and about the federal government's initiative to prevent and reduce the problem. You not only will learn about the consequences of drug abuse to individuals and to society, but also will learn about the importance of each of the four components of an effective program creating a drug-free workplace: (1) education, (2) an employee assistance program, (3) supervisor training, and (4) drug testing.

## Application

Due to the threat of wrongful discharge suits in which juries are awarding damages in six, seven, and occasionally even eight figures, supervisors need to be certain that they are handling correctly the behavioral problems of their employees. The goal of proper discipline is not to discharge problem employees, but to correct the problem behavior in order to retain the employee.

Here are some questions to determine whether you know how to properly handle disciplinary matters. Circle the letter of the best choice.

1. An employee caught stealing should be subject to discipline for:

   a. Unauthorized removal of company property.
   b. Theft.
   c. Dishonesty.
   d. Felonious theft.
   e. Any of the above.

2. Someone who intentionally damages valuable property should be disciplined for:

   a. Gross destruction of company property.
   b. Deliberate destruction of company property.
   c. Felonious destruction of company property.
   d. Damaging company property.
   e. Any of the above.

3. If efforts to help an employee with an alcohol problem are unsuccessful, the employee should be subject to discipline for:

   a. Intoxication.
   b. Reporting to work under the influence of alcohol or drugs.
   c. Reporting to work in an unsafe and unproductive condition.
   d. Work-related alcohol abuse.
   e. Any of the above.

4. An employee who is disciplined for a minor infraction should be given progressively more serious discipline if he or she is again guilty of that infraction within:

   a. Three months or less.
   b. Six months or less.
   c. Twelve months or less.
   d. Eighteen months or less.
   e. Any length of time.

5. Giving long-service employees more chances to correct unacceptable behavior prior to discharge:

   a. Is discriminatory because it does not treat all employees equally.
   b. Is discriminatory but not illegal because it's not based on race, creed, color, age, sex, or national origin.
   c. Is not discriminatory because discrimination is unequal treatment of equals.
   d. Is discriminatory and unwise because long-service employees should know better and be subject to even more serious discipline for misconduct.

Source: Caleb S. Atwood, "Managers Score Poorly on Disciplining Employees, Survey Finds," *Consensus* 3, no. 3, pp. 2–4.

# 14

*A person who has not done one-half his day's work by 10 o'clock runs a chance of leaving the other half undone.*

—**Emily Brontë, nineteenth-century English author**

# Managing Time and Stress

## LEARNING OBJECTIVES

After you have studied this chapter, you should be able to:

14.1 Discuss how supervisors can evaluate their use of time.

14.2 Describe ways to plan the use of time.

14.3 Identify some time wasters and how to control them.

14.4 List factors that contribute to stress among employees.

14.5 Summarize consequences of stress.

14.6 Explain how supervisors can manage their own stress.

14.7 Identify ways organizations, including supervisors, can help their employees manage stress.

Source: © David Young-Wolff/Tony Stone Images

## PRIORITIZING GETS AN "A"

Allen E. Barken is principal of a vocational high school where he supervises 110 employees, including 47 teachers and 23 nursing instructors as well as assistant principals, counselors, and other support staff. Many students perform six to eight grades below their grade level, and a number of students have been identified as having learning or behavior disorders. Besides the standard high-school education, the school offers a program to train high schoolers and adults to become licensed practical nurses.

Juggling the complex and diverse needs of this group of employees and students would overwhelm many people, but Barken emphasizes that he keeps on top of his responsibilities through planning. Barken sets priorities and schedules his activities according to what is most important; the top priority is to "stay focused on the children." In addition, previous training in the military taught Barken to expect the unexpected and be ready for crises.

Barken's organized approach to the way he uses time allows him not only to fulfill his role as principal but also to spend time with his family and to coach semipro football. That well-rounded approach to life also helps him cope with the stresses of the job. He tries to leave the tensions of the workplace behind when he leaves each day, and he works off stress through physical activity such as swimming and power walking.

A supervisor who has a bad day may feel as though everything is out of control. Instead of working on what he or she wants, the supervisor attempts to solve unexpected problems and to soothe upset employees and customers. While workdays like this affect employees and managers at all levels, they are a particular problem for supervisors because a supervisor's people-oriented job means solving many needs and conflicts. To minimize and cope with these difficulties, supervisors must manage time and stress.

This chapter describes basic techniques of time management and stress management. It identifies ways supervisors can control how they use time. Then it defines stress and describes its consequences. Finally, the chapter suggests ways supervisors themselves can cope with stress and also help employees to do so.

# Time Management

Sean Mulligan's typical day is hectic. Just when he gets on the telephone, someone is at the door with a problem; he almost never finds the time to sit down and ponder the problem. By the end of the day, Sean is exhausted, but he would be hard-pressed to say what he accomplished. Lisa Ng's days are also busy, but when someone interrupts her, Lisa pulls out her calendar and makes an appointment for later. She starts out each day knowing what tasks are essential, and she always manages to complete them.

Which kind of supervisor would you rather have working for you? Which kind would you rather be? Time is the only resource we all have in equal shares: Everyone gets 24-hour days. To evaluate your own responses to time pressures, take the Self-Quiz on page 428.

Supervisors who are in control of their time find that their jobs are easier and that they can get more done. Needless to say, getting a lot done is a good way to impress higher-level management. The practice of controlling the way you use time is known as **time management.**

**time management**
The practice of controlling the way you use time.

Time management techniques can be as simple as putting things away as soon as you are done with them, using an appointment calendar to keep track of your schedule, and getting all the information you need *before* you start on a project.[1] While this chapter provides broad guidelines for time management, each supervisor must work out the details. Lisa Kanarek, a Dallas-based professional organizer who gives seminars and individual advice on getting organized, says, "There's not just one way to get organized . . . because no two people can work the same way."[2]

## Understanding How You Use Time

Before you can take control over the way you use time, you have to understand what you already are doing. A practical way to learn about your use of time is to keep a **time log.** This is a record of what activities you are doing hour by hour throughout the workday. Figure 14.1 provides an example. Each half-hour during the day, write down what you did during the previous half-hour. Do not wait until the end of the day; this level of detail is too difficult to remember.

**time log**
A record of what activities a person is doing hour by hour throughout the day.

After you have kept a time log for at least one typical week, review your log. Ask yourself the following questions:

- How much time did I spend on important activities?
- How much time did I spend on activities that did not need to get done?

### ▨ FIGURE 14.1
## Format for a Time Log

| Date _____ | | | |
|---|---|---|---|
| **Time** | **Activity** | **Others Involved** | **Location** |
| 7:30–8:00 | | | |
| 8:00–8:30 | | | |
| 8:30–9:00 | | | |
| 9:00–9:30 | | | |
| 9:30–10:00 | | | |
| 10:00–10:30 | | | |
| 10:30–11:00 | | | |
| 11:00–11:30 | | | |
| 11:30–12:00 | | | |
| 12:00–12:30 | | | |
| 12:30–1:00 | | | |
| 1:00–1:30 | | | |
| 1:30–2:00 | | | |
| 2:00–2:30 | | | |
| 2:30–3:00 | | | |
| 3:00–3:30 | | | |
| 3:30–4:00 | | | |
| 4:00–4:30 | | | |
| 4:30–5:00 | | | |
| 5:00–5:30 | | | |

## ■ FIGURE 14.2

**A Superhuman Level of Time Management**

Source: © 1992 by Nicole Hollander. Reprinted with permission.

- How much time did I spend on activities that someone else could have done (perhaps with some training)?
- What important jobs did I not get around to finishing?

From your review, you may see some patterns. Do you have a certain time of day for telephone calls or meetings? Do you frequently interrupt what you are doing to solve a problem or move on to something more interesting? Do you tackle the most important jobs first or the easiest ones? The answers to these and similar questions will help you see where you need to change. After you have tried applying the principles in this chapter for a while, you might want to try keeping a time log again to see how you have improved.

Keeping a time log is also helpful for people who feel out of control of their personal time. For example, if you are frustrated at how little time you spend with loved ones or if you cannot find the time for charitable work, keep a log of how you use your hours outside of work. You may find that you are spending a lot of time on an unimportant activity that you can relinquish to free time for something else.

### *Planning Your Use of Time*

Based on what you learned from keeping a time log, you can plan how to use your time better. Although few of us would want to achieve the level of time management portrayed in Figure 14.2, you need to make sure that the most important things get done each day before you move on to less important activities. You must set priorities. Thus, your planning consists of deciding what you need to do and which activities are most important. This is the practice recommended by principal Allen E. Barken in the description at the beginning of this chapter.

Planning your use of time begins with the planning process described in Chapter 6. If you follow the guidelines in that chapter, you will routinely establish objectives for the year, specifying when each must be completed. With these yearly objectives in mind, you can figure out what you need to accomplish in shorter time periods—each quarter, month, and week. Review your objectives regularly, and use them to plan what you will need to accomplish each week and day.

### Making a "To Do" List

Many people find it helpful to spend a few minutes at the end of each week writing a list of things to do—what they must accomplish during the next week. When you have made your list, write an *A* next to all the activities that must be completed that week; these are your top priorities. Then write a *B* next to all the activities that are important but can be postponed if necessary. Label everything else *C*; these are your lowest priorities for the week. Schedule times for doing your A-level and B-level activities. If you have more time, work on your C-level activities. As you complete each activity on the "to do" list, check it off.

How do you know when is the best time to do the activities on your list? Here are some guidelines to follow for creating weekly and daily schedules:

- First, record all the activities that must take place at a set time. For example, you do not have any choice about when to schedule your regular Monday morning staff meeting or the appointment you made with your manager for three o'clock on Thursday.
- Next, find times for your remaining A-level activities. Try to avoid scheduling them at the end of the day (on a daily plan) or week (on a weekly plan). If a crisis comes up, you will need another chance to finish these activities. Schedule your B-level activities next.
- Schedule the most challenging and most important activities for the times of day when you are at your best. If you are sleepy after lunch or get off to a slow start in the morning, schedule top-priority activities for times when you are more alert. Consultant Tom Peters reports that when writing a book, he worked from 4:00 A.M. to 7:30 A.M., napped for an hour, and then returned to work. He thus benefited from his most creative time, between 4:00 A.M. and 11:00 A.M.[3]
- Schedule time for thinking, not solely for doing. Remember that the creative process requires time for reflection (see Chapter 9).
- Do not fill up every hour of the day and week. Leave some time free to handle unexpected problems and questions from your employees and others. If problems do not occur, so much the better. You will have time for the C-level activities.

### Planning with a Computer

A supervisor who has access to a computer will be able to benefit from time-management software. For example, PowerCore's Network Scheduler 3 allows users of a computer network (personal computers linked together to share information) to plan their own time and to coordinate their time with others on the network. Among its many features, the program lets each user fill in information on calendars and "to do" lists and review it later, as well as look at multiple calendars to see when everyone is available for a meeting or other group activity. (A security feature enables individual users to keep their peers from reading private information.) The user can look at a calendar for a month, a week, or a single day and can have the computer emit an alarm when it is time for a specified appointment.

## FIGURE 14.3

**Common Time Wasters**

Meetings
Phone calls
Paperwork
Unscheduled Visitors

Procrastination
Perfectionism
Failure to Delegate
Inability to Say No

Other kinds of software also can help a supervisor with time management. A type of program known as a desktop organizer can dial the telephone and keep records of calls made, let the supervisor take notes and print them out later, and perform a number of calendaring functions similar to those described for Network Scheduler 3. Some desktop organizer programs are Sidekick, Agenda, and Word-Perfect Library/Office. In addition, the Windows operating system includes some desktop organizer features.

### Controlling Time Wasters

Many supervisors find that certain activities and attitudes are what most often leads them to waste time. Figure 14.3 identifies the most common time wasters: meetings, telephone calls, paperwork, unscheduled visitors, procrastination, perfectionism, failure to delegate, and inability to say no. Some of the activities are necessary, but a supervisor does not always manage the time spent on them wisely.

#### Meetings
The main reason many supervisors hate meetings is that meetings often waste time. People slowly drift into the room, then devote time to chatting while waiting for latecomers. When the formal meeting finally gets under way, the discussion may drift off onto tangents, and the group may never complete the task that it gathered to carry out. Meetings like these are understandably a source of frustration.

When you attend a meeting chaired by someone else, it is hard to control wasted time. You can encourage careful use of time by being prompt. If meetings tend to start late, you might bring along some reading material or other work to do while you wait. If the discussion at the meeting seems irrelevant, you might try tactfully asking the speaker to explain how the current discussion will help in accomplishing the goal of the meeting.

## TIPS FROM THE FIRING LINE

### *Making Meetings Productive*

Meetings are time wasters when they take longer than necessary to get the job done. But if the supervisor or other person in charge plans the meeting agenda carefully and insists that participants stick to it, the meeting can be productive. When Fedco Automotive Components hosted a multicompany networking meeting, participants were impressed by how well the meeting was organized and how much they gained from attending. Here are a few rules of thumb followed by the Fedco meeting organizers:

- Set the schedule, then stick to it. "We emphasize the time limits when we're planning, and then again two minutes before the meeting starts," says Frederick DeJohn, director and facilitator for the Western New York Technology Development Center. "In some sessions we have timekeepers who will clink a glass when there are two minutes left for each section."
- Build a bathroom break into the schedule for long meetings.
- Establish a focus and stay with it.
- Work through conventional meal times. "After four or five hours, people are ready

to go. To spend 45 minutes on lunch and then try to do the critique afterward would really make for a long day," notes Wally Kensy, Fedco manager.
- Encourage meeting participants to plan what they want to say. "There's a great payoff to having people prepare their own presentations: explaining what they're doing to an outside group lends it credibility," comments Gary Moose, Fedco president.
- Rehearse your presentation.
- Send out a follow-up letter, set of minutes, or the like to tie everything together. "After each networking meeting, I put together a package for everyone who was there, which includes an attendance sheet and other materials the company didn't pass out but wanted people to have. . . . The formal feedback process tells the audience that we're interested in their input—and we do get some valuable suggestions," says Frederick DeJohn.

Source: *Inc.*, July 1994, pp. 78–79.

When you call a meeting, you can use time wisely by starting promptly. If the discussion veers off course, politely remind participants about the subject at hand. It is also smart to set an ending time for the meeting. If you cannot solve the problem in the time allotted, schedule a follow-up meeting. (Chapter 3 and "Tips from the Firing Line" provide more ideas for holding effective meetings.)

### *Telephone Calls*

When other people call you, they usually have no way of knowing whether the time is convenient. Consequently, most of us get telephone calls when we are busy with something else. When they interrupt the work flow, telephone calls are time wasters.

One way to take control of your time is to remember that you are not a slave to the telephone. If you are fortunate to have a secretary to screen your calls, have that person answer your telephone when you are working on top-priority jobs. If you answer the telephone while you are in a meeting or doing something important, explain to the caller that you cannot give the call the attention it deserves at that time, and schedule a convenient time to call back. Of course, you have to use this approach carefully. If the person calling is your manager or a customer, the telephone call may be your top priority.

When you are placing calls yourself, think ahead. Schedule time for making calls each day, bearing in mind different time zones when calling long distance. Before you call someone, make sure you have the information you need close at hand; it does not make sense to place a client on hold while you fetch the file containing the answers he or she wanted. Not only does that waste time, it annoys the person who has to wait. If the person you are calling is not available, ask when you can reach him or her instead of simply leaving a message. That way, you have control over when the call will be made.

The telephone can be a time-saver as well as a time waster. When you have a meeting or appointment on your calendar, call to confirm it. If you need to meet with someone away from the workplace, call to get directions rather than waste time by driving around and looking for the meeting place.[4]

### Paperwork and Reading Material

Supervisors spend a lot of time reading and writing. They receive mail, reports, and magazines to read, and they must prepare reports, letters, and memos to send to others. Reading and writing are not necessarily a waste of time, but many supervisors do these activities inefficiently.

Most advice on how to manage paperwork is based on the principle of handling each item only once. Set aside specific time to read all the papers that cross your desk. At that time, decide whether each item is something you need to act on. If not, throw it away immediately. If you must act, then determine the most efficient response. An efficient way to respond to a memo is to write a brief response across the top and return the memo to the sender. If you have a secretary, you can keep a tape recorder by your side and dictate responses to letters as you read them. Or consider whether you can respond to a letter with a telephone call. If you learn that you must set time aside to do research or prepare a report, then schedule that time immediately.

Most supervisors have a multitude of magazines, newsletters, and newspapers to choose from. Each supervisor will find that some of these are very helpful, others somewhat helpful, and still others not relevant at all. To cut the time spent poring over the unhelpful publications, a supervisor should decide which ones are useful and cancel subscriptions to the rest. It is wise to look at the table of contents in the somewhat helpful publications for relevant information rather than to turn every page. A supervisor who finds that an internal company report he or she receives provides little useful information might ask to be taken off the distribution list.

### Unscheduled Visitors

Supervisors are interrupted at times by unscheduled visitors: customers, peers, employees, salespeople, or anyone else who turns up without an appointment. Because seeing these people is an unplanned use of time, the interruptions can interfere with getting the job done. Figure 14.4 shows some broad guidelines for handling this potential problem.

When a supervisor regularly spends time with unscheduled visitors on unimportant matters, a lot of time gets wasted. The key is to know which interruptions are important. For example, when an angry customer demands to see the manager and interrupts a supervisor in a store, an important part of the supervisor's job is to make that customer happy. When a supervisor's manager occasionally drops in to discuss an idea, the supervisor will probably have to work around the manager's

**FIGURE 14.4**

Handling
Unscheduled
Visitors

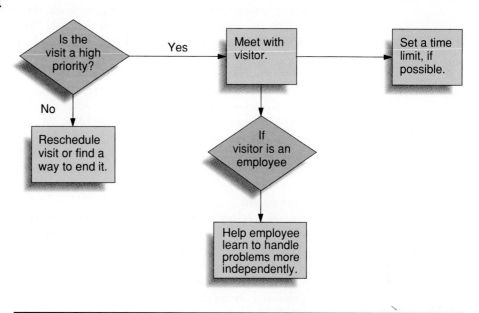

schedule. But when a co-worker in another department stops in to report on his vacation or a salesperson shows up unannounced, the interruption does not carry a high priority.

With low-priority interruptions, the supervisor needs to take control over his or her time diplomatically. The supervisor might say to the co-worker back from vacation, "It's great to hear you had fun last week. Let's have lunch together so you can tell me about it." When salespeople call without an appointment, a supervisor can ask them simply to leave some literature. Another response to unscheduled visitors is to set a time limit. For example, the supervisor might say, "I've got five minutes. What's on your mind?" If the problem seems to deserve more time, the supervisor can arrange to meet the visitor later.

A similar tactic applies when people stop at a supervisor's desk and ask, "Can you spare a minute?" The request sounds slight, but the minute can soon grow to an hour as the supervisor listens to the person and tries to help with the problem. A supervisor's defense can be to take the request literally: "Sure, I can spare a minute," then look at a watch. When the minute is up, the supervisor can say, "I'm sorry, but I really can't spend more than a minute on this now. Let's schedule another time to talk." Then do so.[5]

Standing is a useful signal. If you see an unwanted visitor heading toward your office, stand and meet the visitor at your door, then talk to the visitor there. This sends a message that you expect the conversation to be brief. Meeting with someone else at his or her desk or a conference room allows you to get up and leave when you have completed your business. If you meet with someone in your office, standing up when you finish sends a signal that the meeting is over.

Interruptions from employees can be tricky to handle because part of a supervisor's job is to listen to employees and help them with work-related problems. At the same time, a constant stream of interruptions could mean that employees have too little training or authority to handle their work. If an employee interrupts with a problem, one approach is to listen and then ask, "What do you suggest we do about that?" This shows that the supervisor expects the employee to participate in finding solutions. With practice, the employee may learn to handle problems more independently.

If the problem is not urgent—for example, if it does not hold up an employee's work—a supervisor may want to schedule a later time when supervisor and employee can meet to work on the problem. At that later time, of course, the supervisor should give priority to the meeting with the employee and discourage interruptions from others. Thus, employees will learn that a supervisor will listen and work with them, though not necessarily on a moment's notice.

### Procrastination

Sometimes it is hard to get around to starting an activity. Maybe you have to write a proposal to buy a new computer system. You are not quite sure how to write that kind of proposal, so you are grateful when the telephone rings. You talk for a while, and that conversation reminds you to follow up on an order with a supplier. So you make another telephone call. You get up to stretch your legs and decide it is a good time to check on how your employees are doing. Bit by bit, you manage to get through the entire day without doing any work on the proposal. This

**procrastination**
Putting off what needs to be done.

process of putting off what needs to be done is called **procrastination.**

Procrastination is a time waster because it leads people to spend their time on low-priority activities while they avoid the higher priorities. The best cure for procrastination is to force yourself to jump in. To do that, focus on one step at a time. Decide what the first step is, then do that step. Then do the next step. You will find that you are building momentum and that the big job no longer seems so overwhelming.

If you need more incentive to get started, set deadlines for completing each step, and give yourself a reward for completing each step. For example, you might decide that as soon as you complete the first step, you will go for a walk in the sunshine, call a customer who loves your product, or take a break to open your mail. If the project seems thoroughly unpleasant, you can concentrate on the rewards. The ultimate reward of course is to finish the job.

### Perfectionism

One reason people put off doing necessary work is that they are afraid what they do will not live up to their standards. Although high standards can inspire high performance, perfectionism can make people afraid to try at all. **Perfectionism** is the attempt to do things perfectly. It may sound like a noble goal, but human beings are imperfect. Expecting to be perfect therefore dooms a person to failure.

**perfectionism**
The attempt to do things perfectly.

Instead of being a slave to perfectionism, determine the highest standard you realistically can achieve. You may be able to meet a higher standard by drawing on the expertise of employees and peers. When you find yourself avoiding a difficult task, remind yourself that your goals are realistic, then give the job your best try.

### Failure to Delegate

Perfectionism often underlies the failure to delegate work. Even when someone else can do a job more efficiently in terms of that person's cost and availability, supervisors may resist delegating because they believe only they can really do the job

The consequences of hiring an incompatible employee for Motherwear, a $5 million catalog company in Northhampton, Massachusetts, caused president Jody Wright (*center*) to delegate the hiring responsibilities. Employees have interviewed and hired more than 60 percent of Motherwear's 40-member staff, including the two employees pictured with Wright.

Source: © Allan Penn

right. This attitude stands in the way of appropriate delegating. In terms of time management, the result is that the supervisor has taken on too much work. Instead, the supervisor should learn to delegate effectively.

Rebecca Liss, a branch operations manager for Kemper Securities, uses delegation as one of her major strategies for time management. Liss's office must cope with a rush of business at the end of each trading day. Offers to buy and sell stock must be placed immediately, before the prices change, but many customers call in their orders during the last 5 or 10 minutes before the stock market closes. To manage under pressure, Liss delegates, realizing also that if her employees make mistakes, that is a way for them to learn. "If you can't manage your time," says Liss, "you can't get the job done."

### Inability to Say No

To control your use of time, you must be able to say no when appropriate. However, it is easy to let other people and their demands control how we use our time, so we end up overextending ourselves by taking on more tasks than we can possibly do well. How do you react when someone asks you to chair a committee, manage a new project, or take an active role in a local charity? Most people are uncomfortable saying no when the opportunity is for a worthwhile project or they do not want to hurt somebody's feelings. But when we take on too many things, we cannot do our best at any of them.

If someone comes to you with an opportunity that will require a significant commitment of time, learn to tell the person politely that you will consider the offer and will reply later at some specific time. Then assess your present commitments and priorities. Decide whether you should take on this new task. You may decide that you have time for it, but in other instances you will have to decline, claiming that you do not have enough time to do justice to the task. If your life is already busy but the opportunity seems important, try asking yourself, "What activity am I willing to give up to make time for this new one?"

Certain occupations, such as air traffic controlling, can generate high levels of stress. Technological advances such as this Hughes-built common controller workstation for the Canadian Automated Air Traffic System are being designed to relieve stress in such occupations.

Source: Courtesy of Hughes Aircraft of Canada, Ltd.

Whatever you decide, this thoughtful approach does both yourself and the other person a favor. If you do not have the time to complete a task well and on schedule, it is better to give the other person a chance to find somebody else. None of us like to find out that the person we have been counting on is overcommitted and doesn't have enough time to do the job well.

## Stress Management

Failure to manage time wisely is one reason supervisors find their jobs difficult. It is frustrating to leave the workplace knowing that you did not accomplish anything you really wanted to that day. Supervisors also have difficulty hearing a lot of complaints, working in a dangerous environment, and trying to live up to unrealistic expectations. To cope, supervisors can use the techniques of stress management.

**stress**
The body's response to coping with environmental demands.

**Stress** refers to the body's response to coping with environmental demands such as change, frustration, uncertainty, danger, or discomfort. Usually when we think of stress, we think of the response to problems—for example, arguments, cold, or long hours of work. Stress also results from the challenges that stimulate us and from the happy changes in our lives. Thus, buying a car is stressful, and so is getting married or promoted. People experiencing stress typically undergo physiological changes such as faster heartbeat, faster breathing, higher blood pressure, greater perspiration, greater muscle strength, and decreased gastric (stomach) functioning, among other changes.

### Causes of Stress

The environmental demands that cause stress may arise in the workplace, in people's personal lives, and in the conflicts that may arise between the two.

**FIGURE 14.5**

**Job Factors Linked to Stress**

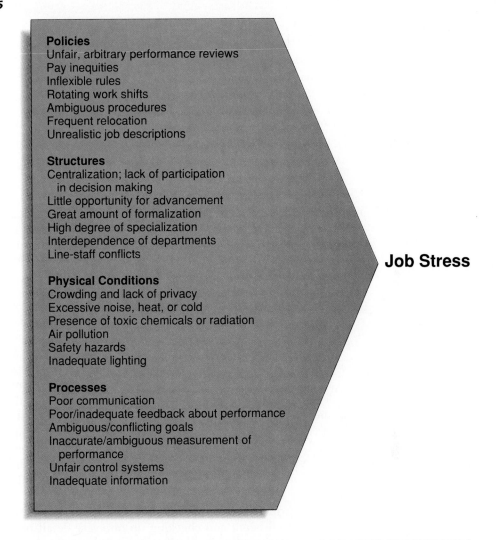

**Policies**
Unfair, arbitrary performance reviews
Pay inequities
Inflexible rules
Rotating work shifts
Ambiguous procedures
Frequent relocation
Unrealistic job descriptions

**Structures**
Centralization; lack of participation
  in decision making
Little opportunity for advancement
Great amount of formalization
High degree of specialization
Interdependence of departments
Line-staff conflicts

**Physical Conditions**
Crowding and lack of privacy
Excessive noise, heat, or cold
Presence of toxic chemicals or radiation
Air pollution
Safety hazards
Inadequate lighting

**Processes**
Poor communication
Poor/inadequate feedback about performance
Ambiguous/conflicting goals
Inaccurate/ambiguous measurement of
  performance
Unfair control systems
Inadequate information

**Job Stress**

Source: Samuel C. Certo, *Modern Management: Quality, Ethics, and the Global Environment*, 6th ed. Copyright © 1994 by Allyn and Bacon. Reprinted by permission of Prentice-Hall, Inc., Upper Saddle River, NJ.

### Work-Related Causes

Job factors linked to stress involve the organization's policies, structures, physical conditions, and processes (the way work gets done). Examples of each type are identified in Figure 14.5. Employees tend to experience the most stress if policies seem unfair and ambiguous, the structure makes jobs relatively unsatisfying, physical conditions are uncomfortable, and processes interfere with employee understanding of what is happening and how well they are doing.

## TABLE 14.1

**Behavior Patterns Associated with Type A and Type B Personalities**

| Type A | Type B |
|---|---|
| Moving, walking, eating rapidly | Having varied interests |
| Feeling impatient with people who move slower than you | Taking a relaxed but active approach to life |
| Feeling impatient when others talk about something that is not of interest to you | |
| Doing two or three things at the same time | |
| Feeling unable to relax or to stop working | |
| Trying to get more and more done in less and less time | |

Source: Adapted from Meyer Friedman and Ray H. Rosenman, *Type A Behavior and Your Heart* (New York: Fawcett Crest, 1974), pp. 100–101, summarized in Jane Whitney Gibson, *The Supervisory Challenge: Principles and Practices* (Columbus, OH: Merrill Publishing, 1990), p. 309.

Recurring efforts at downsizing have contributed to a great deal of employee stress. Many employees see job cuts as a long-term trend that prevails without regard to whether they do their best or the organization earns a profit. A case in point is Pam Cromer, who worked for Westinghouse Electric Corporation in Pittsburgh. She worked up to 80 hours a week when the company was struggling during the early 1990s. One night part of her face went numb, which Cromer learned was caused from clenching her teeth too hard—the result of tension. Despite Cromer's willingness to sacrifice, she was laid off in cutbacks that occurred after she had been with Westinghouse 22 years. At a going-away party, her co-workers observed, "The winners get to leave, and the losers get to stay."[6]

A supervisor's own behavior also can be a source of stress for employees. A supervisor who communicates poorly, stirs up conflict, and metes out discipline arbitrarily is creating stressful working conditions. Other supervisory behaviors that can contribute to employee stress are demonstrating a lack of concern for employee well-being and checking up on every detail of an employee's work. If you've ever typed while someone peered over your shoulder, you know that you can almost feel your blood pressure rise.

### Personal Factors

Even when faced with similar job factors and supervisory behavior, some employees will have a greater stress response than others. General feelings of negativism, helplessness, and low self-esteem can contribute to stress. In addition, some medical researchers have observed that the people who are more likely to have heart disease (presumably a sign of stress) tend to share a similar pattern of behavior, which the researchers named the Type A personality. A **Type A personality** refers to the behavior pattern of constantly trying to get a lot done in a hurry. It includes the behaviors listed in Table 14.1. Research suggests that some Type A people seem to thrive on their approach to life, whereas others—those prone to heart disease—have an excess amount of hostility along with the basic Type A characteristics. To help those at risk, physicians often recommend adopting contrasting behaviors, known collectively as a Type B personality (see Table 14.1).

**Type A personality**
A pattern of behavior that involves constantly trying to accomplish a lot in a hurry.

**FIGURE 14.6**

Stress Levels and
Performance

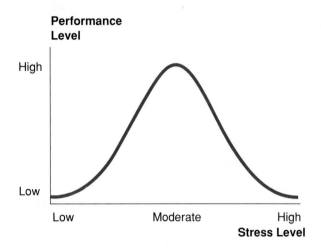

*Work-Family Conflict*

Stress also can be great for people who experience conflict between the demands of work and home. Women have traditionally borne the primary responsibility for homemaking and the family's well-being, so as a group they are particularly vulnerable to this source of stress. A survey of 311 female nurses aged 50 to 70 found that women who feel tension between demands from work and demands from home are at higher risk than other women of having serious heart disease. The risk was not associated with what the women achieved or how hard they worked, but with the degree to which they felt a conflict between career and family. At greatest risk were the women who believed that having a family interfered with advancement in their careers.[7]

## Consequences of Stress

Stress is a fact of life. Indeed, life would be boring without some sources of stress, and most people seek out some degree of stress. Some people even are attracted to jobs billed as challenging or exciting—those likely to be most stressful. On the job, employees tend to perform best when they are experiencing a moderate degree of stress (see Figure 14.6).

However, too much stress brings problems, especially when the sources of stress are negative (e.g., a critical manager or unsafe working conditions). As Figure 14.6 indicates, performance falls when the amount of stress moves from moderate to high. In a highly stressful environment, people are more apt to come down with heart disease, high blood pressure, ulcers, and possibly other diseases. Because of illness and unhappiness, they take more time off from work. When employees are at work, the sources of stress may distract them from doing their best and may make them prone to having accidents. As a result of these consequences, stress costs U.S. organizations an estimated $200 billion each year.[8]

Besides hurting the organization through poor performance and attendance, excess stress can hurt employees as individuals. People experiencing stress tend to feel anxious, aggressive, frustrated, tense, and moody. They may be overly sensitive to

---

**TABLE 14.2**

**Possible Signs of Excess Stress**

Decline in work performance.

Increase in use of sick days.

Increase in number of errors and accidents.

Moodiness and irritability.

Fatigue.

Loss of enthusiasm.

Aggressive behavior.

Difficulty making decisions.

Family problems.

Apparent loss of concern for others and their feelings.*

Feeling that it's impossible to help other people.*

Feeling of inability to get your job done fully or well.*

---

*Possible signs of burnout.

criticism, have trouble making decisions, and be more likely to have trouble maintaining mutually satisfying relationships with loved ones. They may be unable to get enough sleep. People under stress are also at risk for abusing drugs and alcohol.

Because of these potential negative consequences of stress, supervisors should notice when employees seem to be experiencing more stress than they can handle effectively. Table 14.2 lists some signs that indicate when employees may be experiencing excess stress. If some of these signs exist, a supervisor should try to reduce the stress employees are experiencing and recommend some coping techniques. (Approaches to stress management are described in the next section.)

### Burnout

**burnout**
The inability to function effectively as a result of ongoing stress.

A person who cannot cope with stress over an extended period of time may experience burnout. **Burnout** is the inability to function effectively as a result of ongoing stress. Employees who are burned out feel drained and lose interest in doing their job. Typically, burnout occurs in three stages:

1. The employee feels emotionally exhausted.
2. The employee's perceptions of others become calloused.
3. The employee views his or her effectiveness negatively.

Burnout is worse than just needing a vacation. Therefore, it is important to cope with stress before it leads to burnout.

Some signs of excess stress that may indicate burnout are indicated in Table 14.2. Supervisors who observe these signs in employees not only should seek to reduce stress, but also should be sure that employees are being rewarded for their efforts. Burnout is especially likely to occur when people feel they are giving of themselves all the time, with little or no return. For that reason, burnout is reported widely among employees in the so-called "helping" professions, such as health care and teaching.

### Personal Stress Management

Because stress arises from both personal and job factors, a full effort at stress management includes actions at both levels. Personal stress management is especially important for people who hold jobs that are by nature highly stressful, such as the supervisor of nurses in a hospital's intensive care unit or the supervisor of a crew of firefighters.

A variety of techniques are available for personal stress management: time management (discussed in the first part of this chapter), positive attitude, exercise, biofeedback, meditation, and well-rounded life activities. Supervisors can use these techniques to improve their own stress levels, and they also can encourage employees to use them.

#### Time Management

Making conscious, reasoned decisions about your use of time helps prevent the stress that can result from wasted time or unrealistic goals. Thus, a good start for handling the stress related to balancing work and family responsibilities is to set priorities. For example, different people will have different views about whether a promotion is worth the price of moving or working weekends. Then set aside time for the things you consider important, scheduling time for friends and family members as well as work-related commitments.

Don't forget to include time for resting and recharging. (See "Meeting the Challenge.") Bolstered by research reports showing a link to improved safety and job performance, some managers are even putting naps on their schedules. Claudio Stampi, a researcher on sleep strategies, explains:

> We've found that you get tremendous recovery of alertness—several hours' worth—out of a 15-minute nap. You can get temporary help through stimulation—coffee, exercise, brighter light, cooler temperatures—but you're actually fixing the problem by taking a nap.[9]

No wonder spending part of your lunch break with your head down on your desk has come to be called "power napping."

Time management principles are also useful for managing the stress of balancing work and home responsibilities. If family activities are on your "to do" list, you have a built-in response when another request conflicts with family time: "I have other commitments at that time." Also, being realistic about time is ultimately less frustrating than expecting yourself to handle everything. Instead of criticizing yourself for what you do not do, make an effort to give yourself a pat on the back for all the times you strike a balance between home and work commitments.[10]

#### Positive Attitude

As mentioned, people with a negative outlook tend to be more susceptible to stress. Thus, supervisors can reduce their stress response by cultivating a positive attitude. Ways to do this are to avoid making negative generalizations and to look for the positives in any situation. Saying to oneself, "This company doesn't care about us; all it cares about is profits," or, "I'll never get the hang of this job," contribute to a negative attitude. A supervisor can consciously replace such thoughts with more positive ones: "The competition is tough these days, but we each can contribute to helping this company please its customers" and "This job is difficult, but I will plan a way to learn how to do it better."

### MEETING THE CHALLENGE

## *Truck Drivers Battle Road Fatigue*

Many people who consistently work long hours—on overtime, double shifts, or to meet deadlines—know how fatigue can slow them down, impair decision-making ability, cause tempers to flare, and so forth. But what about workers whose fatigue endangers not only their own safety but also the safety of others?

Fatigue is a significant source—and consequence—of stress. Among truck drivers in recent years, it has led to an increase in fatalities on the road. According to the National Transportation Safety Board, 58 percent of 113 single-vehicle heavy truck accidents (in which the driver survived) in one year were linked to tired truck drivers, of which 25 percent had violated rules pertaining to sleep. Most of the drivers involved in the accidents got only about five hours of sleep a night.

When interviewed anonymously, drivers admit to falsifying their log books, which document more sleep than they actually get. Some keep two sets of log books—one accurate, the other for inspectors. Although this practice is clearly unethical, the drivers claim they must stay on the road longer hours—and deliver for their companies or customers—or lose their jobs. Oliver Patton, editor of *Transport Topics* magazine, claims that government deregulation of the trucking industry "took trucking out of its protective envelope and plunged it into a market-based business." Thus, drivers work longer and often for less money.

There are some possible solutions to the sleep problem. One may come from the research being done for NASA by Dr. Claudio Stampi of the Institute for Circadian Studies, who is studying the positive effects of napping rather than long, uninterrupted hours of sleep. Nappers don't fall into deep sleep, he says, and thus awake more refreshed than people who sleep for many hours at a time. "The challenge is to train rescue workers or astronauts to adapt quickly to [a nap] schedule," says Stampi. Truck drivers could benefit, too.

Technology may also help. Satellites and cellular tracking could be used to track the progress of trucks, from their speed to the amount of time they spend on the road. In addition, inspectors may be able to use certain video games to measure alertness and agility among drivers on the road. In the meantime, most of us hope that truck drivers will have the good sense to pull over when they are tired, and grab a nap—or at least a cup of coffee.

Sources: Richard Saltus, "Study on Nap-Based Survival Could Be Workaholic's Dream," *Boston Globe*, Sept. 4, 1995, pp. 17, 24; "Highway to Nod," *The Economist*, Apr. 8, 1995, p. 28.

In the positive examples, a supervisor is focusing on the areas over which he or she has control. This helps to defuse the sense of helplessness that can increase stress and contributes to a positive outlook.[11]

Maintaining a sense of humor also is important to a positive attitude. Consultant Diane C. Decker explains, "If we can laugh at ourselves and see the humor in situations, then we don't feel it's the end of the world."[12] Decker recommends developing a list of things that bring you joy, then cultivating those areas of your life. She arrived at this idea through her own experiences as manager with a manufacturer that was experiencing production problems. She worried about her own future and that of her employees; to beat the stress, she signed up for a class in being a clown. Spending time getting others to laugh helped Decker to relax and put her problems into perspective.

### *Exercise*

Experts on stress believe that the human body long ago developed a stress response to help people handle dangerous situations. Early peoples had to face storms or attacks by wild animals and human enemies. The basic responses are either to fight the danger or to run away. For this reason, the physical changes in response to stress are known as the "fight-or-flight syndrome."

Because the body's response to stress is to get ready for physical action, a logical way to respond to workplace stress is to look for an outlet through physical activity. Although it is never appropriate to punch your manager when he or she criticizes you or to run away when clients complain, other forms of exercise can provide a similar release without negative social consequences. Some people enjoy running, walking, or riding a bicycle before or after work—or as a way to get to work. Others prefer to work out at a health club, participate in sports, or dance. Besides letting off steam, exercising strengthens the body's organs so that they can better withstand stress.

### Biofeedback

People who have devoted time to developing their awareness of such automatically controlled bodily functions as pulse rate, blood pressure, body temperature, and muscle tension have learned to control these functions. Developing an awareness of bodily functions in order to control them is known as **biofeedback.** People use biofeedback to will their body into a more relaxed state.

**biofeedback**
Developing an awareness of bodily functions in order to control them.

### Meditation

While meditation has religious overtones for many people, in its general form it is simply a practice of focusing one's thoughts on something other than day-to-day concerns. The person meditating focuses on breathing, on a symbol, or on a word or phrase. People who practice regular meditation find that it relaxes them and that the benefits carry beyond the time spent meditating.

### Well-Rounded Life Activities

For someone who gets all of his or her satisfaction and rewards from working, job-related stress is more likely to be overwhelming. No job is going to be rewarding all the time, so some of your satisfaction should come from other areas of life. For instance, if your manager is impatient and fails to praise you for completing an important project, you can offset those frustrations by enjoying the love of friends and family members or hearing the cheers of your softball teammates when you make a good play.

In other words, people who lead a well-rounded life are more likely to experience satisfaction in some area of life at any given time. This satisfaction can make stress a lot easier to cope with. Leading a well-rounded life means not only advancing your career but also devoting time to social, family, intellectual, spiritual, and physical pursuits. One person might choose to read biographies, join a volleyball team, and volunteer in a soup kitchen. Another person might take bicycle trips with the kids on weekends and be active in a religious congregation and a professional organization. These varied pursuits not only help people manage stress, they also make life more enjoyable.

## Organizational Stress Management

Although employees can take many actions to cope with stress, a significant reduction in stress requires attacking it at its source. Many sources of stress may arise from the policies and practices of the organization and its management. Therefore, any serious effort at stress management must include organizational interventions.

Organizational stress management can operate on several levels. Supervisors can adjust their behavior so that they do not contribute unnecessarily to employee stress. Also, many organizations have helped employees manage stress through means such as job redesign, environmental changes, and wellness programs. Although a supervisor rarely can carry out all of these measures single-handedly, he or she may be in a position to recommend them to higher-level managers. Also, a supervisor who knows about any stress management measures offered by the organization is in a better position to take advantage of them and to recommend them to employees.

### Behavior of the Supervisor

Understanding sources of stress can help supervisors behave in a manner that minimizes unnecessary stress and enhances employee confidence. Supervisors should avoid behavior that contributes to raising employee stress levels. For instance, knowing that feelings of helplessness and uncertainty contribute to stress, supervisors can minimize such feelings through clear communication and regular feedback. Where possible, supervisors also can empower employees to make decisions and solve problems, thereby giving them more control. Table 14.3 summarizes some basic approaches to reducing stress in the workplace.

As noted earlier, employees with low self-esteem tend to be more susceptible to stress than those with high self-esteem. Therefore, supervisors should avoid behavior that can damage self-esteem; for example, put-downs and criticism with no clue about how to improve. Better still, supervisors should behave in esteem-enhancing ways, including the generous use of praise (when it can be offered sincerely) and feedback to employees about how their efforts add value to the work group or the organization as a whole.

### Changes in the Job

Recall from Figure 14.5 that many characteristics of a job can be sources of stress. Just a few of the job factors linked to stress are unfair policies, ambiguous procedures, lack of opportunities for advancement, and poor communication. A supervisor has at least some control over many of these matters. For example, supervisors can improve their ability to be fair and to communicate instructions clearly and precisely.

In general, an important part of stress management involves identifying job factors linked to stress and then modifying those factors when possible. Sometimes a supervisor cannot act alone to make a change; for example, he or she may not be powerful enough to resolve conflicts with another department. In such cases, a supervisor should be sure that higher-level management knows about the stress-related job factors and how they are affecting employees.

When the sources of stress include boring or overly difficult jobs, the organization may be able to change the job requirements to make them less stressful. As described in Chapter 11, a routine job can be made more interesting through job enlargement or job enrichment. An overly difficult job can be made less so by giving employees further training or by reassigning some responsibilities so that the work is divided more realistically.

### Environmental Changes

As shown in Figure 14.5, some characteristics of the job environment can add to employee stress. For example, it is a strain on employees to cope with noise, poor lighting, uncomfortable chairs, and extremes of heat and cold. When possible, an organization should reduce stress by fixing some of these problems. A supervisor

## TABLE 14.3

**How Supervisors Can Minimize Organizational Stressors**

| Prepare employees to cope with change. | • Communicate thoroughly.<br>• Provide adequate training to handle any new work demands.<br>• Skip unnecessary changes during times of transition. |
|---|---|
| Foster a supportive organizational climate. | • Make policies and procedures flexible.<br>• Establish fair policies and administer them fairly.<br>• Investigate whether work can be done in more efficient ways that reduce work overload.<br>• Make sure employees understand what is expected of them.<br>• Praise individual and group successes. |
| Make work interesting. | • Give employees some control over decisions and work processes.<br>• Match the challenge level to employees' abilities.<br>• Assign a variety of tasks. |
| Encourage career development. | • Communicate with employees about their career prospects in the organization.<br>• Encourage employees to take advantage of any career counseling programs available through the organization.<br>• Make time to discuss career goals with employees. |

Source: Based on information in Samuel C. Certo, *Modern Management*, 6th ed. (Boston: Allyn and Bacon, 1994), pp. 308–10; Fred Luthans, *Organizational Behavior* (New York: McGraw-Hill, 1985), pp. 146–48.

is frequently in an excellent position to identify needed environmental changes and to report them to the managers who can make the changes. That is likely to be the case when employees complain about uncomfortable chairs or dark work areas. (Chapter 19 discusses changes to improve the physical work environment.)

### Wellness Programs

**wellness program**
Organizational activities designed to help employees adopt healthy practices.

Most organizations provide their employees with health insurance, and many also take an active role in helping employees stay well. The usual way to do this is to provide a **wellness program**, or organizational activities designed to help employees adopt healthful practices. These activities might include exercise classes, stop-smoking clinics, nutrition counseling, and health screening such as cholesterol and blood-pressure tests. Some organizations even have constructed exercise facilities for employees. Aetna, the life insurance company, has five modern health clubs. Steelcase, the maker of office furniture, has six wellness workers on its staff, including an exercise physiologist and three health educators.[13]

At the Symmetrix consulting firm in Lexington, Massachusetts, Alice Domar, a staff psychologist from a Boston hospital, teaches stress-reduction techniques to employees.

Source: © 1996 Bob Sacha

At Union Pacific, the wellness program identifies employees at high risk for health problems, then teaches them how to gradually shed unhealthy habits. The program, run by Kersh Wellness Management, measures cholesterol and blood pressure. Employees at high risk are counseled individually in how to reduce fat and add exercise. For instance, counselor Patsy Parker has helped one employee make one change a month, such as substituting mustard for mayonnaise on sandwiches and extending his nightly walk by 15 minutes.[14]

Big companies aren't the only ones with wellness programs. Highsmith, a supplier of library products, invites each of its 240 employees and their spouses to participate in annual screenings measuring cholesterol, blood pressure, percentage of body fat, and general fitness. Based on how well the employee scores, he or she receives a 50, 25, or 12.5 percent reduction in health insurance premiums. (Doctors may sign waivers for employees with conditions beyond their control.) To help employees improve their scores, the company provides on-site instruction in exercise, weight control, nutrition, and smoking cessation.[15]

Highsmith, Union Pacific, and the other companies with wellness programs aren't just bringing down stress levels. They are also slashing costs related to unhealthy employees. Highsmith's president reports that savings in health insurance and related costs completely cover the expenses of its wellness program. According to Union Pacific, the $1.2 million a year it spends on promoting healthy behavior saves the company three times that amount in reduced medical costs alone. Aetna reports that employees who exercise cost the company $282 a year less to insure than its other employees. Steelcase estimates its wellness program has saved $20 million over a decade.[16]

Given the benefits of wellness programs, it makes sense for supervisors to participate in and support them. When possible, supervisors can avoid scheduling activities that conflict with participation in the programs. They can encourage employees to participate and they can set a good example by their own participation. However, supervisors should focus on encouraging all employees to participate in the program instead of singling out employees and encouraging them to make specific changes such as losing weight or cutting out cigarettes. After all, having a specialist conduct the wellness program frees the supervisor to concentrate on work-related behaviors—and avoid charges that the supervisor has discriminated against an employee with a disability such as obesity or addiction to nicotine.

# A Word about Personality

The guidelines given in this chapter for managing time and stress have worked for many people. However, the degree to which a person will succeed at using any particular technique depends in part on that person's personality. This text does not explore psychological theory, but a brief look at one approach to understanding personality types may be helpful. The Myers-Briggs Type Indicator is a test that classifies people into 16 personality types based on the work of psychiatrist Carl Jung.[17] These 16 personality types describe the traits a person has along four dimensions (see Figure 14.7). For example, one person might be an extrovert, an intuitive, a feeler, and a perceiver. Another person will have a different combination of four traits. These traits are not considered good or bad; each has its own strengths and weaknesses.

Knowing your personality type suggests suitable techniques for managing your own time and stress. Thus, an introvert may find that meditation is a pleasant way to relieve stress, whereas an extrovert may find meditation impossible but dancing with friends refreshing. Judgers have an easy time applying such time management aids as "to do" lists. Perceivers also make those lists, but they lose them and cannot seem to make time to find them. To manage their time, these personality types need heroic amounts of self-discipline—or maybe a job that requires flexibility more than structure.

When you discern that a particular way of behavior does not fit your personality type, you have a choice. You can make the effort to develop the contrasting trait. For instance, a feeler might list logical criteria for making a decision that must be objective. Or you can avoid situations that require you to behave in ways unsuited to your personality. If the feeler in the previous example really hates making decisions objectively, this person might seek out a job or organization where highly subjective decisions are valued.

In addition, recognizing different personality types can help you understand the behavior of other people. For example, if you think your manager's head is always in the clouds, perhaps he or she is an intuitive and you are a sensor. Such insights alone can ease a great deal of stress.

■ **FIGURE 14.7**

**A Basis for Categorizing Personality Types**

According to the Myers-Briggs Type Indicator, a person's personality traits fall somewhere along each of these four dimensions.

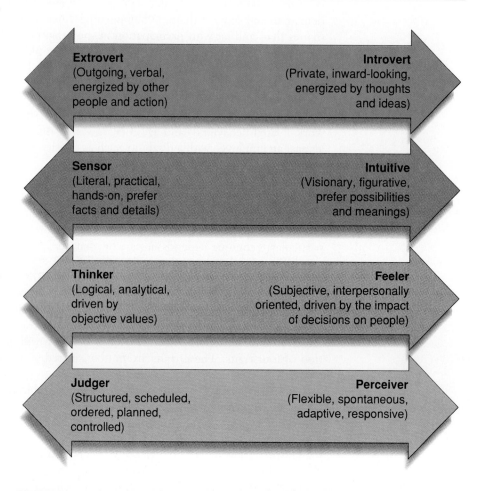

Source: Adapted from Otto Kroeger and Janet M. Thuesen, "It Takes All Types," *Newsweek*, Management Digest advertising section, Sept. 7, 1992, pp. 8–10.

## Summary

**14.1   Discuss how supervisors can evaluate their use of time.**

A practical way to evaluate time use is to keep a time log. A supervisor enters his or her activities for half-hour periods throughout the workday. After a week or two of keeping the time log, a supervisor reviews the information to see whether the time is being used efficiently.

**14.2   Describe ways to plan the use of time.**

A supervisor can plan the use of time by making a list of things to do for the day or week, then rate each item on the list as A (things that must be done), B (things that are important but can be postponed if necessary), or C (everything else). A supervisor then schedules specific times for completing the A- and B-level activities. When time permits, a supervisor works on the C-level activities. A supervisor should not fill up every hour of the day, so that free time is available to handle unexpected problems. A supervisor can plan his or her time with the help of a variety of computer software programs designed specifically for time management. A supervisor also can use programs called desktop organizers.

### 14.3 Identify some time wasters and how to control them.

Many meetings waste time. The supervisor who calls a meeting can start the meeting on time, keep the discussion on track, and end it on time. A supervisor can control telephone calls by having someone screen them, by returning calls at the same time every day, by preparing for calls to be made, and by scheduling calls instead of leaving messages. To handle paperwork and reading material, a supervisor should handle each item only once, decide which items are essential, dictate responses or make telephone calls when possible, and designate a time for reading. With unscheduled visitors, a supervisor can schedule a later meeting, stand to signal that a meeting is ending or will be short, or specify a time limit for the discussion.

The best way to handle procrastination is to tackle the project one step at a time, giving oneself rewards along the way. To combat perfectionism, a supervisor should set high but reasonable standards. Perfectionism is a cause of failure to delegate, so a supervisor must strive to delegate work effectively. Finally, supervisors sometimes find themselves taking on too many projects. The solution is to say no to projects they do not have time to complete properly.

### 14.4 List factors that contribute to stress among employees.

Certain job factors linked to stress involve the organization's policies, structures, physical conditions, and processes. Notably, when employees feel out of control and if the workplace is unsafe or unpredictable, employees will suffer more from the effects of stress. Personal factors also can make a person more vulnerable to stress. Such factors include general feelings of negativism, helplessness, low self-esteem, and a Type A personality—constantly trying to get a lot done in a hurry. Conflicts between work and personal life may be a further source of stress.

### 14.5 Summarize consequences of stress.

Stress is the body's response to coping with environmental demands. These demands can come from change, frustration, uncertainty, danger, and discomfort. Stress can be stimulating, but an excessive amount of it leads to illness and lowered performance. People under stress feel anxious, aggressive, frustrated, tense, and moody, and they may overreact to criticism. They are also at risk for abusing drugs and alcohol. When a person cannot cope with stress over an extended period of time, the person may experience burnout.

### 14.6 Explain how supervisors can manage their own stress.

Supervisors and others can manage stress by using time management, having a positive attitude, getting exercise, using biofeedback, meditating, and leading a well-rounded life. These actions do not reduce the amount of stress the person is under, but they do make a person better able to handle it.

### 14.7 Identify ways organizations, including supervisors, can help employees manage stress.

Supervisors and other managers can seek to eliminate or minimize the job factors linked to stress. They should communicate clearly, give regular feedback to employees, and empower workers to make decisions and solve problems. Supervisors also should behave in ways that enhance employees' self-esteem. In addition, they can make jobs more interesting through job enlargement or job enrichment, and make certain that the work environment is safe and comfortable. Organizations also can offer wellness programs that provide services such as health clinics, instruction in exercise and weight control, and nonsmoking programs.

# Key Terms

| | | |
|---|---|---|
| time management | perfectionism | burnout |
| time log | stress | biofeedback |
| procrastination | Type A personality | wellness program |

# Review and Discussion Questions

1. For one week keep a time log of your activities at work or at school. Follow the format of Figure 14.1. What does it tell you about your own time management habits?

2. Refer to the cartoon in Figure 14.2. Describe an experience in which you succeeded in turning a delay (or other frustrating setback, such as a person not showing up for an appointment with you) into a positive use of your time.

3. Demetrius Jones prepared the following list of things to do:

   | | |
   |---|---|
   | Performance appraisal for Angela | A |
   | Clean out files | C |
   | Finish report due Wednesday | A |
   | Prepare a plan for training employees | B |
   | Find out why Kevin has been making more errors lately | B |
   | Read professional journals | C |

   a. Which activities does Demetrius consider most important? Least important?
   b. Which activities should Demetrius schedule for times when he is at his best?
   c. If Demetrius fits all these activities onto his weekly schedule and finds he has time left over, what should he do about the "free" time?

4. Assume you are the supervisor of social workers at a hospital. One of your co-workers, a nursing supervisor, asks you to meet with him in his office to discuss a mutual problem. When you arrive at the agreed-upon time, he says, "I'll be right back as soon as I deliver these instructions to one of the nurses and grab a cup of coffee." After you get started 10 minutes later, the supervisor takes several telephone calls, interrupting the meeting for 5 minutes at a time. "Sorry," he says after each call, "but that call was important." An hour into the meeting, you have not made much progress toward solving your problem.

   a. How would you feel in a situation like this? How does your co-worker's behavior affect your performance? How does it affect his performance?
   b. How could you react in this situation to improve your use of time?

5. Imagine that you came to work an hour early so that you could get started on a large proposal that you have due in a week. Fifteen minutes into the project, a co-worker stops by to tell you about her recent vacation. After she leaves, your manager pokes his head into your office and asks if you can spare a minute. Finally, you settle into your proposal. Five minutes after the official start of the workday, one of your employees comes into your office and informs you that she wants to resign. What is the best way to handle each of these unscheduled visitors?

6. You know that you have an important assignment to complete by the end of the week, but you put off starting it on Monday because you want to get everything else out of the way first. In addition, you want a clean slate so that you can concentrate and do a perfect job. Suddenly on Thursday, you realize you can't possibly finish the assignment by the next day. You've procrastinated all week. What steps could you have taken to avoid procrastinating and thus complete the assignment on schedule?

7. Which of the following are sources of stress? Explain.

    *a.* A supervisor who gives you vague and confusing instructions and then criticizes your results.
    *b.* Buying a house.
    *c.* Working at a boring job.
    *d.* Getting a promotion to a supervisory position you have wanted for a year.

8. Sales supervisor Anita Feinstein does not understand all the fuss about stress. She feels stimulated by a job that is exciting and contains many challenges. Does her attitude show that stress is not harmful? Explain.

9. Describe the signs of burnout. Describe the three stages of burnout. What should a supervisor do when he or she observes burnout in an employee?

10. Name five job factors linked to stress over which a supervisor could have some control.

11. How do the following responses help a person cope with stress?

    *a.* Exercising.
    *b.* Using biofeedback.
    *c.* Meditating.
    *d.* Participating in a wellness program.

## A SECOND LOOK

Of the job factors linked to stress that are identified in Figure 14.6, which do you think Allen E. Barken would encounter on his job as principal of a vocational high school? (Refer to the story at the beginning of this chapter.) Over which of the factors you have identified do you think Barken might have some control?

# APPLICATIONS MODULE

## CASE

### *Time and Stress: When Is a Vacation Not a Vacation?*

Most of us think of vacation as a time to rest and recharge, away from the daily demands of work. We might want to lie on a beach, take a bicycling tour, travel to a foreign country, or perhaps just stay home and read a book. We don't think about taking our jobs along with us. Or do we?

According to experts like Eileen Canty, an organizational psychologist and principal at William M. Mercer Inc. (a human resources consulting firm), people *are* taking their work on vacation. "More and more I hear about, and see, people taking their PCs, which have electronic mail capability and fax capability, wherever they go, even to the beach," says Canty. A survey conducted for Hilton Hotels discovered that almost 20 percent of those surveyed phoned in to the office during their vacations, 13 percent took work with them, and more than 25 percent said they were anxious that "something would go wrong" at their jobs while they were out. Perhaps this last finding is the most important.

Telecommunications was supposed to free workers, allow them to be mobile, to use their workday more efficiently. (For instance, a sales rep no longer has to waste time driving to visit all customers; with a cellular phone, many business calls can be made from the road.) But in a competitive work environment, in which layoffs often loom in workers' minds, technology can tie them to the workplace 24 hours a day, including vacation time. Employees are *afraid* to be out of touch with the office.

"The boundaries between work and vacation have become more permeable, primarily because of technology," notes Brad Googins, director of Boston University's Center on Work and Family. "Technology has made it so easy to communicate with work that it has also made it almost impossi-

ble to get away." Without a real break from work, secure in the knowledge that the job will be waiting upon the employee's return, workers are bound to experience stress.

Among industrialized nations, the United States has one of the lowest number of average vacation days per year in the world. U.S. workers get around 10 working days of vacation per year; Austria and Brazil's workers get 30. Scandinavian and European workers average around 20 to 25; but interestingly enough, Japanese workers, whose organizations espouse many progressive management principles, get only 10.

Bruce O'Hara, author of *Put Work in Its Place* and *Working Harder Isn't Working*, notes that the Europeans recognize vacation as a valuable use of time in the reduction of stress. "They have never quite let go of older traditions of leisure," he observes. "The history both Canada and the U.S. have is of a pioneer nation where there was always work to be done."

California attorney Richard Such tried to put an initiative on the statewide ballot mandating six weeks of vacation a year to full-time employees. But no one jumped on the bandwagon. "It became almost hollow to say workers should be given more vacation time when workers were saying, 'I am lucky to have a job,' " says Such.

However the survey for Hilton Hotels showed that 65 percent of American workers would take a pay cut in return for more time off. The problem is, they already are taking cuts in pay—or doing more work for the same money as a result of downsizing—but they aren't getting the time off. And when they do take a vacation, they are swamped with more work when they return, creating more time-management difficulties and more stress. So they take their faxes, their laptops, and their cellular phones to the beach, to the cabin, to the campground—a working vacation.

1. Do you think that failure to delegate and an inability to say no contribute to the need for some employees to take their work on vacation? Why or why not? If so, what steps might they take to make better use of work time and vacation time?

2. Do you believe that telecommunications technology has freed workers or further entrapped them? Explain your opinion, giving at least one example.

3. How might U.S. workers use personal stress management to get the most out of their vacation time?

4. Do you think that U.S. workers should have more vacation time per year? Why or why not? If so, how many days should they have?

Source: Scot Lehigh, "Vacation Fax," *Boston Globe*, July 30, 1995, pp. 71–72.

### SELF-QUIZ

## *How Does Time Pressure Affect You?*

To assess the degree to which time pressure influences your life, answer all questions by circling the number of the best alternative, even if no single answer seems exactly right.

1. In a typical week, how often do you wear a watch?

   (1) regularly      (2) part of the time      (3) occasionally      (4) almost never

2. How many hours do you sleep during an average week night?

   (1) 5 or less      (2) 6      (3) 7      (4) 8 or more

3. When driving, how often do you speed?

   (1) regularly      (2) often      (3) seldom      (4) almost never

4. While driving, as you approach a green traffic signal that is turning to yellow, you are most likely to:

   (1) speed up to get through before it turns to red

   (4) slow down and wait for it to turn green

5. (1) When I have a train or plane to catch, I like to arrive as close as possible to the departure time so I won't have to waste time sitting around. (4) I always try to leave extra time to get to an airport or train station so I won't have to worry about missing a flight or train.

6. (1) At a restaurant, I like my food served as soon as possible after I've ordered.

   (4) I don't mind waiting a few minutes for the food I've ordered.

7. (1) I like microwave ovens because they cut down on meal preparation time.

   (4) I'd rather spend extra time preparing meals than use a microwave oven regularly.

8. (1) I often use a remote-control device to scan a lot of television channels to see what's on.

   (4) To me, a remote-control is a convenient tool for turning the TV on or off from a distance, adjusting the volume, or occasionally changing channels.

9. (1) With so many other demands on my time, I find it hard to keep up friendships.

   (4) I try to make time to see my friends regularly.

10. Compared with your life 10 years ago, would you say you have more or less leisure time?

    (1) less      (2) about the same      (3) slightly more      (4) much more

11. How would you compare the amount of time you spend running errands today with the amount you spent 10 years ago?

    (1) more      (2) about the same      (3) somewhat less      (4) much less

12. During the past year, how many books have you read for pleasure from beginning to end?

    (1) 0–2     (2) 3–5     (3) 6–10     (4) 11 or more

13. How good are you at glancing at your watch or a clock without anyone noticing?

    (1) very good     (2) good     (3) fair     (4) poor

14. How would you rate your ability to conduct a conversation and appear to be paying attention while thinking about something else at the same time?

    (1) excellent     (2) good     (3) fair     (4) poor

15. How often do you find yourself interrupting the person with whom you're talking?

    (1) regularly     (2) often     (3) occasionally     (4) rarely

16. When talking on the telephone, do you:

    (1) do paperwork, wash dishes, or do some other chore?

    (2) straighten up the surrounding area?

    (3) do small personal tasks (e.g., file nails, reset watch)?

    (4) do nothing else?

17. In an average week, how many evening or weekend hours do you spend working overtime or on work you've brought home?

    (1) 16 or more     (2) 11–15     (3) 6–10     (4) 0–5

18. On a typical weekend, do you engage primarily in:

    (1) work for income?     (2) errands, household chores, and child care?     (3) leisure activities?     (4) catching up on sleep and relaxation?

19. In a typical year, how many weeks of paid vacation do you take?

    (1) 1 or less     (2) 2     (3) 3     (4) 4 or more

20. On the whole, how do you find vacations?

    (1) frustrating     (2) tedious     (3) relaxing     (4) rejuvenating

21. How often do you find yourself wishing you had more time to spend with family and friends?

    (1) constantly     (2) often     (3) occasionally     (4) almost never

22. During a typical day, how often do you feel rushed?

    (1) constantly     (2) often     (3) occasionally     (4) almost never

23. Which statement best describes your usual daily schedule?

    (1) There aren't enough hours in the day to do everything I have to do.

    (2) On the whole I have enough time to do what I have to do.

    (3) I can usually do the things I have to do with time left over.

    (4) The day seems to have more hours than I'm able to fill.

24. During the past year, how would you say your life has grown?

    (1) busier      (2) about the same

    (3) somewhat less busy      (4) much less busy

Add the total of all numbers circled. A score of 25–40 indicates you are timelocked; 41–55, pressed for time; 56–71, in balance; 72–86, time on hands.

Source: "How Does Time Pressure Affect You?" from *Timelock* by Ralph Keyes. Copyright © 1991 by Ralph Keyes. Adapted by permission of HarperCollins Publishers, Inc.

## Class Exercise

Each student, in turn, tells the class how he or she wastes time. The instructor lists the ways on the chalkboard or overhead projector. Then the class discusses the list.

- Which time wasters are most common?

- Are they really just time wasters, or are they also stress reducers?

Source: The idea for this exercise was provided by Sylvia Ong, Scottsdale Community College, Scottsdale, Arizona.

## Team-Building Exercise

# What Kind of Team Member Are You?

Divide the class into teams of four or five students. Assign each team an imaginary project with a completion date (or have the teams come up with one on their own). Suggested projects are cleaning up one of the common areas used by students at the school, recruiting classmates to participate in a fund-raising activity, or developing publicity for an upcoming arts event. Then have the teams (1) make a "to do" list outlining how they plan to set priorities for the project and use their time; (2) note how they plan to control time wasters; and (3) describe how they plan to manage any stress associated with trying to complete the project properly and on schedule.

At the end of the exercise, have students identify themselves as Type A or Type B personalities and discuss how this contributes to the way they approach getting things done as team members.

# Video Exercise 14: *Managing Time and Stress*

### Video Summary

This video program illustrates the challenges supervisors face in finding the optimal balance between productivity and wellness. Guidelines for handling stress effectively are suggested, and seminars as well as fitness, wellness, and employee assistance programs available for employees at Cummins Engine Company and the Chicago Tribune are featured.

### Application

Begin by taking a quiz to help you answer the question, "How stressed am I?"

## Stress Quiz

Rate how closely you agree with each of the following statements by filling in the blank before each statement with a number from 1 to 10 based on the table.

| Strongly Disagree | Agree Somewhat | Strongly Agree |
|---|---|---|
| 1    2    3 | 4    5    6 | 7    8    9    10 |

| | |
|---|---|
| _____ | 1. I can't honestly say what I really think or get things off my chest at work, school, or home. |
| _____ | 2. I seem to have lots of responsibilities but little authority. |
| _____ | 3. I seldom receive adequate acknowledgment or appreciation when I do a good job. |
| _____ | 4. I have the impression that I am repeatedly picked on or discriminated against. |
| _____ | 5. I feel I am unable to use my talents effectively or to their full potential. |
| _____ | 6. I tend to argue frequently with co-workers, customers, teachers, and other people. |
| _____ | 7. I don't have enough time for family and social obligations or personal needs. |
| _____ | 8. Most of the time I have little control over my life at work, school, or home. |
| _____ | 9. I rarely have enough time to do a good job or accomplish what I want to. |
| _____ | 10. In general, I'm not particularly proud of or satisfied with what I do. |
| _____ | **Total stress score** |

Source: Quiz developed by the American Institute of Stress, a nonprofit clearinghouse for information about stress, *USA WEEKEND*, Dec. 31, 1993–Jan. 2, 1994.

*Indications from Your Score*

If you scored between:

*10 and 39:*   You have little stress and handle it well. You still could benefit from trying out some of the stress-busting tips that follow.

*40 and 69:*   You have moderate stress and handle it OK. You would probably benefit from choosing several of the stress-busting tips.

*70 and 100:*   You are overstressed and may encounter problems that need to be resolved. The stress-busting tips could serve as the first step.

Stress specialists and other stress experts from stress clinics, employee assistance programs, and research organizations have identified some concrete steps you can take to help you deal more effectively with stress. Check the boxes of two or three tips that you believe would help you to manage your stressors more effectively.

## 20 Stress-Busting Tips from the Pros

- Take a warm bath.
- Write a nasty letter to the person stressing you out—then tear it up.
- Play with a pet.
- Make decisions based as much on your heart as on your head.
- Don't eat unless you're hungry.
- Volunteer to do good. You'll feel better about what you've done and who you are.
- If your company's employee assistance program offers a stress-reduction program, sign up for it.
- Cultivate a sense of humor, and smile.
- Unplug the telephone, send the family to a movie, and listen uninterruptedly to your favorite music.
- Remember, while you can't control the timing of stressful events, you're in complete control of the way you react to them.
- Don't be afraid to say no. You are in charge of your time.
- Reduce your sugar consumption. Excess sugar can heighten your stress response.
- Set a comfortable, steady pace at work, then focus totally on the task at hand to improve productivity.
- Eat lots of fiber and starches; complex carbohydrates tend to calm you down.
- Eat breakfast, so you start the day on a full tank. Avoid big meals late at night; they can disrupt your sleep and cause stress.
- Don't be afraid of your tears. Sometimes a good cry is called for; it releases anxiety.
- Schedule time for fun. It's as vital to your well-being as work.
- Leave the job at work. Leave family pressures at home.
- Remember that some things don't have to be done perfectly.
- Lighten up! Once you have examined a perceived failing from the past, let it go and focus on the future.

# 15

*[Supervisors have] to adjust constantly the objectives of any change program to conform to what a company can learn and absorb.*

**—Shikhar Ghosh, CEO of EDS Personal Communications Program**

# Managing Conflict and Change

## LEARNING OBJECTIVES

After you have studied this chapter, you should be able to:

15.1 List positive and negative aspects of conflict.

15.2 Define types of conflict.

15.3 Describe strategies for managing conflict.

15.4 Explain how supervisors can initiate conflict resolution, respond to a conflict, and mediate conflict resolution.

15.5 Identify sources of change, and explain why employees and supervisors resist it.

15.6 Discuss how supervisors can overcome resistance and implement change.

15.7 Identify the types of power supervisors can have.

15.8 Describe common strategies for organization politics.

Source: Courtesy of the 1811 House.

## A RECIPE FOR CHANGE

Marnie Duff operates The 1811 House, an inn located in Manchester, Vermont, which provides guests with lodging and breakfast. As manager of the inn, Duff supervises four employees, including a cook.

The cook at The 1811 House had worked for the previous owner and was used to preparing pancakes using a mix. Duff preferred that he make them from scratch, but the cook resisted the change. However, one day the mix ran out, and Duff gave the cook a recipe for pancakes.

The cook tried the pancake recipe, but, according to Duff, the first trial was "awful." The cook had added far too much liquid and used the turner to pat down the pancakes on the griddle. The pancakes were thin, flat, and unattractive. The guests did not complain, but it was the only breakfast for which they did not visit the kitchen with compliments.

Clearly, the cook needed more help with this change in procedure. Duff gave an on-the-spot lesson in pancake making. She showed him how to fold in the dry ingredients and made sure he did not beat the batter too much. The cook's initial reaction was to feel somewhat hurt and to doubt that Duff knew a better way. But he followed her instructions, and the next pancakes he made were much lighter and fluffier.

Guests started going to the kitchen to compliment the cook on his pancakes. He would take a bow, with a salute of recognition to Duff. Thanks to the positive response, it was easy to make sure the cook followed this new procedure. He now makes all his pancakes from scratch.

In any organization, conflicts and changes are bound to occur. Whether these are constructive or destructive depends significantly on the supervisor's ability to manage them.

This chapter addresses conflict management by examining the nature of conflict and ways to respond to conflict constructively. The chapter also discusses the role of change in the workplace and how supervisors can implement it. Finally, the chapter discusses an aspect of organizational behavior that often affects the management of both conflict and change—organization politics—describing how supervisors can use politics ethically and effectively.

# Conflict

**conflict**
The struggle that results from incompatible or opposing needs, feelings, thoughts, or demands within a person or between two or more people.

In the context of this book, **conflict** refers to the struggle that results from incompatible or opposing needs, feelings, thoughts, or demands within a person or between two or more people. If supervisor Janet Speers sees that an employee she likes is taking home office supplies, her feelings for the employee come into conflict with her belief that stealing is wrong. If her feelings and belief are both strong, she will have difficulty resolving the issue. Likewise, if two employees disagree over how to fill out time sheets for sick days, there is a conflict between the employees. In this case, the organization should have a clear procedure to make the conflict easy to resolve.

## Positive and Negative Aspects of Conflict

Sometimes conflict is a positive force that can bring about necessary changes. Imagine that a business that develops computerized information systems has hired a new systems analyst, Jordan Walsh, the first African American in the company. Jordan gets all the boring and routine jobs—filing, running errands, proofreading the documentation. If he acts cheerful, the other employees will assume there is no conflict (although he may feel one internally). Of course, this situation is not good for Jordan; he feels insulted, is bored every day, and misses out on the experience he needs to develop his career. This arrangement is also bad for the employer, who is paying for a systems analyst but not benefiting from his talents. Furthermore, Jordan may quit, and the company will have to bear the expense of repeating the hiring process. However, if Jordan complains to his supervisor about his limited role, the conflict will surface, and the resolution may leave everyone, including Jordan, better off. Thus, when conflict serves as a signal that a problem exists, it can stimulate a creative response.

Ongoing conflict also has negative consequences. People who are engaged in disputes are under stress, which takes a physical toll. In addition, people who are busy arguing and trying to persuade others to take their side are not involved in more productive activities. Finally, depending on the source of the conflict, the people involved may be angry at management or the organization, so they may vent their anger in ways that are destructive to the organization, such as taking extra time off or sabotaging equipment.

The consequences of conflict may depend partly on the way that it is resolved. If people treat a conflict as an opportunity for constructive problem solving and change, the outcomes may well be positive. If people routinely see conflict as a

## TIPS FROM THE FIRING LINE

### Managing Conflict in Teams

As a team member or team leader, at some point you will encounter conflict. Not all conflict is bad, but if conflict is to be positive, it must be managed rather than avoided or smoothed over. Diane Willis Zoglio, founder of the Institute for Planning and Development, notes some signs of negative conflict to look for in a team: gossip and tension among members, back-stabbing, little trust, and petty criticism or complaints. Conversely, teams that have learned how to manage conflict exhibit playfulness among members, lack of gossip, a win-win focus on problems, orientation toward issues, and direct communication. Zoglio offers three tools that can help teams turn negative conflict into positive conflict:

- *Reframing.* Look at the conflict in another light, or from another perspective—a positive one. For instance, instead of thinking, "If I give in and do what she wants me to do, she'll view me as weak and take me for granted," think "If I honor her request, she may view me more positively, and we will be able to talk more easily."
- *Shifting shoes.* Take the other person's point of view. Think about how that person is affected by what you say.
- *Affirmations.* Make positive statements or consciously think positive thoughts. Instead of thinking, "The minute I see him, I'll explode," think, "I can handle seeing him in a calm manner."

Zoglio offers one final, important point: Teams must establish ground rules for resolving conflict. The rules might include how long the resolution may take or who makes a tie-breaking vote. Then the team should stick to the rules.

Source: Suzanne Willis Zoglio, "Team Conflict Can Be a Constructive Force When It's Properly Managed," *Total Quality*, Dec. 1994, p. 7.

---

**frustration**
Defeat in the effort to achieve desired goals.

need for someone to win at someone else's expense, or for a manager to impose control, the conflict is more likely to have negative consequences. (See "Tips from the Firing Line" for ways teams can turn negative conflict into positive conflict.)

Most notably, when conflict is viewed as a win-lose proposition, the loser will experience **frustration;** that is, defeat in the effort to achieve desired goals. An employee who has her request for a flextime arrangement turned down experiences frustration. So does an employee who can't convince a prospective customer to return his phone calls. Most of us can handle a little frustration philosophically, with words such as "Oh, well, I can't always have my own way" or "No one can have it all." However, repeated frustration tends to generate anger. A frustrated employee may engage in destructive behavior such as sabotage, aggression, insubordination, and absenteeism. (Chapter 13 covers the supervision of employees who engage in such behaviors.) To head off problems arising from frustration, this chapter will emphasize those forms of conflict resolution aimed at finding a solution satisfactory to all parties.

### Types of Conflict

Before a supervisor can respond effectively to a conflict, he or she needs to understand the real nature of that conflict. Who is involved? What is the source of the conflict? A supervisor is likely to respond differently to a conflict that results from a clash of opinions than to one stemming from frustration over limited resources.

**FIGURE 15.1**

**Types of Conflict**

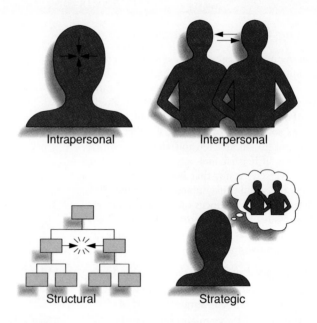

As defined, conflict may arise within an individual (intrapersonal) or between individuals or groups. The basic types of conflict involving more than one person are called interpersonal, structural, and strategic (see Figure 15.1).

### Intrapersonal Conflict

An intrapersonal conflict arises when a person has trouble selecting from among goals. Choosing one of two possible goals is easy if one is good and the other bad. For example, would you rather earn $1 a year as a drug dealer or $1 million a year as the microbiologist who discovered a cure for cancer? Of course, we rarely are faced with such unrealistically easy choices. Most choices fall into three categories:

1. A choice between two good possibilities (e.g., having a child or taking an exciting job that requires travel year-round).
2. A choice between two mixed possibilities (e.g., accepting a promotion that involves moving away from your family or keeping your current, but monotonous, job to be near your family).
3. A choice between two bad possibilities (e.g., reorganizing your department in a way that requires either laying off two employees or eliminating your own position).

Because these choices are not obvious, they result in conflict.

Supervisors should consider whether they or their organization are contributing unnecessarily to intrapersonal conflicts. For example, do they reward unethical behavior or pressure employees to behave unethically? If so, they are setting up conflicts between employees' values and their desire to be rewarded.

The Davis-Bacon Act requires union-scale wages on federally funded construction projects. Adopted in 1931, the Act prevents unorganized construction workers from competing with the organized construction unions. Some believe that this creates labor union gains and great losses for the low-wage minorities. On many New York construction sites, the ongoing battle between these two groups has reached a state of near warfare.

Source: © Les Stone/Sygma

Similarly, Felice Schwartz, founder and retired president of Catalyst, a research and advisory firm, maintains that measuring employees' worth in terms of how many hours they work creates conflicts between commitment to family and commitment to work. In the years immediately following World War II, many people accepted the expectation that women would resolve this conflict by always putting family first, and men by always putting work first. Today, however, fewer employees will settle for these extreme choices. Schwartz recommends that managers be more realistic and measure employee contributions in terms of productivity, not hours spent at the workplace.[1]

In many cases, a supervisor lacks the expertise to resolve an intrapersonal conflict. When supervisors notice that an employee is struggling with an intrapersonal conflict, they should consider who might be able to help. People with skills in handling various types of intrapersonal conflicts include psychologists, religious advisers, and career counselors.

### Interpersonal Conflict

Conflict between individuals is called interpersonal conflict. Supervisors may be involved in interpersonal conflicts with their manager, an employee, a peer, or even a customer. In addition, they may have to manage conflicts between two or more of their employees. Interpersonal conflicts may arise from differing opinions, misunderstandings of a situation, or differences in values or beliefs. Sometimes two people just rub each other the wrong way.

Andrew S. Grove, chief executive of Intel Corporation, contends that a supervisor is not exercising enough leadership when employees are engaged in constant interpersonal conflict such as bickering and complaining about one another.[2] Grove says that a supervisor might be listening to complaints with too much sympathy, for example, or watching disruptive conduct too passively. Instead, a supervisor should establish, communicate, and enforce guidelines for acceptable behavior and set an example by living up to them. (Chapter 8 provides an in-depth discussion of leading employees, and a section later in this chapter describes some approaches to managing interpersonal conflict.)

### Structural Conflict

Conflict that results from the way the organization is structured is called structural conflict. Conflict often arises between line and staff personnel, and production and marketing departments are often at odds. In the latter example, marketing wants to give customers whatever they ask for, and production wants to make what it can easily and well.

Structural conflict often arises when various groups in the organization share resources, such as the services of a word-processing or maintenance department. Each group wants its jobs handled first, but the support department obviously cannot help everyone first. According to Xerox vice-president Richard Palermo, persistent long-term problems are usually the result of structural conflict.[3]

When structural conflict arises between two groups of employees reporting to a supervisor or between a supervisor's group and another group, the supervisor may be able to help minimize or resolve it by providing opportunities for the two groups to communicate and get to know each others' viewpoints, having them collaborate on achieving a mutually desirable goal, and giving each group training or experience in what the other group does.

To help his office employees appreciate the efforts of his blue-collar workers, Oil Changers CEO Larry Read requires each white-collar employee (including all managers) to work on the shop floor one day each month, greeting customers and performing nontechnical tasks as a part of a shop team. According to Read, this improves communication between the two groups of employees and helps the office staff see the practical impact of their decisions.[4]

If some employees involved in a structural conflict report to another supervisor, managing the conflict requires the cooperation of the two supervisors. Engaging that cooperation may require appropriate use of political tactics, discussed in the last section of this chapter.

Because supervisors do not establish an organization's structure, they have limited impact on the sources of structural conflict. However, they do need to be able to recognize it. Knowing that a conflict is structural frees a supervisor from taking the issue personally and alerts him or her to situations that require extra diplomacy. A supervisor also may be able to understand the other party's point of view and communicate it to his or her employees.

### Strategic Conflict

Most of the conflicts described so far arise unintentionally when people and groups try to work together. However, sometimes management or an individual intentionally will bring about a conflict to achieve an objective. This is referred to as a strategic conflict. For instance, a sales department might hold a contest for the highest sales volume and the most impressive example of delighting a customer. Or a manager might tell two employees that they are both in the running for a retiring supervisor's job. In both examples, the intent is to use competition to motivate employees to do exceptional work.

**FIGURE 15.2**

Strategies for
Conflict
Management

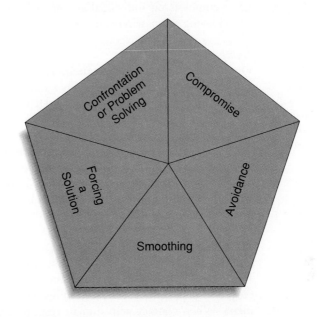

## Managing Interpersonal Conflict

Restaurant manager Phyllis Jensen schedules the hours each server will work during the upcoming week. She has noticed that one of the servers, Rich Yakima, scowls when he gets his assignments and does so for hours afterward. Phyllis asked Rich about it, and he replied, "You know just what the problem is. You know I've been wanting an evening off every weekend so I can go out with my girlfriend, but every week you have me working Friday and Saturday nights. And I've noticed that Rita and Pat always get the hours they want." Responding to problems such as this is known as **conflict management.**

**conflict management**
Responding to problems
stemming from conflict.

### Strategies

How can Phyllis manage the conflict involving Rich? She can begin by recognizing the various strategies available for conflict management: compromise, avoidance, smoothing, forcing a solution, and confrontation or problem solving (see Figure 15.2). Based on her understanding of these strategies, Phyllis can choose the most appropriate one for the circumstances. To see which conflict management strategy you tend to select most frequently, take the Self-Quiz on page 463.

In selecting a strategy, supervisors should be aware that cultural differences sometimes influence their relative success. A manager saw two Arab American employees arguing. He decided to let them work it out. Instead, the incident exploded. The manager did not realize that the two employees expected a third party to intervene. Whereas the predominant culture in the United States places great emphasis on individual action and privacy, Arab culture places more value on achieving a win-win result, often with the aid of mediation.[5]

### Compromise

**compromise**
Settling on a solution that gives each person part of what he or she wanted; no one gets everything, and no one loses completely.

One conflict management strategy is to reach a **compromise,** which means that the parties to the conflict settle on a solution that gives both of them part of what they wanted. No party gets exactly what it wanted, but neither loses entirely either. Both parties presumably experience a degree of frustration—but at a level they are willing to live with.

People who choose to compromise are assuming they cannot reach a solution completely acceptable to everyone, but they would rather not force someone to accept a completely disagreeable choice. In that sense, compromise does not really solve the underlying problem; it works best when the problem is relatively minor and time is limited.

### Avoidance and Smoothing

Conflict is unpleasant, so people sometimes try to manage conflict by avoiding it. For example, if sales supervisor Jeanette Delacroix finds the people in the human resources department stuffy and inflexible, she can avoid dealing with that department. When contact with human resources is absolutely necessary, Jeanette can delegate the responsibility to a member of the sales force. A related strategy is **smoothing,** or pretending that no conflict exists.

**smoothing**
Managing a conflict by pretending it does not exist.

These strategies make sense if you assume that all conflict is bad. If you successfully avoid or smooth over all conflicts, life looks serene on the surface. However, people do disagree, and sometimes people with opposing viewpoints have important ideas to share. Avoiding those conflicts does not make them go away, nor does it make opposing points of view any less valid or significant. Therefore, it is important to be selective in avoiding or smoothing over conflicts. These strategies are most useful for conflicts that are not serious and for which a solution would be more difficult than the problem justifies.

This point is especially important with regard to today's diverse workforce. A person's point of view often seems puzzling, irritating, or downright incorrect to someone of another race, age, or sex. It takes extra work to understand people who are different from us. However, a supervisor must give equal attention to the views of all employees, not only those the supervisor understands best. Pretending that everyone is looking at a situation the same way does not make it so. It can even foster a belief among some employees that the supervisor is discriminating against them.

At the same time, people in many non-Western cultures believe it is best to avoid conflicts, placing a higher value on harmony than on "telling it like it is."[6] People with these values are less likely than employees from Western cultures to complain to their supervisor or to deliver bad news. Thus, a supervisor may not realize there is a problem, such as a dispute between employees or a possibility that a task will be completed late. A supervisor must tactfully ensure that employees know that the supervisor wants to be aware of any problems in order to help resolve them.

### Forcing a Solution

Because ignoring or avoiding a problem does not make it go away, a supervisor may want to try a more direct approach to ending a conflict. One possibility is to force a solution. This means that a person or group with power decides what the outcome will be. For example, if machinist Pete Desai complains to his supervisor that he never gets overtime assignments, the supervisor can respond, "I make the assignments, and your job is to do what you're told. This weekend it's going to be Sue and Chuck, so make the best of it." Or if two supervisors present conflicting proposals for allocating space among their departments, a committee of higher-level managers could select one proposal, allowing no room for discussion.

In an organization with self-managed work teams, another twist on forcing a solution is more likely. The team may decide that instead of reaching a consensus on some issue, the team will simply vote on what to do. The majority makes the decision.

Forcing a solution is a relatively fast way to manage a conflict, and it may be the best approach in an emergency. Reaching consensus, for example, tends to be difficult and time consuming, whereas a team can vote on an issue quickly. However, forcing a solution can cause frustration. In organizations seeking teamwork and employee empowerment, forcing a solution works against those objectives by shutting off input from employees with a minority viewpoint.[7] The bad feelings that accompany frustration and exclusion from decision making may lead to future conflict.

### Confrontation or Problem Solving

The most direct—and sometimes the most difficult—way to manage conflict is to confront the problem and solve it. This is the conflict management strategy called **conflict resolution.** Confronting the problem requires listening to both sides and attempting to understand rather than to place blame. Next, the parties should identify the areas on which they agree and the ways they can both benefit from possible solutions. Both parties should examine their own feelings and take their time at reaching a solution. (Chapter 9 provides further guidelines for problem solving.)

**conflict resolution**
Managing a conflict by confronting the problem and solving it.

Confronting and solving a problem makes a different assumption about the conflict than other strategies for conflict management, which tend to assume that the parties have a *win-lose conflict.* In other words, the outcome of the conflict will be that one person wins (i.e., achieves the desired outcome), and the other person must lose. In contrast, conflict resolution assumes that many conflicts are *win-win conflicts*, in which the resolution can leave both parties better off. Frustration is avoided and both sides feel like winners.

## Initiating Conflict Resolution

When a supervisor has a conflict with another person, he or she needs to resolve that conflict constructively. Otherwise, the conflict is unlikely to go away on its own. When initiating conflict resolution, a supervisor should act as soon as he or she is aware of the problem. As the problem continues, a supervisor is likely to get increasingly emotional about it, which only makes resolution more difficult.

**FIGURE 15.3**

**Initiating Conflict Resolution**

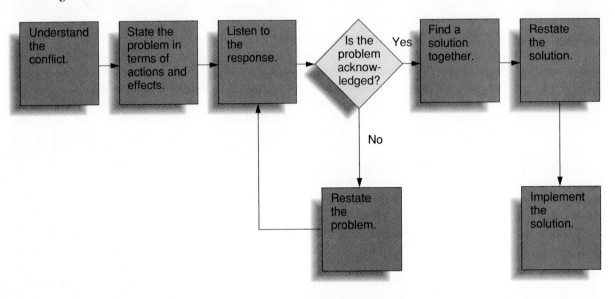

Prepare for conflict resolution by understanding what the conflict is. Focus on behavior (which people can change), not on personalities (which they cannot change). What is the action that is causing the problem, and how does that action affect you and others? For example, you might tell a supervisor in another department, "I haven't been getting the weekly sales figures until late Friday afternoon. That means I have to give up precious family time to review them over the weekend, or else I embarrass myself by being unprepared at the Monday morning staff meetings."

When used politely, this type of approach even works with one's manager. You might say, "I haven't heard from you concerning the suggestions I made last week and three weeks ago. That worries me, because I think maybe I'm giving you too many ideas or not the right kind."

After you have stated the problem, listen to how the other person responds. If the other person does not acknowledge there is a problem, restate your concern until the other person understands or until it is clear that you cannot make any progress on your own. Often a conflict exists simply because the other person has not understood your point of view or your situation. When you have begun communicating about the problem, the two of you can work together at finding a solution. Restate your solution to be sure that both of you agree on what you are going to do (see Figure 15.3).

## Responding to a Conflict

Sometimes a supervisor is party to a conflict that is bothering someone else. When the other person makes the supervisor aware of the conflict, it is up to the supervisor to respond in a way that makes a solution possible. If an employee says, "You always give me the dirty assignments," it is not helpful to get angry or defensive.

## FIGURE 15.4

**Responding to a Conflict**

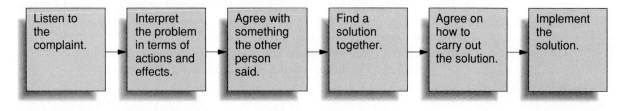

| Listen to the complaint. | Interpret the problem in terms of actions and effects. | Agree with something the other person said. | Find a solution together. | Agree on how to carry out the solution. | Implement the solution. |

### Understand the Problem

The constructive way to respond to a conflict is first to listen to the other person and try to understand what the problem is really about. If the other person is emotional, let that person vent those feelings, then get down to discussing the problem. Try to interpret the problem in the terms you would use to express the problem yourself. Avoid statements of blame, and find out what specific actions the other person is referring to. For example, when an employee says, "You always give me the dirty assignments," you can ask the employee to give specific examples and then describe how he or she feels about the behavior.

Understanding the problem can be complicated if one of the people involved has a "hidden agenda"—a central concern that is left unstated. Typically, a person with a hidden agenda is angry or upset about something but directs those feelings toward some other issue. For example, a colleague in another department explodes, "What's wrong with you? The numbers in your report are off by a mile!" Your colleague is not really angry because you made a mistake. He is nervous because he has to make a presentation to the board of directors, and he wonders if the incorrect numbers are your way to mislead him, so that he looks uninformed and you get the promotion he wants. Or maybe your colleague simply has had a frustrating day, and your mistake is the last straw.

If another person's feelings seem to be out of proportion to the problem he or she is describing, look for a hidden agenda. Finding one can save you from trying to resolve the wrong conflict. In addition, when you are upset about something yourself, it is usually more constructive to describe the problem directly than to leave others guessing at your hidden agenda.

### Work on a Solution

When you understand the problem, build an environment of working together on a solution. To do this, agree with some aspect of what the other person has said. In the example, you might say, "You've really disliked your last three assignments." Then you and the other person should be ready to begin identifying possible solutions. The final step is to agree on what the solution will be and how you will carry it out. Figure 15.4 summarizes this approach.

### *Mediating Conflict Resolution*

Sometimes a supervisor is not personally involved in a conflict, but the parties ask the supervisor to help resolve it. If the parties to the conflict are peers of the supervisor, getting involved can be risky, and the supervisor might be wiser to tactfully refer the peers to a higher-level manager. If the parties to the conflict are the supervisor's employees, then mediating the conflict is part of the supervisor's job and an important way to keep the department functioning as it should.

To mediate a conflict, a supervisor should follow these steps:

1. Begin by establishing a constructive environment. If the employees are calling each other names, have them focus on the issue instead of such destructive behavior.
2. Ask each person to explain what the problem is. Get each person to be specific and to respond to the others' charges.
3. When all parties understand what the problem is, have them state individually what they want to accomplish or what will satisfy them.
4. Restate in your own words what each person's position is. Ask the employees if you have understood them correctly.
5. Have all participants suggest as many solutions as they can. Begin to focus on the future.
6. Encourage the employees to select a solution that benefits all of them. They may want to combine or modify some of the ideas suggested.
7. Summarize what has been discussed and agreed on. Make sure all participants know what they are supposed to do in carrying out the solution, and ask for their cooperation.

Throughout this process, continue your efforts to maintain a constructive environment. Keep the emphasis off personalities and blame; keep it on your mutual desire to find a solution.

## Change in the Workplace

Conflict is both a cause and a consequence of change. When people experience a conflict, they manage it by making changes to the situation or to their attitudes. When change occurs—in the workplace and elsewhere—conflict accompanies the need to let go of familiar behaviors and attitudes.

When the conflicts are between the demands of work and family, the growing desire of employees to balance the two rather than choose one over the other has forced organizations to consider the adoption of policies and values that are more family-friendly.[8] So far, many organizations have concluded that because the labor pool is large, they simply will hire those people who are willing to work the 50 hours or more a week often required for a high-powered career. However, some employees will leave or choose a less prestigious career path within an organization if their work responsibilities heavily conflict with family demands. Perhaps organizations should consider whether they would benefit if people who insist on making time for their families held a greater number of key decision-making positions.

The greater desire to balance work and home life is only one of many sources of change in the workplace today. A recent survey of U.S. companies found that 84 percent were undergoing at least one major business change, such as adopting innovative information technology or reengineering business processes.[9] External sources of change include higher expectations for quality and stiffer foreign competition.

**FIGURE 15.5**

**Sources of Change**

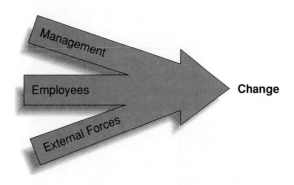

Because of these and many other changes, the success of organizations (i.e., profitability, in the case of businesses) depends on how well they adapt to changes in their environment. For example, an organization must respond when a new competitor enters the marketplace or a new law limits how it may operate.

Change is a fact of organizational life, so supervisors do not decide *whether* organizations should change but *how* to make the changes work. They can do this better if they recognize the various factors that can affect the success of a change:

- *The change agent*—The person trying to bring about the change should have skills in implementing change and solving the related problems, as well as expertise in the area affected.
- *Determination of what to change*—Any changes should make the organization more effective in delivering high quality.
- *The kind of change to be made*—The change can involve process and equipment; policies, procedures, and job structure; and people-related variables such as attitudes and communication skills.
- *Individuals affected*—Some people are more open to change than others. Also, people will see some changes as beneficial to them but other changes as harmful.
- *Evaluation of change*—An evaluation can indicate whether it is necessary to modify the change process or make further changes.

Supervisors are the organization's primary link to operative employees, so they must understand how employees are likely to respond to changes, be able to communicate information about the changes to employees, and help employees respond positively. A good way to begin is to understand what causes management to see a need for change.

## Sources of Change

Changes can originate with management, employees, or external forces (see Figure 15.5). Organizations change when management sees an opportunity or a need to do things better. A need may arise because performance is inadequate (see the story about the flat pancakes at The 1811 House at the beginning of this chapter). Examples of an opportunity are a new computer system that is more efficient or a new procedure that can lead to higher-quality service.

### FIGURE 15.6

**A Change That Leaves Employees Worse Off**

Source: Reprinted by permission: Tribune Media Services.

Even an organization's employees may bring about changes. Forming a union could lead to changes in the way management reaches agreements with employees and the conditions under which employees work. Many organizations actively respond to employee suggestions on how to improve quality and cut costs.

As the U.S. workforce becomes increasingly diverse in terms of age, race, and sex, the forces for change from employees are likely to strengthen. People of diverse backgrounds can offer a greater variety of creative solutions. In addition, the challenge of working harmoniously with different kinds of people can itself lead to a push for changes, such as provisions for different religious holidays or guidelines on how to treat people fairly.

Other changes are imposed from outside. New laws and regulations often lead to changes within organizations. A local government organization might have to make changes in response to voters' refusal to approve a tax increase. A series of lawsuits might cause an organization to reexamine how it makes a product. The size and composition of the workforce may affect whom the organization hires and how much training it provides. Economic trends also are important. For example, businesses usually are able to seek growth more aggressively when the economy is expanding.

### Resistance to Change

In Chapter 12, you read that employees tend to be fearful about productivity-related changes. Any kind of change is uncomfortable to some degree. Management consultant Ken Blanchard writes, "If you don't feel awkward when you're trying something new, you're probably not really doing anything differently."[10] Any change, such as the adoption of a new procedure in the workplace or the completion of a major training program, requires work. People also are fearful because change carries the risk of making them worse off, as happened to the staffers laid off by the politician in Figure 15.6. At a financial services company,

## Engelhard Engineers Change Through Teams

Faced with the hard business realities of the 1980s, Engelhard, a large, New Jersey–based chemical and engineered materials company, decided that reengineering was the answer. To reduce costs and increase production speed, the organization forced its own solution by laying off 500 salaried employees from corporate staff to operations management. And Engelhard found itself no better off. L. Donald LaTorre, president and chief operating officer, now admits, "We learned that we really didn't change the work, we just eliminated people. This made us realize that we had to change the work as well."

LaTorre still wanted to cut costs and boost production. The petroleum catalyst division of the company found a way to do it, but this required a multimillion-dollar plant expansion. LaTorre OK'd the proposal, but said that the expansion had to pay for itself. The plant needed new customers. Thus, the cross-functional sales teams charged with change were born.

Teams included members from sales, distribution, and manufacturing, so that the teams would benefit from different viewpoints. For instance, someone in distribution might learn from someone in sales how customers wanted products packaged and delivered.

The teams were so effective that the increased capacity in the new plant was sold out within six months.

The teams did not always operate smoothly, however. Conflict was a natural part of the process, and not everyone in the division bought in to the new ideas and changes brought about by team decisions. The greatest resistance actually came from middle managers, who felt threatened by changes. "We've had to move some of our resisters out," notes LaTorre, "but we got such good early results that there's been a lot of peer pressure to go along with the change."

Ultimately, the petroleum catalyst division of Engelhard increased its global market share by 35 percent. That's a success story, but it is important to recognize that change—even successful change—is difficult for everyone involved. At Engelhard, those who could not accept change were forced to look for other jobs, but this also points to the important role of all employees, both managers and hourly workers: For an organization to change, people must be willing to change it.

Source: Michael Hammer and Steven A. Stanton, "Beating the Risks of Reengineering," from *The Reengineering Revolution*, excerpted in *Fortune*, May 15, 1995, pp. 108–109, 114.

the announcement of a reengineering effort quickly was followed by widespread rumors predicting massive layoffs, bankruptcy, and a dramatic increase in employee workloads.[11]

Supervisors themselves may have misgivings about some of the changes they must introduce. (See "Meeting the Challenge" to learn how one company dealt with change—and managers who resisted it.) Supervisors' fears are sometimes well founded. For example, Eastman Kodak Company eliminated 30 percent of the managers of its apparatus division, doing away with four levels of management. As a result, first-line supervisors, who in the past simply had carried out orders, had to begin setting goals and making strategies. According to Frank Zaffino, who heads the division, some of the supervisors could not handle the new responsibility. Zaffino said, "They were used to being star technicians, not communicators or leaders."[12]

People's resistance to change is greatest when they are not sure what to expect or why the change is necessary. Change stirs up fear of the unknown, another normal human response. Furthermore, when people do not understand the reasons for change, the effort to change does not seem worthwhile. Before the cook at The 1811 House could appreciate the benefits of no longer using a mix, Marnie Duff had to help him discover the superior quality of pancakes made from scratch.

██ **FIGURE 15.7**

**Lewin's Model of Change**

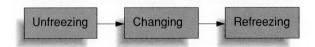

## Implementing Change

To implement change, a supervisor must overcome resistance to it, ensure that the change is made, and create the conditions in which the change is likely to last. Noted behavioral scientist Kurt Lewin has set forth a model for this process (see Figure 15.7). [13] Lewin's model indicates that a successful change has three phases:

1. *Unfreezing*—People recognize a need for change.
2. *Changing*—People begin trying to behave differently.
3. *Refreezing*—The new behavior becomes part of employees' regular processes.

This model makes two assumptions about the change process. First, before a change can occur, employees must see the status quo as less than ideal. Second, when employees begin changing, the organization must provide a way for the new behavior to become established practice.

### Unfreezing

In the unfreezing phase, the supervisor or other person responsible for implementing the change must spell out clearly why a change is needed. AlliedSignal's CEO, Lawrence Bossidy, describes this step colorfully, as the "burning platform theory of change":

> When the roustabouts are standing on the offshore oil rig and the foreman yells, "Jump into the water," not only won't they jump but they also won't feel too kindly toward the foreman. There may be sharks in the water. They'll jump only when they themselves see the flames shooting up from the platform. . . . The leader's job is to help everyone see that the platform is burning, whether the flames are apparent or not. [14]

In essence, then, unfreezing means overcoming resistance to change.

According to Ken Blanchard, a primary reason many efforts to change fail is that management does not consider the employees' point of view. [15] Many changes require not only performing new tasks but also adopting new attitudes, such as a willingness to assume decision-making responsibility and a strong commitment to customer value. Employees may have difficulty changing their attitudes, especially if they are unsure about management's sincerity. [16] Also, management needs to address employee resistance arising from fears about the change. The organization relies heavily on supervisors— as management's link to operative employees— to carry out this responsibility, for which they need good communication skills (see Chapter 10). The following guidelines may help as well:

- Tell employees about a change as soon as you learn about it.
- Make sure employees understand what the change is, then explain how the change is likely to affect them.

- Be as positive about the change as possible, citing any benefits to the employees. These might include more interesting jobs or bigger bonuses. At the same time, don't get caught up in parroting the company's point of view. People need emotional support during periods of change, and they won't take kindly to an insensitive stream of platitudes.[17]
- Describe how the organization will help employees cope. Will there be training in how to follow new procedures? Will the organization provide counseling or other assistance to employees being laid off?
- Do not try to hide bad news, including the possibility that some employees will lose their jobs.
- Give employees plenty of opportunity to express concerns and ask questions. It is better for a supervisor to hear concerns and questions than to let them circulate in the rumor mill, where information may be misleading or incorrect.
- Answer as many questions as you can and get the answers to the rest as soon as possible.
- When employees are upset, listen to expressions of sadness and anger without argument. It is unfair and unwise to tell employees they are overreacting. "People 'overreact' to a change when they're reacting more than we are," says change expert William Bridges. He explains that people experience change subjectively, and one subjective experience is as valid as another. Furthermore, he says, discounting people's feelings shuts off further communication.[18]

In listening to and answering questions, bear in mind that some employees will not think of questions until some time has passed. Therefore, provide opportunities for employees to ask questions on an ongoing basis, not just at the time a change is announced.

### Changing

When employees appreciate the need for a change and have received any necessary training, they are ready to begin altering their behavior. The key to implementing change is to build on successes. A supervisor should determine those aspects of the change over which he or she has control, then seek to carry them out successfully. A supervisor should point out each success the group achieves along the way. As employees see the change achieving desirable results, they are more likely to go along with it and even embrace it.

On a practical level, building on successes generally entails starting with basic changes in behavior, rather than beginning with an effort to change values. Values, by their nature, are more resistant to change. To induce changes in behavior, the change effort should include tangible or intangible rewards for the desired behavior. As employees experience positive outcomes, their attitudes become more positive, and their values may shift as well.

This was the process AT&T followed when it wanted its research staff to be more oriented toward customer needs. The company charged the first-level manager of each research group with fulfilling the company's technology needs in a particular business area instead of focusing strictly on excellence in terms of a particular scientific discipline. Success would be measured in terms of how well the group satisfied customers by helping to meet their needs. The scientists at first viewed the new approach as a lowering of standards, but gradually they saw that useful advances in technology were at least as significant as achievements that won the admiration of their scientific colleagues.[19]

Change can bring positive results. When the organizational structure of Kodak's black-and-white film manufacturing was changed from a vertical/departmental form to a horizontal/self-directed team form, these "zebras" saw dramatic results. Productivity, profitability, and morale soared.

Source: © John Abbot

A supervisor who has control over scheduling a change should establish reasonable deadlines. As employees meet each deadline, the supervisor can point out their on-time achievements. For example, imagine that an accounting department is installing a new computer system. Instead of focusing simply on whether everyone is using the system properly, a supervisor can establish dates for setting up various pieces of equipment and learning to operate different parts of the system. Then the supervisor can note that the terminals arrived on time, that everyone learned how to log on and enter their password in a single training session, and so on.

A supervisor also might have control over which people are directly involved in the change or the order in which people get involved. The supervisor of the accounting department might recognize that some employees are already enthusiastic about the new system or are flexible and open to change. These people should learn the system first; then they can spread their enthusiasm around and help other employees when it is their turn to learn.

Similarly, if a group of employees work well together and enjoy each other's company, a sensible approach is to keep these employees together. For example, the change of adding another shift might proceed more smoothly if informal groups are not split into different shifts. In contrast, when a change involves bringing together two groups of employees from different organizations, locations, or shifts, a supervisor might build cooperation by teaming up employees from each group.[20]

### Refreezing

The change process is complete only when employees make the new behavior part of their routine. However, because new procedures are less comfortable than the old and familiar ones, employees may revert to their old practices when the initial pressure for change eases.[21] In organizations that do not manage change effectively, managers may assume a change effort has succeeded simply because employees modified their behavior according to instructions. But if employees merely fulfill the basic requirements of a change without adjusting their attitudes, and if the organization has not arranged to reinforce and reward the change, backsliding is likely.[22]

Backsliding is a natural response among employees, but it can become a problem unless a supervisor acts to get everyone back on track. A supervisor should remind employees about what they have achieved so far and what is expected of them in the future (see the principles of motivation described in Chapter 11). An important part of refreezing is for employees to be rewarded for behavior that shows they have made the desired change.

### Proposing Change

In many situations, a supervisor wants to make a change but needs to ask higher-level management for authority to implement it. A supervisor also is wise to ask his or her manager about changes that are controversial, difficult to implement, or of major importance. These situations require a supervisor to make a proposal to higher-level management.

To propose a change effectively, the supervisor should begin by analyzing it. How will it help the organization better achieve its goals? Will it improve quality or productivity? What steps are required to carry it out? How much will it cost? Who will carry it out? What training will be required? Only when the answers to these questions confirm that the change is beneficial and feasible is the supervisor in a valid position to continue with the proposal.

Recall that the change process begins with convincing others of the need for a change (unfreezing, in Lewin's model). Some organizations actively cultivate suggestions for improvement, making it relatively easy for a supervisor to sell a change. In other organizations, management may view change more cautiously. Thus, it is often important for a supervisor to begin by helping management see the situation giving rise to the need for a change. A supervisor may have to do this before he or she even mentions changing something.

Once a supervisor's groundwork has prepared management for the proposal, a supervisor should have one ready to submit. Except for simple changes, a supervisor should make proposals in writing. The beginning of a proposal should contain a brief summary of what the change is and why it is desirable. Then the supervisor can provide details about the procedure for change and the costs and benefits involved. (For more suggestions about upward communication and reports, see Chapter 10; for guidelines on maintaining good relations with your manager, see Chapter 8.)

## Organization Politics and Power

**organization politics**
Activities by which people seek to improve their position within the organization, generally by gaining power.

**power**
The ability to influence people to behave in a certain way.

Implementing change and resolving conflicts are easier for a person who has a relatively strong position in the organization. Thus, supervisors can most effectively manage conflict and change if they are able to improve their position with an organization. Together, the activities through which people do this are called **organization politics.** Improving one's position is not in itself good or bad; therefore, politics also is not innately good or bad. Political skills *are* important, however. They help a supervisor obtain the cooperation and support of others in the organization.

The usual way that people use politics to improve their position is by gaining power. **Power** is the ability to influence people to behave in a certain way. For instance, one supervisor says, "I wish everyone would be at work on time," yet employees continue to come in late. Another supervisor gets employees so excited about their contribution to the company that they consistently arrive at work on time and perform above what is required of them. The second supervisor has more power than the first.

## Sources of Power

Editorial supervisor Stan Bakker has a decade-long track record of turning manuscripts into best-sellers. When he tells one of the editors on his staff how to handle a particular author or manuscript, the editor invariably follows Stan's directions. Why? Partly because Stan is the boss, and partly because the editors respect his expertise. Thus, Stan's power comes both from his position in the company and from his personal characteristics.

**position power**
Power that comes from a person's formal role in an organization.

Power that comes from a person's formal role in an organization is known as **position power.** Every supervisor has some position power with the employees he or she supervises. Higher-level managers, in turn, have a greater degree of position power.

**personal power**
Power that arises from an individual's personal characteristics.

In contrast, **personal power** is power that arises from an individual's personal characteristics. Because a person does not need to be a manager in an organization to have personal power there, employees sometimes view a co-worker as an informal leader of their group. If a supervisor announces a reorganization, one employee may successfully urge everyone to rally around the new plan—or may undermine morale by making fun of the changes. The informal leader in a group could be someone that other employees see as having expertise or being fun to work with.

Supervisors cannot eliminate personal power in subordinates, but they should be aware of it so they can use it to their advantage. A supervisor can watch for problems that might arise when the supervisor and an informal leader have conflicting goals. Perhaps more important, a supervisor can seek ways to get an informal leader on his or her side; for example, a supervisor might announce a decision to the informal leader first or discuss plans with that person. When Marie Davis, marketing manager at IDS Financial Services, learned that she and her department would be reporting to a new vice-president, she persuaded the department's informal leaders to help make the change as easy as possible.[23]

## Types of Power

Because power comes from their personal characteristics as well as their position in the organization, supervisors can have a variety of types of power. A supervisor who has less position power than he or she would like might consider the following types of power to see whether some can be developed. These types are summarized in Table 15.1.

*Legitimate power* comes from the position a person holds. Thus, a supervisor has legitimate power to delegate tasks to employees. To exercise legitimate power effectively, a supervisor needs to be sure employees understand what they are directed to do and are able to do it.

*Referent power* comes from the emotions a person inspires. Some supervisors seem to light up the room when they enter; they have a winning personality that includes enthusiasm, energy, and genuine enjoyment of the job. People like working for such a

| ■ **TABLE 15.1** | | |
|---|---|---|
| **Types of Power** | **Power Type** | **Arises from** |
| | Legitimate | The position a person holds |
| | Referent | The emotions a person inspires |
| | Expert | A person's knowledge or skills |
| | Coercive | Fear related to the use of force |
| | Reward | Giving people something they want |
| | Connection | A person's relationship to someone powerful |
| | Information | Possession of valuable information |

supervisor and often perform beyond the call of duty because they want the supervisor to like them. A person with referent power is often called "charismatic."

*Expert power* arises from a person's knowledge or skills. Employees respect a supervisor who knows the employees' jobs better than they do. Their respect leads them to follow the supervisor's instructions. For example, the head of a company's research and development team might be a scientist who is well regarded in the field. Researchers could be expected to ask for and rely on this supervisor's advice.

*Coercive power* arises from fear related to the use of force. A supervisor who says, "Be on time tomorrow, or you're fired!" is using coercive power. This type of power may get results in the short run, but in the long run employees come to resent and may try to get around this supervisor. A supervisor who often relies on coercive power should consider whether he or she is doing so at the expense of developing other, more appropriate types of power.

*Reward power* arises from giving people something they want. The reward given by a supervisor might be a raise, recognition, or assignment to a desired shift. A supervisor who plans to rely on reward power to lead employees had better be sure that he or she is able to give out rewards consistently. Often supervisors are limited in this regard. Company policy may put a ceiling on the size of raises to be granted or there may be only a few assignments that really thrill employees.

*Connection power* is power that stems from a person's relationship to someone powerful. Imagine that two supervisors are golfing buddies. One of them gets promoted to the job of manager of purchasing. The other supervisor has connection power stemming from his relationship to the new manager. Similarly, if one of the organization's employees is the daughter of a vice-president, she has connection power as a result of that family relationship. Connection power can be a problem for the organization and its managers when the people who have it place the interests of their relationship ahead of the interests of the organization. However, it is a fact of organizational life.

*Information power* is power that arises from possessing valuable information. Someone who knows which employees are targeted in the next round of layoffs or when the department manager will be out of town has information power. The secretaries of top managers have information power as well as connection power.

## Political Strategies

A person's political strategies are the methods the person uses to acquire and keep power within the organization. Depending on the particular strategies a person chooses and how he or she uses those strategies, they may be ethical or unethical. The following strategies commonly are used in organizations:[24]

- *Doing favors*—People remember favors and generally are willing to help out or say a good word in return. However, doing favors solely to create an obligation is unethical.
- *Making good impressions*—Those who are skilled at organization politics know that it is important to create a positive image of themselves. Not only do they look their best, but they make sure their accomplishments are visible.
- *Cultivating the grapevine*—The saying "knowledge is power" applies to one's position in the organization. Therefore, power is greater for those who are connected to the grapevines that carry information in the organization (see Chapter 10). Ways to get connected include serving on committees and developing friendships and informal contacts.
- *Supporting the manager*—The supervisor's manager can be a powerful ally. Therefore, it is important to help the manager look good.
- *Avoiding negativism*—People have more respect for those who propose solutions than for those who merely criticize.
- *Giving praise*—People like to be praised, and written compliments are especially valuable. As long as the praise is sincere, the supervisor can offer it to anyone, even his or her manager.

## Building a Power Base

At the heart of organization politics is building a base of power. The particular approach used varies with the kinds of power an employee or manager might acquire. Figure 15.8 summarizes some possible approaches. Some people take on more responsibility in an effort to become needed in the organization. Others seek control over resources; the supervisor with more employees or a bigger budget is considered to be more powerful.

An important way supervisors can build their power base is to please their manager. Peers and subordinates who recognize that a supervisor has a close relationship with the manager tend to treat the supervisor carefully to avoid antagonizing the manager.

To do favors so that others will be in one's debt is yet another approach. Bribery of course is unethical, but there are many ethical ways to do favors for others. A supervisor might offer to stay late to help a co-worker finish a project or jump-start the co-worker's car on a cold day. When the supervisor needs help or a favorable word from someone, the co-worker probably will be happy to return the favor.

Doing favors can help a supervisor with one of the other techniques for building a power base: developing alliances with others in the organization. A supervisor who has many people on his or her side is able to get more done and to build a good reputation. This does not mean supervisors have to hang around with greedy, pushy, or unethical co-workers. Instead, they should identify people they admire as potential allies.[25] Alliances can be built with these people by earning their trust, keeping them informed, and developing comfortable relationships through common interests.[26]

**FIGURE 15.8**

Approaches to Building a Power Base

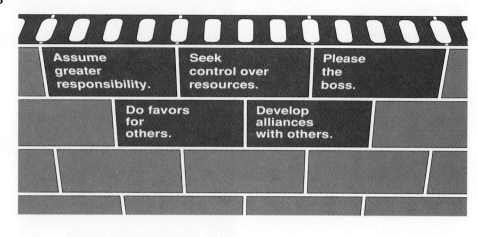

- Assume greater responsibility.
- Seek control over resources.
- Please the boss.
- Do favors for others.
- Develop alliances with others.

### Establishing a Competitive Edge

On the assumption that there are limits to the number of promotions and other goodies available, organization members seek to gain a competitive edge. They try to stand out so that when raises, promotions, and choice assignments are handed out, they will be the recipients. Ethical efforts to establish a competitive edge generally are based on trying to do an exceptional job. For example, a sales manager who works for a U.S. subsidiary of a Mexican conglomerate says, "Learning the language and customs [of Mexico] enabled me to impress the players in our parent company in Mexico. They now respond quickly to my requests."[27]

Some unethical approaches to establishing a competitive edge are spreading lies and rumors about peers and taking credit for the ideas and work of subordinates. Trying to look good at the expense of someone else may be effective at first, but when the truth comes out the person who uses this tactic winds up the biggest loser. Other people learn to distrust such a person. In the long run, the most successful way to look exceptional is to produce exceptional results.

### Socializing

At many organizations, part of the game of getting ahead includes socializing with co-workers. Perhaps the people who get promoted the fastest are those who on occasion play golf with the boss or go out for a drink after work. Depending on a supervisor's behavior in these situations, socializing can be helpful or it can put an end to an employee's career growth.

Common sense can help the supervisor handle socializing appropriately. For example, a supervisor who gets drunk at a party is likely to behave foolishly. Likewise, dating a subordinate is an invitation to trouble. If the relationship lasts, other employees are likely to be jealous of the subordinate and to doubt the supervisor's ability to be fair. If the relationship does not work out, the supervisor could be set up—justly or unjustly—for charges of sexual harassment by an angry subordinate. (For an explanation of sexual harassment, see Chapter 19.)

If handled appropriately, socializing with other employees in activities such as golf can be helpful to a supervisor's career.

Source: © Dick Luria/Tony Stone Images

In general, the wisest course is to be sensible but natural. For example, a supervisor should not push to become a buddy of the manager or of subordinates. Nor should a supervisor use social occasions as an opportunity to make a big impression; showing off is hardly an effective way to build relationships. A more positive approach was that of a marketing coordinator who succeeded with a simple demonstration of interest in her company's president. She learned he likes rhubarb, so she made a rhubarb pie to take to an office party. "The boss had a piece [of the pie], and now he acknowledges me," reported this marketing coordinator.[28] When she needs help with a conflict or wants to propose a change, the marketing coordinator may be able to benefit from this and other positive relationships she has cultivated.

# Summary

**15.1 List positive and negative aspects of conflict.**

When it leads to necessary changes, conflict is a positive force because it signals that a problem exists. However, ongoing conflict puts people under stress and takes up time that could be spent more productively. When conflict involves anger at management or the organization, it may lead to destructive behavior.

**15.2 Define types of conflict.**

Conflict may be intrapersonal, taking place within one person. Conflict between individuals is called interpersonal. Structural conflict results from the way the organization is structured. Strategic conflict is brought about intentionally to achieve some goal, such as motivating employees.

**15.3   Describe strategies for managing conflict.**
One strategy is to compromise, or agree to a solution that meets only part of each party's demands. Another approach is to avoid the conflict or to pretend it does not exist (smoothing). Forcing a solution occurs when a person with power selects and imposes the outcome. None of these strategies tries to solve the underlying problem, and all assume that the situation is win–lose for those involved. Confronting and solving the problem, called conflict resolution, assumes that a conflict can be a win–win situation.

**15.4   Explain how supervisors can initiate conflict resolution, respond to a conflict, and mediate conflict resolution.**
To initiate conflict resolution, a supervisor must begin by understanding what the conflict is. The supervisor then states the problem and listens to the response; when the parties are communicating, they can find a solution and agree upon what each person will do.

To respond to a conflict, a supervisor should listen to the other person and try to understand the problem. Then the supervisor can build cooperation by agreeing with part of the statement and working with the other person to reach a solution.

To mediate conflict resolution, a supervisor begins by establishing a constructive environment, then asks each person to explain what the problem is and state what he or she wants. Next the supervisor restates each position, asks for suggested solutions, and encourages the parties to select a mutually beneficial solution. Finally, the supervisor summarizes what course of action has been agreed upon.

**15.5   Identify sources of change, and explain why employees and supervisors resist it.**
Change can come from management in response to an opportunity or need to do things better. It can come from employees in the form of unioniz-

ing or making suggestions. Change can be imposed by external forces such as the government. Employees and supervisors resist change because it typically requires extra effort and sometimes leaves people worse off. Other reasons for resisting change are fear of the unknown and worry that one is incapable of making the change.

**15.6   Discuss how supervisors can overcome resistance and implement change.**
To overcome resistance to change, supervisors can recognize and respond to employees' feelings. They also can keep employees informed about the change, being realistic but emphasizing any benefits. The supervisor should give employees opportunities to ask questions about the change. To implement change, the supervisor should build on successes. This includes communicating successes as they occur, setting reasonable deadlines for the steps that must be taken, and involving first the people who are most likely to be enthusiastic about the change.

**15.7   Describe the types of power supervisors can have.**
Supervisors can have legitimate power, which comes from their position in the organization; referent power, which comes from the emotions they inspire in others; expert power, which comes from their knowledge or skills; coercive power, which comes from fear related to their use of force; reward power, which comes from giving people something they want; connection power, which comes from their relationships to people in power; and information power, which comes from the possession of valuable information.

**15.8   Identify common strategies for organization politics.**
Political strategies commonly used in organizations include doing favors, making good impressions, cultivating the grapevine, supporting the manager, avoiding negativism, and giving praise.

# Key Terms

| | | |
|---|---|---|
| conflict | compromise | power |
| frustration | smoothing | position power |
| conflict management | conflict resolution | personal power |
| | organization politics | |

# Review and Discussion Questions

1. On her first day on the job, Jenna's supervisor introduces her incorrectly to her co-workers, mispronouncing her name. For several weeks after that, Jenna's co-workers, intending to be friendly, pronounce her name incorrectly. Jenna goes along with it, not wanting to jeopardize her new relationships. Finally, feeling uncomfortable about the situation, Jenna approaches her supervisor about the mistake. Is this a positive or negative conflict? Why?

2. Imagine that you are a production supervisor at a hand-tool manufacturer such as Snap-On Tools. Your manager says, "I know you were looking forward to your trip to Hawaii next month, but we will be stepping up production, and three new employees will be joining your group. I wish you would consider staying to make sure everything goes smoothly."

   a. What is the nature of the conflict in this situation? In other words, what two goals is it impossible for you to achieve at the same time?

   b. List as many possible solutions as you can think of to resolve this conflict.

   c. Which solution do you prefer? How could you present it to your manager?

3. Identify each of the following conflicts as interpersonal, structural, or strategic.

   a. The production department's goal is to make parts faster, and the quality-control department wants slower production to reduce the rate of defects.

   b. A salesperson does not take telephone messages for her co-workers because she believes she has a better chance of being the department's top performer when her co-workers do not return their calls.

   c. One cashier at a supermarket is much older than the others, and he does not spend much time talking to them. The other cashiers criticize him for not being a team player.

4. Why does compromise generally leave both parties feeling frustrated?

5. Rachel Gonzalez supervises servers at a restaurant. She knows that many of them are upset about the hours she has scheduled for them, but she believes that people should not argue. So she avoids discussing the subject, and she posts the following week's schedule just before leaving for the day. What is wrong with Rachel's approach to conflict management? What would be a better way to manage this conflict?

6. Ron Herbst is a supervisor in a clinical laboratory. He has noticed that one employee regularly comes to work in a surly mood. The employee is getting his work done on time, but his attitude seems to be affecting other employees.

   a. How can Ron initiate conflict resolution with this employee? How should he describe the problem?

   b. If the employee responds to Ron's statement of the problem by saying, "I'm fine. Don't worry about me," what should the supervisor do and say?

7. The managers of a soft-drink bottling company decide that production workers will each learn several jobs and rotate among those jobs. They have read that this technique improves productivity, and they believe that workers will be happier because their jobs will be more interesting. However, many of the employees and their supervisors are reluctant to make the change. What could explain their resistance?

8. What are the factors that can affect the success of a change?

9. How can a supervisor overcome resistance to change?

10. What is the primary reason that efforts for change within an organization fail? What can a supervisor do to avoid this failure and to ensure that change will be successful?

11. What are the two basic sources of power available to a supervisor? Which do you think is more important to the supervisor's effectiveness? Why?

12. Which type(s) of power is the supervisor exerting in each of the following situations?

   a. A sales supervisor promises a $50 bonus to the first salesperson to close a sale this week.
   b. One day a month, a supervisor orders in pizza and joins her employees for lunch. The employees look forward to these gatherings because the supervisor joins them in recounting funny stories, and she usually is able to fill them in on some management plans.
   c. A supervisor in the bookkeeping department got his job thanks to a referral from his father, who regularly plays racquetball with the company's president. Since the supervisor was hired, the president has visited the bookkeeping department a couple of times to see how he is doing. The manager of the department is very diplomatic in his criticism of the supervisor.
   d. When the employees in a word-processing department make many errors per page or a particularly glaring error, their supervisor posts the offending pages on the department bulletin board to shame the employees into performing better.

13. A sales supervisor believes she could be more effective if she had more cooperation from the company's credit department. If the credit of potential customers could be approved faster, her salespeople could close more sales. What political tactics would you recommend that the sales supervisor consider to get more cooperation from the credit department?

## A SECOND LOOK

Recall the story about the cook at the beginning of this chapter. Why do you think the cook resisted changing the way he made pancakes? How did his supervisor, Marnie Duff, overcome that resistance?

# APPLICATIONS MODULE

## CASE

*Conflict and Change: Breyers Ice Cream Melts in Philadelphia*

Ice cream used to be one of those unchanging symbols of American life, like baseball or the Sears catalog. But baseball went on strike, and the original Sears catalog folded. And in Philadelphia, the traditional scoop of vanilla fell off the cone when 130-year-old Breyers (now owned by Kraft) announced that it was closing its 71-year-old plant, leaving 240 workers without jobs.

"This has always seemed like the perfect job for me," laments Frank Avent, a 53-year-old Breyers employee facing the layoff. "[Breyers ice cream] has always been my favorite dessert. Until now." Avent worked at the plant for 25 years.

The situation at Breyers is the same one many American companies have had to face in recent years. Operating in a city with high business taxes, an aging infrastructure, and high crime rates, Breyers management concluded it must leave the city where the company was founded. In addition, modernizing the existing plant would have cost $15 million. Trying to get the public and employees to see the benefits of the change, John Gould, Jr., spokesman for Good Humor–Breyers (now based in Wisconsin) claims, "We believe the Philadelphia operation is one that we can close without adversely affecting production."

But the closing does affect jobs, often ones held by people for many years or from one generation to the next. "It's a shame they're leaving Philly. It really is," comments Rich Hunter, a mechanic who has been with Breyers for 12 years. "My father used to work here, too. We've got pictures of this place from [the time] when horse-and-buggies used to deliver the ice cream."

If some workers seem nostalgic, others are angry and mistrustful of the organization. "They knew what they were getting when they bought this place," observes Roney Brabham, a production worker for 18 years, "but they never even tried to fix it up. Where does that leave us?"

Union representatives agree. "Big business once again shows its concern for the bottom line and its lack of concern for working men and women," notes Edward Henderson, head of the Teamsters Local 463, which represents 184 workers at the plant.

If these workers and their union reps resist change, it is understandable: People are losing jobs. Implementing change will not be easy for supervisors, who must deal with the reality of layoffs—and may face layoffs themselves. In this case, the freeze-unfreeze-refreeze model of change may be more difficult to carry out than usual: It's nearly impossible to get the ice cream back into the cone.

1. What three points of view are expressed in this case?
2. Is there any way to initiate some type of conflict resolution in the Breyers case? If so, how?
3. Do the workers have any potential power? If so, what type(s) might they have? How could they use it?
4. What steps might supervisors take to implement the change as painlessly as possible?

Source: "Closing of Breyers Is a Bitter Chapter for Employees, City," *Boston Globe*, Sept. 5, 1995, p. 41.

### SELF-QUIZ

## *What Is Your Conflict-Handling Style?*

Everyone has a basic style for handling conflicts. To identify the strategies you rely upon most, indicate how often each of the following statements applies to you. Next to each statement, write *5* if the statement applies often, *3* if the statement applies sometimes, and *1* if the statement applies never.

When I differ with someone. . .

_____ 1. I explore our differences, not backing down, but not imposing my view either.

_____ 2. I disagree openly, then invite more discussion about our differences.

_____ 3. I look for a mutually satisfactory solution.

_____ 4. Rather than let the other person make a decision without my input, I make sure I am heard and also that I hear the other person out.

_____ 5. I agree to a middle ground rather than look for a completely satisfying solution.

_____ 6. I admit I am half wrong rather than explore our differences.

_____ 7. I have a reputation for meeting a person halfway.

_____ 8. I expect to say about half of what I really want to say.

_____ 9. I give in totally rather than try to change another's opinion.

_____ 10. I put aside any controversial aspects of an issue.

_____ 11. I agree early on, rather than argue about a point.

_____ 12. I give in as soon as the other party gets emotional about an issue.

_____ 13. I try to win the other person over.

_____ 14. I try to come out victorious, no matter what.

_____ 15. I never back away from a good argument.

_____ 16. I would rather win than end up compromising.

To score your responses, add your total score for each of the following sets of statements:

Set A: statements 1–4       Set C: statements 9–12

Set B: statements 5–8       Set D: statements 13–16

A score of 17 or more on any set is considered high. Scores of 12 to 16 are moderately high. Scores of 8 to 11 are moderately low. Scores of 7 or less are considered low.

Each set represents a different strategy for conflict management:

- Set A = Collaboration (I win, you win)
- Set B = Compromise (Both win some, both lose some)
- Set C = Accommodation (I lose, you win)
- Set D = Forcing/domination (I win, you lose)

Source: Adapted from Stephen P. Robbins, *Training in Interpersonal Skills* (Englewood Cliffs, NJ: Prentice Hall, 1989), pp. 214–16.

## *Class Exercise*

This exercise is based on role playing. One class member takes the role of a supervisor, and two class members act as the employees. The supervisor leaves the room for five minutes as the employees act out the following scenario:

> Pat and Chris work in a word-processing department, preparing reports and letters on computer terminals. Pat trips on the cord to Chris's computer, shutting it off and erasing the project Chris was working on. Chris is upset. If Chris does not finish the job by the end of the day, the failure to meet a deadline will show up on Chris's performance records and hurt Chris's chances for getting a raise. In addition, the manager who requested the work will be upset, because this is an important project.

This is a basic scenario; the employees should be creative in adding details. For example, they can address the following questions:

- Did Pat erase the files on purpose?
- Has Pat ever done something like this before?

## *Team-Building Exercise*

## Role Playing Types of Power

Divide the class into teams of five or more students. Each student receives a card marked with the type of power he or she possesses: legitimate, referent, expert, coercive, reward, connection, or information. (If the group is small, some students may have two types of power.) Students should not show other team members which card they have. Each team has a goal: to convince the rest of the class

- Do these employees otherwise get along?
- Are communications in general and this conflict in particular complicated by some difference between the employees (age, sex, race, etc.)?

After the two class members have acted out the scene, the supervisor returns to the room, and the role playing continues as the employees bring their conflict to the supervisor. The supervisor should try to manage the conflict.

When the supervisor is satisfied with how the conflict has been handled (or when 10 minutes have elapsed), the class discusses the following questions:

1. Did the supervisor understand the real problem? If not, what was the real problem?
2. Did the supervisor and employees solve the problem? Was the solution a good one?
3. In what ways was the supervisor effective in resolving the conflict? How could the supervisor improve his or her approach?
4. What other possible solutions might the supervisor and employees have considered?

that changing something (e.g., holding class in the evening instead of the afternoon) is a good idea.

Using the different kinds of power, each team presents its idea to the class. Afterward, the class should discuss how effective each team was, how effective individual team members were, and what type of power was most effective in getting people to respond positively to the idea of change.

# Video Exercise 15: *Managing Conflict and Change*

## *Video Summary*

A supervisor's job increasingly requires knowing how to manage change. In this video, you will learn how Marshall Industries, a leading distributor of electronic components, has managed change within the organization. Specific techniques using Lewin's Model of Change (see Figure 15.7) are illustrated.

## *Application*

The issue of power contributes substantially to this chapter's discussion of managing conflict and change. You can assess yourself on five of the types of power discussed in the chapter by completing the following profile, which has a list of statements that may be used to describe behaviors that leaders in work organizations can direct toward their subordinates. Read each descriptive statement carefully, thinking in terms of *how you prefer to influence others.* Using the following scale, mark the number that most closely represents how you feel:

1 = Strongly disagree

2 = Disagree

3 = Neither agree nor disagree

4 = Agree

5 = Strongly agree

| To influence others, I would prefer to: | Strongly Disagree | Disagree | Neither Agree nor Disagree | Agree | Strongly Agree |
|---|---|---|---|---|---|
| 1. Increase their pay level | 1 | 2 | 3 | 4 | 5 |
| 2. Make them feel valued | 1 | 2 | 3 | 4 | 5 |
| 3. Give undesirable job assignments | 1 | 2 | 3 | 4 | 5 |
| 4. Make them feel that I approve of them | 1 | 2 | 3 | 4 | 5 |
| 5. Make them feel that they have commitments to meet | 1 | 2 | 3 | 4 | 5 |
| 6. Make them feel personally accepted | 1 | 2 | 3 | 4 | 5 |
| 7. Make them feel important | 1 | 2 | 3 | 4 | 5 |
| 8. Give them good technical suggestions | 1 | 2 | 3 | 4 | 5 |
| 9. Make the work difficult for them | 1 | 2 | 3 | 4 | 5 |
| 10. Share my experience and/or training | 1 | 2 | 3 | 4 | 5 |
| 11. Make things unpleasant here | 1 | 2 | 3 | 4 | 5 |
| 12. Make being at work distasteful | 1 | 2 | 3 | 4 | 5 |
| 13. Influence their getting a pay increase | 1 | 2 | 3 | 4 | 5 |
| 14. Make them feel that they should satisfy their job requirements | 1 | 2 | 3 | 4 | 5 |
| 15. Provide them with sound job-related advice | 1 | 2 | 3 | 4 | 5 |

| To influence others, I would prefer to: | Strongly Disagree | Disagree | Neither Agree nor Disagree | Agree | Strongly Agree |
|---|---|---|---|---|---|
| 16. Provide them with special benefits | 1 | 2 | 3 | 4 | 5 |
| 17. Influence their getting a promotion | 1 | 2 | 3 | 4 | 5 |
| 18. Give them the feeling that they have responsibilities to fulfill | 1 | 2 | 3 | 4 | 5 |
| 19. Provide them with needed technical knowledge | 1 | 2 | 3 | 4 | 5 |
| 20. Make them recognize that they have tasks to accomplish | 1 | 2 | 3 | 4 | 5 |

### Scoring

Insert your number scores from the 20 statements in the table below. After summing the numbers in each column, divide by 4 as indicated. This final number represents your score for each of the forms of power that you should use to interpret your score.

| Reward | Coercive | Legitimate | Referent | Expert |
|---|---|---|---|---|
| 1 ____ | 3 ____ | 5 ____ | 2 ____ | 8 ____ |
| 13 ____ | 9 ____ | 14 ____ | 4 ____ | 10 ____ |
| 16 ____ | 11 ____ | 18 ____ | 6 ____ | 15 ____ |
| 17 ____ | 12 ____ | 20 ____ | 7 ____ | 19 ____ |
| Totals ____ | ____ | ____ | ____ | ____ |
| Divide by 4 ____ | ____ | ____ | ____ | ____ |

### Interpretation

A high score (4 and greater) on any of the five dimensions of power implies that you prefer to influence others by employing that particular form of power. A low score (2 and less) implies that you prefer not to employ this particular form of power to influence others. This represents your power profile.

Your overall power position is not reflected by the simple sum of the power derived from each of the five sources. Instead, some combinations of power are synergistic in nature—they are greater than the simple sum of their parts. For example, referent power tends to magnify the impact of other power sources because these other attempts to influence are coming from a "respected" person. Reward power often increases the impact of referent power because people generally tend to like those who give them things that they desire. Some power combinations, however, tend to produce the opposite of synergistic effects, so that the total is less than the sum of the parts. Power dilution frequently accompanies the use of (or threatened use of) coercive power.

Source: Modified version of T. R. Hinkin & C. A. Schriesheim (1989), "Development and application of new scales to measure the French and Raven (1959) bases of social power," *Journal of Applied Psychology* 74, pp. 561–7.

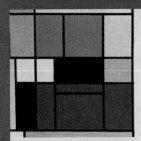

## PART FIVE

# *Supervision and Human Resources*

# 16

*We want to find people who've worked in different industries or companies, who can give us different perspectives, and not just do our own thing over and over and over again.*
**—Mary Eckenrod, director of human resources development, Allen-Bradley Co.**

# Selecting Employees

## CHAPTER OUTLINE

Roles in the Selection Process

Selection Criteria

Recruitment
*Looking Inside the Organization*
*Looking Outside the Organization*

The Selection Process
*Screening from Employment Applications and Résumés*
*Interviewing Candidates*
*Administering Employment Tests*
*Conducting Background and Reference Checks*
*Making the Selection Decision*
*Requesting a Physical Examination*

Legal Issues
*Antidiscrimination Laws*
*Workplace Accessibility*
*Immigration Reform and Control Act*

## LEARNING OBJECTIVES

After you have studied this chapter, you should be able to:

16.1 Discuss common roles for supervisors in the selection process.

16.2 Distinguish job descriptions and job specifications, and explain how they help in selecting employees.

16.3 List possible sources of employees.

16.4 Identify the steps in the selection process.

16.5 Discuss how supervisors should go about interviewing candidates for a job.

16.6 Define types of employment tests.

16.7 Summarize the requirements of antidiscrimination laws.

16.8 Explain how hiring decisions are affected by the Americans with Disabilities Act (ADA).

16.9 Describe the requirements of the Immigration Reform and Control Act (IRCA) of 1986.

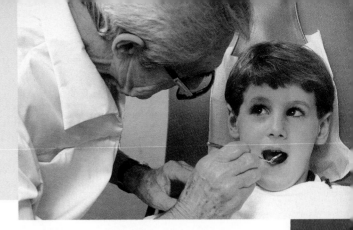

Source: © 1994, Comstock, Inc.

## HARD WORKERS WANTED

As communications supervisor in the office of a pediatric dentist in Tempe, Arizona, Jill Strode supervises four employees: a secretary, an insurance coordinator, and two business assistants. Under her direction, these employees handle the business end of running a dental practice. Their tasks include doing insurance paperwork and communicating information to patients and their parents.

When there is a job opening among these positions, Strode is responsible for all aspects of hiring a replacement. To find qualified candidates, she places an advertisement in the newspaper or talks to her colleagues in the field. When she has identified people who might be suitable for the job, she interviews them. She selects the candidate who seems best qualified, obtains the approval of her employer, Dr. Longfellow, and then makes an offer.

Interviewing job candidates is one of Strode's favorite tasks. She views the interview as a meeting between equals, not an occasion to test the candidate. Strode, says, "If you use too much control, you don't get the best information." Instead, Strode tries to put the candidate at ease and to create an environment where the interviewer and candidate can talk about "the good and the bad."

Once, frustrated by "a string of bad hires," Strode interviewed a young woman she had talked to previously but not hired. She showed the woman a statement she had prepared that spelled out the qualifications she was looking for. The statement focused on attitude and the employee's conduct with patients and co-workers. The candidate reacted to the statement by saying, "That's the *least* you should expect from an employee!" Strode hired that candidate, who proved to be a hard worker and a loyal employee.

An organization's employees can make or break the quality of its goods or services and, in the case of a business, determine the size of its profits. Enthusiastic, well-qualified people are more likely to deliver high quality than indifferent, unqualified people. This is especially true in today's leaner organizations; when fewer employees are getting the work done, each employee has a greater impact on the organization's overall performance. Thus, it is in the supervisor's best interests to do a good job in helping to select employees.

This chapter addresses the supervisor's role in selecting employees, which often entails working with the organization's human resources (or personnel) department. The chapter explains how supervisors define needed qualities of jobs and employees by preparing job descriptions and job specifications. It describes how organizations can recruit candidates and decide whom to hire. Finally, it addresses some legal issues that supervisors and others in the organization must be aware of when hiring.

## Roles in the Selection Process

A supervisor's role in the selection process can vary greatly from one organization to another. In small organizations, such as the dental practice Jill Strode works for, a supervisor may have great latitude in selecting employees to fill vacant positions. Other organizations have formal procedures that require the human resources department to do most of the work, with the supervisor simply approving the candidates recommended. In most cases, a supervisor works to some extent with a human resources department. In this way, a supervisor benefits from that department's skills in screening and interviewing candidates, and from its familiarity with laws regarding hiring practices.

As described in Chapter 3, a growing number of organizations expect employees to work on teams. At the least, the use of teamwork requires the selection of employees who will be effective team members. A supervisor might therefore try to identify candidates who are cooperative and skilled in problem solving or who have helped a team achieve good results in the past. In other cases, the use of teamwork dramatically changes a supervisor's role in the selection process. When teamwork takes the form of self-managing work teams, a team generally interviews candidates and recommends or selects new team members. A supervisor, as team leader, needs to understand the principles of selection so that he or she can coach employees in carrying out the process. The organization's human resources staff supports the team, rather than the individual supervisor.

## Selection Criteria

To select the right employees, the supervisor, team (if applicable), and human resources department have to be clear about what jobs need to be filled and what kind of people can best fill those jobs. A supervisor or self-managed team provides this information by preparing job descriptions and job specifications, consulting with the human resources department as needed. Table 16.1 details basic kinds of information to include in job descriptions and job specifications.

**TABLE 16.1**

**Contents of the Job Description and Job Specification**

| Job Description | Job Specification |
| --- | --- |
| Job title | Education |
| Location | Experience |
| Job summary | Availability to work overtime |
| Duties, including backup functions during peak periods | Skills—technical, physical, communication, and interpersonal |
| Productivity and quality standards | Training |
| Machines, tools, and equipment | Judgment and initiative |
| Materials and forms used | Emotional characteristics |
| Relationships—supervision and teams, if any | Physical effort |
| Working conditions | Unusual sensory demands (sight, smell, hearing, etc.) |

Sources: Samuel C. Certo, *Modern Management*, 6th ed. (Boston: Allyn and Bacon, 1994), p. 265; and J. E. Osborne, "Job Descriptions Do More than Describe Duties," *Supervisory Management*, Feb. 1992, p. 8.

**job description**
A listing of the characteristics of a job, including the job title, duties involved, and working conditions.

A **job description** is a listing of the characteristics of the job—that is, the observable activities required to carry out the job. A written job description typically includes the title of the job, a general description, and details of the duties involved. As you will see later in this chapter, it is important for the job description to spell out the essential duties of the job. When appropriate, a job description may also describe working conditions. Figure 16.1 shows a sample job description for a maintenance technician.

**job specification**
A listing of the characteristics desirable in the person performing a given job, including educational and work background, physical characteristics, and personal strengths.

A **job specification** is a listing of the characteristics desirable in the person performing the job. These include four types of characteristics:[1]

1. *Knowledge*—Information required to perform tasks in the job description.
2. *Skills*—Proficiency in carrying out tasks in the job description.
3. *Abilities*—General enduring capabilities required for carrying out tasks in the job description.
4. *Other characteristics*—Any additional characteristics related to successful performance of the essential tasks (e.g., personality characteristics).

A job specification for the maintenance technician's position therefore would include characteristics such as knowledge about the company's vehicles and shop equipment, skills in repairing these things, broad mechanical abilities, and a commitment to high-quality work.

A supervisor (or team with the supervisor's coaching) should provide the information that applies to the particular job. If a job description and job specification already exist for a position, a supervisor should review them to make sure they reflect current needs. Preparing and using these materials helps a supervisor

### FIGURE 16.1

**Sample Job Description: Maintenance Mechanic**

**General Description of Job:** General maintenance and repair of all equipment used in the operations of a particular district. Includes the servicing of company vehicles, shop equipment, and machinery used on job sites.

1. *Essential Duty (40%): Maintenance of Equipment*

   Tasks: Keep a log of all maintenance performed on equipment. Replace parts and fluids according to maintenance schedule. Regularly check gauges and loads for deviances that may indicate problems with equipment. Perform nonroutine maintenance as required. May involve limited supervision and training of operators performing maintenance.

2. *Essential Duty (40%): Repair of Equipment*

   Tasks: Requires inspection of equipment and a recommendation that a piece be scrapped or repaired. If equipment is to be repaired mechanic will take whatever steps are necessary to return the piece to working order. This may include a partial or total rebuilding of the piece using various hand tools and equipment. Will primarily involve the overhaul and troubleshooting of diesel engines and hydraulic equipment.

3. *Essential Duty (10%): Testing and Approval*

   Tasks: Ensure that all required maintenance and repair has been performed and that it was performed according to manufacturer specifications. Approve or reject equipment for readiness to use on a job.

4. *Essential Duty (10%): Maintain Stock*

   Tasks: Maintain inventory of parts needed for the maintenance and repair of equipment. Responsible for ordering satisfactory parts and supplies at the lowest possible cost.

*Nonessential Functions*

   Other duties as assigned.

Source: Raymond A. Noe, John R. Hollenbeck, Barry Gerhart, and Patrick M. Wright, *Human Resource Management: Gaining a Competitive Advantage*, Austen Press. © Richard D. Irwin, Inc., 1994 p. 208.

base hiring decisions on objective criteria—how well each candidate matches the requirements of the job. Without them, a supervisor risks hiring people solely because he or she likes them better than others.

# Recruitment

To select employees, the supervisor and human resources department need candidates for the job. Identifying people interested in holding a particular job or working for the organization is known as **recruitment,** which involves looking for candidates from both inside and outside the organization.

**recruitment**
A process of identifying people interested in holding a particular job or working for the organization.

## Looking Inside the Organization

Many employees are eager to accept a promotion. Less commonly, employees welcome the variety of working in a new department or at a different task even when the transfer does not involve more money or prestige. These changes can be a source of motivation for employees.

Increased motivation is only one way the organization benefits from promotions and transfers. In addition, the promoted or transferred employees start the new job already familiar with the organization's policies and practices. It may be easier to train new people for entry-level jobs than to hire outsiders to fill more complex positions.

To find employees who are interested in and qualified for a vacant position, a supervisor or human resources department recruits within the organization. Internal recruitment is conducted in two basic ways: through job postings and employee referrals. A job posting is a list of the positions that are vacant in the organization. Typically, a job posting gives the title of the job, the department, and the salary range. In addition, a supervisor's employees may be able to recommend someone for the job—friends or relatives who do not currently work for the organization or qualified candidates they have met through trade or professional groups. Some organizations pay employees a bonus for referrals if the candidate is hired.

## Looking Outside the Organization

A growing organization will especially need to look outside the organization for at least some of its employees. New hires are less familiar with the organization, but they bring fresh ideas and skills that the organization currently lacks. The basic ways to identify qualified candidates outside the organization are through advertising, employment agencies, and schools.

Help-wanted advertisements are a popular way to recruit candidates for a job. Most people at some time or another read the want ads in their local newspaper to see what jobs are available. Organizations also can advertise in journals and magazines directed toward a specialized audience. For example, a research laboratory looking for a writer might advertise in *Technical Communications* and a manufacturer looking for an engineer to develop new products might advertise in *Design News*. Advertising in these kinds of specialized publications limits the recruiting to candidates with a background (or at least an interest) in the relevant field.

Employment agencies seek to match people looking for a job with organizations looking for employees. These agencies may be government run, in which case they do not charge for their services, or private. Many private agencies charge the employer for locating an employee while some charge the person searching for a job. In either case, the agency collects a fee only when someone is hired. Using an agency makes sense when the organization lacks the time or expertise to carry out an effective recruiting effort. (In addition, organizations are increasingly relying on agencies to recruit all types of temporary employees. See "Meeting the Challenge.") Agencies also help screen candidates, a step in the selection process described in the next section.

Depending on the requirements of the job, a supervisor might want employees who recently have graduated from high school, a community college, a trade school, a prestigious university, or some other type of school. In such cases, the organization might seek job candidates through schools of the desired type. Large organizations that expect to hire many recent graduates sometimes send recruiters to talk to students at the targeted schools. Many schools also arrange various kinds of listings of employers who are interested in hiring. Recruiting through schools is a way to limit candidates to those with the desired educational background.

Duplex Products is one company that has benefited from this source of job candidates. The Southfield, Michigan, company gives college placement officers a

## MEETING THE CHALLENGE

### Employers Find a New Source for Employees

In a changing economy, faced with constant pressures to cut costs and still maintain high quality, savvy organizations who know that their best resource is their employees are turning to employment agencies for temporary help. These employment agencies—and the employees they place in jobs—no longer refer to themselves as "temps." Instead, they use the terms "freelancers," "consultants," "self-employed," even "hourly partners," because temporary jobs are no longer confined to typing and bookkeeping. Temporary jobs today run the gamut from law practice to accounting to stock trading to executive positions. Andrea Meltzer of Executive Options, an executive temporary employment agency, notes that her clients are "middle-management people on up. We've been in business for four years, and our growth has been exponential." Executive Options has 6,000 professionals and executives in its database of workers.

The new type of temporary work is competitive. Organizations aren't looking only for recent graduates. For instance, Co-Counsel, a firm that places lawyers in temporary jobs, finds that most companies want attorneys with some working experience. "Every six months, when there's a new swearing-in ceremony [of lawyers], we get a raft of new applications," says Co-Counsel's national sales director Frank Troppe. "These beginners usually are turned down because they lack the necessary experience."

Andrea Meltzer observes that many companies "want to keep a core of full-time people, keeping just enough [supervisor staff] to get by, and augmenting them with a ring of temporary professionals." Thus, a company might hire a stock trader, an accountant, or a lawyer to fill certain temporary needs. The goal is to keep the quality of work high and expenses down.

The flip side, of course, is insecurity for workers. C. J. Meyer, author of *Executive Blues*, writes:

> Peel away the uplifting rhetoric about the exciting workplace of the future and what you're left with is an America in which stability, continuity and security—the basic elements of a coherent life—are going to be beyond the grasp of all but an increasingly small, increasingly isolated minority. . . . Our lives will become a jumble of brief encounters. The man in the gray flannel suit . . . is transmogrified into a soldier of fortune.

But plenty of workers are happy with the arrangement, including increasing numbers of parents who want to work part time to meet family obligations. One accountant who now freelances comments, "I'm making six digits comfortably and I have freedom. When the good weather hits and the golf course beckons . . ." Peter Craig, who became a freelance advertising executive when he was laid off in a downsizing crunch, says that he makes more money now than he did as a full-time employee. "From what I understand, I'm the wave of the future," he observes. These are the winners of the revised game of employment.

Sources: R. C. Longworth and Sharman Stein, "Temp Jobs Gaining Permanence," *Chicago Tribune*, Aug. 21, 1995, Sec. 1, pp. 1, 8; R. C. Longworth, "Cut Adrift, Worker Sees Freelancing as Wave of the Future," *Chicago Tribune*, Aug. 21, 1995, p. 8.

description of the kind of person it wants, and the placement officers send Duplex résumés of students who meet those requirements. Duplex reviews the résumés, then the placement officers set up appointments for the students Duplex wants to interview. Craig Johnson, a regional manager for Duplex, claims that the company found one of its best salespeople through that process.[2]

## The Selection Process

In recent years, organizations typically have had many more candidates than they have needed to fill their vacant positions. Thus, once an organization has identified candidates for a job, it begins the major work: the selection process. Through this process, the supervisor and human resources department seek the

**FIGURE 16.2**

**The Selection
Process**

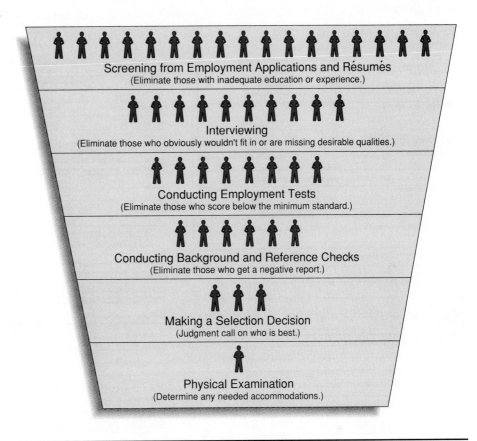

Screening from Employment Applications and Résumés
(Eliminate those with inadequate education or experience.)

Interviewing
(Eliminate those who obviously wouldn't fit in or are missing desirable qualities.)

Conducting Employment Tests
(Eliminate those who score below the minimum standard.)

Conducting Background and Reference Checks
(Eliminate those who get a negative report.)

Making a Selection Decision
(Judgment call on who is best.)

Physical Examination
(Determine any needed accommodations.)

person who is best qualified to fill a particular job. Figure 16.2 shows how the various steps in the selection process narrow the field of candidates. Usually the human resources department does the initial screening, and the supervisor makes the final decision.

### Screening from Employment Applications and Résumés

Candidates for a job respond to recruitment by filling out an employment application or sending in a résumé. Figure 16.3 shows a sample employment application. (Résumés are discussed in the Reference Guide.) The first stage of the selection process is to review the applications or résumés to screen out candidates who are unqualified or less qualified than others. The objective of screening is to narrow the pool of applicants to the number that the supervisor or human resources department wants to interview for the job.

Usually someone in the human resources department takes care of the screening process, comparing the applications or résumés with the job description prepared by the supervisor and eliminating the candidates who obviously fail to meet the qualifications called for in the job description.

**FIGURE 16.3**

**Sample Employment Application**

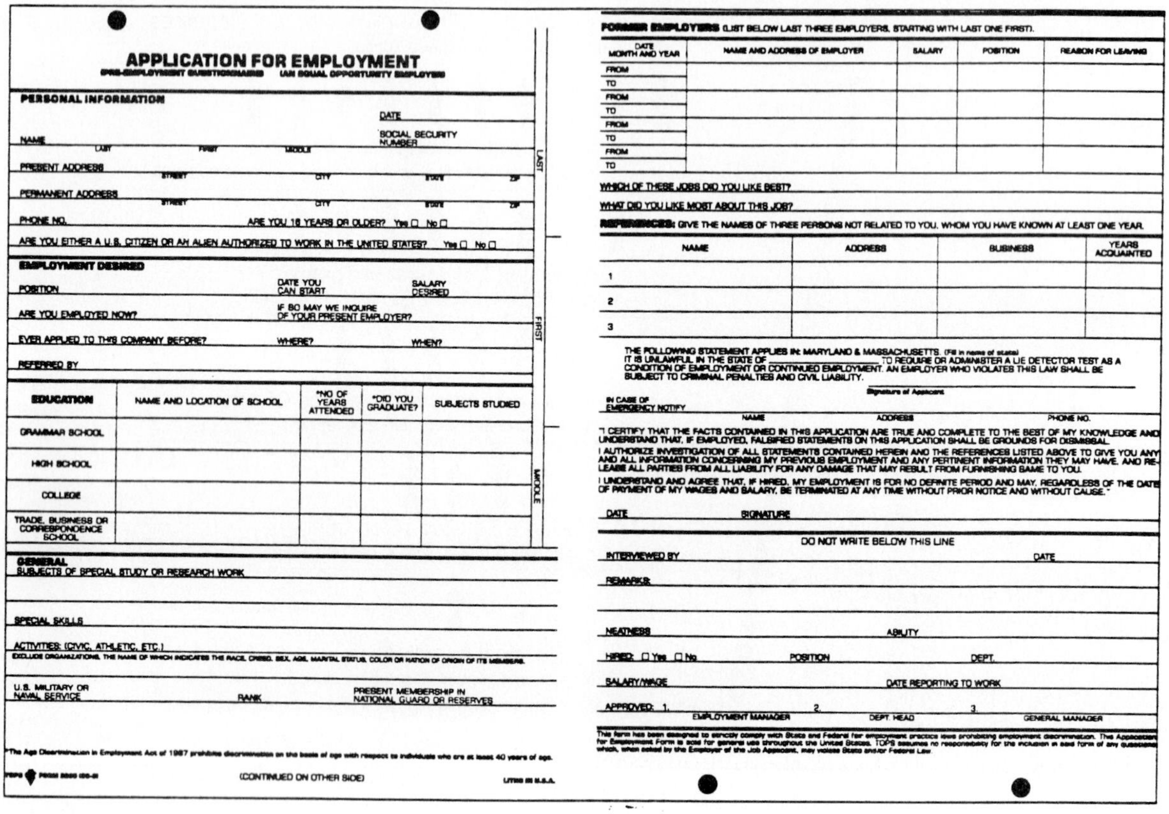

**APPLICATION FOR EMPLOYMENT**
(PRE-EMPLOYMENT QUESTIONNAIRE) (AN EQUAL OPPORTUNITY EMPLOYER)

**PERSONAL INFORMATION**

DATE

NAME (LAST, FIRST, MIDDLE) SOCIAL SECURITY NUMBER

PRESENT ADDRESS (STREET, CITY, STATE, ZIP)

PERMANENT ADDRESS (STREET, CITY, STATE, ZIP)

PHONE NO. ARE YOU 18 YEARS OR OLDER? Yes ☐ No ☐

ARE YOU EITHER A U.S. CITIZEN OR AN ALIEN AUTHORIZED TO WORK IN THE UNITED STATES? Yes ☐ No ☐

**EMPLOYMENT DESIRED**

POSITION DATE YOU CAN START SALARY DESIRED

ARE YOU EMPLOYED NOW? IF SO MAY WE INQUIRE OF YOUR PRESENT EMPLOYER?

EVER APPLIED TO THIS COMPANY BEFORE? WHERE? WHEN?

REFERRED BY

| EDUCATION | NAME AND LOCATION OF SCHOOL | *NO OF YEARS ATTENDED | *DID YOU GRADUATE? | SUBJECTS STUDIED |
|---|---|---|---|---|
| GRAMMAR SCHOOL | | | | |
| HIGH SCHOOL | | | | |
| COLLEGE | | | | |
| TRADE, BUSINESS OR CORRESPONDENCE SCHOOL | | | | |

LAST FIRST MIDDLE

**GENERAL**
SUBJECTS OF SPECIAL STUDY OR RESEARCH WORK

SPECIAL SKILLS

ACTIVITIES: (CIVIC, ATHLETIC, ETC.)
EXCLUDE ORGANIZATIONS, THE NAME OF WHICH INDICATES THE RACE, CREED, SEX, AGE, MARITAL STATUS, COLOR OR NATION OF ORIGIN OF ITS MEMBERS.

U.S. MILITARY OR NAVAL SERVICE RANK PRESENT MEMBERSHIP IN NATIONAL GUARD OR RESERVES

*The Age Discrimination in Employment Act of 1967 prohibits discrimination on the basis of age with respect to individuals who are at least 40 years of age.

TOPS FORM 3300 (05-91) (CONTINUED ON OTHER SIDE) LITHO IN U.S.A.

**FORMER EMPLOYERS** (LIST BELOW LAST THREE EMPLOYERS, STARTING WITH LAST ONE FIRST).

| DATE MONTH AND YEAR | NAME AND ADDRESS OF EMPLOYER | SALARY | POSITION | REASON FOR LEAVING |
|---|---|---|---|---|
| FROM<br>TO | | | | |
| FROM<br>TO | | | | |
| FROM<br>TO | | | | |
| FROM<br>TO | | | | |

WHICH OF THESE JOBS DID YOU LIKE BEST?

WHAT DID YOU LIKE MOST ABOUT THIS JOB?

**REFERENCES:** GIVE THE NAMES OF THREE PERSONS NOT RELATED TO YOU, WHOM YOU HAVE KNOWN AT LEAST ONE YEAR.

| | NAME | ADDRESS | BUSINESS | YEARS ACQUAINTED |
|---|---|---|---|---|
| 1 | | | | |
| 2 | | | | |
| 3 | | | | |

THE FOLLOWING STATEMENT APPLIES IN: MARYLAND & MASSACHUSETTS. (Fill in name of state)
IT IS UNLAWFUL IN THE STATE OF ______________ TO REQUIRE OR ADMINISTER A LIE DETECTOR TEST AS A CONDITION OF EMPLOYMENT OR CONTINUED EMPLOYMENT. AN EMPLOYER WHO VIOLATES THIS LAW SHALL BE SUBJECT TO CRIMINAL PENALTIES AND CIVIL LIABILITY.

Signature of Applicant

IN CASE OF EMERGENCY NOTIFY (NAME, ADDRESS, PHONE NO.)

"I CERTIFY THAT THE FACTS CONTAINED IN THIS APPLICATION ARE TRUE AND COMPLETE TO THE BEST OF MY KNOWLEDGE AND UNDERSTAND THAT, IF EMPLOYED, FALSIFIED STATEMENTS ON THIS APPLICATION SHALL BE GROUNDS FOR DISMISSAL.

I AUTHORIZE INVESTIGATION OF ALL STATEMENTS CONTAINED HEREIN AND THE REFERENCES LISTED ABOVE TO GIVE YOU ANY AND ALL INFORMATION CONCERNING MY PREVIOUS EMPLOYMENT AND ANY PERTINENT INFORMATION THEY MAY HAVE, AND RELEASE ALL PARTIES FROM ALL LIABILITY FOR ANY DAMAGE THAT MAY RESULT FROM FURNISHING SAME TO YOU.

I UNDERSTAND AND AGREE THAT, IF HIRED, MY EMPLOYMENT IS FOR NO DEFINITE PERIOD AND MAY, REGARDLESS OF THE DATE OF PAYMENT OF MY WAGES AND SALARY, BE TERMINATED AT ANY TIME WITHOUT PRIOR NOTICE AND WITHOUT CAUSE."

DATE SIGNATURE

DO NOT WRITE BELOW THIS LINE

INTERVIEWED BY DATE

REMARKS:

NEATNESS ABILITY

HIRED: ☐ Yes ☐ No POSITION DEPT.

SALARY/WAGE DATE REPORTING TO WORK

APPROVED: 1. EMPLOYMENT MANAGER 2. DEPT. HEAD 3. GENERAL MANAGER

This form has been designed to strictly comply with State and Federal fair employment practice laws prohibiting employment discrimination. This Application for Employment Form is sold for general use throughout the United States. TOPS assumes no responsibility for the inclusion in said form of any questions which, when asked by the Employer of the Job Applicant, may violate State and/or Federal Law.

Supervisors seldom participate actively in this process, but sometimes they know of a candidate that they would like to consider. In such cases, the name of this person is sent to the human resources department with the request that the person be included in the selection process. Rarely does the human resources department screen out a person that a supervisor wants included.

### *Interviewing Candidates*

When the human resources department has narrowed the list of candidates to a few people, the next step is to interview them. Objectives of interviewing include narrowing the search for an employee by assessing each candidate's interpersonal and communication skills, seeing whether the supervisor and employee are comfortable with one another, and learning details about the information the

Anthony Coppola, owner of DC Mechanical Corporation in Hauppauge, New York, believes his small business is able to attract and keep employees because it offers opportunity for professional growth. In keeping with this value, selection interviews at DC Mechanical emphasize planning career paths and identifying growth opportunities.

Source: © Wayne Sorce

candidate has provided on the application or résumé. In addition, each candidate has an opportunity to learn about the organization, which helps in the decision about accepting a job offer.

Learning and carrying out effective interviewing practices sometimes may seem like a lot of trouble to a supervisor. When tempted to look for shortcuts, a supervisor should bear in mind the significance of selection interviews. For any new employee, the organization will spend tens, maybe hundreds, of thousands of dollars on salary, benefits, and training. Thus, collecting the information needed for making the right hiring decision is at least as important as doing the research for making other investments of comparable size. Viewed in this light, carefully preparing for and conducting a selection interview is well worth the time and effort.

### Who Should Interview?

The initial interview with a job candidate frequently is conducted by someone in the human resources department. Depending on an organization's policies and practices, a supervisor may participate in later interviews. For this reason, a supervisor can benefit from understanding how to interview effectively.

An organization may support the use of teamwork by having teams (or several team members) interview job candidates. According to James H. Shonk, president of the Team Center in Ridgefield, Connecticut, team input into the selection process can contribute to lower turnover among team members.[3] Team interviews also provide evidence of how a candidate interacts with a team. At Gates Rubber's plant in Siloam Springs, Arkansas, a job candidate meets first with the personnel department, then with a group of three people from different parts of the plant. Plant manager Burt Hoefs explains, "We're evaluating communications skills, work attitudes, and general confidence levels. Since all the work of the plant is done in teams, we're also focusing on an applicant's ability to respond well in a group setting."[4] When interviews are conducted by teams, a supervisor needs to combine skills in interviewing with skills in facilitating group processes (see Chapters 3 and 9).

### Preparation for the Interview

To prepare for an interview, an interviewer should review the job description and develop a realistic way to describe the job to candidates. An interviewer also should review an applicant's résumé or job application, and consider whether the information given there suggests some specific questions to ask. Suppose the interviewer wants to know why a candidate chose a particular major in school or switched fields—say, leaving a job as a salesperson to become a mechanic. The interviewer also will want to inquire about any time gaps between jobs. Finally, the interviewer should arrange for an interview location that meets the conditions described in the next section.

### Interview Conditions

Most job candidates feel at least a little nervous. This can make it hard for an interviewer to tell what a person would be like on the job. Therefore, it is important for an interviewer to conduct the interview under conditions that put a candidate at ease. Good interview conditions include privacy and freedom from interruptions. Seating should be comfortable. Some interviewers sit next to the candidate at a small table, rather than behind a desk, to create a less formal, more equal setting. Candidates also can be put at ease by offering them a cup of coffee and taking a minute or two for comments on a general, noncontroversial topic such as the weather.

Privacy is sometimes difficult for a supervisor to arrange. Many supervisors do not have an office with a door to close. If possible, a supervisor should arrange to use a conference room or someone else's office. At the very least, a supervisor interviewing in a cubicle should hang a Do Not Disturb sign outside.

### Content of the Interview

After making the candidate comfortable, an interviewer should begin by asking general questions about the candidate's background and qualifications. An interviewer should also ask a candidate about his or her goals and expectations concerning the job. The following questions are among those most commonly asked:[5]

- Why do you want to work for our organization?
- What kind of career do you have planned?
- What have you learned in school to prepare for a career?
- What are some of the things you are looking for in an organization?
- How has your previous job experience prepared you for a career?
- What are your strengths? weaknesses?
- Why did you choose the school you attended?
- What do you consider to be your most worthwhile achievement?
- Are you a leader? Explain.
- How do you plan to continue developing yourself?
- Why did you select your major?
- What would you like to know about the organization?

## TIPS FROM THE FIRING LINE

### Interview Questions That Are Easy to Ask

Interviews can be just as stressful for supervisors as they are for job candidates. A supervisor may feel that he or she has to wade through a minefield of questions that are acceptable and unacceptable (even illegal). *Maintenance Management* offers eight standard questions that supervisors are "free to ask any applicant for any job," thus reducing interview stress. The editors emphasize, however, that if these questions are asked of one applicant, they must be asked of all applicants.

- *Do you understand what this job entails?* Discussing the job itself helps both interviewer and job candidate relax, and can lead to insights about a candidate's abilities, experience, and motivation.
- *Why do you think you are well suited for this job?* This question provides further insight into the applicant's perception of and qualifications for the job.
- *Can you describe any extracurricular activities that have provided you with experience that would help on the job?* Another opportunity for candidate and interviewer to relax; a candidate can talk about something that interests him or her deeply, providing further insight. For instance, a candidate might describe performing with a local theater group as evidence that he or she has no trouble speaking in front of groups.
- *Have you had any jobs like this before?* A chance for the candidate to shine.
- *What can you tell me about yourself that makes you think you would be good at this job?* A little

different from the question about being "well suited" for the job. A person might be good at a job, but not particularly suited to it, and vice versa.
- *From what I have told you about it, do you think you would like working at this company?* Few candidates would answer no, but if one gives you this honest answer, at least you can part honestly and amicably; or you can try to make adjustments to the working conditions to accommodate the candidate's wishes.
- *How do you feel about our hours of business?* Don't get into issues surrounding religious holidays. But if an applicant is unable to obtain transportation to work at the specified hours, he or she may want to apply elsewhere, look harder for transportation, or the company may make adjustments to accommodate him or her.
- *Do you have any other information about yourself that you think would help me make a decision regarding your candidacy?* This gives an applicant a final opportunity to make whatever positive points he or she feels have not already been covered.

Source: "Reduce *Your* Interview Stress," *Maintenance Management*, Bureau of Business Practice, July 10, 1995, p. 8. Copyrighted material reprinted with permission of Bureau of Business Practice, 24 Rope Ferry Road, Waterford, CT 06386.

When the interviewer has asked enough questions to gauge the candidate's suitability for the position, he or she should give the candidate a chance to ask questions. This not only can help the candidate learn more, but it can give the interviewer insight into the candidate's understanding and areas of concern. (See "Tips from the Firing Line" for more questions that not only provide insight, but also put both interviewer and candidate at ease.)

The interviewer should close the session by telling the candidate what to expect regarding the organization's decision about the job, such as a telephone call in a week or a letter by the end of the month. As soon as the candidate has left, the

### FIGURE 16.4

**The Interviewing Process**

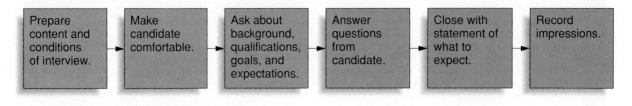

Prepare content and conditions of interview. → Make candidate comfortable. → Ask about background, qualifications, goals, and expectations. → Answer questions from candidate. → Close with statement of what to expect. → Record impressions.

interviewer should jot down notes of impressions about the candidate. Memories fade fast, especially when the interviewer meets many candidates. Figure 16.4 summarizes the steps in the interviewing process.

The questions an interviewer asks must be relevant to performance of the job. This means that an interviewer may not ask questions about the candidate's age, sex, race, marital status, children, religion, and arrest (as opposed to conviction) record. For example, an interviewer may not ask, "So, are you planning to have any children?" or "What nationality is that name?" Such questions violate antidiscrimination laws, described later in this chapter. Table 16.2 (on pages 482–483) identifies many permissible and impermissible questions. A supervisor who is in doubt about whether a particular question is allowable should check with the human resources department before asking it.

### Interviewing Techniques

The person who conducts the interview may choose to make it structured, unstructured, or a combination of the two. A **structured interview** is one based on questions an interviewer has prepared in advance. By referring to the list of questions, the interviewer covers the same material with each candidate. In an **unstructured interview,** an interviewer has no list of questions prepared in advance but thinks of questions based on an applicant's responses. An unstructured interview gives an interviewer more flexibility but makes it harder to be sure that each interview covers the same material.

A practical way to combine these two approaches is to prepare a list of questions that must be covered with each candidate. Then, an interviewer who wants the candidate to clarify a response to a particular question asks a follow-up question such as "Please tell me about your reasons for handling the problem that way." An interviewer need not ask the questions in the order written so long as all of them are covered eventually. Based on a candidate's comments, an interviewer may want to move to a question further down on the list. Even though the format varies somewhat from candidate to candidate, this approach ensures that an interviewer does not omit important topics from some interviews.

Within either a structured or an unstructured interview, an interviewer may ask questions that are open-ended or closed-ended. An **open-ended question** is

**structured interview**
An interview based on questions the interviewer has prepared in advance.

**unstructured interview**
An interview in which the interviewer has no list of questions prepared in advance but asks questions based on the applicant's responses.

**open-ended question**
A question that gives the person responding broad control over the response.

**closed-ended question**
A question that requires a simple answer, such as yes or no.

one that gives the person responding broad control over the response. A **closed-ended question** is one that requires a simple answer, such as yes or no. An example of an open-ended question is "What experiences in your past job will help you carry out this one?" Examples of closed-ended questions are "Did you use a Macintosh computer on your last job?" and "Which shift do you prefer to work?"

Open-ended questions tend to be more useful in interviewing, because they lead a candidate to provide more information. For example, to learn how thoroughly a candidate has researched the job—an indication of how serious he or she is about the position—an interviewer might ask, "What would you look for if you were hiring a person for this position?"[6] Loretta M. Flanagan, who directs Westside Future, an organization dedicated to reducing infant mortality, uses open-ended questions to learn about the human relations and problem-solving skills of job candidates. For example, she might pose this question to a candidate for a case worker position:

> A high, drug-using pregnant woman comes into the office, wanting immediate help. She has missed two previously scheduled appointments. The case manager is busy with another client and has a second client arriving in 20 minutes. How do you handle such competing demands?

Of course, there is no single correct answer. Flanagan looks for candidates who show an ability to set priorities and to justify the course of action selected.

Because the candidate decides how to answer an open-ended question, the answer sometimes is not clear enough or specific enough. Then, the interviewer will want to probe for more details, possibly saying, "Can you give me an example of that?" or "What do you mean when you say your last job was 'too stressful'?"

### Problems to Avoid

When conducting an interview, a supervisor needs to avoid some common errors in judgment. One of these is making decisions based on personal biases. For example, a supervisor may dislike earrings on men or certain modish hairstyles worn by women. However, these characteristics are unlikely to indicate how well a candidate would carry out a job. Likewise, being a friend or relative of a supervisor is not a good predictor of job performance. Making a hiring decision based on these and other biases can lead an interviewer to exclude the person who is best qualified.

**halo effect**
The practice of forming an overall opinion on the basis of one outstanding characteristic.

Another source of errors is the **halo effect,** which means forming an overall opinion on the basis of one outstanding characteristic. For example, many people will evaluate someone's personality on the basis of the person's handshake. "She has a firm grasp," an interviewer might think with regard to a candidate. "I can tell that she's energetic, decisive, and gets along well with people," when the candidate might not have any of those desirable traits. An interviewer needs to look for evidence of each trait, not just lump them all together.

In making judgments based on a handshake, an interviewer is drawing conclusions about personality based on the candidate's body language. A study by Robert Gifford of the University of Victoria suggests that this is a risky approach.[7] Gifford asked 18 experienced interviewers to watch videotapes of selection interviews and to rate the candidates on several traits. Gifford compared the experts' ratings with the results of written tests measuring the same traits. The experts were not

███ **TABLE 16.2**

## Permissible and Impermissible Questions for Selection Interviews

| Category | Interviewer May Ask | Interviewer May Not Ask |
|---|---|---|
| Name | Current legal name; whether candidate has ever worked under another name | Maiden name; whether candidate has ever changed his or her name; preferred courtesy title (e.g., Ms., Miss, Mrs.) |
| Address | Current residence; length of residence | Whether candidate owns or rents home, unless it is a bona fide occupational qualification (BFOQ) for the job; name and relationship of person with whom applicant resides |
| Age | Whether the candidate meets a minimum age requirement set by law (e.g., being 21 to serve alcoholic beverages) | Candidate's age; to see a birth certificate; how much longer candidate plans to work before retiring; dates of attending elementary or high school; how applicant feels about working for a younger (or older) boss |
| Sex | Candidate's sex if it is a BFOQ (e.g., a model or rest-room attendant) | Candidate's sex if it is not a BFOQ |
| Marital and family status | Whether the candidate can comply with the work schedule (must be asked of both sexes if at all) | Candidate's marital status; whether the candidate has or plans to have children; other family matters; information about child-care arrangements; questions about who handles household responsibilities; whether candidate is seeking work just to supplement the household income |
| National origin, citizenship, race, color | Whether the candidate is legally eligible to work in the United States; whether the candidate can prove this, if hired | Candidate's national origin, citizenship, race, or color (or that of relatives); how candidate feels about working with or for people of other races |
| Language | List of languages the candidate speaks or writes fluently; whether the candidate speaks or writes a specific language if it is a BFOQ | Language the candidate speaks off the job; how the candidate learned a language |

always on target. For example, they considered an applicant to be highly motivated if he or she smiled, gestured, and talked a lot. However, the written tests did not support a link between this kind of behavior and motivation.

A supervisor also needs to avoid giving candidates a misleading picture of the organization. If a candidate seems desirable, it can be tempting to describe the organization in glowing terms so that the candidate will want to work there. But if the reality is not so wonderful, the new employee is bound to be disappointed and angry. He or she may even quit. On the other hand, within the bounds of realism, a supervisor should give a good impression of the organization and its people. Even a candidate who is not the best person for the job may someday be a customer or be in a position to influence other people's views about the organization.

| Category | Interviewer May Ask | Interviewer May Not Ask |
|---|---|---|
| Arrests and convictions | Whether the candidate has been convicted of a felony; other information if the felony is job related | Whether the candidate has ever been arrested; information about a conviction that is not job related |
| Height and weight | No questions | Candidate's height or weight |
| Health history and disabilities | Whether the candidate is able to perform the essential functions of the job; how (with or without accommodation) the candidate can perform essential job functions | Whether the candidate is disabled or handicapped; how candidate became disabled; health history; whether the candidate smokes; whether the candidate has AIDS or is HIV positive |
| Religion | Whether the candidate is a member of a specific religious group when it is a BFOQ; whether the candidate can comply with the work schedules | Religious preference, affiliations, or denomination; name of applicant's priest, pastor, rabbi, or other religious leader |
| Personal finances | Credit rating if it is a BFOQ | Candidate's credit rating; other information about personal finances, including assets, charge accounts; whether candidate owns a car |
| Education and work experience | Job-related education and experience | Education and experience that are not job related |
| References | Names of people willing to provide references; names of people who suggested that the candidate apply for the job | Reference from a religious leader |
| Military service | Information about job-related education and experience; whether candidate was dishonorably discharged | Dates and conditions of discharge; eligibility for military service; experience in foreign armed services |
| Organizations | List of memberships in job-related organizations such as unions or professional or trade associations | Memberships in any organizations that are not job related and would indicate race, religion, or other protected group; candidate's political affiliation |

Sources: Richard D. Irwin, Inc., "Management Guidelines," Appendix 2, Dec. 1, 1991; Robert N. Lussier, *Supervision: A Skill-Building Approach* (Homewood, IL: Irwin, 1989), pp. 254–55; and Janine S. Pouliot, "Topics to Avoid with Applicants," *Nation's Business*, July 1992, pp. 57–58.

## Administering Employment Tests

From a résumé or employment application, it is relatively easy to see where a candidate worked and went to school, but how can you tell whether a candidate really has the skills to do the job? Just because Pete Wong works for the marketing division at a candy company does not mean he knows how to sell candy (maybe that is why he wants to leave). Just because Ruth Petersen got a college degree in engineering does not mean she can apply her knowledge to working with a team to prepare the layout of an actual plant.

Giftware maker Will Knecht (*left*), vice president of Wendell August Forge, uses personality testing developed by Management Development Group, Inc., of Cleveland as a tool in hiring, promoting, training, and other personnel decisions. The personality test measures 86 worker attributes such as patience, independence, and exactitude.

Source: © Scott Goldsmith

One way to see whether employees have the necessary skills is to administer an employment test. A variety of employment tests are available:

**aptitude test**
A test that measures a person's ability to learn skills related to the job.

- Tests that measure an applicant's ability to learn skills related to the job are known as **aptitude tests.**
- An applicant may take a **proficiency test** to see whether he or she has the skills needed to perform a job. An example is a word-processing test for a secretarial position.

**proficiency test**
A test that measures whether the person has the skills needed to perform a job.

- For jobs that require physical skills, such as assembling, an applicant may take a **psychomotor test,** which measures a person's strength, dexterity, and coordination.
- Sometimes organizations also use personality tests, which identify various personality traits. Psychologist Martin Seligman maintains that optimism is associated with successful performance of sales jobs. He tested his theory at MetLife by conducting an experiment in which the hiring of one group of salespeople was based on traditional measures, while that of another group was based on their high scores on a test measuring optimism. According to Seligman, the optimists outperformed not only the control group but also MetLife's entire sales force.[8] Similarly, someone who focuses on the big picture instead of on details might excel in many jobs but probably is not suited to keeping track of a large inventory.[9]

**psychomotor test**
A test that measures a person's strength, dexterity, and coordination.

- Finally, some organizations test for drug use, especially where the use of drugs by employees poses a serious safety risk, as in the case of machine operators or pilots. Such tests are controversial, but they are legal in most states.[10]

Usually the human resources department handles the testing of applicants.

Some tests contain language or other biases that make them easier for employees of one ethnic group than another. Using these tests could violate antidiscrimination laws, described later in this chapter. If a supervisor wants to use employment tests, the tests should be reviewed by the human resources department or an outside expert to ensure that they are not discriminatory.

Despite these restrictions, employers can be creative in devising employment tests. At Flash Creative Management, an information technology company, owner David Blumenthal instructs each job candidate to "check the company's references" by calling a list of customers and asking them what type of company Flash is. He then asks the companies to indicate their impression of the candidate—whether the person asked intelligent questions, whether the customer would like working with the candidate, and so on. Blumenthal believes this source of information is critical because each of Flash's employees has direct contact with clients. In addition, the process tests a candidate's willingness and ability to follow through with the assignment. An added benefit is that the practice communicates to a candidate the strength of Flash's commitment to customer service; a candidate who isn't interested in working for such a company can opt out during the selection process.[11]

## Conducting Background and Reference Checks

According to Carl King, president of Team Building Systems of Houston, Texas, 30 percent of all résumés contain false information.[12] A basic way to verify that the information on a job application or résumé is correct is to check references. Not only can checking an employee's background save the organization from hiring an unqualified person, but it can protect the organization from lawsuits. The courts have held employers responsible for crimes committed by an employee whose background at the time of hire was not investigated reasonably, so that the organization hired someone with a history of misdeeds for a position where he or she could do harm.[13]

A supervisor or a member of the human resources department may call or write to schools and former employers, or the organization may pay an employee screening company to do a background check. The $100 or so per candidate that it costs to use one of these companies can be money well spent by an organization that is too small for a human resources staff.[14]

Applicants may give several kinds of references:

- Personal references—people who will vouch for the applicant's character.
- Academic references—teachers or professors who can describe the applicant's performance in school.
- Employment references—former employers who can verify the applicant's work history.

Most people can think of a friend or teacher who can say something nice about them, so the main use of personal and academic references is to screen out the few cases of people who cannot do so.

Previous employers are in the best position to discuss how an applicant has performed in the past. However, to avoid lawsuits from former employees, many organizations have a policy of giving out very little information about past employees. Often a background check will yield only that the applicant did in fact hold the stated position during the dates indicated. Some employers may be willing to discuss the applicant's performance, salary, promotions, and demotions. Because previous employers are cautious about what they disclose, a telephone call to a former supervisor may be more fruitful than a written request for information. People are often willing to make statements over the telephone that they will not commit to writing.

By conducting over-the-phone initial screenings that utilize role playing, managers at Ace Personnel in Overland Park, Kansas, have increased efficiency by hiring about 75 percent of applicants who interview well. After presenting a short history of Ace, candidates are asked how they would contribute to the company's growth and what makes them best for the job. By using a phone interview, "We catch them off guard. We see who can perform under pressure," says Ace owner Shane Jones. Ace gives points for poise and imagination and subtracts points for timidity, canned answers, or a "sense of entitlement."

Source: © 1996, Comstock, Inc.

## Making the Selection Decision

The final decision of whom to hire is usually up to the supervisor. Typically, more than one person will survive all the preceding steps of the screening process. As a result, the final decision is usually a judgment call. Jill Strode, the communications supervisor discussed at the beginning of this chapter, once resolved such a dilemma by paying each of two candidates to work for one day (on separate days). Observing them on the job made the selection easier.

Like Jill Strode, a supervisor can handle the dilemma of several well-qualified people being considered for a position by looking for additional relevant selection criteria. In practice, skillful hiring decisions often reflect a variety of issues, from how the decision will be perceived by higher-level managers to how comfortable a supervisor feels with the candidate.[15] Supervisors sometimes choose an employee like themselves, so they will feel comfortable; they also might select a person whose strengths differ from and thus balance their own strengths. A supervisor can improve his or her selections by applying the principles of effective decision making covered in Chapter 9.

When a supervisor has selected the candidate to hire, the human resources department or supervisor offers the job to the candidate. The person who offers the job is responsible for negotiating pay and fringe benefits and for settling on a starting date. If none of the candidates a supervisor has identified seem satisfactory, no candidate has to be picked and the recruiting process can be repeated. Perhaps the organization can look in new places or try to attract better candidates by offering more money.

## Requesting a Physical Examination

In the past, many organizations have required that job candidates pass a physical examination. However, since Congress passed the Americans with Disabilities Act (described later in this chapter), experts have advised that employers request a physical exam only after a job offer is made.[16] A physical examination after the job offer helps the organization determine whether the person physically is able to fulfill job requirements, yet the timing of the exam reduces the risk that someone will sue the company for refusing to hire him or her because of a disability. Another use of the physical exam is to determine whether the person is eligible for any life, health, and disability insurance that the company offers as benefits.

An illness, disability, or pregnancy may not be used as the basis for denying a person a job unless it makes the person unable to perform the essential functions of the job. If a physical examination suggests a condition that may interfere with the person's ability to perform these essential functions, the company—very likely someone in the human resources department—should ask the candidate how it can adapt the equipment or job to accommodate that person. Because of these limitations on the use of information from physical examinations, most organizations will want the human resources department to handle the exams and the issue of how to accommodate employees with disabilities. A supervisor can then focus on a candidate's experience and talents.

# Legal Issues

Congress has passed laws that restrict employment decisions. Most of these laws are designed to give people fair and equal access to jobs based on their skills, not on their personal traits such as race or physical disabilities. Whatever a supervisor's role in selecting employees, he or she must be aware of the laws affecting hiring in order to help ensure that the organization's actions are legal.

## Antidiscrimination Laws

Certain federal laws prohibit various types of employment discrimination.

**Equal Employment Opportunity Commission (EEOC)**
The federal government agency charged with enforcing Title VII of the Civil Rights Act.

- Under Title VII of the Civil Rights Act of 1964 (commonly known as Title VII), employers may not discriminate on the basis of race, color, religion, sex, or national origin in recruiting, hiring, paying, firing, or laying off employees, or in any other employment practices. The government agency charged with enforcing this law is the **Equal Employment Opportunity Commission (EEOC).** The EEOC investigates charges of discrimination and may pursue a remedy in court or arrange for mediation (which means an impartial third party hears both sides and decides how to resolve the dispute).
- The Age Discrimination in Employment Act of 1967, as amended in 1978 and 1986, prohibits employers from discriminating on the basis of age against people over 40 years old.
- The Rehabilitation Act of 1973 makes it illegal to refuse a job to a disabled person because of the disability, if the disability does not interfere with the person's ability to do the job.
- The Pregnancy Discrimination Act of 1978 makes it unlawful to discriminate on the basis of pregnancy, childbirth, or related medical conditions.
- Disabled veterans and veterans of the Vietnam War receive protection under the Vietnam Era Veterans Readjustment Act of 1974, which requires federal contractors to make special efforts to recruit these people. (This is a type of affirmative action, described shortly.) In deciding whether a veteran is qualified, an employer may consider the military record only to the extent it is directly related to the specific qualifications of the job.

**FIGURE 16.5**

Categories of
Workers
Protected by
Antidiscrimination
Laws

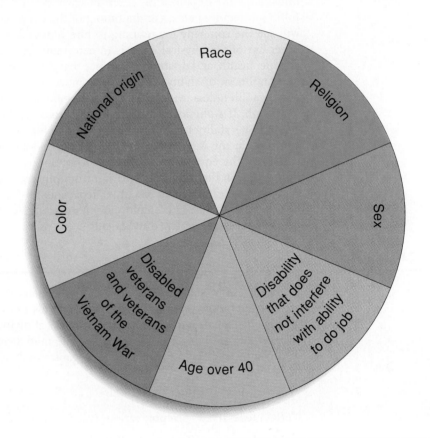

Figure 16.5 illustrates the categories of workers protected by the antidiscrimination laws.

Although some people criticize these laws as a burden on employers, bear in mind that organizations should benefit from making employment decisions on the basis of people's knowledge, skills, and abilities instead of incidental personal traits such as race, age, or sex.

As the managers of many organizations have observed the growing diversity of the workforce and their customers, they have decided that simply avoiding discrimination is too limited a policy. They have adopted policies called "managing diversity." A report by the Society of Human Resource Managers and Commerce Clearing House defined managing diversity as "the management of an organization's culture and systems to ensure that all people are given the opportunity to contribute to the business goals of the company."[17] At an organization that effectively manages diversity, managers and employees create a climate in which all employees feel respected and able to participate.

Managing diversity implies that the organization is hiring and promoting a variety of people. For this and other purposes, many organizations have established

**affirmative action**
Plans designed to increase opportunities for groups that traditionally have been discriminated against.

affirmative action programs. **Affirmative action** refers to plans designed to increase opportunities for groups that traditionally have been discriminated against. In effect, these plans are an active attempt to promote diversity in the organization, not just to treat everyone the same way.

Kansas City Power & Light (KCPL) and Penn Valley Community College developed a program designed to give women and minorities a chance to learn the lineworker's trade. The program includes academic classes in relevant technologies coupled with hands-on experience, including climbing 45-foot utility poles. KCPL has committed to hiring 14 of the program's graduates each year; the other graduates are well qualified for jobs at other utilities. KCPL benefits from having a pool of well-qualified potential employees, while women and minorities gain access to well-paying jobs.[18]

Some people mistakenly think that affirmative action means setting up artificial quotas that favor some groups at the expense of others. However, as the preceding example shows, organizations can increase opportunities in other ways. Besides using training to create a pool of qualified applicants, some companies make a point of doing some of their recruiting at schools where many students are members of racial minorities.

People who favor affirmative action policies argue that because several candidates often have the qualifications to fill any given job, intentionally giving some jobs to people from disadvantaged groups is not only ethical but supports the achievement of the benefits related to diversity. Whatever your opinion of affirmative action, it is important to note that—except for employers that have federal contracts or subcontracts—organizations are not required by law to set up these programs. Rather, affirmative action programs are one possible response to laws against discrimination.

## Workplace Accessibility

In 1990 Congress passed the Americans with Disabilities Act (ADA), which prohibits employers with more than 15 employees from discriminating on the basis of mental or physical disability in hiring and promotion. A person who can perform the essential functions of a job may not be prevented from doing so simply because the person has a mental or physical disability. Table 16.3 summarizes criteria for disability status under the ADA. Organizations also must avoid discrimination in public accommodations, transportation, government services, and telecommunications.

One benefit to organizations that comply with the ADA is that it encourages employers to take advantage of a large pool of potential workers whose talents are often ignored. Larry Gorski, director of the City of Chicago Office for People with Disabilities, estimates that 67 percent of the nation's 43 million disabled people are unemployed.[19] Hiring a disabled person has proved worthwhile for Dow Corning, which more than 25 years ago hired George Gant, who has multiple sclerosis. To enable him to work at Dow, the company installed ramps, made bathrooms accessible, and provided parking. Gant, in turn, has blessed the company by developing many chemical patents, training other employees, and establishing processes to improve the commercialization of Dow's products and services.[20]

**TABLE 16.3**

**Disability Status under the Americans with Disabilities Act**

| "Disability" Includes | "Disability" Does Not Include |
| --- | --- |
| Substantial limitation preventing a person from conducting a major life activity | Cultural and economic disadvantages |
| Physical and mental impairments | Common personality traits, such as impatience |
| History of using drugs as the result of an addiction | Pregnancy |
| Severe obesity (weight in excess of 100 percent of the norm or that arises from a medical disorder) | Normal deviations in weight, height, or strength |
| | Temporary or short-term problems |
| | Illegal drug users disciplined for current abuse |
| | Illegal drug use that is casual (not related to addiction) |

Note: People with disabilities are protected from employment discrimination only to the extent that their disability does not prevent them from performing the essential functions of the job.

Source: Based on "What Constitutes a Disability?" *Nation's Business*, June 1995, p. 39. Summary of EEOC guidelines released in March 1995.

### *Accommodations for Employees with Disabilities*

To comply with the ADA, employers must make accommodations for employees with disabilities if the necessary accommodations are "readily achievable"—that is, easy to carry out and possible to accomplish without much difficulty or expense. Businesses may receive a tax credit of up to $15,000 to help offset the cost of making their establishments accessible.

This law extends beyond wheelchair accessibility to require accommodations for any eligible disabled employee. This means accommodating a variety of disabilities, including impaired sight and hearing. Among people outside of institutions, the four most common disabilities are arthritis, high blood pressure, hearing impairment, and heart disease.[21] Thus, accommodations might include door handles that are easy to manipulate and TDD telephones for hearing-impaired employees. For employees with mental disabilities, appropriate accommodations may include the following measures:[22]

- Modifications to work areas to permit maximum concentration and minimum distraction.
- Flexible schedules to counteract fatigue (e.g., longer and more frequent rest breaks).
- Time off to receive treatment for their disability.

In addition, organizations can head off many problems related to mental disabilities by making extra coaching and counseling available to employees as needed.

A number of ways to accommodate disabled workers draws on computer technology. Julie Wilkinson, a computer analyst with American National Bank, is blind. Using a computer that has a Braille display and allows her to give voice commands, Wilkinson can read her mail and print out documents. She can take notes on a portable Braille unit that can later enter the information into the computer. Other computer systems have been designed for a Colorado accountant who can only move one eyebrow, an Allstate computer worker who has no use of his hands and legs, and a meteorologist who has cerebral palsy and operates the system with his toe.[23]

### What Supervisors Can Do

Supervisors can take several steps to comply with the ADA. One is to review and revise job descriptions.[24] Because an organization cannot discriminate against those who can perform the essential functions of the job, each job description should indicate what is essential. It should focus on the results the employee must achieve instead of the process for achieving those results. For example, a job description for a telephone lineworker might say "Repair telephone lines located at the top of a pole" but not "Climb telephone poles."[25] In addition, supervisors should make sure that production standards are reasonable; current employees should meet those standards.

When interviewing candidates, a supervisor should be careful not to ask whether they have a physical or mental condition that would prevent them from performing the job. Rather, after making a job offer, the organization will seek to accommodate any impairments the person may have. Similarly, the supervisor should not ask for candidates' health history, including any on-the-job injuries that candidates have suffered.

## Immigration Reform and Control Act

By passing the Immigration Reform and Control Act (IRCA) of 1986, Congress gave employers responsibility for helping to discourage illegal immigration. IRCA forbids employers from hiring illegal immigrants and requires them to screen candidates to make sure that they are authorized to work in the United States. At the same time, however, employers may not use these requirements as a rationale for discriminating against candidates because they look or sound "foreign."

This means that the employer must verify the identity and work authorization of *every* new employee. To do this, the employer can ask each new employee to show such documentation as a valid U.S. passport, unexpired Immigration Authorization Service document, unexpired work permit, birth certificate, driver's license, or social security card.[27] In large organizations, this law primarily affects the human resources department, giving it an extra task in the hiring process. In small organizations, however, a supervisor may be responsible for verifying that all his or her new employees are authorized to work in the United States.

# Summary

### 16.1  Discuss common roles for supervisors in the selection process.

In most cases, a supervisor works with a human resources department in the selection process. If the organization depends on teams, a supervisor might try to identify candidates who are cooperative and skilled in problem solving or who have helped a team achieve good results in the past. If a team is making the selection, the supervisor as team leader needs to understand the principles of selection so that he or she can coach employees in carrying out the selection process. A supervisor also prepares job descriptions and job specifications, consulting with the human resources department as needed.

### 16.2  Distinguish between job descriptions and job specifications, and explain how they help in selecting employees.

A job description is a listing of the characteristics of the job—observable activities required to carry out the job. A job specification is a listing of characteristics desirable in the person performing the job. The two forms help show how well each candidate matches the job requirements.

### 16.3  List possible sources of employees.

An organization may recruit inside and outside the organization. Current employees may be promoted or transferred to fill job openings, or they may recommend people for jobs at the organization. Outside the organization, employees can be recruited through help-wanted advertisements, employment agencies, and schools.

### 16.4  Identify the steps in the selection process.

Based on employment applications or résumés, the staff of the human resources department screens out unqualified candidates. Next, the human resources department or the supervisor interviews candidates. An organization may administer employment tests. Background and reference checks are conducted on candidates in whom the organization is still interested. A supervisor makes a selection decision, after which a candidate may be asked to take a physical examination.

### 16.5  Discuss how a supervisor should go about interviewing candidates for a job.

First, a supervisor should prepare for the interview by reviewing the job description and each applicant's résumé or job application, planning questions, and arranging for a place to conduct the interview that offers privacy and freedom from interruptions. When a candidate arrives, a supervisor should make him or her comfortable and then ask about the candidate's goals and expectations for the job. Questions must be relevant to performance of the job and should include both open-ended and closed-ended questions. The interviewer should avoid making common errors in judgment, such as personal biases, or offering misleading information about the organization. Then a candidate should have a chance to ask questions. A supervisor should close the interview by telling a candidate what to expect. As soon as the candidate leaves, the supervisor should make notes of his or her impressions.

### 16.6  Define types of employment tests.

Aptitude tests measure a person's ability to learn job-related skills. Proficiency tests measure whether a person has the skills needed to perform a job. Psychomotor tests measure strength, dexterity, and coordination. Personality tests identify personality traits. Some organizations also test for drug use. Physical examinations may be required after a job offer is made.

### 16.7  Summarize the requirements of antidiscrimination laws.

The organization, including the supervisor, must avoid actions that discriminate on the basis of race, color, religion, sex, national origin, age over 40 years, or physical or mental disability, including pregnancy-related disabilities. These laws apply to recruiting, hiring, paying, firing, and laying off employees and to any other employment practice. In addition, federal contractors and subcontractors must use affirmative action to encourage the employment of minorities and veterans of the Vietnam War. When evaluating veterans' qualifications, an employer may use only the portions of the military record that are related to job requirements.

**16.8 Explain how hiring decisions are affected by the Americans with Disabilities Act (ADA).**

The ADA prohibits discrimination on the basis of mental or physical disability against people who can perform the essential functions of a job. Instead, employers must make accommodations for employees with disabilities if the necessary accommodations are readily achievable. To comply with the law, supervisors should review and revise job descriptions to make sure they indicate what functions of the job are essential. When interviewing candidates, a supervisor should avoid asking about disabilities and a candidate's health history.

**16.9 Describe the requirements of the Immigration Reform and Control Act (IRCA) of 1986.**

Under IRCA, employers are responsible for helping to discourage illegal immigration. They may not hire people who are not authorized to work in the United States, yet they may not discriminate against people who simply appear to be foreigners. Thus, employers must verify the identity and work authorization of every new employee.

## Key Terms

| | | |
|---|---|---|
| job description | unstructured interview | proficiency test |
| job specification | open-ended question | psychomotor test |
| recruitment | closed-ended question | Equal Employment Opportunity Commission (EEOC) |
| structured interview | halo effect | affirmative action |
| | aptitude test | |

## Review and Discussion Questions

1. Think of your current job or a job you recently held. Write a job description and a job specification for the job. How well do (or did) you match the requirements of the job?
2. A business executive said that people tend to make the mistake of hiring in their own image. What does this mean? How does this tendency make it more difficult for an organization to build a diverse workforce?
3. In recruiting for each of the following positions, what source(s) of candidates would you recommend using? Explain your choices.

    a. A receptionist for a city government office.
    b. A printing press operator.
    c. A graphic artist for an advertising agency.
    d. A nurse for an adult day care facility.

4. Describe what happens during the screening process. What does the human resources department look for when reading employment applications and résumés?

5. Supervisor Lisa Kitzinger is interviewing candidates for a computer operator job. Lisa works in a cubicle, and she has a secretary who could help during the interview process. What can Lisa do to put candidates at ease?
6. Which of the following questions is (are) appropriate for a job interview for the position of office manager for an automobile dealership?

    a. "Do you attend church regularly?"
    b. "Do you know how to use our computer and telecommunications systems?"
    c. "Are you familiar with our line of cars?"
    d. "Are you married?"
    e. "Aren't you close to retirement age?"
    f. "What skills did you develop at your previous job that you feel would be helpful in this job?"

7. How can an interviewer combine the techniques of the structured and unstructured interview?

8. Donald Menck, the foreman on a boatbuilding line, interviews a male job candidate who comes to the interview dressed in a jacket and tie. Menck is surprised by the candidate's clothing, which is more formal than what is needed on the job; he is also impressed. He assumes that the candidate is intelligent and motivated. What common error in judgment is Menck making? What steps should he take during the interview to overcome it?

9. An airline has a policy that all its employees must receive a physical examination before they start working for the company. At what point in the selection process should the company request the examination? How may the airline use this information?

10. Which of the following actions would be considered discriminatory under federal laws? Explain your answers.

   a. A company creates a policy that all employees must retire by age 65.
   b. A supervisor gives the biggest raises to men, because they have families to support.
   c. A company that recruits at colleges and universities makes at least 20 percent of its visits to schools that are historically black.
   d. In a department where employees must do a lot of overtime work on Saturdays, a supervisor avoids hiring Jews because Saturday is their day of rest and worship.

11. Joel Trueheart supervises customer service representatives for a toy company. The employees handle complaints and questions from customers calling the company's toll-free telephone number. To fill a vacancy in the department, Joel has reviewed many résumés and is in the process of interviewing a few candidates. One of the most impressive résumés is that of Sophia Ahmad, but when Joel meets her, he is startled to observe that she is wearing dark glasses and carrying a white cane. What should Joel do to make sure he is complying with the Americans with Disabilities Act?

12. What steps must employers take to ensure that they are complying with the Immigration Reform and Control Act?

## A SECOND LOOK

Jill Strode, whose story began the chapter, made a final employee selection after observing two candidates work in the office for a day. What kinds of information could she gather from this observation? Can you suggest any ways to gather the same or similar kinds of information during a selection interview?

# APPLICATIONS MODULE

## CASE

### *In Search of Skilled Laborers*

During the recent years of recession and unemployment, it might seem amazing that manufacturing companies had trouble finding skilled workers to fill entry-level jobs. The number of entry-level jobs for skilled laborers has not exactly skyrocketed, but the desire to do such work has fallen. People entering today's job market are less interested than past generations in holding jobs as laborers and craftspeople.

For example, Ingersoll Milling Machine Company's personnel director, Brian Howard, thought it would be easy to fill blue-collar jobs with candidates who lived near the company's location in Rockford, Illinois. But he was disappointed with the kinds of candidates who applied. In desperation, Howard traveled to northern Wisconsin to find qualified candidates at a two-year technical school in Chippewa Falls.

Part of the difficulty is that today's manufacturing jobs often require more skills than in the past. Formerly, a blue-collar worker would punch the clock and then operate a single machine all day long. Today, however, workers are expected to participate in problem-solving meetings, to suggest improvements, and to handle a variety of tasks as part of a team. Consequently, "we hire people for their heads as well as their hands and arms," says Don Rice, vice-president of human resources for Torrington Company, a manufacturer of bearings.

Other companies are broadening the search. Some are establishing apprenticeships to train people in machining, welding, and other trades. Some are visiting high schools and even grade schools to talk about the advantages of a career in manufacturing. These recruiting efforts sometimes prove disappointing. Ron Bullock, the president of Bison Gear & Engineering Corporation, visited a career night for manufacturers at a high school in Downers Grove, Illinois. The total turnout of students was two boys.

1. What sources of job candidates are mentioned in this case? What other sources might these companies use?
2. In the past, when manufacturing jobs were relatively simple and routine, what kinds of characteristics would you, as a supervisor, look for in a job candidate?
3. How would your requirements be different today at a company such as Torrington, which expects employees to participate in decision making?

Source: Michael Arndt, "Wanted: Skilled Labor; Will Educate," *Chicago Tribune*, Apr. 26, 1992, sec. 7, pp. 1, 5.

**SELF-QUIZ**

## *What Kinds of Questions Are Appropriate for an Interviewer to Ask?*

Mark yes or no on the line before each of the following to indicate whether you believe it is an appropriate question to ask a job candidate.

_____  1. "What nationality is your last name?"

_____  2. "Can you provide documentation of your eligibility to work in the United States if you are hired for this job?"

_____  3. "Do you have any health problems?"

_____  4. "What language do you speak at home?"

_____  5. "This job requires extensive travel to Spain. Do you speak Spanish?"

_____  6. "Would you show me a picture of your children?"

_____  7. "Why did you apply for this job?"

_____  8. "Do you plan to retire in a few years?"

_____  9. "What are your career goals?"

_____  10. "Are our hours of business suitable to you?"

_____  11. "Are you married?"

_____  12. "Do you mind working for someone who is younger than you are?"

Scoring: Questions 2, 5, 7, 9, and 10 are appropriate interview questions. The others are not.

## Class Exercise

This chapter ("Selecting Employees") covered the steps involved in making sound employee selection decisions. Finding employees who have the necessary skills to meet today's workplace challenges is not an easy task. Most organizations are facing similar challenges: adapting to technological changes, improving quality, dealing with workforce diversity, reorganizing work around teams, and empowering employees at all levels to improve customer service. This exercise focuses on the skills employers are looking for in today's job candidates, and it provides practice in developing interview questions that will help you in your evaluation of prospective employees.

### Instructions:
1. Study Table 1.
2. Match the letter of each specific skill from Table 1 with the appropriate descriptor in Table 2. (Each answer will be used only once. The first two have been done for you.)
3. In the space in Table 2 after each descriptor, write an interview question to ask job candidates that will give you insight into their abilities in each area; assume you are interviewing job candidates to fill a job as bank teller. (The first two are already filled in, to give you an idea of some sample questions.)

---

**TABLE 1: Sixteen Job Skills Crucial to Success**

| Category of Skill | Specific Skills in Each Category |
|---|---|
| **Foundation** | *a* Knowing how to learn |
| **Competence** | *b* Reading |
| | *c* Writing |
| | *d* Computation |
| **Communication** | *e* Listening |
| | *f* Oral communication |
| **Adaptability** | *g* Creative thinking |
| | *h* Problem solving |
| **Personal management** | *i* Self-esteem |
| | *j* Goal setting and motivation |
| | *k* Personal/career development |
| **Group effectiveness** | *l* Interpersonal skills |
| | *m* Negotiation |
| | *n* Teamwork |
| **Influence** | *o* Organizational effectiveness |
| | *p* Leadership |

Source: Adapted from Anthony P. Carnevale, *America and the New Economy* (San Francisco: Jossey-Bass, 1991), pp. 165–82.

### ▌ TABLE 2 : Descriptors of Specific Skills

| Answer | Descriptor and Interview Question |
|:---:|:---|
| i | 1.  Employers want employees who have pride in themselves and their potential to be successful.<br>*Question: Can you describe a task or project you completed in your last job that you were particularly proud of?* |
| h | 2.  Employers want employees who can think on their feet when faced with a dilemma.<br>*Question: If you had a customer return to your teller window and claim, in a rather loud and irritated voice, that you had made a mistake, how would you handle the situation?* |
|  | 3.  Employers want employees who can assume responsibility and motivate co-workers when necessary.<br>*Question:* |
|  | 4.  Employers want employees who will hear the key points that make up a customer's concerns.<br>*Question:* |
|  | 5.  Employers want employees who can learn the particular skills of an available job.<br>*Question:* |
|  | 6.  Employers want employees who can resolve conflicts to the satisfaction of those involved.<br>*Question:* |

| **Answer** | **Descriptor and Interview Question** |
|---|---|
| | 7.  Employers want employees who have some sense of the skills needed to perform well in their current jobs and who are working to develop skills to qualify themselves for other jobs.<br>*Question:* |
| | 8.  Employers want employees with good mathematics skills.<br>*Question:* |
| | 9.  Employers want employees who can work with others to achieve a goal.<br>*Question:* |
| | 10.  Employers want employees who can convey an adequate response when responding to a customer's concerns.<br>*Question:* |
| | 11.  Employers want employees who have some sense of where the organization is headed and what they must do to make a contribution.<br>*Question:* |
| | 12.  Employers want employees who can come up with innovative solutions when needed.<br>*Question:* |
| | 13.  Employers want employees who can clearly and succinctly articulate ideas in writing.<br>*Question:* |

| Answer | Descriptor and Interview Question |
|---|---|
| | 14.  Employers want employees who know how to get things done and have the desire to complete tasks. *Question:* |
| | 15.  Employers want employees who can get along with customers, suppliers, and co-workers. *Question:* |
| | 16.  Employers want employees to be analytical, to summarize information, and to monitor their own comprehension of the reading task. *Question:* |

The Class Exercise was prepared by Corinne Livesay, Belhaven College, Jackson, Mississippi.

## *Team-Building Exercise*

## Role-Playing the Selection Process

This exercise simulates an abbreviated version of the selection process. Imagine that the manager of a family-style restaurant such as Denny's needs to hire a server. Working together, the class develops a job description and job specification. The instructor records them on the chalkboard or overhead projector. When in doubt about the details, class members should use their imaginations. The objective is for the class to agree that these two lists are reasonable and complete.

When the job description and job specification are complete, the class develops a list of interview questions that would indicate whether a candidate is appropriate for this job. Besides creating questions to ask, the class also might consider other ways to determine this information during an interview (e.g., observing some aspects of the candidates' behavior).

Next, four class members take on the following parts for a role play:

1.  Restaurant manager.
2.  Candidate 1: a college student with eagerness but no restaurant experience.
3.  Candidate 2: a woman who appears to be about 60 years old and has eight years' experience as a server during the 1950s.
4.  Candidate 3: a man with four years' experience as a server in five different restaurants.

The class members taking these roles should feel free to add details to these descriptions of "themselves." The person acting as the restaurant manager interviews each candidate for no more than five minutes each. (A real interview would probably last much longer.)

The role-playing interviews could be videotaped and then played back during the discussion.

Finally, the class discusses one or both of these topics:

1. *Selecting a candidate:* By a show of hands, the class votes for which candidate they would recommend hiring. What are your reasons for choosing that particular candidate?

2. *Interviewing techniques:*

   - Did the restaurant manager interview objectively, based on the criteria determined at the beginning of the exercise?
   - Did the interview cover all the important points?

- Did the manager use open-ended or closed-ended questions?
- How did the manager's style of questioning help or hurt the information-gathering process?
- Did the candidates have a chance to ask questions?
- Did the manager obey the antidiscrimination laws?
- How did the interviewing experience feel to the candidates? to the manager?

# Video Exercise 16: *Selecting Employees*

### *Video Summary*

This video program features Nucor Steel, the fastest growing and most profitable steel company in the world. Nucor's success is based on a philosophy of teamwork and a very lucrative incentive compensation program. The task of finding technically qualified people who can work well with teams and within this unusual compensation plan is a challenge for Nucor's managers and supervisors.

### *Application*

Based on what you have just learned from the video program about Nucor Steel and its hiring process, assume that you are a supervisor who is scheduled to interview job candidates for an opening in your department. From the following entry-level interview skeleton, place a check mark in the box next to the questions that you think would be most important to ask the candidates. Be prepared to explain the reasons for your opinions.

## Entry-Level Interview Skeleton

### *Educational Background*

- ❏ What school year was most difficult, and why?
- ❏ What changes would you make in your school?
- ❏ What are your plans for further education?
- ❏ What extracurricular activities did you enjoy?
- ❏ How do you think your educational experiences have contributed to your overall development?

### *Work History*

- ❏ How would you describe the ideal job for you?
- ❏ What kind of work interests you most?
- ❏ How many levels of management did you interact with?
- ❏ What has been your least valuable work experience?
- ❏ How would your references describe you?

### *Willingness, Leadership Potential*

- ❏ What have you done that shows initiative and willingness to work?
- ❏ What experience have you had in leadership positions?

### Future Career

- ❑ Why are you interviewing with us?
- ❑ What do you know about our company?
- ❑ What do you expect out of this job?
- ❑ How will this job help you reach your long-term personal and career goals?
- ❑ What is more important at the start of your career—money or the job?
- ❑ What do you feel are the disadvantages of this field?
- ❑ Where do you think you could make the biggest contribution to this organization?
- ❑ How do you define a successful career?

### Goals, Organization

- ❑ How do you plan your day? your week?
- ❑ How do you determine your priorities?
- ❑ An overwhelming, time-sensitive task has just been assigned to you. How do you plan strategy for meeting your deadline?
- ❑ What happens when two priorities compete for your time?

### Oral Communication

- ❑ Getting the job done involves gathering information and input from others. How do you do this?
- ❑ Tell me how you have orally convinced someone of an approach or an idea.
- ❑ Give me an example of a time when you have compromised successfully.
- ❑ How do you overcome objections to your ideas?

### Written Communication

- ❑ When have your oral communications been important enough to follow up in writing?
- ❑ Are there situations better suited to written communication? If yes, name some examples.
- ❑ What is the most difficult paper you have written?

### Stress, Flexibility

- ❑ Tell me about a time when someone lost his or her temper with you in a business environment.
- ❑ What makes you feel tense or nervous?
- ❑ What do you do when you are being pressed for a decision?

### Decision Making

❏ How will you evaluate the company for which you hope to work?
❏ Do you take an intuitive or a logical approach to solving problems?
❏ What kinds of decisions are toughest for you?

### Developmental Areas

❏ What do you see as some of your most pressing developmental needs?
❏ What is the biggest single mistake you have made?
❏ What have the disappointments of life taught you?

### Teamwork

❏ Define cooperation.
❏ Can you think of a time when you have successfully motivated friends or colleagues to achieve a difficult goal?
❏ How will you establish a working relationship with the employees in this company?
❏ Define a good work atmosphere.

### Manageability

❏ What qualities should a successful manager possess?
❏ What do you feel should be the relationship between the manager and the staff?
❏ Describe the toughest manager you ever had.
❏ Give me an example of how you have responded to criticism.
❏ Tell me about an occasion when school or employer policies have been unfair to you.

Source: Adapted from Martin Yate, *Hiring the Best: How to Staff Your Department Right the First Time* (Holbrook, MA: Bob Adams, 1990), pp. 248–51.

# 17

*We now believe that learning and knowledge are our only sustainable competitive advantage.*

**—W. G. High, manager of human resource development, Saturn Corporation**

# Providing Orientation and Training

## CHAPTER OUTLINE

Orientation of New Employees
*Benefits of Orientation*
*The Supervisor's Role*
*Orientation Topics*
*Orientation Methods*

Training
*The Training Cycle*
*Assessment of Training Needs*
*Types of Training*

Coaching to Support Training

Evaluation of Training

## LEARNING OBJECTIVES

After you have studied this chapter, you should be able to:

17.1 Summarize reasons for conducting an orientation for new employees.

17.2 Discuss how a supervisor and the human resources department can work together to conduct an orientation.

17.3 Identify methods for conducting an orientation.

17.4 Describe the training cycle.

17.5 Explain how supervisors can decide when employees need training.

17.6 Define major types of training.

17.7 Describe how a supervisor can use coaching and mentoring to support training.

17.8 Discuss how a supervisor can evaluate the effectiveness of training.

## BACK TO THE BASICS

Source: Courtesy of NCSU Information Services.

In Raleigh, North Carolina, Charles Weathersby supervises 34 maintenance workers at North Carolina State University (NCSU). His challenges include responding to situations in which workers are not able to read well enough to do their jobs. This inability is costly and risky because employees who cannot read are more likely to make mistakes or cause injuries. Weathersby's solution is to train employees in the reading skills they lack.

The first step is to identify which employees need help, a challenging step because people who lack basic skills are often ashamed and try to hide their illiteracy. "There've been times I haven't realized an employee couldn't read or write," says Weathersby. "Then when I hand an individual a work order and see his or her face go blank, I get the message." Another indication of reading problems is making mistakes in following written orders. Weathersby says, "We use special chemical-resistant epoxies in the veterinary school and in laboratories. Workers have applied them in the wrong place, and we've spent two days scraping off the coating."

Then comes what Weathersby considers the hardest part of training employees who need help in basic skills: getting employees to participate in training. NCSU offers employees a literacy training program through Wake Technical Community College. To persuade employees to enroll in this program, Weathersby points out what they are missing by their inability to read well. He also explains that more education can lead to promotions.

After employees decide to participate in the training program, Weathersby's job turns to helping them succeed. "Scheduling poses problems," explains Weathersby, "because we have to make transportation arrangements. I'm running my own school-bus shuttle here because our maintenance facilities are so spread out." Class sessions run from 11:00 A.M. to 1:30 P.M. (paid time), and the workday ends two hours later. To fill the two-hour time slot at the end of the day, Weathersby assigns employees in training to tasks near the classes. Besides being flexible with employees, Weathersby helps by informally tutoring them when they come to him with questions about their course work. And when co-workers make fun of employees in the program, Weathersby puts an end to this destructive behavior.

Weathersby believes that the literacy training is well worth the time and effort required. "I end up with better employees," he explains. "If nothing else, the time loss is more than made up by cutting down on the extra supervisory time that's needed by nonreaders."

Source: "In-House Schoolhouse: Build Reading Skills on the Job," *Maintenance Supervisor's Bulletin*, June 10, 1992, pp. 1–4.

Supervisors are responsible for making sure their employees know what to do and how to do it. Good selection practices ensure that employees are capable of learning their jobs and perhaps already know how to carry out many of the tasks they were hired to perform. However, especially in view of the intense change faced by most organizations, even the best employees need some degree of training. In this context, **training** refers to increasing the skills that will enable employees to better meet the organization's goals.

**training**
Increasing the skills that will enable employees to better meet the organization's goals.

Businesses in the United States spend $50 billion a year on formal employee training.[1] They do so because it meets important needs. New employees need a chance to learn the specific ways things are done in the organization. In addition, employees are best equipped to contribute in a changing workplace when they have an opportunity to learn new skills and improve existing ones through a variety of training programs. Well-trained employees can deliver higher quality than poorly trained people. Training can improve productivity by holding down a variety of costs: overtime pay for employees unfamiliar with their jobs, workers' compensation and lost time of employees injured when they fail to follow safe practices, lawsuits arising from misconduct such as sexual harassment (discussed in Chapter 19), and much more. Finally, well-trained employees are likely to be more satisfied because they know what they are doing and how it contributes to achieving the organization's goals. Figure 17.1 shows areas in which U.S. companies were conducting training, according to a recent survey.

This chapter describes types of training for employees and how supervisors can participate. It begins by laying out the supervisor's role in orientation, the employees' first learning experience. Next, the chapter discusses types of training available once employees are on board and explains how supervisors can assess when training is needed. The chapter also addresses the growing expectation that supervisors supplement formal training with coaching or mentoring. Finally, the chapter describes why and how to evaluate training efforts.

## Orientation of New Employees

Do you remember your first day at your current or most recent job? When you arrived, you might not have known where you would be working or where the rest rooms were. You probably did not know your co-workers or how they spent their lunch hour. You might not have known the details of how to carry out your job, including where and how to get the supplies or materials you would need.

**orientation**
The process of giving new employees the information they need to do their work comfortably, effectively, and efficiently.

The uncertainty you felt is common to new employees in all kinds of organizations. For that reason, supervisors should assume that all employees need some form of orientation. In this context, **orientation** refers to the process of giving new employees the information they need to do their work comfortably, effectively, and efficiently. A survey by *Training* magazine found that 85 percent of companies with more than 100 employees offer a formal orientation program.[2] Even in organizations where someone else is responsible for carrying out a formal orientation program, supervisors themselves must ensure that their employees begin their job with all the information they need.

**FIGURE 17.1**

**Areas of Training Provided by U.S. Companies**

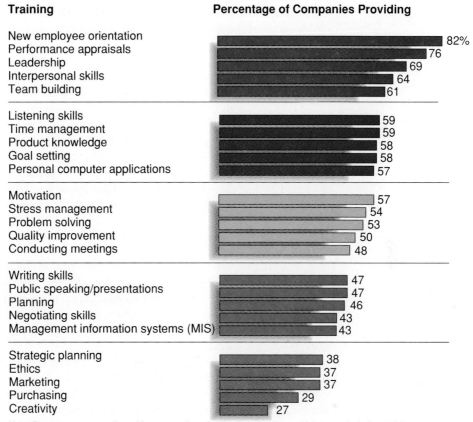

| Training | Percentage of Companies Providing |
| --- | --- |
| New employee orientation | 82% |
| Performance appraisals | 76 |
| Leadership | 69 |
| Interpersonal skills | 64 |
| Team building | 61 |
| Listening skills | 59 |
| Time management | 59 |
| Product knowledge | 58 |
| Goal setting | 58 |
| Personal computer applications | 57 |
| Motivation | 57 |
| Stress management | 54 |
| Problem solving | 53 |
| Quality improvement | 50 |
| Conducting meetings | 48 |
| Writing skills | 47 |
| Public speaking/presentations | 47 |
| Planning | 46 |
| Negotiating skills | 43 |
| Management information systems (MIS) | 43 |
| Strategic planning | 38 |
| Ethics | 37 |
| Marketing | 37 |
| Purchasing | 29 |
| Creativity | 27 |

Note: Responses were gathered from a number of different industries and job types, including training, human resources, sales and marketing, and customer service.

Source: Reprinted with permission from the October 1991 issue of *Training* magazine. © 1991, Lakewood Publications, Minneapolis, MN. All rights reserved.

## Benefits of Orientation

An employee who spends the day hunting for the photocopier, trying to figure out how to operate a cash register, or looking for someone to explain how to fill out a purchase order is not working efficiently. The primary reason organizations have orientation programs is that the sooner employees know basic information related to doing their job, the sooner they can become productive. They can work faster and with fewer errors, and their co-workers and supervisor can spend less time helping them.

Not only does orientation give new employees the knowledge they need to carry out their work, it also reduces their nervousness and uncertainty. This frees new employees to focus on their jobs rather than their worries, which not only boosts employee efficiency but also reduces the likelihood they will quit.

Another reason for conducting orientation is to encourage employees to develop a positive attitude. The time spent on an orientation session shows that the organization values the new employees. This will almost certainly add to employees' feelings of satisfaction and desire to cooperate as part of the organization. It can make new employees feel more confident that joining the organization was a good idea. In addition, work is more satisfying when we know how to do it well. The organization benefits because employees with positive attitudes tend to be more highly motivated, so they are more likely to do good work.

The benefits to employees' attitudes are among the reasons that Great Plains Software in Fargo, North Dakota, went from a one-day to a three-month orientation program. When employees join Great Plains, they take eight formal classes on topics ranging from E-mail to employee benefits to the company's vision. Each employee is assigned to a mentor, who provides personal coaching. (Mentoring is discussed later in this chapter.) Great Plains found that after it started the more intense orientation program, new employees had a better opinion of the company.[3]

### The Supervisor's Role

In a small organization, supervisors often are responsible for conducting the orientation of their employees. If you are one of those supervisors, look for ways to adapt the principles in this chapter to your group's particular needs.

Large organizations more often have a formal orientation program conducted by the human resources department. Even so, supervisors have a role in orientation. While the formal orientation program focuses on information pertaining to the organization as a whole, supervisors still must convey information about the specifics of holding a particular job in a particular department. If you are a supervisor under these circumstances, learn which of the topics and methods your human resources department already covers, then consider ways you and your employees can handle any remaining ones.

### Orientation Topics

When the human resources department and supervisor share responsibility for conducting an orientation, the human resources department typically covers topics related to the organization's policies and procedures, including hours of work and breaks, location of company facilities such as the lunchroom and exercise facilities, procedures for filling out time sheets, and policies regarding performance appraisals, pay increases, and time off. The human resources department also handles the task of having new employees fill out the necessary paperwork such as enrollment forms for insurance policies and withholding forms for tax purposes. The person conducting the orientation should explain each of these forms to new employees.

A supervisor is responsible for orientation topics related to performing a particular job in a particular department. A supervisor explains what the department does and how these activities contribute to the goals of the organization. A supervisor who covered this information in the selection interview should repeat it during the orientation process. As described later, the supervisor's orientation should point out the locations of facilities the employee will need to use and explain any of the department's own policies and procedures.

At W. W. Grainger, Inc., new branch employees attend the "College of Customer Contact" program. Graduates of the one-week program are estimated to gain the equivalent of three to six months of work experience.

Source: Courtesy of W. W. Grainger, Inc.

A supervisor's orientation also should provide instructions on how to perform the job. A supervisor may be able to explain a simple job at one time, but most jobs are more complex and will require a supervisor to first give an overview of the job's responsibilities and then, over the course of days or weeks, show the employee how to perform different aspects of the job. To build morale while training, a supervisor also can explain why the employee's job is important—that is, how it contributes to meeting department and organizational objectives.

A supervisor should prepare and follow a checklist of the topics to cover during orientation of new employees. Figure 17.2 is adapted from a checklist distributed to supervisors at Swift and Company; it is printed on a two-by-three-inch card so supervisors can easily refer to it. In preparing a checklist, a supervisor should include items that fit his or her particular situation.

## Orientation Methods

The methods a supervisor uses will depend on the organization's policies and resources. For example, a large organization with a human resources department may provide a handbook of information for new employees and spell out orientation procedures to follow. A small organization may expect individual supervisors to develop their own orientation methods. Some common methods include using an employee handbook, conducting a tour of the facilities, and encouraging the involvement of co-workers.

### Employee Handbook

**employee handbook**
A document that describes an organization's conditions of employment, policies regarding employees, administrative procedures, and related matters.

If the organization publishes an employee handbook, a new employee should be introduced to this document during the orientation. An **employee handbook** describes an organization's conditions of employment (e.g., attendance, behavior on the job, performance of duties), policies regarding employees (e.g., time off, hours

## FIGURE 17.2

### Sample Checklist for Orientation

**SUPERVISORS' CHECKLIST**
**The Right Start for New Hourly Paid Employees**

A. Explain (before employee starts the job):
1. Rate of pay, including overtime.
2. Pay day.
3. Initial job or assignment.
4. Hours—call out—holiday pay—no tardiness.
5. Starting and quitting time.
6. Lunch period—relief periods.
7. Whom to call if unable to come to work (give name and phone number on card).
8. Work clothes arrangement—laundry.
9. No smoking areas.
10. Safety rules—no running—mesh gloves—reporting all accidents, etc.
11. Sanitation—this is a food factory.
12. Name benefits (will explain later).
13. Possible job difficulties—sore muscles, hands, dizziness, nausea, etc. (encourage to stick it out).
14. Buying of company products.
15. Nothing from plant without order.
16. Importance of quality product.

B. Show:
1. Locker—rest rooms.
2. Lunch room.
3. Where employee will work—introduce to supervisor and immediate co-workers.
4. Explain the job—use JIT.

C. Talk to new employee (to encourage):
1. Twice first day.
2. Once each day the next four days.

D. After one week, explain:
1. Vacation.
2. S & A.
3. Hospitalization.
4. EBA—Group.
5. Pension.
6. Suggestion plan.
7. Union contract, if organized plant (probationary period).

Source: Adapted from a Swift and Company document.

of work, benefits), administrative procedures (e.g., filling out time sheets and travel expense reports), and related matters. A supervisor should show a new employee what topics are covered in the handbook and explain how to use it to find answers to questions. For example, an employee might use the handbook to learn how long he or she must work to qualify for three weeks' vacation.

### Tour of Facilities

Another important orientation method is to give the employee a tour. The tour might start with the employee's own work area, which should already be prepared with the supplies, tools, or equipment the employee will need. The supervisor then shows the employee the locations of physical facilities he or she will need to know about, including rest rooms, water fountain, coffee station, and photocopier, and where to get supplies, parts, or other materials needed to do the job.

During the tour, the supervisor should introduce the new employee to the people he or she will be working with. Friendly, positive words during introductions can help make the new employee part of the team. In introducing a new nurse to her colleagues in the hospital, a supervisor might say, "This is Janet Strahn. She's one of the top graduates from Northern, and I know we're all going to appreciate her help." In introducing a new maintenance mechanic to a machine operator in the department, a supervisor might say, "Pedro is the guy you'll need if your machine goes down." In both examples, the supervisor is emphasizing the importance of the new employee to the department.

### Involvement of Co-Workers

A new employee's co-workers have an important role to play in orientation. Their behavior goes a long way toward making the new employee feel either welcome or like an outsider. Therefore, a supervisor should ask all employees to help welcome newcomers. If the organization tries to build team spirit through activities such as clubs and sports teams, a supervisor should see that these are well publicized so that new employees can participate easily. A supervisor may encourage co-workers to invite a new employee to join them on breaks and at lunch. On the employee's first day, a supervisor can help a new employee feel welcome by inviting him or her to lunch.

### Follow-Up

Besides the initial information giving, orientation should involve follow-up. A supervisor should check with new employees at the end of their first day and their first week to make sure they understand what they are supposed to be doing and know where to get what they need. At all times, a supervisor should encourage employees to ask questions.

Of course, a supervisor should not stop following up after one week. Regularly checking on the performance and progress of employees is part of a supervisor's control responsibilities.

## Training

As mentioned earlier, employees need continued training even after they have worked for the organization for years. Training shows employees how to do the basics of their jobs and then helps them improve their skills. It also helps employees adapt to changes in the workplace. Because change occurs in every organization, the need for training continues (see Chapter 15).

The Xerox Corporation appreciates the importance of training, spending $250 million to $300 million (about 4 percent of its payroll cost) each year on training its employees. The training covers a variety of areas including sales, service, and technical courses.[4] Federal Express also places heavy emphasis on training. To support

**FIGURE 17.3**

**The Training Cycle**

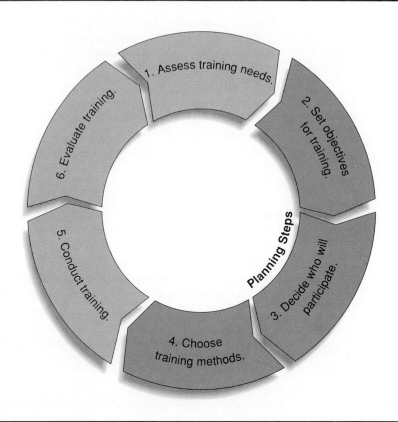

The process of providing training takes place in a cycle of steps (see Figure 17.3). The first step is to assess needs for training. As described in the next section, assessment of training needs is part of a supervisor's job. In addition, higher-level management or the human resources department may identify a need for various kinds of training. The next three steps involve planning the training. Then someone conducts the training as planned. Finally, the training should be evaluated. (See "Tips from the Firing Line" for suggestions on how to plan and implement successful training for new employees.)

the company's concern for quality and its reliance on technology, Federal Express trains customer service people for five to six weeks before they begin work. Couriers train for three to four weeks before beginning to make deliveries.[5]

## The Training Cycle

The process of providing training takes place in a cycle of steps (see Figure 17.3). The first step is to assess needs for training. As described in the next section, assessment of training needs is part of a supervisor's job. In addition, higher-level management or the human resources department may identify a need for various kinds of training. The next three steps involve planning the training. Then someone conducts the training as planned. Finally, the training should be evaluated. (See "Tips from the Firing Line" for suggestions on how to plan and implement successful training for new employees.)

### Planning Steps

A supervisor or other person proposing the training begins the planning stage by setting objectives for it. These objectives are based on a comparison of the current level and the desired level of performance and skills. In other words, they specify progress from the current level to the desired level. The training objectives should meet the criteria for effective objectives (see Chapter 6). Thus, they should be

## TIPS FROM THE FIRING LINE

### Giving New Employees a Good Start

Human resources experts agree that good training gives new employees the best chance for succeeding at their jobs. Audrey Choden, president of Training by Design in Kansas City, observes that new employees usually decide within the first 30 to 90 days whether they will stay on the job. A number of companies and consultants who believe strongly in the value of training offer the following tips for supervisors and other managers who want to develop training programs:

- *List the key points of the job.* The list isn't a job description; instead, it's a checklist for both supervisor and employer to refer to whenever necessary. "Make sure someone covers those points with a new hire because otherwise important duties can fall through the cracks," advises Kate Beauchemin of Training and Communications Group, Inc.
- *Make sure new employees know which tasks have the highest priority.* New employees sometimes feel overwhelmed by the information that is thrown at them when they start a job. Help them sort out what is most important and what they should do first.
- *Choose a valued worker to spend time one-on-one with a new employee.* Audrey Choden recommends selecting someone who has a system for doing the job that can function as on-the-job training. "This is the employee who knows the job best and who does it the best, rather than someone who just happens to be available," Choden explains.

- *Provide new employees with a great deal of feedback.* Give feedback on what is being done well and what needs improvement.
- *Establish a sequence for training.* Create specific blocks of time for training in each task or area.
- *Set goals.* These should be specific and measurable, like any other performance goals.
- *Expose new employees to all aspects of the company.* "All our new hires, no matter who they are—top manager or general factory worker—get exposure for the first couple of weeks to all aspects of manufacturing," says Bob Frey, president of Cin-Made. "We encourage employees to learn everything they can about what makes our company tick." This way, employees learn how they fit in with the rest of the company and why their contribution is so important.
- *Monitor new employees' performance.* Supervisors should check frequently on new employees, especially during the first few days.
- *If your training doesn't seem to be effective, ask for help.* There are many sources of training help, such as industry organizations and business groups. In addition, nonprofit groups such as the American Society for Training and Development, and the Center for Management Effectiveness, can provide useful information and ideas on training.

Source: Bob Kronemeyer, "Basic Training," *Business News*, Fall 1995, pp. 42–43.

written, measurable, clear, specific, and challenging but achievable. Training objectives also should support the organization's goals by helping to develop the kind of employees who can make the organization more competitive. At Welch's Inc., a sizable portion of training funds are devoted to developing interpersonal skills such as decision making, teamwork, and conflict resolution. These skills support the organization's need to have employees who are flexible and responsive to change.[6]

A supervisor also decides who will participate in the training program. For example, training how to prevent and avoid sexual harassment applies to all employees, so

In corporate America, team building is affecting even sales forces, which are competitive by nature. Jack Pohanka, one of 180 Saturn dealers in the United States, is turning his salespeople into team players. He sent his employees off-site for training that included the "trust fall," a backward leap off a 12-foot stepladder into the arms of fellow workers. A Saturn team is shown at right.

Source: © David Graham

everyone in the department would participate. But training how to operate a new piece of equipment would include only those who would use that equipment. This decision may take into account the interests and motivation levels of employees, as well as their skills. For example, an employee who is eager to advance in the organization will want to participate in many training activities to develop a variety of skills. An employee who is interested primarily in job security will probably want just enough training to keep up to date on how to perform the job.

The last step in planning training is to choose the training methods. Some training methods are described later in this chapter. If selecting a training method is part of a supervisor's role, he or she may wish to consult with the human resources department or a training expert to learn which techniques will best meet the objectives of the training.

### Implementation

Once the training has been planned, someone conducts it. In some cases, the trainer may be a supervisor. A department's employees may be qualified to conduct some kinds of training, such as demonstrating how to use a computer system. In other cases, a professional trainer is more appropriate. The choice depends on the expertise of a supervisor or employee, the content and type of training, and the time and money available for training. A supervisor with a big budget and little expertise in a particular area of training is most likely to use an in-house or outside expert. Training topics most often tackled by a supervisor are those about the specific job or department instead of company policies and values, interpreting the company's performance, or working effectively as a team.

When a supervisor is conducting the training, he or she can benefit from applying principles of learning.[7] One of these principles is that adults generally get the most out of training if they are taught a little at a time over a long period, especially if the training is seeking to change behavior rather than merely add to the learner's store of knowledge. Thus, shutting down for a day of training would be less effective than scheduling a half hour every week or so. According to educators, another learning principle is that people retain only the following percentages of what is taught:[8]

- 10 percent of what they read.
- 20 percent of what they hear.
- 30 percent of what they see.
- 50 percent of what they see and hear.
- 70 percent of what they see and describe.
- 90 percent of what they describe while doing.

The implication, of course, is that supervisors and other trainers need to supplement or replace reading assignments and lectures with more effective means of teaching, particularly those that get the learner actively involved. That is most likely to occur when classes are small—no more than about 25 people. Finally, motivation is as important to successful learning as it is to other employee activities. Training will therefore be most effective when it reflects the principles of motivation discussed in Chapter 11.

### Evaluation

After the training is over, the supervisor evaluates the results. Did it meet the objectives? The last section of this chapter discusses the evaluation of training in greater detail. Evaluation completes the training cycle by helping the supervisor identify needs for additional training.

## Assessment of Training Needs

Whether or not supervisors conduct much of their employees' formal training, they are still responsible for recognizing needs for training. With input from the employees, supervisors should determine the areas of training that employees will need and schedule the times for them to receive it. Supervisors make these decisions because they observe employees in action.[9]

Needs assessment should be an ongoing, not an occasional, concern of supervisors. Change is such a dominant force today that organizations depend on a workforce that continually learns and develops to give them a competitive edge.

A supervisor has several ways to identify training needs. First, a supervisor can observe problems in the department that suggest a need for training. For example, if a restaurant's customers are complaining about the quality of service, the manager might conclude that some or all of the staff needs training in how to satisfy customers. Or if forms sent from one department to another frequently contain a similar type of error, the department's supervisor should investigate why the people filling out the forms are making this type of mistake. Although frequent questions from employees are not necessarily a "problem," they do indicate that employees may need training in some area.

Certain areas of change also signal a need for training, and a supervisor should pay attention to them and consider what new knowledge and skills employees will need to keep abreast. If an organization encourages employee empowerment and teamwork, employees will need to know how to make decisions, evaluate team efforts, and listen to team members. When new technology (from a competitor, supplier, or elsewhere) affects an organization or the individuals in it, employees will need to learn about that technology and gain skill in applying it. If a department or its base of customers is becoming more diverse, employees will need to learn how to respect, communicate with, and achieve objectives with different cultures.

Another way to obtain information about training needs is to ask employees. Employees frequently have opinions about what they must learn to do a better job. At a minimum, supervisors and employees should discuss training needs during performance appraisals (see Chapter 18). In addition, a supervisor should encourage employees to communicate their needs as they arise.

Finally, a supervisor can identify training needs when carrying out the planning function. Executing plans often requires that employees receive training in new skills or procedures. For example, if the organization will be introducing a new product, salespeople will have to be able to communicate its benefits to customers, and customer service staff will have to be able to answer questions about it.

Besides recognizing these signals, a supervisor also should evaluate them. Do they indicate a need for training or for something else? Sometimes poor performance is not a training problem, but a motivation problem. Errors or defects may be a symptom that employees lack resources or cooperation from elsewhere in the organization. Frequent questions may signal a need for better communication instead of (or in addition to) training. Before spending money on training, a supervisor should consider whether it is the best response to these signals. A good place to begin may be to ask the relevant employees to help find the underlying issue (see Chapter 9).

### Mandatory Training

A supervisor is not the only one to decide when training is required. Government regulations, union work rules, or company policy may dictate training in certain circumstances. If the state mandates a number of continuing education classes for teachers, if the union requires an apprenticeship of so many months for pipefitters, or if the company's top managers decide that everyone should take a class in total quality management, the supervisor's job is to make sure that his or her employees get the required training. The supervisor does so primarily through decisions related to scheduling and motivation.

### Learning Environment

Along with planning for formal training sessions, supervisors can help organizations meet the need for training by fostering a climate that values learning. This kind of climate has been called a "learning environment." One way to foster a learning environment is to set a good example. Supervisors should develop their own knowledge and skills through a variety of means, from reading to attending seminars. Also, supervisors should share information generously with employees. They can enable employees to learn from one another by encouraging them to exchange what they have learned through their education, training activities, and experience. When employees request time and other resources for training, a supervisor should view the training as an investment to be evaluated, not merely a distraction from the "real work" of the organization.

**FIGURE 17.4**

**Types of Training**

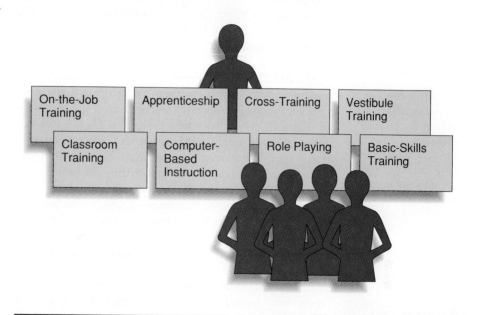

## Types of Training

A variety of types of training are available for employees (see Figure 17.4). Most organizations use a variety of training methods. When BMW planned a new factory in Spartanburg, South Carolina, it also planned a combination of classroom and on-the-job training. In the classroom setting, employees learn the skills required for working on a team: communications, participation in a diverse workforce, and facilitating group processes.[10]

In selecting or recommending a type of training, a supervisor should consider the expense relative to the benefits, the resources available, and trainees' needs for practice and individualized attention. No matter what type of training is used, a supervisor should be sure that the trainer understands the objectives of the training and how to carry it out. A supervisor also should counsel employees who seem discouraged and praise them when they show progress.

### On-the-Job Training

In many cases, the easiest way to learn how to perform a job is to try it. Teaching a job while trainer and trainee do the job at the work site is called **on-the-job training.** The trainer—typically a co-worker or supervisor—shows the employee how to do the job, and then the employee tries it.

An employee who learns in this way benefits from being able to try out the skills and techniques being taught. The results tell immediately whether the employee understands what the trainer is trying to teach. However, on-the-job training carries the risk that an inexperienced employee will make costly and even

**on-the-job training**
Teaching a job while trainer and trainee perform the job at the work site.

dangerous mistakes. Thus, this type of training is most suitable when the tasks to be learned are relatively simple or the costs of an error are low. For more complex or risky tasks, it may be wiser to use other forms of training before or instead of on-the-job training.

### Apprenticeship

**apprenticeship**
Training that involves working alongside an experienced person, who shows the apprentice how to do the various tasks involved in a job or trade.

Many tradespeople learn their trade through an **apprenticeship.** This involves working alongside an experienced person, who shows the apprentice how to do the various tasks involved in the trade. Thus, apprenticeship is a long-term form of on-the-job training. (Many apprenticeship programs also require that apprentices complete classroom training.) Most apprenticeships are in the building trades, such as carpentry and pipefitting. However, Fuchs Copy Systems of West Allis, Wisconsin, uses an apprenticeship program to attract and retain qualified service technicians for the copiers it sells. Fuchs hires high-school and college students to work during the summer or part-time during the school year doing actual repairs—specifically, rebuilding the developer units of the copiers.[11]

Only 2 percent of U.S. high-school graduates complete apprenticeships.[12] Reasons for this low rate include union work rules and the American emphasis on a college education as opposed to learning a trade. An apprenticeship program is more complicated to set up than simple on-the-job training for individual tasks. However, it is one way to help a supervisor meet training needs that require months or years of learning.

### Cross-Training

As you learned in Chapter 11, an increasing number of organizations are using job rotation, meaning that employees take turns performing various jobs. Job rotation requires that employees learn to perform more than one job. Teaching employees another job so that they can fill in as needed is known as cross-training. Employees who have completed cross-training can enjoy more variety in their work, and their supervisor has more flexibility in making assignments. The resulting flexibility also makes cross-training necessary for many forms of teamwork.

Cross-training does not apply only to operating various machines in a factory. An international mail delivery firm, Global Mail Ltd. based in Sterling, Virginia, uses cross-training with its newly hired salespeople. Before they begin sales training, they spend one to three days apiece working in customer service, accounting, operations, and telephone sales. Handling the paperwork and customer complaints shows the salespeople the consequences of writing up an order incorrectly or promising a customer too much.[13]

In planning cross-training, a supervisor should make sure that employees spend enough time practicing each job to learn it well. Some jobs are more complex than others and will require more training time. Also, some employees will learn a given job faster than others.

### Vestibule Training

**vestibule training**
Training that takes place on equipment set up in a special area off the job site.

While on-the-job training is effective, it is not appropriate as initial training for jobs that have no room for errors, such as piloting or nursing. In those cases, people learn principles or techniques before doing the actual job. A type of training that allows employees to practice using equipment off the job is called **vestibule training.** The employees undergoing vestibule training use procedures and equipment set up in a special vestibule school. For example, a large retail store might set up a training room containing cash registers, or an airline might use a simulated cabin for training flight attendants.

Vestibule training is appropriate when the organization hires people who do not already know how to use its equipment. Employees learn to operate the equipment without the pressure of accidents occurring, customers getting impatient, or other employees depending on a minimum amount of output. The expense of vestibule training or other off-the-job training is higher because employees are not producing goods or services for the organization while they undergo the training. However, if the organization hired only people who already had all the necessary skills, it would probably have to pay more and might have difficulty finding enough qualified candidates.

### Classroom Training

Other than vestibule training, most off-the-job training involves some form of classroom instruction. This training takes place in a class or seminar where one or more speakers lecture on a specific topic. Seminars are available from a variety of sources on many topics, so a supervisor who is considering attending or sending employees to a seminar should first make sure that the topic will be relevant to job performance. Classroom training also can occur at the workplace, even if the organization lacks the time or facilities for formal classes. For example, during monthly staff meetings at Phelps County Bank in Rolla, Missouri, each department took turns giving a one-hour presentation about its functions and products.[14]

The main advantage of classroom training is that the person conducting it can deliver a large quantity of information to more than one person in a relatively short span of time. Depending on the format and trainer, it can be a relatively inexpensive way to convey information. A disadvantage is that most of the communication travels in one direction—from the lecturer to the audience. One-way communication is less engaging and memorable. In addition, classroom training rarely allows the learners to practice what they are learning. Classroom training can be more effective when it includes computer-based instruction and role playing.

### Computer-Based Instruction

At a growing number of organizations, computer software is taking the place of classroom-based trainers. Computer-based instruction typically uses a computer to present information, generate and score test questions, keep track of the trainee's performance, and tell the trainee what activities to do next. This type of training is a common way of learning to use a new computer program; the software comes with a series of lessons that give the user a chance to try using it.

**interactive multimedia**
Computer software that brings together sound, video, graphics, animation, and text and adjusts content based on user responses.

Computer-based instruction is becoming more engaging and widespread because of the growing affordability of **interactive multimedia.** This is software that brings together sound, video, graphics, animation, and text. The best interactive multimedia programs adjust the course content based on the student's responses to questions. Interactive multimedia typically is delivered on CD-ROM, a storage medium that many personal computers can use. By a recent count, 80 percent of *Fortune* 500 companies were using interactive multimedia training.[15] Andersen Consulting uses interactive multimedia to create simulations in which trainees practice answering questions and otherwise interacting with digitized images of clients. Retailer J. C. Penney uses interactive multimedia to train customer

**TABLE 17.1**

**Interactive Multimedia Training Programs: Desirable Features**

| | | |
|---|---|---|
| **Consistency** | The method for navigating through the program and getting help should be consistent throughout the program. |
| **Nonlinear design** | The program should adjust for the trainee's progress, allowing the trainee to move into new areas at his or her own pace. |
| **Information** | The program should teach useful material, not simply present catchy music, images, and other gimmicks. |
| **Fun** | The program should draw on its multimedia capabilities in a way that makes the material enjoyable to learn. |
| **Relevance** | The program should realistically reflect the actual job requirements. |

Source: Based on Wendy Marx, "The New High-Tech Training," *Management Review*, Feb. 1995, pp. 57–60.

service representatives in its credit card division. The computer simulates phone calls from customers, so the reps can actually practice handling irate (and reasonable) customers. Supervisors interested in using interactive multimedia should look for the features described in Table 17.1.

Some computer-based training uses simulations. The computer displays conditions that an employee might have to face. For example, a flight simulator would show pilot trainees the cockpit and the view from the window. Another simulation might be of dials and other readouts monitoring the performance of machinery. A trainee uses the computer's keyboard or some other device to respond to the situation displayed by a computer, and the simulator responds by showing the consequences of the trainee's actions. This enables the trainee to practice responding to conditions without suffering the real consequences of a mistake, such as a plane crashing or a boiler exploding.

Computer-based instruction has a significant cost advantage over other methods when there are many trainees. An organization may not have to pay a trainer. In addition, trainees can work at their own pace, eliminating the frustration that arises from a class moving too fast for them to understand material or too slow to maintain their interest. A good training program can help trainees learn faster or better than they might through another training technique. At J. C. Penney, customer service representatives trained with interactive multimedia reach peak proficiency in one-third less time than employees who had more traditional training. Andersen Consulting credits interactive multimedia for employees having "deeper competencies, more skill and knowledge."[16]

Some people, however, are nervous about using a computer. A supervisor or other trainer must serve as a source of encouragement and help for these people. Also, some forms of computer-based instruction do not allow employees to work as a team, ask questions, or exchange ideas. When these features of training are important, a supervisor should choose software that offers these capabilities, supplement the computer-based training, or select other training methods.

High-tech training teaches people complex tasks. Here, a pilot uses a dual touch-sensitive video screen inside a Saab 340A/B simulator at Flight-Safety International in New York.

Source: Courtesy of Flight-Safety International.

**role playing**
A training method in which roles are assigned to participants, who then act out the way they would handle a specific situation.

### Role Playing

To teach skills in working with other people, an organization may use **role playing.** This method involves assigning roles to participants, who then act out the way they would handle a specific situation. Some of the exercises in this book use role playing. A technique that enhances the usefulness of role playing is to videotape the session and play it back so participants can see how they looked and sounded.

Role playing gives people a chance to practice the way they react to others, making it especially useful for training in human relations skills such as communicating, resolving conflicts, and working with people of other races or cultures. People who have acted out a particular role—for example, the role of supervisor—generally have more sympathy for that person's point of view. The major potential drawback of role playing is that, to be most useful, it requires a trainer with expertise in conducting it.

A variation on the standard type of role playing is the use of board games that have been developed to teach by showing the consequences of various decisions under different conditions. For example, the Society of Manufacturing Engineers markets a game called the Competitive Manufacturing Game, which teaches modern techniques for improving quality and productivity. Players make decisions related to running a manufacturing operation, such as laying out equipment and investing in improvements, to see who can come up with the most profitable strategy. Or an organization can use a customized game, such as those created by Corporate Games based in Union City, California. The company's games, drawn from client-supplied information, include indoor and outdoor team competitions, game-show activities, adventure hunts, and murder mysteries.[17]

### Basic-Skills Training

An often-heard complaint among employers today is that it is increasingly difficult to find enough employees with the basic skills necessary to perform modern jobs. Robert Fowler, president of Hampden Papers in Holyoke, Massachusetts, says,

"There used to be a time when we had plenty of jobs for people who were functionally illiterate, but today our machines are very complex."[18] Despite the need for sophisticated employees, many employers cannot assume that employees can read and do basic arithmetic. Indications that employees cannot read or perform other basic tasks include recurrent accidents and mistakes.

An increasing number of employers are responding to this problem by conducting their own training in basic skills. North Carolina State University, described in the story at the beginning of this chapter, is one of these employers. The Armenian Nursing Home in Jamaica Plains, Massachusetts, offers its 75 employees classes in English as a second language; classes in basic reading, writing, and arithmetic; a program leading to a high school diploma; and a course leading to a practical-nursing certificate.[19] In 1991 alone, White Storage and Retrieval Systems, based in Kenilworth, New Jersey, offered 7,000 hours of training in subjects ranging from English as a second language to the use of small tools.[20]

Organizations that offer such programs not only improve the skills of their workers but also attract and keep employees who are highly motivated. At White Storage and Retrieval Systems, for example, employee turnover fell from 25 percent before the company began its training program to only 10 percent a few years later.[21] However, basic-skills education offers some challenges to the employer. One is that employees may resist attending because they are embarrassed or afraid the organization will punish them if it finds out they do not have basic skills. To address this challenge, an organization should name the program carefully, calling it something like "workplace education" or "skills enhancement." Supervisors and other managers should reassure employees that participating in the program does not place their jobs in danger. In addition, experts recommend rewarding employees for participating in a basic-skills program. At Loxcreen Company, a South Carolina manufacturer of screen doors, employees are paid at half of their basic wage rate for their time in class.[22]

# Coaching to Support Training

**coaching**
Guidance and instruction in how to do a job so that it satisfies performance goals.

After employees have received training, a supervisor should take on the role of coach to help them maintain and use the skills they have acquired. **Coaching** is guidance and instruction in how to do a job so that it satisfies performance goals. The concept comes from sports, where a coach constantly observes team members in action, identifies each player's strengths and weaknesses, and works with each person to help him or her capitalize on the strengths and improve on the weaknesses. The most respected coaches generally encourage their team members and take a personal interest in them.

In a business context, coaching involves similar activities. As coach, a supervisor engages in regular observation, teaching, and encouragement to help employees develop so that they in turn can help the team succeed. Much of this coaching is done informally to back up the more formal training process.

In this role, a supervisor observes employees' performances daily and provides feedback. To encourage employees, a supervisor should praise them when they meet or exceed expectations. A supervisor should consider whether good performance is evidence that the employees can be given key responsibilities or have strengths that should be further developed. When an employee makes a mistake, the supervisor should work with the employee, focusing on the problem itself, rather than any perceived deficiencies in the employee's character. Together, the

**FIGURE 17.5**

**The Coaching Process**

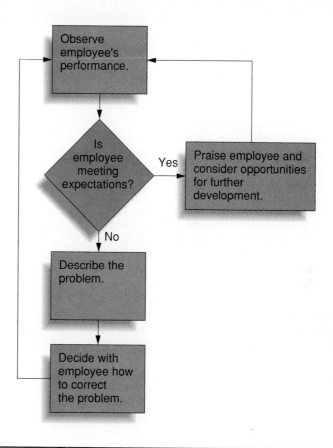

supervisor and employee should decide how to correct the problem—perhaps through more training, a revised assignment, or more reliable access to resources. A supervisor and employee should work on only one problem at a time, with the supervisor continually looking for signs of employee progress. Figure 17.5 summarizes the process of coaching.

The process of coaching is different from simply telling employees what to do. It emphasizes learning about employees, then drawing on and developing their talents. (The Self-Quiz on page 532 can help you evaluate your coaching potential.) Acting as a coach is especially appropriate for supervisors in organizations that encourage employees to participate in decision making and teamwork.

### Mentoring

In some cases, a supervisor may focus coaching efforts on one employee. This practice is called **mentoring,** or providing guidance, advice, and encouragement through an ongoing one-on-one work relationship. A supervisor should not use a mentoring relationship as an excuse for failure to encourage all employees in the work group. However, mentoring may be an appropriate way to support the training of an employee who has especially great potential, needs extra attention to contribute fully, or has been assigned to the supervisor for that purpose. Some organizations use mentoring of minority and female employees to help them learn

**mentoring**
Providing guidance, advice, and encouragement through an ongoing one-on-one work relationship.

## MEETING THE CHALLENGE

### *Training Puts Women to Work*

Training doesn't serve only people who already have jobs; good training can help people get jobs in the first place. In an age of conservative economic thinking, training not only serves a positive purpose for society but also makes good monetary sense. That's what Women Work!, the National Network for Women's Employment, discovered in its study that evaluated the success of job training for women who otherwise might be on welfare.

Currently, the federal government distributes $70 million in funds to individual training programs designed to get displaced homemakers, single parents, and other unemployed women into jobs. State and local groups pick up the rest of the tab. Women Work! functions as a national clearinghouse for women who are looking for help through these programs. The individual programs vary. In Memphis, Women in the Preparation for Employment trains and places participants in nontraditional jobs, while in Maine Women, Work and Community emphasizes training for self-employment.

The study surveyed 6,500 participants and graduates of the various programs to see how they felt about the effectiveness of their training. More than

85 percent rated their training "excellent" or "very good"; 96 percent said they would recommend the training to a friend.

But those are numbers. Here are the names and occupations of some of the graduate trainees: Maria Santos Padillo of Alameda, California, owns her own desktop publishing company; Beverly Craig of Topeka, Kansas, works at a Goodyear tire plant; Debbie Strickland of Skowhegan, Maine, works as a receptionist; Ruth Cord of Springfield, Illinois, works at a social service agency that helps families who are victims of domestic violence.

"The training programs help women become economically independent, reduce their reliance on public assistance, and help them to qualify for higher wages," notes Jill Miller, co-executive director of Women Work! Her comment reflects the good ethics and the positive social purpose of this type of training. What about good monetary sense? All the women who graduate from the training become taxpayers.

Source: Carol Kleiman, "Training Programs Work for Women's Financial Well-Being," *Chicago Tribune*, July 13, 1995, Sec. 3, p. 3.

to navigate in a setting where communications styles, values, expectations, and so on differ from what they are used to. (A supervisor, too, may benefit from having a mentor. See the Reference Guide.)

## Evaluation of Training

A supervisor is often in the best position to determine whether training is working. The most basic way to evaluate training is to measure whether the training is resolving the problem. Are new employees learning their job? Is the defect rate falling? Do employees use the new computer system properly? Are customers now praising the service instead of complaining about it? Looking for answers to such questions is central to the control process, described in Chapter 6.

Other people, including the employees who have participated in the training, also can provide information to help evaluate training (see "Meeting the Challenge"). They might fill out a questionnaire (see Figure 17.6) or the organization might set up a team of people to evaluate the organization's training methods and content. The latter approach has been used at Kansas Gas and Electric Company (KG&E) of Wichita, Kansas.[23] KG&E's power generation department set up a task force—consisting of one plant operator, two mechanics, one electrician, one technician, and the training supervisor—to meet on an as-needed basis and review the department's apprenticeship program. The team surveyed the department's

**FIGURE 17.6**

**Questionnaire for Evaluating Training**

**Title of Program** _____

**Date** _____ **Job Title** _____

Directions: Please indicate your response to each question and return this questionnaire to the program leader. Your responses are confidential. DO NOT SIGN YOUR NAME ON THIS EVALUATION INSTRUMENT.

1. In my opinion, this program was: (check one)
   ____ Excellent  ____ Very good  ____ Good  ____ Fair  ____ Poor

2. Did the program meet the objectives stated in the outline given to you? (check one)
   ____ Yes  ____ No

3. Did the program meet *your* expectations? (Check one)
   ____ Yes  ____ No     If you checked no, please explain _____
   _____

4. Were the training facilities adequate? (Check one)
   ____ Yes  ____ No     If you checked no, please explain _____
   _____

5. In my opinion, the instructor was: (check one)
   ____ Excellent  ____ Very good  ____ Good  ____ Fair  ____ Poor

6. How important was each of these training elements?
   (check one for each element)
   Videotapes          ____ Very important  ____ Worthwhile  ____ Not important
   Role playing        ____ Very important  ____ Worthwhile  ____ Not important
   Lecture             ____ Very important  ____ Worthwhile  ____ Not important
   Handouts            ____ Very important  ____ Worthwhile  ____ Not important
   Group discusssion   ____ Very important  ____ Worthwhile  ____ Not important

7. To what extent did you participate in the program? (check one)
   ____ A lot  ____ Just enough  ____ Somewhat  ____ Not at all

8. How much will the content of this program help you to perform your job responsibilities? (check one)
   ____ A lot  ____ Just enough  ____ Somewhat  ____ Not at all

9. What other types of training programs are of interest to you? Indicate your preferences. _____
   _____

10. How can this program be improved? Indicate your suggestions. _____
    _____

11. Other comments and suggestions. Please indicate any other comments/ suggestions that you feel will be useful in planning future training programs.
    _____
    _____
    _____
    _____
    _____

Source: Donald S. Miller and Stephen E. Catt, *Human Relations: A Contemporary Approach* (Homewood, IL: Richard D. Irwin, 1989), p. 330. Used by permission of Donald S. Miller.

supervisors and trade workers to learn what skills were necessary. Based on the results of that survey, the team modified the information covered in the apprenticeship program so that it includes all the skills actually used by employees.

If the evaluation suggests that training is not meeting its objectives—as was the case with KG&E—the training may have to be modified or expanded. The type of training may not be appropriate for the training needs. For example, new employees who are having difficulty learning job skills may not have enough opportunity to practice what they are being taught. To identify what kinds of changes to make, the supervisor can ask questions such as the following:

- Was the trainer well prepared?
- Did the trainer communicate the information clearly and in an interesting way?
- Did the training include visual demonstrations in addition to verbal descriptions of how to do the task?
- Were the employees well enough prepared for the training program?
- Did the employees understand how they would benefit from the training?
- Did employees have a chance to ask questions?
- Did the employees receive plenty of praise for their progress?

Whatever the outcome, training represents a cost to the organization. Consequently, it is worth conducting only when it leads to improved performance, as measured by increased quantity, quality, or both. Training that does not produce results should be changed or discontinued. In organizations where supervisors and others are selective and use only training that meets evaluation criteria, training programs are not just an expense, but a valuable investment in the organization's human resources.

## Summary

**17.1 Summarize reasons for conducting an orientation for new employees.**
The primary reason to conduct an orientation is that the sooner new employees know basic information related to their job, the sooner they can become productive. Orientation also reduces the nervousness and uncertainty of new employees, and it helps them to develop a positive attitude by boosting job satisfaction.

**17.2 Discuss how a supervisor and the human resources department can work together to conduct an orientation.**
In a small organization, a supervisor may conduct most or all of the orientation. In a large organization, the human resources department may handle most of the task. In either case, it is up to the supervisor to convey information about the specifics of holding a particular job in a particular department. This includes explaining what the department does and what the new employee's job entails. Typically, the human resources department covers topics related to the organization's policies and procedures.

**17.3 Identify methods for conducting an orientation.**
During the orientation, a new employee should be introduced to the organization's employee handbook. A supervisor (or someone else) should give the employee a tour of the workplace, pointing out facilities the employee will need to use. During the tour, the employee should be introduced to the people with whom he or she will be working. A supervisor should instruct other employees in their role of welcoming a new employee. At the end of the first day and the first week, the supervisor should follow up to make sure the new employee understands the new job.

**17.4 Describe the training cycle.**
First, a supervisor (or someone else) assesses training needs. The next three steps cover planning the training: setting objectives, deciding who will participate, and choosing the training method. Then someone (a supervisor, an employee, or a professional trainer) conducts the training. The last step is to evaluate the success of the training. Evaluation sometimes suggests needs for additional training.

**17.5 Explain how supervisors can decide when employees need training.**

A supervisor may observe problems in the department that indicate a need for training. Areas of change may signal training needs. A supervisor may ask employees about the kinds of training they need or may identify training needs when carrying out the planning function. Finally, some training may be mandated by government regulations, union work rules, or company policy.

**17.6 Define major types of training.**

The organization may use on-the-job training, which involves learning while performing a job. Related training methods are apprenticeship and cross-training (i.e., training employees in more than one job). The training also may take place off-site through vestibule training or in a classroom. Classroom training can be more effective when it includes computer-aided instruction (particularly interactive multimedia) and role playing. Some computer-aided instruction involves simulations. Finally, in an organization where employees lack basic skills such as the ability to read directions or work with numbers, the organization may offer basic-skills training.

**17.7 Describe how a supervisor can use coaching and mentoring to support training.**

To help employees maintain and use the skills they have acquired, a supervisor takes on the role of coach, guiding and instructing employees in how to do a job so that it satisfies performance goals. The supervisor observes employee performance and provides feedback on it. Supervisor and employee work together to devise a solution to any problem. Then the supervisor reviews the employee's performance to make sure the employee understood what to do and is doing it. A supervisor may act as a mentor to an employee, providing guidance, advice, and encouragement through an ongoing one-on-one work relationship. Some organizations use mentoring of minority and female employees as a way to help them learn to navigate unfamiliar work situations.

**17.8 Discuss how a supervisor can evaluate the effectiveness of training.**

To evaluate training, a supervisor measures whether the problem addressed by the training is being solved. In addition, participants in the training may fill out a questionnaire in which they evaluate their experience. When training is not producing the desired results, a supervisor should attempt to find out why and then correct the problem.

# Key Terms

| | | |
|---|---|---|
| training | on-the-job training | role playing |
| orientation | apprenticeship | coaching |
| employee handbook | vestibule training | mentoring |
| | interactive multimedia | |

# Review and Discussion Questions

1. Describe a job or activity for which you received training. What was the purpose of this training?

2. Describe a situation in which you received an orientation. What did the orientation consist of? How was the orientation different from training?

3. When Al DeAngelis started his new job as a computer programmer, he arrived in his department at 9:30 A.M., after having spent time in the human resources department filling out forms. Marcia Eizenstadt, Al's supervisor, shook his hand and said, "Al, I'm so glad you're starting with us today. We need your talents tremendously." Then, explaining that she would be tied up all day in important planning meetings, Marcia showed Al to his desk and gave him an employee handbook to look at. "Read this carefully," said Marcia. "It'll tell you everything you need to know about working here. By tomorrow or the next day, I hope we'll be able to sit down and go over your first assignment." Al spent the rest of the day reading the manual, wishing for a cup of coffee, and trying to smile pleasantly in response to the quizzical looks he was getting from other employees passing by and glancing into his cubicle.

    a. What aspects of Al's orientation were helpful?

    b. How could it have been improved?

4. What are the steps in the training cycle?

5. Who determines when training is needed? What are some indications of a need for training?

6. Phil Petrakis supervises the housekeepers at a hotel in a big city. Phil has found that the easiest and fastest way to train his staff is to give them a memo describing whatever new policy or procedure he wants to teach. When the employees have read the memo, the training is complete—it is as simple as that. What is wrong with this approach?

7. Which type(s) of training would you recommend in each of the following situations? Explain your choices.

    a. Teaching air-traffic controllers how to help pilots land planes safely.

    b. Improving the decision-making skills of production workers so they can better participate in the company's employee involvement program.

    c. Teaching a plumber how to replace sewer lines.

    d. Teaching a receptionist how to operate the company's new telephone system.

8. At a department meeting, production supervisor Lenore Gibbs announced, "Starting next month the company will be offering a class for any of you who can't read. It will take place after work in the cafeteria." How do you think employees with reading difficulties would react to Lenore's announcement? How can she phrase the announcement so that employees will be more likely to attend the class?

9. What is coaching? Why is it especially appropriate in organizations that encourage employee involvement and teamwork?

10. What is a mentor? What steps might a mentor take to help a Japanese employee who has been transferred from the Tokyo office to company headquarters in the United States? How might these actions help the employee and the organization?

11. Think back to the training you described in question 1. Evaluate its effectiveness. In what ways might it have been improved?

## A SECOND LOOK

The story at the beginning of this chapter describes basic-skills training for employees of North Carolina State University. The training itself is provided by the local community college. What activities in the training cycle does supervisor Charles Weathersby carry out?

# APPLICATIONS MODULE

## CASE

### Orientation at Web Industries

Web Industries is a small company known as a converter. It cuts materials into smaller sizes for use by manufacturers. Until recently, Web's new employees got the same training as new employees at many small companies: next to nothing. A supervisor would show a new employee how to operate machines and someone would describe the company's benefits package. It was up to the employee to sink or swim.

That changed as the company's managers began to recognize that although they thought they were too busy to train employees, they were spending just as much time fixing problems caused by the lack of training. Charles Edmunson, Web's vice-president of manufacturing, gathered a cross-section of employees to brainstorm about the company's training needs. He then devised an orientation plan that calls for 20 hour-long sessions, which take place daily for four weeks.

The trainers are Web employees, including general managers, plant managers, customer service representatives, machine operators, maintenance workers, and office workers. Each trainer of a new employee covers an aspect of the orientation with which he or she is familiar. Trainers follow an outline prepared by Edmunson. They may add examples but not skip any section of the outline. Involving employees in the training builds a sense of commitment to the company and responsibility for the success of new employees. This approach is consistent with the company's overall emphasis on teamwork and employee involvement.

The orientation program covers the topics shown in Table A. According to Edmunson, some of the most important material is the information about the company, its goals, and employees' future with Web. Edmunson believes that this kind of information is easy to forget if it is not part of a formal orientation program. To make sure that all existing employees are familiar with the information, some Web plants started having all employees participate in the training.

Other topics covered in the orientation show employees how to help the company meet its goals. For example, making employees aware of the value of parts enables them to treat the parts with the care necessary to keep costs under control. Explains Edmunson, "We've got spacers for the machines that are an eighth of an inch wide and precision-ground, and they might be worth 25 or 30 bucks. They just look like little washer tubes. A new guy, if he's not aware that this is an expensive piece, may end up tossing it in the trash dumpster." Similarly, by explaining that the company competes for business by providing customized service, the trainers let new employees know the importance of catering to customers' demands.

When employees have completed the four weeks of orientation, they evaluate the program, indicating areas that need improvement. As a result, the orientation program has been updated once so far, and additional improvements are being considered.

1. Based on the information in Table A, does Web's orientation program appear to cover all the relevant topics? If not, what is missing?
2. What aspects of orientation should Web's supervisors handle? Consider that supervisors can both supplement and repeat what is covered during the formal orientation.
3. If you were a production supervisor at Web, how would you feel about having one of your machine operators taking an hour or two each month to conduct training for new employees? Explain.

Source: Leslie Brokaw, "The Enlightened Employee Handbook," *Inc.,* Oct. 1991, pp. 49–51.

## TABLE A

**Topics Covered in Web Industries Orientation**

| Week | Topics |
|---|---|
| 1 | Welcome; Your Job; The Work Orders; Record Keeping; Your Benefits |
| 2 | Our Business; Teamwork; Math for Converting; Packaging Standards; Maintenance Awareness |
| 3 | Growing Our Company; Safety; Work Order Review; Record Keeping Review; How We Compete for Customers |
| 4 | Your Future at Web; Constant Improvement; Math Review; Packaging Review; The ESOP (employee stock ownership plan) |

Source: Adapted from Leslie Brokaw, "The Enlightened Employees Handbook," *Inc.*, Oct. 1991, pp. 50-51

## SELF-QUIZ

### *Could You Coach Someone?*

This quiz is designed to evaluate your potential for acting as a coach in support of training. Write "True" or "False" before each of the following statements.

_____  1. The best way to get something done is to do it yourself.

_____  2. If I give someone clear instructions, I know that person will get the job done without my checking on him or her.

_____  3. I don't mind if someone asks me questions about how to do a job.

_____  4. If I give someone instructions on how to perform a task, it's that individual's responsibility to complete it.

_____  5. I like to let people know when they've done something right.

_____  6. If someone makes a mistake, we focus on solving the problem together.

_____  7. If someone makes a mistake, I correct the problem myself.

_____  8. If someone doesn't follow company procedures, I assume he or she hasn't read the company handbook.

_____  9. I think that interactive multimedia software is the best form of training for everyone.

_____ 10. Training a new employee shouldn't last more than a week.

Scoring: "True" responses to statements 2, 5, and 6 show good potential for coaching. "True" responses to the other statements show that you need to become aware of the needs of individuals, then work on drawing on and emphasizing their talents.

## Class Exercise

One or more students volunteer to teach the class a skill. If possible, the volunteers should have time to prepare their "training session" before the class meets. Some "trainers" might like to work as a team. Suggestions for skills to teach follow; use your creativity to add to the list:

- Folding paper hats.
- Doing a card trick.
- Communicating a message in sign language.
- Making punch for a party.
- Setting the clock on a VCR.

## Team-Building Exercise

### Orienting a New Team Member

Divide the class into teams of four or five. Select (or ask for a volunteer) one member of each team to play the role of a newcomer to the school (the newcomer might pose as a transfer student, a student from another country, or the like). The rest of the team will do its best to orient the newcomer to the school. Team members might want to take responsibility for different areas of knowledge; for

After the training session(s), the class discusses the following questions:

1. How can you evaluate whether this training was successful? If possible, try conducting an evaluation of what the class learned. What do the results of this evaluation indicate?
2. What training techniques were used? Would additional or alternative techniques have made the skill easier to learn? What changes would have helped?

example, one might draw a map of campus and town for the newcomer, pointing out bus routes and important or useful locations; another might volunteer information on study groups or social activities. At the end of the session, the newcomer should evaluate and discuss how effective the orientation was.

# Video Exercise 17: *Providing Orientation and Training*

### *Video Summary*

Classroom and on-the-job training are two of the most common methods of training. Karen Lohss, professional trainer at LaMarsch & Associates, will demonstrate how she applies both techniques when training visually impaired supervisors. The University of Michigan Hospital recently became the first medical institution to adopt the concepts of total quality management. The secret to this successful venture was the extensive training program through which every individual in the hospital went.

### *Application*

Because on-the-job training (OJT) usually is conducted by or overseen by an employee's supervisor, this application will examine the OJT process in detail.

The following model shows how educators describe the learning process as having four steps: (1) motivation, (2) understanding, (3) participation, and (4) application. Those conducting OJT, whether it be the supervisor or an employee assigned by the supervisor, should make certain his or her training encompasses all four steps in the learning sequence. The right-hand column identifies how the OJT sequence should parallel the learning sequence by including the four steps: (1) prepare, (2) present, (3) try out, and (4) follow up.

Within each of the four steps of OJT instruction are smaller training elements that help the trainers to accomplish each step of the process. Those smaller training elements are listed alphabetically below. Transfer each of the training elements next to the correct bullet in the OJT Training Model that follows. Also try to get the elements within each step correctly ordered. For example, "Demonstrate," "Explain," and "Tell" are the three elements in Step 2. In what order should they be placed?

- Break down job.
- Check progress as necessary.
- Demonstrate.
- Develop instruction plan.
- Explain.
- Learner does the job while trainer gives feedback.
- Put learner at ease.
- Tell.
- Tell learner where to go for help.

## OJT Training Model

| Learning Sequence | Trainer Conducting OJT Should: |
|---|---|
| Step 1: Motivation | Step 1: Prepare |

- _____
- _____
- _____

| Learning Sequence | Trainer Conducting OJT Should: |
|---|---|
| Step 2: Understanding | Step 2: Present |

- _____
- _____
- _____

| Learning Sequence | Trainer Conducting OJT Should: |
|---|---|
| Step 3: Participation | Step 3: Try Out |

- _____

| Learning Sequence | Trainer Conducting OJT Should: |
|---|---|
| Step 4: Application | Step 4: Follow Up |

- _____
- _____

# 18

*There is no security on this earth; there is only opportunity.*
—**Douglas MacArthur, general of the army, U.S. Army**

# Appraising Performance

## LEARNING OBJECTIVES

After you have studied this chapter, you
should be able to:

18.1 Summarize benefits of conducting
performance appraisals.

18.2 Identify the steps in appraising
performance systematically.

18.3 Discuss guidelines for avoiding
discrimination in performance
appraisals.

18.4 Compare types of appraisals.

18.5 Describe sources of bias in
appraising performance.

18.6 Explain the purpose of conducting
performance appraisal interviews.

18.7 Tell how supervisors should
prepare for a performance
appraisal interview.

18.8 Describe guidelines for
conducting the interview.

Source: Courtesy of Nancy Acedo.

## HOW EMPLOYEES RATE

Nancy Maria Acedo is a supervisor with the Fleet Management Program for the State of Colorado. The Fleet Management Program purchases and leases to state agencies pickups, trucks, station wagons, vans, and sedans. The program is also responsible for maintaining the vehicles and providing replacement when necessary. The program's customers are the state employees who lease its cars and trucks.

Once a year Acedo must conduct a formal performance appraisal on each of the five employees she supervises. Using an appraisal form provided by the state, she rates employees in specific areas such as customer service and job performance. The possible ratings are *outstanding, commendable, good, needs improvement*, and *unacceptable*. Acedo gives employees a progress review at least once during the appraisal year to let them know if there are any areas in which they need improvement. She gives specific examples of how to perform in those areas.

One of Acedo's employees was doing a poor job of completing work on time and keeping good records. Besides pointing out this problem, Acedo helped in developing the solution. She prepared a log sheet for the employee to use. On the log sheet, the employee would record who called, when the call was made, and other information such as whether the employee mailed to a customer the maintenance card used to pay for maintenance on certain vehicles. The additional information on the log sheet turned out to be helpful. Customers had sometimes complained about not receiving a customer card, and the log sheets provided useful information for resolving such problems.

**performance appraisal**
Formal feedback on how well an employee is performing his or her job.

Formal feedback on how well an employee is performing on the job is known as a **performance appraisal** (or a performance review or performance evaluation). Like the State of Colorado, most organizations require that supervisors conduct a performance appraisal on each of their employees regularly, typically once a year. Therefore, supervisors need to know how to appraise performance fairly.

This chapter discusses reasons for conducting performance appraisals and describes a process for appraising performances systematically. It describes various types of appraisals used by organizations today. It tells how to avoid biases and how to conduct an appraisal interview.

## Purposes of Performance Appraisal

Performance appraisals provide the information needed by employees to improve the quality of their work. To improve, employees need to hear how they are doing. As described in Chapters 6 and 10, a supervisor should provide frequent feedback. Performance appraisals supplement this informal information with a more thought-out, formal evaluation. (Employees who get enough informal feedback probably will not be surprised by the results of the appraisal.) A formal performance appraisal ensures that feedback to an employee covers all important aspects of the employee's performance.

Based on this information, the employee and supervisor can plan how to improve weak areas. In this way, performance appraisals support the practice of coaching, described in Chapter 17. One company that actively uses this benefit of performance appraisals is Datatec Industries of Fairfield, New Jersey, which installs computer systems in stores. At Datatec, all employees rate each other's performance monthly or quarterly. The frequency of these appraisals helps employees to see problem areas early, when they are easier to resolve.[1]

An appraisal also can help motivate employees. Most people appreciate the time their supervisor spends discussing their work, as well as praise for good performance; just hearing the supervisor's viewpoint can be motivating. Employees also tend to put forth the greatest effort in the areas that get appraised. Therefore, by rating employees on the kinds of behavior it considers important, an organization encourages them to try hard in those areas.

Com-Corp Industries, a Cleveland metal stamper that makes lightbulb shields for General Motors, wants its employees to participate in making suggestions and to develop skills that will improve the company's competitiveness. Therefore, the company's performance appraisals include a section in which employees are rated on "making the company a better place to work" through such activities as suggesting improvements or actually making improvements in their work area.[2]

Finally, performance appraisals provide important records for the organization. They are a useful source of information when deciding on raises, promotions, and discipline, and they provide evidence that these were administered fairly. A performance appraisal also provides documentation on employees whose behavior or performance is a problem. (For more on supervising problem employees, see Chapter 13.)

**FIGURE 18.1**

**The Process of Performance Appraisal**

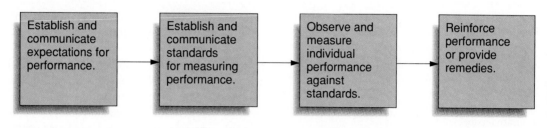

## A Systematic Approach to Appraising Performance

To deliver their potential benefits, appraisals must be completely fair and accurate. Supervisors therefore should be systematic in appraising performance. They should follow a thorough process, use objective measures when possible, and avoid discrimination.

### The Appraisal Process

The appraisal process takes place in four steps (see Figure 18.1). A supervisor establishes and communicates expectations for performance and standards for measuring performance. A supervisor also observes individual performance and measures it against the standards. Based on this information, a supervisor reinforces performance or provides remedies.

#### Establish and Communicate Expectations for Performance

During the planning process, a supervisor determines what the department or work group should accomplish (see Chapter 6). Through action plans, a supervisor spells out who is to do what to accomplish those objectives. From this information, it is relatively easy to specify what each employee must do to help the department or work group meet its objectives. One approach is to list the three to five major responsibilities of each position; the appraisal then focuses on these responsibilities.[3]

For example, suppose Francine Bloch supervises the delivery personnel for a chain of appliance stores in Dallas. Each driver is expected to operate the vehicle safely, deliver every appliance without damaging anything, and be polite to customers.

A supervisor must make sure employees know and understand what is expected of them. To do this, a supervisor should make sure that objectives for the employees are clear, and he or she should communicate them effectively (see Chapter 10).

## TIPS FROM THE FIRING LINE

### The Four Elements of Feedback

Feedback is perhaps the most important aspect of a performance appraisal; without it, an employee would never know what he or she was doing right or wrong. Without feedback, there can be no change. According to Mary Mavis, director of professional development for Sibson & Company, breaking the process into four elements helps the supervisor give accurate feedback:

- *Observations.* A supervisor must base feedback on observable behavior or the results of that behavior. Before a supervisor and employee can discuss interpretations of behavior or any necessary changes, the supervisor must be able to cite examples of certain behavior.
- *Assessment.* An assessment is a value judgment based on a certain standard. For instance, if an employee misses every staff meeting during a single month, the supervisor's assessment might be that the employee is unreliable about attending

meetings. The standard might be that missing one staff meeting is excusable, but missing them all is a problem. The assessment must be based on observations.
- *Consequences.* Consequences are the results of the behavior being observed by the supervisor. Consequences may be either negative (e.g., a reprimand) or positive (e.g., a promotion). During feedback, a supervisor and employee should discuss the consequences of both types of behavior.
- *Development.* Development involves a supervisor and an employee devising a plan for change, improvement, career advancement, and so forth. The plan should include a goal: reduction in tardiness, learning a new skill, a promotion.

Source: Mary Mavis, "Painless Performance Evaluations," *Training & Development*, Oct. 1994, pp. 40–44.

Employees are most likely to understand and be committed to objectives when they have a say in developing them. At Eastman Chemical Company, supervisors meet with each employee to establish mutually acceptable performance goals and expectations.[4]

### Establish and Communicate Standards for Measuring Performance

Because expectations for performance are objectives, each expectation should be measurable (see Chapter 6). In appraising performance, a supervisor's task includes deciding how to measure employees' performance and then making sure employees know what will be measured. With Francine's employees, the standards would include delivering all appliances without damage, having zero accidents or traffic tickets, and receiving no complaints from customers about service.

### Observe and Measure Individual Performance against Standards

Through the control process, a supervisor should continuously gather information about each employee's performance. (See "Tips from the Firing Line" for information needed for feedback.) This is an ongoing activity, not something the supervisor saves to do when filling out appraisal forms. When preparing a performance appraisal, a supervisor compares this information with the standards for the employee being appraised. In the example, Francine would keep records of uncompleted deliveries, damage, accidents, traffic tickets, and customer complaints (and compliments). When appraising a particular employee's performance, she can see how often those problems arose with the employee.

To motivate and encourage the right attitude, Jim Rosen, president of Fantastic Foods, a dry-soup manufacturer in Petaluma, California, helps employees to build self-esteem. One method he uses is self-appraisal, made possible by posting daily production goals in the factory. The employees are able to evaluate themselves. "It's automatic feedback, and it's impersonal," says Rosen. "The clarity takes away stress, and we want to get rid of all the stress we can."

Source: © Gary Laufman

### Reinforce Performance or Provide Remedies

To keep employees motivated and informed, a supervisor needs to tell them when they are doing something right, not just when they are making a mistake. Thus, the final step of the appraisal process includes reinforcement for good performance. This can be as simple as pointing out to employees where they have performed well. For example, Francine might compliment one of the drivers on a letter of praise from a customer. A supervisor might want to comment that this information will be placed in the employee's permanent record with the organization.

Where performance falls short of the standards, an employee needs to know how to improve. A supervisor may state a remedy, but asking the employee to help solve the problem is often more effective. In the case of a driver who has received two traffic tickets for illegal left turns, Francine might point out this situation and ask the driver for an explanation. The driver might reply that he was confused because he was lost. With that information, Francine and the driver can work together to get the driver better acquainted with finding his way around Dallas.

Francine and the driver are treating the underlying problem (the driver's difficulty in finding his way around), rather than the symptom (the traffic tickets). Therefore, the driver's performance in this area can improve in the future. In general, to move beyond discussing symptoms to uncover the underlying problems, a supervisor and employee can ask which of the following kinds of causes led to the poor performance:

- *Inadequate skills*—If the problem is the employee's lack of certain skills, a supervisor should see that the employee gets the necessary training, as described in the previous chapter.
- *Lack of effort*—If the problem is a lack of effort on the employee's part, a supervisor may need to apply the principles of motivation discussed in Chapter 11.
- *Shortcomings of the process*—If organizational or job-related policies and procedures reward inefficient or less than high-quality behavior, the supervisor and employee may be able to change the way work is done.

- *External conditions*—If the problem is something beyond the control of supervisor and employee (e.g., a poor economy, lack of cooperation from another department, or a strike by suppliers), the appraisal standards and ratings should be adjusted so that they are fair to the employee.
- *Personal problems*—If performance is suffering because the employee has personal problems, a supervisor should handle the situation with counseling and discipline (see Chapter 13).

In investigating the underlying problem, a supervisor may gain important insights by asking what can be done to help the employee reach goals.[5] Before the appraisal is over, an employee should have a clear plan for making necessary changes.

## What to Measure in an Appraisal

Waitress Kelly O'Hara was furious as she walked out of her performance appraisal interview. "Irresponsible!" she muttered to herself, "Lazy! Who does he think he is, calling me those things? He doesn't know what he's talking about." Kelly's reaction shows that labeling people with certain characteristics is not a constructive approach to conducting an appraisal. Labels tend to put people on the defensive, and they are difficult, if not impossible, to prove.

Instead, a performance appraisal should focus on *behavior* and *results*. Focusing on behavior means that the appraisal should describe specific actions or patterns of actions. Focusing on results means describing the extent to which an employee has satisfied the objectives for which he or she is responsible. If Kelly's supervisor had noted that he had received several complaints about slow service, he and Kelly could have worked on a plan to minimize these complaints. Perhaps the problem was not even Kelly's behavior, but recurrent backlogs in the kitchen. The focus on meeting objectives would be more constructive than simply evaluating Kelly as "lazy," because it tells an employee exactly what is expected. This focus is also more fair, especially if the employee helped to set the objectives.

In many cases, a supervisor uses an appraisal form that requires drawing conclusions about the employee's personal characteristics. For example, a supervisor might need to rate an employee's dependability or attitude. Although such ratings are necessarily subjective, a supervisor can try to base them on observations about behavior and results. One approach is to record at least one specific example for each category rated. A rating on a personal characteristic seems more reasonable when a supervisor has evidence supporting his or her conclusion.

## EEOC Guidelines

As described in Chapter 16, the Equal Employment Opportunity Commission (EEOC) is the government agency charged with enforcing federal laws against discrimination. The EEOC has published the Uniform Guidelines on Employee Selection Procedures, which include guidelines for designing and implementing performance appraisals. In general, the behaviors or characteristics measured by a performance appraisal should be related to the job and to succeeding on the job. For example, if the appraisal measures "grooming," then good grooming should be important for success in the job. Because of this requirement, a supervisor and others responsible for the content of performance appraisals should make sure that what they measure is still relevant to a particular job.

Just as hiring should be based on a candidate's ability to perform the essential tasks of a particular job, so appraisals should be based on the employee's success in carrying out those tasks. The ratings in a performance appraisal should not be discriminatory; that is, they should not be based on an employee's race, sex, or other protected category but on an employee's ability to meet standards of performance. Furthermore, an employee should know in advance what those standards are, and the organization should have a system in place for employees to ask questions about their ratings.

### Performance Appraisals and Pay Reviews

Many organizations review an employee's wage or salary level at the time of the performance appraisal. This reinforces the link the company makes between performance and pay increases. An employee with an excellent rating would be eligible to receive the largest allowable increase, whereas someone rated as a poor worker might not get any raise or only a cost-of-living increase.

However, reviewing pay and performance at the same time presents a potentially serious drawback.[6] Employees tend to focus on the issue of money, so a supervisor has more difficulty using the performance evaluation as an opportunity for motivating and coaching. Thus, many experts recommend conducting the two types of reviews at separate times. A supervisor of course has little choice in this matter. A supervisor who must review pay rates at the same time as performance should make an extra effort to emphasize performance, and it is especially important to provide coaching and feedback about performance throughout the year.

## Types of Appraisals

Many techniques have been developed for appraising performance. The human resources department or higher-level management usually dictate which type the supervisor will use. An organization that has all supervisors use the same approach establishes a way to keep records showing performance over time, especially when an employee reports to more than one supervisor during his or her employment. Although a supervisor has to use the appraisal format selected for the whole organization, he or she may be able to supplement it with other helpful information. A supervisor can use the "Comments" section of a preprinted form or attach additional information to it, as Nancy Acedo does when appraising the employees of Colorado's Fleet Management Program.

### Graphic Rating Scales

**graphic rating scale**
A performance appraisal that rates the degree to which an employee has achieved various characteristics.

The most commonly used type of appraisal is the **graphic rating scale,** which rates the degree to which an employee has achieved various characteristics, such as job knowledge or punctuality. The rating is often scored from 1 to 5, for example, with 5 representing excellent performance and 1 representing poor performance. Some appraisal forms include space for comments, so that a supervisor can provide support for his or her ratings. Figure 18.2 is a sample appraisal form using a graphic rating scale.

The main advantage of a graphic rating scale is that it is relatively easy to use. In addition, the scores provide a basis for deciding whether an employee has improved in various areas. However, the ratings themselves are subjective; what one

### ■ FIGURE 18.2

## Sample Graphic Rating Scale

| Name_____ | Dept._____ | Date_____ | | | | |
|---|---|---|---|---|---|---|
| | | **Outstanding** | **Good** | **Satisfactory** | **Fair** | **Unsatisfactory** |
| **Quantity of work** | Volume of acceptable work under normal conditions | ☐ | ☐ | ☐ | ☐ | ☐ |
| | Comments: | | | | | |
| **Quality of work** | Thoroughness, neatness, and accuracy of work | ☐ | ☐ | ☐ | ☐ | ☐ |
| | Comments: | | | | | |
| **Knowledge of job** | Clear understanding of the facts or factors pertinent to the job | ☐ | ☐ | ☐ | ☐ | ☐ |
| | Comments: | | | | | |
| **Personal qualities** | Personality, appearance, sociability, leadership, integrity | ☐ | ☐ | ☐ | ☐ | ☐ |
| | Comments: | | | | | |
| **Cooperation** | Ability and willingness to work with associates, super-visors, and subordinates toward common goals | ☐ | ☐ | ☐ | ☐ | ☐ |
| | Comments: | | | | | |
| **Dependability** | Conscientious, thorough, accurate, reliable with respect to attendance, lunch periods, reliefs, etc. | ☐ | ☐ | ☐ | ☐ | ☐ |
| | Comments: | | | | | |
| **Initiative** | Earnestness in seeking increased responsibilities. Self-starting, unafraid to proceed alone | ☐ | ☐ | ☐ | ☐ | ☐ |
| | Comments: | | | | | |

Source: John M. Ivancevich, *Human Resource Management: Foundations of Personnel*, 5th ed. (Homewood, IL: Richard D. Irwin, 1992), p. 307.

supervisor considers "excellent" may be only "average" to another. Also, many supervisors tend to rate everyone at least a little above average. Some appraisal forms attempt to overcome these problems by containing descriptions of excellent or poor behavior in each area. Other rating scales pose a different problem by labeling performance in terms of how well an employee "meets requirements." Presumably, the supervisor wants *all* employees to meet the requirements of the job. However, scoring everyone high on this scale may be seen as a rating bias (on the assumption that not everyone can be a "top performer"), rather than successful management of human resources.[7]

## Paired-Comparison Approach

**paired-comparison approach**
A performance appraisal that measures the relative performance of employees in a group.

The **paired-comparison approach** measures the relative performance of employees in a group. A supervisor lists the employees in the group and then ranks them. One method is to compare the performance of the first two employees on the list. A supervisor places a checkmark next to the name of the employee whose performance is better, then repeats the process, comparing the first employee's performance with that of the other employees. Next, the supervisor compares the second employee on the list with all the others, and so on until each pair of employees has been compared. The employee with the most checkmarks is considered the most valuable.

A supervisor also can compare employees in terms of several criteria, such as work quantity and quality. For each criterion, a supervisor ranks the employees from best to worst, assigning a 1 to the lowest-ranked employee and the highest score to the best employee in that category. Then all the scores for each employee are totaled to see who has the highest total score.

The paired-comparison approach is appropriate when a supervisor needs to find one outstanding employee in a group. It can be used to identify the best candidate for a promotion or special assignment. However, paired comparison makes some employees look good at the expense of others, which makes this technique less useful as a means of providing feedback to individual employees. It is especially inappropriate as a routine form of appraisal in situations calling for cooperation and teamwork.[8]

## Forced-Choice Approach

**forced-choice approach**
A performance appraisal that presents an appraiser with sets of statements describing employee behavior; the appraiser must choose which statement is most characteristic of the employee and which is least characteristic.

In the **forced-choice approach,** the appraisal form gives a supervisor sets of statements describing employee behavior. For each set of statements, a supervisor must choose one that is most characteristic and one that is least characteristic of the employee. Figure 18.3 illustrates part of an appraisal form using the forced-choice approach.

These questionnaires tend to be set up in a way that prevents a supervisor from saying only positive things about employees. Thus, the forced-choice approach is used when an organization determines that supervisors have been rating an unbelievably high proportion of employees as above average.

**FIGURE 18.3**

Sample Forced-
Choice Appraisal

| Instructions: | Rank from 1 to 4 the following sets of statements according to how they describe the manner in which_____ performs |
|---|---|

the job. A rank of 1 should be used for the most descriptive statement, and a rank of 4 should be given for the least descriptive. No ties are allowed.

1. _____ Does not anticipate difficulties
   _____ Grasps explanations quickly
   _____ Rarely wastes time
   _____ Easy to talk to
2. _____ A leader in group activities
   _____ Wastes time on unimportant things
   _____ Cool and calm at all times
   _____ Hard worker

Source: John M. Ivancevich, *Human Resource Management: Foundations of Personnel,* 5th ed. (Homewood, IL: Richard D. Irwin, 1992), p. 310.

## Essay Appraisal

Sometimes a supervisor must write a description of the employee's performance, answering questions such as "What are the major strengths of this employee?" or "In what areas does this employee need improvement?" Essay appraisals often are used along with other types of appraisals, notably graphic rating scales. They provide an opportunity for a supervisor to describe aspects of performance that are not thoroughly covered by an appraisal questionnaire. The main drawback of essay appraisals is that their quality depends on a supervisor's writing skills.

## Behaviorally Anchored Rating Scales (BARS)

**behaviorally anchored rating scales (BARS)**
A performance appraisal in which an employee is rated on scales containing statements describing performance in several areas.

Some organizations pay behavioral scientists or organizational psychologists to create **behaviorally anchored rating scales (BARS).** These scales rate employee performance in several areas, such as work quantity and quality, using a series of statements that describe effective and ineffective performance in each area. In each area, a supervisor selects the statement that best describes how an employee performs. The statements in the rating scales are different for each job title in the organization. Figure 18.4 shows a behaviorally anchored rating scale measuring the performance area of engineering competence.

The major advantage of using BARS is that they can be tailored to the organization's objectives for employees. In addition, the BARS approach is less subjective than some other approaches because it uses statements describing behavior. However, developing the scales is time-consuming and therefore relatively expensive.

**FIGURE 18.4**

**Sample Behaviorally Anchored Rating Scale (BARS)**

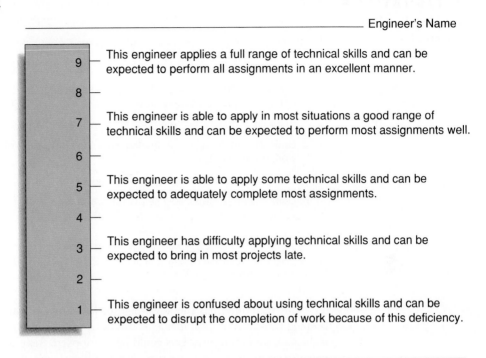

———————————————————————————— Engineer's Name

9 — This engineer applies a full range of technical skills and can be expected to perform all assignments in an excellent manner.

8 —

7 — This engineer is able to apply in most situations a good range of technical skills and can be expected to perform most assignments well.

6 —

5 — This engineer is able to apply some technical skills and can be expected to adequately complete most assignments.

4 —

3 — This engineer has difficulty applying technical skills and can be expected to bring in most projects late.

2 —

1 — This engineer is confused about using technical skills and can be expected to disrupt the completion of work because of this deficiency.

Source: John M. Ivancevich, *Human Resource Management: Foundations of Personnel,* 5th ed. (Homewood, IL: Richard D. Irwin, 1992), p. 312.

## Checklist Appraisal

A checklist appraisal contains a series of questions about an employee's performance. Figure 18.5 shows the format for this kind of appraisal. A supervisor answers yes or no to the questions. Thus, a checklist is merely a record of performance, not an evaluation by a supervisor. The human resources department has a key for scoring the items on the checklist; the score results in a rating of an employee's performance.

While the checklist appraisal is easy to complete, it has several disadvantages. The checklist can be difficult to prepare, and each job category will probably require a different set of questions. Also, a supervisor has no way to adjust the answers for any special circumstances that affect performance.

## Critical-Incident Appraisal

**critical-incident appraisal**
A performance appraisal in which a supervisor keeps a written record of incidents that show positive and negative ways an employee has acted; the supervisor uses this record to assess the employee's performance.

To conduct a **critical-incident appraisal,** a supervisor keeps a written record of incidents that show positive and negative ways an employee has acted. The record should include dates, people involved, actions taken, and any other relevant details. At the time of the appraisal, a supervisor reviews the record to reach an overall evaluation of an employee's behavior. During the appraisal interview, a supervisor should give an employee a chance to offer his or her views of each incident recorded.

**FIGURE 18.5**

**Sample Checklist Appraisal**

|  | Yes | No |
|---|---|---|
| 1. Does the employee willingly cooperate with others in completing work assignments? | _____ | _____ |
| 2. Does the employee have adequate job knowledge to perform duties in a satisfactory manner? | _____ | _____ |
| 3. In terms of quality, is the employee's work acceptable? | _____ | _____ |
| 4. Does the employee meet deadlines for the completion of work assignments? | _____ | _____ |
| 5. Does the employee's record indicate unexcused absences? | _____ | _____ |
| 6. Does the employee follow safety rules and regulations? | _____ | _____ |

Source: Stephen E. Catt and Donald S. Miller, *Supervision: Working with People*, 2nd ed. (Homewood, IL: Richard D. Irwin, 1991), p. 374.

This technique has the advantage of focusing on actual behaviors. However, keeping records of critical incidents can be time-consuming and, even if a supervisor is diligent, important incidents could be overlooked. Also, supervisors tend to record negative events more than positive ones, resulting in an overly harsh appraisal.

### Work-Standards Approach

**work-standards approach**
A performance appraisal in which an appraiser compares an employee's performance with objective measures of what the employee should do.

To use the **work-standards approach,** a supervisor tries to establish objective measures of performance. A typical work standard would be the quantity produced by an assembly-line worker. This amount should reflect what a person normally could produce. A supervisor then compares an employee's actual performance with the standards.

Although the work-standards approach has been applied largely to production workers, the principle of objectively measuring outcomes make sense for a variety of jobs. A recent review of performance appraisals recommends describing each job in terms of 6 to 16 results that the organization wants accomplished.[9] The job results associated with customer service positions, for instance, might include "Serves customers by providing service requested." Then quality standards are established for achieving each result. The quality standard for the previous example might be "Customers are treated with courtesy at all times. Questions and requests are responded to promptly."[10] Under this system, performance appraisals would focus on two issues: Did the employee meet the quality standards? If not, what changes are required to the work process, access to resources, training, motivation, and so on?

### Management by Objectives (MBO)

Chapter 6 introduced management by objectives (MBO) as a planning tool. In an organization that uses MBO, a supervisor will also use this approach for appraising performance. A supervisor compares each employee's accomplishments with

The Circle of Excellence award reinforces excellent performance at Fleetwood Enterprises. Fleetwood produces recreational vehicles and manufactured housing. It presents the award to the retailer that best achieves outstanding levels of customer satisfaction.

Source: Courtesy of Fleetwood Enterprises, Inc.

the objectives for that employee. If the employee has met or exceeded his or her objectives, the appraisal will be favorable. The main advantages of this system are that an employee knows what is expected and a supervisor focuses on results rather than more subjective criteria.

### Assessments by Someone Other than the Supervisor

Supervisors cannot know how an employee behaves at all times or in all situations. Nor can supervisors always appreciate the full impact of an employee's behavior on people inside and outside the organization. To supplement what supervisors do know, other people might offer insights into an employee's behavior. For this reason, supervisors may combine their appraisals with self-assessments by the employee or with appraisals by peers and customers. Appraisals of supervisors and other managers also may come from their subordinates. Combining several sources of appraisals is called **360-degree feedback**.[11]

To use self-assessments, a supervisor can ask each employee to complete an assessment before the appraisal interview. Then the supervisor and employee compare the employee's evaluation of his or her own behavior with the supervisor's evaluation. This can stimulate discussion and insights in areas where the two are in disagreement.

Appraisals by peers—often called **peer reviews**—are less common, but their use is growing. Com-Corp Industries uses peer reviews to balance an appraisal that is affected by a supervisor's feelings about an employee. If the peer reviews conflict with a supervisor's appraisal, the company's human resources director investigates the source of the discrepancy.[12] At Eastman Chemical, employees who work in teams appraise the performance of their team members. The teams do this in meetings, where they discuss each team member's strengths and areas needing improvement.[13] Presumably, employees will react more positively to peer reviews in which all employees participate in the appraising on an equal basis than to peer reviews used occasionally for selected employees.

**360-degree feedback**
Performance appraisal that combines assessments from several sources.

**peer reviews**
Performance appraisals conducted by an employee's co-workers.

## MEETING THE CHALLENGE

### Companies Boost Quality with Customer Feedback

It's an idea that is rapidly spreading among large and small companies: Ask customers what they think of employees' performance. After all, satisfied customers keep a company in business. And ultimately, in some way, it is the job of every employee to keep customers satisfied.

National Fuel Gas Corporation uses telephone surveys to learn how happy customers are with the service they get from sales reps. (If customers prefer to respond in writing, the company mails out questionnaires.) Teleport Communications Group (TCG) sends customers questionnaires that ask: "Does your sales rep know your industry?" "Has your sales rep promised anything he or she hasn't delivered?" IBM uses a combination of blind telephone surveys and person-to-person meetings to learn more about sales reps' service. In all of these cases, customer ratings are tied to the overall performance review (it counts for 15 percent of the review at National Fuel Gas and TCG) and subsequently to pay raises and bonuses (up to 20 percent of base pay at TCG and 20 percent of commissions at IBM). Serving customers has taken on a new importance for many of these employees.

Initially, the sales forces at these organizations did not meet this new twist in the performance review with enthusiasm. "I was very angry," recalls Maryann Cirenza, senior account executive at TCG. She felt betrayed by her own company. "I thought the com-

pany was checking up on me. The questions were very leading, leading customers to say critical things about the reps. It was a total interrogation. I felt there was no trust." Bruce Hale, senior vice-president at National Fuel Gas, notes, "Poor performers are not in love with [the new system], and the marginal ones are scared to death." The flip side, however, is that top performers actually like the plan because "it gives them additional clout to do their jobs."

They also are finding out that the new system can help them improve their performance—and earn heftier pay raises and bonuses. Maryann Cirenza comments that once she got used to it, the customer satisfaction measure "made me focus." When some of her customers noted that she could benefit from a greater knowledge of her industry, she subscribed to trade magazines, read her customers' newsletters, and listened harder to her customers. Recently, she banked a bonus of 20 percent of her base pay.

IBM salesman Greg Buseman sums up the impact of the new type of performance review: "People hate change, but we're transforming this business. I've been liberated from selling boxes. Now I can really focus on understanding the customer's business. I can make the technical calls when something goes wrong. I can see that the problem gets fixed."

Source: Lisa Holton, "Look Who's in on Your Performance Review," *Selling*, Jan.–Feb. 1995, pp. 47–56.

The drive to please customers in a highly competitive market, coupled with a desire for practical information on performance, has encouraged some companies to institute programs in which customers appraise employees' performance. (See "Meeting the Challenge.") Major companies using customer appraisals include IBM, Sears, Ameritech, and Motorola. National Fuel Gas Distribution Corporation, headquartered in Buffalo, New York, asks its major customers to assess salespeople's performance in several areas, including product knowledge and problem-solving ability.[14]

At an increasing number of major corporations, including Amoco, Cigna, and Du Pont, subordinates rate how well their bosses manage.[15] Typically, ratings are anonymous, to protect the workers. The purpose of these subordinate appraisals is to give managers information they can use to supervise more effectively and to make their organization more competitive. The appraisals also support the trend toward giving operative employees a greater voice in how an organization is run.

### Benefits of 360-Degree Feedback

Combining several sources of performance appraisal can correct for some of the appraisal biases described in the next section. It also can provide information that is more useful for problem solving and employee development than the typical results of a traditional top-down appraisal. After New York–based Teleport Communications Group had customers rate the performance of its salespeople, sales rep Maryann Cirenza learned of shortcomings that helped her refocus on activities the customers found more valuable.[16] Similarly, Joe Malik, who manages a team of engineers at AT&T, was surprised to learn from a subordinate review that his employees were not focused merely on day-to-day challenges, but expected him to communicate a vision and a mission for his group.[17] Coming from one person, such challenges can be easy to ignore. When combined voices force a person to listen, the resulting improvements can enhance the person's long-term career prospects.

### Guidelines for 360-Degree Feedback

For 360-feedback to be effective, the person managing the review process should ensure that the responses are anonymous. Subordinates especially may be afraid to respond honestly if they think that the person being reviewed will retaliate for negative comments. Anonymity is greater if the responses are pooled into a single report rather than presented one by one. Collecting appraisals from more than three or four people also increases the likelihood of protecting respondents' privacy.[18]

## Sources of Bias

Ideally, supervisors should be completely objective in their appraisals of employees. Each appraisal should directly reflect an employee's performance, not any biases of a supervisor. Of course, this is impossible to do perfectly. We all make compromises in our decision-making strategies and have biases in evaluating what other people do. Supervisors need to be aware of these biases, so that their effect on the appraisals can be limited or eliminated. Figure 18.6 shows some sources of bias that commonly influence performance appraisals.

Some supervisors are prone to a **harshness bias,** that is, rating employees more severely than their performance merits. New supervisors are especially susceptible to this error, because they may feel a need to be taken seriously. Unfortunately, the harshness bias also tends to frustrate and discourage workers, who resent the unfair assessments of their performance.

At the other extreme is the **leniency bias.** Supervisors with this bias rate their employees more favorably than their performance merits. A recent study suggests that the leniency bias is widespread; in 70 percent of the appraisals, managers inflated their ratings of employees.[19] A supervisor who does this may want credit for developing a department full of "excellent" workers. Or the supervisor may simply be uncomfortable confronting employees with their shortcomings. The leniency bias may feel like an advantage to the employees who receive the favorable ratings, but it cheats the employees and department of the benefits of truly developing and coaching employees.

**harshness bias**
Rating employees more severely than their performance merits.

**leniency bias**
Rating employees more favorably than their performance merits.

**FIGURE 18.6**

**Sources of Bias in Performance Appraisals**

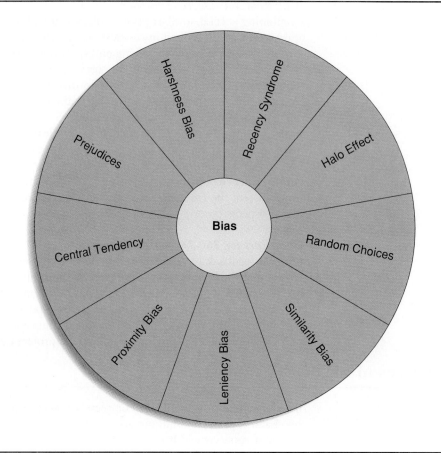

**central tendency**
The tendency to select employee ratings in the middle of a scale.

**proximity bias**
The tendency to assign similar scores to items that are near each other on a questionnaire.

A bias that characterizes the responses to many types of questionnaires is **central tendency,** which is the tendency to select ratings in the middle of the scale. People seem more comfortable on middle ground than taking a strong stand at either extreme. This bias causes a supervisor to miss important opportunities to praise or correct employees.

*Proximity* means nearness. The **proximity bias** refers to the tendency to assign similar scores to items that are near each other on a questionnaire. If a supervisor assigns a score of 8 to one appraisal item, this bias might encourage the supervisor to score the next item as 6 or 7, even though a score of 3 is more accurate. Obviously, this can result in misleading appraisals.

When using a type of appraisal that requires answers to specific questions, a supervisor might succumb to making *random choices*. A supervisor might do this when uncertain how to answer or when the overall scoring on the test looks undesirable. For example, if a supervisor thinks an appraisal is scoring an employee too low, he or she might give favorable ratings in some areas where the supervisor has no strong feelings. Supervisors who catch themselves making random choices should slow down and try to apply objective criteria.

**similarity bias**
The tendency to judge others more positively when they are like yourself.

The **similarity bias** refers to the tendency to judge others more positively when they are like ourselves. Thus, we tend to look more favorably on people who share our interests, tastes, background, or other characteristics. For example, in appraising performance, a supervisor risks viewing a person's performance in a favorable light because the employee shares his or her flair for dressing in the latest fashions. Or a supervisor might interpret negatively the performance of an employee who is much shyer than the supervisor.

As described in Chapter 9, the *recency syndrome* refers to the human tendency to place the most weight on events that have occurred most recently. In a performance appraisal, a supervisor might give particular weight to a problem the employee caused last week or an award the employee just won whereas he or she should be careful to consider events and behaviors that occurred throughout the entire period covered by the review. The most accurate way to do this is to keep records throughout the year, as described earlier with conducting a critical-incident appraisal.

The *halo effect*, introduced in Chapter 16, refers to the tendency to generalize one positive or negative aspect of a person to the person's entire performance. Thus, if supervisor Ben Olson thinks that a pleasant telephone manner is what makes a good customer service representative, he is apt to give high marks to a representative with a pleasant voice, no matter what the employee actually says to the customers or how reliable the performance.

Finally, the supervisor's *prejudices* about various types of people can unfairly influence a performance appraisal. A supervisor needs to remember that each employee is an individual, not merely a representative of a group. A supervisor who believes that African Americans generally have poor skills in using Standard English needs to recognize that this is a prejudice about a group, not a fact to apply to actual employees. Thus, before recommending that a black salesperson needs to improve her speaking skills, a supervisor must consider whether the salesperson really needs improvement in that area or whether the supervisor's prejudices are interfering with an accurate assessment. This is especially important in light of the EEOC guidelines discussed earlier in the chapter.

# The Performance Appraisal Interview

The last stage of the appraisal process—the stage at which a supervisor reinforces performance or provides remedies—occurs in an interview between supervisor and employee. At this time, a supervisor describes what he or she has observed and discusses this appraisal with the employee. Together they agree on areas for improvement and development. The Self-Quiz on page 561 lets you test your own interviewing skills. If you have never been a supervisor, apply the questions to the way your current or most recent supervisor has appraised your performance.

Supervisors often dread conducting appraisal interviews. Pointing out another person's shortcomings can be an unpleasant experience. To overcome these feelings, it helps to focus on the benefits of appraising employees. Supervisors can cultivate a positive attitude by viewing the appraisal interview as an opportunity to coach and develop employees.

Positively reinforcing employee performance during an appraisal review can be key to good ongoing employee relations. A recent issue of *Food Industry News* stated that one of the seven most common reasons for employees leaving their jobs was poor feedback; they received no guidance or reassurance from supervisors about the quality of their performance on the job.

Source: © Bruce Ayres/Tony Stone Images

### Purpose of the Interview

Quite simply, the purpose of holding an appraisal interview is to communicate information about an employee's performance. Once a supervisor has evaluated an employee's performance, the supervisor needs to convey his or her thoughts to the employee. An interview is an appropriate setting for doing so because it sets aside time to focus on and discuss the appraisal in private. The interview is also an opportunity for upward communication from the employee. By contributing his or her viewpoints and ideas, an employee can work with the supervisor on devising ways to improve performance. (Chapter 10 provides guidelines for communicating effectively.)

### Preparing for the Interview

Before the appraisal interview, a supervisor should allow plenty of time for completing the appraisal form. The form should be completed carefully and thoughtfully, not in a rush during the hour before the interview. Besides filling out the form, a supervisor should think about the employee's likely reactions to the appraisal and should plan how to handle them. A supervisor also should be ready with some ideas for correcting problems noted in the appraisal.

A supervisor should notify the employee about the appraisal interview ahead of time. Giving a few days' or a week's notice allows the employee to think about his or her performance. Then the employee can contribute ideas during the interview.

In addition, a supervisor should prepare an appropriate meeting place. The interview should take place in an office or other room where supervisor and employee will have privacy. The supervisor should arrange to prevent interruptions such as telephone calls.

## Conducting the Interview

At the beginning of the interview, a supervisor should try to put an employee at ease. Employees are often uncomfortable at the prospect of discussing their performance. An offer of coffee and a little small talk may help to break the ice.

The supervisor can begin by reviewing the employee's self-appraisal, if one was completed, with the employee, asking him or her to give reasons for the various ratings. Then a supervisor describes his or her rating of the employee and how he or she arrived at it. A supervisor can start by describing overall impressions and then explain the contents of the appraisal form. A supervisor should explain the basis for the ratings, using specific examples of the employee's behavior and results. Most employees are waiting for the "bad news," so it is probably most effective to describe areas for improvement first, followed by the employee's strengths. People need to know what they are doing well so that they will continue on that course, realizing that their efforts are appreciated.

After describing the evaluation of the employee's performance, a supervisor should give the employee time to offer feedback. The employee should be able to agree or disagree with the supervisor's conclusions, as well as to ask questions. This is an important time for the supervisor to keep an open mind and apply the listening skills discussed in Chapter 10. Hearing the employee's reactions is the first step toward resolving any problems described in the appraisal.

### Problem Solving and Coaching

When the supervisor and employee understand each other's point of view, they should reach a decision on how to solve problems described in the appraisal. Together they can come up with a number of alternatives and select the solutions that seem most promising. Sometimes the best solution is for the employee to make behavioral changes; at other times, the supervisor may need to make changes, such as keeping the employee better informed or improving work processes.

Proponents of quality management—notably W. Edwards Deming—have criticized performance appraisals for connecting rewards mainly to individual performance.[20] The problem, they say, is that how well employees perform depends mainly on the organization's systems. Quality work can't be performed by an employee who lacks needed information, authority, or materials. With this in mind, supervisors should be open to ways in which improving performance is a mutual effort. (Chapter 9 provides further guidelines for decision making and problem solving.)

Besides problem solving, appraisal interviews often include time for discussion related to coaching the employee and helping the employee to develop a career with the organization. Strengths and shortcomings identified in the performance appraisal often provide indications of areas in which the supervisor and employee could work together to develop desirable skills through further training or experience. Discussing employees' potential for growth and improvement is essential. As AlliedSignal's Lawrence A. Bossidy once told a manager, "You have to keep growing just to stay where you are," much less to advance in the organization.[21] However, employees tend to have difficulty shifting their focus away from pay and past performance especially when performance appraisals are directly or

### FIGURE 18.7

**The Process of Conducting a Performance Appraisal Interview**

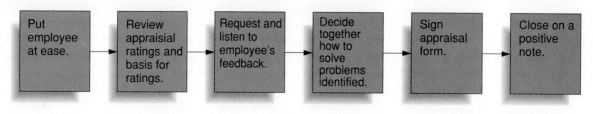

indirectly tied to pay levels.[22] A supervisor therefore should not use performance appraisal interviews as a substitute for coaching on a continuing basis.

### Signatures

At the end of the interview, the supervisor and employee usually are required to sign the appraisal form. By doing so, they acknowledge that the interview has been conducted and that the employee has read and understood the form. If the employee refuses to sign, the supervisor can explain that this is all the employee's signature means. If that explanation does not persuade the employee to sign, the supervisor can note on the appraisal form that the employee refused to sign and can check with the human resources department regarding what procedures to follow next. The employee should receive a copy of the appraisal form.

The supervisor should close the interview on a positive note, with a comment such as, "You've been doing a great job," or, "I think that with the plans we've made, your work will soon be up to standards." Figure 18.7 summarizes the interviewing process.

### Follow-Up

Even after the interview is over, a supervisor continues appraising performance. He or she needs to follow up on any actions planned during the interview. Is the employee making the promised changes? Is the supervisor providing the resources, such as training, that are necessary for improvements to occur? This follow-up should be an ongoing process, not an activity left for the next year's performance appraisal.

## Summary

**18.1   Summarize benefits of conducting performance appraisals.**

Performance appraisals provide information necessary for employees to improve the quality of their work. Appraisals can motivate employees by demonstrating the interest of the supervisor and the organization in them, keeping them informed, and indicating the important areas of performance. Performance appraisals also provide important records for the company, which managers use to make decisions on raises, promotions, and discipline.

**18.2   Identify the steps in appraising performance systematically.**

First, a supervisor establishes and communicates expectations for performance; then he or she establishes and communicates standards for measuring performance. A supervisor observes each employee's performance, measuring it against the standards. Finally, a supervisor provides reinforcement for acceptable or excellent performance and works with the employee to develop remedies for inadequate performance.

**18.3    Discuss guidelines for avoiding discrimination in performance appraisals.**

As much as possible, an appraisal should focus on objective measures of behavior and results—specifically, how well an employee carries out the essential tasks of the job. The behaviors and employee characteristics measured should be related to the job and to succeeding on the job.

**18.4    Compare types of appraisals.**

Graphic rating scales rate the degree to which an employee has achieved various characteristics, such as job knowledge and punctuality. The paired-comparison approach measures the relative performance of employees in a group. The forced-choice approach presents a supervisor with sets of statements describing employee behavior, and the supervisor chooses the statements which are most characteristic of the employee and which are least. An essay appraisal includes one or more paragraphs describing an employee's performance. Behaviorally anchored rating scales (BARS) rate employee performance in several areas by using a series of statements that describe effective and ineffective performance in each area. A checklist appraisal consists of a series of yes-or-no questions about an employee's performance. A critical-incident appraisal is based on an ongoing record of incidents in which an employee has behaved positively or negatively. The work-standards approach is based on establishing objective measures of performance, against which an employee's performance is compared. Management by objectives is a system of developing goals with employees and comparing their performance to those goals. In addition, a supervisor may combine several sources of appraisal in 360-degree feedback, having employees prepare self-assessments, obtaining peer assessments and customer assessments, or asking for appraisals (usually anonymous) of the supervisor.

**18.5    Describe sources of bias in appraising performance.**

Supervisors who want to prove they are tough may succumb to the harshness bias, rating employees too severely; supervisors who hate to deliver bad news may succumb to the leniency bias, rating employees too favorably. The central tendency leads some supervisors to give their employees rankings in the middle of the scale. The proximity bias refers to the tendency to assign similar scores to items that are near each other on a questionnaire. Random choices sometimes are made when an appraiser is uncertain about answers or uncomfortable with an overall rating. The similarity bias is the tendency of people to judge others more positively when they are like themselves. The recency syndrome may lead a supervisor to give too much weight to events that have occurred recently. The halo effect leads an appraiser to use one positive or negative trait to describe a person's entire performance. Finally, people are influenced by their prejudices about groups.

**18.6    Explain the purpose of conducting performance appraisal interviews.**

The purpose of conducting an interview is to communicate the supervisor's impressions of an employee's performance to that employee. In addition, it is an opportunity for an employee to present his or her viewpoint and ideas so that supervisor and employee can work together on improving performance.

**18.7    Tell how supervisors should prepare for a performance appraisal interview.**

A supervisor should take as much time as necessary to complete an appraisal form thoughtfully. A supervisor also should think about how the employee is likely to react and should plan how to handle his or her reactions. A supervisor should be ready with ideas for resolving problems noted in the appraisal. A supervisor should notify the employee about the interview ahead of time and should prepare an appropriate place to meet without interruptions.

**18.8    Describe guidelines for conducting the interview.**

First, a supervisor should attempt to put the employee at ease. Then the supervisor and employee should go over the self-appraisal, if any, and the supervisor's appraisal of the employee. A supervisor should focus first on areas for improvement and next on areas of strength. The employee should have time to give feedback; then the supervisor and employee should work together to develop solutions to any problems identified. The supervisor and employee sign the appraisal form, and then the supervisor closes with a positive comment. After the interview, the supervisor needs to follow up to make sure that planned actions are taken.

## Key Terms

performance appraisal

graphic rating scale

paired-comparison approach

forced-choice approach

behaviorally anchored rating scales (BARS)

critical-incident appraisal

work-standards approach

360-degree feedback

peer reviews

harshness bias

leniency bias

central tendency

proximity bias

similarity bias

## Review and Discussion Questions

1. What is a performance appraisal? How do organizations benefit from using performance appraisals?

2. June Pearson was just promoted to supervisor of the bookkeeping department at an insurance company. Based on the company's schedule for appraising performance, she needs to conduct an appraisal of Ron Yamamoto, one of the employees, only a month after she started the job. June cannot find any records of goals established for Ron, so she asks his peers and others with whom he has contact to describe Ron's performance. Based on this information, June completes an appraisal form and conducts an interview.

   a. Which steps of the systematic approach to appraising performance has June omitted?
   b. How do you think Ron will react to this interview?
   c. Can you think of anything else June could have done to improve this particular appraisal? Explain.

3. Name and describe briefly the five kinds of causes of poor performance.

4. Which of the following are appropriate ways to measure an employee's performance?

   a. Day after day, more than three customers are lined up at Janet's cash register, so her supervisor concludes that she is a slow worker.
   b. Jonathan smiles a lot, so his supervisor assumes he is happy.
   c. Wesley is late to work every Wednesday morning, so his supervisor plans to find out the cause.

   d. Nick habitually takes longer to deliver pizzas than his company promises its customers, so his supervisor notes that he is inefficient.
   e. Production in the group that Caitlin oversees has fallen off somewhat in the last two months, so her supervisor discusses with her the possible reasons.

5. How can a supervisor avoid illegal discrimination in performance appraisals?

6. At a manufacturing company in a south suburb of Chicago, one policy stated that each manager and employee must be appraised at one-year intervals. At the same time, the company conducts a review of the person's wages or salary, usually giving at least a small raise. In recent years, like many manufacturers, this company has become concerned about reducing costs. The policy about conducting performance appraisals has been modified: managers' appraisals now must be conducted *at least* a year after the manager's salary was last reviewed. One supervisor was reviewed in December of one year, then in February (14 months later), and then in May of the third year.

   a. What reasons do you think the supervisor's manager had for delaying the performance appraisals so that they were more than a year apart?
   b. What effects do you think the delays had on the supervisor?

7. What type of performance appraisal is used most frequently? What are advantages and disadvantages of this approach?

8. What type of performance appraisal was (or is) used at your most recent job? How effective do you think it is? Why?

9. At a company that sells X-ray equipment, an important new sales territory is opening up. Patrick O'Day, the supervisor of the company's sales force, wants to assign the territory to the best-qualified salesperson. How can Patrick compare the performance of the members of the sales force to select the best candidate for the job?

10. Give an advantage and a disadvantage of using each of the following types of appraisals:

    *a.* Essay appraisal
    *b.* Behaviorally anchored rating scale (BARS)
    *c.* Checklist
    *d.* Critical-incident appraisal

11. Which type of bias does each of the following situations illustrate?

    *a.* Anne Compton is a new supervisor. To make sure that her employees and her manager take her judgments seriously, she gives each of her employees a lower rating than the previous supervisor did.
    *b.* Ron is late in completing Noreen's written performance appraisal. To finish it as quickly as possible, he looks it over and adds some negative ratings to an overall positive review so that it looks balanced.

    *c.* Renee really likes her new employee, Joan. Recently, Joan and her family moved to the same town in which Renee lives; their children attend the same school; Renee and Joan even enjoy lunchtime shopping together. When it comes time for Joan's performance review, Renee rates Joan high in every category.

12. Reginald DeBeers hates conducting appraisal interviews, so he has the process down to a science. Fifteen minutes before the end of the workday, he meets with the employee who is to be appraised. He gets right down to business, explaining what the employee's ratings are and how he arrived at each number. Then the employee and supervisor sign the form. By then, it is quitting time, and Reginald rises to shake hands with the employee, saying either, "Keep up the good work," or, "I'm sure you'll do better next time."

    What parts of the interviewing process does Reginald omit? What are the consequences of leaving out these steps?

## A SECOND LOOK

Based on the information given in the story about the Fleet Management Program for the State of Colorado at the beginning of this chapter, what type(s) of appraisal does Nancy Acedo use?

# APPLICATIONS MODULE

## CASE

### Appraising Employees in a Dental Office

The story at the beginning of Chapter 16 introduced Jill Strode, who supervises the office staff in a dental office. One of Strode's accomplishments was to develop a system for appraising the performance of the employees she supervises.

For each employee, Strode spells out the specific areas of responsibility that will be evaluated. The areas she evaluates match the responsibilities stated in the employee's job description. Thus, for the check-out receptionist, Jill indicates that she will evaluate how that person handles five areas of responsibility, including check-out procedures and telephone communications. In evaluating how an employee handles each area, Strode looks for specific traits, such as knowledge, initiative, innovation, and courtesy. The following excerpts from an appraisal of the check-out receptionist illustrate the format of the appraisals:

JOB RESPONSIBILITY: Check-Out Procedures and Folder Routing . . .

*Accuracy:* Very good overall. Attention to details is superb in all areas. Seldom forgets any part of the "check-out" procedure.

Example: Ability to pick up on errors made in charting, double-checking folders for missed steps (insurance, scheduling, etc.), thoroughness.

*Innovation:* Below average. This area has remained unchanged since we installed the system. Procedural changes have been suggested by supervisor and implemented by check-out receptionist. Needs improvement.

Example: Complaints with folder errors and patient flow have been verbalized; however, no suggestions for changes or improvement in

procedures have been offered. Space limitations in check-out area still a concern . . . suggestions for improvements?

To review the performance appraisal with the employee, Strode sets up a formal appraisal meeting. She has developed the following agenda list of topics to cover during the meeting:

1. Review specific areas of responsibility that will be evaluated. Make any changes or additions if needed.
2. Appraisal for each specific area.

   *a.* Set goals for improvement and change (at least two improvements/changes for each).
   *b.* Set training dates, if needed.
   *c.* Get feedback from staff on appraisal from supervisor.

3. Overall appraisal of traits as exemplified in daily activities and actions.
4. Review goals and training dates.
5. Questions and answers from list.
6. Open forum for discussion: employee to supervisor.

Strode then follows up to make sure that the employee and supervisor carry through on the goals and plans they established during this interview.

1. Based on the information given, what type of performance appraisal has Strode developed?
2. Would you consider this a useful type of appraisal for clerical employees in a dental practice? Can you suggest any additions or improvements?
3. Based on the agenda Strode uses for appraisal interviews, what principles of effective appraisals does she follow?

Source: Jill Strode.

**SELF-QUIZ**

## *Your Appraisal Interview Technique*

This scale is designed to help you improve your performance appraisal interviews and discussions with employees. Circle the number that best reflects where you currently fall on the scale. When you have finished, total the numbers circled in the space.

|  | Agree Strongly | | | | | Disagree Strongly | | | | |
|---|---|---|---|---|---|---|---|---|---|---|
| 1. I let the employee do most of the talking. | 10 | 9 | 8 | 7 | 6 | 5 | 4 | 3 | 2 | 1 |
| 2. I make an intense effort to listen to the employee's ideas. | 10 | 9 | 8 | 7 | 6 | 5 | 4 | 3 | 2 | 1 |
| 3. I am prepared to suggest solutions to problems and development needs but let the employee contribute first. | 10 | 9 | 8 | 7 | 6 | 5 | 4 | 3 | 2 | 1 |
| 4. My statements about performance are descriptive and specific, not judgmental. | 10 | 9 | 8 | 7 | 6 | 5 | 4 | 3 | 2 | 1 |
| 5. I reinforce the positives inperformance and seek ways to improve below-standard performance. | 10 | 9 | 8 | 7 | 6 | 5 | 4 | 3 | 2 | 1 |
| 6. I try to encourage the employee's ideas about expanding performance. | 10 | 9 | 8 | 7 | 6 | 5 | 4 | 3 | 2 | 1 |
| 7. I invite alternatives rather than assume there is only one way to approach an issue. | 10 | 9 | 8 | 7 | 6 | 5 | 4 | 3 | 2 | 1 |
| 8. I use open-ended, reflective, and directive questions to stimulate discussion. | 10 | 9 | 8 | 7 | 6 | 5 | 4 | 3 | 2 | 1 |
| 9. I am specific and descriptive when I express a concern about performance. | 10 | 9 | 8 | 7 | 6 | 5 | 4 | 3 | 2 | 1 |
| 10. My employees know I want them to succeed. | 10 | 9 | 8 | 7 | 6 | 5 | 4 | 3 | 2 | 1 |

Total ———

A score between 90 and 100 indicates you should be leading successful discussions. A score between 70 and 89 indicates significant strengths plus a few improvement needs. A score between 50 and 69 reflects some strengths, but a significant number of problem areas as well. A score below 50 calls for a serious effort to improve in several categories. Make a special effort to grow in any area where you scored 6 or less, regardless of your total score.

Source: *Supervisor's Survival Kit: Your First Step Into Management,* p. 145, by Elwood N. Chapman., © 1993. Reprinted by permission of Prentice-Hall, Inc., Upper Saddle River, NJ.

## Class Exercise

Figure 18.1 provides an overview of how supervisors conduct performance appraisals. This exercise elaborates on that model by showing you how you can use *ManagePro* (trademark of Avantos Performance Systems)—the first product of its kind in a new category of business productivity software: goal and people management (GPM)—to improve your performance management skills.*

### Instructions:

You are one of 17 supervisors at Tybro, a major toy manufacturer in the Midwest. Place yourself in the following scenario:

**Scenario** During a meeting with your boss, he shows you an article from *The Wall Street Journal*, "PC Program Lets Machines Help Bosses Manage People," and says to you, "I want to find out more about whether *ManagePro*, the software program reviewed in this article, could help our Tybro supervisors and managers, and I'd like you to be the one to answer that question for me. Probably the best way for you to find out is to register to attend the one-day *ManagePro* seminar, and then you can make your recommendation when you return, based on your hands-on experience."

You attend the seminar and learn a great deal about the performance management process. Following are some of the highlights of what you learned about *ManagePro*.

**Overview of ManagePro** The seminar trainer explained that *ManagePro* is based on fundamental, proven management processes that meet the basic performance needs that your employees have (see table).

| Employees' Performance Needs | Management Process |
|---|---|
| "Tell me what we're trying to achieve, and let's agree on what is expected of me." | *Set clear, measurable goals* that support the key business objectives with specific checkpoints and due dates. |
| "Let's discuss how I'm doing." | *Monitor progress* on each goal at a frequency determined by the capability of the people involved. |
| "Help me to improve." | *Provide adequate feedback and coaching* to keep people informed and help them improve performance. Surveys consistently show that employees have very little sense of what their boss thinks of their performance. Giving regular feedback to your people and helping them through coaching are critical parts of managing. |
| "Reward me for my contribution." | *Evaluate, recognize, and reward people's contributions.* If people feel that performance pays off, they will work harder to achieve success. |

*Permission granted by Avantos Performance Systems, Inc., to include the *ManagePro* information contained in this exercise. For further information on *ManagePro*, contact Avantos Performance Systems, 5900 Hollis Street, Suite C, Emeryville, CA 94608, or call 1-800-AVANTOS.

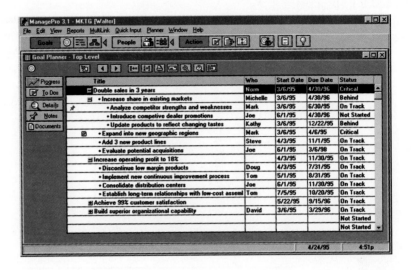

**FIGURE A**

**Stay Organized**

Throughout the day you learned how these processes are reinforced throughout *ManagePro* in (1) the way the program is structured, (2) the tools it provides, and (3) the advice available in the Management Advisor.

*Program Structure* As you try out the program, you find that information is simple to enter using fill-in-the-blank forms, outlines, and spreadsheet-like tables. Information is also easy to view and manipulate at multiple levels of detail. You find yourself quickly manipulating the program, using your mouse and pointing and clicking at the icons of what you need. Everything is very intuitive and easy to follow. Changes made through any part of the program at any level are reflected automatically reflected throughout the program. For example, if you reorganize your goals in the Goal Planner/Outliner, the changes automatically are reflected in the People Status Board.

Some of the key features of *ManagePro* include the following:

- The Goal Planner/Outliner allows you to organize your goals. Goals can be divided into layers of subgoals, given start and due dates, and delegated to a person or team. Click-and-drag movements makes it easy to organize and reorganize goals. (See Figure A.)
- The Goal Status Board gives a view of pending goals and their progress. Color-light indicators alert you to items that require action. For example, yellow means at least one subgoal is behind schedule. (See Figure B.)
- The People/Team Planner allows you to organize people, track goals associated with people, and manage information on feedback, coaching, and performance reviews.

### FIGURE B
**Stay on Top of
Your Goals**

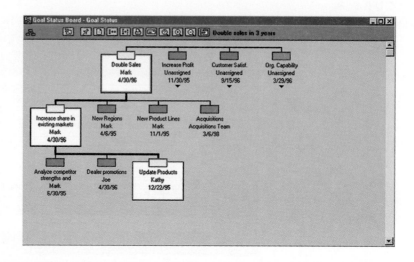

- The People Status Board prompts you periodically to consider getting updates on goal progress and to consider giving feedback, coaching, and recognition at a frequency determined by you for each individual or team. For example, you can have *ManagePro* remind you to give a certain employee feedback every three months. This will help you build up your people management discipline so that important activities and processes do not fall between the cracks. (See Figure C.)

*Tools*   Some of *ManagePro's* support tools include the following:

- The **Calendar** displays year-, month-, week-, and day-at-a-glance graphic views of events and deadlines.
- The **Action List** provides a customizable view of action items and status relating to all goals and actions in *ManagePro*, including people management actions such as progress reviews.
- The **Reports** allow you to generate a variety of standard reports on goals, planning, calendars, action lists, and people management information.

*Management Advisor*   One other major component of the program is accessed by selecting the Management Advisor button, which allows you to receive context-sensitive management tips and techniques compiled by experts. The Management Advisor helps new supervisors learn and apply management processes on the job; it also provides a refresher and specific diagnostic support for the experienced supervisor.

### *Conclusion*
You return to your office the following day and sit down at your desk to prepare your recommendation to your boss on *ManagePro*. You definitely are sold on the idea that Tybro supervisors (and for that matter, all levels of management at Tybro) would benefit greatly by using this GPM software. In support of your recommendation, you will answer the following questions:

1. What management processes does *ManagePro* support?
2. What three features of *ManagePro* most impressed you as beneficial to improving your performance management and that of your company as a whole? Why?

**FIGURE C**

**Effectively Manage Your People**

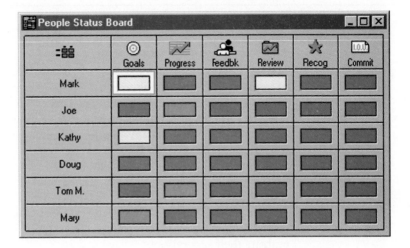

## Team-Building Exercise

### Designing an Appraisal

Divide the class into teams of four or five students. Each team will design a performance appraisal intended to evaluate the performance of either the president of the university or the president of the United States (or some other prominent person chosen by the class or the instructor). First, each team should choose which type of appraisal is best suited to evaluate the person's performance. Next, team members decide the content of the appraisal (what questions should be asked). Finally, the class as a whole should discuss which types of appraisals were selected and why, and why certain questions were chosen.

# Video Exercise 18: *Appraising Performance*

### Video Summary

Having a thorough understanding of an employee's job is a necessary condition of a supervisor performing an effective performance appraisal. This video program examines how the job redesign process at Detroit Diesel Corporation, a manufacturer of high-horsepower diesel engines, contributed to a remarkable turnaround for the company—an improvement in job performance, quality, and job satisfaction.

### Application

The focus in this chapter has been on the appraising of employees' performance by their supervisors. Let's turn the tables and think about how employees would evaluate their supervisors.

If you are in a supervisory position, give a copy of the following Supervisor Review to each of your employees to fill out anonymously concerning your performance as their supervisor. If you are not in a supervisory position but have worked or are currently working under a supervisor, complete the review according to how you would evaluate that supervisor. As you go through the review questions, consider the many factors employees consider when they determine the effectiveness of their supervisor's performance.

## Supervisor Review

1. What is your level of satisfaction when you discuss areas of your work with your supervisor that he or she will have, or will have access to, the necessary information and knowledge to give you an accurate solution to your problem?

   ❏ No opinion    ❏ Very satisfied    ❏ Satisfied    ❏ Dissatisfied    ❏ Very dissatisfied

2. What is your level of satisfaction with your supervisor's *ability* to teach you the things you do not know? (Are you learning more?)

   ❏ No opinion    ❏ Very satisfied    ❏ Satisfied    ❏ Dissatisfied    ❏ Very dissatisfied

3. What is your level of satisfaction with your supervisor's *willingness* to teach you the things you do not know? (Are you learning more?)

   ❏ No opinion    ❏ Very satisfied    ❏ Satisfied    ❏ Dissatisfied    ❏ Very dissatisfied

4. What is your level of satisfaction over how accessible your supervisor is to you?

   ❏ No opinion    ❏ Very satisfied    ❏ Satisfied    ❏ Dissatisfied    ❏ Very dissatisfied

5. What is your level of satisfaction over how approachable your supervisor is to you? Is your supervisor intimidating? Are you made to feel like an annoyance? Are your comments and problems welcomed?

   ❏ No opinion    ❏ Very satisfied    ❏ Satisfied    ❏ Dissatisfied    ❏ Very dissatisfied

6.  What is your level of satisfaction with your supervisor over the amount of feedback you receive?

    ❏ No opinion        ❏ Very satisfied        ❏ Satisfied        ❏ Dissatisfied        ❏ Very dissatisfied

7.  What is your level of satisfaction with your supervisor over the accuracy of the feedback you receive?

    ❏ No opinion        ❏ Very satisfied        ❏ Satisfied        ❏ Dissatisfied        ❏ Very dissatisfied

8.  What is your level of satisfaction with your supervisor's responsiveness to your needs? Does he or she get back to you in a timely manner on questions or concerns?

    ❏ No opinion        ❏ Very satisfied        ❏ Satisfied        ❏ Dissatisfied        ❏ Very dissatisfied

9.  What is your level of satisfaction regarding your supervisor's sense of fairness?

    ❏ No opinion        ❏ Very satisfied        ❏ Satisfied        ❏ Dissatisfied        ❏ Very dissatisfied

10. What is your level of satisfaction that your supervisor will keep confidential any matters that you want kept confidential?

    ❏ No opinion        ❏ Very satisfied        ❏ Satisfied        ❏ Dissatisfied        ❏ Very dissatisfied

11. What is your level of satisfaction with your supervisor's manner of conducting him- or herself? Is he or she unprofessional, offensive, or annoying?

    ❏ No opinion        ❏ Very satisfied        ❏ Satisfied        ❏ Dissatisfied        ❏ Very dissatisfied

12. What is your level of confidence in your supervisor's administrative ability? Are reviews, sick days, vacations, and other forms kept current and delivered in a timely manner? Do you receive memos on time?

    ❏ No opinion        ❏ Very satisfied        ❏ Satisfied        ❏ Dissatisfied        ❏ Very dissatisfied

13. What is your level of satisfaction about the environment your supervisor has created? Is it an open, relaxed, enjoyable atmosphere or hostile and tense?

    ❏ No opinion        ❏ Very satisfied        ❏ Satisfied        ❏ Dissatisfied        ❏ Very dissatisfied

14. What is your level of confidence in how much your supervisor is "in touch" with what is really going on in your department?

    ❏ No opinion        ❏ Very satisfied        ❏ Satisfied        ❏ Dissatisfied        ❏ Very dissatisfied

15. What is your level of satisfaction that your supervisor is trying to be a good supervisor?

    ❏ No opinion        ❏ Very satisfied        ❏ Satisfied        ❏ Dissatisfied        ❏ Very dissatisfied

16. What is your overall level of satisfaction with your immediate supervisor?

    ❏ No opinion        ❏ Very satisfied        ❏ Satisfied        ❏ Dissatisfied        ❏ Very dissatisfied

17. Do you have any suggestions that may improve your work area or your supervisor's skills?

    _____

    _____

Source: Scott Warrick, "Supervisor Review Sheds Light on Blind Spots," *HR Magazine*, June 1992, pp. 112–13.

# 19

*[During the Industrial Revolution] the people who came into the cities to work in the sweatshops were entering the highest pay, the best working conditions they'd ever had in their lives. As bad as it was in the cities, poverty in the rural areas was even worse.*
—**Senator Phil Gramm**

# The Impact of the Law

## LEARNING OBJECTIVES

After you have studied this chapter, you should be able to:

19.1 Summarize the basic purpose of the OSHAct and describe the supervisor's responsibilities under the act.

19.2 Identify basic categories of health and safety hazards in the workplace.

19.3 Discuss common safety and health concerns and how employers are addressing them.

19.4 Describe workplace safety and health programs, including their benefits and the supervisor's role in them.

19.5 Explain the supervisor's role during a union organization drive and collective bargaining.

19.6 Provide guidelines for working with a union steward and handling grievances.

19.7 Explain the supervisor's role in preventing strikes and operating during a strike.

19.8 Discuss how supervisors should respond to charges of sexual harassment and prevent it from occurring.

Source: Courtesy of DuPont Company Inc.

## PUTTING A STOP TO HAZARDS

According to Du Pont senior development specialist Anthony Cantarella, safety has been a concern at Du Pont for almost 200 years. It had to be, because the company started out as a manufacturer of explosives. The focus on safety has improved continually through teamwork and employee involvement. In the 1950s, the company assigned a group of plant managers to find out why some plants had a better safety record than others. The managers learned that at the most successful plants, managers spent more time observing the safety practices of their employees.

As a result of this investigation, Du Pont launched a program it calls STOP, which stands for Safety Training Observation Program. While management treats safety as a concern that each facility must address individually, the corporation does provide training that covers two levels: STOP for Supervisors and STOP for Employees.

According to a STOP brochure, STOP for Supervisors is based on the view that supervisors have "a primary responsibility for on-the-job safety." The program trains supervisors to take a systematic approach to observing, correcting, and reporting unsafe acts in the workplace and preventing them from recurring. The idea is to make supervisors better observers, not to make them catch and punish employees.

A supervisor approaching an employee who is working observes the employee from head to toe, thinking about all the ways the employee could be injured. For example, the employee might not be wearing a necessary hard hat. The supervisor talks to the employee about what he or she has observed, making sure the employee understands the job and safety procedures. This positive approach is considered more effective than simply punishing employees who engage in unsafe practices.

STOP training also covers how supervisors should handle employee reactions. For example, some employees may take safety precautions only when they notice the supervisor observing them. A supervisor who thinks the employee is following safety precautions simply in response to being observed discusses this with the employee. Again, the objective is to be sure that employees understand the need for the safety precautions.

The Du Pont program also includes STOP for Employees, which emphasizes that safety is the responsibility of everyone. This program trains operative employees to recognize and eliminate unsafe acts and conditions from their work areas. They do this by observing their work areas and identifying ways to replace unsafe acts with safe ones. As part of their training, employees visit a work site within their plant and look for ways to improve safety there.

STOP appears to be a success at Du Pont. In a recent year the company's 120,000 employees experienced fewer than 40 lost-time injuries.

Source: "One Company's Technique Takes Hold: Putting a STOP to Unsafe Behaviors," *OSHA Compliance Advisor*, Sept. 23, 1991, pp. 3–6.

Good-quality air to breathe is essential for the health of all workers. Because the exhaust from automobiles used for transportation to work sites is a major cause of air pollution, the 1990 Clean Air Act required large- and medium-sized companies in several states to develop plans to discourage employees from driving their own cars to work. Alaska Biological Research, near Fairbanks, began its own program offering $1.50 to $3.00 per day as a cash incentive for those who did not drive to work. Some employees walk, some bicycle even in winter, and one employee (*photo*) skies six miles each way, mushing two dogs in front of him.

Source: © Geoffrey Orth

Du Pont's supervisors are well aware that maintaining the safety and health of employees is a major task. This responsibility is just one of many imposed by the federal government on organizations operating in the United States. Other chapters have addressed some additional responsibilities. Chapter 3 discussed labor laws that limit the ways in which organizations can use teamwork. Chapter 11 introduced the impact of the law on the scope of benefits organizations must offer employees. Chapters 16 and 18 explored laws intended to ensure fair employment practices.

This chapter covers three areas in which federal laws govern the actions of organizations. First, it describes the role of the federal government in regulating safety and health in the workplace. It then describes safety and health hazards, organizational programs for promoting safety and health, and the role of the supervisor in this area. Next, the chapter discusses unions—their impact and the laws governing the interaction of organizations with unions and unionizing efforts. Finally, the chapter examines sexual harassment. It suggests ways to prevent sexual harassment and appropriate responses when an employee claims sexual harassment has occurred.

## Government Regulation of Safety and Health

According to the Bureau of Labor Statistics, in 1989 more than 6.5 million occupational injuries and illnesses occurred among the almost 79 million workers in the private sector.[1] Furthermore, these problems are not limited to factory settings. For example, the industry with the greatest number of job-related injuries in 1989 was restaurant work, where employees are especially at risk for sprains, falls, and burns.[2] Not only is the challenge of preventing these problems widespread, but many injuries and illnesses reported today are newly recognized—complaints such as injuries related to repetitive motion and the less-than-optimal design of workstations.

Many organizations recognize that safeguarding the well-being of employees in the workplace is not only ethical but also essential to attracting and keeping qualified personnel. Unfortunately, this view has not always prevailed. As a result, the government has stepped in to regulate the safety and health of the workplace.

Terrible accidents occurred when the Industrial Revolution brought together inexperienced workers with new and unfamiliar machinery. Beginning primarily in the early 1900s, state governments passed inspection laws and set up workers' compensation programs to provide benefits for employees injured on the job. In 1913 Congress created the Department of Labor, whose duties include the improvement of working conditions. In spite of such actions, however, public sentiment in favor of further protection continued to grow.

### Occupational Safety and Health Act (OSHAct) of 1970

**Occupational Safety and Health Act (OSHAct) of 1970**
The federal law that sets up government agencies to conduct research on occupational health and safety, set health and safety standards, inspect workplaces, and penalize employers that do not meet standards.

The most far-reaching of the laws regulating workplace safety and health is the **Occupational Safety and Health Act (OSHAct) of 1970**. The law is intended "to assure so far as possible every working man and woman in the nation safe and healthful working conditions and to preserve our human resources." The OSHAct sets up government agencies to conduct research regarding occupational health and safety, set health and safety standards, inspect workplaces, and penalize employers that do not meet standards. Penalties can be severe, including fines of $7,000 per day for failure to correct a violation and jail terms of six months for falsifying records to deceive inspectors.

### OSHA and NIOSH

**Occupational Safety and Health Administration (OSHA)**
The agency of the federal government charged with setting and enforcing standards for workplace health and safety.

The OSHAct established two government agencies to see that employers carry out its provisions. The **Occupational Safety and Health Administration (OSHA)**, a part of the U.S. Department of Labor, is the government agency charged with setting and enforcing standards for workplace health and safety. People often think of OSHA standards as pertaining mainly to such factory-related issues as personal protective equipment (e.g., gloves, safety shoes) and guards on machinery. However, many OSHA standards pertain to health and safety issues that arise in offices, including recently proposed standards for air quality and prevention of repetitive-motion injuries. (These topics are discussed further later in the chapter.)

To see that organizations are meeting its standards, OSHA's inspectors may visit companies but must show a search warrant before conducting an inspection. In a recent year, over half of OSHA's inspections were in the construction field; inspections of manufacturing facilities were next most common.[3] OSHA also operates a program of free on-site consultations through which independent consultants evaluate an organization's work practices, environmental hazards, and health and safety program. If an organization follows the consultant's recommendations, it bears no penalties for the shortcomings identified.[4]

OSHA's regulations have been criticized as excessively far-reaching and even petty. As a result, the agency in 1978 eliminated over 1,000 of its standards to focus on the most significant concerns. Many standards remain, and whatever a supervisor and other managers think of them, it is important that the organization comply with the standards.

**National Institute for Occupational Safety and Health (NIOSH)** The agency of the federal government responsible for conducting research related to workplace safety and health.

The **National Institute for Occupational Safety and Health (NIOSH)** is the government agency responsible for conducting research related to workplace safety and health. It is a part of the Department of Health and Human Services. NIOSH provides OSHA with information necessary for setting standards.

### The Supervisor's Responsibility under the OSHAct

Given the extent of OSHA regulations and the thousands of pages interpreting those regulations, supervisors cannot be familiar with every regulation. However, supervisors do need to understand what kinds of practices are required to preserve health and safety in their department. In addition, the OSHAct imposes some specific responsibilities that apply to supervisors.

The OSHAct requires that supervisors keep records of occupational injuries and illnesses. They must record these on OSHA forms within six working days after learning of the injury or illness. Figure 19.1 details which types of accidents and illnesses must be recorded.

A supervisor also may have to accompany OSHA officials when they conduct an inspection. These inspections occur in response to a request by an employer, a union, or an employee, or when OSHA's own schedule calls for them. (An employer may not penalize an employee for requesting an investigation or reporting a possible violation.) During the inspection, it is important to be polite and cooperative. This is not always as easy as it sounds because the inspection may come at an inconvenient time, and a supervisor may view it as unwanted interference. However, being uncooperative is no way to foster good relations with the agency and could even lead the inspectors to be tougher than they otherwise might be.

Because chemical hazards are widespread in the modern workplace, OSHA has issued a right-to-know rule requiring that employees be informed about the chemicals used where they work. Each organization must have available information about what chemical hazards exist in the workplace and how employees can protect themselves against those hazards. The information must include labels on containers of chemicals and hazardous materials, as well as Material Safety Data Sheets (MSDSs), both of which identify the chemicals, describe how to handle them, and identify the risks involved. A supervisor should make certain that this information is available for all chemicals that are brought into, used in, or produced at the workplace he or she supervises. If a supervisor finds that some information still is needed, the suppliers of the chemicals and other hazardous substances should be able to provide it.

## Types of Safety and Health Problems

Because supervisors have an important role to play in maintaining a safe and healthy workplace, they need to be aware of problems that commonly arise, including health hazards and safety hazards. People tend to associate both classes of hazards with factory settings, but hazards can arise in any work setting, from offices to police cars.

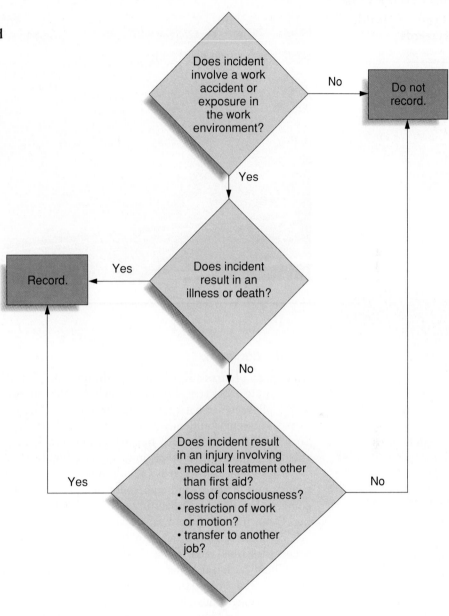

**FIGURE 19.1**

**Accidents and Illnesses
That Must Be Recorded
under OSHAct**

**FIGURE 19.2**

**Types of Health Hazards**

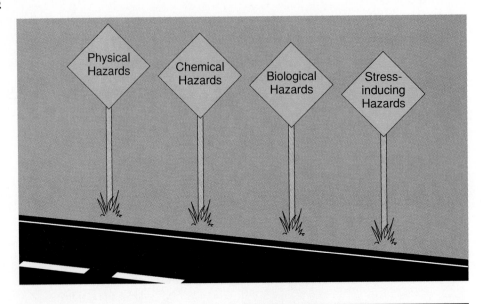

## Health Hazards

As a result of stressful working conditions, an air-traffic controller developed a stomach ulcer. A clerical employee believes that sharing a poorly ventilated room with a photocopier has caused her dizzy spells. These are examples of conditions in the work environment that may gradually hurt the health of the people there. Such conditions are **health hazards.** In general, health hazards may be physical, chemical, biological, or stress-inducing (see Figure 19.2).

Physical health hazards include noise, vibration, radiation, temperature extremes, and furniture and equipment that are not designed properly for the user's comfort. For instance, operating noisy equipment can impair an employee's hearing. Exposure to radiation can make a person more vulnerable to cancer. Improperly designed furniture can contribute to muscle aches and repetitive-motion disorders (described later in this chapter).

Chemical hazards may be present in dusts, fumes, and gases. They include chemicals that are carcinogenic (causes of cancer). Examples of chemical hazards are asbestos, coal dust, lead, and benzene. According to a recent study, women who handled certain chemicals used in making microchips had miscarriages at a rate more than twice that of women who had no contact with those chemicals.[5] People in office buildings may be exposed to chemicals from synthetic carpeting, tobacco smoke, and other sources. OSHA has proposed regulations for indoor air quality. The research into the sources of such pollution is incomplete, so the proposed standards emphasize providing adequate ventilation and separate smoking rooms.[6]

Biological hazards include bacteria, fungi, and insects associated with risks to people's health. Modern office buildings, which tend to be sealed tight against the elements, can be fertile ground for such health hazards. Thus, at a financial services company in the Northeast, employees complained of feeling sick, and the

**health hazards**
Conditions in the work environment that may gradually hurt the health of the people there.

FIGURE 19.3

**FIGURE 19.3**

**Causes of
On-the-Job Accidents**

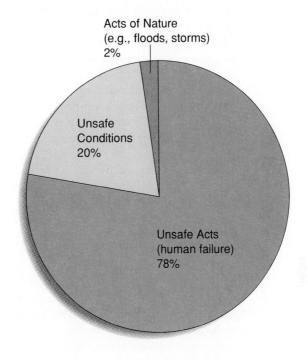

Acts of Nature
(e.g., floods, storms)
2%

Unsafe
Conditions
20%

Unsafe Acts
(human failure)
78%

Source: Data from *The Front Line Supervisor's Standard Manual* (Bureau of Business Practice, 1989), p.155.

cause turned out to be microbes in the air-conditioning system.[7] Likewise, over-watering plants can encourage the growth of molds in the standing water, and those molds can circulate on air currents, making employees ill.

Stressful working conditions also may harm the health of employees. For example, employees may be more apt to suffer from stress-related illnesses if their work requires them to take risks, please an unpredictable supervisor, or witness a lot of suffering. (Chapter 14 describes the consequences of stress and ways to manage it.)

### Safety Hazards

**safety hazards**
Conditions in the workplace that may lead to an injury-causing accident.

A **safety hazard** is a condition in the workplace that may lead to an injury-causing accident. Common types of injuries include cuts, broken bones, burns, and electric shocks. At their most serious, injuries can lead to death. The National Safety Council reported that the costs related to deaths and injuries caused by on-the-job accidents in 1994 equaled the combined profits of the 50 largest U.S. corporations.[8] In general, safety hazards arise from personal behavior (i.e., unsafe acts) or conditions of the physical environment. As Figure 19.3 shows, unsafe acts cause the majority of accidents.

### Types of Safety Hazards

Personal behavior as a safety hazard refers to practices by managers and employees that create an environment in which accidents may occur. This behavior may be as basic as carelessness or as obvious as drinking on the job. Sometimes employees cause a safety hazard by refusing to follow proper procedures or use safety equipment such as goggles or gloves. Supervisors and other managers can contribute by failing to enforce safety measures or requiring employees to work such long hours that they do not get enough rest to think clearly. Requiring employees to work rotating shifts also is associated with greater accident rates.[9] Transportation accidents are the leading cause of accidental deaths on the job, accounting for 40 percent of fatal work injuries in 1993.[10] Therefore, supervisors should be especially concerned about encouraging safe behavior among employees who spend work time in vehicles—delivery personnel, salespeople, employees who take business trips, and so on.[10]

Some employees are said to be accident-prone—that is, more likely to have accidents than other people. These employees tend to act on impulse, without careful thought, and do not concentrate on their work. Many employees who are vulnerable to accidents have negative attitudes about their job, co-workers, or supervisor. Perhaps they find the work boring. Sometimes people who are otherwise careful are vulnerable to accidents. When people are struggling with personal problems or do not get enough sleep, they may become accident-prone. Therefore, a supervisor needs to pay attention to the behavior of all employees in order to recognize which of them are especially at risk for causing an accident on any given day. A supervisor may need to restrict the activities of an employee who is temporarily accident-prone or even to send that person home. If the problem continues, a supervisor may have to use the counseling and discipline procedures described in Chapter 13.

Hazardous working conditions that can lead to accidents are as varied as a messy work environment, electrical cords lying where people might trip over them, poor lighting, and a lack of protective devices on machinery. David Cooper fell and injured his knee when he slipped on a grease spot near the grill at the McDonald's restaurant where he was working. Explained Cooper, "It's not like they're unclean with the floor, but when things get busy, it gets slippery with grease and sauce."[11]

### Responses

A supervisor who observes unsafe conditions should take one of the following actions, listed in order of priority:

1. Eliminate the hazard.
2. If the hazard cannot be eliminated, use protective devices such as guards on machinery.
3. If the hazard cannot be guarded, provide warnings, such as labels on the hot parts inside photocopiers.
4. If you cannot remove or guard the hazard on your own, notify the proper authority. Recommend a solution, then follow up to make sure that the condition has been corrected.

This is essentially the approach used at Frontier Enterprises in San Antonio, Texas, which runs restaurant chains. The most common accidents at the restaurants were slips and falls, so employees now receive instructions to mark any spill with a cone bearing a "caution" message and then to clean up the spill immediately.[12]

Back and neck injuries account for one-fifth of all workplace injuries,[13] so a supervisor should especially seek measures to prevent and correct safety hazards causing such injuries. Ways to prevent back injuries include designing the job to minimize injuries, training employees to use lifting techniques that minimize strain on the back, reducing the size or weight of objects to be lifted, using mechanical aids, and making sure that workers assigned to do a job are strong enough to do it safely. The position that puts the most stress on the back is sitting.[14] Supervisors of office employees therefore should be sure that employees have comfortable chairs and enough opportunities to stand up and move around.

## Common Concerns

Several common concerns about safety and health in the workplace are especially significant because they are widely occurring, or at least widely discussed. These include smoking, alcoholism and drug abuse, problems related to the use of computers, repetitive-motion disorders, and AIDS.

### Smoking

An estimated 22 to 27 percent of all U.S. workers smoke cigarettes.[15] According to a report by the Surgeon General of the United States, cigarette smoking causes more death and disability among U.S. workers than exposure to work-related hazardous substances. Smoking has been associated with cancer, heart disease, and lung diseases such as emphysema. A recent study found that the overall health costs for smokers are 18 percent higher than for nonsmokers.[16] In addition, people who smoke may be more vulnerable to the effects of other hazards than people who do not smoke. Nonsmokers exposed to secondhand smoke can suffer some of the ill effects of smoking; this exposure is often called "passive smoking." Besides being a health hazard, cigarette smoking is a safety hazard; lit cigarettes can cause fires or explosions when handled carelessly or near flammable substances.

Because the consequences of cigarette smoking are potentially serious, many organizations have restricted the amount of smoking allowed in the workplace. In many locations, the restrictions also are required by state or local law. A survey by the Society for Human Resource Management found that 85 percent of companies had imposed some restrictions on smoking, with more than one-third banning it from the premises altogether.[17] Supervisors can help to minimize the effects of smoking in the workplace by enforcing the organization's restrictions and by providing encouragement and recognition to employees who are trying to quit smoking.

### Alcoholism and Drug Abuse

Alcoholism and drug abuse are serious problems in the workplace and can be costly to the organization. One reason is that people who are under the influence of these substances are more likely to be involved in accidents. Many organizational policies therefore call for strong action when an employee is found to be under the influence.

Part of the supervisor's role in promoting safety involves counseling and disciplining employees with these problems. (For more information on how supervisors should respond, refer to Chapter 13.)

Portable personal computers (PCs), which account for about one-quarter of all PC sales, provide the necessary compact size and light weight for carrying in a briefcase and computing on the go. The ergonomics of the keyboard, pointing device, and monitor, however, must be considered. Features such as wrist rests, legs to adjust a keyboard to a comfortable angle, and space bars that respond reliably to a sideways thumb motion become very important for the comfort of the employee after many hours of work.

Source: © Dan Bosler/Tony Stone Images

**video display terminal (VDT)**
The screen on which a computer displays information.

**virtual reality**
A three-dimensional computer-generated environment that gives the user a sensation of being part of that environment.

### Problems Related to Computer Use

Nearly half of U.S. workers now use computers on the job.[18] As computers have become increasingly common in all kinds of work environments, people have attributed some health problems to computer use. Many of the concerns involve the use of **video display terminals (VDTs),** the screens on which computers display information. Users of VDTs have complained that working with or near these screens causes a variety of health problems. A Louis Harris poll found that eyestrain was the most common complaint among office workers, almost half of whom named it as a serious concern.[19] Working for extended periods in front of a VDT also can lead to sore muscles in the back, arms, legs, and neck. Some reports have suggested that VDT use also is linked to pregnancy problems, notably miscarriages, through the radiation emitted by the VDTs. At this time, research results neither support nor refute a link between VDT use and pregnancy risks.

Fortunately, the problems associated with VDT use can be reduced or eliminated. A workstation that includes VDTs should be well designed for comfort, including features such as an adjustable screen, a wrist rest, a device to minimize glare on the screen, and an adjustable chair and worktable. Employees who use VDTs should take rest breaks. NIOSH recommends a 15-minute break after two continuous hours of VDT use, or after one hour if the use involves intense concentration. One way to provide breaks is to rotate assignments so that employees spend only part of the day working with a VDT. To minimize the possible risks of radiation, VDTs should be at least four feet from one another, and employees should sit at least two feet from the sides and back of any screen.[20] Those who are concerned about radiation also may wish to install radiation shields on their computer or to use only low-emission VDTs.

Instead of staring at a standard VDT, a growing number of computer users are pulling on headsets to take advantage of a new technology called virtual reality. **Virtual reality** is a three-dimensional computer-generated environment that gives the user a sensation of being part of that environment.[21] The technology is fairly new, but employees already are using it to test products and receive training. Although learning to fly a new jet aircraft with virtual reality avoids some of the obvious safety hazards of actually piloting the jet, it does involve some health hazards. The use of virtual reality, especially for extended periods, has been associated with nausea and headaches. A few users even experience flashbacks hours or days later. Prairie Virtual Systems used virtual reality to test office spaces being designed for people in wheelchairs. Even though the motions were small—such as picking up a telephone or pulling out a desk drawer—up to 5 percent of the people experienced symptoms akin to motion sickness.[22] The design of virtual reality systems may eventually reduce some of this "cybersickness," and supervisors can help by providing frequent breaks for employees using these systems.

People who type into computers for long stretches of time may also be susceptible to repetitive-motion disorders, discussed next.

### Repetitive-Motion Disorders

**repetitive-motion disorders**
Injuries that result from repeatedly applying force to the same muscles or joints.

Advances in machinery and electronic equipment have enabled workers to perform repetitive functions at an increasingly rapid pace. Unfortunately, the repeated application of force to the same muscles or joints can result in injuries known as **repetitive-motion disorders.** According to the Bureau of Labor Statistics, there were six times as many reports of repetitive-motion disorders in 1990 as in 1982. As a result, these disorders have come to account for half of all occupational illnesses in the United States.[23]

An example of these disorders is carpal tunnel syndrome, which involves pain in the wrist and fingers. This is a common complaint among those who type at a keyboard all day or perform other tasks involving the wrist, such as making the same cut in chickens all day long at a poultry processor. *Los Angeles Times* columnist Bob Jones took time off after years of working at a computer left him in a constant state of pain that no therapy seemed able to alleviate. Jones said, "If this disease was a matter of just enduring pain when I typed, that would be one thing. But I can't garden, cook, play sports, or pick up and play with my 11-month-old son when I want."[24] Some people in the newspaper business have speculated that stiff competition for jobs in that field has forced many reporters and columnists to try to cope with the pain rather than complain about it.

**ergonomics**
The science concerned with the human characteristics that must be considered in designing tasks and equipment so that people will work most effectively and safely.

To prevent repetitive-motion disorders, an organization can take several measures, including designing jobs and workstations to allow for rests, using adjustable furniture, and avoiding awkward movements and bad posture. This type of response to the problem is an application of **ergonomics,** the science concerned with the human characteristics that need to be considered in designing tasks and equipment so that people will work most effectively and safely. While supervisors need not be experts in ergonomics, they can cultivate an awareness of these issues. M. Franz Schneider of Humantech proposes a straightforward way to determine whether a job or equipment is ergonomically designed: Simply ask, "Would I do it that way?" According to Schneider, "If you can answer yes, then [the job or equipment] passes the ergonomics test. If you say, 'Thank God I'm in management,' then it doesn't."[25] Another measure is to encourage employees who are in pain to seek medical attention right away. Supervisors should never tell their employees to work through pain, as this may aggravate an existing injury. (See "Tips from the Firing Line.")

## TIPS FROM THE FIRING LINE

### Reducing the Risk of CTDs

CTDs—cumulative trauma disorders—aren't as dramatic as a single blow or a frightening fall. Instead, these injuries creep into a person's soft tissue and slowly but steadily weaken it. CTDs in the workplace come from a variety of sources and can cost an employer a lot of money. The National Council on Compensation Insurance estimates that the average cost of a CTD is about $27,500. CTDs often can be prevented through ergonomics. Eric Cady, a consultant with Lynch, Ryan & Associates, recommends that employers reduce the risks by evaluating the workplace to identify problems, analyzing each employee's job, brainstorming potential solutions, and following through. According to Cady, the elements of risk to watch for are:

- *Repetition*. Repetitive tasks wear down soft tissue because they focus movement on a specific body part.
- *Posture*. Unnatural body positions, such as bending the wrist while typing, strain muscles and tendons and compress nerves.

- *Force*. Incorrectly lifting or carrying heavy objects, such as bending over to pick up a heavy item, strains muscles and tendons.
- *Lack of rest*. The human body needs sleep, a time to recuperate from stresses. A lack of rest can enhance the effects of repetition, posture, and force. Without adequate rest, a person is likely to feel CTD pain most acutely at the end of the work week.
- *Temperature*. Temperatures that drop below 50 degrees can cause muscles to contract more, which increases the chances that they will tear.
- *Vibration*. Vibrations from jackhammers or other tools can cause blood vessels to constrict, reducing the blood supply to tendons. Muscles and tendons rely on blood for the nourishment that helps the healing process when there is an injury. Thus, continued exposure to vibrations can inhibit the healing of muscles and tendons.

Source: Eric Cady, "Is Your Workplace a Trauma Center?", *Small Business Reports*, Oct. 1994, pp. 14–16.

### AIDS

**AIDS (acquired immune deficiency syndrome)**
The incurable and fatal illness that is caused by the HIV virus.

Although other illnesses are more widespread, probably the most feared is **AIDS,** caused by the HIV virus. The biggest reason for the fear is that AIDS remains incurable and fatal. Fortunately, people cannot catch it from touching a person with AIDS or sharing a drinking fountain or rest room; the HIV virus is transmitted through the exchange of bodily fluids, which can occur through sexual activity, blood transfusions, and the sharing of contaminated hypodermic needles, as well as between an infected mother and a fetus.

Most of the activities involving the transmission of HIV would not occur in the workplace. The major exception is health care institutions where hypodermic needles are used. These institutions should have procedures for the proper handling and disposal of the needles to prevent the spread of AIDS and other serious diseases such as hepatitis.

In most work settings, the major concern about AIDS is how to treat employees who are HIV-positive or who have AIDS. Fairness and federal antidiscrimination laws both dictate treating these employees in the same way as anyone else with a disability. As long as the employees can perform their job, they should be allowed to remain. At some point, an organization may have to make reasonable accommodations to allow them to continue working, such as allowing an ill employee to complete job assignments at home.

When an employee has AIDS, a supervisor must confront the fears that other employees are likely to have about working with that employee. With help from the human resources department, a supervisor may need to educate other employees about AIDS and how it is transmitted. Despite these efforts, some employees may shun a co-worker with AIDS. Therefore, the supervisor and others in the organization must do their best to protect the confidentiality of a person with AIDS. If an employee with AIDS or the employee's co-workers are having trouble coping, the supervisor may wish to refer them to the organization's employee-assistance program, if one exists. (These programs are described in Chapter 13.)

## Workplace Programs to Promote Safety and Health

Many employers have instituted formal programs to promote the safety and health of employees. The program may include training, safety meetings, posters, awards for safe performance, and safety and health committees. A typical committee includes operative employees and managers, perhaps with a membership that rotates among the employees. The safety committees at Frontier Enterprises' restaurants include employees from each area of the restaurant.[26] The duties of this committee can include regularly inspecting work areas, reviewing employees' suggestions for improving health and safety, and promoting awareness about safety. The committee also might sponsor the organization's contests or awards for safe practices.

Some organizations have extended their safety and health programs to cover off-duty conduct by employees that contributes to health problems. These efforts may be part of a *wellness program* (see Chapter 14). For example, some wellness programs seek to discourage employees from smoking altogether (not just restricting smoking at work), and others seek to teach healthy eating and exercise habits.

### Benefits

By reducing the number and severity of work-related injuries and illnesses, safety and health programs can cut the costs to organizations in a number of areas. (See "Meeting the Challenge.") These include health and workers' compensation insurance, defense of lawsuits, repair or replacement of equipment damaged in accidents, and wages paid for lost time. The savings can be significant; for every car they make, the Big Three automakers spend $900 to care for an occupational illness or injury.[27] In addition, safety and health programs can motivate employees, reduce turnover, and help prevent pain and suffering among employees and their families. Finally, an organization that is a safe and healthy place to work is more likely to enjoy good relations with the government and community and should have an easier time recruiting desirable employees.

### Characteristics of an Effective Program

A safety and health program is effective when it succeeds in minimizing the likelihood that people will be injured or become ill as a result of conditions in the workplace, when all levels of management demonstrate a strong commitment to the program, and when employees believe that the program is worthwhile. In addition, all employees need to be trained in the importance of safety and ways to promote health and safety in the workplace. This training should give employees an ongoing awareness of the need to behave in safe ways. Finally, an organization should have a system for identifying and correcting hazards before they do damage.

## MEETING THE CHALLENGE

### *The Lower Cost of Good Health and Safety Practices*

It's no revelation that workplace accidents cause companies money. Insuring against those accidents may cost even more. (Nationally, workers' compensation premiums cost businesses about $65 billion per year.) For small companies, trying to find an affordable workers' compensation insurance plan (which covers employees injured or rendered ill on the job) can be a nightmare. (Larger companies can foot the bill for their own self-insurance plans; smaller companies can't.) Ethically—and in some states, legally—companies must take care of their employees through some type of disability or workers' compensation insurance, no matter how difficult the task may be.

Recently, more small businesses have turned to self-insured groups, or SIGs. Some even have launched these groups themselves. For instance, a group of 70 small jewelry manufacturers and related businesses pooled their resources in a nonprofit trust to pay their own workers' comp bills. The Jewelry Industry Risk Management Association now has 144 members. Most of the growth in self-insurance has come from groups like this.

These groups don't just pay bills; they encourage their members to develop safe workplaces so that the bills diminish. Here's the financial incentive for this practice: Because each SIG holds its own funds in reserve, any surplus received from premiums and not spent on medical bills is returned as a "dividend" to the members.

SIGs hire administrators to manage their operations, develop safety training for workers, manage cases and claims, and oversee the finances. Mike Follick, president of Abacus Management Group Inc., in Rhode Island, describes the philosophy of a successful SIG: "I look at this not just as a way of helping with workers' comp costs but also helping small business develop certain problem-solving and management skills, which can then be applied to other areas." Abacus as well as other SIG administrators teach injury prevention and other methods for reducing the need for workers' comp claims. Once a case is taken on, Abacus follows the worker's recuperation closely.

At the encouragement of Abacus, SIG member Greylawn Foods, a distributor of refrigerated foods that employs 45 people, gives new hires a B200 back exam, which measures how much weight a person can lift safely. Because most jobs at Greylawn require a lot of lifting, the company needs to establish a baseline for workers' capacity to lift. That way, if an employee gets hurt lifting on the job, there is a record of how much weight he or she reasonably could have been expected to handle. "The B200 is expensive, but it is worth every penny," comments Greylawn president Sidney Goldman.

SIG members and their administrators know that keeping their employees healthy and safe translates to greater productivity—something on which most workers and employers agree. "You *must* care about the employees," declares Jack Curley of Steve Connolly Seafood in Boston. "You want them to get better from any type of injury. You want to preserve their paycheck for them, to the extent possible, to bring them back for 'light duty' at the earliest moment." (Light duty is less demanding work at full pay while a worker is recovering to full health.) For workers and their employers, even light duty is better than no duty at all.

Source: Roberta Reynes, "Do-It-Yourself Workers' Comp," *Nation's Business*, Apr. 1995, pp. 26–28.

### *Role of the Supervisor*

Top management's support of safety measures is important; the organization may even have a safety director or other manager responsible for safety programs. Nevertheless, it is up to supervisors to see that employees follow safety precautions. After all, it is the supervisors who observe and are responsible for the day-to-day performance of employees. Unfortunately, some supervisors must witness a serious injury before they appreciate why they must enforce safety rules and procedures. Supervisors who avoid enforcing these rules because they are afraid employees will react negatively are missing the point of why the rules exist. They also are failing to recognize that they have an important role in maintaining a safe and healthy workplace.

### Training and Hazard Prevention

A supervisor needs to see that employees understand and follow all procedures designed to maintain safety and health. New employees must be well trained in how to do their job safely; more experienced employees need training when they take on new responsibilities or when the organization introduces new procedures, materials, or machinery. In addition, employees need reminders about safe practices. Besides comments from the supervisor, the reminders can include posters, items in the company or department newsletter, and presentations by one employee to the others. Statistics about the department's performance, such as number of accidents during this year compared with last year, can be posted on bulletin boards or reported in the newsletter. In addition, OSHA requires that companies with more than 10 employees display the safety and health poster shown in Figure 19.4, which provides information about employees' rights and responsibilities under the OSHAct.

Some special concerns arise with regard to educating workers who are or may become pregnant. A Supreme Court ruling prohibits employers from forbidding pregnant workers from holding hazardous jobs, a policy that, if permitted, could force women to choose between holding a job and having a baby. Nevertheless, women who remain in these jobs may sue an employer for damages if a child is born with injuries caused by hazardous working conditions.[28] The acceptable way to protect women employees of childbearing age is to emphasize information. They should be informed of any pregnancy-related risks of work assignments. A supervisor also may encourage employees to ask for a reassignment to a less hazardous job if they become pregnant. (The organization may not reduce the employee's pay, benefits, or seniority rights.) If the employee cannot be reassigned, the organization can give the employee leave during her pregnancy, including full pay and a guarantee of getting the job back after the baby is born.

Another situation calling for special attention is the supervision of shift workers, who also need additional guidance in safe practices.[29] Employees will be more alert and better able to concentrate if they adapt their overall lifestyle to working night shifts or rotating shifts. They must make an extra effort to get enough quality sleep during the day, seeking out a quiet, dark, cool place for doing so. People who are naturally alert late at night will probably sleep best if they do so right after working at night, whereas others will do better if they sleep just before going in to work at night. People who work a night shift also will be more comfortable if they eat relatively light foods during their shift, avoiding heavy, greasy items.

A supervisor should encourage all employees to participate in the promotion of safe and healthy conditions. One way to do this is to emphasize that employees share in the responsibility for creating a safe work setting. Du Pont's Anthony Cantarella uses the example of an electrical cord on which an employee tripped and injured herself. Cantarella says, "The cord didn't get there by itself. Somebody put it there. You might call the cord an 'unsafe condition,' but it was really

**FIGURE 19.4**

OSHA Safety and
Health Poster

# JOB SAFETY & HEALTH PROTECTION

The Occupational Safety and Health Act of 1970 provides job safety and health protection for workers by promoting safe and healthful working conditions throughout the Nation. Provisions of the Act include the following:

## EMPLOYERS

All employers must furnish to employees employment and a place of employment free from recognized hazards that are causing or are likely to cause death or serious harm to employees. Employers must comply with occupational safety and health standards issued under the Act.

## EMPLOYEES

Employees must comply with all occupational safety and health standards, rules, regulations and orders issued under the Act that apply to their own actions and conduct on the job.

The Occupational Safety and Health Administration (OSHA) of the U.S. Department of Labor has the primary responsibility for administering the Act. OSHA issues occupational safety and health standards, and its Compliance Safety and Health Officers conduct jobsite inspections to help ensure compliance with the Act.

## INSPECTION

The Act requires that a representative of the employer and a representative authorized by the employees be given an opportunity to accompany the OSHA inspector for the purpose of aiding the inspection.

Where there is no authorized employee representative, the OSHA Compliance Officer must consult with a reasonable number of employees concerning safety and health conditions in the workplace.

## COMPLAINT

Employees or their representatives have the right to file a complaint with the nearest OSHA office requesting an inspection if they believe unsafe or unhealthful conditions exist in their workplace. OSHA will withhold, on request, names of employees complaining.

The Act provides that employees may not be discharged or discriminated against in any way for filing safety and health complaints or for otherwise exercising their rights under the Act.

Employees who believe they have been discriminated against may file a complaint with the nearest OSHA office within 30 days of the alleged discriminatory action.

## CITATION

If upon inspection OSHA believes an employer has violated the Act, a citation alleging such violations will be issued to the employer. Each citation will specify a time period within which the alleged violation must be corrected. The OSHA citation must be prominently displayed at or near the place of alleged violation for three days, or until it is corrected, whichever is later, to warn employees of dangers that may exist there.

## PROPOSED PENALTY

The Act provides for mandatory civil penalties against employers of up to $7,000 for each serious violation and for optional penalties of up to $7,000 for each nonserious violation. Penalties of up to $7,000 per day may be proposed for failure to correct violations within the proposed time period and for each day the violation continues beyond the prescribed abatement date. Also, any employer who willfully or repeatedly violates the Act may be assessed penalties of up to $70,000 for each such violation. A minimum penalty of $5,000 may be imposed for each willful violation. A violation of posting requirements can bring a penalty of up to $7,000.

There are also provisions for criminal penalties. Any willful violation resulting in the death of any employee, upon conviction, is punishable by a fine of up to $250,000 (or $500,000 if the employer is a corporation), or by imprisonment for up to six months, or both. A second conviction of an employer doubles the possible term of imprisonment. Falsifying records, reports, or applications is punishable by a fine of $10,000 or up to six months in jail or both.

## VOLUNTARY ACTIVITY

While providing penalties for violations, the Act also encourages efforts by labor and management, before an OSHA inspection, to reduce workplace hazards voluntarily and to develop and improve safety and health programs in all workplaces and industries. OSHA's Voluntary Protection Programs recognize outstanding efforts of this nature.

OSHA has published Safety and Health Program Management Guidelines to assist employers in establishing or perfecting programs to prevent or control employee exposure to workplace hazards. There are many public and private organizations that can provide information and assistance in this effort, if requested. Also, your local OSHA office can provide considerable help and advice on solving safety and health problems or can refer you to other sources for help such as training.

## CONSULTATION

Free assistance in identifying and correcting hazards and in improving safety and health management is available to employers, without citation or penalty, through OSHA-supported programs in each State. These programs are usually administered by the State Labor or Health department or a State university.

## POSTING INSTRUCTIONS

Employers in States operating OSHA approved State Plans should obtain and post the State's equivalent poster.

*Under provisions of Title 29, Code of Federal Regulations, Part 1903.2 (a) (1) employers must post this notice (or facsimile) in a conspicuous place where notices to employees are customarily posted.*

**More Information**

Additional information and copies of the Act, specific OSHA safety and health standards, and other applicable regulations may be obtained from your employer or from the nearest OSHA Regional Office in the following locations:

To report suspected fire hazards, imminent danger, safety and health hazards in the workplace, or other job safety and health emergencies, such as toxic waste in the workplace, call OSHA's 24-hour hotline: 1-800-321-OSHA

| | |
|---|---|
| Atlanta, GA | (404) 347-3573 |
| Boston, MA | (617) 565-7164 |
| Chicago, IL | (312) 353-2220 |
| Dallas, TX | (214) 767-4731 |
| Denver, CO | (303) 844-3061 |
| Kansas City, MO | (816) 426-5861 |
| New York, NY | (212) 337-2378 |
| Philadelphia, PA | (215) 596-1201 |
| San Francisco, CA | (415) 744-6670 |
| Seattle, WA | (208) 442-5930 |

This information will be made available to sensory impaired individuals upon request. Voice phone (202) 523-8615; TDD message referral phone: 1-800-326-2577

Washington, D.C.
1991 (Reprinted)
OSHA 2203

*Lynn Martin*

Lynn Martin, Secretary of Labor
**U.S. Department of Labor**
Occupational Safety and Health Administration

someone's unsafe act that led to that condition."[30] In addition, a supervisor should be responsive to employee complaints related to safety, seeing that the health and safety committee or the appropriate individual investigates these complaints. Any hazardous conditions should be corrected immediately.

### Prompt Responses

A supervisor who observes a violation of health and safety guidelines should respond immediately and consistently. Failure to react is a signal to employees that the guidelines are not really important. First, a supervisor should determine why the violation occurred. Does the employee understand what the proper procedures are? If the employee understands the procedures but still resists following them, the supervisor should try to find out why. For example, if an employee complains that some safety equipment is uncomfortable to use, investigating the complaint may turn up a more effective alternative, such as a greater selection of safety glasses or a way to set up a job so that less safety equipment is required. Despite complaints, however, a supervisor must insist that employees follow safety procedures, even when they seem inconvenient. If the safety rules are violated, a supervisor may have to take disciplinary action. (See Chapter 13 for a discussion of discipline.)

### Quality of Work Life

By combating fatigue, boredom, and dissatisfaction, which can make an employee accident-prone, a supervisor can promote safety and health. These efforts may include improving the quality of work life by making jobs more interesting and satisfying. Although no one has proved that there is a link between quality of work life and employee safety and health, it seems reasonable to assume that interested, satisfied employees will tend to be healthier and more careful. (Chapter 11 offers some guidelines for expanding and enriching jobs.)

In the case of shift workers, a supervisor can help minimize fatigue by encouraging the organization to place employees on a single shift or to rotate shifts so that employees go to work later and later, rather than earlier and earlier or in no steady pattern. Making sure there is bright lighting also will help employees stay alert at night.

### Setting an Example

As with any other area where the supervisor wants employees to behave in a certain way, the supervisor must set a good example and follow safe practices. For example, a supervisor who uses tools improperly, creates a tower of soft-drink cans on a filing cabinet, or tries to troubleshoot a photocopier without first turning off the power is voiding the effect of even the most eloquent lecture on safety in the workplace.

## Labor Relations: The Supervisor's Role

Concerns related to health and safety are among those that spurred the formation of unions as we know them in the United States during the late 1800s. Employees, who then worked as long as 12 hours each day, banded together to persuade employers to shorten work hours, pay higher wages, and improve safety. Today unions continue to negotiate with organizations over similar issues.

■ **FIGURE 19.5**

**Union Membership as a Percentage of the Employed U.S. Workforce**

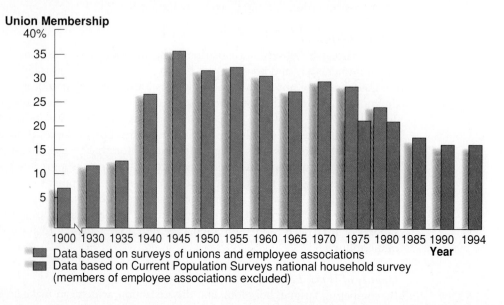

Sources: C. Chang and C. Sorrentino, "Union Membership in 12 Countries," *Monthly Labor Review* 114, no. 12 (1991), pp. 46–53; L. Troy and N. Sheflin, *Union Sourcebook* (West Orange, N.J.: Industrial Relations Data and Information Services, 1985); Bureau of Labor Statistics, *Handbook of Labor Statistics* (Washington, D.C., 1992); *Statistical Abstract of the United States: 1995* (Washington, D.C., 1995), p. 444.

**Wagner Act**
Federal law intended to define and protect the rights of workers and employers, encourage collective bargaining, and eliminate unfair labor practices.

In 1935 the federal government passed the **Wagner Act** (also called the National Labor Relations Act). This law aims to define and protect the rights of workers and employers, encourage collective bargaining, and eliminate unfair practices (e.g., violence and threatening to fire employees who join a union). Following passage of the Wagner Act, union membership tripled (see Figure 19.5). As a percentage of the total workforce, union membership peaked in the 1940s.

Union membership has since fallen to under 16 percent of the workforce in the mid-1990s.[31] This drop accompanies a decline in the industrial sector of the economy, where membership was traditionally strongest. The power of unions has also declined along with the numbers. During the 1980s, many unions made major concessions in negotiations with employers. Wage increases to union members were less than the Consumer Price Index in all but one year between 1983 and 1990.[32]

**labor relations**
Management's role in working constructively with unions that represent the organization's employees.

The processes by which supervisors and other managers work constructively with unions constitute the management discipline of **labor relations.** Effective labor relations cannot eliminate all conflicts between labor and management, but it does provide a relatively low-cost means of resolving conflict through discussion rather than confrontation. Labor relations take place through activities such as organization drives and collective bargaining.

## The Organization Drive

An organization drive is the union's method of getting its members elected to represent the workers in an organization. Management typically resists these drives because it believes that a union will interfere with managers' ability to make decisions in the best interests of the company. Managers also fear that the union will convert employees' loyalty to the company into loyalty to the union. The union tries to persuade employees that management has never had their interests at heart and that they will be better off if they let the union bargain collectively with management.

The process of organizing begins when a few employees decide they want to be represented by a union or when union leaders target an organization as a likely candidate. Union representatives then go to the company to organize. If at least 30 percent of the employees sign an authorization card stating they want the union to represent them, the union may request an election. The employees vote by secret ballot. If a majority of the voting employees favor the union, the union becomes the representative of *all* employees in the bargaining unit.

Although managers generally want to keep unions out, federal law says supervisors and other managers may not restrain employees from forming or joining a union. Supervisors are allowed to state their views about unions, but they may not threaten employees with punishment for forming or joining a union, and they may not promise rewards for working against the union. A supervisor who is unsure about what kinds of comments are permitted should consult with the organization's human resources department. A union in turn may not try to pressure employees into joining. Supervisors who think the union is violating this law should inform the human resources department.

## Collective Bargaining

**collective bargaining**
The process of seeking to reach a contract spelling out the rights and duties of unionized workers and their employer.

Typically, workers and managers have differing views on a variety of issues; after all, the fundamental reason for unions is to give workers a stronger voice when differences arise. The basic process for resolving such differences is **collective bargaining**—the process of seeking to reach a contract spelling out the rights and duties of unionized workers and their employer. Typically, bargaining begins when the union and management set forth their demands. Because the two parties usually differ on what is acceptable, they discuss how to resolve the major areas of conflict. If they need help in resolving a conflict, they may call in a **mediator,** or **conciliator,** a neutral person who helps the two sides reach agreement.

**mediator or conciliator**
A neutral person who helps opposing parties in an organization reach agreement.

A supervisor seldom has a direct role in collective bargaining. However, management may ask a supervisor to provide information that will help during the bargaining process. This is another reason why the supervisor should keep careful records concerning employees.

## The Labor Contract

A typical labor contract contains provisions such as guidelines for union membership; procedures for handling grievances; policies about regular and overtime pay, benefits (including vacations and holidays), and work hours; and agreements concerning safety and health. A supervisor must abide by the terms of this contract, so he or she must be familiar with it. A supervisor who is unfamiliar with the labor contract may unintentionally cause a problem by, for example, asking an employee to do something forbidden by the contract or using a procedure for discipline that is prohibited. Ignoring a provision in the contract, such as the length of rest periods, may be interpreted as an agreement to change the contract. A supervisor also should treat all employees fairly and consistently. Not only is this good practice whether or not there is a union, but federal law prohibits supervisors and other managers from discriminating against union members.

### Working with the Union Steward

**union steward**
An employee who is the union's representative in a particular work unit.

Part of a supervisor's job under a labor contract is to maintain a good relationship with the union steward. A **union steward** is an employee who serves as the union's representative in a particular work unit. Employees go to the union steward with their contract-related questions and complaints.

To minimize conflict and to resolve problems that arise, a supervisor needs to cooperate with the union steward. The supervisor should treat a union steward with respect and tell him or her about problems and upcoming changes. If the supervisor and union steward have a cooperative relationship, they often can resolve problems themselves rather than subject the organization and its employees to the cost and stress of an ongoing dispute.

### Grievances

**grievance**
A formal complaint that the terms of a labor contract have been violated.

Employees who believe they have been treated unfairly under the terms of the labor contract may bring a formal complaint, or **grievance.** Typically, when an employee brings a grievance, he or she first meets with the supervisor and union steward to look for a solution. Most of the time, the three of them can resolve the problem. If not, higher-level managers and union representatives meet to seek a solution. If they cannot reach an agreement, both parties might agree to bring in an outside **arbitrator,** a neutral person who reaches a decision on how to resolve a conflict. Both parties must adhere to the terms set by the arbitrator.

**arbitrator**
A neutral person who reaches a decision on the resolution of a conflict; both parties must adhere to the decision.

To avoid this costly and time-consuming process, supervisors should make sure that employees have a chance to be heard. In many cases, a supervisor can resolve conflicts before an employee even files a grievance. When a grievance is filed, a supervisor should take it seriously. This means gathering complete information and trying to resolve the problem as quickly as possible. Conflicts that are allowed to continue are likely to seem more significant to both parties.

According to arbitrator Arthur J. Hedges, the supervisor's role is particularly important in arbitration cases involving employees who were discharged because their job performance was declining.[33] Frequently, a supervisor put up with the employee as long as he or she could. Then the employee had a particularly bad day and was fired by the supervisor. The union filed a grievance claiming that the employee was discharged without just cause and that the employer failed to give corrective discipline and warning notices so that the employee could correct the problem. Hedges says, "First-line supervisors are key to winning such cases," because the supervisor is the person responsible for making sure the employee is aware of any performance problems and the consequences of failing to improve.

After the Air Line Pilots Association (ALPA) won the right to represent the 2,800 pilots for Federal Express Corporation (FedEx), negotiations between ALPA and Federal Express stretched into a two-year period. Major issues included representation of foreign-based pilots, use of nonunion pilots to fly leased planes, pensions, and pay hikes. Even a federally mandated cooling-off period did not bring agreement. In the photo is Joseph DePete, head of ALPA's FedEx unit.

Source: © Lisa Waddell

**strike**
Refusal by employees to work until there is a contract.

**wildcat strike**
Refusal by employees to work during the term of a labor contract.

### Strikes

Occasionally, the parties are unable to reach an agreement during collective bargaining, so the employees vote to go on strike. During a **strike,** employees leave their jobs and refuse to come back until there is a contract. The use of strikes has been declining in recent decades. According to the U.S. Department of Labor, there were 381 major strikes in 1970, 187 in 1980, and only 40 in 1991.[34] In general, striking during the term of a contract—a **wildcat strike**—is illegal.

### The Supervisor's Role in Preventing Strikes

Although a supervisor has little control over any agreement reached during collective bargaining by union and management representatives, he or she does have a role in minimizing the likelihood of a strike. Treating employees fairly and reasonably fosters good relations between employees and management. In this kind of climate, employees are less likely to desire a strike. Good communication practices also enable employees to understand management's point of view and give them a chance to vent their frustrations while staying on the job.

### The Supervisor's Role during a Strike

Once the employees have voted to strike, there is little a supervisor can do to resolve the conflict. If the circumstances of the strike do not involve unfair labor practices by an employer, the employer may hire replacement workers. Then the supervisor must tackle the challenge of training and getting to know a new workforce. The supervisor will have to adjust goals and expectations to allow for the new employees' inexperience.

When a wildcat strike takes place, a supervisor should follow the practices listed in Table 19.1, notably, to observe carefully what is occurring and to encourage employees to abide by the contract and return to work. At no time should the supervisor make agreements or even discuss the problem that led to the wildcat strike.

## ■ TABLE 19.1

**Guidelines for Supervising during a Wildcat Strike**

Stay on the job.

Notify higher management by telephone or messenger.

Carefully record the events as they happen.

Pay strict attention to who the leaders are, and record their behavior.

Record any lack of action by union officials.

Report all information as fully and as soon as possible to higher management.

Encourage employees to go back to work.

Ask union officials to instruct employees to go back to work.

Do not discuss the cause of the strike.

Do not make any agreements or say anything that might imply permission to leave work.

Make it clear that management will discuss the issue when all employees are back at work.

Source: Leslie W. Rue and Lloyd L. Byars, *Supervision: Key Link to Productivity*, 4th ed. (Homewood, IL: Richard D. Irwin, 1993), p. 325.

## Sexual Harassment

**sexual harassment**
Unwelcome sexual advances, requests for sexual favors, and other sexual conduct that interferes with work performance or creates a hostile work environment.

In days of testimony before the Senate Judiciary Committee in October 1991, law professor Anita Hill accused her former boss, Justice Clarence Thomas, of sexual harassment, and Thomas refuted her charges. While neither of them ever fully proved their case, the controversy dramatically highlighted the issue of sexual harassment, a category of behavior prohibited by laws against sex discrimination. As defined by the Equal Employment Opportunity Commission (EEOC), **sexual harassment** is "unwelcome sexual advances, requests for sexual favors, and other verbal and physical conduct of a sexual nature" that "has the purpose or effect of unreasonably interfering with an individual's work performance or creating an intimidating, hostile, or offensive work environment." It may include any of the behaviors listed in Table 19.2. The perpetrator and victim may be either male or female. (About 10 percent of all complaints filed with the EEOC involve a version of harassment other than a man harassing a woman.[35]) The victim does not need to prove that sexual harassment caused psychological harm, only that it was unwelcome. (The Self-Quiz on page 597 can help you determine how well you understand sexual harassment and what to do about it.)

In the wake of the Hill-Thomas hearings, the number of sexual harassment charges filed with the EEOC increased dramatically.[36] For example, the number of claims of sexual harassment filed in the fourth quarter of 1991 was 71 percent higher than a year earlier—1,244 compared with 728 in 1990. These numbers suggest that the problem is persistent and extensive.

### Responding to Charges of Sexual Harassment

A charge of sexual harassment is a serious one. Court decisions have held employers liable for the misdeeds of their employees unless an organization actively tries to prevent the misbehavior and responds effectively when it does occur. Therefore,

**TABLE 19.2**

**Behaviors that May Constitute Sexual Harassment**

Suggestive remarks.

Teasing or taunting of a sexual nature.

Unwelcome physical conduct or sexual advances.

Continual use of offensive language.

Sexual bantering.

Bragging about sexual prowess.

Office or locker-room pinups.

"Compliments" with sexual overtones.

A demand for sex in return for retaining a job or being promoted.

Source: Based on Michael A. Verespej, "New-Age Sexual Harassment," *Industry Week*, May 15, 1995, p. 66.

when an employee charges a member of an organization with sexual harassment, a supervisor must take the problem seriously.[37] There are no exceptions to this rule—not the attractiveness of the victim nor the supervisor's opinion of a man who is offended by centerfold pictures.

A supervisor must see that the complaint is investigated properly. Generally, the investigation involves a third party, such as a personnel official, interviewing everyone involved. This official, the supervisor, and the parties involved should keep the investigation confidential. The supervisor must avoid also expressing an opinion or imposing his or her interpretation on the situation.

Whether harassment occurs depends on how the behavior affects the recipient, not on the intent of the person performing the behavior. Thus, if lewd jokes and pornographic pictures create a climate that feels hostile and intimidating to an employee, it does not matter that the person who told the jokes and hung up the pictures thought only that they were funny. Not surprisingly, perceptions vary from one person to another.

If the investigation indicates that sexual harassment did occur, the problem must be corrected. One approach that does *not* work is ignoring the offensive behavior in the hope that it will go away. The victim telling the offender to stop is effective more than half the time. Because of differences in perceptions, it may be helpful to describe not only the offending behavior but the kind of behavior that would be acceptable. In addition, a supervisor needs to work with the human resources department to identify a prompt and firm response to charges that are proven. The response might be to move the employee to another department or shift, or even to fire him or her. In any case, discipline should be appropriate and swift, occurring the same day if possible or at least within a week.

### Preventing Sexual Harassment

An employee who sexually harasses another employee hurts the organization in several ways. First, the person who is being harassed is upset and unable to work as effectively as possible. If that person complains, disciplining the harasser may involve transferring or dismissing him or her, resulting in the loss of an otherwise qualified employee. And if the harassed person sues, the company faces the embarrassment and expense of defending itself in court. It is clearly in the organization's best interests to prevent harassment.

According to George Stillman of BNA Communications in Rockville, Maryland, most instances of sexual harassment result from ignorance.[38] In other words, people of the opposite sex tend to interpret words and actions differently. For example, men more often than women view a proposition as flattering. Likewise, when women behave in a way they view as simply friendly, men sometimes interpret their behavior as a come-on. Such differences in perception also occur among people of different cultures. To make sure employees know how to avoid harassment, an increasing number of organizations are providing training about it.

David P. Tulin, president and lead trainer of Tulin DiversiTeam Associates, based in Philadelphia, offers the following lessons in avoiding sexual harassment:[39]

- When in doubt, do not say or do it.
- When in doubt, ask if it is all right.
- If the behavior is unwanted, stop the behavior.
- Do not assume that friendliness equals sexual interest.

Tulin emphasizes that sexual harassment is not defined by the intent of the actor but by the effect of his or her behavior on the person being harassed.

Some people have complained that concern about sexual harassment has poisoned the workplace—that they no longer feel safe paying friendly compliments. However, respecting the viewpoints and emotional comfort of all employees simply makes sense. The same is true of ensuring employees' safety and health, and of practicing good labor relations. In each case, a supervisor is recognizing that good employee relations is at the heart of cultivating the organization's most important resources: its employees.

# Summary

**19.1  Summarize the basic purpose of the OSHAct, and describe the supervisor's responsibilities under the act.**

OSHAct set up two government agencies (OSHA and NIOSH) to conduct research regarding occupational health and safety, set health and safety standards, inspect workplaces, and penalize employers that do not meet standards. According to OSHAct, a supervisor must keep records of occupational injuries and illnesses, accompany OSHA officials on inspections of the workplace, and disseminate information about chemicals used in the workplace.

**19.2  Identify basic categories of health and safety hazards in the workplace.**

Health hazards may be physical, chemical, biological, or stress inducing. Safety hazards include personal behavior (i.e., unsafe acts) and unsafe conditions of the physical environment.

**19.3  Discuss common safety and health concerns and how employers are addressing them.**

Cigarette smoke can cause a variety of illnesses in smokers and the people who breathe secondhand smoke. As a result, many organizations have banned or limited smoking in the workplace. The abuse of alcohol and other drugs can be costly, so organizations have policies for responding to employees with these problems. Extended use of video display terminals can result in eyestrain and muscle aches, and they possibly contribute to miscarriages among pregnant employees. Organizations can address these problems with rest breaks, ergonomically designed workstations, and seating that places employees a safe distance from the screen. Repetitive-motion disorders can result when employees repeatedly apply force to the same muscles or joints. Applying ergonomics to the design of jobs and workstations can minimize such problems. Many employees are afraid of working near someone with AIDS; however, the means of transmitting this disease are limited. A supervisor may need to provide an employee who has AIDS with reasonable accommodations and educate the employee's co-workers about this disease.

### 19.4 Describe workplace safety and health programs, including their benefits and the supervisor's role in them.

Workplace safety and health programs may include training, safety meetings, posters, awards for safe performance, and safety and health committees. These programs can cut costs by reducing work-related injuries and illnesses. In addition, safety and health programs can motivate employees, reduce turnover, and help prevent pain and suffering for employees and their families. A supervisor needs to make sure that employees understand and follow safety measures, and should encourage all employees to participate in the promotion of these measures. A supervisor must respond immediately to a violation of health and safety guidelines. A supervisor also should set a good example for employees.

### 19.5 Explain a supervisor's role during a union organization drive and collective bargaining.

During an organization drive, a supervisor may state his or her views about the union. However, a supervisor may not threaten employees about forming or joining a union and may not promise rewards for working against the union. If the union tries to coerce employees into supporting the union, the supervisor should report those activities. During collective bargaining, a supervisor provides management with information that will help it bargain.

### 19.6 Provide guidelines for working with a union steward and handling grievances.

A supervisor should cooperate with the union steward and treat that person with respect. He or she should tell the steward about problems and upcoming changes and should try to resolve problems with the steward rather than let them escalate. A supervisor should try to avoid grievances by giving employees a chance to be heard and trying to resolve conflicts. When a grievance is filed, a supervisor should take it seriously, gathering information and trying to resolve the problem as quickly as possible.

### 19.7 Explain a supervisor's role in preventing strikes and operating during a strike.

A supervisor should foster good relations with employees by treating them fairly and communicating effectively. This minimizes the chance that employees will want to strike. During a strike, a supervisor may have to train and oversee replacement workers. During a wildcat strike, a supervisor should observe carefully what is occurring and encourage employees to go back to work. A supervisor should not make agreements or even discuss the problem that led to the wildcat strike.

### 19.8 Discuss how a supervisor should respond to charges of sexual harassment and prevent it from occurring.

When an employee charges a member of the organization with sexual harassment, a supervisor must take the problem seriously, without exception. He or she must see that the complaint is investigated properly and avoid expressing an opinion or imposing an interpretation on the situation. A supervisor should work with the human resources department to identify a prompt and firm response to charges that are proven true. In many cases, sexual harassment can be prevented through training and greater awareness of different points of view between men and women.

# Key Terms

Occupational Safety and Health Act (OSHAct) of 1970

Occupational Safety and Health Administration (OSHA)

National Institute for Occupational Safety and Health (NIOSH)

health hazards

safety hazards

video display terminal (VDT)

virtual reality

repetitive-motion disorders

ergonomics

AIDS (acquired immune deficiency syndrome)

Wagner Act

labor relations

collective bargaining

mediator or conciliator

union steward

grievance

arbitrator

strike

wildcat strike

sexual harassment

# Review and Discussion Questions

1. Describe the two government agencies established by the Occupational Safety and Health Act of 1970. What is their role in promoting safety and health in the workplace?

2. Keith Navarro is a new supervisor at a supermarket. He is worried that OSHA has so many regulations that it is impossible to keep track of them all. What general guidelines can you give Keith about his responsibilities under the OSHAct?

3. Give an example of the following types of health and safety hazards:

   *a.* Physical
   *b.* Chemical
   *c.* Biological
   *d.* Stressful working conditions
   *e.* Personal behavior

4. Betsy Lee is the supervisor of the central files department of a large professional association. She is concerned about the number of minor injuries caused by employees tripping, dropping stacks of files, and colliding. Two employees have complained that lighting is often poor because lightbulbs are not immediately replaced when they burn out. What actions should Betsy take to minimize the safety hazards in her department?

5. What can supervisors do to minimize the effects of each of the following hazards?

   *a.* Cigarette smoking in the workplace.
   *b.* Extended use of video display terminals.

6. What are the benefits of workplace health and safety programs?

7. A clothing manufacturer wants to set up a safety and health program. What characteristics should this program have to be effective?

8. Julie Lindholm supervises a shift of workers who sew together teddy bears for a toy manufacturer. What steps should she be taking to implement her company's health and safety measures?

9. A foreman notices that an employee is not wearing the safety goggles required for operating a piece of grinding equipment. How should the foreman respond? What actions should he take?

10. Supervisor Sandy Berkmann recently learned that several of his employees approached a union to conduct an organization drive. Sandy feels somewhat hurt by their action, believing that it is a reflection on his supervisory skills. He also thinks the union will be a disruptive force among his workers. By law, what may Sandy do or not do during the organization drive? What do you think would be the best way for Sandy to behave, so that the process is beneficial to everyone?

11. During the term of a labor contract, a group of employees becomes angry about a new policy they believe is unfair, and they leave their work areas to walk off the job. In an effort to keep them working, their supervisor calls out, "Hey, not so fast! Why don't you tell me what the problem is, and we'll work out a solution." Is this an acceptable way for the supervisor to handle the situation? Explain.

12. One of Jim Seifert's women employees tells him that a male supervisor—a good friend of Jim's—has repeatedly made sexually explicit comments to her that embarrass and offend her. What should Jim do about the situation?

## A SECOND LOOK

The story at the beginning of this chapter described how supervisors at Du Pont promote safety. Besides observing employees and teaching them about safe practices, how else might supervisors promote safety?

# APPLICATIONS MODULE

## CASE

### Promoting Safety at Pacific Lumber Company

Several years ago, the management of Pacific Lumber Company (PALCO), located in Scotia, California, decided the company needed a comprehensive safety program that would go beyond its existing efforts to avoid safety violations. The company sought to improve its program not only to meet OSHA regulations but also to cut the rising number of work-related injuries.

Part of the expanded efforts involve training supervisors in conducting safety meetings. PALCO's director of accident prevention, Jeff A. Ringwald, explains:

> I've found that it's easier to *tell* a supervisor to have a safety meeting than it is to actually have them *do* it. Most of the supervisors can run their crews and keep the production end of things going, but they find it difficult to talk to their crew from a public speaking standpoint.

Training is a hands-on activity, supplemented with written materials. The company assigns an experienced worker to help each new employee until the new person is ready to do the job alone.

To help management and all employees see how their efforts are working, the company tries to provide feedback. Ringwald explains, "The program's no good if you don't communicate after you try something." Each month, the company updates a graph of lost-time injuries and first-aid cases so that everyone can compare the current year's performance with that of past years. So far the news has been good; lost-time injuries have fallen by 52 percent.

The company also rewards employees for safe performance. At the end of every year, employees with both perfect attendance and no injuries are eligible to participate in a drawing for cash prizes. The grand prize is $15,000 toward the purchase of a U.S.-made car of the employee's choice. Ten smaller prizes also are awarded. Furthermore, every employee who qualifies for the drawing receives a company jacket bearing the year's safety slogan, which was chosen in a contest among employees.

A separate program recognizes supervisors and their departments. Departments compete to see which will have the year's most significant decline in accidents, measured in terms of lost time compared with the previous year. Employees in the winning department and their guests enjoy a group dinner at a local restaurant.

PALCO has found that several resources are available to help in the effort to improve the company's safety program. For example, the Timber Operators Council has a safety specialist, safety training consultants, and resources for training in conducting safety meetings. Every year PALCO invites one of the organization's training consultants to focus on a particular area of safety concerns. Other resources include information from the National Safety Council and a training program from the California Lumbermen's Accident Prevention Association.

1. What health hazards and safety hazards would you expect to be concerns at PALCO?
2. Review the characteristics of an effective safety and health program described in the chapter. Which of these characteristics does PALCO's safety program include?
3. Based on the information given, what safety-related duties do the supervisors have at PALCO? What else might PALCO's supervisors do to promote safety in the workplace?

Source: Gina C. Wilson, " 'Safety Sense—Your Best Defense,' " *Quality Digest*, July 1992, pp. 40–46.

### SELF-QUIZ

## How Well Do You Understand Sexual Harassment?

Mark each of the following statements True or False.

_____ 1. Sexual harassment applies only to comments or actions made by men toward women.

_____ 2. There are no laws defining sexual harassment.

_____ 3. If I intend my remarks to be friendly, they cannot be interpreted as sexual harassment.

_____ 4. A court may find a company legally responsible for sexual harassment by one of its employees.

_____ 5. Sometimes the best way to deal with sexual harassment is to ignore it.

_____ 6. To keep things from escalating, a supervisor should personally investigate an employee's charge of sexual harassment.

_____ 7. A supervisor's opinion of both the victim and the person charged can provide valuable information in a sexual harassment investigation.

_____ 8. Discipline for sexual harassment should take place as soon as possible.

_____ 9. Showing someone pornographic pictures at the workplace does not constitute sexual harassment.

_____ 10. Because men and women often interpret behavior differently, education about sexual harassment could help prevent it.

Scoring: The correct response to statements 4, 8, and 10 is "true"; to all other statements, "false."

## Class Exercise

Suppose students could be represented by a union. How might they benefit? How would this change their relationship with their instructors and the university? Appoint someone in the class to play the role of union representative and someone to play the role of "supervisor." Hold an organization drive meeting, in which students as well as the union rep and supervisor participate. At the end of the meeting, allow students to vote on whether they want the union to represent them. (Note: Course grades or other benefits can be considered "pay" if issues of compensation are discussed.)

## Team-Building Exercise

### Conducting a Safety Inspection

Divide the class into teams of two to four members each. At the end of the class session or between sessions, the teams will look for and list health and safety hazards on campus or in some other prescribed area. Team members may choose the area of campus to visit and investigate, or the instructor may assign the teams to specific areas (e.g., parking lots, recreation areas, bookstore, classrooms). Before the teams begin, it may be helpful for the class as a whole to discuss what kinds of hazards they expect to find—wet floors, dangerous intersections, unmarked fire extinguishers, uncomfortable chairs at VDTs, sources of stress, and so on.

At the next class session, each team reports its findings to the class. The instructor may invite the campus security director to sit in on this discussion.

Source: This exercise is based on ideas submitted by Debbie Jansky, Milwaukee Area Tech Institute, Milwaukee, Wisconsin; James Mulvihill, Mankato Technical Institute, Mankato, Minnesota; and Sylvia Ong, Scottsdale Community College, Scottsdale, Arizona.

# Video Exercise 19: *The Impact of the Law*

## Video Summary

In 1985 General Motors announced that it intended to build a world-class car—the Saturn—that would be a leader in quality, cost, and customer satisfaction. The new manufacturing facility, located in Spring Hill, Tennessee, would build cars a "whole new way" thanks to the innovative partnership arrangement between General Motors and the United Auto Workers union. They believed that their unique agreement would become a model of manufacturing excellence in that workers at every level of the organization would be truly involved in all decision-making as coequals.

## Application

After viewing the video, form groups of three to five students to discuss the following questions:

1. What is the role of a union in an organization such as Saturn Corporation? If there is truly shared consensus-based decision making, is a union needed?

   _____

   _____

   _____

2. What arguments exist against an arrangement such as that at Saturn Corporation? Is such a system in the best interests of the employees? List arguments for and against such a shared partnership arrangement.

   | Pros of Shared Partnership | Cons of Shared Partnership |
   |---|---|
   |  |  |
   |  |  |
   |  |  |

3. What skills do supervisors and union leaders need to develop to make such a cooperative, shared system work successfully? Would these skills also be needed on the shop floor?

   _____

   _____

   _____

4. What is the difference between the union acting as an "adversary" and acting as an "advocate"?

_____

_____

_____

Source: Adapted from Noe, Hollenbeck, Gerhart, and Wright, *Human Resource Management: Gaining a Competitive Advantage* (Burr Ridge, IL: Austen Press/Irwin, 1994), p. 753.

# Notes

**CHAPTER 1**

1. "A Challenge for the 1990s —Managing the Diverse Workforce," in *The Challenge of Diversity: Equal Employment Opportunity and Managing Differences in the 1990's* (Rockville, MD: BNA Communications, N.d.).

2. Jolie Solomon, "As Cultural Diversity of Workers Grows, Experts Urge Appreciation of Differences," *The Wall Street Journal*, September 12, 1990, pp. B1, B8.

3. Thomas G. Exter, "In and Out of Work," *American Demographics*, June 1992, p. 63.

4. Exter, "In and Out of Work."

5. See, for example, "The Spare Sex," *The Economist*, March 28, 1992, p. 20.

6. William P. Anthony, "Managing Diversity, Then and Now," *The Wall Street Journal*, July 3, 1992, p. A6.

7. Audrey Edwards, "The Sting of the Subtle Snub," *Working Woman*, January 1992, pp. 53, 55.

8. Abby Livingston, "What YOUR Department Can Do," *Working Woman*, January 1991, pp. 59, 61.

9. "Improving Your Supervisory Skills: The Basics Plus," *Maintenance Supervisor's Bulletin* (Bureau of Business Practice), January 10, 1992, p. 2.

10. "The Salaryman Rides Again," *The Economist*, February 4, 1995, p. 64.

11. Carol Hymowitz, "When Firms Cut Out Middle Managers, Those at the Top and Bottom Often Suffer," *The Wall Street Journal*, April 5, 1990, pp. B1, B4.

12. Noel M. Tichy and Ram Charan, "The CEO as Coach: An Interview with Allied Signal's Lawrence A. Bossidy," *Harvard Business Review*, March-April 1995, pp. 69–78.

13. Frank Quisenberry, "World-of-Work Changes Signal New Roles for Service Supervisors," *The Service Edge*, November 1994, p. 7.

14. Story adapted from Bill Kelley, "From Salesperson to Manager: Transition and Travail," *Sales & Marketing Management*, February 1992, pp. 32–36.

15. See Connie Wallace, "Sizing Up Your New Staff," *Working Woman*, May 1990, pp. 29–31.

16. Wallace, "Sizing Up Your New Staff," p. 30.

17. Kelley, "From Salesperson to Manager," p. 34.

18. "Moving on Up: Handling Your Own Promotion," *Maintenance Supervisor's Bulletin* (Bureau of Business Practice), December 10, 1991, pp. 1–4.

19. This paragraph is based on ideas in Roberta Maynard, "How to Be a Great Boss," *Nation's Business*, December 1991, pp. 44–45.

**CHAPTER 2**

1. "Marketing Services: Cable Industry Forges Service Guarantees to Shore Up Its Weak Ratings with Customers," *The Service Edge*, February 1995, p. 4.

2. Ulf Dreber, John Condon, Bjorn Thunqvist, and Darlene Meskell, "Cost of Quality: Sweden Post Increases Customer Service *and* Saves Millions," *Quality Digest*, May 1992, pp. 45–51.

3. Taken from "Critical Quality," *Total Quality Newsletter*, January 1992, p. 8.

4. Ronald E. Yates, "Managing Quality: Certainty Not Part of the Equation," *Chicago Tribune*, January 27, 1992, sec. 4, pp. 1–2.

5. Aaron Bernstein, "Quality Is Becoming Job One in the Office, Too," *Business Week*, April 29, 1992, pp. 52–53, 56.

6. Steve Mitra, "Hospitals Try Treating Their Patients Like Customers," *Chicago Tribune*, August 2, 1992, sec. 7, p. 2.

7. Roy Duff, "Why TQM Fails—and What Companies Can Do about It," *Quality Digest*, February 1995, pp. 50–52.

8. Joshua Hyatt, "Surviving on Chaos," *Inc.*, May 1990, pp. 60–62ff.

9. "TQM and the Bottom Line," *Supervisory Management*, July 1992, p. 12.

10. "TQM 101: The Basics of Total Quality Management," *Commitment Plus* (Quality and Productivity Management Association), November 1991, pp. 1–4.

11. "The Straining of Quality," *The Economist*, January 14, 1995, pp. 55–56.

12. Mitra, "Hospitals Try Treating Their Patients Like Customers."

13. "TQM 101."

14. "The 'Heart' of TQM," *Commitment Plus* (Quality & Productivity Management Association), October 1991, pp. 1, 4.

15. Bernstein, "Quality Is Becoming Job One," p. 53.

16. "Making the Quality Connection," *Front Line Supervisor's Bulletin*, April 25, 1992, pp. 1–2.

17. "The Straining of Quality," p. 55.

18. Marion Harmon, "Internal Award Programs: Benchmarking the Baldrige to Improve Corporate Quality," *Quality Digest*, May 1992, pp. 20–24ff.

19. Jeremy Main, "Is the Baldrige Overblown?" *Fortune*, July 1, 1991, pp. 62–65.

20. This paragraph is based on information in Eugene Sprow, "Insights into ISO 9000," *Manufacturing Engineering*, September 1992, pp. 73–77.

21. Jerry G. Bowles, "Quality '92: Leading the World-Class Company," *Fortune*, September 21, 1992, special advertising section, p. 63.

22. John Guaspari, "A Cure for 'Initiative Burnout,'" *Management Review*, April 1995, pp. 45–49.

23. Oren Harari, "Why Don't Things Change?" *Management Review*, February 1995, pp. 30–32.

24. Keith H. Hammonds, "Corning's Class Act," *Business Week*, May 13, 1991, p. 70.

25. "Changes in Satisfaction Demands and Technology Alter the How's, What's, Why's of Measurement," *The Service Edge*, January 1995, pp. 1–3, 5.

26. "Making the Quality Connection."

27. James L. Heskett, W. Earl Sasser, Jr., and Leonard A. Schlesinger, "How to Improve Service to Improve Profits," *Boardroom Reports*, September 1, 1992, p. 8.

28. "Tips from a Pro: Getting People to Care about Quality," *Practical Supervision*, sample issue, p. 6.

29. Anne London and Richard L. Daft, *Managing Employee Diversity Supplement* (Fort Worth, TX: Dryden Press), pp. 22–23 (supplementing Richard L. Daft, *Management*, 2nd ed.).

30. Tom Salemme, "Lessons Learned from Employees about Quality Improvement Efforts," *Tapping the Network Journal*, Fall–Winter 1991, pp. 2–6.

31. Hyatt, "Surviving on Chaos."

32. Ibid.

33. Dennis Sowards, "TQM Is a Journey: So Where Do We Begin?" *Industrial Engineering*, January 1992, pp. 24–28.

34. "Quality Improvement Requires Continuing Employee Participation," *NIBA News Bulletin* (Northern Illinois Business Association), March 1992, p. 10.

35. Ronald E. Yates, "For Motorola, Quality an Olympian Effort," *Chicago Tribune*, January 27, 1992, sec. 4, pp. 1–2.

## CHAPTER 3

1. Bradford McKee, "Turn Your Workers into a Team," *Nation's Business*, July 1992, pp. 36–38.

2. Dorothy Miller, "Group Dynamics: Handling Subgroups," *Nursing Management*, December 1991, pp. 33–35.

3. Julia Lawlor, "Diversity Provides Rewards," *USA Today*, April 24, 1992.

4. R. B. Lacoursiere, *The Life Cycle of Groups: Group Development Stage Theory* (New York: Human Service Press, 1980).

5. William G. Dyer, *Team Building: Issues and Alternatives*, 2nd ed. (Reading, MA: Addison-Wesley, 1987), p. 24.

6. George Milite, "The Supervisor's Role in a Project Team," *Supervisory Management*, May 1992, pp. 10–11.

7. "The Trouble with Teams," *The Economist*, January 14, 1995, p. 61.

8. S. C. Gwynne, "The Right Stuff," *Time*, October 29, 1990, pp. 74–84.

9. Cathy Hyatt Hills, "Making the Team," *Sales & Marketing Management*, February 1992, pp. 54, 56–57.

10. Jon Van, "Mass Production Is Out; Quality, Skills Are In," *Chicago Tribune*, November 3, 1991, sec. 1, pp. 1, 12.

11. Edward E. Lawler III, Susan Albers Mohrman, and Gerald E. Ledford, Jr., "Study Shows Strong Evidence that Participatory Management Pays Off," *Total Quality*, September 1992, pp. 1–4.

12. Barbara B. Buchholz and Margaret Crane, "Nurturing the Team Spirit at Growing Green," *Your Company*, Spring 1995, pp. 10–11, 14–16.

13. See, for example, "The Trouble with Teams."

14. "F. Suzanne Jenniches: Sharp Isn't Strong Enough to Describe Her," *Industry Week*, March 2, 1992, pp. 32–33, 36.

15. "Guidelines for Implementing Self-Directed Work Teams," *Supervisory Management*, March 1995, p. 10.

16. "Guidelines for Implementing Self-Directed Work Teams."

17. "What Mentors Shouldn't Do," *Supervisory Management*, March 1995, p. 5.

18. Alfredo S. Lanier, "Alex Warren: Bridging the Gap between Cultures and Technologies," *GSB Chicago* (University of Chicago Graduate School of Business), Winter 1991, pp. 9–13.

19. Dyer, *Team Building*, p. 23.

20. Edward Glassman, "Self-Directed Team Building without a Consultant," *Supervisory Management*, March 1992, p. 6.

21. Rebecca J. Johnson, "Deep Sinkers," *Journal of Business Strategy*, May–June 1995, pp. 62–63.

22. "The Trouble with Teams."

23. "The Dream Team," Supervisory Management, May 1995, p. 10.

24. Donald J. McNerney, "Team Compensation," *Management Review*, February 1995, p. 16.

25. Hills, "Making the Team."

26. Aaron Bernstein, "Putting a Damper on That Old Team Spirit," *Business Week*, May 4, 1992, p. 60.

27. Michael P. Cronin, "Team Penalty," *Inc.*, May 1993, p. 29.

28. David F. Girard-diCarlo, Michael J. Hanlon, and Caren E. I. Naidoff, "Legal Traps in Employee Committees," *Management Review*, November 1992, pp. 27–29.

29. Cronin, "Team Penalty."

30. "Avoid Labor Law Violations in Employee Involvement Programs," *NIBA News Bulletin* (Northern Illinois Business Association), March 1992, p. 11; Bernstein, "Putting a Damper on That Old Team Spirit."

31. Roderick Wilkinson, "Forget That Meeting!" *Nursing Management*, December 1991, p. 42.

32. "Holding Meetings that Motivate," *Supervisory Management*, July 1991, p. 9 (quoting "Meetings that Motivate," *Supervisor Sense*, February 1990).

33. George Milite, "Communicating One-on-One with Members," *Supervisory Management*, May 1992, p. 11.

## CHAPTER 4

1. Pat Widder, "More Corporations Learning That Ethics Are Bottom-Line Issue," *Chicago Tribune*, June 7, 1992, sec. 7, pp. 1, 6.

2. Rushworth M. Kidder, "Ethics: A Matter of Survival," *The Futurist*, March–April, 1992, pp. 10–12.

3. "Good Grief," *The Economist*, April 8, 1995, p. 57.

4. Quoted in "The Holiday Spirit," *Total Quality Newsletter*, December 1992, p. 8.

5. Robert McGarvey, "Do the Right Thing," *Entrepreneur*, October 1992, pp. 138–143.

6. Matt Murray, "Wounded Phar-Mor Found a Healer in Antonio Alvarez," *The Wall Street Journal*, May 26, 1995, pp. B1, B6.

7. Matt Murray, "Former Phar-Mor President Guilty in Fraud Case," *The Wall Street Journal*, May 26, 1995, p. B6.

8. "Good Grief."

9. Kenneth Labich, "The New Crisis in Business Ethics," *Fortune*, April 20, 1992, pp. 167–168ff.

10. Reported on "60 Minutes," October 4, 1992.

11. "Hard Graft in Asia," *The Economist*, May 27, 1995, p. 61.

12. Sondra Thiederman, *Bridging Cultural Barriers for Corporate Success: How to Manage the Multicultural Work Force* (New York: Lexington Books, 1991), pp. 125–126.

13. "Hard Graft in Asia."

14. Karen Berney, "Finding the Ethical Edge," *Nation's Business*, August 1987, pp. 18–19, 22–24.

15. "Doing the Right Thing," *The Economist*, May 20, 1995, p. 64.

16. Adapted from Laura Nash, "Ethics without the Sermon," *Harvard Business Review*, November–December 1981, p. 81.

17. Andrew S. Grove, "What's the Right Thing? Everyday Ethical Dilemmas," *Working Woman*, June 1990, pp. 16–18.

18. Example from Grove, "What's the Right Thing?" p. 18.

19. Widder, "More Corporations Learning," p. 6.

20. Robert A. Mamis, "Don't Copy That Floppy," *Inc.*, June 1992, p. 127.

21. Cynthia Berryman-Fink, *The Manager's Desk Reference* (New York: American Management Association, 1989), pp. 342–343.

22. Tim Smart, "This Man Sounded the Silicone Alarm—in 1976," *Business Week*, January 27, 1992, p. 34.

23. Berryman-Fink, *The Manager's Desk Reference*, p. 343.

## CHAPTER 5

1. Randall Fields and Nicholas Imparato, "Cost, Competition & Cookies," *Management Review*, April 1995, pp. 57–61.

2. Dennis Kneale, "Unleashing the Power," *The Wall Street Journal*, June 27, 1994, pp. R1, R6–R7; Ralph T. King, Jr., "High-Tech Edge Gives U.S. Firms Global Lead in Computer Networks," *The Wall Street Journal*, September 9, 1994, pp. A1, A10.

3. James Coates, "A Mailbox in Cyberspace Brings World to Your PC," *Chicago Tribune*, March 26, 1995, sec. 19, p.1.

4. John W. Verity, "Planet Internet," *Business Week*, April 3, 1995, pp. 118–124.

5. Dave Zielinski, "On-Line Customer Support Offers Potent Complement to Phone, Mail Feedback Tools," *The Service Edge*, November 1994, pp. 1–3.

6. Verity, "Planet Internet," p. 119.

7. "How Various Industries Use Technology to Create Customer Intimacy," *The Service Edge*, November 1994, pp. 3, 5.

8. Laurie Freeman, "Getting More Owners to Compute," *Crain's Chicago Business*, May 22, 1995, p. 31.

9. Scott Heimes, "Changes in Satisfaction Demand and Technology Alter the How's, What's, Why's of Measurement," *The Service Edge*, January 1995, pp. 1–3, 5.

10. Joshua Macht, "An Electronic Field Day," *Inc. Technology*, no. 2 (1995), pp. 88–89.

11. Nilly Landau, "Holistic Salespeople," *International Business*, April 1995, pp. 50–52.

12. Macht, "An Electronic Field Day," p. 88.

13. Macht, "An Electronic Field Day," p. 88.

14. William A. Faunce, *Problems of an Industrial Society* (New York: McGraw-Hill, 1968).

15. H. P. Capron, *Instructor's Guide* for *Computers and Data Processing*, 2nd ed. (Menlo Park, CA: Benjamin Cummings Publishing, 1983), p. 4.

16. "PC I Love You," *Entrepreneur*, December 1992, p. 53.

17. "A World Without Jobs?" *The Economist*, February 11, 1995, pp. 21–22.

18. William R. Page, "Far Out," *Inc. Technology*, no 2. (1995), pp. 21–23.

## CHAPTER 6

1. *Fortune*, December 2, 1991, p. 59.

2. Christina Duff and Bob Ortega, "How Wal-Mart Outdid a Once-Touted Kmart in Discount-Store Race," *The Wall Street Journal*, March 24, 1995, pp. A1, A4.

3. James E. Ellis, "Monsanto's New Challenge: Keeping Minority Workers," *Business Week*, July 8, 1991, pp. 60–61.

4. "Planning for Success," *Front Line Supervisor's Bulletin* (Bureau of Business Practice), February 25, 1992, pp. 1–2.

5. Henry Fersko-Weiss, "Project Managers: A New Focus on Graphics and Resource Controls," *PC Magazine*, February 11, 1992, p. 39.

6. William Keenan, Jr., "Numbers Racket," *Sales & Marketing Management*, May 1995, pp. 46–66ff.

7. Marshall Loeb, "Jack Welch Lets Fly on Budgets, Bonuses, and Buddy Boards," *Fortune*, May 29, 1995, pp. 1345–47.

8. Scott Heimes, "Changes in Satisfaction Demands and Technology Alter the How's, What's, Why's of Measurement," *The Service Edge*, January 1995, pp. 1–3, 5.

9. "Is Maintenance Really Doing Its Job?" *Maintenance Management*, June 10, 1995, pp. 1–3, 7.

10. Privileged Information," *Boardroom Reports*, September 1, 1992, p. 2, citing T. Scott Gross, *Positively Outrageous Service: New and Easy Ways to Win Customers for Life* (New York: MasterMedia, Ltd.).

11. Ellis, "Monsanto's New Challenge."

12. Ellis, "Monsanto's New Challenge."

13. Duff and Ortega, "How Wal-Mart Outdid a Once-Touted Kmart," p. A4.

14. Cynthia Crossen, "No Place Like Home," *The Wall Street Journal*, June 4, 1990, pp. R6–R8ff; and David Foster, "Workers Stay Home, Keep Jobs," *Chicago Tribune*, April 19, 1992, sec. 7, p. 9A.

## CHAPTER 7

1. "Sales Systems Help Digital Move to Account Based Selling," advertisement in *Sales & Marketing Management*, Jan. 1992, p. 32.

2. "After Re-engineering, What's Next?" *Supervisory Management*, May 1995, pp. 1, 6.

3. "Another New Model . . . ," *The Economist*, Jan. 7, 1995, pp. 52–53.

4. See, for example, Peter F. Drucker, "The Network Society," *The Wall Street Journal*, Mar. 29, 1995, p. A14.

5. Barbara Bobo, "Building a Business Using Contractors," *Nation's Business*, June 1995, p. 6.

6. Joel Kotkin and David Friedman, "Why Every Business Will Be Like Show Business," *Inc.*, Mar. 1995, pp. 64–66.

7. John Grossmann, "Kevin Iverson: Simply the Best," *American Way*, Aug. 1, 1987, pp. 23–25; Richard Preston, "American Steel," *American Way*, Dec. 15, 1991, pp. 79–82.

8. James B. Treece, "Will GM Learn from Its Own Role Models?" *Business Week*, Apr. 9, 1990, p. 62.

9. "Shhh . . . the Best Kept Secret at The Ritz-Carlton Is . . . ," *Re-designing Customer Service*, May 1995, pp. 1–2.

10. Brad Lee Thompson, *The New Manager's Handbook* (Burr Ridge, IL: Irwin, 1995) p. 42.

11. "The Best Kept Secret at The Ritz-Carlton."

12. Norma Jean Schmieding, "The Complexity of an Authority Role," *Nursing Management*, Jan. 1992, p. 58.

13. The factors described in this paragraph are based on Harold Koontz, "Making Theory Operational: The Span of Management," *Journal of Management Studies*, Oct. 1966, pp. 229–43; and Raymond L. Hilgert and Theo Haimann, *Supervision: Concepts and Practices of Management*, 5th ed. (Cincinnati, OH: South-Western Publishing, 1991), pp. 189–90.

14. DeAnne Rosenberg, "Delegation Is *Not* a Dirty Word," *Quality Digest*, Sept. 1992, pp. 51–53.

15. Mark Henricks, "Who's the Boss?" *Entrepreneur*, Jan. 1995, pp. 54–55.

16. "Getting Things Done through People," *Front Line Supervisor's Bulletin* (Bureau of Business Practice), July 10, 1992, pp. 1–2.

17. Geoffrey Brewer, "The New Managers," *Sales & Marketing Management—Performance*, Mar. 1995, pp. 31–35.

18. Peter F. Drucker, "Management Lessons of Irangate," *The Wall Street Journal*, Mar. 24, 1987.

19. "Managers Who Type Too Much," *Sales & Marketing Management*, Jan. 1992, p. 48.

20. Alex Markels, "A Power Producer Is Intent on Giving Power to Its People," *The Wall Street Journal*, July 3, 1995, pp. A1, A12.

## CHAPTER 8

1. *Boardroom Reports*, August 15, 1992, p. 2, citing Paul B. Malone III, *Abuse 'Em and Lose 'Em* (Annandale, VA: Synergy Press).

2. James M. Kouzes and Barry Z. Posner, "The Credibility Factor: What Followers Expect from Their Leaders," *Management Review*, January 1990, pp. 29–33.

3. Roger Ailes, "Lighten Up! Stuffed Shirts Have Short Careers," *Newsweek*, Management Digest special advertising section, May 18, 1992, p. 10.

4. Peter L. Thigpen, "Creating the Covenant," *Quality Digest*, August 1992, pp. 63–64.

5. Geoffrey Brewer, "The New Managers," *Sales & Marketing Management— Performance*, March 1995, pp. 31–35.

6. See Charlotte Taylor, "Taking the Lead," *Entrepreneurial Woman*, April 1992, pp. 42–47.

7. Sondra Thiederman, *Bridging Cultural Barriers for Corporate Success: How to Manage the Multicultural Work Force* (Lexington, MA: Lexington Books, 1991), p. 80.

8. Jeff Weinstein, "Service Lessons from Most-Admired Companies," *Restaurants and Institutions*, December 15, 1994, pp. 34, 38.

9. Bradford McKee, "A Business in Crisis Has No Time for Democracy," *Nation's Business*, July 1992, pp. 8, 17.

10. Walter Kiechel III, "The Boss as Coach," *Fortune*, November 4, 1991, pp. 201, 204.

11. Joseph Lipsey, personal correspondence.

12. For these and other questions for employee appraisal of a manager, see Adele Scheele, "Are You a Bad Boss?" *Working Woman*, April 1992, p. 32.

13. Elwood N. Chapman, *Your Attitude Is Showing: A Primer of Human Relations*, 6th ed. (New York: Macmillan, 1991), p. 5.

14. Kouzes and Posner, "The Credibility Factor," p. 30.

15. Jim Kouzes, "The 10 Commitments of Leadership," *Quality Digest*, July 1992, pp. 47–49.

### CHAPTER 9

1. Clark Wigley, "Working Smart on Tough Business Problems," *Supervisory Management*, February 1992, p. 1.

2. Noel M. Tichy and Ram Charan, "The CEO as Coach: An Interview with AlliedSignal's Lawrence A. Bossidy," *Harvard Business Review*, March–April 1995, pp. 69–78.

3. This section is based largely on the excellent discussion of stereotypes in Sondra Thiederman, *Bridging Cultural Barriers for Corporate Success: How to Manage the Multicultural Work Force* (New York: Lexington Books, 1991), pp. 11–22.

4. This paragraph is based on *The Front Line Supervisor's Standard Manual* (Waterford, CT: Bureau of Business Practice, 1989), p. 55.

5. "Parts Problems—Detecting Product Defects," *Maintenance Management*, June 10, 1995, p. 6.

6. Lee Thé, "Organize Your E-MailBag," *Datamation*, March 1, 1992, p. 74.

5. Wigley, "Working Smart," p. 1.

6. See Irving L. Janis, *Groupthink: Psychological Studies of Policy Decisions and Fiascoes*, 2nd ed. (Boston: Houghton Mifflin, 1982).

7. Aimee L. Stern, "Why Good Managers Approve Bad Ideas," *Working Woman*, May 1992, pp. 75, 104.

8. Andrew S. Grove, "In Search of Big Ideas," *Working Woman*, June 1992, pp. 22, 24.

9. David M. Armstrong, "Management by Storytelling," *Executive Female*, May–June 1992, pp. 38–41ff.

10. Joseph Alan Redman, "Nine Creative Brainstorming Techniques," *Quality Digest*, August 1992, pp. 50–51.

11. James Webb Young, *A Technique for Producing Ideas* (Chicago: Crain Communications, 1975).

12. Young, *A Technique for Producing Ideas*, pp. 59–60.

13. Magaly Olivero, "Get Crazy! How to Have a Breakthrough Idea," *Working Woman*, September 1990, pp. 145–147ff.

14. Magaly Olivero, "Some Wacko Ideas That Worked," *Working Woman*, September 1990, pp. 147, 222.

15. Stratford P. Sherman, "America Won't Win Till It Reads More," *Fortune*, November 18, 1991, pp. 201–204.

### CHAPTER 10

1. Philip R. Harris and Robert T. Moran, *Managing Cultural Differences*, 3rd ed. (Houston: Gulf Publishing, 1991), p. 28.

2. Linnet Myers, "U.S. Agent Tried to Stop First Waco Raid," *Chicago Tribune*, July 25, 1995, sec. 1, pp. 1, 7.

3. George Gendron, "FYI," *Inc.*, February 1992, p. 11.

4. Michael P. Cronin, "You Gotta Get a Gimmick," *Inc.*, November 1994, p. 134.

5. Carl R. Rogers and Richard E. Farson, "Active Listening," reprinted in William V. Haney, *Communication and Interpersonal Relations: Text and Cases*, 6th ed. (Homewood, IL: Richard D. Irwin, 1992), pp. 158–159.

6. This section is based on Rose Knotts and Sandra J. Hartman, "Communication Skills in Cross-Cultural Situations," *Supervisory Management*, March 1991, p. 12; and Sondra Thiederman, *Bridging Cultural Barriers for Corporate Success: How to Manage the Multicultural Work Force* (New York: Lexington Books, 1991).

7. Haney, *Communication and Interpersonal Relations*, p. 286.

8. Tony Mauro, "Justice's Gentle Reminder: She's Not a He," *USA Today*, November 14, 1991, p. 3A.

9. Deborah Tannen, *Talking from 9 to 5* (New York: William Morrow, 1994).

10. This example is taken from Thiederman, *Bridging Cultural Barriers*, p. 24.

11. Thiederman, *Bridging Cultural Barriers*, p. 136.

12. The ideas in this paragraph are based on Catherine R. Benson and Arlene M. Sperhac, "Image Building: Putting Your Best Foot Forward," *Healthcare Trends & Transition*, January 1992, pp. 26–29ff.

13. David Jackson, "Memos an Art Form at City Hall," *Chicago Tribune*, April 26, 1992, sec. 1, pp. 1, 16.

14. The ideas in this paragraph are drawn from Mary Rowland, "Shedding the Fear of Speaking," *New York Times*, May 17, 1992, p. F5; Bristol Voss, "Speak for Yourself," *Sales & Marketing Management*, January 1992, pp. 77–82; Katherine Griffin, "Beating Performance Anxiety," *Working Woman*, July 1995, pp. 62–65, 76.

15. Ripley Hotch, "How to Stay in Touch over the Network," *Nation's Business*, July 1992, p. 60.

16. William R. Pape, "Beyond E-mail," *Inc. Technology*, Summer 1995, pp. 27–28.

17. Pape, "Beyond E-mail," p. 27.

18. Dave Zielinski, "On-Line Customer Support Offers Potent Complement to Phone, Mail Feedback Tools," *The Service Edge*, November 1994, pp. 1–3.

19. William Keenan, Jr., "The Man in the Mirror," *Sales & Marketing Management*, May 1995, pp. 95–97.

20. Carrie A. Miles and Jean M. McCloskey, "People: The Key to Productivity," *HRMagazine*, February 1993, pp. 40–45.

21. Patti Doten, "Flying Rumors May Mean a Crash Landing," *Chicago Tribune*, January 14, 1992, sec. 5, pp. 1, 7.

22. Based on *The Front Line Supervisor's Standard Manual* (Waterford, CT: Bureau of Business Practice, 1989), pp. 42–43.

23. Based on Mortimer R. Feinberg, "How to Get the Grapevine on Your Side," *Working Woman*, May 1990, p. 23.

24. Donna Fenn, "Out to Lunch," *Inc.*, June 1995, p. 89.

**CHAPTER 11**

1. See, for example, Abraham Maslow, *Eupsychian Management* (Homewood, IL: Richard D. Irwin, 1965); and C. P. Alderfer, "An Empirical Test of a New Theory of Human Needs," *Organization Behavior and Human Performance* 4 (1969), pp. 142–175.

2. Michael P. Cronin, "Piquing Employee Interest," *Inc.*, August 1992, p. 83.

3. Eileen Ogintz, "Quaker Takes Hand in Helping Families," *Chicago Tribune*, September 23, 1992, sec. 3, pp. 1, 4.

4. Alessandra Bianchi, "The Strictly Business Flextime Request Form," *Inc.*, May 1995, pp. 79–81.

5. Carol Kleiman, "Survey Says Personal Friends Can Be Perk for Women Personnel," *Chicago Tribune*, March 30, 1995, sec. 3, p. 3.

6. John R. Schermerhorn, Jr., William N. Gardner, and Thomas N. Martin, "The Trouble with Bob: A Drama in Managerial Life," *Executive Female*, September–October 1991, pp. 42–47.

7. Noel M. Tichy and Ram Charan, "The CEO as Coach: An Interview with AlliedSignal's Lawrence A. Bossidy," *Harvard Business Review*, March–April 1995, pp. 69–78.

8. Bianchi, "The Strictly Business Flextime Request Form."

9. "Study: More Companies Link Compensation to Quality," *Total Quality*, April 1992, p. 6.

10. Andrea Gabor, "After the Pay Revolution, Job Titles Won't Matter," *New York Times*, May 17, 1992, p. F5.

11. Ellyn E. Spragins, "The All-Purpose Incentive System," *Inc.*, February 1992, pp. 103–104.

12. Susan Greco, "Great Pay for Great Service," *Inc.*, September 1992, p. 27.

13. Susan Greco and Phaedra Hise, "How to Unite Field and Phone Sales," *Inc.*, July 1992, p. 115.

14. Nucor Corporation brochure.

15. Aldo J. Massaferro, Jr., J. Clarence Morrison, and John C. Tumazos, "Lessons from Nucor," *Boardroom Reports*, December 1, 1991, pp. 7–8.

16. John A. Parnell, "Five Reasons Why Pay Must Be Based on Performance," *Supervision*, February 1991, pp. 6–8.

17. Rosemary F. Lyons, "Cross-Training: A Richer Staff for Leaner Budgets," *Nursing Management*, January 1992, pp. 43–44.

18. George Gendron, "FYI: Schwarzkopf on Leadership," *Inc.*, January 1992, p. 11.

19. Gabor, "After the Pay Revolution."

20. Will Kaydos, "Motivating by Measuring Performance," *Quality Digest*, May 1992, pp. 53–54, 75.

21. Mary Peterson Kauffold, "Taking Care of Business," *Chicago Tribune*, February 26, 1995, sec. 18, pp. 1–2.

22. Bianchi, "The Strictly Business Flextime Request Form," p. 79.

23. George Gendron, "FYI: The First Annual *301 Great Management Ideas* Sweepstakes," *Inc.*, September 1992, p. 11.

**CHAPTER 12**

1. See Myron Magnet, "The Truth About the American Worker," *Fortune*, May 4, 1992, pp. 48–51ff; Thomas A. Stewart, "U.S. Productivity: First but Fading," *Fortune*, October 19, 1992, pp. 54–57; and "Today's U.S. Worker," *Fortune*, May 4, 1992, pp. 60–61.

2. Myron Magnet, "The Productivity Payoff Arrives," *Fortune*, June 27, 1994, pp. 79–82, 84.

3. Ralph T. King, Jr., "High-Tech Edge Gives U.S. Firms Global Lead in Computer Networks," *The Wall Street Journal*, September 9, 1994, pp. A1, A10.

4. Magnet, "The Productivity Payoff Arrives"; "What Computers Are For," *The Economist*, January 22, 1994, p. 74; Erik Brynjolfsson and Lorin Hitt, "The Productivity Paradox of Information Technology," *Communications of the ACM*, December 1993, 66–77.

5. "Nicely Does It," *The Economist*, March 19, 1994, p. 84.

6. Sondra Thiederman, *Bridging Cultural Barriers for Corporate Success: How to Manage the Multicultural Work Force* (New York: Lexington Books, 1991), pp. 5–10.

7. Robert Frank, "Efficient UPS Tries to Increase Efficiency," *The Wall Street Journal*, May 24, 1995, pp. B1, B4.

8. Marie Manthey, "Staffing and Productivity," *Nursing Management*, December 1991, pp. 20–21.

9. Frank Voehl, "Avoid Business Suicide," *Quality Digest*, September 1992, pp. 20, 78.

10. Jon Van, "Involved at IBM: Errors Drop after Workers Get Big Picture," *Chicago Tribune*, July 26, 1992, sec. 7, pp. 1–2.

11. "Frugality in the Air at American," *Chicago Tribune*, January 19, 1992, sec. 7, p. 5.

12. "Winners Announced in Cost Reduction Contest," *Advance Digest* (Advance Transformer Company), Fall 1991, pp. 1, 6.

13. Joshua Hyatt, "Ideas at Work," *Inc.*, May 1991, pp. 59–60ff.

14. Teri Lammers Prior, "If I Were President," *Inc.*, April 1995, pp. 56–61.

15. Mary Crabtree Tonges, "Work Designs: Sociotechnical Systems for Patient Care Delivery," *Nursing Management*, January 1992, pp. 27–31.

16. Michael Hammer and Steven A. Stanton, "Beating the Risks of Reengineering," *Fortune*, May 15, 1995, pp. 105–106*ff*.

17. Frank, "Efficient UPS Tries to Increase Efficiency."

18. "Cutting Down on Unnecessary Paperwork," *Maintenance Supervisor's Bulletin* (Bureau of Business Practice), July 25, 1992, pp. 1–4.

19. Jon Van, "Old Manufacturing Ideas Crippling U.S.," *Chicago Tribune*, November 3, 1991, sec. 1, pp. 1, 12–13.

20. Stewart, "U.S. Productivity," p. 55.

21. Jon Van, "At Ingersoll, Flexibility, Change Are a Way of Life," *Chicago Tribune*, November 5, 1991, sec. 1, p. 12.

22. Robert F. Huber, "Can You Afford Not to Buy This Justification Software?" *Production*, 1992.

23. Stewart, "U.S. Productivity," p. 57.

24. Joseph Kahn, "China's New Slogan: Workers of the World Take the Day Off!" *The Wall Street Journal*, May 4, 1995, p. A9.

25. Kenneth B. Hamlet, "Slowing the Service Sector's Revolving Door," *The Wall Street Journal*, August 14, 1989, p. A8.

26. Eileen Ogintz, "The Bottom Line Is Benefits," *Chicago Tribune*, March 7, 1990, sec. 5, pp. 1, 3.

27. Bruce G. Posner, "Role Changes," *Inc.*, February 1990, pp. 95, 98.

28. Stephen Franklin, "Technology Puts AT&T Jobs on Hold," *Chicago Tribune*, March 23, 1992, sec. 4, pp. 1–2.

29. Franklin, "AT&T Jobs on Hold."

30. Van, "Ingersoll," p. 12.

## CHAPTER 13

1. John R. Schermerhorn, Jr., William N. Gardner, and Thomas N. Martin, "The Trouble with Bob: A Drama in Managerial Life," *Executive Female*, September–October 1991, pp. 42–47.

2. Michael Barrier, "The Enemy Within," *Nation's Business*, February 1995, pp. 18–24.

3. Beth Lorenzini and Brad A. Johnson, "Restaurant Wars," *Restaurants and Institutions*, May 1, 1995, pp. 148*ff*.

4. Jim Braham, "Difficult Employees," *Industry Week*, June 19, 1989, pp. 30–35.

5. Michael Karol, "The Lows of Being High," *Graphic Arts Monthly*, September 1990, pp. 101–107.

6. William C. Symonds, "Is Business Bungling Its Battle with Booze?" *Business Week*, March 25, 1991, pp. 76–78.

7. John Horgan, "Your Analysis Is Faulty," *The New Republic*, April 2, 1990, pp. 22–24.

8. Karol, "The Lows of Being High."

9. Symonds, "Is Business Bungling Its Battle with Booze?" p. 77.

10. "Substance Abuse on the Job," *Maintenance Supervisor's Bulletin*, January 10, 1992, pp. 3–4.

11. "Preventing Crime on the Job," *Nation's Business*, July 1990, pp. 36–37.

12. Phyllis Gillespie, "Stolen Trust: Employee Theft Costs $320 Billion," *Arizona Republic*, May 4, 1992, pp. E1, E8.

13. Gerald Graham, "Reducing Staff Theft Possible: U.S. Losses Total $40 Billion a Year," *Arizona Republic*, March 19, 1989, p. E6.

14. Gillespie, "Stolen Trust," p. E8.

15. "Curbing Crime in the Workplace," *Nation's Business*, July 1990, p. 37.

16. Joseph T. Straub, "Dealing with Complainers, Whiners, and General Malcontents," *Supervisory Management*, July 1992, pp. 1–2.

17. List of rights provided by Corinne R. Livesay, Liberty University, Lynchburg, VA.

18. Andrew S. Grove, "Personal Problems in the Office," *Working Woman*, April 1992, pp. 36, 38.

19. Donald H. Weiss, "How to Deal with Unpleasant People Problems," *Supervisory Management*, March 1992, pp. 1–2.

20. Lorenzini and Johnson, "Restaurant Wars," p. 158.

21. Barrier, "The Enemy Within."

22. William C. Symonds, "How to Confront—and Help—an Alcoholic Employee," *Business Week*, March 25, 1991, p. 78.

23. Symonds, "How to Confront." See also Sara J. Harty, "Training Required to Spot Addicts," *Business Insurance*, June 24, 1991, pp. 12–13.

24. Deborah Shalowitz, "Employee Assistance Plan Trends," *Business Insurance*, June 24, 1991, pp. 24–25.

## CHAPTER 14

1. "How Jim Howard Gets So Much Done," *Boardroom Reports*, September 1, 1992, pp. 13–14.

2. Michael Barrier, "How a Dallas Consultant Helps Managers Attack the Paper Piled on Their Desks," *Nation's Business*, January 1992.

3. Tom Peters, "You, Too, Can Manage without a Time Manager," *Chicago Tribune*, August 3, 1992, sec. 4, p. 5.

4. "How Jim Howard Gets So Much Done," p. 14.

5. "Foil the Time Grabbers," *Executive Female*, July–August 1992, pp. 9–10.

6. Frank Grazian, "Are You Coping with Stress?" *Communication Briefings*, vol. 14, no. 1, p. 3.

7. Matt Murray, "Amid Record Profits, Companies Continue to Lay Off Employees," *The Wall Street Journal*, May 4, 1995, pp. A1, A4.

8. Marilyn Elias, "Women's Job, Home Conflicts Raise Heart Risk," *USA Today*, March 3, 1992, p. 1D.

9. Alex Markels, "Shhh! Napping Is Trying to Tiptoe into the Workplace," *The Wall Street Journal*, June 26, 1995, pp. A1, A6.

10. Daniel D. Shade, "Balancing Work and Family: Suggestions from a Tightrope Walker," *Healthcare Trends & Transition*, January 1992, p. 55.

11. Grazian, "Are You Coping with Stress?"

12. Carol Kleiman, "Turning Stress Control into a Laughing Matter," *Chicago Tribune*, August 6, 1995, sec. 8, p. 1.

13. Shawn Tully, "America's Healthiest Companies," *Fortune*, June 12, 1995, pp. 98–100*ff*.

14. Tully, "America's Healthiest Companies," p. 104.

15. Donna Fenn, "Healthy Workers Cost Less," *Inc.*, May 1995, p. 137.

16. Tully, "America's Healthiest Companies."

17. This discussion of the Myers-Briggs Type Indicator is based largely on Otto Kroeger and Janet M. Thuesen, "It Takes All Types," *Newsweek*, Management Digest advertising section, September 7, 1992, pp. 8–10.

**CHAPTER 15**

1. Sue Shellenbarger, "Felice Schwartz: From the Mommy Track to the Zigzag Track," *The Wall Street Journal*, May 3, 1995, p. B1.

2. Andrew S. Grove, "How to Manage Office Friction," *Working Woman*, August 1990, pp. 24, 26.

3. Thomas A. Stewart, "The Search for the Organization of Tomorrow," *Fortune*, May 18, 1992, pp. 92–98.

4. Michael P. Cronin, "No More 'Us versus Them,'" *Inc.*, May 1994, p. 150.

5. Jolie Solomon, "As Cultural Diversity of Workers Grows, Experts Urge Appreciation of Differences," *The Wall Street Journal*, September 12, 1990, pp. B1, B8.

6. The ideas in this paragraph are from Sondra Thiederman, *Bridging Cultural Barriers for Corporate Success: How to Manage the Multicultural Work Force* (New York: Lexington Books, 1991), pp. 83–88.

7. Jerry Wisinski, "What to Do about Conflicts?" *Supervisory Management*, March 1995, p. 11.

8. See, for example, Sharman Stein, "Making a Life or a Living?" *Chicago Tribune*, May 18, 1995, sec. 1, pp. 1, 12.

9. Catherine Romano, "Managing Change, Diversity and Emotions," *Management Review*, July 1995, pp. 6–7.

10. Ken Blanchard, "The Seven Dynamics of Change," *Quality Digest*, May 1992, pp. 18, 78.

11. Michael Hammer and Steven A. Stanton, "Beating the Risks of Reengineering," *Fortune*, May 15, 1995, pp. 105–106*ff*.

12. Carol Hymowitz, "When Firms Cut Out Middle Managers, Those at Top and Bottom Often Suffer," *The Wall Street Journal*, April 5, 1990, pp. B1, B4.

13. Kurt Lewin, "Frontiers in Group Dynamics: Concept, Method, and Reality of Social Sciences—Social Equilibrium and Social Change," *Human Relations*, June 1947, pp. 5–14.

14. Noel M. Tichy and Ram Charan, "The CEO as Coach: An Interview with AlliedSignal's Lawrence A. Bossidy," *Harvard Business Review*, March–April 1995, pp. 69–78.

15. Ken Blanchard, "Six Concerns in the Change Process," *Quality Digest*, June 1992, pp. 14, 62.

16. Hammer and Stanton, "Beating the Risks of Reengineering," p. 106.

17. Elaine Gregg, "How to Be a Great Boss in Bad Times," *Black Enterprise*, April 1991, p. 72.

18. Betsy Wiesendanger, "Bad News Meetings," *Sales & Marketing Management*, November 1992, pp. 66–68ff.

19. Arno Penzias, "New Paths to Success," *Fortune*, June 12, 1995, pp. 90–92, 94.

20. See Gregg, "How to Be a Great Boss," p. 72.

21. Blanchard, "The Seven Dynamics of Change," p. 78.

22. Barry K. Spiker and Eric Lesser, "We Have Met the Enemy . . . ," *Journal of Business Strategy*, pp. 17–21.

23. Connie Wallace, "Sizing Up Your New Staff," *Working Woman*, May 1990, pp. 29–30*ff*.

24. Donald S. Miller and Stephen E. Catt, *Human Relations: A Contemporary Approach* (Homewood, IL: Richard D. Irwin, 1989), pp. 200–202.

25. George Milite, "Office Politics: It's Still Out There," *Supervisory Management*, July 1992, pp. 6–7.

26. Elizabeth Leech, "Working Smart: Take Care to Build Alliances If You're Headed for the Top," *Chicago Tribune*, September 20, 1992, sec. 6, p. 9.

27. Bristol Voss, "Office Politics: A Player's Guide," *Sales & Marketing Management*, October 1992, pp. 47–52.

28. Voss, "Office Politics," p. 49.

## CHAPTER 16

1. Raymond A. Noe, John R. Hollenbeck, Barry Gerhart, and Patrick M. Wright, *Human Resource Management: Gaining a Competitive Advantage* (Burr Ridge, IL: Austen Press, 1994), p. 207.

2. "Finding Top Reps on Campus," *Sales & Marketing Management*, March 1995, p. 38.

3. "Experts Discuss Pitfalls, Advantages of Team-Based Systems," *Employee Relations Weekly*, April 18, 1994, pp. 415–16.

4. "Best Practices: Hiring," *Inc.*, March 1994, p. 10.

5. John M. Ivancevich, *Human Resource Management: Foundations of Personnel*, 5th ed. (Homewood, IL: Irwin, 1992), p. A20.

6. "Brainstorming … on Personnel," *Boardroom Reports*, September 1, 1992, p. 15.

7. Martin Everett and Betsy Wiesendanger, "What Does Body Language *Really* Say?" *Sales & Marketing Management*, April 1992, p. 40.

8. John Anderson, "Don't Leave Home Without It," *Selling*, March 1995, pp. 68-71.

9. Ellyn E. Spragins, "Hiring without the Guesswork," *Inc.*, February 1992, pp. 83*ff*.

10. Melissa Wahl, "Navigating the Maze of Employee Rights," *Executive Female*, September–October 1992, pp. 103–104.

11. Donna Fenn, "Check My References—Please!" *Inc.*, April 1995, p. 111.

12. Ellyn E. Spragins, "Screening New Hires," *Inc.*, August 1992, p. 82.

13. "Workers' Crimes Become Companies' Concerns," *Nation's Business*, March 1990, p. 8.

14. Spragins, "Screening New Hires."

15. Susan Kostal, "Picking the Best Person for a Key Job," *Working Woman*, December 1994, pp. 54, 56, 58.

16. See Ivancevich, *Human Resource Management*, p. 274; Bob McDonald, "Better Take the Americans with Disabilities Act Very Seriously," *Boardroom Reports*, August 15, 1992, pp. 3–4; and Ellyn E. Spragins, "Preparing for the Americans with Disabilities Act," *Inc.*, January 1992, pp. 99–100.

17. Sharon Nelton, "Nurturing Diversity," *Nation's Business*, June 1995, pp. 25–27.

18. John Dralus and Jan Sokoloff Harness, "Working Together," *Training & Development*, December 1991, p. 16.

19. Wilma Randle, "Opening Opportunities for Disabled: Confusion, Debate Still Trail New Law," *Chicago Tribune*, December 1, 1991, sec. 7, pp. 1, 4.

20. Hugh H. McDonough, "Hiring People with Disabilities," *Supervisory Management*, February 1992, p. 11.

21. Ellyn E. Spragins, "Tapping Workers with Disabilities," *Inc.*, November 1992, p. 33.

22. "Accommodations for Employees with Mental Disability," *Supervisory Management*, April 1995, p. 5.

23. Eileen Ogintz, "Technology Sees Beyond Disabilities," *Chicago Tribune*, March 8, 1992, sec. 7, p. 3.

24. These guidelines are taken from Spragins, "Preparing for the Americans with Disabilities Act."

25. McDonald, "Better Take the ADA Very Seriously," p. 4.

26. Ivancevich, *Human Resource Management*, p. 215.

## CHAPTER 17

1. Edward Shaw, "The Training-Waste Conspiracy," *Training*, April 1995, pp. 59–60*ff*.

2. Reported in Nancy K. Austin, "Giving New Employees a Better Beginning," *Working Woman*, July 1995, pp. 20–21, 74.

3. Austin, "Giving New Employees a Better Beginning," p. 20.

4. Carol Kleiman, "Employer-Based Training Is a Growing Job Source," *Chicago Tribune*, January 12, 1992, sec. 8, p. 1.

5. Patricia A. Galagan, "Training Delivers Results to Federal Express," *Training and Development*, December 1991, pp. 27–33.

6. Eileen Davis, "What's on American Managers' Minds?" *Management Review*, April 1995, pp. 14–20.

7. A number of these points are mentioned in Shaw, "The Training-Waste Conspiracy."

8. David L. Goetsch, *Industrial Supervision in the Age of High Technology* (New York: Merrill, 1992), p. 407.

9. See George Piskurich, "Training: The Line Starts Here," *Training and Development*, December 1991, pp. 35–37.

10. "Experts Discuss Pitfalls, Advantages of Team-Based Systems," *Employee Relations Weekly*, April 18, 1994, pp. 415–16.

11. Ellyn E. Spragins, "Lowering Turnover by Using Apprentices," *Inc.*, May 1992, p. 145.

12. Janet Novack, "Earning and Learning," *Forbes*, May 11, 1992, pp. 150, 154.

13. Susan Greco, "A 'Finishing School' for Sales Reps," *Inc.*, October 1992, p. 30.

14. Ellyn E. Spragins, "Turning Education into a Game," *Inc.*, September 1992, p. 34.

15. Wendy Marx, "The New High-Tech Training," *Management Review*, February 1995, pp. 57–60.

16. Marx, "The New High-Tech Training."

17. Alessandra Bianchi, "New Businesses: Corporate Games," *Inc.*, July 1992, p. 20.

18. Ellyn E. Spragins, "Employee Illiteracy," *Inc.*, August 1992, p. 81.

19. Joan C. Szabo, "Boosting Workers' Basic Skills," *Nation's Business*, January 1992, pp. 38–40.

20. "What It Takes," *Inc.*, November 1992, pp. 105–107ff.

21. "What It Takes," p. 110.

22. Szabo, "Boosting Workers' Basic Skills."

23. "Apprenticeship Training: Time for an Update!" *Maintenance Supervisor's Bulletin*, June 25, 1992, pp. 1–4.

**CHAPTER 18**

1. Ellyn E. Spragins, "How to Fire," *Inc.*, May 1992, pp. 66–68, 72.

2. Susan Greco, "The Interactive Employee Review," *Inc.*, November 1991, pp. 73–75.

3. "Performance Reviews: Take a Positive Approach," *Front Line Supervisor's Bulletin* (Bureau of Business Practice), June 10, 1992, pp. 1–2.

4. Nancy K. Austin, "Updating the Performance Review," *Working Woman*, November 1992, pp. 32, 34–35.

5. Patricia Buhler, "Evaluating an Employee's Performance," *Supervision*, April 1991, pp. 17–19.

6. See, for example, Edward E. Lawler III, "Performance Management: The Next Generation," *Quality Digest*, February 1995, pp. 29–31.

7. Greg Boudreaux, "What TQM Says about Performance Appraisal," *Quality Digest*, February 1995, pp. 32–35.

8. Lawler, "Performance Management"; Boudreaux, "What TQM Says about Performance Appraisal."

9. Boudreaux, "What TQM Says about Performance Appraisal."

10. Boudreaux, "What TQM Says about Performance Appraisal," p. 34.

11. Brian O'Reilly, "360 Feedback Can Change Your Life," *Fortune*, October 17, 1994, pp. 93–94ff; Marcie Schorr Hirsch, "360 Degrees of Evaluation," *Working Woman*, August 1994, pp. 20–21.

12. Teri Lammers Prior, "If I Were President . . . ," *Inc.*, April 1995, pp. 56–61.

13. Austin, "Updating the Performance Review," p. 34.

14. Lisa Holton, "Look Who's in on Your Performance Review," *Selling*, January/February 1995, pp. 47–48ff.

15. Antony J. Michels, "More Employees Evaluate the Boss," *Fortune*, July 29, 1991, p. 13.

16. Holton, "Look Who's in on Your Performance Review."

17. O'Reilly, "360 Feedback Can Change Your Life," pp. 94, 96.

18. Hirsch, "360 Degrees of Evaluation."

19. Claire McIntosh and Laurel Touby, "Appraisals: Are You Giving A's to 'B' Employees?" *Working Woman*, May 1990, pp. 23–23.

20. Boudreaux, "What TQM Says about Performance Appraisal"; Lawler, "Performance Management."

21. Noel M. Tichy and Ram Charan, "The CEO as Coach: An Interview with AlliedSignal's Lawrence A. Bossidy," *Harvard Business Review*, March–April 1995, pp. 69–78.

22. Lawler, "Performance Management," p. 29.

**CHAPTER 19**

1. David Warner, "Ways to Make Safety Work," *Nation's Business*, December 1991, pp. 25–27.

2. Merrill Goozner, "Expanding Fast-Food Industry Growing More Accident-Prone," *Chicago Tribune*, July 15, 1991, sec. 4, pp. 1–2.

3. "OSHA Penalties Hit Record High in 1994," *Supervisory Management*, April 1995, p. 4.

4. Warner, "Ways to Make Safety Work," p. 25.

5. "Chemical Caution," *Time*, October 26, 1992, p. 27.

6. Mitchell Pacelle, "Plan to Clear the Office Air Spurs a Battle," *The Wall Street Journal*, December 6, 1994, pp. B1, B4.

7. Doreen Mangan, "Avoid 'Sick Building' Syndrome," *Your Company*, Spring 1992, p. 7.

8. "On-the-Job Accidents' Cost Put at $120 Billion," *Chicago Tribune*, August 31, 1995, sec. 3, p. 3.

9. See Ron Kotulak and Jon Van, "Rotating Shifts Raise Chances of Accidents," *Chicago Tribune*, July 12, 1992, sec. 5, p. 6; and "Shiftwork: Staying Alert and Vigilant around the Clock," *Maintenance Supervisor's Bulletin*, September 10, 1992, pp. 1–4.

10. "On-the-Job Accidents' Cost Put at $120 Billion."

11. Goozner, "Expanding Fast-Food Industry," p. 1.

12. Ellyn E. Spragins, "Take Charge," *Inc.*, December 1992, pp. 122–125ff.

13. "OSHA Cites Back Injuries as Top Workplace Safety Problem," *NIBA Bulletin* (Northern Illinois Business Association), March 1992, p. 13.

14. Robert A. Mamis, "Oh, That Aching Back," *Inc.*, October 1992, p. 53.

15. Christine Woolsey, "Linking Wellness to Health Care Costs," *Business Insurance*, February 17, 1992, p. 12.

16. Christine Woolsey, "Employers Monitor Lifestyles," *Business Insurance*, February 17, 1992, pp. 4–6.

17. Doreen Mangan, "When It's Time to Ban Smoking," *Your Company*, Spring 1992, p. 6.

18. Christopher Conte, "Labor Letter," *The Wall Street Journal*, November 19, 1991, p. A1.

19. Patricia Fernberg, "Is Your Terminal Ill?" *Health*, March 1991, pp. 36, 38.

20. Paula M. Noaker, "The Search for Agile Manufacturing," *Manufacturing Engineering*, November 1994, pp. 40–43.

21. Jon Van, "Actual Side Effects from Virtual Reality," *Chicago Tribune*, August 14, 1995, sec. 4, pp. 1, 3.

22. Jon Van, "Carpal Syndrome Reports Rise Sharply," *Chicago Tribune*, February 12, 1992, sec. 3, p. 3.

23. James Warren, "Typing Trauma: Computer-Related Injury Forces L.A. Times Columnist to the Sidelines," *Chicago Tribune*, April 5, 1992, sec. 5, p. 2.

24. Louise Kertesz, "Human 'Machines' Need Good Workplace Design," *Business Insurance*, April 13, 1992, p. 30.

25. Spragins, "Take Charge."

26. Kertesz, "Human 'Machines' Need Good Workplace Design."

27. See, for example, Woolsey, "Linking Wellness to Health Care Costs."

28. Deborah L. Jacobs, "Pregnant Workers and the Law," *Your Company*, Spring 1992, p. 15.

29. The suggestions in this paragraph are adapted from "Shiftwork: Staying Alert and Vigilant around the Clock."

30. "One Company's Technique Takes Hold: Putting a STOP to Unsafe Behaviors," *OSHA Compliance Advisor*, September 23, 1991, pp. 3–6.

31. Robert L. Rose, "Federal Labor Board Gets More Aggressive, to Employers' Dismay," *The Wall Street Journal*, June 1, 1995, pp. A1, A5.

32. Aaron Bernstein, "Been Down So Long…," *Business Week*, January 14, 1991, pp. 30–31.

33. Arthur J. Hedges, "Reflections of an Arbitrator," *Discipline and Grievances* (Bureau of Business Practice), 1986, p. 9.

34. Robert L. Rose, "Caterpillar's Success in Ending Strike May Curtail Unions' Use of Walkouts," *The Wall Street Journal*, April 20, 1992, p. A3.

35. Michael A. Verespej, "New-Age Sexual Harassment," *Industry Week*, May 15, 1995, pp. 64, 66, 68.

36. Carol Kleiman, "Sex Harassment Complaints on the Rise," *Chicago Tribune*, March 7, 1992, sec. 1, pp. 1, 12; Charlene Marmer Solomon, "Sexual Harassment after the Thomas Hearings," *Personnel Journal*, December 1991, pp. 32–37.

37. The guidelines in this section are based on Alan Deutschman, "Dealing with Sexual Harassment," *Fortune*, November 4, 1991, pp. 145, 148; Robert T. Gray, "How to Deal with Sexual Harassment," *Nation's Business*, December 1991, pp. 28, 30–31; Janice Murphy, "Sexual Harassment at Work," *Healthcare Trends & Transition*, January 1992, pp. 45–48; Verespej, "New-Age Sexual Harassment," p. 68.

38. Peggy Stuart, "Prevent Sexual Harassment in Your Work Force," *Personnel Journal*, December 1991, p. 34.

39. Stuart, "Prevent Sexual Harassment in Your Work Force."

# Glossary

**accountability** The practice of imposing penalties for failing to adequately carry out responsibilities and of providing rewards for meeting responsibilities. 14

**action plan** The plan for how to achieve an objective. 150

**active listening** Hearing what the speaker is saying, seeking to understand the facts and feelings the speaker is trying to convey, and stating what you understand that message to be. 284

**affirmative action** Plans designed to increase opportunities for groups that traditionally have been discriminated against. 489

**agenda** A list of the topics to be covered at a meeting. 79

**AIDS acquired immune deficiency syndrome** The incurable and fatal illness that is caused by the HIV virus. 580

**apprenticeship** Training that involves working alongside an experienced person, who shows the apprentice how to do the various tasks involved in a job or trade. 520

**aptitude test** A test that measures a person's ability to learn skills related to the job. 484

**arbitrator** A neutral person who reaches a decision on the resolution of a conflict; both parties must adhere to the decision. 588

**authoritarian leadership** A leadership style in which the leader retains a great deal of authority. 217

**authority** The right to perform a task or give orders to someone else. 190

**average rate of return (*ARR*)** A percentage that represents the average annual earnings for each dollar of a given investment. 359

**behavior modification** The use of reinforcement theory to motivate people to behave in a certain way. 322

**behaviorally anchored rating scales (BARS)** A performance appraisal in which an employee is rated on scales containing statements describing performance in several areas. 546

**benchmarking** Identifying the top performer of a process, then learning and carrying out the top performer's practices. 46

**biofeedback** Developing an awareness of bodily functions in order to control them. 417

**brainstorming** An idea-generating process in which group members state their ideas, a member of the group records them, and no one may comment on the ideas until the process is complete. 262

**budget** A plan for spending money. 154

**burnout** The inability to function effectively as a result of ongoing stress. 414

**central tendency** The tendency to select employee ratings in the middle of a scale. 552

**chain of command** The flow of authority in an organization from one level of management to the next. 196

**closed-ended question** A question that requires a simple answer, such as yes or no. 481

**coaching** Guidance and instruction in how to do a job so that it satisfies performance goals. 524

**cohesiveness** The degree to which group members stick together. 69

**collective bargaining** The process of seeking to reach a contract spelling out the rights and duties of unionized workers and their employer. 587

**commissions** Payment linked to the amount of sales completed. 325

**communication** The process by which people send and receive information. 280

**compromise** Settling on a solution that gives each person part of what he or she wants; no one gets everything, and no one loses completely. 442

**conceptual skills** The ability to see the relation of the parts to the whole and to one another. 4

**concurrent control** Control that occurs while the work takes place. 165

**conflict** The struggle that results from incompatible or opposing needs, feelings, thoughts, or demands within a person or between two or more people. 436

**conflict management** Responding to problems stemming from conflict. 441

**conflict resolution** Managing a conflict by confronting the problem and solving it. 443

**contingency planning** Planning what to do if the original plans don't work out. 151

**controlling** Monitoring performance and making needed corrections. 10

**controlling** The management function of making sure that work goes according to plan. 159

**counseling** The process of learning about an individual's personal problem and helping him or her resolve it. 376

**creativity** The ability to bring about something imaginative or new. 263

**critical-incident appraisal** A performance appraisal in which a supervisor keeps a written record of incidents that show positive and negative ways an employee has acted; the supervisor uses this record to assess the employee's performance. 547

**cross-training** Training in the skills required to perform more than one job. 328

**decision** A choice from among available alternatives. 246

**decision tree** A graph that helps decision makers use probability theory by showing the expected values of decisions under varying circumstances. 257

**decision-making leave** A day off during which a problem employee is supposed to decide whether to return to work and meet standards or to stay away for good. 385

**decision-making skills** The ability to analyze information and reach good decisions. 5

**decision-making software** A computer program that leads the user through the steps of the formal decision-making process. 259

**delegating** Giving another person the authority and responsibility to carry out a task. 197

**democratic leadership** A leadership style in which the leader allows subordinates to participate in decision making and problem solving. 217

**demotion** Transfer of an employee to a job involving less responsibility and usually lower pay. 381

**department** A unique group of resources that management has assigned to carry out a particular task. 185

**departmentalization** Setting up departments in an organization. 185

**detour behavior** Tactics for postponing or avoiding work. 356

**directive counseling** An approach to counseling in which the supervisor asks the employee questions about the specific problem; when the supervisor understands the problem, he or she suggests ways to handle it. 378

**discipline** Action taken by the supervisor to prevent employees from breaking rules. 379

**dismissal** Relieving an employee of his or her job. 381

**downtime** Time during which employees or machines are not producing goods or services. 356

**downward communication** Organizational communication that involves sending a message to someone at a lower level. 300

**employee assistance program (EAP)** A company-based program for providing counseling and related help to employees whose personal problems are affecting their performance. 389

**employee handbook** A document that describes an organization's conditions of employment, policies regarding employees, administrative procedures, and related matters. 511

**employee involvement teams** Teams of employees who plan ways to improve quality in their area of the organization. 38

**Equal Employment Opportunity Commission (EEOC)** The federal government agency charged with enforcing Title VII of the Civil Rights Act. 487

**ergonomics** The science concerned with the human characteristics that must be considered in designing tasks and equipment so that people will work most effectively and safely. 579

**ethics** The principles by which people distinguish what is morally right. 96

**exception principle** The control principle stating that a supervisor should take action only when a variance is meaningful. 163

**feedback** The way the receiver of a message responds or fails to respond to the message. 281

**feedback control** Control that focuses on past performance. 165

**financial incentives** Payments for meeting or exceeding objectives. 324

**forced-choice approach** A performance appraisal that presents the appraiser with sets of statements describing employee behavior; the appraiser must choose which statement is most characteristic of the employee and which is least characteristic. 545

**formal communication** Organizational communication that is work-related and follows the lines of the organization chart. 301

**formal groups** Groups set up by management to meet organizational objectives. 63

**functional authority** The right given by higher management to specific staff personnel to give orders concerning an area in which the staff have expertise. 192

**functional groups** Groups that fulfill ongoing needs in the organization by carrying out a particular function. 63

**gainsharing** A group incentive plan in which the organization encourages employees to participate in making suggestions and decisions, then rewards the group with a share of improved earnings. 326

**Gantt chart** Scheduling tool that lists the activities to be completed and uses horizontal bars to graph how long each activity will take including its starting and ending dates. 155

**goals** Objectives, often those with a broad focus. 147

**grapevine** The path along which informal communication travels. 302

**graphic rating scale** A performance appraisal that rates the degree to which an employee has achieved various characteristics. 543

**grievance** A formal complaint that the terms of a labor contract have been violated. 588

**group** Two or more people who interact with one another, are aware of one another, and think of themselves as a group. 62

**group incentive plan** A financial incentive plan that rewards a team of workers for meeting or exceeding an objective. 326

**groupthink** The failure to think independently and realistically as a group because of the desire to enjoy consensus and closeness. 260

**halo effect** The practice of forming an overall opinion on the basis of one outstanding characteristic. 481

**harshness bias** Rating employees more severely than their performance merits. 551

**health hazards** Conditions in the work environment that may gradually hurt the health of the people there. 574

**homogeneity** The degree to which the members of a group are the same. 70

**human relations skills** The ability to work effectively with other people. 4

**idle time** Time during which employees or machines are not producing goods or services. 356

**inference** A conclusion drawn from the facts available. 290

**informal communication** Organizational communication that is directed toward individual needs and interests and does not necessarily follow formal lines of communication. 301

**informal groups** Groups that result when individuals in the organization develop relationships to meet personal needs. 63

**insubordination** Deliberate refusal to do what the supervisor or other superior asks. 373

**internal locus of control** The belief that you are the primary cause of what happens to yourself. 214

**ISO 9000** A series of standards adopted by the International Organization of Standardization to spell out acceptable criteria for quality systems. 46

**job description** A listing of the characteristics of a job, including the job title, duties involved, and working conditions. 471

**job enlargement** An effort to make a job more interesting by adding more duties to it. 328

**job enrichment** The incorporation of motivating factors into a job—in particular, giving the employee more responsibility and recognition. 329

**job rotation** Moving employees from job to job to give them more variety. 328

**job specification** A listing of the characteristics desirable in the person performing a given job, including educational and work background, physical characteristics, and personal strengths. 471

**labor relations** Management's role in working constructively with unions that represent the organization's employees. 586

**laissez-faire leadership** A leadership style in which the leader is uninvolved and lets subordinates direct themselves. 217

**lateral communication** Organizational communication that involves sending a message to a person at the same level. 300

**leading** The management function of influencing people to act or not act in a certain way. 214

**leniency bias** Rating employees more favorably than their performance merits. 551

**line authority** The right to carry out tasks and give orders related to the organization's primary purpose. 190

**Malcolm Baldrige National Quality Award** An annual award administered by the U.S. Department of Commerce and given to the company that shows the highest-quality performance in seven categories. 45

**management by objectives (MBO)** A formal system for planning in which managers and employees at all levels set objectives for what they are to accomplish; their performance is then measured against those objectives. 152

**mediator or conciliator** A neutral person who helps opposing parties in an organization reach agreement. 587

**mentor** A higher-level manager who takes the role of showing a lower-level employee how to get along in the organization and making sure that the employee gets recognized by other managers. 608

**motivation** Giving people incentives that cause them to act in desired ways. 316

**National Institute for Occupational Safety and Health (NIOSH)** The agency of the federal government responsible for conducting research related to workplace safety and health. 572

**nepotism** The hiring of one's relatives. 102

**networking** The process of developing a variety of contacts inside and outside the organization. 609

**nondirective counseling** An approach to counseling in which the supervisor primarily listens, encouraging the employee to look for the source of the problem and to propose possible solutions. 378

**nonverbal message** A message conveyed without using words. 292

**norms** Group standards for appropriate or acceptable behavior. 68

**objectives** The desired accomplishments of the organization as a whole or of part of the organization. 147

**Occupational Safety and Health Act (OSHAct) of 1970** The federal law that sets up government agencies to conduct research on occupational health and safety, set health and safety standards, inspect workplaces, and penalize employers that do not meet standards. 571

**Occupational Safety and Health Administration (OSHA)** The agency of the federal government charged with setting and enforcing standards for workplace health and safety. 571

**on-the-job training** Teaching a job while trainer and trainee perform the job at the work site. 519

**open-ended question** A question that gives the person responding broad control over the response. 480

**operational planning** The development of objectives that specify how divisions, departments, and work groups will support organizational goals. 148

**organization politics** Activities by which people seek to improve their position within the organization, generally by gaining power. 453

**organizing** The management function of setting up the group, allocating resources, and assigning work to achieve goals. 184

**orientation** The process of giving new employees the information they need to do their work comfortably, effectively, and efficiently. 508

**overhead** Expenses not related directly to producing goods and services; examples are rent, utilities, and staff support. 356

**paired-comparison approach** A performance appraisal that measures the relative performance of employees in a group. 545

**parity principle** The principle that personnel who are given responsibility must also be given enough authority to carry out that responsibility. 195

**payback period** The length of time it will take for the benefits generated by an investment (such as cost savings from machinery) to offset the cost of the investment. 359

**perceptions** The ways people see and interpret reality. 290

**perfectionism** The attempt to do things perfectly. 408

**performance appraisal** Formal feedback on how well an employee is performing his or her job. 538

**performance report** A summary of performance and comparison with performance standards. 110

**personal power** Power that arises from an individual's personal characteristics. 454

**piecework system** Payment according to the quantity produced. 324

**planning** The management function of setting goals and determining how to meet them. 146

**policies** Broad guidelines for how to act. 150

**position power** Power that comes from a person's formal role in an organization. 454

**positive discipline** Discipline designed to prevent problem behavior from beginning. 384

**power** The ability to influence people to behave in a certain way. 56

**precontrol** Efforts aimed at preventing behavior that may lead to undesirable results. 166

**prejudices** Negative conclusions about a category of people based on stereotypes. 291

**probability theory** A body of techniques for comparing the consequences of possible decisions in a risk situation. 256

**problem** A factor in the organization that is a barrier to improvement. 164

**procedures** The steps that must be completed to achieve a specific purpose. 150

**process control** Quality control that emphasizes how to do things in a way that leads to better quality. 35

**procrastination** Putting off what needs to be done. 408

**product quality control** Quality control that focuses on ways to improve the product itself. 34

**productivity** The amount of results (output) an organization gets for a given amount of inputs. 346

**proficiency test** A test that measures whether the person has the skills needed to perform a job. 484

**profit-sharing plan** A group incentive plan under which the company sets aside a share of its profits and divides it among employees. 326

**program evaluation and review technique (PERT)** Scheduling tool that identifies the relationships among tasks as well as the amount of time each task will take. 156

**proximity bias** The tendency to assign similar scores to items that are near each other on a questionnaire. 552

**psychomotor test** A test that measures a person's strength, dexterity, and coordination. 484

**punishment** An unpleasant consequence given in response to undesirable behavior. 322

**Pygmalion effect** The direct relationship between expectations and performance; high expectations lead to high performance. 329

**quality control** An organization's efforts to prevent or correct defects in its goods or services or to improve them in some way. 33

**recency syndrome** The tendency to more easily remember events that have occurred recently. 251

**recruitment** Identifying people interested in holding a particular job or working for the organization. 472

**reinforcement** Encouragement of a behavior by associating it with a reward. 163

**reinforcement** A desired consequence or the ending of a negative consequence, either of which is given in response to a desirable behavior. 322

**repetitive-motion disorders** Injuries that result from repeatedly applying force to the same muscles or joints. 579

**résumé** A summary of work-related skills and experience. 608

**role conflicts** Situations in which a person has two different roles that call for conflicting types of behavior. 68

**role playing** A training method in which roles are assigned to participants, who then act out the way they would handle a specific situation. 523

**roles** Patterns of behavior related to employees' positions in a group. 67

**rules** Specific statements of what to do or not to do in a given situation. 150

**safety hazards** Conditions in the workplace that may lead to an injury-causing accident. 575

**scheduling** Setting a precise timetable for the work to be completed. 155

**self-concept** A person's self-image. 229

**self-managing work teams** Groups of 5 to 15 members who work together to produce an entire product. 72

**similarity bias** The tendency to judge others more positively when they are like yourself. 553

**smoothing** Managing a conflict by pretending it does not exist. 442

**span of control** The number of people a manager supervises. 197

**staff authority** The right to advise or assist those with line authority. 190

**staffing** Identifying, hiring, and developing the necessary number and quality of employees. 9

**standards** Measures of what is expected. 159

**statistical process control (SPC)** A statistical quality-control technique using statistics to monitor production quality on an ongoing basis and making corrections whenever the results show the process is out of control. 36

**statistical quality control** Looking for defects in parts or finished products selected through a sampling technique. 36.

**status** A group member's position in relation to others in the group. 68

**strategic planning** The creation of long-term goals for the organization as a whole. 147

**stress** The body's response to coping with environmental demands. 410

**strike** Refusal by employees to work until there is a contract. 589

**structured interview** An interview based on questions the interviewer has prepared in advance. 480

**supervisor** A manager at the first level of management. 4

**suspension** Requirement that an employee not come to work for a set period of time; the employee is not paid for the time off. 381

**symptom** An indication of an underlying problem. 164

**task groups** Groups that are set up to carry out a specific activity and then disband when the activity is completed. 63

**team** A group of people who must collaborate to some degree to achieve common goals. 72

**team building** Developing the ability of team members to work together to achieve common objectives. 76

**technical skills** The specialized knowledge and expertise used to carry out particular techniques or procedures. 4

**Theory X** A set of management attitudes based on the view that people dislike work and must be coerced to perform. 218

**Theory Y** A set of management attitudes based on the view that work is a natural activity and that people will work hard and creatively to achieve objectives they are committed to. 219

**Theory Z** A set of management attitudes that emphasizes employee participation in all aspects of decision making. 219

**time log** A record of what activities a person is doing hour by hour throughout the day. 400

**time management** The practice of controlling the way you use time. 400

**total quality management (TQM)** An organizationwide focus on satisfying customers by continuously improving every business process for delivering goods or services. 40

**training** Increasing the skills that will enable employees to better meet the organization's goals. 508

**turnover** The rate at which employees leave an organization. 360

**Type A personality** A description of someone who is constantly trying to get a lot done in a hurry. 412

**union steward** An employee who is the union's representative in a particular work unit. 588

**unity of command** The principle that each employee should have only one supervisor. 196

**unstructured interview** An interview in which the interviewer has no list of questions prepared in advance but asks questions based on the applicant's responses. 480

**upward communication** Organizational communication that involves sending a message to someone at a higher level. 300

**variance** The size of the difference between actual performance and a performance standard. 162

**verbal message** A message that consists of words. 292

**vestibule training** Training that takes place on equipment set up in a special area off the job site. 520

**video display terminal (VDT)** The screen on which a computer displays information. 578

**wellness program** Organizational activities designed to help employees adopt healthy practices. 419

**whistle blower** Someone who exposes a violation of ethics or law. 105

**wildcat strike** Refusal by employees to work during the term of a labor contract. 589

**work-standards approach** A performance appraisal in which the appraiser compares an employee's performance with objective measures of what the employee should do. 548

**zero-defects approach** A quality-control technique based on the view that everyone in the organization should work toward the goal of delivering such high quality that all aspects of the organization's goods and services are free of problems. 37

# Index